CURRENT LAW STATUTES ANNOTATED
1987

VOLUME TWO

AUSTRALIA AND NEW ZEALAND
The Law Book Company Ltd.
Sydney : Melbourne : Perth

CANADA AND U.S.A.
The Carswell Company Ltd.
Agincourt, Ontario

INDIA
N. M. Tripathi Private Ltd.
Bombay
and
Eastern Law House Private Ltd.
Calcutta and Delhi

M.P.P. House
Bangalore

ISRAEL
Steimatzky's Agency Ltd.
Jerusalem : Tel Aviv : Haifa

CURRENT LAW
STATUTES
ANNOTATED
1987

VOLUME TWO

EDITOR IN CHIEF
PETER ALLSOP, C.B.E., M.A.
Barrister

GENERAL EDITOR
KEVAN NORRIS, LL.B.
Solicitor

ASSISTANT GENERAL EDITORS
GILLIAN BRONZE, LL.B.
SUSAN SHUAIB, B.A.

LONDON

SWEET & MAXWELL   STEVENS & SONS

EDINBURGH

W. GREEN & SON

1988

Published by
SWEET & MAXWELL LIMITED
and STEVENS & SONS LIMITED
of 11 New Fetter Lane, London,
and W. GREEN & SON LIMITED
of St. Giles Street, Edinburgh,
and Printed in Great Britain
by The Eastern Press Ltd.,
London and Reading

ISBN This Volume only : 0 421 39660 1
As a set : 0 421 39680 6

CONTENTS

CHRONOLOGICAL TABLE

VOLUME TWO

STATUTES

c.26. Housing (Scotland) Act 1987
27. Fire Safety and Safety of Places of Sport Act 1987
28. Deer Act 1987
29. Agricultural Training Board Act 1987
30. Northern Ireland (Emergency Provisions) Act 1987
31. Landlord and Tenant Act 1987
32. Crossbows Act 1987
33. AIDS Control Act 1987
34. Motor Cycle Noise Act 1987
35. Protection of Animals (Penalties) Act 1987
36. Prescription (Scotland) Act 1987
37. Access to Personal Files Act 1987
38. Criminal Justice Act 1987
39. Parliamentary and Health Service Commissioners Act 1987
40. Registered Establishments (Scotland) Act 1987
41. Criminal Justice (Scotland) Act 1987

INDEX OF SHORT TITLES

VOLUME TWO

References are to chapter numbers of 1987

HOUSING (SCOTLAND) ACT 1987

(1987 c.26)

A table showing the derivation of the provisions of this consolidation Bill will be found at the end of the Bill. The table has no official status.

ARRANGEMENT OF SECTIONS

PART I

PROVISION OF HOUSING

Part IX

Government Grants and Subsidies

Part X

Housing Accounts of Local Authorities

Part XI

Rents and Service Charges

Part XII

House Loans and other Financial Assistance

Part XV

Compensation Payments

Part XVI

General and Miscellaneous

An Act to consolidate with amendments to give effect to recommendations of the Scottish Law Commission, certain enactments relating to housing in Scotland.

[15th May 1987]

PART I

PROVISION OF HOUSING

Duties and powers of local authorities

Duty of local authority to consider needs of their area for further housing accommodation

1.—(1) Every local authority shall consider the housing conditions in their area and the needs of the area for further housing accommodation.

(2) For that purpose they shall review any information which has been brought to their notice, including in particular information brought to their notice as a result of a survey or inspections made under section 85(3).

(3) If the Secretary of State gives them notice to do so, they shall, within 3 months after such notice, prepare and submit to him proposals for the provision of housing accommodation.

(4) In considering the needs of their area for further housing accommodation under subsection (1), every local authority shall have regard to the special needs of chronically sick or disabled persons; and any proposals prepared and submitted to the Secretary of State under subsection (3) shall distinguish any houses which they propose to provide which make special provision for the needs of such persons.

Powers of local authority to provide housing accommodation

2.—(1) A local authority may provide housing accommodation—
    (a) by the erection of houses on any land acquired or appropriated by them;

    (b) by the conversion of any buildings into houses;
    (c) by acquiring houses;
    (d) by altering, enlarging, repairing or improving any houses or other buildings which have, or a right or interest in which has, been acquired by the local authority.

(2) For the purpose of supplying the needs for housing accommodation in its area, a local authority may exercise any of its powers under subsection (1) outside that area.

(3) A local authority may alter, enlarge, repair or improve any house provided by them under subsection (1).

(4) For the purposes of this Part the provision of housing accommodation includes the provision of—

    (a) a cottage with a garden of not more than one acre;
    (b) a hostel.

(5) In this section "hostel" means—

    (a) in relation to a building provided or converted before 3 July 1962, a building in which is provided, for persons generally or for any class or classes of persons, residential accommodation (otherwise than in separate and self-contained dwellings) and board;
    (b) in relation to a building provided or converted on or after 3 July 1962, a building in which is provided, for persons generally or for any class or classes of persons, residential accommodation (otherwise than in houses) and either board or common facilities for the preparation of food adequate to the needs of those persons or both.

Power of local authority to provide shops, etc., in connection with housing accommodation

3.—(1) Subject to the provisions of this section, a local authority may provide and maintain—

    (a) any building adapted for use as a shop;
    (b) any recreation grounds;
    (c) such other buildings or land as are referred to in subsection (2),

in connection with housing accommodation provided by them under this Part.

(2) The buildings or land referred to in subsection (1)(c) are buildings or land which in the opinion of the Secretary of State will serve a beneficial purpose in connection with the requirements of the persons for whom the housing accommodation is provided.

(3) The provision and maintenance of any building or land under this section—

    (a) requires the consent of the Secretary of State;
    (b) may be undertaken jointly with any other person.

(4) The Secretary of State may, in giving his consent to the provision of any building or land under this section, by order apply, with any necessary modifications, to that building or land any statutory provisions which would have been applicable to it if the building or land had been provided under any enactment giving any local authority powers for that purpose.

Power of local authority to provide furniture, etc.

4.—(1) A local authority—

    (a) may fit out, furnish and supply any house erected, converted or acquired by them under section 2 with all requisite furniture, fittings and conveniences;
    (b) shall have power to sell, or to supply under a hire-purchase

agreement, furniture to the occupants of houses provided by the local authority and, for that purpose, to buy furniture.

(2) In this section "hire-purchase agreement" means a hire-purchase or conditional sale agreement within the meaning of the Consumer Credit Act 1974.

Power of local authority to provide board and laundry facilities

5.—(1) The power of a local authority under this Part to provide housing accommodation shall include power to provide, in connection with the provision of such accommodation for any persons, such facilities for obtaining meals and such laundry facilities and services as accord with the needs of those persons.

(2) A local authority may make such reasonable charges for meals provided by them by virtue of this section, and such reasonable charges to persons availing themselves of laundry facilities or services so provided, as the authority may determine.

(3) This section shall not authorise the grant of a licence under the Licensing (Scotland) Act 1976 for the sale of alcoholic liquor in connection with the provision under this section of facilities for obtaining meals.

Duty of local authority to have regard to amenities of locality, etc.

6.—(1) A local authority, in preparing any proposals for the provision of houses or in taking any action under this Act, shall have regard to artistic quality in the lay-out, planning and treatment of the houses to be provided, the beauty of the landscape or countryside and the other amenities of the locality, and the desirability of preserving existing works of architectural, historic or artistic interest.

(2) For their better advice in carrying out the requirements of subsection (1), a local authority may appoint a local advisory committee including representatives of architectural and other artistic interests.

Execution of works by local authority in connection with housing operations outside their area

7. Where any housing operations under this Part are being carried out by a local authority outside their own area, that authority shall have power to execute any works which are necessary for the purposes, or are incidental to the carrying out, of the operations, subject to entering into an agreement with the local authority of the area in which the operations are being carried out as to the terms and conditions on which any such works are to be executed.

Adjustment of differences between local authorities as to carrying out of proposals for provision of housing accommodation

8. Where a local authority are providing houses in the area of another local authority, any difference arising between those authorities with respect to the carrying out of the proposals may be referred by either authority to the Secretary of State, and the Secretary of State's decision shall be final and binding on the authorities.

Acquisition and disposal of land

Power of local authority to acquire land for, or in connection with, provision of housing accommodation

9.—(1) A local authority may acquire—
    (a) any land as a site for the erection of houses;

(b) land proposed to be used for any purpose authorised by section 3 or section 5;

(c) subject to subsection (2),

    (i) houses, and

    (ii) buildings other than houses, being buildings which may be made suitable as houses,

together with any lands occupied with the houses or buildings, or any right or interest in the houses or buildings;

(d) land for the purposes of—

    (i) selling or leasing the land under the powers conferred by this Act, with a view to the erection on the land of houses by persons other than the local authority;

    (ii) selling or leasing, under the powers conferred by this Act, any part of the land acquired, with a view to the use of that land for purposes which in the opinion of the local authority are necessary or desirable for, or incidental to, the development of the land as a building estate;

    (iii) carrying out on the land works for the purpose of, or connected with, the alteration, enlargement, repair or improvement of an adjoining house;

    (iv) selling or leasing the land under the powers conferred by this Act, with a view to the carrying out on the land by a person other than the local authority of such works as are mentioned in sub-paragraph (iii).

(2) Nothing in subsection (1)(c) shall authorise a local authority to acquire otherwise than by agreement any house or other building which is situated on land used for agriculture, and which is required in connection with that use of that land.

Procedure for acquiring land

10.—(1) Land for the purposes of this Part may be acquired by a local authority by agreement under section 70 of the Local Government (Scotland) Act 1973.

(2) A local authority may be authorised by the Secretary of State to purchase land compulsorily for the purposes of this Part, and the Acquisition of Land (Authorisation Procedure) (Scotland) Act 1947 shall apply in relation to any such compulsory purchase as if this Act had been in force immediately before the commencement of that Act.

(3) A local authority may acquire land by agreement, or may be authorised by the Secretary of State to purchase land compulsorily, for the purpose of this Part, notwithstanding that the land is not immediately required for those purposes.

(4) Where land is purchased compulsorily by a local authority for the purposes of this Part, the compensation payable in respect thereof shall be assessed by the Lands Tribunal in accordance with the Land Compensation (Scotland) Act 1963, subject to the rules set out in Schedule I.

Local authority may take possession of land to be acquired by agreement or appropriated for purposes of this Part

11.—(1) Where a local authority have agreed to purchase, or have determined to appropriate, land for the purposes of this Part, subject to the interest of the person in possession of the land, and that interest is not greater than that of a tenant for a year or from year to year, then, at any time after such agreement has been made, or such appropriation takes effect, the authority may, after giving to the person in possession not less than 14 days' notice and subject to subsection (2), enter on and take possession of the land or such part of it as is specified in the notice without previous consent.

(2) The powers conferred by subsection (1) are exercisable subject to payment to the person in possession of the like compensation and interest on the compensation awarded, as if the authority had been authorised to purchase the land compulsorily and that person had in pursuance of such power been required to give up possession before the expiration of his term or interest in the land, but without the necessity of compliance with sections 83 to 88 of the Lands Clauses Consolidation (Scotland) Act 1845.

Powers of dealing with land acquired or appropriated for purposes of this Part

12.—(1) Where a local authority have acquired or appropriated any land for the purposes of this Part, then, without prejudice to any of their other powers under this Act, the authority may—

(a) lay out and construct roads and open spaces on the land;

(b) subject to subsection (5), sell or lease the land or part of the land to any person under the condition that that person will erect on it in accordance with plans approved by the local authority, and maintain, such number of houses of such types as may be specified by the authority, and when necessary will lay out and construct public streets or roads and open spaces on the land, or will use the land for purposes which, in the opinion of the authority, are necessary or desirable for, or incidental to, the development of the land as a building estate in accordance with plans approved by the authority;

(c) subject to subsection (5), sell or lease the land or excamb it for land better adapted for those purposes, either with or without paying or receiving any money for equality of exchange;

(d) subject to subsections (5) and (7), sell or lease any houses or any part share thereof on the land or erected by them on the land, subject to such conditions, restrictions and stipulations as they may think fit to impose in regard to the use of the houses or any part share thereof, and on any such sale they may agree to the price being secured by standard security over the subjects sold.

(2) Where a local authority sell or lease land under subsection (1), they may contribute or agree to contribute towards the expenses of the development of the land and the laying out and construction of roads on the land, subject to the condition that the roads are dedicated to the public use.

(3) Where a local authority have acquired a building which may be made suitable as a house, or a right or interest in such a building, they shall forthwith proceed to secure that it is so made suitable either by themselves executing any necessary work or by selling or leasing it to some person subject to conditions for securing that he will so make it suitable.

(4) Where a local authority acquire any land for the purposes of section 9(1)(d)(iv), they may, subject to subsection (5), sell or lease the land to any person for the purpose and under the condition that that person will carry out on the land, in accordance with plans approved by the authority, the works with a view to the carrying out of which the land was acquired.

(5) A local authority shall not, in the exercise of their powers under subsection (1)(b), (c) or (d), or subsection (4), dispose of land which consists or forms part of a common or open space or is held for use as allotments, except with the consent of the Secretary of State.

(6) For the purposes of subsection (5), the consent of the Secretary of State may be given either generally to all local authorities, or to any class

of local authorities, or may be given specifically in any particular case, and (whether given generally or otherwise) may be given either unconditionally or subject to such conditions as the Secretary of State may consider appropriate.

(7) Notwithstanding anything in section 27(1) of the Town and Country Planning (Scotland) Act 1959 (power of local and other public authority to dispose of land without consent of a Minister), a local authority shall not, in the exercise of their powers under subsection (1)(d), sell or lease any house or any part thereof to which the housing revenue account kept under section 203 relates except with the consent of the Secretary of State unless it is a house to which section 14 applies; and, in giving his consent to such transactions as are referred to in this subsection, the Secretary of State may make general directions or a direction related to a specific transaction.

(8) Subsection (7) shall not apply where—
  (a) the house is being sold to a tenant or to a member of his family who normally resides with him (or to a tenant together with members of his family, as joint purchasers); or
  (b) the requirements of section 14(2)(b) are satisfied.

(9) Subject to the provisions of the Town and Country Planning (Scotland) Act 1959, section 74 of the Local Government (Scotland) Act 1973 (which makes provision as to price and other matters relating to the disposal of land by local authorities) shall, subject to subsection (10), apply to any disposal of land by a local authority in the exercise of their powers under subsection (4), as it applies to the like disposal of land by a local authority within the meaning of the said Act of 1973 in the exercise of any power under Part VI of that Act.

(10) The said section 74 shall not apply to the disposal of a house by a local authority, being a disposal in relation to which subsection (7) has effect.

(11) For the purposes of this section land shall be taken to have been acquired by a local authority in the exercise (directly or indirectly) of compulsory powers if it was acquired by them compulsorily or was acquired by them by agreement at a time when they were authorised by or under any enactment to acquire the land compulsorily; but the land shall not be taken to have been so acquired, if the local authority acquired it (whether compulsorily or by agreement) in consequence of the service in pursuance of any enactment (including any enactment contained in this Act) of a notice requiring the authority to purchase the land.

Power of Secretary of State in certain cases to impose conditions on sale of local authority's houses, etc.

13. If any house, building, land or dwelling in respect of which a local authority are required by section 203 to keep a housing revenue account is sold by the authority with the consent of the Secretary of State, the Secretary of State may in giving consent impose such conditions as he thinks just.

Powers of local authorities to sell certain houses without consent of Secretary of State

14.—(1) Subject to section 74(2) of the Local Government (Scotland) Act 1973 (restriction on disposal of land) but notwithstanding anything contained in section 12(6) or in any other enactment, a local authority may sell any house to which this section applies without the consent of the Secretary of State.

(2) This section applies to a house provided for the purposes of this Part, where—

(a) the house is being sold to a tenant or to members of his family who normally reside with him (or to a tenant together with such members of his family, as joint purchasers); or

(b) the house is unoccupied and—
  (i) it is not held on the housing revenue account maintained in terms of section 203; or
  (ii) it is held on the housing revenue account and it is, in the opinion of the local authority, either surplus to its requirements or difficult to let, because it has been continuously vacant for a period of not less than 3 months immediately prior to the date of the sale and during that period it has been on unrestricted offer to any applicant on the local authority's housing list (within the meaning of section 19 (admission to housing list)).

Power of local authority to enforce obligations against owner for time being of land

15.—(1) Where—

(a) a local authority have sold or excambed land acquired by them under this Act, and the purchaser of the land or the person taking the land in exchange has entered into an agreement with the authority concerning the land; or

(b) an owner of any land has entered into an agreement with the local authority concerning the land for the purposes of any of the provisions of this Act;

then, if the agreement has been recorded in the General Register of Sasines, or, as the case may be, registered in the Land Register for Scotland, it shall, subject to subsection (2), be enforceable at the instance of the local authority against persons deriving title from the person who entered into the agreement.

(2) No such agreement shall at any time be enforceable against any party who has in good faith onerously acquired right (whether completed by infeftment or not) to the land prior to the recording of the agreement or against any person deriving title from such party.

Disposal of land for erection of churches, etc.

16. Where a local authority, in the exercise of any power conferred on them by this Act, dispose of land to any person for the erection of a church or other building for religious worship or buildings ancillary thereto, then, unless the parties otherwise agree, such disposal shall be by way of feu.

Management and allocation of local authority's houses

General management and inspection of local authority's houses

17.—(1) The general management, regulation and control of houses held for housing purposes by a local authority shall be vested in and exercised by the authority.

(2) A house held for housing purposes by a local authority shall be at all times open to inspection by the local authority for the area in which it is situated or by any officer duly authorised by them.

Byelaws for regulation of local authority's houses

18. A local authority may make byelaws for the management, use and regulation of houses held by them for housing purposes.

Admission to housing list

19.—(1) In considering whether an applicant for local authority housing is entitled to be admitted to a housing list, a local authority shall take no account of—

(a) the age of the applicant provided that he has attained the age of 16 years; or

(b) the income of the applicant and his family; or

(c) whether, or to what value, the applicant or any of his family owns or has owned (or any of them own or have owned) heritable or moveable property; or

(d) any outstanding liability (for payment of rent or otherwise) attributable to the tenancy of any house of which the applicant is not, and was not when the liability accrued, a tenant; or

(e) whether the applicant is living with, or in the same house as—
    (i) his spouse; or
    (ii) a person with whom he has been living as husband and wife.

(2) Where an applicant—

(a) is employed in the area of the local authority; or

(b) has been offered employment in the area of the local authority; or

(c) wishes to move into the area of the local authority and the local authority is satisfied that his purpose in doing so is to seek employment; or

(d) has attained the age of 60 years and wishes to move into the area of the local authority to be near a younger relative; or

(e) has special social or medical reasons for requiring to be housed within the area of the local authority,

admission to a housing list shall not depend on the applicant being resident in the area.

(3) Where a local authority has rules which give priority to applicants on its housing list it shall apply those rules to an applicant to whom subsection (2) above applies no less favourably than it applies them to a tenant of the local authority whose housing needs are similar to those of the applicant and who is seeking a transfer to another house belonging to the local authority.

(4) In this section and in section 21 of this Act, "housing list" means a list of applicants for local authority housing which is kept by a local authority in connection with the allocation of housing.

Persons to have priority on housing list and allocation of housing

20.—(1) A local authority shall, in relation to all houses held by them for housing purposes, secure that in the selection of their tenants a reasonable preference is given—

(a) to persons who—
    (i) are occupying houses which do not meet the tolerable standard; or
    (ii) are occupying overcrowded houses; or
    (iii) have large families; or
    (iv) are living under unsatisfactory housing conditions; and

(b) to persons to whom they have a duty under sections 31 to 34 (homeless persons).

(2) In the allocation of local authority housing a local authority—

(a) shall take no account of—
    (i) the length of time for which an applicant has resided in its area; or
    (ii) any outstanding liability (for payment of rent or otherwise) attributable to the tenancy of any house of which

the applicant is not, and was not when the liability accrued, a tenant; or

    (iii) any of the matters mentioned in paragraphs (a) to (c) of section 19(1); and

  (b) shall not impose a requirement—

    (i) that an application must have remained in force for a minimum period; or

    (ii) that a divorce or judicial separation be obtained; or

    (iii) that the applicant no longer be living with, or in the same house as, some other person,

before the applicant is eligible for the allocation of housing.

Publication of rules relating to the housing list and to transfer of tenants

21.—(1) It shall be the duty of every local authority, the Scottish Special Housing Association and development corporations (including urban development corporations) to publish in accordance with subsection (2), and within 6 months of any alteration of the rules, any rules which it may have governing—

  (a) admission of applicants to any housing list;

  (b) priority of allocation of houses;

  (c) transfer of tenants from houses owned by it to houses owned by other bodies;

  (d) exchanges of houses.

(2) It shall be the duty of every registered housing association—

  (a) within the period of 6 months commencing on 7th January 1987 to make rules governing the matters mentioned in paragraphs (a) to (d) of subsection (1) (unless it has, in accordance with subsections (4) and (5), published such rules before that date and those rules remain current);

  (b) within 6 months of the making of rules under paragraph (a), and within 6 months of any alteration of such rules (whether or not made under that paragraph)—

    (i) to send a copy of them to each of the bodies mentioned in subsection (3); and

    (ii) to publish them in accordance with subsections (4) and (5).

(3) The bodies referred to in subsection (2)(b)(i) are—

    (i) the Housing Corporation; and

    (ii) every local authority within whose area there is a house let, or to be let, by the association under a secure tenancy.

(4) The rules to be published by a body in accordance with subsection (1) or (2) shall be—

  (a) available for perusal; and

  (b) on sale at a reasonable price; and

  (c) available in summary form on request to members of the public,

at all reasonable times—

    (i) in a case where the body is a local authority or a development corporation, at its principal offices and its housing department offices; and

    (ii) in any other case, at its principal and other offices.

(5) Rules sent to a local authority in accordance with subsection 2(b) shall be available for perusal at all reasonable times at its principal offices.

(6) An applicant for housing provided by a body mentioned in subsection (1) or (2) shall be entitled on request to inspect any record kept by that body of information furnished by him to it in connection with his application.

Housing co-operatives

Agreements for exercise by housing co-operatives of local authority housing functions

22.—(1) A local authority may make an agreement with a society, company or body of trustees for the time being approved by the Secretary of State for the purposes of this section (in this section called a "housing co-operative")—

(a) for the exercise by the co-operative, on such terms as may be provided in the agreement, of any of the local authority's powers relating to land or any interest in land held by them for the purposes of this Part, and the performance by the co-operative of any of the local authority's duties relating to such land or interest; or

(b) for the exercise by the co-operative, in connection with any such land or interest, of any of the local authority's powers under section 4 or 5 (powers to provide furniture, board and laundry facilities).

(2) An agreement to which this section applies may only be made with the approval of the Secretary of State.

(3) The Secretary of State's approval to the making of such an agreement may be given either generally or to any local authority or description of local authority or in any particular case, and may be given unconditionally or subject to any conditions.

(4) A housing association is not entitled under the Housing Associations Act 1985 to housing association grant, revenue deficit grant or hostel deficit grant in respect of land comprised in an agreement to which this section applies.

(5) Houses on land included in an agreement to which this section applies shall continue to be included in the local authority's housing revenue account; and neither the fact that the authority have made the agreement nor any letting of land in pursuance of it shall be treated as a ground for the reduction, suspension or discontinuance of any Exchequer contribution or subsidy under section 202.

Powers of Scottish Special Housing Association

Compulsory purchase of land by Scottish Special Housing Association

23.—(1) Where the Scottish Special Housing Association (hereafter in this section referred to as "the Association") desire to acquire any land for—

(a) the provision of new houses by the Association under the terms of an agreement between them and the Secretary of State, or

(b) the provision of housing accommodation by the Association under a scheme submitted by them to the Secretary of State under section 196(1)(b),

and the Association have made an application to the local authority in whose district the land is situated requesting them to acquire the land under this Part for the purpose of selling it or leasing it to the Association, then if the authority have power so to acquire the land and the Association are satisfied, after consultation with the authority, that the authority are unwilling to acquire the land for that purpose or that the footing on which they are willing to do so involves the sale or leasing of the land to the Association subject to conditions which are unacceptable to the Association, the Association may themselves acquire the land compulsorily.

(2) The Association may, at the request of the Housing Corporation made in accordance with section 88(5) of the Housing Associations Act 1985, acquire land compulsorily.

(3) The power of the Association to acquire any land compulsorily under subsection (1) or subsection (2) shall be exercisable in any particular case on their being authorised to do so by the Secretary of State, and in relation to the compulsory purchase the Acquisition of Land (Authorisation Procedure) (Scotland) Act 1947 shall apply as if the Association were a local authority within the meaning of that Act, as if this Act had been in force immediately before the commencement of that Act, and in relation to the exercise of the Association's powers under subsection (1) of this section as if in Part I of Schedule 1 to that Act (procedure for authorising compulsory purchases) references to an owner of any land comprised in the compulsory purchase order included references to the local authority in whose district the land is situated.

(4) The Association may not dispose of any land acquired by them compulsorily under this section which is not required for the purposes for which it was acquired without the consent in writing of the Secretary of State.

(5) In the case of land which is situated partly in the district of one local authority and partly in the district of another, references in this section to the local authority in whose district the land is situated shall be construed as references to each of those local authorities.

(6) The Association may, for the purpose of securing the improvement of the amenities of a predominantly residential area within a district in which it has an interest as owner of land—

(a) carry out any works on land owned by them;

(b) with the agreement of the owner of any land, carry out or arrange for the carrying out of works on that land at his expense, or at the expense of the Association, or in part at the expense of both;

(c) acquire any land by agreement.

(7) Subsection (6) applies to a development corporation in respect of its designated area as it applies to the Association in respect of a district in which it has an interest as owner of land, and in addition to the powers conferred by that subsection, a development corporation may assist (whether by grants or loans or otherwise) in the carrying out of works on land not owned by them.

PART II

HOMELESS PERSONS

Main definitions

Homeless persons and persons threatened with homelessness

24.—(1) A person is homeless if he has no accommodation in Scotland, or England or Wales.

(2) A person is to be treated as having no accommodation if there is no accommodation which he, together with any other person who normally resides with him as a member of his family or in circumstances in which the local authority consider it reasonable for that person to reside with him—

(a) is entitled to occupy by virtue of an interest in it or by virtue of an order of a court, or

(b) has a right or permission, or an implied right or permission to occupy, or in England and Wales has an express or implied licence to occupy, or

(c) occupies as a residence by virtue of any enactment or rule of law giving him the right to remain in occupation or restricting the right of any other person to recover possession.

(3) A person is also homeless if he has accommodation but—
  (a) he cannot secure entry to it, or
  (b) it is probable that occupation of it will lead to violence from some other person residing in it or to threats of violence from some other person residing in it and likely to carry out the threats, or
  (c) it consists of a movable structure, vehicle or vessel designed or adapted for human habitation and there is no place where he is entitled or permitted both to place it and to reside in it; or
  (d) it is overcrowded within the meaning of section 135 and may endanger the health of the occupants.

(4) A person is threatened with homelessness if it is likely that he will become homeless within 28 days.

Priority need for accommodation

25.—(1) The following have a priority need for accommodation—
  (a) a pregnant woman or a person with whom a pregnant woman resides or might reasonably be expected to reside;
  (b) a person with whom dependent children reside or might reasonably be expected to reside;
  (c) a person who is vulnerable as a result of old age, mental illness or handicap or physical disability or other special reason, or with whom such a person resides or might reasonably be expected to reside;
  (d) a person who is homeless or threatened with homelessness as a result of an emergency such as flood, fire or any other disaster.

(2) The Secretary of State may by order made by statutory instrument—
  (a) specify further descriptions of persons as having a priority need for accommodation, and
  (b) amend or repeal any part of subsection (1).

(3) Before making such an order the Secretary of State shall consult such associations representing relevant authorities, and such other persons, as he considers appropriate.

(4) No such order shall be made unless a draft of the order has been laid before and approved by resolution of each House of Parliament.

Becoming homeless intentionally

26.—(1) A person becomes homeless intentionally if he deliberately does or fails to do anything in consequence of which he ceases to occupy accommodation which is available for his occupation and which it would have been reasonable for him to continue to occupy.

(2) A person becomes threatened with homelessness intentionally if he deliberately does or fails to do anything the likely result of which is that he will be forced to leave accommodation which is available for his occupation and which it would have been reasonable for him to continue to occupy.

(3) For the purposes of subsection (1) or (2) an act or omission in good faith on the part of a person who was unaware of any relevant fact shall not be treated as deliberate.

(4) Regard may be had, in determining for the purpose of subsections (1) and (2) whether it would have been reasonable for a person to continue to occupy accommodation, to the general circumstances prevailing in relation to housing in the district of the local authority to whom he applied for accommodation or for assistance in obtaining accommodation.

Meaning of "local connection"

27.—(1) Any reference in this Part to a person having a local connection with a district is a reference to his having a connection with that district—

(a) because he is, or in the past was, normally resident in it and his residence in it is or was of his own choice; or

(b) because he is employed in it, or

(c) because of family associations, or

(d) because of any special circumstances.

(2) Residence in a district is not of a person's own choice for the purposes of subsection (1) if he became resident in it—

(a) because he or any person who might reasonably be expected to reside with him—

(i) was serving in the regular armed forces of the Crown, or

(ii) was detained under the authority of any Act of Parliament, or

(b) in such other circumstances as the Secretary of State may by order specify.

(3) A person is not employed in a district for the purposes of subsection (1)—

(a) if he is serving in the regular armed forces of the Crown, or

(b) in such other circumstances as the Secretary of State may by order specify.

(4) An order under subsections (2) or (3) shall be made by statutory instrument which shall be subject to annulment in pursuance of a resolution of either House of Parliament.

Duties of local authorities with respect to homelessness and threatened homelessness

Inquiry into cases of possible homelessness or threatened homelessness

28.—(1) If a person ("an applicant") applies to a local authority for accommodation, or for assistance in obtaining accommodation, and the authority have reason to believe that he may be homeless or threatened with homelessness, they shall make such inquiries as are necessary to satisfy themselves as to whether he is homeless or threatened with homelessness.

(2) If the authority are so satisfied, they shall make any further inquiries necessary to satisfy themselves as to—

(a) whether he has a priority need, and

(b) whether he became homeless or threatened with homelessness intentionally;

and if the authority think fit, they may also make inquiries as to whether he has a local connection with the district of another local authority in Scotland, England or Wales.

Interim duty to accommodate in case of apparent priority need

29.—(1) If the local authority have reason to believe that an applicant may be homeless and have a priority need, they shall secure that accommodation is made available for his occupation pending any decision which they may make as a result of their inquiries under section 28.

(2) This duty arises irrespective of any local connection which an applicant may have with the district of another local authority.

Notification of decision and reasons

30.—(1) On completing their inquiries under section 28, the local authority shall notify the applicant of their decision on the question whether he is homeless or threatened with homelessness.

(2) If they notify him that their decision is that he is homeless or threatened with homelessness, they shall at the same time notify him of their decision on the question whether he has a priority need.

(3) If they notify him that their decision is that he has a priority need, they shall at the same time notify him—

(a) of their decision on the question whether he became homeless or threatened with homelessness intentionally, and

(b) whether they have notified or propose to notify any other local authority under section 33 that his application has been made.

(4) If they notify him—

(a) that they are not satisfied—

    (i) that he is homeless or threatened with homelessness, or

    (ii) that he has a priority need, or

(b) that they are satisfied that he became homeless or threatened with homelessness intentionally, or

(c) that they have notified or propose to notify another local authority under section 33 that his application has been made,

they shall at the same time notify him of their reasons.

(5) The notice required to be given to a person under this section shall be given in writing and shall, if not received by him, be treated as having been given to him only if it is made available at the authority's office for a reasonable period for collection by him or on his behalf.

Duties to persons found to be homeless

31.—(1) This section applies where a local authority are satisfied that an applicant is homeless.

(2) Where they are satisfied that he has a priority need and are not satisfied that he became homeless intentionally, they shall, unless they notify another local authority in accordance with section 33 (referral of application on ground of local connection) secure that accommodation becomes available for his occupation.

(3) Where they are satisfied that he has a priority need but are also satisfied that he became homeless intentionally, they shall—

(a) secure that accommodation is made available for his occupation for such period as they consider will give him a reasonable opportunity of himself securing accommodation for his occupation; and

(b) furnish him with advice and such assistance as they consider appropriate in the circumstances, in any attempts he may make to secure that accommodation becomes available for his occupation.

(4) Where they are not satisfied that he has a priority need they shall furnish him with advice and such assistance as they consider appropriate in the circumstances, in any attempts he may make to secure that accommodation becomes available for his occupation.

Duties to persons found to be threatened with homelessness

32.—(1) This section applies where a local authority are satisfied that an applicant is threatened with homelessness.

(2) Where they are satisfied that he has a priority need and are not satisfied that he became threatened with homelessness intentionally they shall take reasonable steps to secure that accommodation does not cease to be available for his occupation.

(3) Where—

(a) they are not satisfied that he has a priority need, or

(b) they are satisfied that he has a priority need, but are also satisfied that he became threatened with homelessness intentionally, they shall furnish him with advice and assistance as they consider appropriate in the circumstances, in any attempts he may make to secure that accommodation does not cease to be available for his occupation.

(4) Nothing in subsection (2) shall affect any right of a local authority to secure vacant possession of accommodation, whether by virtue of a contract or of any enactment or rule of law.

(5) In section 31 and in this section, "accommodation" does not include accommodation that is overcrowded within the meaning of section 135 or which may endanger the health of the occupants.

Referral of application to another local authority

33.—(1) If a local authority—

(a) are satisfied that an applicant is homeless and has a priority need, and are not satisfied that he became homeless intentionally, but

(b) are of opinion that the conditions are satisfied for referral of his application to another local authority,

they may notify that other local authority in Scotland, England or Wales of the fact that his application has been made and that they are of that opinion.

(2) The conditions of referral of an application to another local authority are—

(a) that neither the applicant nor any person who might reasonably be expected to reside with him has a local connection with the district of the authority to whom his application was made,

(b) that the applicant or a person who might reasonably be expected to reside with him has a local connection with that other local authority's district, and

(c) that neither that applicant nor any person who might reasonably be expected to reside with him will run the risk of domestic violence in that other local authority's district.

(3) For the purposes of this section a person runs the risk of domestic violence—

(a) if he runs the risk of violence from a person with whom, but for the risk of violence, he might reasonably be expected to reside, or from a person with whom he formerly resided, or

(b) if he runs the risk of threats of violence from such a person which are likely to be carried out.

(4) The question whether the conditions for referral of an application are satisfied shall be determined by agreement between the notifying authority and the notified authority, or in default of agreement, in accordance with such arrangements as the Secretary of State may direct by order made by statutory instrument.

(5) An order may direct that the arrangements shall be—

(a) those agreed by any relevant authorities or association of relevant authorities, or

(b) in default of such agreement, such arrangements as appear to the Secretary of State to be suitable, after consultation with such associations representing relevant authorities, and such other persons, as he thinks appropriate.

(6) No order shall be made unless a draft of the order has been laid before and approved by resolution of each House of Parliament.

Duties to persons whose applications are referred

34.—(1) Where, in accordance with section 33(1), a local authority notify another authority of an application, the notifying authority shall secure that accommodation is available for occupation by the applicant until it is determined whether the conditions for referral of his application to the other authority are satisfied.

(2) If it is determined that the conditions for referral are satisfied, the notified authority shall secure that accommodation becomes available for occupation by the applicant; if it is determined that the conditions are not satisfied, the notifying authority shall secure that accommodation becomes available for occupation by him.

(3) When the matter has been determined, the notifying authority shall notify the applicant—

  (a) whether they or the notified authority are the authority whose duty it is to secure that accommodation becomes available for his occupation, and

  (b) of the reasons why the authority subject to that duty are subject to it.

(4) The notice required to be given to a person under subsection (3) shall be given in writing and shall, if not received by him, be treated as having been given to him only if it is made available at the authority's office for a reasonable period for collection by him or on his behalf.

Supplementary provisions

35.—(1) A local authority may perform any duty under section 31 or 34 (duties to persons found to be homeless to secure that accommodation becomes available for the occupation of a person)—

  (a) by making available accommodation held by them under Part I (provision of housing) or under any other enactment,

  (b) by securing that he obtains accommodation from some other person, or

  (c) by giving him such advice and assistance as will secure that he obtains accommodation from some other person.

(2) Without prejudice to section 210(1), a local authority may require a person to whom they were subject to a duty under section 29, 31 or 34 (interim duty to accommodate pending inquiries and duties to persons found to be homeless)—

  (a) to pay such reasonable charges as they may determine in respect of accommodation which they secure for his occupation (either by making it available themselves or otherwise), or

  (b) to pay such reasonable amount as they may determine in respect of sums payable by them for accommodation made available by another person.

Protection of property of homeless persons and persons threatened with homelessness

36.—(1) This section applies where a local authority have reason to believe that an applicant is homeless or threatened with homelessness (or, in the case of an applicant to whom they owe a duty under section 29 (interim duty to accommodate pending inquiries), that he may be homeless) and that—

  (a) there is a danger of loss of, or damage to, any moveable property of his by reason of his inability to protect it or deal with it, and

  (b) no other suitable arrangements have been or are being made.

(2) If the authority have become subject to a duty towards the applicant under section 29, 31(2) or (3)(a), 32(2) or 34 (duty to accommodate during inquiries and duties to persons found to be homeless or threatened with homelessness), then, whether or not they are still subject to such a duty, they shall take reasonable steps to prevent the loss of the moveable property or prevent or mitigate damage to it; and if they have not become

subject to such a duty, they may take any steps they consider reasonable for that purpose.

(3) The authority may for the purposes of this section—

    (a) enter, at all reasonable times, any premises which are the usual place of residence of the applicant or which were his last usual place of residence, and

    (b) deal with any moveable property of his in any way which is reasonably necessary, in particular by storing it or arranging for its storage.

(4) The authority may decline to take action under this section except upon such conditions as they consider appropriate in the particular case, which may include conditions as to—

    (a) the making and recovery by the authority of reasonable charges for the action taken, or

    (b) the disposal by the authority, in such circumstances as may be specified, of moveable property in relation to which they have taken action.

(5) When in the authority's opinion there is no longer any reason to believe that there is a danger of loss of or damage to a person's moveable property by reason of his inability to protect it or deal with it, the authority shall cease to have any duty or power to take action under this section; but property stored by virtue of their having taken such action may be kept in store and any conditions upon which it was taken into store shall continue to have effect, with any necessary modifications.

(6) Where the authority—

    (a) cease to be subject to a duty to take action under this section in respect of an applicant's moveable property, or

    (b) cease to have power to take such action, having previously taken such action,

they shall notify the applicant of that fact and of the reason why they are of opinion that there is no longer any reason to believe that there is a danger of loss of or damage to his moveable property by reason of his inability to protect it or deal with it.

(7) The notification shall be given to the applicant—

    (a) by delivering it to him, or

    (b) by leaving it, or sending it to him, at his last known address.

(8) References in this section to moveable property of the applicant include moveable property of any person who might reasonably be expected to reside with him.

Administrative provisions

Guidance to authorities by the Secretary of State

37.—(1) In relation to homeless persons and persons threatened with homelessness, a relevant authority shall have regard in the exercise of their functions to such guidance as may from time to time be given by the Secretary of State.

(2) The Secretary of State may give guidance either generally or to specified descriptions of authorities.

Co-operation between authorities

38. Where a local authority—

    (a) request another local authority in Scotland or England or Wales, a development corporation, a registered housing association or the Scottish Special Housing Association to assist them in the discharge of their functions under sections 28, 29, 31 to 33 and 34(1) and (2) (which relate to the duties of local

     authorities with respect to homelessness and threatened home-
     lessness as such),

   (b) request a social work authority in Scotland or a social services
       authority in England or Wales to exercise any of their functions
       in relation to a case which the local authority are dealing with
       under those provisions, or

   (c) request another local authority in Scotland or England or
       Wales to assist them in the discharge of their functions under
       section 36 (protection of property of homeless persons and
       persons threatened with homelessness),

the authority to whom the request is made shall co-operate in rendering
such assistance in the discharge of the functions to which the request
relates as is reasonable in the circumstances.

Assistance for voluntary organisations

Financial and other assistance for voluntary organisations concerned with homelessness

39.—(1) The Secretary of State, with the consent of the Treasury, may,
upon such terms and subject to such conditions as he may determine, give
to a voluntary organisation concerned with homelessness, or with matters
relating to homelessness, assistance by way of grant or loan or partly in
the one way and partly in the other.

(2) A local authority may, upon such terms and subject to such
conditions as they may determine, give to such a voluntary organisation
such assistance as is mentioned in subsection (1), and may also assist such
an organisation by—

   (a) permitting them to use premises belonging to the authority upon
       such terms and subject to such conditions as may be agreed,

   (b) making available furniture or other goods, whether by way of gift,
       loan or otherwise, and

   (c) making available the services of staff employed by the authority.

(3) No assistance shall be given under subsection (1) or (2) unless the
voluntary organisation first give an undertaking—

   (a) that they will use the money, furniture or other goods or premises
       made available to them for a specified purpose, and

   (b) that they will, if the person giving the assistance serves notice on
       them requiring them to do so, furnish, within the period of 21 days
       beginning with the date on which the notice is served, a certificate
       giving such information as may reasonably be required by the
       notice with respect to the manner in which the assistance given to
       them is being used.

(4) The conditions subject to which assistance is given under this section
shall in all cases include, in addition to any conditions determined or
agreed under subsection (1) or (2), conditions requiring the voluntary
organisation to—

   (a) keep proper books of account and have them audited in such
       manner as may be specified,

   (b) keep records indicating how they have used the money, furniture
       or other goods or premises made available to them, and

   (c) submit the books of account and records for inspection by the
       person giving the assistance.

(5) If it appears to the person giving the assistance that the voluntary
organisation have failed to carry out their undertaking as to the purpose
for which the assistance was to be used, he shall take all reasonable steps
to recover from the organisation an amount equal to the amount of the
assistance; but no sum is so recoverable unless he has first served on the

voluntary organisation a notice specifying the amount which in his opinion is recoverable and the basis on which that amount has been calculated.

Supplementary provisions

False statements, withholding information and failure to disclose change of circumstances

40.—(1) If a person, with intent to induce a local authority to believe, in connection with the exercise of their functions under this Part, that he or another person—

(a) is homeless or threatened with homelessness, or

(b) has a priority need, or

(c) did not become homeless or threatened with homelessness intentionally,

knowingly or recklessly makes a statement which is false in a material particular, or knowingly withholds information which the authority have reasonably required him to give in connection with the exercise of those functions, he shall be guilty of an offence.

(2) If before an applicant receives notification of the local authority's decision on his application there is any change of facts material to his case, he shall notify the authority as soon as possible; and the authority shall explain to every applicant, in ordinary language, the duty imposed on him by this subsection and the effect of subsection (3).

(3) A person who fails to comply with subsection (2) commits an offence unless he shows that he was not given the explanation required by that subsection or that he had some other reasonable excuse for non-compliance.

(4) A person guilty of an offence under this section shall be liable on summary conviction to a fine not exceeding level 5 on the standard scale.

Meaning of accommodation available for occupation

41. For the purposes of this Part accommodation shall be regarded as available for a person's occupation only if it is available for occupation both by him and by any other person who might reasonably be expected to reside with him; and references to securing accommodation for a person's occupation shall be construed accordingly.

Application of this Part to cases arising in England or Wales

42.—(1) Sections 33 and 34 (referral of application to another local authority and duties to persons whose applications are referred) apply—

(a) to applications referred by a local authority in England or Wales in pursuance of section 67(1) of the Housing Act 1985, and

(b) to persons whose applications are so transferred,

as they apply to cases arising under this Part.

(2) Section 38 (duty of other authorities to co-operate with local authority) applies to a request by a local authority in England or Wales under section 72 of the Housing Act 1985 as it applies to a request by a local authority in Scotland.

(3) In this Part, in relation to England and Wales—

(a) "local authority" means a local housing authority within the meaning of section 1(1) of the said Act of 1985 and references to the district of such an authority are to the area of the council concerned,

(b) "social work authority" means a social services authority for the purposes of the Local Authority Social Services Act 1970, as defined in section 1 of that Act;

and in section 38(a) (requests for co-operation) "development corporation" means a development corporation established by an order made or having effect as if made under the New Towns Act 1981 or the Commission for the New Towns.

Minor definitions

43. In this Part—
"accommodation available for occupation" has the meaning assigned to it by section 41;
"applicant (for housing accommodation)" has the meaning assigned to it by section 28(1);
"homeless" has the meaning assigned to it by section 24(1) to (3);
"homeless intentionally or threatened with homelessness intentionally" has the meaning assigned to it by section 26;
"local connection (in relation to the district of a local authority)" has the meaning assigned to it by section 27;
"priority need (for accommodation)" has the meaning assigned to it by section 25;
"relevant authority" means a local authority or social work authority;
"securing accommodation for a person's occupation" has the meaning assigned to it by section 41;
"social work authority" means a local authority for the purposes of the Social Work (Scotland) Act 1968, that is to say, a regional or islands council;
"threatened with homelessness" has the meaning assigned to it by section 24(4);
"voluntary organisation" means a body, not being a public or local authority, whose activities are carried on otherwise than for profit.

PART III

RIGHTS OF PUBLIC SECTOR TENANTS

Security of tenure

Secure tenancies

44.—(1) Subject to subsection (4) and to section 45 and section 52(6), a tenancy (whenever created) of a house shall be a secure tenancy if—
(a) the house is let as a separate dwelling;
(b) the tenant is an individual and the house is his only or principal home; and
(c) the landlord is one of the bodies mentioned in subsection (2).
(2) The bodies referred to in subsections (1)(c) and (7) are the bodies mentioned in section 61(2)(a) and any housing trust which was in existence on 13th November 1953.
(3) Where a tenancy of a house is held jointly by two or more individuals, the requirements of subsection (1)(b) shall be deemed to be satisfied if all the joint tenants are individuals and at least one of the joint tenants occupies the house as his only or principal residence.
(4) A tenancy shall not be a secure tenancy if it is a tenancy of a kind mentioned in Schedule 2.
(5) Where the tenancy of a house is excluded from being a secure tenancy by reason only of the operation of paragraph 1 or 8 of Schedule 2, sections 53 to 60 shall nevertheless apply to that tenancy as if it were a secure tenancy.

(6) A tenancy which has become a secure tenancy shall continue to be a secure tenancy notwithstanding that the requirements of subsection (1)(b) may have ceased to be fulfilled.

(7) Where a tenant under a secure tenancy is accommodated temporarily in another house of which the landlord is a body mentioned in subsection (2), while the house which he normally occupies is not available for occupation, the other house shall be deemed for the purposes of this Part, except sections 46 and 47, to be the house which he normally occupies.

Special provision for housing associations

45.—(1) A tenancy shall not be a secure tenancy at any time when the interest of the landlord belongs to a registered housing association which is a co-operative housing association.

(2) Sections 44, 46 to 50, 51, 52, and 82 to 84 shall apply to a tenancy at any time when the interest of the landlord belongs to a housing association which is a co-operative housing association and is not registered.

(3) If a registered housing association which is a registered co-operative housing association ceases to be registered, it shall notify those of its tenants who thereby become secure tenants.

(4) Notice under subsection (3) shall be given in writing to each tenant concerned, within the period of 21 days beginning with the date on which the association ceases to be registered.

(5) In this section—
  (a) references to registration in relation to a housing association are to registration under the Housing Associations Act 1985;
  (b) "co-operative housing association" has the same meaning as in section 300(1)(b).

Restriction on termination of secure tenancy

46.—(1) Notwithstanding any provision contained in the tenancy agreement, a secure tenancy may not be brought to an end except—
  (a) by the death of the tenant (or, where there is more than one, of any of them), where there is no qualified person within the meaning of section 52;
  (b) by operation of section 52(4) or (5);
  (c) by written agreement between the landlord and the tenant;
  (d) by operation of section 50(2);
  (e) by an order for recovery of possession under section 48(2); or
  (f) by 4 weeks' notice given by the tenant to the landlord.

(2) If, while the house which the tenant under a secure tenancy normally occupies is not available for occupation, the tenant is accommodated temporarily in another house of which the landlord is a body mentioned in section 44(2), either—
  (a) by agreement; or
  (b) following an order under section 48(2) (in a case where an order has also been made under subsection (5) of that section),
the landlord shall not be entitled to bring the tenant's occupation of the other house to an end before the house which he normally occupies is available for occupation unless the secure tenancy has been brought to an end.

Proceedings for possession

47.—(1) The landlord under a secure tenancy may raise proceedings for recovery of possession of the house by way of summary cause in the sheriff court of the district in which it is situated.

(2) Proceedings for recovery of possession of a house subject to a secure tenancy may not be raised unless—

(a) the landlord has served on the tenant a notice complying with subsection (3);

(b) the proceedings are raised on or after the date specified in the said notice; and

(c) the notice is in force at the time when the proceedings are raised.

(3) A notice under this section shall be in a form prescribed by the Secretary of State by statutory instrument, and shall specify—

(a) the ground, being a ground set out in Part I of Schedule 3, on which proceedings for recovery of possession are to be raised; and

(b) a date, not earlier than 4 weeks from the date of service of the notice or the date on which the tenancy could have been brought to an end by a notice to quit had it not been a secure tenancy, whichever is later, on or after which the landlord may raise proceedings for recovery of possession.

(4) A notice under this section shall cease to be in force 6 months after the date specified in it in accordance with subsection (3)(b), or when it is withdrawn by the landlord, whichever is earlier.

Powers of sheriff in proceedings

48.—(1) The court may, as it thinks fit, adjourn proceedings under section 47 on a ground set out in any of paragraphs 1 to 7 and 16 of Part I of Schedule 3 for a period or periods, with or without imposing conditions as to payment of outstanding rent or other conditions.

(2) Subject to subsection (1), in proceedings under section 47 the court shall make an order for recovery of possession if it appears to the court that the landlord has a ground for recovery of possession, being—

(a) a ground set out in any of paragraphs 1 to 7 of that Part and specified in the notice required by section 47 and that it is reasonable to make the order; or

(b) a ground set out in any of paragraphs 8 to 15 of that Part and so specified and that other suitable accommodation will be available for the tenant when the order takes effect; or

(c) the ground set out in paragraph 16 of that Part and so specified and both that it is reasonable to make the order and that other suitable accommodation will be available as aforesaid.

(3) Part II of Schedule 3 shall have effect to determine whether accommodation is suitable for the purposes of subsection (2)(b) or (c).

(4) An order under subsection (2) shall appoint a date for recovery of possession and shall have the effect of—

(a) terminating the tenancy; and

(b) giving the landlord the right to recover possession of the house, at that date.

(5) Where, in proceedings under section 47 on the ground set out in paragraph 10 of Part I of Schedule 3, it appears to the court that it is the intention of the landlord—

(a) that substantial work will be carried out on the building (or a part of the building) which comprises or includes the house; and

(b) that the tenant should return to the house after the work is completed,

the court shall make an order that the tenant shall be entitled to return to the house after the work is completed; and subsection (4)(a) shall not apply in such a case.

Rights of landlord where a secure tenancy appears to have been abandoned

49.—(1) This section shall have effect where a landlord who has let a house under a secure tenancy has reasonable grounds for believing that—

(a) the house is unoccupied; and

(b) the tenant does not intend to occupy it as his home.

(2) The landlord shall be entitled to enter the house at any time for the purpose of securing the house and any fittings, fixtures or furniture against vandalism.

(3) For the purposes of subsection (2), the landlord and its servants or agents may open, by force if necessary, doors and lockfast places.

(4) The landlord may take possession of the house in accordance with section 50.

Repossession

50.—(1) A landlord wishing to take possession of a house under section 49(4) shall serve on the tenant a notice—

(a) stating that the landlord has reason to believe that the house is unoccupied and that the tenant does not intend to occupy it as his home;

(b) requiring the tenant to inform the landlord in writing within 4 weeks of service of the notice if he intends to occupy the house as his home; and

(c) informing the tenant that, if it appears to the landlord at the end of the said period of 4 weeks that the tenant does not intend so to occupy the house, the secure tenancy will be terminated forthwith.

(2) Where the landlord has—

(a) served on the tenant a notice which complies with subsection (1); and

(b) made such inquiries as may be necessary to satisfy the landlord that the house is unoccupied and that the tenant does not intend to occupy it as his home,

and at the end of the period of 4 weeks mentioned in subsection (1)(c) is so satisfied, it may serve a further notice on the tenant bringing the tenancy to an end forthwith.

(3) Where a tenancy has been terminated in accordance with this section the landlord shall be entitled to take possession of the house forthwith without any further proceedings.

(4) The Secretary of State may by order made by statutory instrument make provision for the landlord to secure the safe custody and delivery to the tenant of any property which is found in a house to which this section applies, and in particular—

(a) for requiring charges to be paid in respect of such property before it is delivered to the tenant; and

(b) for authorising the disposal of such property, if the tenant has not arranged for its delivery to him before the expiry of such period as the order may specify, and the application of any proceeds towards any costs incurred by the landlord and any rent due but unpaid by the tenant to the landlord.

Tenant's right of recourse to sheriff

51.—(1) A tenant under a secure tenancy who is aggrieved by termination of the tenancy by the landlord under section 50(2) may raise proceedings by summary application within 6 months after the date of the termination in the sheriff court of the district in which the house is situated.

(2) Where in proceedings under this section it appears to the sheriff that—
(a) the landlord has failed to comply with any provision of section 50; or
(b) the landlord did not have reasonable grounds for finding that the house was unoccupied, or did not have reasonable grounds for finding that the tenant did not intend to occupy it as his home; or
(c) the landlord was in error in finding that the tenant did not intend to occupy the house as his home, and the tenant had reasonable cause, by reason of illness or otherwise, for failing to notify the landlord of his intention so to occupy it,

he shall—
(i) where the house has not been let to a new tenant, make an order that the secure tenancy shall continue; or
(ii) in any other case, direct the landlord to make other suitable accommodation available to the tenant.

(3) Part II of Schedule 3 to this Act shall have effect to determine whether accommodation is suitable for the purposes of subsection (2)(ii).

Succession

Succession to secure tenancy

52.—(1) On the death of a tenant under a secure tenancy, the tenancy shall pass by operation of law to a qualified person, unless—
(a) there is no qualified person, or the qualified person declines the tenancy under subsection (4); or
(b) the tenancy is terminated by operation of subsection (5).

(2) For the purposes of this section, a qualified person is—
(a) a person whose only or principal home at the time of the tenant's death was the house and who was at that time either—
(i) the tenant's spouse; or
(ii) living with the tenant as husband and wife; and
(b) where the tenancy was held jointly by two or more individuals, a surviving tenant where the house was his only or principal home at the time of the tenant's death;
(c) where there is no person falling within paragraph (a) or (b), a member of the tenant's family who has attained the age of 16 years where the house was his only or principal home throughout the period of 12 months immediately preceding the tenant's death.

(3) Where there is more than one qualified person, the benefit of the provisions of subsection (1) or, as the case may be, of subsection (6) shall accrue—
(a) to such qualified person; or
(b) to such two or more qualified persons as joint tenants,
as may be decided by agreement between all the qualified persons or, failing agreement within 4 weeks of the death of the tenant, as the landlord shall decide.

(4) A qualified person who is entitled to the benefit of subsection (1) may decline the tenancy by giving the landlord notice in writing within 4 weeks of the tenant's death, and—
(a) he shall vacate the house within 3 months thereafter;
(b) he shall be liable to pay rent which becomes due after the said death only in respect of any rental period (that is to say, a period in respect of which an instalment of rent falls to be paid) during any part of which he has occupied the house after the said death.

(5) A secure tenancy which has passed under subsection (1) to a qualified person shall not, on the death of a tenant (or one of joint tenants) so pass on a second occasion, and accordingly the secure tenancy shall be terminated when such a death occurs; but the provisions of this subsection shall not operate so as to terminate the secure tenancy of any tenant under a joint tenancy where such a joint tenant continues to use the house as his only or principal home.

(6) Where a secure tenancy is terminated by operation of subsection (5) and there is a qualified person, he shall be entitled to continue as tenant for a period not exceeding 6 months, but the tenancy shall cease to be a secure tenancy.

(7) Where a tenant gives up a secure tenancy in order to occupy another house which is subject to a secure tenancy, whether by agreement or following termination of the first tenancy by an order under section 48(2)(b), for the purposes of subsections (2) and (5) those tenancies shall be treated as being a single secure tenancy.

Leases

Tenant's right to written lease

53.—(1) Every secure tenancy shall be constituted by writing which shall be probative or holograph of the parties.

(2) It shall be the duty of the landlord under a secure tenancy to draw up the documents required to comply with subsection (1), to ensure that they are duly executed before the commencement of the tenancy and to supply a copy of the documents to the tenant.

(3) A tenant shall not be required to pay any fees in respect of anything done under subsection (2).

Restriction on variation of terms of secure tenancies

54.—(1) Notwithstanding anything contained in the tenancy agreement, the terms of a secure tenancy may not be varied, except—

  (a) by agreement between the landlord and the tenant; or

  (b) under subsection (2) or (4).

(2) The rent or any other charge payable under a secure tenancy may, without the tenancy being terminated, and subject to section 58 of the Rent (Scotland) Act 1984, be increased with effect from the beginning of any rental period (that is to say, a period in respect of which an instalment of rent falls to be paid) by a written notice of increase given by the landlord to the tenant not less than 4 weeks before the beginning of the rental period (or any earlier day on which the payment of rent in respect of that period falls to be made).

(3) Where—

  (a) a landlord wishes to vary the terms or conditions of a secure tenancy, but the tenant refuses or fails to agree the variation; or

  (b) a tenant wishes to vary any term of a secure tenancy which restricts his use or enjoyment of the house, on the ground that—

    (i) by reason of changes in the character of the house or of the neighbourhood or other circumstances which the sheriff may deem material, the term is or has become unreasonable or inappropriate; or

    (ii) the term is unduly burdensome compared with any benefit which would result from its performance; or

    (iii) the existence of the term impedes some reasonable use of the house,

but the landlord refuses or fails to agree the variation,
the landlord or, as the case may be, the tenant may raise proceedings by
way of summary application in the sheriff court of the district in which the
house is situated.

(4) In proceedings under subsection (3), the sheriff may make such
order varying any term of the tenancy (other than a term relating to the
amount of rent or of any other charge payable by the tenant) as he thinks
it reasonable to make in all the circumstances, having particular regard to
the safety of any person and to any likelihood of damage to the house or
to any premises of which it forms part, including if the sheriff thinks fit an
order that the tenant shall pay to the landlord such sum as the sheriff
thinks just to compensate him for any patrimonial loss occasioned by the
variation; and such an order shall not have the effect of terminating the
tenancy.

(5) At any time before he grants an order in proceedings under
subsection (3)(b), the sheriff may order the tenant to serve a copy of his
application on any person who, in the capacity of owner or tenant of any
land—

(a) appeals to the sheriff to benefit from the term of which variation
is sought; or

(b) appears to him to be adversely affected by the proposed variation.

(6) An agreement under subsection (1)(a) shall be in writing which is
probative or holograph of the parties, and it shall be the duty of the
landlord to draw up the said writing and to ensure that it is duly executed.

Subletting

No subletting by secure tenant without landlord's consent

55.—(1) It shall be a term of every secure tenancy that the tenant shall
not assign, sublet or otherwise give up to another person possession of
the house or any part thereof or take in a lodger except with the consent
in writing of the landlord, which shall not be unreasonably withheld.

(2) The landlord may refuse consent under this section if it appears to
it that a payment other than—

(a) a rent which is in its opinion a reasonable rent; or

(b) a deposit returnable at the termination of the assignation, subletting
or other transaction given as security for the subtenant's obligations
for accounts for supplies of gas, electricity, telephone or other
domestic supplies and for damage to the house or contents, which
in its opinion is reasonable,

has been or is to be received by the tenant in consideration of the
assignation, subletting or other transaction.

(3) This section shall not apply to any assignation, subletting or other
transaction entered into before 3rd October 1980 provided that the
consent of the landlord to the transaction and to the rent which is being
charged has been obtained.

(4) An assignation, subletting or other transaction to which this section
applies shall not be a protected tenancy or a statutory tenancy within the
meaning of the Rent (Scotland) Act 1984, nor shall Part VII of that Act
apply to such an assignation, sublet or other transaction.

(5) In this section and in section 56, "subtenant" means a person
entitled to possession of a house or any part thereof under an assignation,
subletting or other transaction to which this section applies, and includes
a lodger.

(6) The provisions of Schedule 4 shall have effect as terms of every
secure tenancy.

Rent payable by subtenants

56.—(1) It shall be a term of every secure tenancy—
    (a) that the tenant shall notify the landlord of any proposed increase in a rent to which this section applies; and
    (b) that no increase shall be made in a rent to which this section applies if the landlord objects.

(2) Where a landlord under a secure tenancy has given consent to an assignation, subletting or other transaction under section 55, subsection (1) shall apply to the rent payable by the subtenant at the commencement of the assignation, subletting or other transaction.

Repairs and improvements

Landlord's consent to work

57.—(1) It shall be a term of every secure tenancy that the tenant shall not carry out work, other than interior decoration, in relation to the house without the consent in writing of the landlord, which shall not be unreasonably withheld.

(2) In this section and in Schedule 5, "work" means—
    (a) alteration, improvement or enlargement of the house or of any fittings or fixtures;
    (b) addition of new fittings or fixtures;
    (c) erection of a garage, shed or other structure,
but does not include repairs or maintenance of any of these.

(3) The provisions of Schedule 5 shall have effect as terms of every secure tenancy.

Reimbursement of cost of work

58.—(1) On the termination of a secure tenancy, the landlord shall have the power (in addition to any other power which it has to make such payments) to make any payment to the tenant which it considers to be appropriate in respect of any work carried out by him (or by any predecessor of his as tenant under the same secure tenancy) with the consent of the landlord under section 57, which has materially added to the price which the house might be expected to fetch if sold on the open market.

(2) The amount of any payment under subsection (1) shall not exceed the cost of the work in respect of which it is made, after deduction of the amount of any grant paid or payable under Part I of the Act of 1974 or under Part XIII.

(3) Where a secure tenancy has been terminated (under section 46(1)(a)) by the death of the tenant, a payment under subsection (1) may be made to the tenant's personal representatives.

Effect of works on rent

59. No account shall be taken at any time in the assessment of rent to be payable under a secure tenancy by a tenant who has carried out work on the house or by a person who has succeeded him in the tenancy or by the spouse of such a person of any improvement in the value or amenities of the house resulting from the work carried out by the tenant.

Scheme giving tenant a right to carry out repairs

60.—(1) The Secretary of State may by regulations make a scheme entitling a tenant under a secure tenancy, subject to and in accordance with the provisions of the scheme—

(a) to carry out to the house which is the subject of the secure tenancy repairs which the landlord is under an obligation to carry out; and

(b) after carrying out the repairs, to recover from the landlord such sums (not exceeding the costs that would have been incurred by the landlord in carrying out the repairs) as may be determined by or under the scheme.

(2) Regulations under this section may make different provision with respect to different cases or descriptions of case and may make such procedural, incidental, supplementary or transitional provision as may appear to the Secretary of State to be necessary or expedient.

(3) Without prejudice to the generality of subsection (2) regulations under this section—

(a) may provide for any question arising under the scheme to be determined in such manner as the regulations may specify; and

(b) may provide that where a tenant under a secure tenancy makes application under the scheme, the obligations of the landlord in respect of repairs to the house shall cease to apply for such period and to such extent as may be determined by or under the scheme.

(4) Regulations under this section shall be made by statutory instrument subject to annulment in pursuance of a resolution of either House of Parliament.

Right to buy

Secure tenant's right to purchase

61.—(1) Notwithstanding anything contained in any agreement, a tenant of a house to which this section applies (or such one or more of joint tenants as may be agreed between them) shall, subject to this Part, have the right to purchase the house at a price fixed under section 62.

(2) This section applies to every house let under a secure tenancy where—

(a) the landlord is either—

(i) an islands or district council, or a joint board or joint committee of an islands or district council or the common good of an islands or district council, or any trust under the control of an islands or district council; or

(ii) a regional council, or a joint board or joint committee of 2 or more regional councils, or any trust under the control of a regional council; or

(iii) a development corporation (including an urban development corporation); or

(iv) the Scottish Special Housing Association; or

(v) the Housing Corporation; or

(vi) a registered housing association; or

(vii) a housing co-operative; or

(viii) a police authority in Scotland; or

(ix) a fire authority in Scotland; and

(b) the landlord is the heritable proprietor of the house or, in the case of a landlord who is a housing co-operative, a body mentioned in paragraph (a)(i) is the heritable proprietor; and

(c) immediately prior to the date of service of an application to purchase, the tenant has been for not less than 2 years in occupation of a house (including accommodation provided as mentioned in subsection (11)(n)) or of a succession of houses provided by any persons mentioned in subsection (11).

(3) This section also applies to a house let under a secure tenancy granted in pursuance of section 282(3) (grant of secure tenancy on

acquisition of defective dwelling), if the tenant would not otherwise have the right to purchase under this Part; and where it so applies—
  (a) paragraph (c) of subsection (2) shall not have effect;
  (b) the words "beyond 2" in section 62(3)(b) shall not have effect.
  (4) This section does not apply—
  (a) to a house that is one of a group which has been provided with facilities (including a call system and the services of a warden) specially designed or adapted for the needs of persons of pensionable age or disabled persons; or
  (b) where a landlord which is a registered housing association has at no time received a grant under—
      (i) any enactment mentioned in paragraph 2 of Schedule 1 to the Housing Associations Act 1985 (grants under enactments superseded by the Housing Act 1974);
      (ii) section 31 of the Housing Act 1974 (management grants);
      (iii) section 41 of the Housing Associations Act 1985 (housing association grants);
      (iv) section 54 of that Act (revenue deficit grants);
      (v) section 55 of that Act (hostel deficit grants); or
      (vi) section 59(2) of that Act (grants by local authorities); or
  (c) where such a landlord has at no time let (or had available for letting) more than 100 dwellings; or
  (d) where such a landlord is a charity—
      (i) entered in the register of charities maintained under the Charities Act 1960 by the Charity Commissioners for England and Wales; or
      (ii) which but for section 4(4) of, and paragraph (g) of the Second Schedule to, that Act (exempt charities) would require to be so entered; or
  (e) where by virtue of section 49(2) of the said Act of 1960 (extent) such a landlord is not one to which Part II of that Act (registration of charities, etc.) applies, but—
      (i) the landlord has, in respect of all periods from 14th November 1985 or from the date of first being registered by the Housing Corporation (whichever is the later) claimed and been granted (whether or not retrospectively), under section 360(1) of the Income and Corporation Taxes Act 1970 (special exemptions for charities), exemption from tax; and
      (ii) where such exemption has not been claimed and granted in respect of all periods from the said date of registration, the rules of the landlord, registered under the Industrial and Provident Societies Act 1965 and in force at that date, were such as would have admitted of such exemption had it been claimed as at that date; or
  (f) where, within a neighbourhood, the house is one of a number (not exceeding 14) of houses with a common landlord, being a landlord so mentioned, and it is the practice of that landlord to let at least one half of those houses for occupation by any or all of the following—
      (i) persons who have suffered from, or are suffering from, mental disorder (as defined in the Mental Health (Scotland) Act 1984), physical handicap or addiction to alcohol or other drugs;
      (ii) persons who have been released from prison or other institutions;
      (iii) young persons who have left the care of a local authority,

and a social service is, or special facilities are, provided wholly or partly for the purpose of assisting those persons.

(5) Where the spouse of a tenant or, where there is a joint tenancy, the spouse of a joint tenant, occupies the house as his only or principal home but is not himself a joint tenant, the right to purchase the house under subsection (1) shall not be exercised without the consent of such spouse.

(6) A tenant may exercise his right to purchase, if he so wishes, together with one or more members of his family acting as joint purchasers, provided—

(a) that such members are at least 18 years of age, that they have, during the period of 6 months ending with the date of service of the application to purchase, had their only or principal home with the tenant and that their residence in the house is not a breach of any obligation of the tenancy; or

(b) where the requirements of paragraph (a) are not satisfied, the landlord has consented.

(7) The Secretary of State may by order made by statutory instrument amend, or add to, the descriptions of persons set out in sub-paragraphs (i) to (iii) of paragraph (f) of subsection (4).

(8) The Commissioners of Inland Revenue shall, as regards any registered housing association, at the request of the Secretary of State, provide him and the Housing Corporation with such information as will enable them to determine whether that association is a landlord in respect of which this section will not, by virtue of subsection (4)(d), apply; and where a registered housing association is refused exemption on a claim under section 360(1) of the Income and Corporation Taxes Act 1970 the Commissioners shall forthwith inform the Secretary of State and the Housing Corporation of that fact.

(9) Where information has been received by the Housing Corporation under subsection (8) and having regard to that information the Corporation is satisfied that the housing association to which it relates is not a landlord in respect of which this section applies, they shall make an entry to that effect in the register of housing associations maintained by them under section 3(1) of the Housing Associations Act 1985; and they shall cancel that entry where subsequent information so received in relation to that housing association is inconsistent with their being so satisfied.

(10) In this section and the following section—

(a) references to occupation of a house include occupation—

(i) in the case of joint tenants, by any one of them;

(ii) by any person occupying the house rent-free;

(iii) as the spouse of the tenant, joint tenant or of any such person;

(iv) as the child, or the spouse of a child, of a tenant or a person occupying the house rent free who has succeeded, directly or indirectly, to the rights of that person in a house occupation of which would be reckonable for the purposes of this section; but only in relation to any period when the child, or as the case may be spouse of the child, is at least 16 years of age; or

(v) in the discretion of the landlord, as a member of the family of a tenant or a person occupying the house rent free who, not being that person's spouse or child (or child's spouse), has succeeded, directly or indirectly, to such rights as are mentioned in paragraph (iv); but only in relation to any period when the member of the family is at least 16 years of age.

(b) for the purpose of determining the period of occupation—

       (i) any interruption in occupation of 12 months or less shall be regarded as not affecting continuity; and

      (ii) any interruption in occupation of more than 12 months and less than 24 months may at the discretion of the landlord be regarded as not affecting continuity.

(11) The persons providing houses referred to in subsection (2)(c) (occupation requirement for exercise of right to purchase) and in section 62(3)(b) (calculation of the discount from the market value) are—

(a) a regional, islands or district council in Scotland; any local authority in England and Wales or in Northern Ireland; and the statutory predecessors of any such council or authority, or the common good of any such council, or any trust under the control of any such council;

(b) the Commission for the New Towns;

(c) a development corporation, an urban development corporation; and any development corporation established under corresponding legislation in England and Wales or in Northern Ireland; and the statutory predecessors of any such authority;

(d) the Scottish Special Housing Association;

(e) a registered housing association;

(f) the Housing Corporation;

(g) a housing co-operative within the meaning of section 22 or a housing co-operative within the meaning of section 27B of the Housing Act 1985;

(h) the Development Board for Rural Wales;

(i) the Northern Ireland Housing Executive or any statutory predecessor;

(j) a police authority or the statutory predecessors of any such authority;

(k) a fire authority or the statutory predecessors of any such authority;

(l) a water authority in Scotland; any water authority constituted under corresponding legislation in England and Wales or in Northern Ireland; and the statutory predecessors of any such authority;

(m) the Secretary of State, where the house was at the material time used for the purposes of the Scottish Prison Service or of a prison service for which the Home Office or the Northern Ireland Office have responsibility;

(n) the Crown, in relation to accommodation provided in connection with service whether by the tenant or his spouse as a member of the regular armed forces of the Crown;

(o) the Secretary of State, where the house was at the material time used for the purposes of a health board constituted under section 2 of the National Health Services (Scotland) Act 1978 or for the purposes of a corresponding board in England and Wales, or for the purposes of the statutory predecessors of any such board; or the Department of Health and Social Services for Northern Ireland, where the house was at the material time used for the purposes of a Health and Personal Services Board in Northern Ireland, or for the purposes of the statutory predecessors of any such board;

(p) the Secretary of State, or the Minister of Agriculture, Fisheries and Food, where the house was at the material time used for the purposes of the Forestry Commission;

(q) the Secretary of State, where the house was at the material time used for the purposes of a State Hospital provided by him under section 90 of the Mental Health (Scotland) Act 1984 or for the purposes of any hospital provided under corresponding legislation in England and Wales;

(r) the Commissioners of Northern Lighthouses;

(s) the Trinity House;
(t) the Secretary of State, where the house was at the material time used for the purposes of Her Majesty's Coastguard;
(u) the United Kingdom Atomic Energy Authority;
(v) the Secretary of State, where the house was at the material time used for the purposes of any function transferred to him under section 1(2) of the Defence (Transfer of Functions) Act 1964 or any function relating to defence conferred on him by or under any subsequent enactment;
(w) such other person as the Secretary of State may by order made by statutory instrument subject to annulment in pursuance of a resolution of either House of Parliament prescribe.

The price

62.—(1) Subject to subsections (7) and (8), the price at which a tenant shall be entitled to purchase a house under this Part shall be fixed by subtracting a discount from the market value of the house.

(2) The market value for the purposes of this section shall be determined by—

(a) a qualified valuer nominated by the landlord and accepted by the tenant; or
(b) the district valuer,

as if the house were available for sale on the open market with vacant possession at the date of service of the application to purchase.

For the purposes of this subsection, no account shall be taken of any element in the market value of the house which reflects an increase in value as a result of work the cost of which would qualify for a reimbursement under section 58.

(3) Subject to subsection (5), the discount for the purposes of subsection (1) shall be—

(a) 32 per cent. of the market value of the house except—
    (i) where the house is a flat, it shall be 44 per cent. of the market value;
    (ii) where the house is one to which section 61(3) applies, it shall be 30 per cent. or, where it is a flat, 40 per cent. of the market value;

together with

(b) an additional one per cent. or, where the house is a flat, two per cent., of the market value for every year beyond 2 of continuous occupation by the appropriate person, immediately preceding the date of service of the application to purchase, of a house (including accommodation provided as mentioned in section 61(11)(n)) or of a succession of houses provided by any persons mentioned in section 61(11),

up to a maximum discount of 60 per cent., or where the house is a flat, 70 per cent. of the market value.

(4) For the purposes of subsection (3), the "appropriate person" is the tenant, or if it would result in a higher discount and if she is cohabiting with him at the date of service of the application to purchase, his spouse; and where joint tenants are joint purchasers the "appropriate person" shall be whichever tenant (or, as the case may be, spouse) has the longer or longest such occupation.

(5) The Secretary of State may by order made with the consent of the Treasury provide that, in such cases as may be specified in the order—

(a) the minimum percentage discount,
(b) the percentage increase for each complete year of the qualifying period after the first two, or

  (c) the maximum percentage discount,
shall be such percentage, higher than that specified in subsection (3), as
may be specified in the order.

  (6) An order under subsection (5)—

   (a) may make different provision with respect to different cases or
descriptions of case,

   (b) may contain such incidental, supplementary or transitional
provisions as appear to the Secretary of State to be necessary
or expedient, and

   (c) shall be made by statutory instrument and shall not be made
unless a draft of it has been laid before and approved by
resolution of each House of Parliament.

  (7) Where the house was first let under a secure tenancy (or under a
tenancy which, if this Part had then been in force, would have been a
secure tenancy) after 31st December 1978, the price fixed under subsection
(1) shall not be less than—

   (a) the outstanding debt incurred after that date (either or both)—

    (i) in providing;

    (ii) in making improvements (other than by way of repair or
maintenance) to,

   the house; or

   (b) the market value of the house determined under subsection (2),
whichever is the lesser, except in such cases as the Secretary of State may,
by order made by statutory instrument subject to annulment in pursuance
of a resolution of either House of Parliament, with the consent of the
Treasury, prescribe.

  (8) Where the house was first let under a tenancy which, if this Part
had then been in force, would have been a secure tenancy, on or before
the date mentioned in subsection (7) but an outstanding debt has been
incurred after that date in making improvements (other than by way of
repair or maintenance) to the house, the price fixed under subsection (1)
shall not be less than—

   (a) that outstanding debt; or

   (b) the market value of the house determined under subsection (2),
whichever is the lesser, except in such cases as the Secretary of State may,
by order made as is mentioned in subsection (7), prescribe.

  (9) In subsections (7) and (8), "outstanding debt" means—

   (a) in relation to subsection (7)(a)(i), any undischarged debt arising
from—

    (i) the cost of the erection or acquisition of the house;
together with

    (ii) the cost of acquisition of the site of the house;

    (iii) the cost of works of improvement, alteration, or major
structural repair;

    (iv) administrative costs attributable to the matters mentioned
in sub-paragraphs (i) to (iii); and

    (v) where the landlord is the Housing Corporation, or a
registered housing association, any proportion of capital
grants which it must repay on the house being sold;

   (b) in relation to subsection (7)(a)(ii) and in subsection (8), any
undischarged debt arising from the cost of works of improvement together with—

    (i) administrative costs attributable to these works; and

    (ii) any proportion of capital grants as mentioned in para-
graph (a)(v) where the landlord is a body mentioned
there.

  (10) Where at the date of service of an offer to sell under section 63
any of the costs referred to in subsection (9) are not known, the landlord

shall make an estimate of such unknown costs for the purposes of that subsection.

(11) The Secretary of State may, with the consent of the Treasury, by order—

(a) substitute a later date in subsection (7);

(b) provide that subsections (7)(a)(ii), (8) and (9) shall apply subject to such modifications as may be specified in the order.

(12) Any such order may—

(a) make different provision in relation to different areas, cases or classes of case;

(b) exclude certain areas, cases or classes of case.

(13) An order under subsection (11) shall be made by statutory instrument and shall be subject to annulment in pursuance of a resolution of either House of Parliament.

Procedure

Application to purchase and offer to sell

63.—(1) A tenant who seeks to exercise a right to purchase a house under section 61 shall serve on the landlord a notice (referred to in this Part as an "application to purchase") which shall be in such form as the Secretary of State shall by order made by statutory instrument prescribe, and shall contain—

(a) notice that the tenant seeks to exercise the right to purchase;

(b) a statement of any period of occupancy of a house on which the tenant intends to rely for the purposes of sections 61 and 62; and

(c) the name of any joint purchaser within the meaning of section 61(6).

(2) Where an application to purchase is served on a landlord, and the landlord does not serve a notice of refusal under sections 68 to 70 it shall, within 2 months after service of the application to purchase, serve on the tenant a notice (referred to in this Part as an "offer to sell") containing—

(a) the market value of the house determined under section 62(2);

(b) the discount calculated under section 62(3);

(c) the price fixed under section 62(1);

(d) any conditions which the landlord intends to impose under section 64; and

(e) an offer to sell the house to the tenant and any joint purchaser named in the application to purchase at the price referred to in paragraph (c) and under the conditions referred to in paragraph (d).

Conditions of sale

64.—(1) Subject to section 75, an offer to sell under section 63(2) shall contain such conditions as are reasonable, provided that—

(a) the conditions shall have the effect of ensuring that the tenant has as full enjoyment and use of the house as owner as he has had as tenant;

(b) the conditions shall secure to the tenant such additional rights as are necessary for his reasonable enjoyment and use of the house as owner (including, without prejudice to the foregoing generality, common rights in any part of the building of which the house forms part) and shall impose on the tenant any necessary duties relative to rights so secured; and

(c) the conditions shall include such terms as are necessary to entitle the tenant to receive a good and marketable title to the house.

(2) A condition which imposes a new charge or an increase of an existing charge for the provision of a service in relation to the house shall provide for the charge to be in reasonable proportion to the cost to the landlord of providing the service.

(3) No condition shall be imposed under this section which has the effect of requiring the tenant to pay any expenses of the landlord.

(4) Subject to subsection (6), no condition shall be imposed under this section which has the effect of requiring the tenant or any of his successors in title to offer to the landlord, or to any other person, an option to purchase the house in advance of its sale to a third party, except in the case of a house which has facilities which are substantially different from those of an ordinary house and which has been designed or adapted for occupation by a person of pensionable age or disabled person whose special needs require accommodation of the kind provided by the house.

(5) Where an option to purchase permitted under subsection (4) is exercised, the price to be paid for the house shall be determined by the district valuer who shall have regard to the market value of the house at the time of the purchase and to any amount due to the landlord under section 72 (recovery of discount on early re-sale).

(6) Subsection (4) shall not apply to houses in an area which is designated a rural area by the islands or district council within whose area it is situated where the Secretary of State, on the application of the islands or district council concerned, makes an order, which shall be made by statutory instrument subject to annulment in pursuance of a resolution of either House of Parliament, to that effect.

(7) An order under subsection (6) may be made where—
    (a) within the said rural area more than one-third of all relevant houses have been sold; and
    (b) the Secretary of State is satisfied that an unreasonable proportion of the houses sold have been resold and are not being used as the only or principal home of the owner.

(8) For the purposes of subsection (7)(a), a "relevant house" is one of which—
    (a) at 3rd October 1980, the council concerned, or
    (b) at 7th January 1987, a registered housing association,
is landlord.

(9) A condition imposed by virtue of subsection (6) shall not have effect in relation to any house for more than 10 years from the date of its conveyance to a tenant in pursuance of his right to purchase under this Part and subsection (5) shall apply to any option to purchase exercised under such a condition.

Variation of conditions

65.—(1) Where an offer to sell is served on a tenant and he wishes to exercise his right to purchase, but—
    (a) he considers that a condition contained in the offer to sell is unreasonable; or
    (b) he wishes to have a new condition included in it; or
    (c) he has not previously notified the landlord of his intention to exercise that right together with a joint purchaser, but now wishes to do so; or
    (d) he has previously notified the landlord of his intention to exercise that right together with any joint purchaser but now wishes to exercise the right without that joint purchaser,
he may request the landlord to strike out or vary the condition, or to include the new condition, or to make the offer to sell to the tenant and the joint purchaser, or to withdraw the offer to sell in respect of the joint

purchaser, as the case may be, by serving on the landlord within one month after service of the offer to sell a notice in writing setting out his request; and if the landlord agrees, it shall accordingly serve an amended offer to sell on the tenant within one month of service of the notice setting out the request.

(2) A tenant who is aggrieved by the refusal of the landlord to agree to strike out or vary a condition, or to include a new condition, or to make the offer to sell to the tenant and the joint purchaser, or to withdraw the offer to sell in respect of any joint purchaser under subsection (1), or by his failure timeously to serve an amended offer to sell under the said subsection, may, within one month or, with the consent of the landlord given in writing before the expiry of the said period of one month, within two months of the refusal or failure, refer the matter to the Lands Tribunal for determination.

(3) In proceedings under subsection (2), the Lands Tribunal may, as it thinks fit, uphold the condition or strike it out or vary it, or insert the new condition or order that the offer to sell be made to the tenant and the joint purchaser, or order that the offer to sell be withdrawn in respect of any joint purchaser, and where its determination results in a variation of the terms of the offer to sell, it shall order the landlord to serve on the tenant an amended offer to sell accordingly within 2 months thereafter.

Notice of acceptance

66.—(1) Where an offer to sell is served on a tenant and he wishes to exercise his right to purchase and—

(a) he does not dispute the terms of the offer to sell by timeously serving a notice setting out a request under section 65(1) or by referring the matter to the Lands Tribunal under subsection (1)(d) of section 71; or

(b) any such dispute has been resolved;

the tenant shall, subject to section 67(1), serve a notice of acceptance on the landlord within 2 months of whichever is the latest of—

(i) the service on him of the offer to sell;

(ii) the service on him of an amended offer to sell (or if there is more than one, of the latest amended offer to sell);

(iii) a determination by the Lands Tribunal under section 65(3) which does not require service of an amended offer to sell;

(iv) a finding or determination of the Lands Tribunal in a matter referred to it under section 71(1)(d) where no order is made under section 71(2)(b);

(v) the service of an offer to sell on him by virtue of subsection (2)(b) of section 71;

(vi) where a loan application under subsection (2)(a)(i) of section 216 (loans) has been served on the landlord, the service of a relative offer or refusal of loan; or

(vii) where section 216(7) (loans) is invoked, the decision of the court.

(2) Where an offer to sell (or an amended offer to sell) has been served on the tenant and a relative notice of acceptance has been duly served on the landlord, a contract of sale of the house shall be constituted between the landlord and the tenant on the terms contained in the offer (or amended offer) to sell.

Fixed price option

67.—(1) Where an offer to sell (or an amended offer to sell) is served on a tenant, but he is unable by reason of the application of regulations made under section 216(3) (loans) to obtain a loan of the amount for which he has applied, he may, within 2 months of service on him of an offer of loan, or (as the case may be) of the date of a declarator by the sheriff under section 216(7) (loans), whichever is the later, serve on the landlord a notice to the effect that he wishes to have a fixed price option, which notice shall be accompanied by a payment to the landlord of £100, and in that event he shall be entitled to serve a notice of acceptance on the landlord at any time within 2 years of the service of the application to purchase:

Provided that where, as regards the house, the tenant has served a loan application in accordance with subsection (2)(a)(ii) of section 216 (loans), he shall be entitled (even if the said period of 2 years has expired) to serve a notice of acceptance on the landlord within 2 months of whichever is the later of—

(a) the service of a relative offer, or refusal, of loan; or
(b) where section 216(7) is invoked, the decision of the court.

(2) The payment of £100 mentioned in subsection (1) shall be recoverable—

(a) by the tenant, when he purchases the house in accordance with that subsection or, if he does not, at the expiry of the period of 2 years mentioned therein;
(b) by the tenant, when the landlord recovers possession of the house under subsection (3); or
(c) by his personal representatives, if he dies without purchasing the house in accordance with that subsection.

(3) The existence of a fixed price option under subsection (1) shall not prevent the landlord from recovering possession of the property in any manner which may be lawful, and in that event the option shall be terminated.

Refusal of applications

68.—(1) Where a landlord on which an application to purchase has been served disputes the tenant's right to purchase a house under section 61, it shall by notice (referred to in this Part as a "notice of refusal") served within one month after service of the application to purchase—

(a) refuse the application; or
(b) offer to sell the house to the tenant under section 14, or under any other power which the landlord has to sell the house.

(2) Where a landlord on which an application to purchase has been served, after reasonable enquiry (which shall include reasonable opportunity for the tenant to amend his application), is of the opinion that information contained in the application is incorrect in a material respect it shall issue a notice of refusal within 2 months of the application to purchase.

(3) A notice of refusal shall specify the grounds on which the landlord disputes the tenant's right to purchase or, as the case may be, the accuracy of the information.

(4) Where a landlord serves a notice of refusal on a tenant under this section, the tenant may within one month thereafter apply to the Lands Tribunal for a finding that he has a right to purchase the house under section 61 on such terms as it may determine.

Houses provided for special purposes

Secretary of State's power to authorise refusal to sell certain houses provided for persons of pensionable age

69.—(1) This section applies to a house which has facilities which are substantially different from those of an ordinary house and which has been designed or adapted for occupation by a person of pensionable age whose special needs require accommodation of the kind provided by the house.

(2) Where an application to purchase a house is served on a landlord and it appears to the landlord that—

(a) the house is one to which this section applies; and

(b) the tenant would, apart from this section, have a right under section 61 to purchase the house,

the landlord may, within one month after service of the application to purchase, instead of serving an offer to sell on the tenant, make an application to the Secretary of State under this section.

(3) An application under subsection (2) shall specify the facilities and features of design or adaptation which in the view of the landlord cause the house to be a house to which this section applies.

(4) Where the Secretary of State has received an application under this section and it appears to him that the house concerned is one to which this section applies, he shall authorise the landlord to serve on the tenant a notice of refusal under this section, which shall be served as soon as is practicable after the authority is given and in any event within one month thereafter.

(5) A notice of refusal served under subsection (4) shall specify the facilities and features specified for the purposes of subsection (3) and that the Secretary of State's authority for service of the said notice has been given.

(6) Where the Secretary of State refuses an application made under subsection (2), the landlord shall serve on the tenant an offer to sell under section 63(2)—

(a) within the period mentioned in that section; or

(b) where the unexpired portion of that period is less than one month or there is not an unexpired portion of that period, within one month of the Secretary of State's refusal.

Power to refuse to sell certain houses required for educational purposes

70.—(1) Where an application to purchase a house is served on an islands council as landlord and—

(a) the house is—

(i) held by the council for the purposes of its functions as education authority; and

(ii) required for the accommodation of a person who is or will be employed by the council for those purposes;

(b) the council is not likely to be able reasonably to provide other suitable accommodation for the person mentioned in paragraph (a)(ii); and

(c) the tenant would, apart from this section, have a right under section 61 to purchase the house,

the landlord may, within one month of service of the application to purchase, serve a notice of refusal on the tenant.

(2) A refusal by the landlord under subsection (1) shall contain sufficient information to demonstrate that the conditions mentioned in paragraphs (a) and (b) of that subsection are fulfilled in relation to the house.

Lands Tribunal

Reference to Lands Tribunal

71.—(1) Where—

(a) a landlord who has been duly served with an application to purchase fails to issue timeously either an offer to sell (even if only such an offer to sell as is mentioned in paragraph (d)) or a notice of refusal; or

   (b) the Lands Tribunal has made a determination under section
      65(3) (variation of terms of offer to sell) and the landlord has
      failed to issue an amended offer to sell within 2 months
      thereafter; or
   (c) the Lands Tribunal has made a finding under section 68(4)
      (refusal of right to purchase) or has made an order under
      subsection (2)(b) of this section and the landlord has not duly
      progressed the application to purchase in accordance with that
      finding or, as the case may be, order, within 2 months there-
      after; or
   (d) a landlord has served an offer to sell whose contents do not
      conform with the requirements of paragraphs (a) to (e) of
      section 63(2) (or where such contents were not obtained in
      accordance with the provisions specified in those paragraphs),
the tenant (together with any joint purchaser) may refer the matter to the
Lands Tribunal by serving on the clerk to that body a copy of any notice
served and of any finding or determination made under this Part, together
with a statement of his grievance.

   (2) Where a matter has been referred to the Lands Tribunal under
subsection (1), the Tribunal shall consider whether in its opinion—
   (a) any of paragraphs (a) to (c) of that subsection apply, and if it so
      finds it may—
     (i) give any consent, exercise any discretion, or do anything which
        the landlord may give, exercise or do under or for the purposes
        of sections 61 to 84; and
     (ii) issue such notices and undertake such other steps as may be
        required to complete the procedure provided for in sections 63
        and 65 to 67;
      and any consent given, any discretion exercised, or anything done,
      under the foregoing provisions of this subsection shall have effect
      as if it had been duly given, exercised or done by the landlord; or
   (b) paragraph (d) of that subsection applies, and if it so finds it may
      order the landlord to serve on the tenant an offer to sell, in proper
      form, under section 63(2) within such time (not exceeding 2
      months) as it may specify.

   (3) Nothing in this section shall affect the operation of the provisions
of any other enactment relating to the enforcement of a statutory duty
whether under that enactment or otherwise.

Recoverability of discount

Recovery of discount on early re-sale

   72.—(1) A person who has purchased a house in exercise of a right to
purchase under section 61, or any of his successors in title, who sells or
otherwise disposes of the house (except as provided for in section 73)
before the expiry of 3 years from the date of service of a notice of
acceptance by the tenant under section 66, shall be liable to repay to the
landlord, in accordance with subsection (3), a proportion of the difference
between the market value determined, in respect of the house, under
section 62(2) and the price at which the house was so purchased.

   (2) Subsection (1) applies to the disposal of part of a house except in
a case where—
   (a) it is a disposal by one of the parties to the original sale to one of
      the other parties; or
   (b) the remainder of the house continues to be the only or principal
      home of the person disposing of the part.

   (3) The proportion of the difference which shall be paid to the landlord
shall be—

(a) 100 per cent. where the disposal occurs within the first year after the date of service of notice,

(b) 66 per cent. where it occurs in the second such year, and

(c) 33 per cent. where it occurs in the third such year.

(4) Where as regards a house or part of a house there is, within the period mentioned in subsection (1), more than one disposal to which that subsection would (apart from the provisions of this subsection) apply, that subsection shall apply only in relation to the first such disposal of the house, or part of the house.

(5) Where a landlord secures the liability to make a repayment under subsection (1) the security shall, notwithstanding section 13 of the Conveyancing and Feudal Reform (Scotland) Act 1970, have priority immediately after—

(a) any standard security granted in security of a loan either—

(i) for the purchase of the house, or

(ii) for the improvement of the house,

and any interest present or future due thereon (including any such interest which has accrued or may accrue) and any expenses or outlays (including interest thereon) which may be, or may have been, reasonably incurred in the exercise of any power conferred on the lender by the deed expressing the said standard security; and

(b) if the landlord consents, a standard security over the house granted in security of any other loan, and in relation thereto any such interest, expenses or outlays as aforesaid.

(6) For the avoidance of doubt, paragraph (a) of subsection (5) applies to a standard security granted in security both for the purpose mentioned in sub-paragraph (i) and for that mentioned in sub-paragraph (ii) as it applies to a standard security so granted for only one of those purposes.

(7) The liability to make a repayment under subsection (1) shall not be imposed as a real burden in a disposition of any interest in the house.

Cases where discount etc. is not recoverable

73.—(1) There shall be no liability to make a repayment under section 72(1) where the disposal is made—

(a) by the executor of the deceased owner acting in that capacity; or

(b) as a result of a compulsory purchase order; or

(c) in the circumstances specified in subsection (2).

(2) The circumstances mentioned in subsection (1)(c) are that the disposal—

(a) is to a member of the owner's family who has lived with him for a period of 12 months before the disposal; and

(b) is for no consideration:

Provided that, if the disponee disposes of the house before the expiry of the 3 year period mentioned in section 72(1), the provisions of that section will apply to him as if this was the first disposal and he was the original purchaser.

Duties of landlords

Duties of landlords

74. It shall be the duty of every landlord of a house to which sections 61 to 84 and section 216 apply to make provision for the progression of applications under those sections in such manner as may be necessary to enable any tenant who wishes to exercise his rights under this Part to do so, and to comply with any regulations which may be made by statutory instrument by the Secretary of State in that regard.

Agreements affecting right to purchase

    75.—(1) Subject to sections 61(1), 67(1) and 72(1)—

        (a) no person exercising or seeking to exercise a right to purchase under section 61(1) shall be obliged, notwithstanding any agreement to the contrary, to make any payment to or lodge any deposit with the landlord which he would not have been obliged to make, or as the case may be lodge, had he not exercised (or sought to exercise) the right to purchase;

        (b) a landlord mentioned in section 61(2)(a)(i) or (ii) is required neither to enter into, nor to induce (or seek to induce) any person to enter into, such agreement as is mentioned in paragraph (a), or into any agreement which purports to restrict that person's rights under this Part.

    (2) Paragraph (a) of subsection (1) does not apply to the expenses in any court proceedings.

Duty of landlords to provide information to secure tenants

    76.—(1) Whenever a new secure tenancy is to be created, if—

        (a) the landlord is not the heritable proprietor of the house; or

        (b) by virtue of section 61(4), the house is not one to which that section applies; or

        (c) section 62(7) or (8) may (assuming no change in the date for the time being specified in the former subsection and disregarding any order made, or which might be made, by the Secretary of State under section 62(11)(b)) affect any price fixed, as regards the house, under section 62(1),

the landlord shall so inform the prospective tenant by written notice.

    (2) Where in the course of a secure tenancy the landlord ceases to be the heritable proprietor of the house or the house, by virtue of section 61(4), ceases to be one to which that section applies, the landlord shall forthwith so inform the tenant by written notice.

    (3) Subsections (1) and (2) do not apply if—

        (a) the landlord is a housing co-operative within the meaning of section 22, and

        (b) the heritable proprietor is a local authority.

Powers of Secretary of State

Secretary of State may make provision for vesting in landlord to bring into being tenant's right to purchase house

    77.—(1) Subject to subsection (2), where, but for the fact that a landlord is not the heritable proprietor of land on which houses have been let (or made available for letting) by it, one or more of its tenants would have a right to purchase under section 61, the Secretary of State may by order made by statutory instrument provide that the whole of the heritable proprietor's interest in the land shall vest in the landlord.

    (2) An order under this section shall only be made where—

        (a) the heritable proprietor is a body mentioned in paragraph (a) of section 61(2); and

        (b) the Secretary of State is of the opinion, after consultation with the heritable proprietor and with the landlord, that the order is necessary if the right to purchase is to come into being.

    (3) An order under this section shall have the same effect as a declaration under section 278 of the Town and Country Planning (Scotland) Act 1972 (general vesting declarations), except that, in relation to such an order, the enactments mentioned in Schedule 6 shall have effect subject to the modifications specified in that Schedule.

(4) Compensation under the Land Compensation (Scotland) Act 1963, as applied by subsection (3) and Schedule 6 shall be assessed by reference to values current on the date the order under this section comes into force.

(5) An order under this section shall have no effect until approved by resolution of each House of Parliament.

(6) An order under this section which would, apart from the provisions of this subsection, be treated for the purposes of the Standing Orders of either House of Parliament as a hybrid instrument shall proceed in that House as if it were not such an instrument.

(7) An order under this section may include such incidental, consequential or supplementary provisions as may appear to the Secretary of State to be necessary or expedient for the purposes of this Act.

Secretary of State may give directions to modify conditions of sale

78.—(1) Where it appears to the Secretary of State that the inclusion of conditions of a particular kind in offers to sell would be unreasonable he may by direction require landlords generally, landlords of a particular description, or particular landlords not to include conditions of that kind (or not to include conditions of that kind unless modified in such manner as may be specified in the direction) in offers to sell served on or after a date so specified.

(2) Where a condition's inclusion in an offer to sell—

  (a) is in contravention of a direction under subsection (1) or

  (b) in a case where the tenant has not by the date specified in such a direction served a relative notice of acceptance on the landlord, would have been in such contravention had the offer to sell been served on or after that date,

the condition shall have no effect as regards the offer to sell.

(3) A direction under subsection (1) may—

  (a) make different provision in relation to different areas, cases or classes of case and may exclude certain areas, cases or classes of case; and

  (b) be varied or withdrawn by a subsequent direction so given.

(4) Section 211 of the Local Government (Scotland) Act 1973 (provision for default of local authority) shall apply as regards a failure to comply with a requirement in a direction under subsection (1) as that section applies as regards such failure as is mentioned in subsection (1) thereof.

Secretary of State may give financial and other assistance for tenants involved in proceedings

79.—(1) Where, in relation to any proceedings, or prospective proceedings, to which this section applies, a tenant or purchaser is an actual or prospective party, the Secretary of State may on written application to him by the tenant or purchaser give financial or other assistance to the applicant, if the Secretary of State thinks fit to do so:

Provided that assistance under this section shall be given only where the Secretary of State considers—

  (a) that the case raises a question of principle and that it is in the public interest to give the applicant such assistance; or

  (b) that there is some other special consideration.

(2) This section applies to—

  (a) any proceedings under sections 61 to 84 and section 216; and

  (b) any proceedings to determine any question arising under or in connection with those sections other than a question as to market value for the purposes of section 62.

(3) Assistance by the Secretary of State under this section may include—
(a) giving advice;
(b) procuring or attempting to procure the settlement of the matter in dispute;
(c) arranging for the giving of advice or assistance by a solicitor or counsel;
(d) arranging for representation by a solicitor or counsel;
(e) any other form of assistance which the Secretary of State may consider appropriate.

(4) In so far as expenses are incurred by the Secretary of State in providing the applicant with assistance under this section, any sums recovered by virtue of an award of expenses, or of an agreement as to expenses, in the applicant's favour with respect to the matter in connection with which the assistance is given shall, subject to any charge or obligation for payment in priority to other debts under the Legal Aid (Scotland) Act 1986 and to any provision of that Act for payment of any sum into the Scottish Legal Aid Fund, be paid to the Secretary of State in priority to any other debts.

(5) Any expenses incurred by the Secretary of State in providing assistance under this section shall be paid out of money provided by Parliament; and any sums received by the Secretary of State under subsection (4) shall be paid into the Consolidated Fund.

Secretary of State may make contributions towards the cost of transfers and exchanges

80.—(1) The Secretary of State may with the consent of the Treasury make grants or loans towards the cost of arrangements for facilitating moves to and from homes by which—
(a) a secure tenant of one landlord (the "first landlord") becomes, at his own request, the secure tenant of a different landlord (whether or not by means of an exchange whereby a secure tenant of the different landlord becomes the secure tenant of the first landlord); or
(b) each of two or more tenants of houses, one at least of which is let under a secure tenancy, becomes the tenant of the other house (or, as the case may be, of one of the other houses).

(2) The grants or loans may be made subject to such conditions as the Secretary of State may determine, and may be made so as to be repayable (or, as the case may be, repayable earlier) if there is a breach of such a condition.

(3) In subsection (1) the reference to a "secure tenant" is to a tenant under a secure tenancy within the meaning of this Act or of the Housing Act 1985 or of Chapter II of Part II of the Housing (Northern Ireland) Order 1983.

Information from landlords in relation to Secretary of State's powers

81.—(1) Without prejudice to section 199 of the Local Government (Scotland) Act 1973 (reports and returns by local authorities etc.), where it appears to the Secretary of State necessary or expedient, in relation to the exercise of his powers under sections 61 to 84 and section 216, he may by notice in writing to a landlord require it—
(a) at such time and at such place as may be specified in the notice, to produce any document; or
(b) within such period as may be so specified or such longer period as the Secretary of State may allow, to furnish a copy of any document or supply any information.

(2) Any officer of the landlord designated in the notice for that purpose or having custody or control of the document or in a position to give that information shall, without instructions from the landlord, take all reasonable steps to ensure that the notice is complied with.

General

Interpretation of this Part

82. In this Part and in sections 14, 19, 20 and 216, except where provision is made to the contrary,

"application to purchase" has the meaning assigned to it by section 63;

"family" and any reference to membership thereof shall be construed in accordance with section 83;

"fire authority" means a fire authority for the purposes of the Fire Services Acts 1947 to 1959 or a joint committee constituted by virtue of section 36(4)(b) of the Fire Services Act 1947;

"heritable proprietor", in relation to a house, includes any landlord entitled under section 3 of the Conveyancing (Scotland) Act 1924 (disposition of the dwelling-house etc. by persons uninfeft) to grant a disposition of the house;

"housing co-operative" has the meaning assigned to it by section 22;

"landlord" means a person who lets a house to a tenant for human habitation, and includes his successors in title;

"offer to sell" has the meaning assigned to it by section 63(2) and includes such offer to sell as is mentioned in section 71(1)(d);

"police authority" means a policy authority in Scotland within the meaning of section 2(1) or 19(9)(b) of the Police (Scotland) Act 1967 or a joint police committee constituted by virtue of subsection (2)(b) of the said section 19 and any police authority constituted in England and Wales or Northern Ireland under corresponding legislation;

"secure tenancy" means a secure tenancy within the meaning of section 44;

"tenancy" means any agreement under which a house is made available for occupation for human habitation, and "leases", "let" and "lets" shall be construed accordingly;

"tenant" means a person who leases a house from a landlord and who derives his right therein directly from the landlord, and in the case of joint tenancies means all the tenants.

Members of a person's family

83.—(1) A person is a member of another's family for the purposes of this Act if—

(a) he is the spouse of that person or he and that person live together as husband and wife; or

(b) he is that person's parent, grandparent, child, grandchild, brother, sister, uncle, aunt, nephew or niece.

(2) For the purposes of subsection (1)(b)—

(a) a relationship by marriage shall be treated as a relationship by blood;

(b) a relationship of the half-blood shall be treated as a relationship of the whole blood;

(c) the stepchild of a person shall be treated as his child; and

(d) a child shall be treated as such whether or not his parents are married.

Service of notices

84.—(1) A notice or other document which requires to be served on a person under any provision of this Part or of section 216 may be given to him—

(a) by delivering it to him;
(b) by leaving it at his proper address; or
(c) by sending it by recorded delivery post to him at that address.

(2) For the purposes of this section and of section 7 of the Interpretation Act 1978 (references to service by post) in its application to this section, a person's proper address shall be his last known address.

PART IV

SUB-STANDARD HOUSES

The tolerable standard

General duty of local authority in respect of houses not meeting tolerable standard

85.—(1) It shall be the duty of every local authority to secure that all houses in their district which do not meet the tolerable standard are closed, demolished or brought up to the tolerable standard within such period as is reasonable in all the circumstances.

(2) In determining what period is reasonable for the purposes of subsection (1), regard shall be had to alternative housing accommodation likely to be available for any persons who may be displaced from houses as a result of any action proposed by the local authority in pursuance of that subsection.

(3) Every local authority shall from time to time cause to be made such a survey or inspection of their district as may be necessary for the performance of the duty imposed on them by subsection (1) or for the purpose of ascertaining the availability of alternative housing accommodation.

Definition of house meeting tolerable standard

86.—(1) Subject to subsection (2), a house meets the tolerable standard for the purposes of this Act if the house—

(a) is structurally stable;
(b) is substantially free from rising or penetrating damp;
(c) has satisfactory provision for natural and artificial lighting, for ventilation and for heating;
(d) has an adequate piped supply of wholesome water available within the house;
(e) has a sink provided with a satisfactory supply of both hot and cold water within the house;
(f) has a water closet available for the exclusive use of the occupants of the house and suitably located within the house;
(g) has an effective system for the drainage and disposal of foul and surface water;
(h) has satisfactory facilities for the cooking of food within the house;
(i) has satisfactory access to all external doors and outbuildings;

and any reference to a house not meeting the tolerable standard or being brought up to the tolerable standard shall be construed accordingly.

(2) The Secretary of State may by order vary or extend or amplify the criteria set out in the foregoing subsection either generally or, after

consultation with a particular local authority, in relation to the district, or any part of the district, of that authority.

(3) This section shall be without prejudice to section 114 (certain underground rooms to be treated as houses not meeting the tolerable standard).

Official representation that house does not meet tolerable standard

87.—(1) The proper officer of the local authority may make an official representation to the authority whenever he is of opinion that any house in their district does not meet the tolerable standard.

(2) A local authority shall as soon as may be take into consideration any official representation which has been made to them.

(3) Every representation made in pursuance of this section by the proper officer of the local authority shall be in writing.

Improvement order

Improvement of houses below tolerable standard outside housing action areas

88.—(1) Subject to subsections (2) and (3), where a local authority are satisfied that a house which is not situated in a housing action area does not meet the tolerable standard, they may by order require the owner of the house within a period of 180 days of the making of the order to improve the house by executing works—

(a) to bring it up to the tolerable standard; and

(b) to put it into a good state of repair;

and where the local authority are satisfied that the house has a future life of not less than 10 years, they may in addition require the execution of such further works of improvement as to ensure that the house will be provided with all of the standard amenities within that period.

(2) In subsection (1), reference to a house which does not meet the tolerable standard includes a reference to a house which does not have a fixed bath or shower and reference to executing works to bring it up to the tolerable standard includes reference to installing a fixed bath or shower.

(3) If the works of improvement required by an order under subsection (1) have not been completed within the said period of 180 days, the local authority may if—

(a) they consider that satisfactory progress has been made on the works, or

(b) they are given an undertaking in writing that the works will be completed by a date which they consider satisfactory,

amend the order to require the works to be completed within such further period as they may determine.

(4) If the works of improvement have not been completed within the period of 180 days or, as the case may be, the further period determined under subsection (3), the local authority, in order that they themselves may carry out the works required by the order under subsection (1), may acquire the house by agreement or may be authorised by the Secretary of State to acquire the house compulsorily; and the Acquisition of Land (Authorisation Procedure) (Scotland) Act 1947 shall apply in relation to any such compulsory purchase as if this Act had been in force immediately before the commencement of that Act.

(5) Paragraphs (a) to (c) of section 118(1) (persons upon whom closing and demolition orders are to be served) shall apply to orders under this section as they apply to orders under that section.

(6) Section 129 (appeals) shall apply to enable an aggrieved person to appeal against an order under this section as it applies to enable an aggrieved person to appeal against a closing order.

(7) A local authority shall make an improvement grant in accordance with Part XIII towards meeting the cost of the works which are required in pursuance of this section.

(8) The owner of the house in respect of which improvement works are required under this section may apply to the local authority for a loan to meet the cost of the works in so far as they are not met by a grant made under subsection (7); and subsections (2) to (9) of section 217 shall apply for the purposes of this subsection as they apply for the purposes of subsection (1) of that section.

Housing action areas

Declaration of housing action areas for demolition

89.—(1) Where a local authority are satisfied—
    (a) that the houses, or the greater part of the houses, in any area in their district do not meet the tolerable standard, and
    (b) that the most effective way of dealing with the area is to apply to the area the provisions of subsection (2),
they may cause the area to be defined on a map and pass a draft resolution declaring the area so defined to be a housing action area for demolition, that is to say, an area which is to be dealt with in accordance with the provisions of subsection (2).

(2) A resolution passed under this section shall provide that a housing action area for demolition shall be dealt with by securing the demolition of all the buildings in the area but—
    (a) such an area shall not include the site of a building unless at least part of the building consists of a house which does not meet the tolerable standard;
    (b) there may be excluded from demolition any part of a building which is used for commercial purposes.

(3) For the purposes of this section and the following two sections, a house in respect of which a closing order has been made and not determined shall be deemed to be a house which does not meet the tolerable standard.

Declaration of housing action areas for improvement

90.—(1) Where a local authority are satisfied—
    (a) that the houses, or the greater part of the houses, in any area in their district lack one or more of the standard amenities or do not meet the tolerable standard, and
    (b) that the most effective way of dealing with the area is to apply to the area the provisions of subsection (2),
they may cause the area to be defined on a map and pass a draft resolution declaring the area so defined to be a housing action area for improvement, that is to say, an area which is to be dealt with in accordance with the provisions of that subsection.

(2) A resolution passed under this section shall provide that a housing action area for improvement shall be dealt with by securing the carrying out of such works on the houses in the area which do not meet the standard specified by the local authority under subsection (3) in respect of the area that on the completion of the works all the houses in the area will meet that standard.

(3) The standard specified by the local authority for the purposes of this section shall be that all the houses in the area—

(a) shall meet the tolerable standard; and

(b) shall be in a good state of repair (disregarding the state of internal decorative repair) having regard to the age, character and locality of the houses,

and, where the local authority are satisfied that the houses in the area have a future life of not less than 10 years, they may in addition specify that all the houses in the area shall be provided with all of the standard amenities.

(4) A housing action area for improvement shall not include the site of a building unless at least part of the building consists of a house which—

(a) lacks one or more of the standard amenities, or

(b) does not meet the tolerable standard, or

(c) is not in a good state of repair (disregarding the state of internal decorative repair) having regard to the age, character and locality of the house.

Declaration of housing action areas for demolition and improvement

91.—(1) Where a local authority are satisfied—

(a) that the houses, or the greater part of the houses, in any area in their district lack one or more of the standard amenities or do not meet the tolerable standard, and

(b) that the most effective way of dealing with the area is to apply to the area the provisions of subsection (2),

they may cause the area to be defined on a map and pass a draft resolution declaring the area so defined to be a housing action area for demolition and improvement, that is to say, an area which is to be dealt with in accordance with the provisions of that subsection.

(2) Subject to subsection (4), a resolution passed under this section shall provide that a housing action area for demolition and improvement shall be dealt with by securing the demolition of some of the buildings in the area and by securing the carrying out of such works on those houses in the area which do not meet the standard specified by the local authority by virtue of subsection (3) in respect of the area, other than the houses in those buildings, that on the completion of the works all the houses then in the area will meet that standard.

(3) For the purposes of specifying the standard mentioned in subsection (2), the provisions of subsection (3) of section 90 shall apply as they apply for the purposes of specifying the standard mentioned in subsection (2) of that section.

(4) A local authority—

(a) shall not secure the demolition of a building in a housing action area for demolition and improvement unless the greater part of the houses in the building are below the tolerable standard, and

(b) may exclude from demolition any part of such a building which is used for commercial purposes.

(5) A housing action area for demolition and improvement shall not include the site of a building unless at least part of the building consists of a house which—

(a) lacks one or more of the standard amenities, or

(b) does not meet the tolerable standard, or

(c) is not in a good state of repair (disregarding the state of internal decorative repair) having regard to the age, character and locality of the house.

Provisions supplementary to sections 89 to 91

92.—(1) In considering whether to take action under sections 89 to 91 with respect to an area, a local authority shall have regard to any directions given by the Secretary of State, either generally or in respect of any particular authority or authorities, with regard to the identification of areas suitable to be declared to be housing action areas.

(2) If, on the application of a local authority, the Secretary of State is satisfied that in all the circumstances it is reasonable to do so, he may give directions as respects the waiving of the requirement in the said section 90(1)(a) or 91(1)(a) that the greater part of the houses in any area of that local authority's district lack one or more of the standard amenities or do not meet the tolerable standard.

(3) A draft resolution passed under the provisions of the said section 89, 90 or 91 shall specify the section under which it was made, be in such form and contain such information about such matters as the Secretary of State may prescribe, and the Secretary of State may prescribe different requirements for the different resolutions.

(4) A draft resolution passed under the said section 90 or 91 shall, without prejudice to the generality of the foregoing provisions of this section, contain a statement as to the standard specified by the local authority under the said section 90 or by virtue of the said section 91 and a draft resolution shall identify—

(a) where it is passed under section 89 or 91, those buildings in the area which consist of a house or houses which, in the opinion of the local authority, should be demolished;

(b) where it is passed under section 90 or 91, those houses in the area which are below the standard specified as aforesaid and which, in the opinion of the local authority, should be brought up to that standard and do not fall within paragraph (c);

(c) where it is passed under section 90 or 91, those houses in the area which form part of a building comprising two or more flats and which, in the opinion of the local authority—

(i) are below the standard specified for the area as aforesaid, and

(ii) require to be integrated with some other part or parts of that building;

and that other part or parts of the building shall also be identified.

Consent to demolition of listed buildings, rehabilitation orders and compensation

93. Schedule 7 (consent to demolition of listed buildings in housing action areas, rehabilitation orders and compensation) shall have effect for the purpose of making provision in relation to houses acquired in housing action areas and subject to rehabilitation orders.

Powers of Secretary of State

Functions of Secretary of State, and duty of local authority to publish information

94.—(1) A local authority shall, as soon as may be after passing a draft resolution under section 89, 90 or 91, submit the draft resolution and a copy of the map to the Secretary of State.

(2) On receiving the draft resolution and a copy of the map, the Secretary of State shall send to the local authority a written acknowledgement of the receipt of the resolution and of the map.

(3) If it appears to the Secretary of State to be appropriate to do so he may, at any time within the period of 28 days beginning with the day on which he sent an acknowledgement under subsection (2)—

(a) direct the local authority to rescind the resolution; or

(b) notify the local authority that he does not propose to direct them to rescind the resolution; or

(c) notify the local authority that he requires a further period for consideration of the resolution and as soon as practicable thereafter direct the local authority as mentioned in paragraph (a) or, as the case may be, notify them as mentioned in paragraph (b).

(4) As soon as may be after the date on which a local authority are notified as mentioned in subsection (3)(a), the local authority shall rescind the draft resolution.

(5) Where the local authority are notified as mentioned in subsection (3)(b) or, if after the expiry of the period of 28 days mentioned in subsection (3), the local authority have received no notification from the Secretary of State, the local authority shall as soon as may be—

(a) publish in two or more newspapers circulating in the locality (of which one shall, if practicable, be a local newspaper) a notice that a draft resolution has been made and naming a place or places and times at which a copy of the resolution and a copy of the map may be inspected; and

(b) serve on every owner, lessee and occupier of any premises to which the draft resolution relates a notice stating the effect of the resolution.

(6) Any notice for the purposes of subsection (5) shall be in such form, contain such information and be served in such manner as the Secretary of State may prescribe; and the Secretary of State may prescribe different requirements for the different resolutions.

(7) Without prejudice to the generality of the provisions of subsection (6), a notice served under subsection (5)(b) shall state that such owner, lessee and occupier may, within two months from the date of service of the notice, make representations to the local authority concerning the draft resolution or any matter contained therein.

Powers of local authority

Further procedure, powers of local authority on acquisition of land, compensation and agricultural holdings

95.—(1) Part I of Schedule 8 shall have effect in relation to the procedure to be followed after publication and service of a draft resolution.

(2) Part II of Schedule 8 shall have effect in relation to the powers of a local authority acquiring land for the purposes of this Part.

(3) Part III of Schedule 8 shall have effect in relation to compensation in respect of land acquired compulsorily.

(4) Part IV of Schedule 8 shall have effect in relation to the adjustment of relations between lessors and lessees where improvements have been carried out on agricultural holdings under this Part.

Power of local authority to retain houses subject to demolition for temporary occupation

96.—(1) A local authority, who in a resolution passed under section 89 or 91 have provided that some or all of the buildings in a housing action area should be demolished, may postpone the demolition of any such building on land purchased by or belonging to the authority within that area, being a building which is, or which contains, a house which in the opinion of the authority must be continued in use as housing accommodation for the time being.

(2) Where the demolition of a building is postponed under subsection (1), the authority shall carry out such works as may in their opinion from

time to time be required for rendering or keeping such house capable of being continued in use as housing accommodation pending its demolition.

(3) In respect of any house retained by a local authority under this section for use for housing purposes, the authority shall have the same powers and duties as they have in respect of houses provided under Part I.

Local authority may control occupation of houses in housing action area

97.—(1) Subject to subsection (3) of this section, a local authority may—

(a) as soon as practicable after they receive notification under section 94(3)(b), or

(b) if after the expiry of the period of 28 days mentioned in section 94(3) they have received no notification from the Secretary of State;

make an order in the prescribed form prohibiting the occupation of the houses in the area which have been identified in accordance with section 92(4)(a) and (c) except with the consent of the authority.

(2) Within 28 days of making an order under this section, the local authority shall serve a notice in the prescribed form in respect of every such house in the housing action area—

(a) upon the person having control of the house, and

(b) upon any other person who is an owner or occupier of the house, stating that the order has been made and indicating the effect of the order.

(3) An order made under this section shall not prohibit the occupation of a house in the area by a person occupying it on the date of the service of the notice in respect of the house under subsection (2).

(4) If any person, knowing that an order has been made under this section, occupies or permits to be occupied a house under subsection (2) in contravention of the order, he shall be guilty of an offence and shall be liable on summary conviction—

(a) to a fine not exceeding level 5 on the standard scale or to imprisonment for a term not exceeding 3 months or to both such fine and such imprisonment; and

(b) in the case of a continuing offence to a further fine of £5 for every day or part of a day which he occupies the house, or permits it to be occupied, after conviction.

(5) Where an owner or a person having control of a house in respect of which an order under this section is served considers that it is unreasonable in all the circumstances of the case that the order should continue to apply to the house, he may apply to the local authority to revoke the order in respect of the house.

(6) Where an applicant for a revocation under subsection (5) is aggrieved by the refusal of the local authority to revoke the order, he may appeal to the sheriff by giving notice of appeal within 21 days of the date of the refusal.

(7) An order made under this section shall cease to have effect in relation to any house affected by any of the following events, that is to say—

(a) on the date on which the local authority revoke an order under subsection (5);

(b) on the date of the passing of a final resolution under paragraph 1 of Schedule 8 identifying a house in accordance with that paragraph as read with section 92(4)(b);

(c) on the date of the rescinding of a draft resolution under paragraph 1 of Schedule 8;

(d) in the case where the Secretary of State, in refusing to confirm an order for compulsory purchase submitted to him under paragraph 5 of Schedule 8, directs that any order made under this section shall cease to apply either generally or in respect of individual houses, on the date of that direction;

(e) in the case where the Secretary of State, in modifying in accordance with the provisions of paragraph 5(3)(e) of Schedule 8 an order for compulsory purchase submitted to him under that paragraph, directs that any order made under this section shall cease to apply either generally or in respect of individual houses, on the date of that direction.

Obligation of local authorities in relation to rehousing in housing action areas

98. Where a person is to be displaced as a result of implementation of the provisions of this Part, and where a local authority are under a duty by virtue of section 36 of the Land Compensation (Scotland) Act 1973 to rehouse him, the authority shall, if so requested by that person and in so far as practicable, secure that he will be provided with suitable alternative accommodation within a reasonable distance from the locality of the house from which he is to be displaced.

Landlords and tenants in housing action areas

Application to sheriff for possession where house is identified in accordance with paragraph 1(1) of Schedule 8 as read with section 92(4)(a)

99.—(1) Where—

(a) an owner of a house has received a notice stating the effect of a final resolution passed under paragraph 1(1) of Schedule 8, which identifies the building of which the house consists or forms part in accordance with that paragraph as read with section 92(4)(a);

(b) the owner of the house is willing to secure the demolition of the building of which the house consists or forms part; and

(c) the owner cannot obtain vacant possession of the house by agreement with the tenant thereof,

then, whether or not the tenancy of that house has been terminated, the owner may apply to the sheriff for an order for possession of that house.

(2) Any such order shall require the tenant to vacate the house within such period, not being less than 4 weeks nor more than 6 weeks from the date of the order, as the sheriff may determine and, where any tenancy of that house has not previously been terminated, such order shall have the effect of terminating that tenancy as from the date of the order.

(3) Any order made under this section may be made subject to such conditions (including conditions with respect to the payment of money by any party to the proceedings to any other party thereto by way of adjustment of rent or compensation for any improvements carried out by the tenant) as the sheriff may think just and equitable, having regard to the respective rights, obligations and liabilities of the parties and to all the circumstances of the case, but no such order shall be made unless the sheriff is satisfied that suitable alternative accommodation on reasonable terms will be available to the tenant.

Application to sheriff for possession where house is identified in accordance with paragraph 1(1) of Schedule 8 as read with section 92(4)(c)

100.—(1) Where—

  (a) an owner of a house has received a notice stating the effect of a final resolution passed under paragraph 1(1) of Schedule 8 which identifies the house in accordance with that paragraph as read with section 92(4)(c);

  (b) the owner of the house is also the owner of the other part or parts of the building of which the house forms part which have been identified as aforesaid as requiring to be integrated with that house, in whole or in part;

  (c) the owner of the house is willing to carry out the necessary works of integration as aforesaid; and

  (d) the owner cannot obtain vacant possession of the house or of the said other part or parts of the building by agreement with any tenant thereof,

then, whether or not the tenancy of that house or of the said other part or parts of the building has been terminated, the owner may apply to the sheriff for an order for possession of that house or of the said other part or parts of the building.

(2) The provisions of section 99(2) and (3) shall apply to an order made under this section as they apply to an order made under that section but, without prejudice to the generality of the provisions of those subsections, the sheriff shall, before imposing any such conditions as are referred to in section 99(3), have regard as to whether the owner has offered to any tenant, who will be required to vacate the house by an order under this section, a tenancy of a house which will include in whole or in part that house.

Application to sheriff for possession where house is identified in accordance with paragraph 1 of Schedule 8 as read with section 92(4)(b)

101.—(1) Where—

  (a) an owner of a house has received a notice stating the effect of a final resolution passed under paragraph 1(1) of Schedule 8, which identifies the house in accordance with that paragraph as read with section 92(4)(b);

  (b) the owner of the house is willing to carry out the necessary works to bring the house up to the standard specified for the area by the local authority under section 90(3) or, as the case may be, by virtue of section 91(3);

  (c) those works cannot be carried out without the consent of the tenant of that house or without the house being vacated temporarily; and

  (d) the tenant refuses to consent to the carrying out of those works or to vacate the house,

then the owner may apply to the sheriff for an order authorising the owner to enter the house and carry out those works, and, on any such application, the sheriff may, if he considers that it is necessary for the house to be vacated to enable the works to be carried out, order the tenant to vacate the house for such period, beginning not less than 4 weeks from the date of the order, as the sheriff may determine.

(2) Any order made under this section may be made subject to such conditions (including conditions with respect to the payment of rent payable under the tenancy during the carrying out of the works and as to the period during which the house is to be vacated) as the sheriff may think just and equitable, having regard to all the circumstances of the case, but no such order shall be made unless the sheriff is satisfied that

suitable alternative accommodation on reasonable terms will be available to the tenant.

Procedure; and application of s.103(1) of Rent (Scotland) Act 1984

102. Any application made to the sheriff under this Part shall be made by way of summary application and the provisions of section 103(1) of the Rent (Scotland) Act 1984 shall apply to any such application as they apply to an application made under any of the provisions referred to in subsection (2) of that section.

Certain provisions of Rent (Scotland) Act 1984 not to apply

103. Nothing in the Rent (Scotland) Act 1984 restricting the power of a court to make an order for possession of a dwelling-house shall apply to any application made to the sheriff or to any order made by the sheriff under this Part.

Effect of refusal to make order on validity of resolution

104. Where, in relation to any application under this Part, the sheriff refuses to make the order sought, that refusal shall not affect the validity of any resolution passed by the local authority under this Part or any rights or obligations of the local authority under this Part or under any other enactment relating to housing.

Miscellaneous

Exclusion of houses controlled by Crown

105.—(1) No order under section 88 nor any notice of a final resolution under Part I of Schedule 8 may be served in respect of a house in which there is a Crown interest except with the consent of the appropriate authority and, where a notice of a final resolution is served with the consent of the appropriate authority, this Part shall apply in relation to the house as it applies in relation to a house in which there is no such interest.

(2) If, after a notice of a final resolution as aforesaid has been served in respect of any house in which there is a Crown interest, the appropriate authority becomes the person having control of the house, any such notice shall cease to have effect.

(3) In this section, "Crown interest" means an interest belonging to Her Majesty in right of the Crown or belonging to a government department, or held in trust for Her Majesty for the purposes of a government department, and "the appropriate authority"—

(a) in relation to land belonging to Her Majesty in right of the Crown and forming part of the Crown Estate, means the Crown Estate Commissioners, and, in relation to any other land belonging to Her Majesty in right of the Crown, means the government department having the management of that land;

(b) in relation to land belonging to a government department or held in trust for Her Majesty for the purposes of a government department, means that department,

and if any question arises as to what authority is the appropriate authority in relation to any land, that question shall be referred to the Treasury, whose decision shall be final.

Power of local authority to arrange for the execution of works of improvement by agreement with the owner

106. A local authority may by agreement with an owner of a house at his expense execute, or arrange for the execution of, any works of improvement or of repair to which this Part or Part V or Part XIII applies which the local authority and the owner agree are necessary or desirable.

Conditions may be attached to sale of below-standard local authority houses

107. Where a house on land acquired or appropriated by a local authority for the purposes of Part I lacks one or more of the standard amenities or does not meet the tolerable standard, the local authority may make the sale by them of that house conditional on the purchaser providing the house with the standard amenities which it lacks or bringing the house up to the tolerable standard.

PART V

REPAIR OF HOUSES

Repair notices

Power of local authority to secure repair of house in state of serious disrepair

108.—(1) Where a local authority are satisfied that any house in their district is in a state of serious disrepair, they may serve upon the person having control of the house a repair notice.

(2) A repair notice shall—

    (a) require that person to execute the works necessary to rectify such defects as are specified in the notice within such reasonable time, being not less than 21 days, as may be specified in the notice, and

    (b) state that, in the opinion of the local authority, the rectification of those defects will bring the house up to such a standard of repair as is reasonable having regard to the age, character and location, and disregarding the internal decorative repair, of the house.

(3) Subject to subsection (5), if a notice under subsection (1) is not complied with, the local authority—

    (a) may themselves execute the works necessary to rectify the defects specified in the notice or in the notice as varied by the sheriff, as the case may be, and

    (b) may in addition execute any further works which are found to be necessary for the purpose of bringing the house up to the standard of repair referred to in subsection (2)(b), but which could not reasonably have been ascertained to be required prior to the service of the notice.

(4) Any question as to whether further works are necessary or could not have been reasonably ascertained under subsection (3)(b) shall be determined by the sheriff, whose decision shall be final.

(5) The local authority shall not execute any works under subsection (3) until—

    (a) the expiration of the time specified in the repair notice; or

    (b) if an appeal against the notice has been made and the notice confirmed with or without variation by the sheriff, the expiration of 21 days from the date of the determination of the appeal or such longer period as the sheriff may order.

(6) Any action taken under this section or under section 109 shall be without prejudice to any other powers of the local authority or any remedy available to the tenant of a house against his landlord under any enactment or rule of law.

(7) Where a local authority are of the opinion that a house in their district is in need of repair although not in a state of serious disrepair and that it is likely to deteriorate rapidly, or to cause material damage to another house, if nothing is done to repair it, they may treat it as being in a state of serious disrepair for the purposes of this Part.

(8) In this Part, "house" includes a building which comprises or includes—

(a) a house or houses; or

(b) a house or houses and other premises.

Recovery by local authority of expenses under s.108

109.—(1) Subject to the provisions of this section, any expenses incurred by a local authority under section 108(3), together with interest from the date when a demand for the expenses is served until payment, may be recovered by the authority from—

(a) the person having control of the house, or

(b) if he receives the rent of the house as trustee, tutor, curator, factor or agent for or of some other person, from him or from that other person, or in part from him and in part from that other person.

(2) A local authority may apportion any such expenses among the persons having control of the houses and other premises comprised in the building.

(3) The local authority may by order declare any such expenses to be payable by weekly, monthly, half-yearly or annual instalments within a period not exceeding 30 years with interest from the date of the service of the demand until the whole amount is paid, and any such instalments and interest, or any part thereof, may be recovered from any owner or occupier of the house, and, if recovered from an occupier, may be deducted by him from the rent of the house.

(4) Any interest payable under subsection (1) or subsection (3) of this section shall be at such reasonable rate as the local authority may determine.

(5) The provisions of Schedule 9 shall have effect for the purpose of enabling a local authority to make a charging order in respect of any expenses incurred by them under section 108(3) in relation to a house or building.

Recovery by lessee of proportion of expenses incurred in repairing house

110.—(1) Where the tenant of a house or his agent has—

(a) incurred expenditure in complying with a repair notice, or in paying the expenses of a local authority who has carried out the works specified in such a notice, and

(b) intimated service of the notice and its purport to the landlord under the lease in writing within 14 days after such service,

the tenant or the landlord may, in the absence of any agreement between them, apply to the sheriff to determine what part, if any, of the expenditure is payable by the landlord to the tenant.

(2) In determining an application under subsection (1), the sheriff shall make such determination as he thinks fit having regard to—

(a) the obligations of the landlord and the tenant under the lease with respect to the repair of the house;

(b) the length of the unexpired term of the lease;

(c) the rent payable under the lease; and

(d) all other relevant circumstances.

(3) Where the sheriff makes an order for payment by the landlord to the tenant, and the landlord in question is himself a tenant of the house

under another lease, he shall be treated for the purposes of this section as being a tenant who has incurred expenditure under subsection (1)(a).

(4) In this section "lease" includes a sublease and any tenancy, and the expressions "landlord" and "tenant" shall be construed accordingly.

Appeals etc.

Appeals under Part V

111.—(1) Any person aggrieved by—
  (a) a repair notice,
  (b) a demand for the recovery of expenses incurred by a local authority in executing works, specified in such a notice,
  (c) an order made by a local authority with respect to any such expenses,
  (d) a charging order made under Schedule 9,
may appeal to the sheriff by giving notice of appeal within 21 days after the date of the service of the notice, demand or order, as the case may be; and no proceedings shall be taken by the local authority to enforce any notice, demand or order while an appeal against it is pending.

(2) On an appeal under paragraph (b), (c) or (d) of subsection (1), no question shall be raised which might have been raised on an appeal against the original notice requiring the execution of the works.

Date of operation of notices, demands and orders subject to appeal

112. Any notice, demand or order against which an appeal might be brought to the sheriff under section 111 shall—
  (a) if no such appeal is brought, become operative on the expiration of 21 days after the date of the service of the notice, demand or order, as the case may be, and shall be final and conclusive as to any matters which could have been raised on such an appeal, and
  (b) if such an appeal is brought shall, if and so far as it is confirmed by the sheriff, become operative as from the date of the determination of the appeal.

Landlord and tenant

Obligations to repair

113. Schedule 10 shall have effect in relation to the landlord's obligation under certain leases to repair the subjects let.

Part VI

Closing and Demolition Orders

Powers of local authority

Closing order

114.—(1) Where a local authority, on consideration of an official representation or a report by the proper officer or other information in their possession, are satisfied that any house does not meet the tolerable standard and that it ought to be demolished and—
  (a) the house forms only part of a building, and
  (b) the building does not comprise only houses which do not meet the tolerable standard,
the local authority may make a closing order prohibiting the use of the house for human habitation.

(2) A closing order shall have effect from such date as may be specified in the order, not being less than 28 days from the date on which it comes into operation.

(3) In this section, "house" includes any room habitually used as a sleeping place, the surface of the floor of which is more than 3 feet below the surface of the part of the street adjoining or nearest to the room (an "underground room").

(4) An underground room does not meet the tolerable standard for the purpose of this section if—

(a) it is not an average of 7 feet in height from floor to ceiling, or

(b) it does not comply with such regulations as the local authority may make for securing the proper ventilation and lighting of such rooms and the protection thereof against dampness, effluvia or exhalation.

(5) If a local authority, after being required to do so by the Secretary of State, fail to make regulations under subsection (4)(b), the Secretary of State may himself make regulations which shall effect as if they had been made by the authority under that subsection.

Demolition order

115. Where a local authority, on consideration of an official representation or a report by the proper officer or other information in their possession, are satisfied that any building comprises only a house which does not meet, or houses which do not meet, the tolerable standard and that the house or, as the case may be, houses, ought to be demolished, they may, subject to section 119, make a demolition order requiring—

(a) that the building shall be vacated within such period as may be specified in the order, not being less than 28 days from the date on which the order comes into operation, and

(b) that the building shall be demolished within 6 weeks after the expiration of that period or, if the building is not vacated before the expiration of the period, within 6 weeks after the date on which it is vacated.

Revocation of closing and demolition order

116. If in the case of a house in respect of which a closing order has been made or a building in respect of which a demolition order has been made the local authority are satisfied, on an application made by any owner of the house or building, or any person appearing to the authority to have reasonable cause for making the application, that the house has, or, as the case may be, the house or houses comprised in the building have, been brought up to the tolerable standard, they shall make an order revoking the closing order or, as the case may be, the demolition order.

Undertakings to bring up to tolerable standard and suspension order

117.—(1) Where a closing order or a demolition order has been made in respect of a house or building and not revoked, any owner of the house or building, or any person holding a heritable security over it, may give to the local authority, within a period of 21 days from the date of service of the order or such longer period therefrom as the authority may, either during or after the expiry of the 21 days, determine to be appropriate, an undertaking in writing—

(a) that he will within a specified period carry out such works as will, in the opinion of the local authority, bring the house or, as the case may be, all the houses in the building, up to the tolerable standard; or

(b) in the case of a building in respect of which a demolition order has been made, that no house in the building will be used for human habitation (unless at any time all the houses therein are brought up to the tolerable standard and the local authority agree that they have been so brought).

(2) If an undertaking is so given the local authority shall as soon as may be either—

(a) accept the undertaking and make in respect of it a suspension order suspending the closing order or, as the case may be, the demolition order, or

(b) reject the undertaking and serve on the person who gave the undertaking notice that they have done so.

(3) A suspension order shall cease to have effect on the expiry of one year from the date of its making unless renewed, at the discretion of the local authority, at the expiry of that year; and this subsection shall apply to any suspension order so renewed as it applies to the original order.

(4) A suspension order made or renewed by a local authority may be revoked by them at any time by order if they have reasonable cause to believe that there has been a breach of the undertaking in respect of which it was made or renewed.

(5) Any period—

(a) between the service of the closing order or demolition order and the service of a suspension order or a notice of rejection under subsection (2), and

(b) while a suspension order is in force,

shall be left out of account in reckoning in relation to the closing order or demolition order in question the period of 21 days referred to in sections 129(1) and 130.

Service

118.—(1) Any order made or notice issued under sections 114 to 117 in respect of a house or building shall be served—

(a) upon the person having control of the house or, as the case may be, the house or houses comprised in the building;

(b) upon any other person who is an owner of the house or, as the case may be, any of those houses;

(c) upon any person holding a heritable security over the house or, as the case may be, any of those houses, unless it appears to the local authority, after exercising their powers under section 325, that there is no such person; and

(d) where an application has been made in relation to the house, or, as the case may be, those houses, under section 116, by a person upon whom the order or notice is not required to be served apart from this paragraph, upon that person.

(2) In subsection (1), references to an owner of, and to any person holding a heritable security over, a building shall be construed as including respectively references to an owner of, and to any person holding a heritable security over, any part of the building.

Listed buildings and houses subject to building preservation orders

119.—(1) Where apart from this section a local authority would be empowered to make a demolition order under this Part with respect to a building—

(a) in relation to which a building preservation notice served under section 56 of the Town and Country Planning (Scotland) Act 1972 is in force, or

(b) which is a listed building within the meaning of section 52(7) of that Act, they shall not make a demolition order but instead may make a closing order or closing orders under this section in respect of the house or houses comprised in the building.

(2) Where a building to which a demolition order made under this Part by a local authority applies (whether or not that order has become operative) becomes—

(a) subject to a building preservation notice served under the said section 56, or

(b) a listed building within the meaning of the said section 52(7),

the local authority shall revoke the demolition order and may make a closing order or closing orders in respect of the house or houses comprised in the building.

(3) The provisions of section 114(1), 116, 117 and 118 shall, subject to any necessary modifications, have effect in relation to a closing order made under this section as they have effect in relation to a closing order made under those sections.

Powers of local authority in relation to building consisting wholly of closed houses

120.—(1) Where a building consists wholly of houses with respect to which closing orders have become operative and none of those orders has been revoked or is subject to a suspension order, then—

(a) the local authority may revoke the closing orders and make a demolition order under section 115 in respect of the whole building, but section 117 shall not apply to the order; or

(b) the local authority may purchase the land by agreement or may, subject to the provisions of this section, be authorised by the Secretary of State to purchase it compulsorily.

(2) The provisions of the Acquisition of Land (Authorisation Procedure) (Scotland) Act 1947 shall apply in relation to the compulsory purchase of land under subsection (1)(b) as if that subsection had been in force immediately before the commencement of that Act.

(3) The compensation to be paid for land purchased compulsorily under this section shall be assessed by the Lands Tribunal in accordance with Land Compensation (Scotland) Act 1963 subject, however, to the provisions of subsections (4) and (5).

(4) The compensation payable under this section shall not (except by virtue of paragraph 3 of Schedule 2 to the said Act of 1963) exceed the value, at the time when the valuation is made, of the site as a cleared site available for development in accordance with the requirements of the building regulations for the time being in force in the district.

(5) The references in subsections (3) and (4) to compensation are references to the compensation payable in respect of the purchase exclusive of any compensation for disturbance or for severance or for injurious affection.

(6) Where a local authority acquire land by virtue of this section, the provisions of paragraph 8(b) of Schedule 8 shall apply as if the land were in a housing action area and had been purchased for the purpose of demolishing the buildings thereon.

Local authority may acquire and repair house or building liable to closing or demolition order

121.—(1) If, in relation to any house or building to which this section applies, it appears to a local authority that having regard to—

(a) its existing condition;

(b) the needs of the area for the provision of further housing accommodation;

the house or building must remain in use as housing accommodation, they may purchase it.

(2) This section applies to any house or building in respect of which the local authority may make—

(a) a closing order under section 114; or

(b) a demolition order under section 115 or 120(1).

(3) Where a local authority determine to purchase a house or building under subsection (1), they shall serve notice of the determination on every person on whom they would be required under section 118(1) to serve a closing order or a demolition order made in respect of the house or building, and at any time after that notice comes into operation the local authority may purchase the house or building by agreement or may be authorised by the Secretary of State to purchase it compulsorily.

(4) The provisions of the Acquisition of Land (Authorisation Procedure) (Scotland) Act 1947 shall apply in relation to the compulsory purchase of a house or building under this section as if this section had been in force immediately before the commencement of that Act.

(5) The compensation to be paid for any house or building purchased compulsorily under this section shall be assessed by the Lands Tribunal in accordance with the Land Compensation (Scotland) Act 1963 subject, however, to the provisions of subsections (6) and (7).

(6) The compensation payable under this section shall not (except by virtue of paragraph 3 of Schedule 2 to the said Act of 1963) exceed the value, at the time when the valuation is made, of the site as a cleared site available for development in accordance with the requirements of the building regulations for the time being in force in the area.

(7) The references in subsections (5) and (6) to compensation are references to the compensation payable in respect of the purchase exclusive of any compensation for disturbance or for severance or for injurious affection.

(8) A local authority by whom a house or building is purchased under this section shall carry out such works as may in the opinion of the authority from time to time be required for rendering or keeping it capable of being continued in use as housing accommodation.

(9) In respect of any house purchased by a local authority under this section, the authority shall have the like powers and duties as they have in respect of houses provided under Part I.

Offences

Penalty for use of premises in contravention of closing order or of undertaking

122.—(1) If any person—

(a) knowing that a closing order made under section 114 or section 119 has become operative and applies to any premises, uses those premises or permits those premises to be used for human habitation without having obtained the consent of the local authority to the use of the premises for that purpose; or

(b) knowing that an undertaking that any premises shall not be used for human habitation has been accepted by the local authority under this Part, uses those premises for human habitation or permits them to be so used,

he shall be guilty of an offence.

(2) Any person guilty of an offence under subsection (1) shall be liable on summary conviction—

(a) to a fine not exceeding level 5 on the standard scale, or to imprisonment for a term not exceeding 3 months or to both such fine and such imprisonment; and

(b) in the case of a continuing offence, to a further fine of £5 for every
day or part of a day on which he so uses those premises, or permits
them to be so used, after conviction.

Powers of local authority following demolition order

Procedure where demolition order made

123.—(1) When a demolition order has become operative, the owner of
the building to which it applies shall demolish the building within the time
limited in that behalf by the order; and, if the building is not demolished
within that time, the local authority may enter and demolish the building
and sell the material thereof.

(2) Any expenses incurred by a local authority under subsection (1),
after giving credit for any amount realised by the sale of materials, may
be recovered by them from the owner of the building, and any surplus in
the hands of the authority shall be paid by them to the owner of the
building.

(3) In the application of this section to a demolition order made in
respect of a building comprising two or more parts separately owned—

(a) any reference to the owner of the building shall be construed as a
reference to the owners of the several parts comprised in the
building;

(b) without prejudice to the powers of the local authority under
subsection (1), the duty imposed by that subsection on the owners
of the several parts comprised in the building to demolish the
building shall be regarded as a duty to arrange jointly for the
demolition of the building; and

(c) subsection (2) shall have effect subject to the proviso that any sum
recoverable or payable by the local authority under that subsection
shall be recoverable from or payable to the several owners in such
proportions as the owners may agree or, failing agreement, as shall
be determined by an arbiter, nominated by the owners or, failing
such nomination, nominated on the application of the authority or
any of the owners, by the sheriff.

**Power of local authority to purchase site of demolished building where
expenses of demolition cannot be recovered**

124.—(1) Where a local authority have demolished a building in exercise
of the powers conferred on them by section 123 and the expenses thereby
incurred by them cannot be recovered by reason of the fact that the owner
of the building cannot be found, the authority may be authorised by the
Secretary of State to purchase compulsorily the site of the building,
including the area of any yard, garden or pertinent belonging to the
building or usually enjoyed therewith.

(2) The provisions of the Acquisition of Land (Authorisation Procedure)
(Scotland) Act 1947 shall apply in relation to a compulsory purchase of
land under subsection (1) as if that subsection had been in force immediately before the commencement of that Act.

(3) A local authority shall be entitled to deduct from the compensation
payable on the compulsory purchase of the site of a building under this
section the amount of the expenses referred to in subsection (1) so far as
not otherwise recovered.

(4) A local authority shall deal with any land purchased by them under
this section by sale, letting or appropriation in accordance with the
provisions of paragraph 8 of Schedule 8.

Demolition of obstructive buildings

Local authority may by resolution require demolition of obstructive building

125.—(1) A local authority may serve upon the owner or owners of a building which appears to the authority to be an obstructive building notice of the time (being some time not less than one month after the service of the notice) and place at which the question of demolishing the building will be considered by the authority.

(2) Where a local authority serve a notice under subsection (1) on an owner of a building, they shall at the same time require him to furnish within two weeks thereafter a written statement specifying the name and address of the superior of whom such owner holds, and of any person holding a heritable security over the owner's interest in the building, and the authority shall as soon as may be after receipt of such statement serve on any person whose name is included therein, notice of the time and place at which the question of demolishing the building will be considered.

(3) Any person on whom a notice is served under subsection (1) or (2) shall be entitled to be heard when the question of demolishing the building to which the notice relates is taken into consideration.

(4) If after so taking the matter into consideration the local authority are satisfied that the building is an obstructive building and that the building or any part thereof ought to be demolished, they may pass a resolution that the building or that part thereof shall be demolished and may, by such resolution, require that the building, or such part thereof as is required to be vacated for the purposes of the demolition, shall be vacated within two months from the date on which the resolution becomes operative, and, if they do so, shall serve a copy of the resolution upon the owner or owners of the building.

(5) If any person fails to give to the local authority any information required by them under subsection (2) or knowingly makes any mis-statement with reference thereto, he shall be guilty of an offence and shall be liable on summary conviction to a fine not exceeding level 1 on the standard scale.

(6) In this section, the expression "obstructive building" means a building which, by reason only of its contact with, or proximity to, other buildings, is injurious or dangerous to health.

(7) This section shall not apply to a building which is the property of public undertakers, unless it is used for the purposes of a dwelling, showroom or office, or which is the property of a local authority.

Effect of resolution for demolition of obstructive building

126.—(1) Subject to the provisions of this section, where a local authority have made a resolution and required a building to be vacated under section 125(4), they shall be bound to purchase the building if the owner offers to sell it to them.

(2) On purchasing a building under this section, the local authority shall demolish it as soon as possible after they obtain possession of it.

(3) A local authority shall only be bound to purchase the building if—
   (a) the offer is made before the expiry of the period within which the resolution requires it to be vacated; and
   (b) the acquisition of the owner's interest would, apart from section 125, enable them to demolish the building.

(4) The offer to sell shall be at a price to be assessed by the Lands Tribunal in accordance with the Land Compensation (Scotland) Act 1963, as modified by Schedule 1, as if it were compensation for compulsory purchase.

(5) If no such offer as is mentioned in subsection (1) is made before the expiry of the said period, the local authority shall, as soon as may be thereafter, carry out the demolition and shall have the like right to sell the materials rendered available thereby as if they had purchased the building.

(6) Where the demolition of a building is carried out under subsection (5), compensation shall be paid by the local authority to the owner in respect of loss arising from the demolition, and that compensation shall, notwithstanding that no land is acquired compulsorily by the authority, be assessed by the Lands Tribunal in accordance with the said Act of 1963, as modified by Schedule I, except that paragraphs (2) to (6) of section 12 of the said Act of 1963 shall not apply and that paragraph (1) of the said section 12 shall have effect with the substitution, for the reference to acquisition, of a reference to demolition.

Possession

Recovery of possession of building or house subject to closing order, etc.

127.—(1) Where a closing order, a demolition order, or a resolution passed under section 125 has become operative, the local authority shall serve on the occupier of any building or house or any part thereof to which the order or resolution relates a notice—

(a) stating the effect of the order or resolution, and

(b) specifying the date by which the order or resolution requires the building or house to be vacated, and

(c) requiring the occupier to remove from the building or house before the said date or before the expiration of 28 days from the service of the notice, whichever may be the later.

(2) If at any time after the date on which a notice under subsection (1) requires a building or house to be vacated, any person is in occupation of the building or house or of any part of it, the local authority or any owner of the building or house may make a summary application for removal and ejection to the sheriff.

(3) The sheriff may, after requiring service of such additional notice (if any) as he thinks fit, grant warrant for ejection giving vacant possession of the building or house or of the part of it in question to the authority or owner, as the case may be, within such period, not being less than 2 weeks nor more than 4 weeks, as the sheriff may determine.

(4) Subject to subsection (5), any expenses incurred by a local authority under this section in obtaining possession of any building or house or part thereof may be recovered by them from the owner of the building or house.

(5) Subsection (4) does not apply to expenses incurred in obtaining possession of—

(a) premises to which a resolution passed under section 125 applies; or

(b) any other premises unless the owner has failed to make within a reasonable time a summary application for removal and ejection to the sheriff or, having made such an application, has failed to take all steps necessary to have the application disposed of within a reasonable time.

(6) Any person who, knowing that a demolition order or a resolution passed under section 125 has become operative and applies to any building or house, enters into occupation of that building or house or any part of it after the date by which the order or resolution requires that building or house to be vacated, or permits any other person to enter into such occupation after that date, shall be guilty of an offence and shall be liable on summary conviction—

(a) to a fine not exceeding level 5 on the standard scale, or to imprisonment for a term not exceeding 3 months or to both such fine and such imprisonment; and

(b) in the case of a continuing offence to a further fine of £5 for every day, or part of a day, on which the occupation continues after conviction.

Recovery of possession of house to which Rent Acts applies

128. Nothing in the Rent (Scotland) Act 1984 shall be deemed to affect the provisions of this Act relating to obtaining possession of a house with respect to which a closing order, or a demolition order has been made or to which a resolution passed under section 125 applies, or to prevent possession being obtained—

(a) of any house possession of which is required for the purpose of enabling a local authority to exercise their powers under any enactment relating to housing;

(b) of any house possession of which is required for the purpose of securing compliance with any byelaws made for the prevention of overcrowding;

(c) of any premises by any owner in a case where an undertaking has been given under this Part that those premises shall not be used for human habitation.

Appeals and date of operation of certain notices, etc.

Appeals

129.—(1) Subject to the provisions of this section and subsections (2), (3) and (4) of section 324 any person aggrieved by—

(a) a closing order made under section 114 or section 119 or a refusal to determine such a closing order;

(b) a demolition order or a refusal to determine a demolition order or a resolution under section 125;

(c) a notice of determination to purchase served under section 121(3);

(d) a notice that no payment falls to be made under section 304(1) served under subsection (2) of that section;

may appeal to the sheriff by giving notice of appeal within 21 days after the date of the service of the notice, or order or resolution, or after the refusal, as the case may be; and no proceedings shall be taken by the local authority to enforce any notice, or order while an appeal against it is pending.

(2) No appeal shall lie under paragraphs (a), (b) or (c) of subsection (1) at the instance of a person who is in occupation of the premises to which the order or resolution or notice relates under a lease or agreement the unexpired term of which does not exceed 6 months.

(3) On an appeal under paragraph (a) or paragraph (b) of subsection (1), the sheriff may consider any undertaking such as is specified in relation to a closing order or a demolition order, as the case may be, in section 117 and, if he thinks it proper to do so having regard to the undertaking, may direct the local authority to make a suspension order under that section.

Date of operation of notices, orders or resolutions subject to appeal

130.—(1) Any notice, or order or resolution against which an appeal might be brought to the sheriff under section 129 shall, if no such appeal is brought, become operative on the expiration of 21 days after the date of the service of the notice, or order or resolution, as the case may be, and shall be final and conclusive as to any matters which could have been raised on such an appeal.

(2) Any such notice or order or resolution against which an appeal is brought shall, if and so far as it is confirmed by the sheriff, become operative as from the date of the determination of the appeal.

Charging orders

Power of local authority to make charging order in favour of themselves

131.—(1) Where a local authority have themselves incurred expenses under section 123 in the demolition of a building, they may make a charging order in favour of themselves in respect of such expenses.

(2) The provisions of Schedule 9 shall, subject to any necessary modifications and to the provisions of subsection (3), apply to a charging order so made.

(3) A charging order so made shall be made in relation to the site of the building demolished, including the area of any yard, garden or pertinent belonging to the building or usually enjoyed therewith.

Supplementary

Protection of superiors and owners

132.—(1) If the superior of any lands and heritages gives notice to the local authority of his right of superiority, the authority shall give to him notice of any proceedings taken by them in pursuance of this Part in relation to the lands and heritages.

(2) Nothing in this Part shall prejudice or interfere with the rights or remedies of any owner for the breach, non-observance or non-performance of any contract or obligation entered into by a tenant or lessee with reference to any house in respect of which an order or resolution is made by a local authority under this Part; and if any owner is obliged to take possession of any house in order to comply with any such order or resolution the taking possession shall not affect his right to avail himself of any such breach, non-observance or non-performance which may have occurred before he so took possession.

Interpretation

133.—(1) In this Part (except sections 125, 126 and 132) any reference to a house, or to a building, includes a reference to premises occupied by agricultural workers although such premises are used for sleeping purposes only.

(2) For the purposes of this Part a crofter or a landholder shall be deemed to be the owner of any house on his croft or holding in respect of which he would, on the termination of his tenancy, be entitled to compensation under the Crofters (Scotland) Acts 1955 and 1961 or, as the case may be, the Small Landholders (Scotland) Acts 1886 to 1931, as for an improvement.

Saving

Saving for telecommunication and gas apparatus

134. Paragraph 23 of Schedule 2 to the Telecommunications Act 1984 (code for cases where works involve the alteration of apparatus), as applied by paragraph 2(7) of Schedule 7 to the Gas Act 1986 to gas apparatus, shall apply to a local authority for the purposes of any works which they are authorised to execute under this Part.

PART VII

OVERCROWDING

Definition of overcrowding

Definition of overcrowding

135.—A house is overcrowded for the purposes of this Part when the number of persons sleeping in the house is such as to contravene—

    (a) the standard specified in section 136 (the room standard), or

    (b) the standard specified in section 137 (the space standard).

The room standard

136.—(1) The room standard is contravened when the number of persons sleeping in a house and the number of rooms available as sleeping accommodation is such that two persons of opposite sexes who are not living together as husband and wife must sleep in the same room.

(2) For this purpose—

    (a) children under the age of 10 shall be left out of account, and

    (b) a room is available as sleeping accommodation if it is of a type normally used in the locality either as a bedroom or as a living room.

The space standard

137.—(1) The space standard is contravened when the number of persons sleeping in a house is in excess of the permitted number, having regard to the number and floor area of the rooms of the house available as sleeping accommodation.

(2) For this purpose—

    (a) no account shall be taken of a child under the age of one and a child aged one or over but under 10 shall be reckoned as one-half of a unit, and

    (b) a room is available as sleeping accommodation if it is of a type normally used in the locality either as a living room or as a bedroom.

(3) The permitted number of persons in relation to a house is whichever is the less of—

    (a) the number specified in Table I in relation to the number of rooms in the house available as sleeping accommodation, and

    (b) the aggregate for all such rooms in the house of the numbers specified in column 2 of Table II in relation to each room of the floor area specified in column 1.

No account shall be taken for the purposes of either Table of a room having a floor area of less than 50 square feet.

Table I

Number of rooms	Number of persons
1	2
2	3
3	5
4	$7\frac{1}{2}$
5 or more	2 for each room

Table II

Floor area of room	Number of persons
110 sq. ft. or more	2
90 sq. ft. or more but less than 110 sq. ft.	$1\frac{1}{2}$
70 sq. ft. or more but less than 90 sq. ft.	1
50 sq. ft. or more but less than 70 sq. ft.	$\frac{1}{2}$

(4) The Secretary of State may prescribe the manner in which the floor area of a room is to be ascertained for the purposes of this section; and the regulations may provide for the exclusion from computation, or the bringing into computation at a reduced figure, of floor space in a part of the room which is of less than a specified height.

(5) Regulations under subsection (4) shall be made by statutory instrument which shall be subject to annulment in pursuance of a resolution of either House of Parliament.

(6) A certificate of the local authority stating the number and floor areas of the rooms in a house, and that the floor areas have been ascertained in the prescribed manner, is evidence for the purposes of legal proceedings of the facts stated in it.

Powers of Secretary of State

Secretary of State may increase permitted number of persons temporarily

138.—(1) The Secretary of State may, subject to the provisions of this section, increase by order the number of permitted persons in relation to houses to which this section applies or a specified class of those houses.

(2) This section applies to houses consisting of a few rooms, or comprising rooms of exceptional floor area.

(3) The Secretary of State may make an order under this section if he is satisfied on the representation of the local authority that such houses constitute so large a proportion of the housing accommodation in their district, or in any part of it, that it would be impracticable to assess the permitted number of persons in accordance with the provisions of section 137(3).

(4) An order under this section may—
- (a) direct that the provisions of section 137(3) are to have effect subject to such modifications for increasing the permitted number of persons as may be specified in the order;
- (b) specify the period not exceeding 3 years during which such modifications are to apply;
- (c) specify different modifications in relation to different classes of houses.

(5) Any period specified in the order may be extended by the Secretary of State on the application of the local authority.

(6) The Secretary of State shall consult the local authority before varying or revoking an order made under this section, and may vary it in respect of the modifications or of the houses to which the modifications apply or to both.

(7) An order made under this section shall be made by statutory instrument.

Responsibility of occupier

Penalty for occupier causing or permitting overcrowding

139.—(1) The occupier of a house who causes or permits it to be overcrowded is guilty of an offence, subject to subsection (2).

(2) The occupier is not guilty of an offence—
- (a) if the overcrowding is within the exceptions specified in sections 140 or 141 (children attaining age of 10 or temporary visitor), or
- (b) by reason of anything done under the authority of, and in accordance with any conditions specified in, a licence granted by the local authority under section 142 or a resolution passed under section 143.

(3) A person committing an offence under this section is liable on summary conviction to a fine not exceeding level 1 on the standard scale.

Exception: children attaining age of 1 or 10

140.—(1) Where a house which would not otherwise be overcrowded becomes overcrowded by reason of a child attaining the age of one or 10, the occupier does not commit an offence under section 139(1) (occupier causing or permitting overcrowding), so long as the condition in subsection (2) is met and the occupier does not fail to accept an offer of suitable alternative accommodation or to secure the removal of any person living in the house who is not a member of his family and whose removal is reasonably practicable.

(2) The condition is that all the persons sleeping in the house are persons who were living there when the child attained that age and thereafter continuously live there, or children born after that date of any of those persons.

Exception: temporary visitor

141.—The occupier of a house shall not be guilty of an offence under section 139(1) in respect of overcrowding if the overcrowding is caused by a temporary resident whose stay does not exceed 16 days and to whom lodging is given by the occupier otherwise than for gain.

Licence of local authority

142.—(1) The occupier or intending occupier of a house may apply to the local authority for a licence authorising him to permit a number of persons in excess of the permitted number to sleep in the house.

(2) The authority may grant such a licence if it appears to them that there are exceptional circumstances and that it is expedient to do so; and they shall specify in the licence the number of persons authorised in excess of the permitted number.

(3) The licence shall be in the prescribed form and may be granted either unconditionally or subject to conditions specified in it.

(4) The local authority may revoke the licence at their discretion by notice in writing served on the occupier and specifying a period (at least one month from the date of service) at the end of which the licence will cease to be in force.

(3) Unless previously revoked, the licence continues in force for such period not exceeding twelve months as may be specified in it.

(6) A copy of the licence and of any notice of revocation shall, within seven days of the issue of the licence or the service of the notice on the occupier, be served by the local authority on the landlord (if any) of the house.

Exception: holiday visitors

143.—(1) A local authority may, for the purpose of providing for a seasonal increase of holiday visitors in their area, pass a resolution authorising—

(a) the occupiers of houses generally;

(b) the occupiers of houses of a specified class,

in their area or any specified part of it to permit such number of persons in excess of the permitted number as may be specified to sleep in those houses during any period it is in force.

(2) Such a resolution—

(a) requires the approval of the Secretary of State;

(b) is subject to such conditions as may be specified in it; and

(c) remains in force during the year in which it is passed for such period or periods not exceeding 16 weeks in the aggregate as it may specify.

Powers and duties of landlord

Offence by landlord not to inform prospective tenant of permitted number of occupants

144.—(1) The landlord of a house is guilty of an offence if he lets or agrees to let it to any person without—

   (a) giving that person a written statement in the prescribed form of the permitted number of persons in relation to the house, and

   (b) obtaining from that person a written acknowledgement in the prescribed form, and

   (c) exhibiting the acknowledgement to the local authority on demand by them.

(2) A person guilty of an offence under subsection (1) shall be liable on summary conviction to a fine not exceeding level 1 on the standard scale.

(3) A written statement given under subsection (1)(a) shall be treated as being sufficient and correct if it agrees with information given by the local authority under section 148.

Recovery of possession of overcrowded house that is let

145. If the occupier of a house is guilty of an offence by reason of it being overcrowded—

   (a) nothing in the Rent (Scotland) Act 1984 shall prevent the landlord from obtaining possession of the house;

   (b) the local authority after giving to the landlord written notice of their intention to do so may take any such steps for the termination of the occupier's tenancy or for his removal or ejection from the house as the landlord could take.

Powers and duties of local authority

Duty of local authority to inspect district and to make reports and proposals as to overcrowding

146.—(1) A local authority shall, subject to the provisions of this section, carry out an inspection of their district or any part of it for the purpose of identifying houses that are overcrowded.

(2) An inspection under subsection (1) shall be carried out at such times as—

   (a) it appears to the local authority that there is occasion to do so, or

   (b) the Secretary of State so directs.

(3) On carrying out such an inspection the local authority shall prepare and submit to the Secretary of State a report indicating—

   (a) the result of the inspection, and

   (b) the additional housing accommodation required to put an end to overcrowding in the area to which the report relates, and

   (c) subject to subsection (5), proposals for its provision, and

   (d) in relation to such proposals, a statement of the steps the local authority propose to take to secure that priority is given to rehousing families living under the worst conditions of overcrowding or otherwise living under unsatisfactory housing conditions.

(4) The report shall give such details as the Secretary of State may direct.

(5) The report shall not require to make proposals for the additional housing accommodation required, if the local authority satisfy the Secretary of State that it will be otherwise provided.

(6) Where the Secretary of State gives a direction under subsection (2), he may fix dates before which the performance of their duties under this section is to be completed.

Power to require information about persons sleeping in house

147.—(1) The local authority may, for the purpose of enabling them to discharge their duties under this Part, serve notice on the occupier of a house requiring him to give them within 14 days a written statement of the number, ages and sexes of the persons sleeping in the house.

(2) The occupier shall be guilty of an offence if—

    (a) he makes default in complying with the requirement, or

    (b) he gives a statement which to his knowledge is false in a material particular,

and shall be liable on summary conviction to a fine not exceeding level 1 on the standard scale.

Duty to give information to landlords and occupiers

148.—(1) A local authority shall inform the landlord and the occupier of a house in writing of the permitted number of persons in relation to the house as soon as they have ascertained the floor area of the rooms.

(2) They shall also so inform the landlord or the occupiers if they apply for the information.

Power to publish information

149. A local authority may publish information for the assistance of landlords and occupiers of houses as to their rights and duties under this Part.

Duty to enforce this Part

150. A local authority shall enforce the provisions of this Part.

Interpretation and applications

151.—(1) In this Part, except where the context otherwise requires—

    "house" means any premises used or intended to be used as a separate dwelling, not being premises which are entered in the valuation roll last authenticated at a rateable value exceeding £45;

    "landlord" means, in relation to any house, the person from whom the occupier derives his right to occupy it;

    "suitable alternative accommodation" means, in relation to the occupier of a house, a house in which the occupier and his family can live without causing it to be overcrowded, being a house which the local authority certify to be suitable to the needs of the occupier and his family as respects security of tenure and proximity to place of work and to be suitable in relation to his means.

(2) The provisions of sections 138(1) to (5), 139(3), 140(1) and (2) and 144(1) and (2) apply only to a locality in respect of which a day has been appointed under section 99 of the Housing (Scotland) Act 1966 or under any enactment referred to in that section.

PART VIII

HOUSES IN MULTIPLE OCCUPATION

Registration schemes

Registration schemes

152.—(1) A local authority may make and submit to the Secretary of State for confirmation by him a registration scheme authorising the authority to compile and maintain a register for their district of—

   (a) houses which, or a part of which, are let in lodgings, or which are occupied by members of more than one family; and
   (b) buildings which comprise separate dwellings, two or more of which lack either or both of the following—
      (i) a sanitary convenience accessible only to those living in the dwelling, and
      (ii) personal washing facilities so accessible,

and the Secretary of State may, if he thinks fit, confirm the scheme, with or without modification.

   (2) A registration scheme need not be for the whole of a local authority's district and need not be for every description of house or building falling within paragraphs (a) and (b) of subsection (1).

   (3) A registration scheme may—

   (a) specify the particulars to be inserted in the register;
   (b) make it the duty of such persons as may be specified by the scheme to notify the local authority of the fact that a house or building appears to be registrable, and to give to the authority as regards the house or building all or any of the particulars specified in the scheme;
   (c) make it the duty of such persons to notify the authority of any change which makes it necessary to alter the particulars inserted in the register as regards any house or building; and
   (d) make a contravention of, or failure to comply with, any provision in the scheme an offence under the scheme, and a person guilty of an offence under the scheme shall be liable on summary conviction to a fine not exceeding level 2 on the standard scale.

   (4) A registration scheme may vary or revoke a previous registration scheme and a local authority may at any time, with the consent of the Secretary of State, by order revoke a registration scheme.

   (5) A registration scheme shall not come into force until it has been confirmed but, subject to that, comes into force on such date as may be fixed by the scheme or, if no date is so fixed, at the expiration of one month after it is confirmed.

Steps to inform the public about scheme

153.—(1) The local authority shall publish notice of their intention to submit a registration scheme to the Secretary of State for confirmation in one or more newspapers circulating in their district at least one month before the scheme is submitted to the Secretary of State for confirmation by him.

   (2) As soon as any such scheme is confirmed by the Secretary of State, the local authority shall publish in one or more newspapers circulating in their district a notice—

   (a) stating the fact that a registration scheme has been confirmed, and
   (b) describing any steps which will have to be taken under the scheme by those concerned with registrable houses and buildings (other

than steps which have only to be taken after a notice from the local authority), and

(c) naming a place where a copy of the scheme may be seen at all reasonable hours.

(3) A copy of a registration scheme confirmed by the Secretary of State—

(a) shall be printed and deposited at the offices of the local authority by whom it was made, and

(b) shall at all reasonable hours be open to public inspection without payment, and

(c) a copy thereof shall on application be furnished to any person on payment of such sum, not exceeding 5p for every copy, as the authority may determine.

(4) If a local authority revoke a registration scheme by order they shall publish notice of the order in one or more newspapers circulating in their district.

Proof of scheme and contents of register

154. The production of a printed copy of a registration scheme purporting to be made by a local authority upon which is endorsed a certificate purporting to be signed by the proper officer of the authority stating—

(a) that the scheme was made by the authority,

(b) that the copy is a true copy of the scheme, and

(c) that on a specified date the scheme was confirmed by the Secretary of State,

shall be prima facie evidence of the facts stated in the certificate, and without proof of the handwriting or official position of the person by whom the certificate purports to be signed.

Power to require information for purposes of scheme

155.—(1) Without prejudice to the provisions of section 325 (power of local authority to require occupier to state interest), a local authority may—

(a) for the purpose of ascertaining whether a house or building is registrable, and

(b) for the purpose of ascertaining the particulars to be entered in the register as regards the house or building,

require any person who has an estate or interest in, or who lives in, the house or building to state in writing any information in his possession which the authority may reasonably require for that purpose.

(2) Any person who, having been required in pursuance of this section to give information to a local authority, fails to give information, or knowingly makes any mis-statement in respect of it, shall be guilty of an offence and shall be liable on summary conviction to a fine not exceeding level 2 on the standard scale.

Management code

Power of Secretary of State to make management code

156.—(1) The Secretary of State may by regulations contained in a statutory instrument with a view to providing a code for the management of houses which may be applied under section 157, make provision for the purpose of ensuring that the person managing a house which, or a part of which, is let in lodgings, or which is occupied by members of more than one family observes proper standards of management.

(2) Without prejudice to the generality of subsection (1), the regulations may, in particular, require the person managing a house to which the regulations apply to ensure the repair, maintenance, cleansing and good order of—

(a) all means of water supply and drainage in the house;

(b) kitchens, bathrooms and water closets used in common by persons living in the house;

(c) sinks and wash-basins used in common by persons living in the house;

(d) the roof and windows forming part of the house;

(e) common staircases, corridors and passage ways;

(f) outbuildings, yards and gardens used in common by persons living in the house;

and to make satisfactory arrangements for the disposal of refuse and litter from the house.

(3) The regulations may—

(a) make different provision for different types of houses;

(b) provide for keeping a register of the names and addresses of those who are managers of houses;

(c) impose duties on persons who have an estate or interest in a house or any part of a house to which the regulations apply as to the giving of information to the local authority, and in particular may make it the duty of any person who acquires or ceases to hold an estate or interest in such a house to notify the authority;

(d) impose duties on persons who live in a house to which the regulations apply for the purpose of ensuring that the person managing the house can effectively carry out the duties imposed on him by the regulations;

(e) authorise the local authority to obtain information as to the number of individuals or households accommodated in the house;

(f) make it the duty of the person managing the house to cause a copy of the order under section 157 and of the regulations, to be displayed in a suitable position in the house;

(g) contain such other incidental and supplementary provisions as may appear to the Secretary of State to be expedient.

(4) If any person knowingly contravenes or without reasonable excuse fails to comply with any regulation under this section as applied under this Act in relation to any house he shall be guilty of an offence and shall be liable on summary conviction to a fine not exceeding level 3 on the standard scale.

(5) In this section, "person managing a house" means—

(a) the person who is an owner or lessee of the house and who, directly or through a trustee, tutor, curator, factor or agent, receives rents or other payments from persons who are tenants of parts of the house, or who are lodgers; and

(b) where those rents or other payments are received through another person as his trustee, tutor, curator, factor or agent, that other person.

(6) Regulations under this section may vary or replace for the purposes of this section and of the regulations made under it the definition of the "person managing a house" in subsection (5).

Power of local authority to apply management code to particular house

157.—(1) If it appears to a local authority that a house which, or a part of which, is let in lodgings, or which is occupied by members of more than one family is in an unsatisfactory state in consequence of failure to maintain proper standards of management and, accordingly, that it is necessary that the regulations made under section 156 should apply to the house, the authority may by order direct that those regulations shall so apply; and so long as the order is in force the regulations shall apply in relation to the house accordingly.

(2) Not less than 21 days before making an order under this section, the local authority shall—

(a) serve on an owner of the house, and on every person who is to their knowledge a lessee of the house, notice of their intention to make the order, and

(b) post such a notice in some position in the house where it is accessible to those living in the house,

and shall afford to any person on whom a notice is served an opportunity of making representations regarding their proposal to make the order.

(3) The order comes into force on the date on which it is made.

(4) The local authority shall within 7 days from the making of the order—

(a) serve a copy of the order on an owner of the house and on every person who is to their knowledge a lessee of the house, and

(b) post a copy of the order in some position in the house where it is accessible to those living in the house.

(5) The local authority may at any time revoke the order on the application of a person having an estate or interest in the house.

Appeal against making of, or failure to revoke, order under s.157

158.—(1) A person on whom a copy of an order is served under section 157(4), and any other person who is a lessee of the house, may, within 14 days from the latest date by which copies of the order are required to be served, appeal to the sheriff on the ground that the making of the order was unnecessary.

(2) On an appeal under subsection (1) the sheriff shall take into account the state of the house at the time when the local authority under section 157 served notice of their intention to make the order, as well as at the time of the making of the order, and shall disregard any improvement in the state of the house between those times unless the sheriff is satisfied that effective steps have been taken to ensure that the house will in future be kept in a satisfactory state.

(3) If the sheriff allows the appeal, he shall revoke the order, but without prejudice to its operation prior to the revocation and without prejudice to the making of a further order.

(4) If a local authority—

(a) refuse an application for the revocation of an order under section 157(5), or

(b) do not within 42 days from the making of the application, or within such further period as the applicant may in writing allow, notify the applicant of their decision on the application,

the applicant may appeal to the sheriff and the sheriff, if of the opinion that there has been a substantial change in the circumstances since the making of the order, and that it is in other respects just to do so, may revoke the order.

Registration of order and of revocation

159.—(1) The local authority shall as soon as practicable after an order under section 157 has come into force cause the order to be recorded in the General Register of Sasines or registered in the Land Register, as the case may be.

(2) If any such order is revoked the authority shall as soon as practicable cause to be recorded in the General Register of Sasines or registered in the Land Register, as the case may be, a notice stating that the order has been revoked.

Powers of local authority to require works to be done

Notice requiring compliance with management code

160.—(1) If in the opinion of the local authority the condition of a house is defective in consequence of—

(a) neglect to comply with the requirements imposed by regulations under section 156 (regulations prescribing management code), or

(b) in respect of a period falling wholly or partly before the regulations applied to the house, neglect to comply with standards corresponding to the requirements imposed by the regulations,

the authority may serve on the person managing the house a notice specifying the works which in the opinion of the authority are required to make good the neglect, and requiring the person on whom the notice is served to execute those works.

(2) If it is not practicable after reasonable inquiry to ascertain the name or address of the person managing the house, the notice under this section may be served by addressing it to him by the description of "manager of the house" (naming the house to which it relates) and by delivering it to some person on the premises.

(3) The notice shall require the execution of the works specified in the notice within such period, being not less than 21 days from the service of the notice, as may be so specified.

(4) That period may from time to time be extended by written permission of the local authority.

(5) Where the local authority serve a notice on any person under this section they shall inform any other person who is to their knowledge an owner or lessee of the house or a person holding a heritable security over the house of the fact that such a notice has been served.

Notice requiring compliance with standards

161.—(1) The local authority may serve a notice under this section where the condition of a house which, or a part of which, is let in lodgings, or which is occupied by members of more than one family is, in the opinion of the authority, so far defective with respect to any of the matters mentioned in subsection (2), having regard to the number of individuals or households, or both, accommodated for the time being on the premises, as not to be reasonably suitable for occupation by those individuals or households.

(2) The matters referred to in subsection (1) are—

natural and artificial lighting,

ventilation,

water supply,

personal washing facilities,

drainage and sanitary conveniences,

facilities for the storage, preparation and cooking of food, and for the disposal of waste water,

installations for space heating or for the use of space heating appliances.

(3) The notice shall specify the works which in the opinion of the authority are required for rendering the premises reasonably suitable—

(a) for occupation by the individuals and households for the time being accommodated there, or

(b) for a smaller number of individuals or households and the number of individuals or households, or both, which, in the opinion of the authority, the premises could reasonably accommodate if the works were carried out.

(4) The notice shall be served either—

    (a) on the person having control of the house, or

    (b) on any person to whom the house is let, or on any person who, as the trustee, tutor, curator, factor or agent for or of a person to whom the house is let, receives rents or other payments from tenants of parts of the house or lodgers in the house.

(5) The notice shall require the person on whom it is served to execute the works specified in the notice within such period (of at least 21 days from the service of the notice) as may be so specified.

(6) That period may from time to time be extended by written permission of the authority.

(7) If the local authority are satisfied that—

    (a) after the service of a notice under this section in respect of any premises the number of individuals living on those premises has been reduced to a level which will make the work specified in the notice unnecessary, and

    (b) that number will be maintained at or below that level whether in consequence of exercise of the authority's powers under section 166 (powers to limit number of occupants of houses) or otherwise,

they may notify in writing the person on whom the notice was served of the withdrawal of the notice, but the withdrawal of the notice shall be without prejudice to the issue of a further notice.

(8) Where the local authority serve a notice on any person under this section they shall inform any other person who is to their knowledge an owner or lessee of the house or a person holding a heritable security over the house of the fact that such a notice has been served.

Notice requiring provision of means of escape from fire

162.—(1) If it appears to a local authority that a house which, or a part of which, is let in lodgings, or which is occupied by members of more than one family is not provided with such means of escape from fire as the authority consider necessary, the authority may, subject to this section, serve on any person on whom a notice may be served under section 161 a notice specifying the works which in the opinion of the authority are required to provide such means of escape, and requiring the person on whom the notice is served to execute those works.

(2) A local authority shall serve such a notice if such house is of such description or occupied in such manner as the Secretary of State may, with the consent of the Treasury, specify by order a draft of which has been approved by the House of Commons.

(3) A local authority shall, before serving a notice under this section, consult with the fire authority concerned.

(4) A notice under this section shall require the execution of the works within such period, being not less than 21 days from the service of the notice, as may be specified in the notice, but that period may from time to time be extended by written permission of the local authority.

(5) Where the local authority serve a notice on any person under this section they shall inform any other person who is to their knowledge an owner or lessee of the house or a person holding a heritable security over the house of the fact that such a notice has been served.

(6) In this section "fire authority" has the same meaning as in section 82.

Appeal against notice requiring execution of works

163.—(1) A person on whom a notice is served under section 160, 161 or 162 or any other person who is an owner or lessee of the house, or a person holding a heritable security over the house, to which the notice relates, may, within 21 days from the service of the notice, or within such longer period as the local authority may in writing allow, appeal to the sheriff on any of the grounds specified in subsection (2).

(2) Those grounds are—

(a) that there has been some informality, defect or error in, or in connection with, the notice;

(b) that the local authority have refused unreasonably to approve the execution of alternative works, or that the works required by the notice to be executed are otherwise unreasonable in character or extent, or are unnecessary;

(c) that the time within which the works are to be executed is not reasonably sufficient for the purpose;

(d) that some person other than the appellant is wholly or in part responsible for the state of affairs calling for the execution of the works, or will as the holder of an estate or interest in the premises derive a benefit from the execution of the works, and that that other person ought to pay the whole or any part of the expenses of executing the works;

(e) in the case of a notice under section 160, that the condition of the house did not justify the local authority in requiring the execution of the works specified in the notice;

(f) in the case of a notice under section 161, that—

(i) having regard to the matters mentioned in subsections (1) and (2) of that section, the condition of the house did not justify the local authority in requiring the execution of the works specified in the notice;

(ii) the number of individuals or households, or both, specified in the notice is unreasonably low;

(g) in the case of a notice under section 162, that the notice is not justified by the terms of that section.

(3) In an appeal on ground (a), the sheriff shall dismiss the appeal if he is satisfied that the informality, defect or error was not a material one.

(4) In an appeal on ground (d)—

(a) the appellant shall serve a copy of his notice of appeal on each other person referred to in that notice, and

(b) on the hearing of the appeal the sheriff may, if satisfied that any other person referred to in the notice of appeal has had proper notice of the appeal, make such order as he thinks fit with respect to the payment to be made by that other person to the appellant or, where the work is executed by the local authority, to the authority.

(5) If on an appeal under this section against a notice under section 161, the sheriff is satisfied that the number of persons living in the house has been reduced, and that adequate steps (whether by the exercise by the exercise* by the local authority of the power conferred by section 166 to limit the number of persons living in the house or otherwise) have been taken to prevent that number being again increased, the sheriff may, if he thinks fit, revoke the notice or vary the list of works specified in the notice.

Carrying out of works by local authority

164.—(1) If a notice under section 160, 161 or 162 (notice requiring the execution of works) is not complied with, the local authority may them-

* Error in H.M.S.O. copy.

selves do the works required by the notice, with any variation made by the sheriff.

(2) Compliance with a notice means the completion of the works specified in the notice within the period for compliance, which is—

    (a) if no appeal is brought against the notice, the period specified in the notice with any extension duly permitted by the local authority;

    (b) if an appeal is so brought, and the notice is confirmed in whole or in part of the appeal, the period of 28 days from the final determination of the appeal, or such longer period as the sheriff in determining the appeal may fix.

(3) If, before the expiration of the period for compliance with the notice, the person on whom the notice was served notifies the local authority in writing that he is not able to do the work in question, the authority may, if they think fit, themselves do the work forthwith.

(4) Part IV of Schedule 11 shall have effect in relation to the recovery by the local authority of expenses reasonably incurred by them under this section.

Penalty for failure to execute works

165.—(1) A person on whom a notice has been served under section 160, 161 or 162 who wilfully fails to comply with the notice, shall be guilty of an offence and shall be liable on summary conviction to a fine not exceeding—

    (a) in the case of a notice under section 160 or 161, level 3 on the standard sale;

    (b) in the case of a notice under section 162, level 4 on the standard scale.

(2) The obligation to execute the works specified in the notice continues notwithstanding that the period for compliance has expired; and a person who wilfully fails to comply with that obligation, after being convicted of an offence in relation to the notice under subsection (1) or this subsection, commits a further summary offence and is liable on conviction to a fine not exceeding level 4 on the standard scale.

(3) References in this section to compliance with a notice and to the period for compliance shall be construed in accordance with section 164(2).

(4) No liability arises under subsection (1) if the local authority, on being notified under section 164(3) by the person on whom any such notice requiring the execution of works was served that he is not able to do the work in question, serve notice that they propose to do the work and relieve the person served with the notice from liability under subsection (1).

(5) Subsection (1) shall be without prejudice to the exercise by the local authority of their powers of carrying out works under section 164.

Overcrowding

Local authority may give directions to prevent or reduce overcrowding in house in multiple occupation

166.—(1) A local authority may, for the purpose of preventing the occurrence of, or remedying, a state of affairs calling for the service of a notice or further notice under section 161, fix as a limit for any house what is in their opinion the highest number of individuals who should, having regard to the considerations set out in subsections (1) and (2) of that section, live in the house in its existing condition, and give a direction applying that limit to the house.

References in this section to a house include references to part of a house, and the local authority shall have regard to the desirability of applying separate limits where different parts of a house are, or are likely to be, occupied by different persons.

(2) The powers conferred by this section shall be exercisable whether or not a notice has been given under section 161 and where a local authority have served a notice under subsection (3) of that section specifying the number of individuals or households, or both, which in the opinion of the authority any premises could reasonably accommodate if the works specified in the notice were carried out, the authority may adopt that number of individuals, or a number of individuals determined by reference to that number of households, in fixing a limit under subsection (1) as respects those premises.

(3) The powers conferred by subsection (1) may be exercised as regards any premises notwithstanding the existence of any previous direction under the subsection laying down a higher maximum.

(4) A direction under subsection (1) shall have effect so as to make it the duty of the occupier for the time being of the house—

(a) not to permit any individual to take up residence in the house so as to increase the number of individuals living in the house to a number above the limit specified in the direction, and

(b) where the number of individuals living in the house is for the time being above the limit so specified and any individual ceases to reside in the house, not to permit any other individual to take up residence in the house.

In this subsection the reference to the occupier for the time being of a house shall include a reference to any person who is for the time being entitled or authorised to permit individuals to take up residence in the house or any part of it.

(5) If any person knowingly fails to comply with the requirements imposed on him by subsection (4) he shall be guilty of an offence and shall be liable on summary conviction to a fine not exceeding level 3 on the standard scale.

Notice of direction

167.—(1) A local authority shall, not less than 7 days before giving a direction under section 166—

(a) serve on an owner of the house, and on every person who is to their knowledge a lessee of the house, notice of their intention to give the direction, and

(b) post such a notice in some position in the house where it is accessible to those living in the house,

and shall afford to any person on whom a notice is so served an opportunity of making representations regarding their proposal to give the direction.

(2) The local authority shall within 7 days from the giving of any such direction—

(a) serve a copy of the direction on an owner of the house and on every person who is to their knowledge a lessee of the house, and

(b) post a copy of the direction in some position in the house where it is accessible to those living in the house.

Power to require information where notice is in force

168.—(1) The local authority may from time to time serve on the occupier of a house or part of a house in respect of which a direction under section 166 is in force a notice requiring him to furnish them within 7 days with a statement in writing giving all or any of the following particulars—

   (a) the number of individuals who are, on a date specified in the notice, living in the house or part of the house, as the case may be;

   (b) the number of families or households to which those individuals belong;

   (c) the names, ages and sex of those individuals and the names of the heads of each of those families or households;

   (d) the rooms used by those individuals and families or households respectively.

(2) If the occupier makes default in complying with the requirements or furnishes a statement which to his knowledge is false in any material particular, he shall be guilty of an offence and shall be liable on summary conviction to a fine not exceeding level 2 on the standard scale.

Revocation and variation

169.—(1) At any time after giving such a direction the local authority may on the application of any person having an estate or interest in the house—

   (a) revoke that direction, or

   (b) vary it so as to allow more people to be accommodated in the house.

(2) In exercising their powers under subsection (1) the local authority shall have regard to—

   (a) any works which have been executed in the house, or

   (b) any other change of circumstances.

Appeal against refusal

170.—(1) If the local authority refuse an application under section 169 or do not within 42 days from the making of such an application, or within such further period as the applicant may in writing allow, notify the applicant of their decision on the application, the applicant may appeal to the sheriff.

(2) The sheriff may revoke the direction or vary it in any manner in which it might have been varied by the authority.

Supplementary

Application of sections 156 to 161 to certain buildings comprising separate dwellings

171.—(1) Subject to the provisions of this section, sections 156 to 161 apply—

   (a) to a building which is not a house but comprises separate dwellings, two or more of which lack either or both of the following—

     (i) a sanitary convenience accessible only to those living in the dwelling, and

     (ii) personal washing facilities so accessible, and

   (b) to a building which is not a house but comprises separate dwellings, two or more of which are wholly or partly let in lodgings or occupied by members of more than one family,

being in either case a building all the dwellings in which are owned by the same person, as if references in those sections to a house which, or part of which, is let in lodgings or which is occupied by members of more than one family included references to any such building.

(2) A notice under section 161(3)(b) shall not by virtue of this section be served in respect of such a building.

(3) A direction under section 166 shall not by virtue of this section be given in relation to such a building.

(4) If a local authority make an order under section 157, as applied by subsection (1), in respect of any building at a time when another order under that section is in force as respects one of the dwellings in the building, they shall revoke the last-mentioned order.

(5) References to a house in sections 163, 164, 175 and 177 shall include references to a building to which this section applies.

Management code to be available for dwellings in certain tenements

172.—(1) If—

(a) all the dwellings in any tenement are owned by the same person, and

(b) all or any of those dwellings are without one or more of the standard amenities,

sections 156 to 160 shall apply to the tenement as if references in those sections to a house which, or a part of which, is let in lodgings, or which is occupied by members of more than one family included references to the tenement.

(2) If a local authority make an order under section 157, as applied by subsection (1), in respect of any tenement at a time when another order under that section is in force as respects one of the dwellings in the tenement, they shall revoke the last-mentioned order.

(3) References to a house in section 163 (so far as relating to appeals against notices under section 160) and in sections 164, 175 and 177 shall include references to a tenement to which this section applies.

(4) In this section—

"dwelling" means a building or part of a building occupied or intended to be occupied as a separate house;

"tenement" means a building which contains two or more flats.

Warrant to authorise entry

173.—(1) Where it is shown to the satisfaction of the sheriff, or of a justice of the peace or magistrate, on sworn information in writing, that admission to premises specified in the information is reasonably required by a person employed by, or acting on the instructions of, a local authority for the purpose—

(a) of survey and examination to determine whether any powers under the foregoing provisions of this Part should be exercised in respect of the premises, or

(b) of ascertaining whether there has been a contravention of any regulations or direction made or given under the foregoing provisions of this Part,

then, subject to this section, the sheriff, justice or magistrate may by warrant under his hand authorise that person to enter on the premises for the purposes mentioned in paragraphs (a) and (b), or for such of those purposes as may be specified in the warrant.

(2) A sheriff, justice or magistrate shall not grant a warrant under this section unless he is satisfied—

(a) that admission to the premises has been refused and, except where the purpose specified in the information—

(i) is the survey and examination of premises to determine whether there has been a failure to comply with a notice under section 160 or section 161 or section 162, or

(ii) is to ascertain whether there has been a contravention of any regulations or direction made or given under the foregoing provisions of this Part,

that admission was sought after not less than 24 hours' notice of the intended entry had been given to the occupier; or

(b) that an application for admission to the premises would defeat the object of the entry.

(3) Every warrant granted under this section shall continue in force until the purpose for which the entry is required has been satisfied.

(4) Any person who, in the exercise of a right of entry under this section, enters any premises which are unoccupied, or any premises the occupier of which is temporarily absent, shall leave the premises as effectually secured against trespassers as he found them.

(5) Any power of entry conferred by this section—

    (a) shall include power to entry, if need be, by force, and

    (b) may be exercised by the person on whom it is conferred either alone or together with any other persons.

Application to sheriff where consent unreasonably withheld

174. If on an application made by any person required by a notice under the foregoing provisions of this Part to execute any works it appears to the sheriff that any other person having an estate or interest in the premises has unreasonably refused to give any consent required to enable the works to be executed, the sheriff may give the necessary consent in place of that other person.

Protection of superiors and owners

175.—(1) If the superior or owner of any lands and heritages gives notice to the local authority of his estate in those lands and heritages, the authority shall give to him notice of any proceedings taken by them in pursuance of the foregoing provisions of this Part in relation to those lands and heritages or any part thereof.

(2) Nothing in the foregoing provisions of this Part shall prejudice or interfere with the rights or remedies of any owner for the breach, non-observance or non-performance of any agreement or stipulation entered into by a lessee with reference to any house in respect of which a notice requiring the execution of works is served by a local authority under the foregoing provisions of this Part, or as respects which regulations made under section 156 are for the time being in force; and if any owner is obliged to take possession of a house in order to comply with any such notice the taking possession shall not affect his right to avail himself of any such breach, non-observance or non-performance which has occurred before he so took possession.

Identity and notice under Part VIII

176.—(1) A local authority shall take reasonable steps to identify the persons mentioned in subsection (2).

(2) Those persons are—

    (a) the person having control of or managing premises;

    (b) the person having an estate or interest in premises or any class of such persons,

upon whom the local authority require to serve a document under this Part.

(3) A person having an estate or interest in premises may for the purposes of this Part give notice to the local authority of his interest in the premises, and the authority shall enter the notice in their records.

Statutory tenant to be regarded as lessee, etc.

177. In this Part—

    (a) references to a lessee of a house and to a person to whom a house is let include references to any person who retains possession of the house by virtue of the Rent (Scotland) Act 1984 and not as being entitled to any tenancy; and

(b) references to a person having an estate or interest in a house include references to any person who retains possession of the house as mentioned in paragraph (a).

Control orders

Making of control order

178.—(1) A local authority may make a control order in respect of a house in their district which, or a part of which, is let in lodgings, or which is occupied by members of more than one family if—

(a) a notice has been served in respect of the house under section 160 or 161 (notices requiring the execution of works),

(b) a direction has been given in respect of the house under section 166 (direction limiting number of occupants),

(c) an order under section 157 is in force in respect of the house (order applying management code), or

(d) it appears to the local authority that the state or condition of the house is such as to call for the taking of action under any of those sections,

and if it appears to the local authority that the living conditions in the house are such that it is necessary to make the control order in order to protect the safety, welfare or health of persons living in the house.

(2) A local authority may exclude from the provisions of a control order any part of the house which, when the control order comes into force, is occupied by a person who has an estate or interest in the whole of the house, and, except where the context otherwise requires, references in this Part to the house do not include references to any part of the house so excluded from the provisions of the control order.

(3) A control order shall come into force when it is made, and as soon as practicable after making a control order the local authority shall, in exercise of the power conferred in the following provisions of this Part and having regard to the duties imposed on them by the said provisions, enter on the premises and take all such immediate steps as appear to them to be required to protect the safety, welfare or health of persons living in the house.

(4) As soon as practicable after making a control order the local authority shall—

(a) post a copy of the control order, together with a notice as described in subsection (5), in some position in the house where it is accessible to those living in the house; and

(b) serve a copy of the control order, together with such a notice, on every person who, to the knowledge of the local authority—

(i) was, immediately before the coming into force of the control order, a person managing the house or a person having control of the house, or

(ii) is an owner or lessee of the house or a person holding a heritable security over the house.

(5) The notice referred to in subsection (4) shall set out the effect of the control order in general terms, referring to the rights of appeal against control orders conferred by this Part and stating the principal grounds on which the local authority consider it necessary to make a control order.

(6) As soon as practicable after making a control order the local authority shall cause the control order to be recorded in the General Register of Sasines or registered in the Land Register, as the case may be.

General effect of control order

179.—(1) While a control order is in force the local authority—
   (a) have the right to possession of the premises, and
   (b) have the right to do, and to authorise others to do, in relation
      to the premises anything which any person having an estate or
      interest in the premises would, but for the making of the
      control order, be entitled to do, without incurring any liability
      to any such person except as expressly provided by this Part.

(2) Subject to subsection (3), the local authority may, notwithstanding that they do not, under this section, have an interest amounting to an estate in the premises, create an interest in the premises which, as near as may be, has the incidents of a lease and, subject to the provisions of section (4) and to any other express provision of this Part, any enactment or rule of law relating to landlords and tenants or leases shall apply in relation to any interest created under this section as if the local authority were the owner of the premises.

(3) Subject to the provisions of paragraphs 5(6) and 6(1) of Schedule 11, the local authority shall not, in exercise of the power conferred by this section, create any right in the nature of a lease or licence which is for a fixed term exceeding one month, on which is terminable by notice to quit (or an equivalent notice) of more than 4 weeks:

Provided that this subsection shall not apply to a right created with the consent in writing of the person or persons who would have power to create that right if the control order were not in force.

(4) On the coming into force of a control order any order under section 157, and any notice or direction under sections 160, 161, 162 or 166, shall cease to have effect as respects the house to which the control order applies, but without prejudice to any criminal liability incurred before the coming into force of the control order, or to the right of the local authority to recover any expenses incurred in carrying out any works.

(5) References in this Act or in any other enactment to housing accommodation provided or managed by a local authority shall not include references to any house which is subject to a control order, but this subsection shall not be taken as restricting the powers of acquiring land by agreement or compulsorily conferred on local authorities by Part I.

Effect of control order on persons occupying house

180.—(1) This section applies to a person who at the time a control order comes into force—
   (a) is occupying any part of the house, and
   (b) does not have an estate or interest in the whole of the house.

(2) Section 179 (general effect of control order) does not affect the rights or liabilities of such a person under any lease, licence or agreement, whether in writing or not, under which that person is occupying any part of the house at the time when the control order comes into force, and—
   (a) any such lease, licence or agreement has effect, while the control
      order is in force, as if the local authority were substituted in it for
      any party to it who has an estate or interest in the house and who
      is not a person to whom this section applies; and
   (b) any such lease continues to have effect as near as may be as a lease
      notwithstanding that the rights of the local authority, as substituted
      for the lessor, do not amount to an estate in the premises.

(3) Subject to the provisions of subsection (4) and to any other express provision of this Part, any enactment or rule of law relating to landlords and tenants or leases shall apply in relation to any lease to which the local authority become a party under this section as if the authority were the owner of the premises.

(4) Section 5 of the Rent (Scotland) Act 1984 (which excludes lettings by local authorities from being protected tenancies within the meaning of the Act) shall not apply to any lease or agreement under which a person to whom this section applies is occupying any part of the house, and if immediately before the control order came into force any person to whom this section applies was occupying part of the house under a protected or statutory tenancy, within the meaning of the Rent (Scotland) Act 1984, nothing in this Part relating to control orders shall prevent the continuance of that protected or statutory tenancy nor affect the continued operation of that Act in relation to that protected or statutory tenancy after the coming into force of the control order.

(5) So much of the regulations made under section 156 as imposes duties on persons who live in a house to which the regulations apply (regulations prescribing management code) also applies to persons who live in a house as respects which a control order is in force.

(6) Without prejudice to the rights conferred on the local authority by section 179, the authority and any person authorised in writing by them, shall have the right at all reasonable times, as against any person having an estate or interest in a house which is subject to a control order, to enter any part of the house for the purpose of—

(a) survey and examination, and
(b) carrying out any works.

(7) The rights conferred by subsection (6) shall, so far as reasonably required for the purpose of survey and examination of a part of a house subject to a control order, or for the purpose of carrying out any works in that part of a house, be exercisable as respects the part of the house which, by virtue of section 178(2), is not subject to the control order.

Effect of control order in relation to furniture in furnished lettings

181.—(1) Subject to this section, if on the date on which a control order comes into force there is any furniture in the house which a resident in the house has the right to use in consideration of periodical payments to the dispossessed proprietor (whether included in the rent payable by the resident or not), the right to possession of the furniture shall, on that date and as against all persons other than the resident, vest in the local authority and remain vested in the authority while the control order remains in force.

(2) The local authority may, on the application in writing of the person owning any furniture to which subsection (1) applies, by notice served on that person not less than 2 weeks before the notice takes effect, renounce the right to possession of the furniture conferred by subsection (1).

(3) In respect of the period during which the local authority have the right to possession of any furniture in pursuance of subsection (1), the authority shall be liable to pay to the dispossessed proprietor compensation in respect of the use of any furniture the right to possession of which vests under that subsection at such rate as the parties may agree or as may be determined by the rent assessment committee constituted under section 44 of the Rent (Scotland) Act 1984 or under any corresponding enactment repealed by that Act for the area in which the house is situated.

(4) If the local authority's right to possession of any furniture conferred by subsection (1) is a right exercisable as against more than one person interested in the furniture, any such person may apply to the sheriff for an adjustment of the rights and liabilities of those persons as regards the furniture, and the sheriff may make an order for any such adjustment of rights and liabilities either unconditionally or subject to such terms and conditions (including terms or conditions with respect to the payment of money by any party to the proceedings to any other party to the

proceedings by way of compensation, damages or otherwise) as he thinks just and equitable.

(5) Compensation due under this section—
  (a) shall be payable by quarterly instalments, the first instalment being payable 3 months after the date when the control order comes into force;
  (b) is to be considered as accruing due from day to day and shall be apportionable in respect of time accordingly.

(6) In this Part "dispossessed proprietor" means the person by whom the rents or other periodical payments to which a local authority become entitled on the coming into force of a control order would have been receivable but for the making of the control order, and the successors in title of that person; and in this section "furniture" includes fittings and other articles.

General duties of local authority when control order in force

182.—(1) The local authority shall—
  (a) exercise the powers conferred on them by a control order so as to maintain proper standards of management in the house,
  (b) take such action as is needed to remedy all the matters which they would have considered it necessary to remedy by the taking of action under any other provision of this Part if they had not made a control order.

(2) The local authority may fit out, furnish and supply any house subject to a control order with such furniture, fittings and conveniences as appear to them to be required.

(3) The local authority shall make reasonable provision for insurance of any premises subject to a control order, including any part of the premises which, by virtue of section 178(2), is excluded from the provisions of the control order, against destruction or damage by fire or other cause, and premiums paid for the insurance of the premises shall, for the purposes of the provisions of this Part, be treated as expenditure incurred by the local authority in respect of the premises.

(4) The local authority shall keep full accounts of their income and expenditure in respect of a house which is subject to a control order, and afford to the dispossessed proprietor, or any other person having an estate or interest in the house, all reasonable facilities for inspecting, taking copies of and verifying those accounts.

(5) While a control order is in force the local authority shall afford to the dispossessed proprietor, or any other person having an estate or interest in the house, any reasonable facilities requested by him for inspecting and examining the house.

Compensation payable to dispossessed proprietor

183.—(1) The local authority shall be liable to pay the dispossessed proprietor compensation in respect of the period during which the control order is in force at an annual rate of an amount equal to one half of the gross annual value for rating purposes of the house as shown in the valuation roll on the date when the control order comes into force.

(2) Compensation due under this section—
  (a) shall be payable by quarterly instalments, the first instalment being payable 3 months after the date when the control order comes into force;
  (b) is to be considered as accruing due from day to day and shall be apportionable in respect of time accordingly.

(3) If at the time when compensation under this section accrues due the estate or interest of the dispossessed proprietor is subject to any

heritable security or charge, the compensation shall be deemed to be comprised in that heritable security or charge.

(4) For the purposes of the references in this section to the gross annual value of a house—

  (a) where after the date on which the control order comes into force the valuation roll is altered so as to vary the gross annual value of the house or of the lands and heritages of which house forms part, and the alteration has effect from a date not later than the date on which the control order comes into force, compensation shall be payable under this section as if the gross annual value of the house or lands and heritages shown in the valuation roll on the date when the control order came into force had been the amount of the value shown on the roll as altered; and

  (b) if the house forms part only of any lands and heritages, such proportion of the gross annual value shown in the valuation roll for those lands and heritages as may be agreed in writing between the local authority and the person claiming the compensation shall be the gross annual value of the house;

and any dispute arising under paragraph (b) shall be determined by the sheriff on the application of either party.

(5) If different persons are the dispossessed proprietors of different parts of any house, compensation payable under this section shall be apportioned between them in such manner as they may agree (or as may, in default of agreement, be determined by the sheriff on the application of any of such persons) according to the proportions of the gross annual value of the house properly attributable to the parts of the house in which they are respectively interested.

(6) In the application of this section to any lands and heritages whose net annual value is ascertained under subsection (8) of section 6 of the Valuation and Rating (Scotland) Act 1956 (and for which there is therefore no gross annual value shown in the valuation roll)—

  (a) in subsection (1), for the words "one half of the gross" there shall be substituted the words "0.625 of the net", and

  (b) in each of subsections (4) and (5), for the word "gross", whenever it occurs, there shall be substituted the word "net".

Duty to prepare management scheme

184.—(1) After a control order has been made, the local authority shall prepare a management scheme and shall, not later than 8 weeks after the date on which the control order comes into force, serve a copy of the scheme on—

  (a) every person who is to the knowledge of the authority—
    (i) a dispossessed proprietor, or
    (ii) an owner or lessee of the house, or
    a person holding a heritable security over the house, and

  (b) on any other person on whom the local authority served a copy of the control order.

(2) Part I of Schedule 11 has effect with respect to the matters to be provided for in a management scheme and for related matters.

(3) This section does not affect the powers conferred on a local authority by section 179 and, accordingly, a local authority may carry out any works in a house which is subject to a control order whether or not particulars of those works have been included in a management scheme.

Power of sheriff to modify or determine lease

185.—(1) Either the lessor or the lessee under any lease of premises which consist of or comprise a house which is subject to a control order, other than a lease to which section 180(2) applies, may apply to the sheriff for an order under this section.

(2) On any such application, the sheriff may make an order for the determination of the lease, or for its variation, and, in either case, either unconditionally or subject to such terms and conditions or subject to such terms and conditions (including terms or conditions with respect to the payment of money by any party to the proceedings to any other party to the proceedings by way of compensation, damages or otherwise) as the sheriff may think just and equitable to impose, regard being had to the respective rights, obligations and liabilities of the parties under the lease and to the other circumstances of the case.

(3) If on any such application the sheriff is satisfied that—

    (a) if the lease is determined and control order is revoked the lessor will be in a position, and intends, to take all such action to remedy the condition of the house as the local authority consider would have to be taken in pursuance of the powers conferred on them under this Part (other than those relating to control orders); and

    (b) the local authority intend, if the lease is determined, to revoke the control order,

the sheriff shall exercise the jurisdiction conferred by this section so as to determine the lease.

Appeals

Appeal against control order

186.—(1) Any person having an estate or interest in a house to which a control order relates, or, subject to subsection (2), any other person, may appeal to the sheriff against the control order at any time after the making of the control order, but not later than the expiry of a period of 6 weeks from the date on which a copy of the relevant scheme is served in accordance with section 184(1).

(2) The sheriff may, before entertaining an appeal by a person who had not, when he brought the appeal, an estate or interest in the house, require the appellant to satisfy the sheriff that he may be prejudiced by the making of the control order.

(3) The grounds of appeal are—

    (a) that (whether or not the local authority have made an order or issued a notice or direction under sections 157, 160, 161 or 166) the state or condition of the house was not such as to call for the taking of action under any of those provisions;

    (b) that it was not necessary to make the control order in order to protect the safety, welfare or health of persons living in the house;

    (c) where part of the house was occupied by the dispossessed proprietor when the control order came into force, that it was practicable and reasonable for the local authority to exercise their powers under section 178(2) so as to exclude from the provisions of the control order a part of the house (or a greater part of the house than has been excluded);

    (d) that the control order is invalid on the ground that any requirement of this Act has not been complied with or on the ground of some informality, defect or error in or in connection with the control order.

(4) In so far as an appeal under this section is based on the ground that the control order is invalid, the sheriff shall confirm the control order unless satisfied that interests of the appellant have been substantially prejudiced by the facts relied on by him.

(5) A control order shall, subject to the right of appeal conferred by this section, be final and conclusive as to any matter which could have been raised on any such appeal.

(6) Where a control order is revoked on an appeal under this section, the local authority shall as soon as practicable thereafter cause to be recorded in the General Register of Sasines or registered in the Land Register, as the case may be, a notice stating that the control order has been revoked as aforesaid.

Control order revoked on appeal

187.—(1) This section shall have effect if a control order is revoked by the sheriff on an appeal against the control order.

(2) If the local authority are in the course of carrying out any works in the house which, if a control order were not in force, the authority would have power to require some other person to carry out under the provisions of this Part or under any other enactment relating to housing or public health, and on the hearing of the appeal the sheriff is satisfied that the carrying out of the works could not be postponed until after the determination of the appeal because the works were urgently required for the sake of the safety, welfare or health of persons living in the house, or of other persons, the sheriff may suspend the revocation of the control order until the works have been completed.

(3) Part II of Schedule 11 has effect in relation to matters arising on the revocation of a control order on appeal.

Expiration and revocation of control order, etc.

Expiration of control order, and earlier revocation by local authority or sheriff

188.—(1) A control order shall cease to have effect on the expiry of a period of 5 years beginning with the date on which it came into force.

(2) The local authority may at any earlier time, either on an application under this section or on their own initiative, by order revoke a control order.

(3) Not less than 21 days before the local authority revoke a control order they shall serve notice of their intention to revoke the control order on the persons occupying any part of the house, and on every person who is to the knowledge of the authority an owner or lessee of the house or a person holding a heritable security over the house.

(4) If any person applies to the local authority requesting the authority to revoke a control order, and giving the grounds on which the application is made, the authority shall, if they refuse the application, inform the applicant of their decision and of their reason for rejecting the grounds advanced by the applicant.

(5) Where the local authority propose to revoke a control order on their own initiative and apply to the sheriff under this subsection, the sheriff may take any of the following steps, to take effect on the revocation of the control order, that is—

(a) approve the making of an order under section 157;

(b) approve the giving of a notice under section 160 or section 161 or section 162; or

(c) approve the giving of a direction under section 166;

and no appeal lies against any order or notice so approved.

Effect of cessation of control order

189. Part III of Schedule 11 (which sets out the consequences of a control order ceasing to have effect) shall have effect for the purposes of this Part.

Interpretation of Part VIII

190.—(1) In this Part of this Act, unless the context otherwise requires—

"dispossessed proprietor" has the meaning given by section 181(6);

"establishment charges" means, in relation to any expenditure incurred by a local authority, the proper addition to be made to that expenditure to take account of overhead expenditure incurred by the authority, and to allow for a proper return of capital;

"lease" includes a sublease or any tenancy, and any agreement for a lease, sublease or tenancy, and references to a lessor or to a lessee or to a person to whom a house is let shall be construed accordingly;

"licence" means any right or permission relating to land but not amounting to an estate or interest therein;

"person managing a house" has the meaning given to it by section 156(5);

"surpluses on revenue account as settled by the scheme" has the meaning given by paragraph 1(3) of Schedule 11.

(2) References in this Part to the net amount of rents or other payments received by a local authority from persons occupying a house are references to the amount of the rent and other payments received by the authority from those persons under leases or licences, or in respect of furniture to which section 181(1) applies, after deducting income tax paid or borne by the authority in respect of those rents and other payments.

(3) References in this Part to expenditure incurred in respect of a house subject to a control order include, in a case where the local authority—

(a) require persons living in a house to vacate their accommodation for any period while the local authority are carrying out works in the house, and

(b) defray all or any part of the expenses incurred by or on behalf of those persons removing from and returning to the house, or provide housing accommodation for those persons for any part of that period,

references to the sums so defrayed by the local authority, and to the net cost to the authority of so providing housing accommodation.

(4) For the purposes of this Part the withdrawal of an appeal shall be deemed the final determination thereof having the like effect as a decision dismissing the appeal.

PART IX

GOVERNMENT GRANTS AND SUBSIDIES

Housing support grants to local authorities

Housing support grants: fixing of aggregate amount

191.—(1) For the purpose of assisting local authorities to meet reasonable housing needs in their areas, the Secretary of State shall make housing support grants in accordance with the provisions of this Part.

(2) Subject to subsection (5), for the purpose of fixing the aggregate amount of the housing support grants for any year, the Secretary of State shall, in respect of all local authorities, estimate the following amounts—

(a) the aggregate amount of eligible expenditure which it is reasonable for local authorities to incur for that year; and

(b) the aggregate amount of relevant income (other than housing support grants) which could reasonably be expected to be credited to the local authorities' housing revenue accounts for that year,

and the amount remaining after deducting the amount mentioned in paragraph (b) from the amount mentioned in paragraph (a) shall, subject to subsection (4) and section 193, be the aggregate amount of the housing support grants for that year.

(3) Before estimating the amounts mentioned in paragraphs (a) and (b) of subsection (2) for any year, the Secretary of State shall consult with such associations of local authorities as appear to him to be concerned and shall take into consideration—

(a) the latest information available to him as to the level of eligible expenditure and relevant income;

(b) the level of interest rates, remuneration, costs and prices which, in his opinion, would affect the amount of eligible expenditure for that year; and

(c) the latest information available to him as to changes in the general level of earnings which would affect the amount of relevant income which could reasonably be expected for that year.

(4) In fixing the aggregate amount of the housing support grants for any year, the Secretary of State may take into account the extent, if any, to which the aggregate amount of eligible expenditure which it was reasonable for local authorities to incur for any previous year differs or is likely to differ from the aggregate amount for that previous year which he estimated or re-estimated under this section or section 193 respectively.

(5) In estimating the amounts mentioned in paragraphs (a) and (b) of subsection (2) the Secretary of State may leave out of account the eligible expenditure and relevant income of a local authority if (either or both)—

(a) he estimates that the amount of that income will exceed the amount of that expenditure;

(b) he determines, under section 192, that no proportion of the aggregate amount of the housing support grants is to be apportioned to that authority.

(6) In subsection (4), "local authorities" does not include an authority whose eligible expenditure was, for the purpose of the estimate, left out of an account under subsection (5).

(7) The aggregate amount of the housing support grants, fixed in accordance with subsection (2) for any year, shall be set out in a housing support grant order made by the Secretary of State with the consent of the Treasury.

(8) A housing support grant order may be made in respect of any year before the beginning of that year.

(9) No housing support grant order shall be made until that order has been laid in draft before the Commons House of Parliament, together with a report of the considerations leading to the provisions of the order, and has been approved by a resolution of that House.

(10) In this Act—

"eligible expenditure", in relation to any year, means the expenditure which a local authority are required to debit to their housing revenue account for that year in pursuance of Schedule 15;

"relevant income", in relation to any year, means the income, payments, contributions (including any rate fund contribution) and receipts which a local authority are required to credit to their housing revenue account for that year in pursuance of that Schedule.

Apportionment of housing support grants

192.—(1) Subject to the provisions of this section, the proportion, if any, of the aggregate amount of the housing support grants payable for any year to a local authority shall be determined by the Secretary of State, after consulting with such associations of local authorities as appear to him to be concerned, by such method as may be prescribed.

(2) A prescribed portion of the aggregate amount may be apportioned to a particular local authority.

(3) The report accompanying a housing support grant order in accordance with section 191(9) shall contain a table showing in respect of each local authority, for the year in question—

(a) the estimated amount of grant payable to that local authority; or

(b) if no amount of grant is so payable, that fact.

(4) In prescribing the method of determining the proportion, if any, of the aggregated amount of the housing support grants payable to a local authority for any year, the Secretary of State may take into account any substantial difference in the actual amount of any element of their eligible expenditure as compared with any estimate of the amount of that element made by him in determining the proportion payable to them for a previous year.

(5) In prescribing the method of determining the proportion mentioned in subsection (1) payable for any year to a local authority the Secretary of State shall have regard to any special needs affecting eligible expenditure.

(6) The Secretary of State may, for any year (in this subsection referred to as "the current year"), prescribe such method of determining that proportion as to secure that no reduction in the amount of housing support grant payable to any local authority for the current year as compared with the amount of housing support grant so payable for the immediately preceding year is so great that there is an unreasonable increase for the current year over that preceding year in the amount of the authority's eligible expenditure which is required to be met by way of rent or rate fund contributions.

(7) In this section "prescribed" means prescribed by a housing support grant order.

Variation of orders

193.—(1) Subject to the provisions of this section, the Secretary of State may re-estimate the aggregate amount of eligible expenditure estimated under section 191.

(2) He shall first consult such associations of local authorities as appear to him to be concerned.

(3) Then if it appears to him—

(a) that after that amount was estimated for any year, the eligible expenditure of local authorities for that year has been, or is likely to be, substantially increased or decreased by means of changes which have taken place or are likely to take place in the level of the matters specified in section 191(3)(b), and

(b) that inadequate account was taken of those changes when that amount was estimated,

he may re-estimate that amount.

(4) On such re-estimate he may, by an order made in the like manner and subject to the same provisions as a housing support grant order, increase or, as the case may be, decrease the amount fixed by the relevant housing support grant order as the aggregate amount of the housing support grants for that year.

(5) An order made under this section with respect to any year may, as respects that year, vary any matter prescribed by the relevant housing support grant order.

Grants to the Scottish Special Housing Association and other bodies

Grants payable to the Scottish Special Housing Association and development corporations

194.—(1) The Secretary of State may each year make grants, of such amount and subject to such conditions as he may determine, to the Scottish Special Housing Association ("the Association") and to development corporations in accordance with the provisions of this section.

(2) Grants under this section shall be payable for any year to the Association and to development corporations in respect of the total net annual expenditure (as approved by the Secretary of State and calculated in accordance with rules made by him with the consent of the Treasury) necessarily incurred for that year by the Association, acting otherwise than as agents, or by any development corporation—

(a) in providing housing accommodation by—
  (i) erecting houses,
  (ii) converting any houses or other buildings into houses,
  (iii) acquiring houses;
(b) in improving housing accommodation so provided;
(c) in managing and maintaining any housing accommodation so provided or improved;
(d) in improving the amenities of a predominantly residential area;
(e) in providing or converting buildings for use as hostels or as parts of hostels, and in improving, managing and maintaining buildings so provided or converted;
(f) in doing anything ancillary to any of the activities mentioned in paragraphs (a) to (e).

(3) In subsection (2) "improving" includes altering, enlarging or repairing.

Grants for affording tax relief to Scottish Special Housing Association

195.—(1) The Secretary of State may, on the application of the Association, make grants to the Association for affording relief from—

(a) income tax (other than income tax which the Association is entitled to deduct on making any payment); and
(b) corporation tax.

(2) A grant under this section shall be of such amount, shall be made at such times and shall be subject to such conditions as the Secretary of State thinks fit.

(3) The conditions mentioned in subsection (2) may include conditions for securing the repayment in whole or in part of a grant made to the Association in the event of tax in respect of which the grant was made subsequently being found not to be chargeable or in such other events as the Secretary of State may determine.

(4) An application under this section shall be made in such manner and shall be supported by such evidence as the Secretary of State may direct.

(5) The Commissioners of Inland Revenue and their officers may disclose to the Secretary of State such particulars as he may reasonably require for determining whether a grant should be made under this section or whether a grant so made should be repaid or the amount of such grant or repayment.

Advances to Scottish Special Housing Association for provision or improvement of housing accommodation

196.—(1) The Secretary of State may make advances, of such amounts, on such terms, and repayable over such periods, as may be approved by the Treasury, to the Scottish Special Housing Association for the purpose of—

(a) enabling or assisting the provision or improvement of housing accommodation by the Association (whether as principals or as agents for a local authority or for any other person);

(b) meeting the whole or any part of the expenditure incurred by the Association in connection with any scheme submitted to the Secretary of State by the Association under which the Association will provide or improve housing accommodation, and as to which the Secretary of State is satisfied that the housing accommodation so provided or improved will be let or kept available for letting except at such times and in such cases as the Secretary of State may approve;

(c) enabling or assisting the Association to carry out such other works in connection with housing accommodation provided or improved by them as the Secretary of State may with the agreement of the Treasury approve;

(d) assisting the Association to acquire any land compulsorily under section 23;

(e) enabling or assisting the Association to purchase, on terms approved by the Secretary of State, all or any of the assets of any housing trust to which section 119 of the Housing (Scotland) Act 1925 applied;

(f) enabling or assisting the Association to make loans, on such terms as the Secretary of State may determine, to persons intending to purchase housing accommodation or a part share of such accommodation provided or improved by the Association;

(g) enabling or assisting the Association to provide or convert buildings for use as hostels:

Provided that—

(i) the aggregate amount of the advances made under this subsection, together with any advances made under section 94(1) of the Housing (Scotland) Act 1950 or section 25(1) of the Act of 1968, shall not exceed six hundred million pounds or such greater sum, not exceeding seven hundred and fifty million pounds, as the Secretary of State may by order specify;

(ii) the aggregate amount of the advances made under paragraph (b) of this subsection shall not exceed one million pounds.

(2) It shall be the duty of the Association, if they accept any advances under paragraph (b) of subsection (1) in connection with a scheme, to comply with any directions which the Secretary of State may give to them with respect to the administration of the scheme and the disposal of the assets provided under the scheme.

(3) The power to make orders conferred on the Secretary of State by paragraph (i) of the proviso to subsection (1) shall be exercisable by statutory instrument, and no order shall be made in the exercise of that power unless a draft of the order has been laid before the House of Commons and has been approved by a resolution of that House.

(4) The Treasury may issue to the Secretary of State out of the National Loans Fund such sums as are necessary to enable him to make advances under this section; and any sums received by the Secretary of State in repayment of such advances shall be paid into the National Loans Fund.

(5) The Secretary of State shall—

(a) prepare in respect of each financial year an account, in such form and manner as the Treasury may direct, of sums issued to him for advances under this section, and of sums received by him under this section, and of the disposal by him of those sums respectively, and

(b) send it to the Comptroller and Auditor-General not later than the end of November in the following financial year;

and the Comptroller and Auditor-General shall examine, certify and report on the account and lay copies of it, together with his report, before each House of Parliament.

(6) In this section—

(a) references to the provision of housing accommodation are references to the provision of housing accommodation whether by building new houses or by the acquisition of houses; and

(b) references to the improvement of housing accommodation are references to the improvement of housing accommodation—

(i) by the provision of dwellings by means of the conversion of houses or other buildings, or

(ii) by the improvement of dwellings.

(7) Any reference in this section to a house shall be construed as including a reference to any residential accommodation provided for occupation by not more than two persons and equipped with cooking facilities for the exclusive use of those persons, notwithstanding that it is not equipped with facilities of other kinds for such exclusive use.

In this subsection the expression "cooking facilities" in relation to any residential accommodation means facilities suitable for the preparation of food for the number of persons for which the accommodation is provided, and if any question arises whether any particular facilities fall within that description it shall be decided by the Secretary of State.

Financial assistance to voluntary organisations concerned with housing

197.—(1) The Secretary of State may, with the consent of the Treasury and upon such terms and subject to such conditions as he may determine, give to a voluntary organisation assistance by way of grant or by way of loan, or partly in the one way and partly in the other, for the purpose of enabling or assisting the organisation to provide training or advice, or to undertake research, or for other similar purposes relating to housing.

(2) In this section "voluntary organisation" means a body the activities of which are carried on otherwise than for profit, but does not include any public or local authority or a registered housing association.

Payment of grants

Payment of grants and accounting provisions

198.—(1) Any grant to be paid by the Secretary of State under this Part shall be payable at such times and in such manner as he may determine and subject to such conditions as he may impose.

(2) Without prejudice to the generality of subsection (1), the making of any such payment shall be subject to the making of an application for the payment in such form, and containing such particulars, as the Secretary of State may from time to time determine.

Termination of certain exchequer payments to housing authorities

199. Schedule 12 shall have effect for the purpose of terminating certain exchequer payments to housing authorities.

Slum clearance subsidy

The slum clearance subsidy

200.—(1) A local authority shall be entitled to slum clearance subsidy in respect of such expenditure incurred by them as may be approved by the Secretary of State which falls within any of the following categories—

(a) any expenses in demolishing a building in pursuance of any provision of Part IV and Part VI less any such expenses which the local authority have recovered from the owner of the building under any such provision and any amount realised by the local authority in the sale of materials of the building;

(b) any expenses in the clearance of the site of any such building as is referred to in paragraph (a);

(c) any payment under section 308 (payments to certain owner-occupiers and others in respect of houses not meeting tolerable standard which are purchased or demolished) other than any such payment in respect of an interest in a house which has been purchased by the local authority for the purpose of bringing that house or another house up to the tolerable standard;

(d) any payment under section 304 (payments in respect of well-maintained houses) other than any such payment in respect of an interest in a house which has been purchased by the local authority for the purpose of bringing that house or another house up to the tolerable standard;

(e) the cost of any works carried out by the local authority under section 121(7) (local authority may acquire and repair a house or building liable to closing or demolition order);

(f) any payment under section 234(5) or (6) (payment of removal and other allowances to person displaced);

(g) such other expenditure as the Secretary of State may direct.

(2) The amount of slum clearance subsidy payment to a local authority shall be an amount equal to 75 per cent. of the annual loan charges referable to the amount of expenditure incurred by them in a year which falls within any of the categories set out in subsection (2), payable annually for the period of 20 years beginning with the year immediately following the year in which the expenditure was incurred.

(3) For the purposes of subsection (2) the annual loan charges referable to the amount of expenditure incurred by the local authority shall be the annual sum which, in the opinion of the Secretary of State, would fall to be provided by the local authority for the payment of interest on, and the repayment of, a loan of that amount repayable over a period of 20 years.

Payment of subsidies

Payment of subsidies and accounting provisions

201.—(1) Any subsidy to be paid by the Secretary of State under this Part shall be payable at such times and in such manner as the Treasury may direct and subject to such conditions as to records, certificates, audit or otherwise, as the Secretary of State may, with the approval of the Treasury, impose.

(2) Without prejudice to the generality of subsection (1), the making of any such payment shall be subject to the making of a claim for the payment in such form, and containing such particulars, as the Secretary of State may from time to time determine.

(3) The aggregate amount of any one subsidy payable under this Part to a housing authority for any year shall be calculated to the nearest

pound, by disregarding an odd amount of 50 pence, or less, and by treating an odd amount exceeding 50 pence as a whole pound.

(4) Subsection (1) applies to Exchequer contributions payable under the enactments specified in Schedule 13 as it applies to subsidies paid under this Part, and Schedule 13 shall have effect for the purposes of this subsection.

(5) Schedule 14 shall have effect for the purposes of specifying such Exchequer contributions as may be reduced, suspended or discontinued under section 202(3).

Secretary of State's power to vary Exchequer contributions

Power of Secretary of State to reduce, suspend, discontinue or transfer particular Exchequer contributions

202.—(1) The Secretary of State may in the circumstances mentioned in subsection (2) reduce the amount of a subsidy to be paid under this Part or suspend or discontinue such payment or part of such payment.

(2) The circumstances are—

(a) where the Secretary of State is satisfied that the local authority has failed to discharge any of their functions;

(b) where the subsidy is payable subject to a condition, and the Secretary of State is satisfied that the condition has not been complied with.

(3) The Secretary of State may, in any of the circumstances mentioned in subsection (5), reduce the amount of any Exchequer contribution being an Exchequer contribution falling to be made under any of the enactments specified in Schedule 14 in respect of a particular subsidised unit, or suspend or discontinue the payment of such Exchequer contributions or part thereof, as he thinks just in those circumstances.

(4) Where an Exchequer contribution is made to a local authority in respect of a subsidised unit in relation to which an annual grant is payable by the authority to a development corporation or a housing association, then, if the amount of the Exchequer contribution is reduced or the payment of the Exchequer contribution or part of it is suspended or discontinued under this section, the authority may reduce the annual grant to a corresponding or any less extent or suspend the payment thereof, for a corresponding period or discontinue the payment, or of a corresponding part, as the case may be.

(5) The circumstances referred to in subsection (3) are—

(a) that the Exchequer contribution is to be made to a local authority and the Secretary of State is satisfied that the authority have failed to discharge any of their duties under this Act or that they have failed to exercise any power mentioned therein in any case where any such power ought to have been exercised;

(b) that the Exchequer contributions fall to be made or the subsidy falls to be paid subject to any conditions and the Secretary of State is satisfied that any of those conditions has not been complied with;

(c) that the subsidised unit has been converted, demolished or destroyed;

(d) that the subsidised unit is not fit to be used or has ceased to be used for the purpose for which it was intended;

(e) that the subsidised unit has been sold or has been leased for a stipulated duration exceeding 12 months;

(f) that the subsidised unit has been transferred, whether by sale or otherwise.

(6) Where the Secretary of State's power under this section to discontinue the payment of the whole or part of any Exchequer contributions to be made to a recipient authority in respect of a particular subsidised unit becomes exercisable in the circumstances mentioned in paragraph (e) or paragraph (f) of subsection (5) and the subsidised unit has become vested in or has been leased to another recipient authority, then, if the Secretary of State exercised that power he may make to that other authority Exchequer contributions of the like amount as he would otherwise have made to the first-mentioned authority if the conditions subject to which the first-mentioned Exchequer contributions fell to be made had been complied with.

(7) In this section—

"recipient authority" means a local authority, a development corporation, a housing association or the Scottish Special Housing Association.

"the subsidised unit" means the house, hostel or other land in respect of which Exchequer contributions fall to be made, whether they fall to be made in respect of it or its site or in respect of land comprising it or in respect of the cost of any houses, or the acquisition of any land, comprising it.

PART X

HOUSING ACCOUNTS OF LOCAL AUTHORITIES

The housing revenue account

203.—(1) A local authority shall keep a housing revenue account of the income and expenditure of the authority for each year in respect of the houses, buildings and land specified in Part I of Schedule 15, and Part I shall have effect for that purpose.

(2) A local authority may, with the consent of the Secretary of State, include in or exclude from the housing revenue account any individual house or other property or categories of houses or other properties.

(3) The Secretary of State may make a direction either generally or in relation to specified properties that any category of house or other properties shall be included in or excluded from the housing revenue account of a local authority.

(4) The land in respect of which the local authority are required by subsection (1) to keep a housing revenue account shall not include any land which the local authority have provided expressly for sale for development by another person.

(5) Part II of Schedule 15 shall have effect in relation to the operation of the housing revenue account.

(6) The Secretary of State may, as respects any year, after consultation with such associations of local authorities as appear to him to be concerned, by order amend Schedule 15.

(7) An order under subsection (6) shall be made by statutory instrument subject to annulment in pursuance of a resolution of either House of Parliament.

Power of Secretary of State to limit estimated rate fund contributions to housing revenue account

204.—(1) The Secretary of State may by order impose, as respects a local authority or class thereof specified in the order, a limit to the amount of contribution out of their general fund which the authority or, as the case may be, an authority of the class may estimate that they will carry to the credit of their housing revenue account for the year specified in the order; and it shall be the duty of the local authority so to estimate that amount as not to exceed that limit.

(2) The limit referred to in subsection (1) may be expressed in whatever way the Secretary of State thinks fit.

(3) An order under this section shall be made by statutory instrument which shall be subject to annulment in pursuance of a resolution of either House of Parliament.

(4) Every local authority shall submit to the Secretary of State an estimate of the income and expenditure an account of which they are obliged, under section 203, to keep in their housing revenue account for the year next following.

(5) In subsection (1), "general fund" means the fund maintained by a local authority under section 93 of the Local Government (Scotland) Act 1973.

The rent rebate account

205.—(1) A local authority shall keep a rent rebate account for each year.

(2) The authority shall—
  (a) credit that account with the amount of rent rebate subsidy payable to them under section 32 of the Social Security and Housing Benefits Act 1982;
  (b) debit that account with—
    (i) the amount of the authority's rent rebates for the year, and
    (ii) the authority's costs of administering their rent rebates for the year.

(3) Where for any year a deficit is shown in the account, the local authority shall credit the account in respect of that year with an amount equal to the amount of the deficit.

The rent allowance account

206.—(1) A local authority shall keep a rent allowance account for each year.

(2) The authority shall—
  (a) credit that account with the amount of rent allowance subsidy payable to them under section 32 of the Social Security and Housing Benefits Act 1982;
  (b) debit that account with—
    (i) the amount of the authority's rent allowances for the year, and
    (ii) the authority's costs of administering their rent allowances for the year.

(3) Where for any year a deficit is shown in the account, the local authority shall credit the account in respect of that year with the amount of the deficit.

The slum clearance revenue account

207.—(1) A local authority shall keep a slum clearance revenue account for each year.

(2) That account shall include—
  (a) the income and expenditure of the authority in respect of houses and other property acquired by them, or appropriated, for the purposes of Parts IV, V or VI other than houses

acquired under Part IV for the purpose of bringing it or another house up to the tolerable standard; and

(b) any expenditure of the authority referred to in section 200 in respect of houses and other property which is not included in paragraph (a) together with any income related to that expenditure.

(3) Schedule 16 shall have effect in relation to the slum clearance revenue account.

Application of receipts from disposal of certain land

208.—(1) Any money received by a local authority from the disposal of land to which this section applies shall be applied for a purpose for which the land which was the subject of the transaction was held.

(2) Subsection (1) shall not have effect if the Secretary of State approves the money being applied for another purpose.

(3) Subsection (1) applies to land in respect of which income and expenditure is accounted for—

(a) in the housing revenue account, or

(b) in the slum clearance account.

Adjustment of accounts on appropriation of land

209.—(1) Where land is appropriated by a local authority for the purposes of Parts I or V or on the discontinuance of use for those purposes, such adjustment shall be made in the accounts of the local authority as the Secretary of State may direct.

(2) Any direction under this section may be either a general direction or a direction for any particular case.

(3) Where this section applies, section 25 of the Town and Country Planning (Scotland) Act 1959 (which also relates to the adjustment of accounts on appropriation of land) shall not apply.

PART XI

RENTS AND SERVICE CHARGES

Rents for public sector housing

210.—(1) Subject to the provisions of this section, a local authority may charge such reasonable rents as they may determine for the tenancy or occupation of houses provided by them.

(2) A local authority shall from time to time review such rents and make such charges either of rents generally or of particular rents as circumstances may require.

(3) In determining standard rents to which their housing revenue account relates, a local authority shall take no account of the personal circumstances of the tenants.

Service charges

211.—(1) A local authority shall make a service charge for each year of such amount as they think reasonable in all the circumstances in respect of the following items to which the housing revenue account relates—

(a) any garage, car-port or other car parking facilities provided by them in so far as not included within the terms of the tenancy of a house;

(b) any service provided by them under the terms of the tenancy of a house;

(c) any other item made available under section 3 or 5 or supplied under section 4 for which a charge was made in the financial year 1971–2 under sections 139 to 141 of the Act of 1966 and which has continued to be made available or supplied after that year.

(2) The Secretary of State may direct in relation to any service provided under paragraph (b) of subsection (1) either generally or in a particular case that no such service charge shall be made.

(3) Before making any such direction the Secretary of State shall consult—

(a) such associations of local authorities as appear to him to be concerned;

(b) any local authority with whom consultation appears to him to be desirable.

Rent increase notice

212.—(1) Where an authority lets a house held by it for housing purposes to a tenant it shall be an implied term of the tenancy that the rent or any other charge payable to the authority under the tenancy may be increased by notice ("rent increase notice") without the tenancy being terminated.

(2) A rent increase notice shall—

(a) be in writing;

(b) specify the increased rent and the date on which it has effect;

(c) be given to the tenant at least 4 weeks before it has effect;

(d) inform the tenant of his right to terminate the tenancy and of the steps to be taken if he wishes to do so;

(e) inform him of the dates by which the notice of removal under section 213 must be received and the tenancy terminated if the increase is not to have effect.

(3) A rent increase notice given in accordance with this section shall have effect unless a removal notice is given in accordance with section 213.

(4) For the purposes of this section an authority is—

(a) a regional, islands or district council;

(b) a joint board or a joint committee;

(c) a development corporation;

(d) the Scottish Special Housing Association;

(e) a water authority or a water development board.

(5) This section does not apply to a secure tenancy.

Removal notice

213.—(1) A tenant who has been given a rent increase notice may give the authority a removal notice terminating the tenancy.

(2) The removal notice shall have effect to terminate the tenancy if—

(a) it is given within 2 weeks of the date on which the rent increase notice was given, or such longer period as the notice may specify;

(b) it specifies a date for the termination of the tenancy within 4 weeks after the date on which it is given.

(3) Nothing in the terms of the tenancy (express or implied) shall prevent a tenant giving a removal notice that complies with subsection (2).

PART XII

HOUSE LOANS AND OTHER FINANCIAL ASSISTANCE

House loans: general

Power of local authority to make advances for the purpose of increasing housing accommodation

214.—(1) A local authority may advance money to any person for the purpose of—

(a) acquiring a house;

(b) constructing a house;

(c) converting another building into a house or acquiring another building and converting it into a house; or

(d) altering, enlarging, repairing or improving a house; or

(e) subject to subsection (4), facilitating the repayment by means of the advance of the amount outstanding on a previous loan made for any of the purposes specified in paragraphs (a) to (d).

(2) The authority may make advances whether or not the houses or buildings are in the authority's area.

(3) In determining whether to advance money under subsection (1), the local authority shall have regard to any advice which may be given from time to time by the Secretary of State.

(4) An advance shall not be made for the purpose specified in paragraph (e) of subsection (1) unless the local authority satisfy themselves that the primary effect of the advance will be to meet the housing needs of the applicant by enabling him either to retain an interest in the house concerned or to carry out such works in relation to that house as would be eligible for an advance by virtue of paragraph (c) or (d) of that subsection.

(5) An advance under this section may be made in addition to assistance given by the local authority in respect of the same house under any other Act or any other provision of this Act.

(6) If it appears to a local authority that the principal effect of the making of an advance under subsection (1) in respect of any premises would be to meet the housing needs of the applicant, they may make the advance notwithstanding that it is intended that some part of the premises will be used or, as the case may be, will continue to be used, otherwise than as a house, and accordingly where, by virtue of this subsection, a local authority propose to make an advance in respect of any premises, the premises shall be treated for the purposes of subsections (1) to (4) as, or as a building to be converted into, a house.

(7) In this section any reference to a house includes a reference to any part share of it.

(8) Schedule 17 shall have effect in relation to the terms of an advance under this section.

Requirements as to meeting tolerable standard

215.—(1) Before advancing money under section 214 for the purpose of acquiring a house, the local authority shall satisfy themselves that the house to be acquired will meet the tolerable standard.

(2) Before advancing money under this section for any of the purposes specified in paragraphs (b) to (d) of subsection (1), the authority shall satisfy themselves that the house to be constructed, altered, enlarged, repaired, improved or into which the building is to be converted, as the case may be, will, when the construction, alteration, enlargement, repair, improvement or conversion has been completed, meet that standard.

House loans: special cases

House loans to tenants exercising right to purchase

216.—(1) A tenant who seeks to exercise his right to purchase a house under Part III and who has received an offer to sell (or, as the case may be, an amended offer to sell) from the landlord shall be entitled, together with any joint purchaser under section 61(6) (and the said tenant and any joint purchaser are referred to in this section as "the applicant") to apply—

    (a) in the case where the landlord is a development corporation (including an urban development corporation) or the Scottish Special Housing Association, to that body; or

    (b) in a case where the landlord is the Housing Corporation or a registered housing association, to the Housing Corporation; or

    (c) in any other case, to the local authority for the area in which the house is situated,

for a loan of an amount not exceeding the price fixed under section 62 to assist him to purchase the house.

(2) A loan application under subsection (1)—

    (a) must be served on the landlord or other body—

        (i) within one month after service on the tenant of the offer to sell (or, where there has been service of one or more amended offers to sell or there has been a determination by the Lands Tribunal under section 65(3) which does not require the issue of an amended offer to sell, of the latest of these); or

        (ii) within one year and 10 months after service of the application to purchase if the tenant has, in terms of section 67, a fixed price option as regards the house;

    (b) shall be in such form as the Secretary of State shall by order made by statutory instrument prescribe, and shall contain—

        (i) the amount of the loan which the applicant seeks;

        (ii) the applicant's annual gross income and his net income after payment of income tax and national insurance contributions;

        (iii) any liabilities in respect of credit sales or other fixed outgoings of the applicant; and

        (iv) a statement that the applicant has applied for and been unable to obtain a sufficient building society loan; and

    (c) shall be accompanied by evidence of the matters referred to in sub-paragraphs (ii) to (iv) of paragraph (b).

(3) Subject to such requirements as the Secretary of State may by order made by statutory instrument impose, a landlord or other body which receives an application under subsection (1) shall, where it is satisfied on reasonable inquiry (which shall include reasonable opportunity for the applicant to amend his application) that the information contained in the loan application is correct, serve on the applicant an offer of loan, which shall specify a maximum amount of loan calculated in accordance with regulations made by statutory instrument by the Secretary of State.

(4) A landlord or other body to which application has been made under subsection (1) shall complete its inquiries and either—

    (a) issue the offer of loan under subsection (3); or

    (b) refuse the application on the ground that information contained in the loan application is incorrect in a material respect,

within 2 months of the date of service of the loan application.

(5) An applicant who wishes to accept an offer of loan shall do so along with his notice of acceptance under sections 66(1) or 67(1).

(6) An offer of loan under subsection (3) together with an acceptance under subsection (5) shall constitute an agreement by the landlord or other body, subject to such requirements as the Secretary of State may by order made by statutory instrument impose, to lend to the applicant for the purpose of purchasing the house—

(a) the maximum amount of loan mentioned in subsection (3); or

(b) the amount of loan sought by the applicant,

whichever is the lesser, on the execution by the applicant of a standard security over the house.

(7) An applicant who is aggrieved by a refusal under subsection (4)(b), or by a failure to comply with the said subsection, or by the calculation of maximum amount of loan mentioned in subsection (3) may, within 2 months of the date of the refusal or failure or of the offer of loan, as the case may be, raise proceedings by way of summary application in the sheriff court for the district in which the house is situated for declarator that he is entitled to a loan in accordance with subsection (3).

(8) Where in proceedings under subsection (7) the sheriff grants declarator that the applicant is entitled to a loan, such declarator shall have effect as if it were an offer of loan of the amount specified in the declarator duly issued under this section by the landlord or other body.

(9) A statutory instrument made under subsection (3) or (6) shall be subject to annulment in pursuance of a resolution of either House of Parliament.

Duty of local authorities to offer loans to meet expenses of improvement of houses in housing action areas

217.—(1) Where the owner or the lessee of a house situated in a housing action area is willing to carry out improvement works which are, in the opinion of the local authority, required in order to bring the house up to the standard specified under section 90(3) or by virtue of section 91(3), he may, not later than 9 months from the date of publication and service of a notice of a final resolution passed under Part I of Schedule 8, apply to the local authority for a loan.

(2) Subject to this section, if the local authority are satisfied that the applicant can reasonably be expected to meet obligations assumed by him in pursuance of this section in respect of a loan of the amount of the expenditure to which the application relates, the authority shall offer to make a loan of that amount to the applicant, the loan to be secured to the authority by a standard security over the premises consisting of or comprising the house.

(3) Subject to this section, if the local authority are not so satisfied, but consider that the applicant can reasonably be expected to meet obligations assumed by him in pursuance of this section in respect of a loan of a smaller amount, the authority may, if they think fit, offer to make a loan of that smaller amount to the applicant, the loan to be secured as aforesaid.

(4) Any offer made by the local authority under this section shall contain a condition to the effect that, if an improvement grant or a repairs grant becomes payable under Part XIII in respect of the expenditure to which the application under this section relates, the authority shall not be required to lend a sum greater than the amount of the expenditure to which the application relates after deduction of the amount of the grant.

(5) The local authority shall not make an offer under the foregoing provisions of this section unless they are satisfied that—

(a) the applicant's estate or interest in the house amounts to ownership or a lease for a period which will not expire before the date for final repayment of the loan, and

(b) according to a valuation made on behalf of the local authority, the amount of the principal of the loan does not exceed the value which it is estimated the subjects comprised in the security will bear after improvement of the house or houses to the standard specified under section 90(3) or by virtue of section 91(3).

(6) The rate of interest payable on a loan under this section shall be a variable rate calculated under section 219.

(7) Subject to this section, the loan offered by the local authority under this section shall be subject to such reasonable terms as the authority may specify in their offer.

(8) The local authority's offer may in particular include any such terms as are described in paragraphs 4 to 7 of Schedule 17 (repayment of principal and interest) and provision for the advance being made by instalments from time to time as the works of improvement progress.

(9) Where an improvement grant or repairs grant is payable partly in respect of expenditure to which the application under this section relates, and partly in respect of other expenditure, the reference in subsection (4) to an improvement grant or repairs grant shall be taken as a reference to the part of the grant which in the opinion of the local authority is attributable to the expenditure to which the application under this section relates.

Duty of local authority to offer loans to meet expenses of repairs

218.—(1) Where the person having control of a house is willing to carry out the works necessary to rectify the defect specified in the notice under section 108(2), he may, not later than 21 days from the date of service of the said notice, or from the date of determination of any appeal, apply to the local authority for a loan.

(2) Subsections (2) to (8) of section 217 shall apply for the purposes of this section as they apply for the purposes of that section, but as if in subsection (5)(b) for the words from "improvement" to the end there were substituted the words "the works necessary to rectify the defects specified in the repair notice have been executed.".

Rates of interest on home loans

Local authority home loan interest rates

219.—(1) Subject to subsections (2) and (3)—
   (a) any advance of money under a power conferred by section 214 or under any other power to make loans for the like purposes; and
   (b) any sum secured under any arrangement by which the price or part of the price of a house sold by a local authority is secured by a standard security; and
   (c) any sum secured under any security which is taken over by a local authority under a power conferred by section 229 (local authority indemnities for building societies, etc.),
is a variable interest home loan for the purposes of this section.

(2) This section does not apply to an advance made before 3rd October 1980 or to a sum secured in respect of the price of a house agreed to be sold before then or (where subsection 1(c) applies) to a security granted before then.

(3) This section shall not apply to an advance made in implement of a contract constituted by an offer of advance made before that date and an unqualified acceptance of that offer thereafter.

(4) Subject to section 220, a local authority shall, in respect of their variable interest home loans, charge a rate of interest which shall be equal to whichever is the higher of the following—

(a) the standard rate for the time being, as declared by the Secretary of State in accordance with subsection (5);

(b) the locally determined rate calculated in accordance with subsection (6).

(5) In considering what rate to declare as the standard rate for the purposes of subsection (4), the Secretary of State shall take into account interest rates charged by building societies in the United Kingdom and any movement in those rates.

(6) The locally determined rate for the purposes of this section shall be the rate which is necessary to service loan charges on money which is to be applied to making variable interest home loans during the relevant period of six months (referred to in subsection (7)), together with the addition of one quarter per cent. to cover the administration cost of making and managing variable interest home loans.

(7) The locally determined rate, for the purposes of this section, shall be determined by each local authority for the period of 6 months not less than one month before the beginning of the relevant period.

(8) Nothing in this or the following two sections shall affect the operation of section 223(1)(b) (under which a part of certain loans may be free of interest for up to 5 years).

Variation of rate by local authority

220.—(1) Where the declaration of a new standard rate or, as the case may be, the determination of a new locally determined rate, affects the rate of interest chargeable under section 219 by a local authority the authority shall, as soon as practicable after such declaration or determination, serve in respect of each of its variable interest home loans a notice on the borrower which shall, as from the appropriate day—

(a) vary the rate of interest payable by him; and

(b) where, as the result of the variation, the amount outstanding under the advance or security would increase if the periodic repayments were not increased, increase the amount of the periodic repayments to such an amount as will ensure that the said outstanding amount will not increase.

(2) In subsection (1), "the appropriate day" means such day as shall be specified in the notice, being—

(a) in the case of a new standard rate, a day not less than 2 weeks, nor more than 6 weeks, after service of the notice; and

(b) in the case of a new locally determined rate, the first day of the relevant period of 6 months.

Variation of rate by Secretary of State

221. Notwithstanding anything contained in sections 219 and 220, but subject to section 230, the Secretary of State may, where he considers that the interest rate charged by a local authority does not satisfy the requirements of section 219(4), direct a local authority—

(a) to charge an interest rate specified in the direction; and

(b) to vary the rate in accordance with the provisions of section 220.

Assistance for first-time buyers

Advances to recognised lending institutions to assist first-time buyers

222.—(1) The Secretary of State may make advances to recognised lending institutions enabling them to provide assistance to first-time purchasers of house property in Great Britain where—

(a) the purchaser intends to make his home in the property,

(b) finance for the purchase of the property (and improvements, if

any) is obtained by means of a secured loan from the lending
institution, and

(c) the purchase price is within the prescribed limits.

(2) In this section "prescribed" means prescribed by order of the
Secretary of State.

(3) An order—

(a) may prescribe different limits for properties in different areas,
and

(b) shall be made by statutory instrument which shall be subject to
annulment in pursuance of a resolution of the House of
Commons.

Forms of assistance and qualifying conditions

223.—(1) Assistance under section 222 (assistance for first-time buyers)
may be given in the following ways—

(a) the secured loan may be financed by the Secretary of State to the
extent of £600 (that amount being normally additional to that which
the institution would otherwise have lent, but not so that the total
loan exceeds the loan value of the property);

(b) £600 of the total loan may be made free of interest, and of any
obligation to repay principal, for up to 5 years from the date of
purchase; and

(c) the institution may provide the purchaser with a bonus on his
savings (which bonus shall be tax-exempt) up to a maximum of
£110, payable towards the purchase or expenses arising in connection with it.

(2) The purchaser qualifies for assistance under subsection (1)(a) and
(b) (interest-free loan) by satisfying the following conditions with respect
to his own savings—

(a) that he has been saving with a recognised savings institution for at
least 2 years preceding the date of his application for assistance,

(b) that throughout the 12 months preceding that date he had at least
£300 of such savings, and

(c) that by that date he has accumulated at least £600 of such savings;
and he qualifies for assistance under subsection (1)(c) (bonus on savings)
by satisfying the conditions specified in paragraphs (a) and (b) above.

(3) The Secretary of State may allow for the conditions to be relaxed or
modified in particular classes of case.

(4) No assistance shall be given in any case unless the amount of the
secured loan is at least £1,600 and amounts to not less than 25 per cent.
of the purchase price of the property.

(5) The Secretary of State may by order made with the consent of the
Treasury—

(a) alter any of the money sums specified in this section;

(b) substitute a longer or shorter period for either or both of the
periods mentioned in subsection (2)(a) and (b) (conditions as to
savings);

(c) alter the condition in subsection (2)(c) so as to enable the purchaser
to satisfy it with lesser amounts of savings and to enable assistance
to be given in such a case according to reduced scales specified in
the order;

(d) alter the percentage mentioned in subsection (4) (minimum secured
loan).

(6) An order shall be made by statutory instrument which shall be
subject to annulment in pursuance of a resolution of the House of
Commons.

Recognised lending institutions

224.—(1) The lending institutions recognised for the purposes of section 222 (assistance for first-time buyers) are—
>   building societies,
>   local authorities,
>   development corporations,
>   The Scottish Special Housing Association,
>   banks,
>   insurance companies, and
>   friendly societies.

(2) The Secretary of State may by order made with the consent of the Treasury—
>   (a) add to the list in subsection (1), or
>   (b) direct that a named body shall no longer be a recognised lending institution;

but before making an order under paragraph (b) he shall give an opportunity for representations to be made on behalf of the body concerned.

(3) An order shall be made by statutory instrument.

Recognised savings institutions

225.—(1) The savings institutions recognised for the purposes of section 223 (qualifying conditions as to savings) are—
>   building societies,
>   local authorities,
>   banks,
>   friendly societies,
>   the Director of Savings, and
>   the Post Office,

and savings institutions recognised for the purposes of the corresponding provisions in force in England or Wales or Northern Ireland.

In this section and in section 227 those corresponding provisions are—
>   (a) in relation to England and Wales, sections 445 to 449 of the Housing Act 1985;
>   (b) in relation to Northern Ireland, Part IX of the Housing (Northern Ireland) Order 1981.

(2) The Secretary of State may by order made with the consent of the Treasury—
>   (a) add to the list in subsection (1), or
>   (b) direct that a named body shall no longer be a recognised savings institution,

but before making an order under paragraph (b) he shall give an opportunity for representations to be made on behalf of the body concerned.

(3) An order shall be made by statutory instrument.

Terms of advances and administration

226.—(1) Advances to lending institutions under section 222 (assistance for first-time buyers) shall be on such terms as to repayment and otherwise as may be settled by the Secretary of State, with the consent of the Treasury, after consultation with lending and savings institutions or organisations representative of them; and the terms shall be embodied in directions issued by the Secretary of State.

(2) The following matters, among others, may be dealt with in directions issued by the Secretary of State—
>   (a) the cases in which assistance is to be provided;

(b) the method of determining the loan value of property for the purpose of section 223(1)(a) (limit on total loan);

(c) the method of quantifying bonus by reference to savings;

(d) the considerations by reference to which a person is or is not to be treated as a first-time purchaser of house property;

(e) the steps which must be taken with a view to satisfying the conditions in section 223(2) (conditions as to purchaser's own savings), and the circumstances in which those conditions are or are not to be treated as satisfied;

(f) the supporting evidence and declarations which must be furnished by a person applying for assistance, in order to establish his qualification for it, and the means of ensuring that restitution is made in the event of it being obtained by false representations;

(g) the way in which amounts paid over by way of assistance are to be repaid to the lending institutions and to the Secretary of State.

(3) The Secretary of State may, to the extent that he thinks proper for safeguarding the lending institutions, include in the terms an undertaking to indemnify the institutions in respect of loss suffered in cases where assistance has been given.

Modifications of building society law and disapplication of provisions of the Restrictive Trade Practices Act 1976 in relation to assistance for first-time buyers

227.—(1) So much of an advance by a building society which is partly financed under section 222 (assistance for first-time buyers) or the corresponding English or Northern Ireland provisions as is so financed shall be treated as not forming part of the advance for the purpose of determining—

(a) whether the advance, or any further advance made within two years of the date of purchase, is beyond the powers of the society, and

(b) the classification of the advance, or any such further advance, for the purposes of Part III of the Building Societies Act 1986.

(2) Section 16(3) and (5) of the Restrictive Trade Practices Act 1976 (recommendations by service supply associations to members) shall not apply to recommendations made to lending institutions and savings institutions about the manner of implementing sections 222 to 226 (assistance for first-time buyers) or the corresponding English or Northern Ireland provisions, provided that the recommendations are made with the approval of the Secretary of State, or as the case may be, the Department of Environment for Northern Ireland, which may be withdrawn at any time on one month's notice.

Exclusion of Restrictive Trade Practices Act: agreements as to loans on security of new houses

228.—(1) In determining for the purposes of the Restrictive Trade Practices Act 1976 whether an agreement between building societies is one to which that Act applies by virtue of an order made, or having effect as if made, under section 11 of that Act (restrictive agreements as to services), no account shall be taken of any term (whether or not subject to exceptions) by which the parties or any of them agree not to grant loans on the security of new houses unless they have been built by or at the direction of a person who is registered with, or has agreed to comply with the standards of house building laid down or approved by, an appropriate body.

(2) In subsection (1)—

"appropriate body" means a body concerned with the specification and control of standards of house building which—

(a) has its chairman, or the chairman of its board of directors or other governing body, appointed by the Secretary of State, and

(b) promotes or administers a scheme conferring rights in respect of defects in the condition of houses on persons having or acquiring interest in them, and

"new house" means a building or part of a building intended for use as a private dwelling and not previously occupied as such.

(3) The reference in subsection (1) to a term agreed to by the parties or any of them includes a term to which the parties or any of them are deemed to have agreed by virtue of section 16 of the Restrictive Trade Practices Act 1976 (recommendations of services supply associations).

Other assistance

Local authority indemnities for building societies, etc.

229.—(1) A local authority may, with the approval of the Secretary of State, enter into an agreement with a building society or recognised body under which the authority binds itself to indemnify the building society or recognised body in respect of

(a) the whole or any part of any outstanding indebtedness of a borrower; and

(b) loss or expense to the building society or recognised body resulting from the failure of the borrower duly to perform any obligation imposed on him by a heritable security.

(2) The agreement may also, where the borrower is made party to it, enable or require the authority in specified circumstances to take an assignation of the rights and liabilities of the building society or recognised body under the heritable security.

(3) Approval of the Secretary of State under subsection (1) may be given generally in relation to agreements which satisfy specified requirements, or in relation to individual agreements, and with or without conditions, as he thinks fit, and such approval may be withdrawn at any time on one month's notice.

(4) Before issuing any general approval under subsection (1) the Secretary of State shall consult with such bodies as appear to him to be representative of local authorities, and of building societies, and also with the Building Societies Commission.

(5) Section 16(3) and (5) of the Restrictive Trade Practices Act 1976 (recommendations by services supply association to members) shall not apply to recommendations made to building societies or recognised bodies about the making of agreements under this section provided that the recommendations are made with the approval of the Secretary of State.

(6) In this section "recognised body" means a body designated, or of a class or description designated, in an order under this subsection made by statutory instrument by the Secretary of State with the consent of the Treasury.

(7) Before making an order under subsection (6) varying or revoking an order previously so made, the Secretary of State shall give an opportunity for representations to be made on behalf of a recognised body which, if the order were made, would cease to be such a body.

Assistance by local authority for acquiring houses in need of repair and improvement

230.—(1) Notwithstanding any other provision of sections 219, 220 and 221, a local authority may, where the conditions set out in subsection (2) are satisfied, give assistance to a person acquiring a house in need of repair or improvement by making provision for waiving or reducing, for a period ending not later than 5 years after the date of an advance of money of the kind mentioned in section 219(1)(a) or of the granting of a security under an arrangement of the kind mentioned in section 219(1)(b), the interest payable on the sum advanced or remaining outstanding under the security, as the case may be.

(2) The conditions mentioned in subsection (1) are that—

    (a) the assistance is given in accordance with a scheme which has been approved by the Secretary of State or which conforms with such requirements as may be specified by the Secretary of State by order made by statutory instrument with the consent of the Treasury; and

    (b) the person acquiring the house has entered into an agreement with the local authority to carry out, within a period specified in the agreement, works of repair or improvement therein specified.

Loans by Public Works Loan Commissioners for provision or improvement of housing accommodation

231.—(1) The Public Works Loan Commissioners may, subject to the provisions of this section, lend money to any person entitled to any land either as owner or as lessee under a lease of which a period of not less than 50 years remains unexpired at the date of the loan for the purpose of constructing or improving, or facilitating or encouraging the construction or improvement of, houses, and any such person may borrow from the Public Works Loan Commissioners such money as may be required for the purposes aforesaid.

(2) A loan for any of the purposes specified in subsection (1) shall be secured with interest by a heritable security over the land and houses in respect of which that purpose is to be carried out and over such other land and houses, if any, as may be offered as security for the loan.

(3) Any such loan may be made whether the person receiving the loan has or has not power to borrow on bond and disposition in security or otherwise, independently of this Act, but nothing in this Act shall affect any regulation, statutory or otherwise, whereby any company may be restricted from borrowing until a definite portion of capital is subscribed for, taken or paid up.

(4) The following conditions shall apply in the case of any such loan—

    (a) the period for repayment shall not exceed 40 years;

    (b) no money shall be lent on the security of any land or houses unless the estate or interest therein proposed to be burdened is either ownership or a lease of which a period of not less than 50 years remains unexpired at the date of the loan;

    (c) the money lent shall not exceed such proportion as is hereinafter authorised of the value, to be ascertained to the satisfaction of the Public Works Loan Commissioners, of the estate or interest in the land or houses proposed to be burdened in pursuance of subsection (2); but loans may be made by instalment from time to time as the building of houses or other work on the land so burdened progresses, so, however, that the total loans do not at any time exceed the amount aforesaid; and the heritable security may be granted accordingly to secure such loans so to be made from time to time.

(5) The proportion of such value as aforesaid authorised for the purpose of the loan shall be three-fourths but if the loan exceeds two-thirds of such value, the Public Works Loan Commissioners shall require, in

addition to such heritable security as is mentioned in subsection (2), such further security as they may think fit.

Powers of court in cases relating to instalment purchase agreements

232.—(1) Where, under the terms of an instalment purchase agreement, a person has been let into possession of a house and, on the termination of the agreement or of his right to possession under it, proceedings are brought for possession of the house, the court may—

    (a) adjourn the proceedings; or

    (b) on making an order for possession of the house, supersede extract or postpone the date of possession;

for such period or periods as the court thinks fit.

(2) On any such adjournment, superseding of extract, or postponement, the court may impose such conditions with regard to the payment by the person in possession in respect of his continued occupation of the house and such other conditions as the court thinks fit.

(3) The court may revoke or from time to time vary any condition imposed by virtue of this section.

(4) In this section "instalment purchase agreement" means an agreement for the purchase of a house under which the whole or part of the purchase price is to be paid in 3 or more instalments and the completion of the purchase is deferred until the whole or a specified part of the purchase price has been paid.

Power of local authority to assist in provision of separate service water pipes for houses

233.—(1) A local authority may if they think fit give assistance in respect of the provision of a separate service pipe for a house in their district which has a piped supply of water from a water main, but no separate service pipe.

(2) Subject to this section, the assistance shall be by way of making a grant in respect of all or any part of the expenses incurred in the provision of the separate service pipe.

(3) The reference to expenses in subsection (2) includes, in a case where all or any part of the works required for the provision of the separate service pipe are carried out by a water authority (whether in exercise of default powers or in any other case), a reference to sums payable by the owner of the house, or any other person, to the water authority for carrying out the works.

Financial assistance towards tenants' removal expenses

234.—(1) A local authority shall, in the performance of the functions of management of houses conferred on them by section 17, have power, subject to subsections (2) and (3), in every case where a tenant of a house held by it for housing purposes moves to another house, whether or not that other house is also owned by the local authority—

    (a) to pay any expenses of the removal;

    (b) where the tenant is purchasing the house, to pay any expenses incurred by him in connection with the purchase other than the purchase price.

(2) Paragraph (b) of subsection (1) shall only apply in a case where a tenant of a house moves to another house of the local authority if that house has never been let.

(3) A local authority may make their payment of expenses in connection with the purchase of a house subject to such conditions as they think fit.

(4) Nothing in this section shall affect the operation of section 34 of the Land Compensation (Scotland) Act 1973 (disturbance payments for persons without compensatable interests).

(5) The power conferred on a local authority by subsection (1) to make allowances towards the expenses incurred in removing by persons displaced in consequence of the exercise by the authority of their powers shall include power to make allowances to persons so displaced temporarily in respect of expenses incurred by them in storage of furniture.

(6) Where, as a result of action taken by a local authority under Part IV, the population of the locality is materially decreased, the authority may pay to any person carrying on a retail shop in the locality such reasonable allowance as they may think fit towards any loss which, in their opinion, he will thereby sustain, so, however, that in estimating any such loss they shall have regard to the probable future development of the locality.

Contributions to assistance for elderly, etc.

Contributions by other local authorities towards expense of housing pensioners and disabled persons

235. A regional or islands council may make any contribution they think fit towards expenditure incurred by a local authority in connection with—

(a) the provision, maintenance and management, under this Act, of housing accommodation for disabled persons and persons of pensionable age; and

(b) the exercise, in relation to housing accommodation so provided, or for the benefit of persons occupying such accommodation, of any of their functions under section 3, 4 or 5.

PART XIII

LOCAL AUTHORITY GRANTS FOR IMPROVEMENT, REPAIR AND CONVERSION

Improvement grants

Power of local authorities to make improvement grants

236.—(1) Subject to the provisions of this Part, a local authority may give assistance by making an improvement grant in respect of—

(a) works required for the provision of houses by the conversion of houses or other buildings;

(b) works required for the improvement of houses.

(2) Subject to subsection (4), in this Part—

(a) "improvement", in relation to a house, includes—
  (i) alteration and enlargement, and
  (ii) in relation to a house for a disabled occupant, the doing of works required for making it suitable for his accommodation, welfare or employment;

(b) any reference to works required for the provision or improvement of a house, whether generally or in any particular respect, includes a reference to any works of repair or replacement needed in the opinion of the local authority paying the grant for the purpose of enabling the house to which the improvement relates to attain a good state of repair,

and "improved" shall be construed accordingly.

(3) In this section—

"disabled occupant" means a disabled person for whose benefit it is proposed to carry out works in respect of which an improvement grant is sought;

"disabled person" means a person who is substantially handicapped by illness, injury or congenital deformity;

"house for a disabled occupant" means a house which—

(a) is a disabled occupant's only or main residence when an application for an improvement grant in respect of it is made; or

(b) is likely in the opinion of the local authority to become a disabled occupant's only or main residence not later than the expiry of a reasonable period after the completion of the works in respect of which an improvement grant is sought.

(4) Any reference in this Part to works required for the improvement of a house does not include a reference to works specified in a notice under section 162 (which empowers a local authority to require the provision of means of escape in the case of fire in a house in multiple occupation) or to works required in connection with works so specified.

Form of application

237. An application for an improvement grant shall be in such form as may from time to time be prescribed and shall contain full particulars of—

(a) the works which are proposed to be or are being carried out together with plans and specifications of the works;

(b) the land on which those works are proposed to be or are being carried out; and

(c) the expenses (including any professional fees) estimated to be incurred in executing the works, and where the application relates to the provision or improvement of more than one house, the estimate shall specify the proportion of the expenses attributable to each house proposed to be provided or improved.

Powers of local authority

238.—(1) Subject to this Part, a local authority may approve, or refuse to approve, such an application.

(2) If it approves the application, it shall make an improvement grant.

Consent of Secretary of State

239.—(1) The Secretary of State may give directions to a local authority or to local authorities generally, requiring that an application for an improvement grant or all such applications of any class specified in the directions shall not be approved except with the consent of the Secretary of State and subject to any conditions which he may impose.

(2) It shall be the duty of any local authority to comply with any such directions.

Conditions for approval of applications for improvement grant other than applications relating exclusively to the provision of standard amenities

240.—(1) A local authority shall not approve an application for an improvement grant—

(a) unless they are satisfied that the owner of every parcel of land on which the improvement works are to be or are being carried out (other than land proposed to be sold or leased under section 9(4)),

has consented in writing to the application and to being bound by any conditions imposed by or under section 246;
(b) if the improvement works specified in it have begun, unless they are satisfied that there were good reasons for beginning the works before the application was approved.

(2) A local authority shall not approve any such application, other than an application to which section 244 (provision of standard amenities) applies—
(a) unless, subject to subsection (6), they are satisfied that—
(i) the house or houses to which the application for an improvement grant relates will provide satisfactory housing accommodation for such period and conform with such requirements with respect to construction and physical condition and the provision of services and amenities as may be specified for the time being for the purposes of this section by the Secretary of State, and
(ii) in a case where the house or houses to which the said application relates is or are comprised in a building containing more than one house, the works to be carried out on the house or houses will not prevent the improvement of any other house in that building;
(b) if the application is in respect of the improvement or conversion of a house provided after 15th June 1964, but the Secretary of State may give directions, either generally or with respect to any particular case, as to the waiving of this provision;
(c) if, subject to subsections (3) to (6), it is made by the owner of the house to which the application relates or by a member of his family and the house or any part thereof is to be occupied by that owner or by a member of his family after completion of the works and—
(i) the rateable value of the occupied premises exceeds the prescribed limit; or
(ii) if it is to be provided by the conversion of two or more houses, the aggregate of the rateable values of those houses exceeds the prescribed limit:
Provided that where sub-paragraph (i) applies, a local authority may approve such an application if it is made in relation to a part of the house which after completion of the works will be self-contained and is not to be occupied by the owner or by a member of his family.

(3) Paragraph (c) of subsection (2) shall not apply—
(a) where the house to which the application relates is in a housing action area for improvement declared under section 90 and is listed in the final resolution under section 92(4)(b) or (c) as requiring improvement or integration;
(b) where the house to which the application relates is subject to an improvement order made under section 88(1);
(c) in relation to an application for an improvement grant for the conversion of a building which does not at the date of the application consist of or include a house; or
(d) to a house which is to be occupied by a disabled person (as defined in section 236(3)) in so far as the application is in respect of works which his disability renders necessary if the house is to be suitable for his accommodation, welfare or employment.

(4) In paragraph (c) of subsection (2)—
"prescribed limit" means such limit of rateable value as the Secretary of State with the consent of the Treasury may prescribe; and different limits may be so prescribed for different cases and for

different classes of cases; and a limit so prescribed shall be prescribed by order of the Secretary of State made by statutory instrument which shall be subject to annulment by resolution of either House of Parliament; and

"rateable value" means the rateable value entered in the valuation roll and in force on the date of the application.

(5) The Secretary of State may by order made in a statutory instrument which shall be subject to annulment by resolution of either House of Parliament vary the provisions of paragraph (c) of subsection (2).

(6) The local authority may, with the approval of the Secretary of State, disregard any requirement specified by him under subsection (2)(a)(i) in any case where, in the opinion of the local authority, conformity with that requirement would not be practicable at a reasonable expense.

Approval of application for improvement grant

241.—(1) Where a local authority approve an application made under the provisions of this Part for an improvement grant, they shall notify the applicant and where appropriate, the owner, of the amount of the expense (as estimated in the application) approved by them as being attributable to each house proposed to be provided or improved (an amount hereinafter referred to in relation to improvement works as the "approved expense" of executing those works), and of the amount payable, expressed as a percentage of the approved expense and as a cash amount.

(2) In approving an application for an improvement grant a local authority may require as a condition of paying the grant that the improvement works are carried out within such period (which must not be less than a period of 12 months) as the local authority may specify or within such further period as the local authority may allow.

(3) Where a local authority—

(a) refuse an application, or

(b) approve an application but fix as the amount of an improvement grant an amount less than that which may be fixed by virtue of section 242 or 244,

they shall notify the applicant in writing of the grounds of their decision.

Amount of improvement grant

242.—(1) Subject to the following provisions of this section, the amount of an improvement grant other than a grant paid under section 244 shall not exceed 50 per cent., or such other percentage as may be prescribed of the approved expense of executing the works, but the approved expense for an improvement grant including any amount allowed for the purposes of subsection (4) shall be subject to a maximum of £10,200 or such other maximum as may be prescribed, in respect of each house to which the application relates.

(2) If, after an application for a grant has been approved by a local authority, the authority are satisfied that owing to circumstances beyond the control of the applicant the expense of the works will exceed the estimate contained in the application, they may, on receiving a further estimate, substitute a higher amount as the amount of the approved expense of executing the works, but that amount shall not exceed the maximum authorised by virtue of subsection (1).

(3) A local authority may allow for works for repair and replacement needed, in their opinion, for the purposes of enabling the house to attain a good state of repair—

(a) where an application for an improvement grant relates wholly or partly to the provision of any or all of the standard amenities and—

   (i) on completion of the works the house is in the opinion of the local authority likely to be available for use as a house for a period of at least 10 years, a maximum approved expense not exceeding £3,000 or such other amount as may be prescribed, or 50 per cent., or such other percentage as may be prescribed of the approved expense of executing the improvement works, whichever is the greater; or

   (ii) on completion of the works the house is in the opinion of the local authority likely to be available for use as a house for a period of less than 10 years, a maximum approved expense not exceeding £300 (or such other amount as may be prescribed) for each standard amenity provided, but subject to a maximum of £1,200 or such other amount as may be prescribed;

  (b) where an application does not so relate, a maximum approved expense not exceeding 50 per cent., or such other percentage as may be prescribed of the approved expense of executing the improvement works.

(4) If the local authority are satisfied that in any particular case—

  (a) there are good reasons for fixing a higher amount than that payable by virtue of subsection (1), that amount may be exceeded by such amount as the Secretary of State may approve; and the approval of the Secretary of State may be given either with respect to a particular case or with respect to a particular class of case;

  (b) the expense of executing the works was materially enhanced by measures taken to preserve the architectural or historic interest of the house or building to which the application relates, the amount payable by virtue of subsection (1) may be exceeded by such amount as the Secretary of State may approve.

(5) In any case where—

  (a) an improvement grant or repairs grant within the meaning of Part I of the Act of 1974, or

  (b) an improvement grant or repairs grant within the meaning of this Part, or

  (c) assistance under either of the following enactments—

     (i) section 1 of the Hill Farming Act 1946,

     (ii) section 22(2) of the Crofters (Scotland) Act 1955;

has been made or given in respect of a house and, within the period of 10 years beginning on the date on which the grant or assistance was paid or, if it was paid by instalments, the date on which the last instalment was paid, an improvement grant under this Part, other than a grant payable under section 244 or in respect of works for the benefit of a disabled occupant within the meaning of section 236, is made in respect of that house, the amount payable in relation to that improvement grant shall, when added to the unrepaid amount, if any, of that previous grant or assistance, not exceed 50 per cent., or such other percentage as may be prescribed in pursuance of subsection (1), of the maximum approved expense so prescribed.

(6) Where by virtue of the making on any occasion of an improvement grant in respect of the improvement of a house, the conditions specified in section 236 are required to be observed with respect to the house before the observance thereof by virtue of the making of an improvement grant on a previous occasion has ceased to be requisite, the provisions of sections 246, 247, 252(4) and Schedule 19 shall apply in relation to the

house as regards each occasion on which an improvement grant is so made as if it were the only occasion on which it was so made.

(7) The percentage of the approved expense that may be prescribed under subsection (1) or (3) shall be prescribed by order of the Secretary of State made with the consent of the Treasury.

(8) An order made under subsection (7) shall be made by statutory instrument and shall not be made unless a draft has been laid before and approved by resolution of the House of Commons.

(9) The maximum approved expense that may be prescribed under subsection (1) or (3) shall be prescribed by order of the Secretary of State made by statutory instrument which shall be subject to annulment in pursuance of a resolution of either House of Parliament.

(10) An order under this section may make different provision with respect to different cases or descriptions of case.

Payment of improvement grant

243.—(1) An improvement grant in respect of the expenses incurred for the purpose of the execution of improvement works shall, subject to the following provisions of this section, be paid—

(a) within one month of the date on which, in the opinion of the local authority, the house first becomes fit for occupation after the completion of the works; or

(b) partly in instalments paid from time to time as the works progress and with a final settlement of the balance within one month of the completion of the works but the aggregate of the instalments paid shall not at any time before the completion of the improvement works exceed 50 per cent., or such other percentage fixed by virtue of section 242(1), or, as the case may be, section 244(6) of the aggregate approved expense of the works executed up to that time.

(2) The payment of an improvement grant or of an instalment or the balance thereof shall be conditional on the improvement works, or, as the case may be, the part of the works which the local authority consider will entitle the applicant to payment of the instalment or of the balance of the grant, being executed to the satisfaction of the local authority.

(3) Where an instalment of an improvement grant is paid before the completion of the works, and the works are not completed within 12 months of the date of payment of the instalment, then that instalment and any further instalment paid by the local authority on account of the grant shall, on being demanded by the authority, forthwith become payable to them by the person to whom the instalments were paid, and the instalments shall carry interest at such reasonable rate as the local authority may determine from the date on which they were paid by the authority until repaid under this subsection.

Duty of local authorities to make improvement grants where an application relates exclusively to the provision of standard amenities or to disabled occupant; and amount thereof

244.—(1) Subject to the provisions of this Part, a local authority shall, where an application in that behalf is made to the local authority, give assistance in respect of the improvement of any house by way of making an improvement grant in respect of the cost of executing works required for the house to be provided with one or more of the standard amenities which it presently lacks, if on completion of the works the house will, in the opinion of the local authority—

(a) be provided with all of the standard amenities for the exclusive use of its occupants; and

(b) meet the tolerable standard.

(2) A local authority shall not make an improvement grant under this section in respect of a house comprised in a building containing more than one house, unless they are satisfied that the works carried out on the house will not prevent the improvement of any other house in the building.

(3) Where an application in that behalf is made to a local authority in relation to any house, an improvement grant shall be made under subsection (1) in respect of the cost of executing works required for the house to be provided with a standard amenity, notwithstanding that the house already has such a standard amenity, if in the opinion of the local authority the additional standard amenity to be provided is essential to the needs of a disabled occupant.

(4) Paragraph (a) of subsection (1) shall not apply where the house in respect of which application for a grant is made is not likely to be available for use as a house for a period of at least 10 years.

(5) Subsection (1) shall not apply in respect of a house which is or forms part of a house or building as regards which the local authority are satisfied that they have power to serve a notice under section 161 (power to require execution of works of descriptions other than work to make good neglect).

(6) Subject to subsection (8), the standard amenities for the purposes of this Part are the amenities which are described in the first column of Part I of Schedule 18 and which will be for the exclusive use of the occupants of the house to which the application relates.

(7) The amount of an improvement grant made under this section shall be 50 per cent. or such other percentage as may be prescribed of the approved expense, which shall be subject to a limit determined in accordance with Part II of Schedule 18.

(8) The Secretary of State may by order vary the provisions of Schedule 18, and any such order may contain such transitional or other supplementary provisions as appear to the Secretary of State to be expedient.

(9) Section 86 shall have effect for determining whether a house meets the tolerable standard for the purposes of subsection (1) as it has effect for determining whether a house meets that standard for the purposes of Part IV.

(10) The Secretary of State may by order—
    (a) vary the requirements of subsection (1)(a) and (b);
    (b) vary the amount specified in subsection (6), so as to provide for different amounts of grant to apply for different classes of cases.

(11) Schedule 18 shall have effect for the purpose of specifying the standard amenities and the maximum eligible amount of improvement grant in respect thereof.

(12) The percentage of the approved expense that may be prescribed under subsection (7) or (10)(b) shall be prescribed by order of the Secretary of State made with the consent of the Treasury.

(13) An order made under subsection (8) or (10)(a) shall be made by statutory instrument which shall be subject to annulment in pursuance of a resolution of either House of Parliament.

(14) An order made under subsection (12) shall be made by statutory instrument and shall not be made unless a draft has been laid before and approved by resolution of the House of Commons.

Grants restricted to applicant and his personal representatives

245. In relation to a grant or an application for a grant, any reference in the preceding provisions of this Part to the applicant shall be construed, in relation to any time after his death, as a reference to his personal representatives.

Conditions to be observed with respect to houses in respect of which an improvement grant has been made, and registration thereof

246.—(1) Where an application for an improvement grant has been approved by a local authority, the provisions of this section shall apply with respect to the house for a period of 5 years beginning with the date on which, in the opinion of the local authority, it first becomes fit for occupation after the completion of the improvement works, and shall, so long as those provisions are required to be so observed, be deemed to be part of the terms of any lease or tenancy of the house and shall be enforced accordingly.

(2) It shall be a condition of the grant that—

    (a) the house shall not be used for the purposes other than those of a private dwelling-house, but a house shall not be deemed to be used for the purposes other than those of a private dwelling-house by reason only that part thereof is used as a shop or office, or for business, trade or professional purposes;

    (b) the house shall not be occupied by the owner or a member of his family except as his only or main residence within the meaning of Part V of the Capital Gains Tax Act 1979;

    (c) all such steps as are practicable shall be taken to secure the maintenance of the house in a good state of repair.

(3) The owner of the house shall, on being required to do so by the local authority, certify that the conditions specified in subsection (2) are being observed with respect to the house, and any tenant of the house shall, on being so required in writing by the owner, furnish to him such information as he may reasonably require for the purpose of enabling him to comply with the provisions of this subsection.

(4) A local authority shall not, as a prerequisite of approving a grant, require any conditions or obligations, other than the conditions mentioned in this Part or other statutory obligations to be observed with respect to a house in respect of which an improvement grant has been made under this Part.

(5) The provisions of Schedule 19 shall have effect in the event of a breach of any of the conditions mentioned in this section at a time when they are required to be observed with respect to a house.

(6) Where a local authority pay an improvement grant or, in a case where an improvement grant is payable partly in instalments as the improvement works progress and the balance after the completion of the works in respect of a house, they shall specify in the notice or record mentioned respectively in subsections (7) and (8) the matters specified in subsection (9).

(7) If subsection (6) applies, the local authority shall, where the applicant for the grant was not a tenant-at-will or was a tenant-at-will who since applying, has acquired his landlord's interest in the tenancy, cause to be recorded in the General Register of Sasines or registered in the Land Register, as the case may be, a notice in such form as may be prescribed.

(8) If subsection (6) applies, the local authority shall, where that applicant was and continues to be a tenant-at-will, keep a written record.

(9) The matters to be specified are—

    (a) the conditions mentioned in this section which are required to be observed with respect to the house;

    (b) the period for which the conditions are to be observed; and

    (c) the provisions of Schedule 19 under which, on a breach of any of the said conditions at a time when they require to be observed, the owner of the house becomes liable to repay to the authority the amount repayable by virtue of that Schedule.

(10) Any expenses incurred under subsection (7) recording the notice in the Register of Sasines or registering it in the Land Register, as the case may be, shall be repaid to the local authority by the applicant.

Voluntary repayment of improvement grants

247.—(1) The owner of a house in respect of the provision or improvement of which an improvement grant has been made or the holder of a heritable security over the house, being a heritable creditor entitled to exercise his power of sale, may, at any time when the conditions specified in section 246 are required to be observed with respect to the house, pay to the local authority the like amount as would become payable to them by virtue of Schedule 19 in the event of a breach of any of the conditions referred to in section 246(2), and on the making of the payment observance with respect to the house of those conditions shall cease to be requisite and the provisions of paragraph 7 of the said Schedule shall apply for the purposes of this subsection as they apply for the purposes of that Schedule.

(2) A sum paid under subsection (1) by a heritable creditor shall be treated as part of the sum secured by the heritable security.

Repairs grants

Repairs grants

248.—(1) Subject to the provisions of this section, where an application for a repairs grant is duly made a local authority—

(a) shall approve the application in so far as it relates to the execution of works required by a notice under section 108(1) (repair notices); and

(b) in so far as it does not so relate, may approve the application in such circumstances as they think fit.

(2) A local authority shall not approve an application under this section unless they are satisfied that the house to which the application relates will provide satisfactory housing accommodation for such period as they consider reasonable.

(3) In considering whether or not to approve an application for a repairs grant, a local authority shall have regard to the question whether, in their opinion, the owner would, without undue hardship, be able to finance the expense of the relevant works without the assistance of a repairs grant:

Provided that this subsection shall not apply in any such case as may be prescribed.

(4) The amount of a repairs grant shall not exceed 50 per cent., or such other percentage as may be prescribed, of the approved expense of the works, but the approved expense shall not exceed £4,800 or such other amount as may be prescribed in respect of each house to which the application relates.

(5) Sections 237 to 247 (other than sections 240, 242(1), (4) and (7)) shall apply to an application for a repairs grant as they apply to an application for an improvement grant, except that for the purposes of the application of section 243(1)(b), for the words "section 242(1) or as the case may be section 244(6)" are substituted the words "section 248(4)":

Provided that section 240(2)(c) shall not apply in relation to an application for a repairs grant in respect of the replacement in a different material of such pipes, cisterns, taps or other equipment used for the supply of water to a house as are wholly or partly made of lead.

(6) References in this section to a house shall, in relation to an application made under this section for a grant in respect of works which are to rectify defects specified in a notice under section 108(1), be construed as including references to premises other than a house; but where such an application relates to such premises—

    (a) the local authority shall not, under subsection (2), approve the application unless they are satisfied that the premises form part of a building which contains a house or houses and that house or, as the case may be, all those houses will provide satisfactory housing accommodation as mentioned in that subsection;

    (b) subsection (4) shall be construed as if the reference in it to each house were a reference to each of the premises other than a house; and

    (c) subsection (5) shall be construed as if the enactments excepted by that subsection included sections 240(2) to (6), 246(1), (2), (3), and (5) to (10).

(7) A case that is prescribed under the proviso to subsection (3) shall be prescribed by order of the Secretary of State made by statutory instrument which shall be subject to annulment in pursuance of a resolution of either House of Parliament.

(8) The percentage of the approved expense that may be prescribed under subsection (4) shall be prescribed by order of the Secretary of State made with the consent of the Treasury.

(9) An order made under subsection (8) shall be made by statutory instrument and shall not be made unless a draft has been laid before and approved by resolution of the House of Commons.

(10) The maximum approved expense that may be prescribed under subsection (4) shall be prescribed by order of the Secretary of State made by statutory instrument which shall be subject to annulment in pursuance of a resolution of either House of Parliament.

Grants for fire escapes

Grants for fire escapes for houses in multiple occupation

249.—(1) Subject to the provisions of this section, where an application for a grant for a fire escape in a house in multiple occupation is duly made, a local authority—

    (a) shall approve the application in so far as it relates to the execution of works specified in a notice served on any person, other than a public body, under section 162 (which empowers a local authority to require the provision of a means of escape from fire in a house in multiple occupation);

    (b) in so far as it is not so specified but is required in connection with works so specified, may approve the application.

(2) A local authority shall not approve an application under this section unless they are satisfied that at the time of completion of the works to which the application relates the house will be in reasonable repair (disregarding the state of internal decorative repair) having regard to its age, character and location.

(3) Where a local authority approve an application under this section they shall determine the maximum amount of expenses which they think proper to be incurred for the relevant works; but so much of such amount as relates to works referred to in—

    (a) paragraph (a) of subsection (1) shall not exceed £8,100 or such other amount as may be prescribed under subsection (8);

    (b) paragraph (b) of that subsection shall not exceed £3,000 or such other amount as may be prescribed under subsection (8).

(4) Subject to subsection (5), the amount of grant payable under subsection (1) above in relation to any application shall be 75 per cent. of the maximum amount determined under subsection (3) above in relation thereto or such other percentage of that maximum amount as may be prescribed under subsection (9).

(5) If, in any case, it appears to the local authority by whom the application is approved that the applicant will not without undue hardship be able to finance the cost of so much of the work as is not met by the grant, they may, as regards that case, increase the percentage referred to in subsection (4) above to such percentage, not exceeding 90 per cent., as they think fit.

(6) Sections 236 to 239 and 241 to 247 (other than section 241(3)(b), section 242(1), (1A), (3), (4), (6) and (7) and section 244) shall apply to an application for a grant under subsection (1) as they apply to an application for an improvement grant, except that for the purposes of the application of section 243(1)(b), for the words "section 242(1) or as the case may be section 244(6)" are substituted the words "section 248(4) or (5) as the case may be".

(7) In subsection (1), "public body" means a regional, islands or district council or such other body as the Secretary of State may by order made by statutory instrument specify.

(8) The maximum amount of expenses prescribed under subsection (3)(a) or (b) shall be prescribed by order of the Secretary of State made by statutory instrument which shall be subject to annulment in pursuance of a resolution of either House of Parliament.

(9) The percentage of the maximum amount that may be prescribed under subsection (4) shall be prescribed by order of the Secretary of State made with the consent of the Treasury.

(10) An order made under subsection (9) shall be made by statutory instrument and shall not be made unless a draft has been laid before and approved by resolution of the House of Commons.

Grants for houses in housing action areas

Application of this Part to houses situated in a housing action area and power of local authority to give repairs grants in such areas and amount thereof

250.—(1) The provisions of this Part shall apply to houses which are to be brought up to the standard specified by a local authority under section 90 or 91 and which are situated in housing action areas for improvement or for demolition and improvement within the meaning of Part IV, but subject to the modifications contained in subsections (2) to (7) below.

(2) In section 242(1), for "not exceed 50 per cent." there shall be substituted "be 75 per cent.".

(3) In section 243(1), for "50 per cent." there shall be substituted "75 per cent.".

(4) In section 254(2), for "75 per cent." there shall be substituted "90 per cent.".

(5) If, in the case of a house which is in a housing action area on the date on which the application is approved for a grant under section 242(1) as read with subsection (2), it appears to the local authority by whom the application is approved that the applicant will not without undue hardship be able to finance the cost of so much of the improvement work as is not met by the grant, they may increase the percentage under the said subsection from 75 per cent. to such percentage, not exceeding 90 per cent., as they think fit; but this subsection shall not apply where an applicant for an improvement grant is not the owner of the land to which the application relates.

(6) Sections 238(1), in so far as it relates to refusal to approve an application, and 244 shall not apply, but a local authority shall make an improvement grant to an owner of a house situated in a housing action area as aforesaid in respect of such improvement works as may, in their opinion, be required for the house to be brought up to the standard specified by the local authority in a resolution passed under section 90 or 91 in relation to that area:

Provided that an improvement grant shall not be made in pursuance of this subsection in respect of a house which is comprised in a building containing more than one house, if the local authority are of the opinion that the improvement works to be carried out on that house would prevent any other house in that building from being brought up to the standard specified as aforesaid.

(7) In section 248—

    (a) for subsections (1) and (2) there shall be substituted the following subsections—

        "(1) Subject to the following provisions of this section, where an application for a repairs grant is duly made, a local authority shall approve the application in so far as it relates to the execution of works to houses to which the provisions of this Part are applied by section 250(1).

        (2) A local authority shall not approve an application under this section unless on completion of the works the house will attain the standard specified in the resolution passed under section 90 or 91.";

    (b) in subsection (4), at the beginning there shall be inserted the words "Subject to section 249(5)" and for the words "50 per cent." there shall be substituted the words "75 per cent.";

    (c) in subsection (5), after the words "section 244" there shall be inserted the words "and subsections (3), (4) and (5) of section 249".

Improvement of amenity grants

Powers of local authority for improvement of amenities

251.—(1) For the purpose of securing the improvement of the amenities of a predominantly residential area within their district, a local authority may—

    (a) carry out any works on land owned by them and assist (whether by grants or loans or otherwise) in the carrying out of any works on land not owned by them;

    (b) with the agreement of the owner of any land, carry out or arrange for the carrying out of works on that land at his expense, or at the expense of the local authority, or in part at the expense of both;

    (c) acquire any land by agreement;

and may be authorised by the Secretary of State to purchase any land compulsorily.

(2) The Acquisition of Land (Authorisation Procedure) (Scotland) Act 1947 shall apply to a compulsory purchase of land under subsection (1) as if that subsection had been in force immediately before the commencement of this Act.

Grants for thermal insulation

Schemes for grants for thermal insulation

252.—(1) Local authorities shall make grants, in accordance with such schemes as may be prepared and published by the Secretary of State and laid by him before Parliament, towards the cost of works undertaken to improve the thermal insulation of dwellings in their district.

(2) Schemes under this section shall specify—

(a) the descriptions of dwelling and the insulation works qualifying for grants, and

(b) the persons from whom applications may be entertained in respect of different descriptions of dwelling.

(3) The grant shall be such percentage of the cost of the works qualifying for grant as may be prescribed, or such money sum as may be prescribed, whichever is the less.

(4) A scheme may provide for grants to be made only to those applying on grounds of special need or to be made in those cases on a prescribed higher scale; and for this purpose "special need" shall be determined by reference to such matters personal to the applicant (such as age, disability, bad health and inability without undue hardship to finance the cost of the works) as may be specified in the scheme.

(5) In this section, "prescribed" means prescribed by order of the Secretary of State made with the approval of the Treasury.

(6) An order shall be made by statutory instrument which shall be subject to annulment in pursuance of a resolution of the House of Commons.

Finance and administration of schemes under s.252

253.—(1) Finance for the making of grants under section 252 shall be provided to local authorities from time to time by the Secretary of State.

(2) A local authority is not required, nor has power, to make grants under section 252 in any year beyond those for which the Secretary of State has notified them that finance is committed for that year in respect of the authority's district.

(3) In the administration of grants under section 252 local authorities shall comply with any directions given to them by the Secretary of State after consultation with their representative organisations.

(4) The Secretary of State may, in particular, give directions as to—

(a) the way in which applications for grants are to be dealt with, and the priorities to be observed between applicants and different categories of applicant, and

(b) the means of authenticating applications, so that grants are only given in proper cases, and of ensuring that the works are carried out to any standard specified in the applicable scheme.

(5) The Secretary of State shall, with the approval of the Treasury, pay such sums as he thinks reasonable in respect of the administrative expenses incurred by local authorities in operating schemes under section 252.

Exchequer contributions

Exchequer contributions towards improvement or repairs grants or grants for fire escapes

254.—(1) The Secretary of State may make Exchequer contributions towards the expense incurred by a local authority in making an improvement grant or a repairs grant or a grant under section 250 (grants for fire escapes).

(2) Subject to any order made by the Secretary of State under subsection (5), an Exchequer contribution under subsection (1) shall be a sum equal to 75 per cent. (in the case of an improvement or repairs grant), or 90 per cent. (in the case of a grant under section 250) of the annual loan charges referable to the amount of the grant, payable for each of the 20 financial years beginning with the year in which were completed the works in respect of which the grant was made.

(3) For the purposes of this section, the annual loan charges referable to the amount of a grant shall (whatever may be the manner in which the local authority have provided or intend to provide the money requisite for making the grant) be the annual sum which, in the opinion of the Secretary of State, would fall to be provided by the authority for the payment of interest on, and the repayment of, an amount of borrowed money equal to the amount of the grant, being money the period for the repayment of which is 20 years.

(4) A local authority shall pay to the Secretary of State such percentage as may have been paid to them by virtue of subsection (2) of any sum—

(a) recovered by them by virtue of section 246 in consequence of a breach of any of the conditions required to be observed with respect to the house, or

(b) paid to them under section 247 in respect of the house.

(5) The Secretary of State may by order made with the consent of the Treasury vary, either generally or in relation to classes of houses, with respect to grants made in pursuance of applications approved by local authorities after such date as may be specified in the order, the percentages fixed by virtue of subsection (2):

Provided that the said percentages shall not be reduced to less than 65 per cent.

(6) An order under subsection (5)—

(a) shall not be made unless a draft thereof has been approved by a resolution of the House of Commons; and

(b) shall not specify under that subsection a date earlier than the date of the laying of the draft;

and before laying such a draft the Secretary of State shall consult with such associations of local authorities as appear to him to be concerned and with any local authority with whom consultation appears to him to be desirable.

Exchequer contributions to local authority towards expenditure incurred for improvement of amenities

255.—(1) Subject to the provisions of this section, the Secretary of State may, subject to any directions of the Treasury, pay an Exchequer contribution to a local authority towards such expenditure incurred by them for improvement of amenities under section 248—

(a) in carrying out works, whether in pursuance of arrangements made or otherwise, or acquiring or appropriating land, or

(b) in making contributions to any other authority or person towards expenses which might be so incurred by the local authority,

as he may approve for the purposes of this section on an application by the local authority.

(2) This section does not apply to land to which the housing revenue account relates.

(3) The approval of the Secretary of State under subsection (1) shall not be given if the works have been begun, unless he is satisfied that there were good reasons for beginning the works before the application had been approved by him.

(4) For the purposes of this section—

(a) the cost of any works shall be taken to be the amount certified by the local authority as appearing to them to be the cost likely to be incurred by them in carrying out those works whether in pursuance of arrangements made or otherwise; and

(b) the cost of any land acquired by a local authority under section 248 shall be taken to be the expenses incurred by the authority in connection with the acquisition, and the cost of any land appropriated by a local authority for the purposes of that section shall be taken to be such amount as the Secretary of State may determine.

(5) An Exchequer contribution under this section shall be a sum payable annually for a period of 20 years beginning with the financial year in which the works are completed and that sum shall be equal to the annual loan charges referable to such percentage of the expenditure approved for the purposes of this section as the Secretary of State shall, with the consent of the Treasury, prescribe by order made by statutory instrument which shall be subject to annulment in pursuance of a resolution of the House of Commons.

(6) The aggregate of any expenditure approved for the purposes of this section (whether on one or more applications) shall not exceed the sum arrived at by taking £600 for each of the dwellings in the area.

(7) The Secretary of State may, with the consent of the Treasury, by order substitute another amount for the amount of £600 mentioned in subsection (6), and any such order shall be made by statutory instrument, which shall be subject to annulment in pursuance of a resolution of the House of Commons.

(8) Without prejudice to subsection (7), the Secretary of State may direct that in the case of a class or classes of predominantly residential areas or in the case of a particular predominantly residential area, subsection (6) shall have effect as if for the amount of £600, or such other amount as may be substituted for that amount under subsection (7), there were substituted a greater amount.

(9) For the purposes of this section, the annual loan charges referable to any amount shall be the annual sum which, in the opinion of the Secretary of State, would fall to be provided by a local authority for the payment of interest on, and the repayment of, a loan of that amount, being money the period for the repayment of which is 20 years.

(10) Where any arrangements made between a local authority and a registered housing association so provide, any expenditure incurred by the housing association in pursuance of the arrangements which might have been incurred by the local authority under section 248 shall be treated for the purposes of subsection (1) as if it were expenditure so incurred by the local authority; and where any such expenditure is approved by the Secretary of State for the purposes of this section—

(a) subsection (9) shall have effect, in relation to it, as if the reference therein to a local authority were a reference to the housing association, and

(b) the local authority shall pay to the housing association by way of annual grant an amount not less than so much of the Exchequer contribution paid to the local authority under this section as is referable to that expenditure.

Agricultural tenants, etc.

Application of this Part to agricultural tenants, etc.

256.—(1) For the purposes of the provisions of this Part, a tenant, crofter, landholder or statutory small tenant shall be deemed to be the owner of any house, building or other land on his farm, croft or holding if in respect of the execution thereon of improvement works he would, on the termination of his tenancy, be entitled to compensation under the Agricultural Holdings (Scotland) Act 1949 or the Crofters (Scotland) Acts 1955 and 1961 or the Small Landholders (Scotland) Acts, 1886 to 1931 (as the case may be) as for an improvement.

(2) Where by virtue of subsection (1) an improvement grant or a repairs grant is made to a crofter, a landholder or a statutory small tenant

in respect of a house on his croft or holding, the local authority shall forthwith intimate to the landlord of the croft or holding that an improvement grant or a repairs grant has been so made, and shall inform him of the amount thereof.

(3) If at any time within the period during which conditions are required by section 246 to be observed with respect to a house provided on a farm, croft or holding otherwise than by the landlord thereof, compensation becomes payable in respect of the house, or of any improvement works executed in relation thereto, as for an improvement under the Agricultural Holdings (Scotland) Act 1949 or the Crofters (Scotland) Acts 1955 and 1961 or the Small Landholders (Scotland) Acts 1886 to 1931 (as the case may be), so much of the value of the house or works as is attributable to the sum paid by way of improvement grant or repairs grant, shall be taken into account in assessing the compensation so payable and shall be deducted therefrom.

(4) The landlord of a farm, croft or holding on which there is a house with respect to which conditions are for the time being required to be observed by virtue of section 246, shall not at any time within the period during which those conditions are so required to be observed be entitled to obtain any consideration by way of rent or otherwise in respect of so much of the value of the house, or of any improvement works executed in relation thereto, as is attributable to the sum paid by way of improvement grant or repairs grant.

PART XIV

ASSISTANCE FOR OWNERS OF DEFECTIVE HOUSING

Eligibility for assistance

Designation of defective dwellings by Secretary of State

257.—(1) The Secretary of State may designate as a class any buildings each of which consists of or includes one or more dwellings if it appears to him that—

  (a) buildings in the proposed class are defective by reason of their design or construction, and

  (b) by virtue of the circumstances mentioned in paragraph (a) having become generally known, the value of some or all of the dwellings concerned has been substantially reduced.

(2) A dwelling which is, or is included in a building in a class so designated is referred to in this Part as a "defective dwelling"; and in this Part in relation to such a dwelling—

  (a) "the qualifying defect" means what, in the opinion of the Secretary of State, is wrong with the buildings in that class; and

  (b) "the cut-off date" means the date by which, in the opinion of the Secretary of State, the circumstances mentioned in subsection (1)(a) became generally known.

(3) A designation shall describe the qualifying defect and specify—

  (a) the cut-off date,

  (b) the date (being a date on or after the cut-off date) on which the designation is to come into operation,

  (c) the period within which persons may seek assistance under this Part in respect of the defective dwellings concerned.

(4) A designated class shall not be described by reference to the area in which the buildings concerned are situated.

(5) Notice of a designation shall be published in the Edinburgh Gazette.

(6) Any question arising as to whether a building is or was at any time in a class designated under this section shall be determined by the Secretary of State.

Variation or revocation of designation

258.—(1) The Secretary of State may—

    (a) vary a designation under section 257, but not so as to vary the cut-off date, or

    (b) revoke such a designation.

(2) The Secretary of State may by a variation of the designation extend the period referred to in section 257(3)(c) (period within which assistance must be applied for) whether or not it has expired.

(3) The variation or revocation of a designation does not affect the operation of the provisions of this Part in relation to a dwelling if, before the variation or revocation comes into operation, the dwelling is a defective dwelling by virtue of the designation in question and an application for assistance under this Part has been made.

(4) Notice of the variation or revocation of a designation shall be published in the Edinburgh Gazette.

Conditions of eligibility

259.—(1) Subject to the following provisions of this Part, a person to whom this section applies is eligible for assistance in respect of a defective dwelling for the purposes of this Part if—

    (a) his interest in the dwelling is that of owner ("the owner's interest"), and

    (b) one of the following sets of conditions is satisfied.

(2) This section applies to—

    (a) an individual who is not a trustee,

    (b) trustees, if all the beneficiaries are individuals, and

    (c) personal representatives.

(3) The first set of conditions is that—

    (a) there was a disposal by a public sector authority of the owner's interest in the dwelling before the cut-off date; and

    (b) there has been no disposal for value by any person of owner's interest in the dwelling on or after the cut-off date;

and for the purposes of this subsection where a public sector authority hold an interest in a dwelling a disposal of that interest by or under any enactment is to be treated as a disposal by the authority.

(4) The second set of conditions is that—

    (a) a person to whom this section applies acquired the owner's interest in the dwelling on a disposal for value occurring within the period of 12 months beginning with the cut-off date;

    (b) on the date of that disposal he was unaware of the association of the dwelling with the qualifying defect;

    (c) the value by reference to which the price for the disposal was calculated did not take any, or any adequate, account of the qualifying defect; and

    (d) if the cut-off date had fallen immediately after the date of the disposal, the first set of conditions would have been satisfied.

Exceptions to eligibility

260. A person is not eligible for assistance in respect of a defective dwelling if the local authority are of the opinion that—

    (a) work to the building that consists of or includes the dwelling has been carried out in order to deal with the qualifying defect, and

(b) on the completion of the work, no further work relating to the dwelling was required to be done to the building in order to deal satisfactorily with the qualifying defect.

Construction of references to disposal, etc.

261.—(1) References in this Part to a disposal include a part disposal; but for the purposes of this Part a disposal of an interest in a dwelling is a disposal of a relevant interest in the dwelling only if on the disposal the person to whom it is made acquires a relevant interest in the dwelling.

(2) Subject to subsection (3), where any interest in land is disposed of, the time at which the disposal is made is, for the purposes of this Part, the time the missives are concluded (and not, if different, the date of entry specified in the missives).

(3) If the missives contain a condition precedent (and in particular if they contain a condition relating to the exercise of an option) the time at which the disposal is made for those purposes is the time when the condition precedent is satisfied.

(4) References in this Part to a disposal of an interest for value are to a disposal for money or money's worth, whether or not representing full value for the interest disposed of.

(5) In relation to a person holding an interest in a dwelling formed by the conversion of another dwelling, references in this Part to a previous disposal of an interest in the dwelling include a previous disposal on which an interest in land which included that part of the original dwelling in which his interest subsists was acquired.

Determination of entitlement

Application for assistance

262. A person seeking assistance under this Part in respect of a defective dwelling shall make a written application to the local authority within the period specified in the relevant designation.

Application not to be entertained where grant application pending or approved

263.—(1) The local authority shall not entertain an application for assistance under this Part if—

(a) an application has been made in respect of the defective dwelling (whether before or after the relevant designation came into operation) for a grant under Part XIII, and

(b) the relevant works in relation to that grant include the whole or part of the work required to reinstate the dwelling,

unless the grant application has been refused or has been withdrawn under subsection (2) or the relevant works have been completed.

(2) Where a person has applied for such a grant in respect of a dwelling and—

(a) the dwelling is a defective dwelling, and

(b) the relevant works include the whole or part of the work required to reinstate it,

he may withdraw his application, whether or not it has been approved, if the relevant works have not been begun.

(3) In this section "relevant works", in relation to a grant, means works of improvement or repair within the meaning of Part XIII.

Determination of eligibility

264.—(1) A local authority receiving an application for assistance under this Part shall as soon as reasonably practicable give notice in writing to the applicant stating whether in their opinion he is eligible for assistance in respect of the defective dwelling.

(2) If they are of opinion that he is not so eligible, the notice shall state the reasons for their view.

(3) If they are of opinion that he is so eligible, the notice shall inform him of his right to make such a claim as is mentioned in section 265(2) (claim that assistance by way of reinstatement grant is inappropriate in his case).

Determination of form of assistance to which applicant is entitled

265.—(1) A local authority receiving an application for assistance under this Part shall, if the applicant is eligible for assistance, determine whether he is entitled to assistance by way of reinstatement grant or by way of repurchase.

(2) If the authority are satisfied, on a claim by the applicant to that effect, that it would be unreasonable to expect him to secure or await the carrying out of the work required to reinstate the defective dwelling, the applicant is entitled to assistance by way of repurchase.

(3) Subject to subsection (2), the applicant is entitled to assistance by way of reinstatement grant if the authority are satisfied that the conditions for such assistance set out in section 266 are met, and otherwise to assistance by way of repurchase.

Conditions for assistance by way of reinstatement grant

266.—(1) The conditions for assistance by way of reinstatement grant are, subject to any order under subsection (2)—

(a) that the dwelling is a house (as defined in section 302);

(b) that if the work required to reinstate the dwelling (together with any other work which the local authority are satisfied the applicant proposes to carry out) were carried out—

(i) the dwelling would be likely to provide satisfactory housing accommodation for a period of at least 30 years, and

(ii) an individual acquiring ownership of the dwelling with vacant possession would be likely to be able to obtain a loan on the security of it on satisfactory terms from a lending institution;

(c) that giving assistance by way of reinstatement grant is justified having regard, on the one hand, to the amount of reinstatement grant that would be payable in respect of the dwelling and, on the other hand, to the likely value of the dwelling with vacant possession after the work required to reinstate it has been carried out; and

(d) that the amount of reinstatement grant would not be likely to exceed the aggregate of the price payable on the acquisition of the applicant's interest in the dwelling in pursuance of this Part and the amount to be reimbursed under section 280 (reimbursement of expenses incidental to repurchase).

(2) The Secretary of State may by order amend the conditions set out in subsection (1) so as to modify or omit any of the conditions or to add or substitute for any of the conditions other conditions.

(3) An order—

(a) may make different provision for different classes of case,

(b) shall be made by statutory instrument, and

(c) shall not be made unless a draft of it has been laid before and approved by a resolution of each House of Parliament.

(4) An order does not affect an application for assistance made before the order comes into force.

Meaning of "work required for reinstatement" and "associated arrangement"

267.—(1) For the purposes of this Part the work required to reinstate a defective dwelling is the work relating to the dwelling that is required to be done to the building that consists of or includes the dwelling in order to deal satisfactorily with the qualifying defect, together with any further work—

(a) required to be done, in order to deal satisfactorily with the qualifying defect, to any garage or outhouse designed or constructed as that building is designed or constructed, being a garage or outhouse in which the interest of the person eligible for assistance subsists and which is occupied with and used for the purposes of the dwelling or any part of it, or

(b) reasonably required in connection with other work falling within this subsection.

(2) In this Part, "associated arrangement" means an arrangement which is entered into in connection with the execution of the work required to reinstate a defective dwelling and is likely to contribute towards the dwelling being regarded as an acceptable security by a lending institution.

Notice of determination

268.—(1) where an applicant is eligible for assistance, the authority to whom the application was made shall as soon as reasonably practicable give him notice in writing (a "notice of determination") stating the form of assistance to which he is entitled.

(2) If, on such a claim by the applicant as is mentioned in section 265(2) (claim that assistance by way of reinstatement grant is inappropriate in his case), the authority are not satisfied that it would be unreasonable to expect him to secure or await the carrying out of the work required to reinstate the defective dwelling, the notice shall state the reasons for their view.

(3) A notice stating that the applicant is entitled to assistance by way of reinstatement grant shall also state—

(a) the grounds for the authority's determination;

(b) the work which, in their opinion, is required to reinstate the defective dwelling;

(c) the amount of expenditure which, in their opinion, may properly be incurred in executing the work;

(d) the amount of expenditure which, in their opinion, may properly be incurred in entering into an associated arrangement;

(e) the condition required by section 270 (execution of work to satisfaction of authority within specified period), including the period within which the work is to be carried out; and

(f) their estimate of the amount of grant payable in respect of the dwelling in pursuance of this Part.

(4) A notice stating that the applicant is entitled to assistance by way of repurchase shall also state the grounds for the authority's determination and the effect of—

(a) paragraphs 1 to 3 of Schedule 20 (request for notice of proposed terms of repurchase), and

(b) sections 281, 283 and 284(1) (provisions for grant of tenancy to former owner-occupier of repurchased dwelling).

(5) References in the following provisions of this Part to a person entitled to assistance by way of reinstatement grant or, as the case may be, by way of repurchase are to a person who is eligible for assistance in respect of the dwelling and on whom a notice of determination has been served stating that he is entitled to that form of assistance.

Assistance by way of reinstatement grant

Reinstatement grant

269.—(1) Where a person is entitled to assistance by way of reinstatement grant, the local authority shall pay reinstatement grant to him in respect of—

(a) the qualifying work, and

(b) any associated arrangement,

subject to and in accordance with the following provisions of this Part.

(2) The "qualifying work" means the work stated in the notice of determination, or in a notice under section 272 (notice of change of work required), to be the work which in the opinion of the local authority is required to reinstate the dwelling.

Conditions of payment of reinstatement grant

270.—(1) It is a condition of payment of reinstatement grant that the qualifying work is carried out—

(a) to the satisfaction of the local authority, and

(b) within the period specified in the notice of determination, or that period as extended.

(2) The period so specified shall be such reasonable period (of at least 12 months), beginning with service of the notice, as the authority may determine.

(3) The authority shall, if there are reasonable grounds for doing so, by notice in writing served on the person entitled to assistance, extend or further extend the period for carrying out the qualifying work (whether or not the period has expired).

(4) Payment of reinstatement grant shall not be subject to any other condition, however expressed.

Amount of reinstatement grant

271.—(1) The amount of reinstatement grant payable is the appropriate percentage of whichever is the least of—

(a) the amount stated in the notice of determination, or in a notice under section 272 (notice of change in work required or expenditure permitted), to be the amount of expenditure which, in the opinion of the local authority, may properly be incurred in executing the qualifying work and entering into any associated arrangement,

(b) the expenditure actually incurred in executing the qualifying work and entering into any associated arrangement, and

(c) the expenditure which is the maximum amount permitted to be taken into account for the purposes of this section.

(2) The appropriate percentage is 90 per cent. or, in a case where the authority are satisfied that the person entitled to assistance would suffer financial hardship unless a higher percentage of the expenditure referred to in subsection (1) were paid to him, 100 per cent.

(3) The Secretary of State may by order vary either or both of the percentages mentioned in subsection (2).

(4) The maximum amount of expenditure permitted to be taken into account for the purposes of this section is the amount specified as the expenditure limit by order made by the Secretary of State, except in a case or description of case in which the Secretary of State, on the application of a local authority, approves a higher amount.

(5) An order under subsection (4) may make different provision for different areas, different designated classes and different categories of dwelling.

(6) An order under this section shall be made by statutory instrument which shall be subject to annulment in pursuance of a resolution of the House of Commons.

Changes in work or expenditure

272. Where the local authority are satisfied that—

    (a) the work required to reinstate the defective dwelling is more extensive than that stated in the notice of determination or in a previous notice under this section, or

    (b) the amount of the expenditure which may properly be incurred in executing that work is greater than that so stated, or

    (c) there is an amount of expenditure which may properly be incurred in entering into an associated arrangement but no such amount is stated in the notice of determination or a previous notice under this section, or

    (d) where such an amount is so stated, the amount of expenditure which may be properly so incurred is greater than that amount,

they shall by notice in writing served on the person entitled to assistance state their opinion as to that amount or, as the case may be, that work and that amount; and the amount of reinstatement grant shall be adjusted accordingly.

Payment of reinstatement grant

273.—(1) The local authority may pay reinstatement grant in respect of the qualifying work in a single sum on completion of the work or by instalments.

(2) No instalment shall be paid if the instalment, together with any amount previously paid, would exceed the appropriate percentage of the cost of so much of the qualifying work as has been executed at that time.

(3) The authority shall pay reinstatement grant in respect of an associated arrangement when payment in respect of the expenditure incurred in entering into the arrangement falls to be made.

Repayment of grant for breach of condition

274.—(1) Where an amount of reinstatement grant has been paid in one or more instalments and the qualifying work is not completed within the period for carrying out the work, the local authority may, if they think fit, require the person who was entitled to assistance to repay that amount to them forthwith.

(2) The amount required to be repaid (or, if it was paid in more than one instalment, the amount of each instalment) shall carry interest, at such reasonable rate as the authority may determine, from the date on which it was paid until repayment.

Assistance by way of repurchase

Repurchase

275. Schedule 20 shall have effect with respect to assistance by way of repurchase, as follows—

    Part I—The agreement to repurchase.

    Part II—Price payable and valuation.

Repurchase by authority other than local authority

276. Where the local authority give a notice of determination to a person stating that he is entitled to assistance by way of repurchase and they are of opinion that—

   (a) a relevant interest in the dwelling was disposed of by a public sector authority mentioned in column 1 of the following Table (or a predecessor mentioned there of such an authority),

   (b) there has been no disposal within paragraph (a) since the time of that disposal, and

   (c) any conditions mentioned in column 2 of the Table in relation to the authority are met,

they shall forthwith give that other authority a notice in writing, together with a copy of the notice of determination, stating that the authority may acquire, in accordance with this Part, the interest of the person entitled to assistance.

Table

Public sector authority	Conditions
1. A registered housing association (other than a co-operative housing association) or a predecessor housing association of that association.	None.
2. The Scottish Special Housing Association.	None.
3. A development corporation.	None.
4. Another local authority or a predecessor of that authority.	The local authority provide housing accommodation in the vicinity of the defective dwelling with which the dwelling may conveniently be managed.
5. Any other public sector authority prescribed by order of the Secretary of State, or a predecessor so prescribed.	Any conditions prescribed by the order.

   (2) The other authority may, within the period of four weeks beginning with the service of the notice on them, give notice in writing to the local authority—

   (a) stating that they wish to acquire the interest, and

   (b) specifying the address of the principal office of the authority and any other address which may also be used as an address for service;

and the local authority shall forthwith give to the person entitled to assistance a transfer notice, that is, a notice in writing of the contents of the notice received by them and the effect of subsection (3).

   (3) After a transfer notice has been given to the person entitled to assistance, the other authority shall be treated as the appropriate authority for the purposes of anything done or falling to be done under this Part, except that—

   (a) a request under paragraph 2 of Schedule 21 (request for notice of proposed terms of acquisition), may be made either to the local authority or to the other authority, and

   (b) any such request given to the local authority (whether before or after the notice) shall be forwarded by them to the other authority;

and references in this Part to "the purchasing authority" shall be construed accordingly.

   (4) An order under this section shall be made by statutory instrument.

Interest subject to right of pre-emption, etc.

   277.—(1) This section applies where a person ("the owner") is entitled to assistance by way of repurchase in respect of a defective dwelling and there is a condition in the title relating to his interest in the dwelling whereby—

  (a) before disposing of the interest he must offer to dispose of it to a public sector authority, or

  (b) in the case of an interest under a lease, he may require a public sector authority who are his landlords to accept a surrender of the lease but is otherwise prohibited from disposing of it.

(2) If the public sector authority are the local authority in whose area the dwelling is situated, the condition in the title shall be disregarded for the purposes of Schedule 20 (repurchase).

(3) If the public sector authority are not the local authority, the provisions of this Part as to repurchase do not apply so long as there is such a condition in the title; but if—

  (a) the owner disposes of his interest to the public sector authority in pursuance of the condition in the title or lease, and

  (b) the interest acquired by that authority on the disposal subsists only in the land affected, that is to say, the defective dwelling and any garage, outhouse, garden, yard and pertinents belonging to or usually enjoyed with the dwelling or any part of it,

the owner is entitled to be paid by the local authority the amount (if any) by which 95 per cent. of the defect-free value exceeds the consideration for the disposal.

(4) For the purposes of this section—

  (a) the "consideration for the disposal" means the amount before any reduction required by section 72 (reduction corresponding to amount of discount repayable) or any provision to the like effect, and

  (b) the "defect-free value" means the amount that would have been the consideration for the disposal if none of the defective dwellings to which the designation in question related had been affected by the qualifying defect.

Compulsory purchase compensation to be made up to 95 per cent. of defect-free value

278.—(1) Where a person ("the owner") has disposed of an interest in a defective dwelling, otherwise than in pursuance of Schedule 20 (repurchase), to an authority possessing compulsory purchase powers and—

  (a) immediately before the time of the disposal he was eligible for assistance under this Part in respect of the dwelling,

  (b) the amount paid as consideration for the disposal did not include any amount attributable to his right to apply for such assistance, and

  (c) on the disposal the authority acquired an interest in any of the affected land, that is to say, the defective dwelling and any garage, outhouse, garden, yard and pertinents belonging to or usually enjoyed with the dwelling or any part of it,

he is entitled, subject to the following provisions of this section, to be paid by the local authority the amount (if any) by which 95 per cent. of the defect-free value exceeds the amount of the compensation for the disposal.

(2) For the purposes of this section—

  (a) the "amount of compensation for the disposal" means the amount that would have been the proper amount of compensation for the disposal (having regard to any relevant determination of the Lands Tribunal) or, if greater, the amount paid as the consideration for the disposal, and

  (b) the "defect-free" value means the amount that would have been the proper amount of compensation for the disposal if none of the defective dwellings to which the designation in question related had been affected by the qualifying defect; but excluding, in either case, any amount payable for disturbance or for any other matter not directly based on the value of land.

(3) For the purposes of this section, it shall be assumed that the disposal occurred on a compulsory acquisition (in cases where it did not in fact do so).

(4) Where the compensation for the disposal fell to be assessed by reference to the value of the land as a site cleared of buildings and available for development, it shall be assumed for the purposes of determining the defect-free value that it did not fall to be so assessed.

(5) The amount payable by the local authority under this section shall be reduced by the amount of any payment made in respect of the defective dwelling under section 304 or 305 (payments for well-maintained houses).

(6) In this section "authority possessing compulsory purchase powers" has the same meaning as in the Land Compensation (Scotland) Act 1963.

Supplementary provisions as to payments under s.277 or 278

279.—(1) The local authority are not required to make a payment to a person under—

(a) section 277 (making-up of consideration on disposal in pursuance of right of pre-emption, etc.), or

(b) section 278 (making up of compulsory purchase compensation),

unless he makes a written application to them for payment before the end of the period of two years beginning with the time of the disposal.

(2) Where the authority—

(a) refuse an application for payment under section 277 on any grounds, or

(b) refuse an application for payment under section 278 on the grounds that the owner was not eligible for assistance in respect of the defective dwelling,

they shall give the applicant written notice of the reasons for their decision.

(3) Any question arising—

(a) under section 277 or 278 as to the defect-free value, or

(b) under section 278 as to the amount of compensation for the disposal,

shall be determined by the district valuer if the owner or the local authority so require by notice in writing served on the district valuer.

(4) A person serving a notice on the district valuer in pursuance of subsection (3) shall serve notice in writing of that fact on the other party.

(5) Before making a determination in pursuance of subsection (3), the district valuer shall consider any representation by the owner or the authority made to him within 4 weeks from the service of the notice under that subsection.

Reimbursement of expenses incidental to repurchase

280.—(1) A person whose interest in a defective dwelling is acquired by the purchasing authority in pursuance of Schedule 20 (repurchase) is entitled to be reimbursed by the purchasing authority the proper amount of—

(a) expenses in respect of legal services provided in connection with the authority's acquisition, and

(b) other expenses in connection with negotiating the terms of that acquisition, being in each case expenses which are reasonably incurred by him after receipt of a notice under paragraph 3 of that Schedule (authority's notice of proposed terms of acquisition).

(2) An agreement between a person and the purchasing authority is void in so far as it purports to oblige him to bear any part of the costs or expenses incurred by the authority in connection with the exercise by him of his rights under this Part.

Effect of repurchase on occupier

Effect of repurchase on certain existing tenancies

281.—(1) Where an authority mentioned in section 44 (authorities satisfying the landlord condition for secure tenancy) acquire an interest in a defective dwelling in pursuance of Schedule 20 (repurchase) and—

(a) the land in which the interest subsists is or includes a house occupied as a separate dwelling, and

(b) the interest of the person entitled to assistance by way of repurchase is, immediately before the completion of the authority's acquisition, subject to a tenancy of the house,

the tenancy shall not, on or after the acquisition, become a secure tenancy unless the conditions specified in subsection (2) are met.

(2) The conditions are—

(a) that the tenancy was a protected tenancy throughout the period beginning with the making of an application for assistance under this Part in respect of the defective dwelling and ending immediately before the authority's acquisition; and

(b) no notice was given in respect of the tenancy in accordance with any of Cases 11 to 14 and 16 to 21 in Schedule 2 to the Rent (Scotland) Act 1984 (notice that possession might be recovered under that Case) or under section 34(1)(d) of the Tenants Rights Etc. (Scotland) Act 1980 (notice that tenancy is to be a protected short tenancy).

Grant of tenancy to former owner-occupier

282.—(1) Where an authority acquire an interest in a defective dwelling in pursuance of Schedule 20 (repurchase), or in the circumstances described in section 277(3) (exercise of right of pre-emption, etc.), and—

(a) the land in which the interest subsists is or includes a house occupied as a separate dwelling, and

(b) an individual is an occupier of the house throughout the period beginning with the making of an application for assistance under this Part in respect of the dwelling and ending immediately before the completion of the authority's acquisition, and

(c) he is a person entitled to assistance by way of repurchase in respect of the defective dwelling, or the persons so entitled are in relation to the interest concerned his trustees,

the authority shall, in accordance with this section, either grant or arrange for him to be granted a tenancy of that house or another on the completion of their acquisition of the interest concerned.

(2) If the authority are among those mentioned in section 44(1) (public sector authorities capable of granting secure tenancies) their obligation is to grant a secure tenancy.

(3) In any other case their obligation is to grant or arrange for the grant of either—

(a) a secure tenancy, or

(b) a protected tenancy other than one under which the landlord might recover possession under one of the cases in Part II of Schedule 2 to the Rent (Scotland) Act 1984 (cases in which the court must order possession).

(4) Where two or more persons qualify for the grant of a tenancy under this section in respect of the same house, the authority shall grant the tenancy, or arrange for it to be granted, to such one or more of them as they may agree among themselves or (if there is no such agreement) to all of them.

Grant of tenancy to former statutory tenant

283.—(1) Where an authority mentioned in section 44 (public sector authorities capable of granting secure tenancies) acquire an interest in a defective dwelling in pursuance of Schedule 20 (repurchase), and—

(a) the land in which the interest subsists is or includes a house occupied as a separate dwelling, and

(b) an individual is an occupier of a house throughout the period beginning with the making of an application for assistance under this Part in respect of the dwelling and ending immediately before the completion of the authority's acquisition, and

(c) he is a statutory tenant of the house at the end of that period, and

(d) no notice was given in respect of the original tenancy in accordance with any of Cases 11 to 14 and 16 to 21 in Schedule 2 to the Rent (Scotland) Act 1984 (notice that possession might be recovered under that Case) or under section 34(1)(d) of the Tenant's Rights Etc. (Scotland) Act 1980 (notice that tenancy is to be a protected shorthold tenancy), and

(e) the interest of the person entitled to assistance would, if the statutory tenancy were a contractual tenancy, be subject to the tenancy at the end of the period mentioned in paragraph (b),

the authority shall grant him a secure tenancy (of that house or another) on the completion of their acquisition of the interest concerned.

(2) Where two or more persons qualifying for the grant of a tenancy under this section in respect of the same house, the authority shall grant the tenancy to such one or more of them as they may agree among themselves or (if there is no such agreement) to all of them.

(3) If at any time after the service of a notice of determination it appears to the purchasing authority that a person may be entitled to request them to grant him a secure tenancy under this section, they shall forthwith give him notice in writing of that fact.

Alternative accommodation under s.282 or 283

284.—(1) The house to be let under the tenancy granted to a person—

(a) under section 282 or 283 (grant of tenancy to former owner-occupier or statutory tenant of defective house acquired by authority), or

(b) under arrangements made for the purposes of section 283,

shall be the house of which he is the occupier immediately before the completion of the authority's acquisition (the "current house"), except in the following Cases—

Case 1

By reason of the condition of any building of which the current house consists or of which it forms part, the house may not safely be occupied for residential purposes.

Case 2

The authority intend, within a reasonable time of the completion of their acquisition of the interest concerned—

    (a) to demolish or reconstruct the building which consists of or includes the defective dwelling in question, or

    (b) to carry out work on any building or land in which the interest concerned subsists,

and cannot reasonably do so if the current house remains in residential occupation.

    (2) In those Cases the house to be let shall be another house which, so far as is reasonably practicable in the case of that authority, affords accommodation which is—

    (a) similar as regards extent and character to the accommodation afforded by the current house,

    (b) reasonably suitable to the means of the prospective tenant and his family, and

    (c) reasonably suitable to the needs of the prospective tenant and his family as regards proximity to place of work and place of education.

Request for tenancy under s.282 or 283

285.—(1) An authority are not required to grant, or arrange for the grant of, a tenancy to a person under section 282 or 283 unless he requests them to do so in writing before—

    (a) in the case of an acquisition under Schedule 20 (repurchase), the service on the person entitled to assistance of an offer to purchase under paragraph 4 of that Schedule, or

    (b) in the case of an acquisition in the circumstances described in section 277(3) (acquisition in pursuance of right of pre-emption, etc.), the time of the disposal.

    (2) An authority receiving a request under subsection (1) shall, as soon as reasonably practicable, give notice in writing to the person making the request stating whether in their opinion either of the Cases in section 284(1) applies (cases in which tenancy may be of a house other than the current house).

    (3) If their opinion is that either Case does apply, the notice shall also state which of the Cases is applicable and the effect of section 284.

Interpretation of ss.281 to 285

286. In sections 281 to 285 (effect of repurchase on occupier)—

    (a) "house" has the same meaning as in Part III (secure tenancies);

    (b) "occupier", in relation to a house, means a person who occupies the house as his only or principal home or (in the case of a statutory tenant) as his residence;

    (c) references to the grant of a secure tenancy are to the grant of a tenancy which would be a secure tenancy assuming that the tenant under the tenancy occupies the house as his only or principal home.

Local schemes

Designation of defective dwellings under local schemes

287.—(1) A local authority may by resolution designate as a class buildings in their area each of which consists of or includes one or more dwellings if it appears to them that—

    (a) buildings in the proposed class are defective by reason of their design or construction, and

    (b) by virtue of the circumstances mentioned in paragraph (a) having become generally known, the value of some or all of the dwellings concerned has been substantially reduced.

(2) Subsection (1) does not apply to a building in a class designated under section 257 (designation by Secretary of State); but a building does not cease to be included in a class designated under this section by virtue of its inclusion in a class designated under that section.

(3) A dwelling which is, or is included in, a building in a class so designated is referred to in this Part as a "defective dwelling"; and in this Part, in relation to such a dwelling—

(a) "the qualifying defect" means what, in the opinion of the authority, is wrong with the buildings in that class, and

(b) "the cut-off date" means the date by which, in the opinion of the authority, the circumstances mentioned in subsection (1)(a) became generally known.

(4) A designation shall describe the qualifying defect and specify—

(a) the cut-off date,

(b) the date (being a date falling on or after the cut-off date) on which the designation is to come into operation, and

(c) the period within which persons may seek assistance under this Part in respect of the defective dwellings concerned.

(5) A designation may not describe a designated class by reference to the area (other than the authority's district) in which the buildings concerned are situated; but may be so described that within the authority's area there is only one building in the class.

(6) Any question arising as to whether a building is or was at any time in a class designated under this section shall be determined by the local authority concerned.

Variation or revocation of designation under local schemes

288.—(1) The local authority may by resolution—

(a) vary a designation under section 287, but not so as to vary the cut-off date, or

(b) revoke such a designation.

(2) The authority may by a variation of the designation extend the period referred to in section 287(4)(c) (period within which assistance must be applied for) whether or not it has expired.

(3) The variation or revocation of a designation does not affect the operation of the provisions of this Part in relation to a dwelling if, before the variation or revocation comes into operation, the dwelling is a defective dwelling by virtue of the designation in question and application for assistance under this Part has been made.

Secretary of State's control over designation, variation or revocation

289.—(1) Where a local authority have passed a resolution under—

(a) section 287 (designation under local scheme), or

(b) section 288 (variation or revocation of designation under local scheme),

they shall give written notice to the Secretary of State of the resolution before the expiry of the period of 28 days beginning with the date on which it is passed.

(2) The designation, variation or revocation shall not come into operation before the expiry of the period of 2 months beginning with the receipt by the Secretary of State of the notice under subsection (1).

(3) If within that period the Secretary of State serves notice in writing to that effect on the authority, the designation, revocation or variation shall not come into operation.

Miscellaneous

Duty of local housing authority to publicise availability of assistance

290.—(1) A local authority shall, within the period of 3 months beginning with the coming into operation of—
  (a) a designation under section 257 (designation of defective dwellings
      by Secretary of State) or section 287 (designation of defective
      dwellings under local scheme), or
  (b) a variation of such a designation,
publish in a newspaper circulating in their area notice suitable for the
purpose of bringing the effect of the designation or variation to the
attention of persons who may be eligible for assistance in respect of such
of the dwellings concerned as are situated within their area.
  (2) No such notice need be published by a local housing authority who
are of opinion—
  (a) that none of the dwellings concerned are situated in their area, or
  (b) that no-one is likely to be eligible for assistance in respect of the
      dwellings concerned which are situated in their area.
  (3) If at any time it becomes apparent to a local authority that a person
is likely to be eligible for assistance in respect of a defective dwelling
within their area, they shall forthwith take such steps as are reasonably
practicable to inform him of the fact that assistance is available.

Duties of public sector authority disposing of defective dwelling

291.—(1) A public sector authority shall, where a person is to acquire
a relevant interest in a defective dwelling on a disposal by the authority,
give him notice in writing before the time of the disposal—
  (a) specifying the qualifying defect, and
  (b) stating that he will not be eligible for assistance under this Part in
      respect of the dwelling.
  (2) A public sector authority shall, before they convey a relevant
interest in a defective dwelling in pursuance of completed missives to a
person on whom a notice under subsection (1) has not been served, give
him notice in writing—
  (a) specifying the qualifying defect,
  (b) stating, where the time of disposal of the interest falls after the
      cut-off date, that he will not be eligible for assistance under this
      Part, and
  (c) stating the effect of subsection (3).
  (3) A person on whom a notice under subsection (2) is served—
  (a) is not obliged to complete the conveyance before the expiry of
      the period of 6 months beginning with the service of that notice
      on him, and
  (b) may within that period withdraw from the transaction by notice
      in writing to the authority to that effect.
  (4) Where a public sector authority are required to serve a notice under
section 63(2), 68, 69 or 70 (landlord's response to notice claiming to
exercise right to buy) in respect of a defective dwelling, the notice under
subsection (1) shall be served with that notice.
  (5) A notice under subsection (1) or (2) shall, (except in the case of a
notice under subsection (1) which is served in accordance with subsection
(4)), be served at the earliest date at which it is reasonably practicable to
do so.

Reinstatement of defective dwelling by local authority

292.—(1) Where a relevant interest in a defective dwelling has been
disposed of by a public sector authority, the local authority may, before

the end of the period within which a person may seek assistance under this Part in respect of the dwelling, enter into an agreement with—

(a) any person holding an interest in the dwelling, or

(b) any person who is a statutory tenant of it,

to execute at his expense any of the work required to reinstate the dwelling.

(2) For the purposes of this section a disposal by or under an enactment of an interest in a dwelling held by a public sector authority shall be treated as a disposal of the interest by the authority.

Death of person eligible for assistance, etc.

293.—(1) Where a person who is eligible for assistance in respect of a defective dwelling—

(a) dies, or

(b) disposes of his interest in the dwelling (otherwise than on a disposal for value) to such a person as is mentioned in section 259(2) (persons qualifying for assistance: individuals, trustees for individuals and personal representatives),

this Part applies as if anything done (or treated by virtue of this subsection as done) by or in relation to the person so eligible had been done by or in relation to his personal representatives or, as the case may be, the person acquiring his interest.

(2) In sections 277 to 279 (subsidiary forms of financial assistance) references to the owner of an interest in a defective dwelling include his personal representatives.

Dwellings included in more than one designation

294. The provisions of Schedule 21 have effect with respect to dwellings included in more than one designation.

Application of Act in relation to lenders on security of defective dwelling

295.—(1) The Secretary of State may by regulations made by statutory instrument subject to annulment by either House of Parliament make provision for the purpose of conferring rights and obligations on any person who has granted a loan on the security of a defective dwelling where—

(a) a power of sale is exercisable by the lender, and

(b) the borrower is eligible for assistance in respect of the defective dwelling.

(2) The rights that may be conferred on a lender by regulations under this section are—

(a) rights corresponding to those conferred by this Part on a person holding a relevant interest in the defective dwelling, and

(b) the right to require the local authority to acquire in accordance with the regulations any interest in the defective dwelling to be disposed of in exercise of the power of sale,   .

and the rights that may be so conferred may be conferred in place of any rights conferred on any other person by this Part.

(3) Regulations under this section may provide that, where the conditions in subsection (1)(a) and (b) are or have been satisfied, this Part, the power of sale and any enactment relating to the power of sale in question shall have effect subject to such modifications as may be specified in the regulations.

(4) Regulations under this section—

(a) may make different provision for different cases, and

(b) may make incidental and consequential provision.

Contributions by Secretary of State

Contributions by Secretary of State

296.—(1) The Secretary of State may, if he thinks fit in any case contribute towards the expense incurred by a local authority—
  (a) in giving assistance by way of reinstatement grant,
  (b) in giving assistance by way of repurchase of a dwelling which is a defective dwelling by virtue of a designation under section 257 (designation by Secretary of State), or
  (c) in making payments under section 277 (making up of consideration on disposal in pursuance of right of pre-emption, etc.) or section 278 (making up of compulsory purchase compensation).
(2) The contributions shall be annual payments—
  (a) in respect of a period of 20 years beginning with the financial year in which, as the case may be, the work in respect of which the grant was payable was completed, the acquisition of the interest concerned was completed or the payment was made, and
  (b) of a sum equal to the relevant percentage of the annual loan charges referable to the amount of the expenses incurred.
(3) The relevant percentage is—
  (a) 90 per cent. in the case of reinstatement grant,
  (b) 75 per cent. in the case of repurchase or a payment under section 277 or 278 where there has at any time been a disposal of a relevant interest in the defective dwelling by the local authority or a predecessor of that authority, and
  (c) 100 per cent. in the case of repurchase or a payment under those sections not within paragraph (b);
or such other percentage as, in any of those cases, may be provided by order under section 297.
(4) The amount of the expense incurred is—
  (a) in the case of reinstatement grant, the amount of the grant,
  (b) in the case of repurchase, the price paid for the acquisition, together with any amount reimbursed under section 280 (incidental expenses), less the value of the interest at the relevant time determined in accordance with paragraph 8 of Schedule 21 (value for purposes of repurchase) but without the assumption required by paragraph 8(1)(a) (assumption that dwelling is defect free),
  (c) in the case of a payment under section 277 or 278, the amount of the payment.
(5) The annual loan charges referable to the amount of the expense incurred means the annual sum which, in the opinion of the Secretary of State, would fall to be provided by a local authority for the payment of interest on, and the repayment of, a loan of that amount repayable over a period of 20 years.
(6) Payment of contributions under this section is subject to the making of a claim in such form, and containing such particulars, as the Secretary of State may determine; and the contributions are payable at such times, in such manner and subject to such conditions, as to records, certificates, audit or otherwise, as the Secretary of State may, with the agreement of the Treasury, determine.

Power to vary relevant percentage

297.—(1) The Secretary of State may by order made with the consent of the Treasury vary all or any of the percentages specified in section 296(3) (relevant percentages for purposes of contribution to expenditure of local authority) in respect of assistance or payments, or a class of assistance or payments specified in the order.

(2) An order—

(a) may make different provision for assistance given or payments made in respect of defective dwellings in different areas or under different provisions or for different purposes of the same provision;

(b) shall be made by statutory instrument, and

(c) shall not be made unless a draft of it has been laid before and approved by a resolution of the House of Commons.

(3) An order applies to assistance given or payments made in pursuance of applications made after such date as may be specified in the order, and the specified date shall not be earlier than the date of the laying of the draft.

Supplementary provisions

Service of notices

298.—(1) A notice or other document under this Part may be given to or served on a person, and an application or written request under this Part may be made to a person—

(a) by delivering it to him or leaving it at his proper address, or

(b) by sending it to him by post,

and also, where the person concerned is a body corporate, by giving or making it to or serving it on the secretary of that body.

(2) For the purposes of this section, and of section 7 of the Interpretation Act 1978 as it applies for the purposes of this section, the proper address of a person is—

(a) in the case of a body corporate or its secretary, the address of the principal office of the body,

(b) in any other case, his last known address,

and also, where an additional address for service has been specified by that person in a notice under section 276(2) (notice of intention to assume responsibility for repurchase), that address.

Jurisdiction of sheriff in Scotland

299.—(1) A sheriff of the sheriff court district within which the defective dwelling is situated has jurisdiction—

(a) to determine any question arising under this Part; and

(b) to entertain any proceedings brought in connection with the performance or discharge of any obligations so arising, including proceedings for the recovery of damages or compensation in the event of the obligations not being performed.

(2) Subsection (1) has effect subject to—

(a) sections 257(6) and 287(6) (questions of designation to be decided by designating authority),

(b) section 279(3) and paragraph (9) of Schedule 21 (questions of valuation to be determined by district valuer).

(3) Where an authority required by section 270(3) or paragraph 7 of Schedule 20 to extend or further extend any period fail to do so, the sheriff may extend or further extend that period until such date as he may specify.

Meaning of "public sector authority"

300.—(1) In this Part—

(a) "public sector authority" means—

a regional, islands or district council (or a predecessor of
    such a council),

a joint board and a joint committee of which every constitu-
    ent member is, or is appointed by, such a council or
    predecessor of such a council,

a water authority,

the Housing Corporation,

the Scottish Special Housing Association,

a registered housing association other than a co-operative
    housing association (or a predecessor housing associ-
    ation of such an association),

a development corporation,

the National Coal Board, or

the United Kingdom Atomic Energy Authority,

or a body corporate or housing association specified by order
of the Secretary of State in accordance with the following
provisions;

(b) "co-operative housing association" means a fully mutual housing association which is a society registered under the Industrial
and Provident Societies Act 1965, and "fully mutual", in
relation to a housing association, means that the rules of the
association—

    (i) restrict membership to persons who are tenants or pro-
        spective tenants of the association, and

    (ii) preclude the granting or assignation of tenancies to per-
        sons other than members.

(2) The Secretary of State may provide that a body corporate shall be
treated as a public sector authority if he is satisfied—

(a) that the affairs of the body are managed by its members, and

(b) that its members hold office by virtue of appointment (to that or
    another office) by a Minister of the Crown under an enactment,

or if he is satisfied that it is a subsidiary of such a body.

(3) The Secretary of State may provide that a housing association shall
be treated as a public sector authority if he is satisfied that the objects or
powers of the association include the provision of housing accommodation
for individuals employed at any time by a public sector authority or
dependants of such individuals.

(4) Where the Secretary of State is satisfied that a body or association
met the requirements of subsection (2) or (3) during any period, he may,
whether or not he makes an order in respect of the body or association
under that subsection, provide that it shall be treated as having been a
public sector authority during that period.

(5) If the Secretary of State is satisfied that a body or association
specified in an order under subsection (2) or (3) has ceased to meet the
requirements of that subsection on any date, he may by order provide
that it shall be treated as having ceased to be a public sector authority on
that date.

(6) An order under this section shall be made by statutory instrument.

**Disposal of certain Crown interests in land treated as disposal by public
    sector authority**

301. References in this Part to a disposal of an interest in a dwelling by
a public sector authority include a disposal of—

(a) an interest belonging to Her Majesty in right of the Crown,

(b) an interest belonging to, or held in trust for Her Majesty for the
    purposes of, a government department or Minister of the Crown.

Meaning of "dwelling" and "house"

302.—(1) In this Part, "dwelling" means any house, flat or other unit designed or adapted for living in.

(2) For the purposes of this Part a building so designed or adapted is a "house" if it is a structure reasonably so called; so that where a building is divided into units so designed or adapted—

(a) if it is so divided horizontally, or a material part of a unit lies above or below another unit, the units are not houses (though the building as a whole may be), and

(b) if it is so divided vertically, the units may be houses.

(3) Where a house which is divided into flats or other units is a defective dwelling in respect of which a person is eligible for assistance, the fact that it is so divided shall be disregarded for the purposes of section 266(1)(a) (first condition for assistance by way of reinstatement: that the dwelling is a house).

Interpretation

303. In this Part—

"associated arrangement" has the meaning given by section 267(2);

"cut-off date" is to be construed in accordance with section 257(2) or, as the case may be, 287(3);

"defective dwelling" is to be construed in accordance with section 257(2) or, as the case may be, 287(3);

"interest in dwelling" includes an interest in land which is or includes the dwelling;

"lending institution" means a building society, a bank or an insurance company;

"person entitled to assistance" (by way of reinstatement grant or repurchase) is to be construed in accordance with section 268(5);

"public sector authority" has the meaning given by section 300;

"purchasing authority" is to be construed in accordance with section 276(3);

"qualifying defect" is to be construed in accordance with section 257(2) or, as the case may be, section 287(3);

"relevant interest" means the interest of the owner;

"work required to reinstate a defective dwelling" is to be construed in accordance with section 267(1).

Part XV

Compensation Payments

Payments for well-maintained houses

Payments in respect of well-maintained houses subject to closing orders etc.

304.—(1) If—

(a) a house has been vacated in pursuance of a closing order or a demolition order, or purchased compulsorily under section 121 instead of the making of a closing order or a demolition order in respect of the building in which it is comprised; and

(b) any person has, within 3 months after the service of the closing order or demolition order, or of the notice of determination to purchase required by section 121(3), or after the confirmation of a compulsory purchase order, made a representation to the local authority that the house has been well maintained and that the good maintenance of the house is attributable wholly or partly to work carried out by him or at his expenses; and

(c) leaving out of account any defects in the house in respect of any such matters as are mentioned in section 86, the representation is correct;

the local authority shall make to that person in respect of that house a payment calculated in accordance with section 306.

(2) If, on receiving a representation under subsection (1), the local authority consider that the condition specified in paragraph (c) of that subsection is not satisfied, they shall serve on the person by whom the representation was made notice that no payment falls to be made to him under that subsection.

(3) For the purposes of this section, a house comprised in a building which might have been the subject of a demolition order but which has, without the making of such an order, been vacated and demolished in pursuance of an undertaking for its demolition given to the local authority shall be deemed to have been vacated in pursuance of a demolition order made and served at the date when the undertaking was given.

Payments in respect of well-maintained houses subject to compulsory purchase as not meeting the tolerable standard

305.—(1) Where as respects a house which is made the subject of a compulsory purchase order under Part IV as not meeting the tolerable standard, the local authority are satisfied that it has been well maintained, they shall make a payment calculated in accordance with section 306 in respect of the house.

(2) A payment under this section shall be made—

(a) if the house is occupied by an owner thereof, to him, or

(b) if the house is not so occupied, to the person or persons liable to maintain and repair the house, and, if more than one person is so liable, in such shares as the local authority think equitable in the circumstances:

Provided that, if any other person satisfies the local authority that the good maintenance of the house is attributable to a material extent to work carried out by him or at his expense, the authority may, if it appears to them to be equitable in the circumstances, make the payment, in whole or in part to him.

(3) The local authority shall, along with the notice which they serve on any person under paragraph 3(b) of Schedule 1 to the Acquisition of Land (Authorisation Procedure) (Scotland) Act 1947 in respect of the compulsory purchase of a house under Part IV, enclose a notice stating, subject to the calculation to be made under section 306, whether or not they intend to make a payment under this section in respect of the house.

(4) Any person aggrieved by a notice under subsection (3) which states that the local authority do not intend to make a payment under this section in respect of a house may, within 21 days of service on him of that notice, refer the matter to the Secretary of State; and the Secretary of State may, if he thinks it appropriate to do so (after, if he considers it necessary, causing the house to be inspected by one of his officers), direct the local authority to make such a payment.

Calculation of amount payable for well-maintained houses

306.—(1) This section shall apply in relation to any payment in respect of a well maintained house under section 304 or section 305.

(2) Subject to subsection (4), a payment to which this section applies shall be of an amount equal to the rateable value of the house multiplied

by such multiplier as may from time to time be specified in an order made by the Secretary of State.

(3) An order made under subsection (2) shall be made by statutory instrument which shall be of no effect unless it is approved by a resolution of each House of Parliament.

(4) A payment to which this section applies shall not in any case exceed the amount (if any) by which the full compulsory purchase value of the house exceeds the restricted value thereof; and any question as to such value shall be determined, in default of agreement, as if it had been a question of disputed compensation arising on such a purchase.

(5) Where a payment falls to be made in respect of any interest in a house under section 308, no payment shall be made in respect of that house under section 304 or 305.

(6) In this section—

"full compulsory purchase value" has the same meaning as in section 311(2);

"rateable value" means the rateable value entered in the valuation roll last authenticated prior to the relevant date;

"restricted value" has the same meaning as in section 311(2); and

"the relevant date" in relation to any payment made with respect to any house means—

(a) if the house was purchased compulsorily in pursuance of a notice served under section 121, the date when the notice was served;

(b) if the house was vacated in pursuance of a demolition order or a closing order, or was declared not to meet the tolerable standard by an order under paragraph 2(1) of Schedule 2 to the Land Compensation (Scotland) Act 1963, the date when the order was made.

Repayment of certain payments

Repayment of payments made in connection with closing or demolition order when revoked

307. Where a payment in respect of a house has been made by a local authority under section 304, 305 or 308 in connection with a demolition order or a closing order and, the demolition order or the closing order is revoked by an order under section 116, then if at any time the person to whom the payment was made is entitled to an interest in the house (within the meaning of section 311(2)), he shall on demand repay the payment to the authority.

Payments for houses not meeting tolerable standard

Right to and amount of payments for house not meeting tolerable standard

308.—(1) Where a house has been purchased at restricted value in pursuance of a compulsory purchase order made by virtue of sections 88 or 121 or paragraph 5 of Schedule 8, or in pursuance of an order under paragraph 2(1) of Schedule 2 to the Land Compensation (Scotland) Act 1963, or has been vacated in pursuance of a demolition order under section 115 or a closing order under section 114 or 119, then if—

(a) on the relevant date and throughout the qualifying period the house was occupied as a private dwelling, and the person so occupying the house (or, if during that period it was so occupied by two or more persons in succession, each of those persons) was a person entitled to an interest in that house or a member of the family of a person so entitled, and

(b) the full compulsory purchase value of the interest is greater than its restricted value,

the authority concerned shall make in respect of that interest a payment of an amount equal to the difference between the full compulsory purchase value and the restricted value.

(2) Any question as to the values referred to in subsection (1) shall be determined, in default of agreement, as if it had been a question of disputed compensation arising on such a purchase.

(3) Where an interest in a house purchased or vacated as described in subsection (1) was acquired by any person (in this subsection referred to as the first owner) on or after 1st August 1968 and less than 2 years before the relevant date, and a payment under the said subsection (1) in respect of that interest would have fallen to be made by the authority concerned had the qualifying period been a period beginning with the acquisition and ending with the relevant date, the authority concerned shall make to the person who was entitled to the interest at the date when the house was purchased or vacated a payment of the like amount, if—

(a) the authority are satisfied that before acquiring the interest the first owner had made all reasonable inquiries to ascertain whether it was likely that the notice, resolution or order, by reference to which the relevant date is defined in section 311 would be served, passed or made within 2 years of the acquisition and that he had no reason to believe that it was likely; and

(b) the person entitled to the interest at the date when the house was purchased or vacated was the first owner or a member of his family.

Right of parties to certain agreements secured on, or related to, houses not meeting the tolerable standard to apply to sheriff for adjustment of the agreements

309.—(1) This section shall apply whether or not a payment falls to be made in respect of an interest in a house under section 308 where a house is purchased at restricted value in pursuance of a compulsory purchase order made by virtue of section 88, 120 or 121, or paragraph 5 of Schedule 8, or in pursuance of an order under paragraph 2(1) of Schedule 2 to the Land Compensation (Scotland) Act 1963, or has been vacated in pursuance of a demolition order or a closing order, and on the date of the making of the compulsory purchase or other order the house is occupied in whole or part as a private dwelling by a person who throughout the relevant period—

(a) holds an interest in the house, being an interest subject to a heritable security or charge, or

(b) is a party to an agreement to purchase the house by instalments.

(2) Where the provisions of subsection (1) apply in the case of any house, any party to the heritable security, charge or agreement in question may apply to the sheriff who, after giving to other parties an opportunity of being heard, may, if he thinks fit, make an order—

(a) in the case of a house which has been purchased compulsorily, discharging or modifying any outstanding liabilities of the person having an interest in the house, being liabilities arising by virtue of any bond or other obligation with respect to the debt secured by the heritable security or charge, or by virtue of the agreement, or

(b) in the case of a house vacated in pursuance of a demolition order, or closing order, discharging or modifying the terms of the heritable security, charge or agreement,

and, in either case, either unconditionally or subject to such terms and conditions, including conditions with respect to the payment of money, as the sheriff may think just.

(3) In determining in any case what order, if any, to make under this section, the sheriff shall have regard to all the circumstances of the case, and in particular—

(a) in the case of a heritable security or charge—

    (i) to whether the heritable creditor or person entitled to the benefit of the charge acted reasonably in advancing the principal sum on the terms of the heritable security or charge; and in relation to this sub-paragraph he shall be deemed to have acted unreasonably if, at the time when the heritable security or charge was created, he knew or ought to have known that in all the circumstances of the case the terms of the heritable security or charge did not afford sufficient security for the principal sum advanced, and

    (ii) where the heritable security or charge secures a sum which represents all or any part of the purchase price payable for the interest, to whether the purchase price was excessive, or

(b) in the case of an agreement to purchase by instalments, to how far the amount already paid by way of principal, or, where the house has been purchased compulsorily, the aggregate of that amount and so much, if any, of the compensation in respect of compulsory purchase as falls to be paid to the seller, represents a fair price for the purchase.

(4) In this section "the relevant period" means the period from the date of the making of the compulsory purchase or other order to—

(a) in the case of a compulsory purchase order, the date of service of notice to treat (or deemed service of notice to treat) for purchase of the house or, if the purchase is effected without service of notice to treat, the date of completion of that purchase, and

(b) in the case of any other order, the date of vacation of the house in pursuance of the order or of an order deemed to have been made and served in the terms of the next following subsection;

or, if the person referred to in subsection (1) dies before the date specified in paragraph (a) or (b), to the date of death.

(5) For the purposes of this section, a house which might have been the subject of a demolition order but which has, without the making of such an order, been vacated and demolished in pursuance of an undertaking for its demolition given to the local authority, shall be deemed to have been vacated in pursuance of a demolition order made and served at the date when the undertaking was given.

Provisions as to house subject to heritable security or purchased by instalments

310. Section 309 (right of parties to certain agreements secured on, or related to, houses not meeting tolerable standard to apply to sheriff for adjustment of agreements) shall apply, whether or not a payment falls to be made in respect of an interest in a house under section 308, where the house not meeting the tolerable standard is purchased at restricted value in pursuance of a compulsory purchase order made by virtue of section 88, 120 or 121 or paragraph 5 of Schedule 8, or in pursuance of an order under paragraph 2(1) of Schedule 2 to the Land Compensation (Scotland) Act 1963, or has been vacated in pursuance of a demolition order or a closing order as it applies where a house has been purchased or vacated before 25th August 1969 as described in section 309.

Interpretation of sections 308 to 310

311.—(1) In section 308, in relation to any house purchased or vacated, "the relevant date" and "the authority concerned" mean respectively—

(a) if the house was purchased compulsorily in pursuance of a notice served under section 121, the date when and the authority by whom the notice was served;

(b) if the house was comprised in an area declared by a final resolution passed under Part IV to be a housing action area, the date when notice of that resolution was published and served in accordance with the provisions of Part I of Schedule 8 and the authority by whom the resolution was passed;

(c) if the house was declared not to meet the tolerable standard by an order under paragraph 2(1) of Schedule 2 to the Land Compensation (Scotland) Act 1963, the date when the order was made and the acquiring authority within the meaning of that Act;

(d) if the house was vacated in pursuance of a demolition order or closing order, the date when and the authority by whom the order was made;

(e) if the house was compulsorily purchased under section 88(4), the date when and the authority by whom the order was served;

and "the qualifying period" means the period of 2 years ending with the relevant date, except that where that date is earlier than 31st July 1970, it means the period beginning with 1st August 1968 and ending with the relevant date.

(2) In sections 308 to 310—

"full compulsory purchase value", in relation to any interest in a house, means the compensation which would be payable in respect of the compulsory purchase of that interest if the house were not being dealt with under Part IV or Part VI as not meeting the tolerable standard, and, in the case of a house subject to a demolition order or closing order, the making of that order were a service of the notice to treat;

"interest" in a house does not include the interest of a tenant for a year or any less period or of a statutory tenant within the meaning of the Rent (Scotland) Act 1984;

"restricted value", in relation to the compulsory purchase of a house, means compensation in respect thereof assessed under or by virtue of section 120 or 121 or Part III of Schedule 8.

(3) For the purposes of section 308, a house which might have been the subject of a demolition order but which has, without the making of such an order, been vacated and demolished in pursuance of an undertaking for its demolition given to the local authority having power to make the order shall be deemed to have been vacated in pursuance of a demolition order made and served by that authority at the date when the undertaking was given.

Payments to other local authorities

Payment of purchase money or compensation by one local authority to another

312.—(1) Any purchase money or compensation payable by a local authority under this Act in respect of any land, right or interest of another local authority which would but for this section be paid into a bank as provided by the Lands Clauses Acts may be otherwise paid and applied as the Secretary of State approves and determines.

(2) A determination of the Secretary of State under this section shall be final and conclusive.

PART XVI

GENERAL AND MISCELLANEOUS

Byelaws

Byelaws with respect to houses in multiple occupation

313.—(1) The power of making and enforcing byelaws under section 72 of the Public Health (Scotland) Act 1897 with respect to houses or parts of houses which are let in lodgings or occupied by members of more than one family shall extend to the making and enforcing of byelaws imposing any duty (being a duty which may be imposed by the byelaws and which involves the execution of work) on the owner within the meaning of that Act of the said house, in addition to or in substitution for any other person having an interest in the premises, and prescribing the circumstances and conditions in and subject to which any such duty is to be discharged.

(2) For the purpose of discharging any duty so imposed, the owner or other person may at all reasonable times enter upon any part of the premises.

(3) Where an owner or other person has failed to carry out any work which he has been required to carry out under the byelaws, the local authority may, after giving to him not less than 21 days' notice in writing, themselves carry out the works and recover the costs and expenses.

(4) For the purpose of subsection (3), the provisions of Part V with respect to the enforcement of notices requiring the carrying out of work and the recovery of expenses by local authorities shall apply with such modifications as may be necessary.

(5) In this section "owner", in relation to a house mentioned in subsection (1), means the person entitled to receive, or who would if the premises were let, be entitled to receive the rents of the premises, and includes a trustee, factor, tutor, or curator, and in the case of public or municipal property applies to the persons to whom the management is entrusted.

Byelaws with respect to accommodation for agricultural workers

314.—(1) A local authority shall make, with respect to bothies, chaumers and similar premises which are used for the accommodation of agricultural workers and are not part of a farmhouse, byelaws regarding any of the following matters—

(a) the provision of a separate entrance in any case where the premises form part of other premises;

(b) the provision of ventilation and floor area;

(c) the provision of adequate heating and lighting;

(d) the prevention of and safety from fire;

(e) the provision of a ventilated larder and a fireplace or stove suitable for cooking food and sufficient cooking utensils;

(f) the provision of furnishing, including the provision of a separate bed and bedding for each worker;

(g) the provision of accommodation for personal clothing, and of facilities for personal ablution;

(h) the painting, whitewashing or other cleansing of the premises at regular intervals;

(i) intimation to the local authority by farmers of the number of workers employed by them who are accommodated in bothies or in chaumers or similar premises;

(j) such other matters as may from time to time be prescribed:

Provided that, if the local authority show to the satisfaction of the Secretary of State that it is unnecessary to make byelaws under this section, the Secretary of State may dispense with the making of such byelaws.

(2) Byelaws regarding the matters specified in paragraph (e) of subsection (1) shall apply only to premises in which the occupants cook their meals.

(3) Byelaws made by a local authority under this section may be limited to particular parts of the authority's area.

(4) Where a local authority fail, within such period as the Secretary of State may allow, to make with respect to any of the matters specified in subsection (1) byelaws which are in the opinion of the Secretary of State sufficient and satisfactory, the Secretary of State may himself make such byelaws which shall be of the like force and effect as if they had been made by the authority and confirmed.

Byelaws with respect to accommodation for seasonal workers

315.—(1) Subject to the provisions of this section, a local authority shall make byelaws for the whole or any part of their area with a view to providing proper accommodation for seasonal workers in respect of—

    (a) intimation to the local authority of the intention to employ seasonal workers;

    (b) the nature and extent of the accommodation to be provided for such workers, including due provision for—

        (i) sleeping accommodation and separation of the sexes;

        (ii) lighting, ventilation, cubic space, cleanliness and furnishing, including beds and bedding and cooking utensils;

        (iii) storage of food, washing of clothes and drying of wet clothes;

        (iv) water closets or privies for the separate use of the sexes; and

        (v) a suitable supply of water;

    (c) determining the persons responsible for the provision of the accommodation required by the byelaws, taking into account the terms of current contracts;

    (d) inspection of the premises;

    (e) exhibition on the premises of the byelaws;

    (f) such other matters relating to the accommodation of seasonal workers (including determining the persons responsible for regulating the use by the workers of the accommodation) as may from time to time be prescribed.

(2) If the local authority show to the satisfaction of the Secretary of State that it is unnecessary to make byelaws under this section, the Secretary of State may dispense with the making of such byelaws.

(3) The Secretary of State may suspend, as respects the area of any local authority or any part of that area, the operation of any byelaw made under this section which affects agricultural interests in cases of emergency.

(4) If in consequence of any byelaws made under this section a farmer or a fruit grower is required to provide accommodation involving the erection of additional buildings, he may require the landlord to erect such buildings on terms and conditions to be determined, failing agreement, by the Secretary of State.

(5) In this section the expression "seasonal workers" includes navvies, harvesters, potato-workers, fruit-pickers, herring-gutters, and such other workers engaged in work of a temporary nature as may from time to time be prescribed.

(6) Where a local authority fail, within such period as the Secretary of State may allow, to make in respect of any of the matters specified in

subsection (1) byelaws which are in the opinion of the Secretary of State sufficient and satisfactory, the Secretary of State may himself make such byelaws which shall have force and effect as if they had been made by the authority and confirmed.

Confirmation of byelaws

316. For the purposes of section 202 of the Local Government (Scotland) Act 1973 (which relates to the procedure and other matters connected with the making of byelaws) the Secretary of State shall be the person by whom byelaws made under this Act are to be confirmed.

Entry

Power of entry for survey, etc.

317.—(1) Subject to the provisions of this section, any person author- ised by a local authority or by the Secretary of State may at all reasonable times enter any house, premises or building—

(a) for the purpose of survey and examination, where it appears to the local authority or the Secretary of State that survey or examination is necessary in order to determine whether any powers under this Act should be exercised in respect of any house, premises or building;

(b) for the purpose of survey and examination, in the case of any house in respect of which a notice under this Act requiring the execution of works has been served or a closing order, or a demolition order has been made;

(c) for the purpose of survey or valuation, in the case of houses, premises or buildings which the local authority are authorised to purchase compulsorily under this Act;

(d) for the purpose of measuring the rooms of a house in order to ascertain for the purposes of Part VII the number of persons permitted to use the house for sleeping;

(e) for the purpose of ascertaining whether there has been a contra- vention of any regulation or direction made or given under Part VIII;

(f) for the purpose of ascertaining whether there has been an offence under section 165.

(2) Any person so authorised shall, except where entry is only for the purpose mentioned in paragraph (e) or paragraph (f) of subsection (1), give 24 hours' notice of his intention to enter any house, premises or building to the occupier thereof and to the owner, if the owner is known.

(3) An authorisation under this section shall be in writing and shall state the particular purpose or purposes for which the entry is authorised.

Offences

Penalty for obstructing execution of Act

318. If any person obstructs any officer of a local authority or any officer of the Secretary of State or any person authorised to enter houses, premises or buildings in pursuance of this Act in the performance of anything which such officer, authority or person is by this Act required or authorised to do, he shall be guilty of an offence and shall be liable on summary conviction to a fine not exceeding level 3 on the standard scale.

Penalty for preventing execution of works, etc.

319.—(1) If any person, after receiving notice of the intended action—

(a) being the occupier of any premises, prevents the owner or other person having control of them, or his officers, agents, servants or workmen from carrying into effect with respect to those premises any of the provisions of Part VIII (other than section 173 and the provisions relating to control orders) or any of the provisions of Part V or any of the provisions of a byelaw made under section 313; or

(b) being the owner or occupier of any premises, or a person having control of any premises, prevents any officers, agents, servants or workmen of the local authority, from so doing; or

(c) being the occupier of any part of a house subject to a control order under Part VIII, prevents any officers, agents, servants or workmen of the local authority from carrying out any works in the house,

the sheriff or any two justices of the peace sitting in open court or any magistrate having jurisdiction in the place on proof thereof may order that person to permit to be done on the premises all things requisite for carrying into effect such provisions with respect to the premises or, in a case falling under paragraph (c), everything which the local authority consider necessary.

(2) If any such person fails to comply with such an order, he shall be guilty of an offence and shall be liable on summary conviction to a fine not exceeding level 3 on the standard scale.

Penalty for damage to houses, etc.

320. Any person who wilfully or by culpable negligence damages or suffers to be damaged any house provided under this Act, or any of the fittings or appurtenances of any such house, including the drainage or water supply and any apparatus connected with the drainage or water supply, and the fence of any enclosure, shall be guilty of an offence and shall be liable on summary conviction to a fine not exceeding level 1 on the standard scale, without prejudice to any remedy for the recovery of the amount of the damage.

Liability of directors, etc. in case of offence by body corporate

321.—(1) Where an offence under this Act committed by a body corporate is proved to have been committed with the consent or connivance of, or to be attributable to any neglect on the part of, a director, manager, secretary or other similar officer of the body corporate, or a person purporting to act in any such capacity, he, as well as the body corporate, is guilty of an offence and liable to be proceeded against and punished accordingly.

(2) Subject to subsection (3), where a person is convicted of an offence under subsection (1) and the body corporate in question is liable under sections 152 to 177 to a higher penalty by reason of a previous conviction than it would have been if not so convicted, that person shall be liable under those sections to the same penalties as the body corporate would be liable if a natural person, including imprisonment.

(3) The person mentioned in subsection (2) shall not be so liable if he shows—

(a) at the time of the offence he did not know of the previous conviction; and

(b) at the time of the previous conviction he was not acting, or purporting to act, as a director, manager, secretary, or other similar officer of the body corporate.

Powers of sheriff for housing purposes

Sheriff may determine lease in certain cases

322.—(1) Where in respect of any premises that are leased—

    (a) a closing order, a demolition order or a resolution passed under section 125 has become operative, and

    (b) the lease is not determined,

the landlord, the tenant, or any other person deriving right under the lease may apply to the sheriff within whose jurisdiction the premises are situated for an order determining the lease.

(2) On any such application the sheriff, after giving to any subtenant or other person whom he considers to be interested in the matter an opportunity of being heard, may, if he thinks fit, order that the lease shall be determined, either unconditionally or subject to such terms and conditions (including conditions with respect to the payment of money by any party to the proceedings to any other party thereto by way of compensation or damages or otherwise) as he may think it just and equitable to impose.

(3) In making an order under subsection (2) the sheriff shall have regard to the respective rights, obligations and liabilities of the parties under the lease and to all the other circumstances of the case.

(4) The sheriff shall not be entitled to order any payment to be made by the landlord to the tenant in respect of the lease of a house.

(5) In this section the expression "lease" includes a sublease and any tenancy or tacit relocation following on a lease.

Sheriff may authorise superior to execute works, etc.

323.—(1) Subject to the provisions of this section, the superior of any lands and heritages may apply to the sheriff for an order entitling him to enter on those lands and heritages to execute works (including demolition works) within such period as may be specified in the order.

(2) The sheriff may make such an order if—

    (a) the following notices or orders under this Act in respect of those lands and heritages are not being complied with—

        (i) a notice requiring the execution of works, or

        (ii) a closing order, or

        (iii) a notice or resolution requiring the demolition of a building under Part VI, and

    (b) the interests of the superior are thereby prejudiced, and

    (c) the sheriff thinks it just to make the order.

(3) Before an order is made under this section notice of the application shall be given to the local authority.

Procedure on applications and appeals to sheriff

324.—(1) An application to the sheriff under paragraph 5 of Schedule 10 (restriction on contracting out) or section 110 (recovery of expenses by lessee) or Part VIII (houses in multiple occupation) shall be made by a summary application, and the sheriff's decision on any such application shall be final.

(2) The Court of Session may prescribe by rules of court the procedure on any appeal to the sheriff under this Act.

(3) The sheriff may, before considering an appeal which may be made to him under this Act, require the appellant to deposit such sum to cover the expenses of the appeal as may be prescribed by rules of court.

(4) The sheriff in deciding an appeal under this Act may make such order as he thinks just.

(5) Any such order shall be final.

(6) In the case of an appeal against a notice given or an order made by a local authority, the sheriff may either confirm, vary or quash the notice or order.

(7) The sheriff—

(a) may at any stage of the proceedings on an appeal under this Act, state a case to the Court of Session on any question of law that arises;

(b) shall do so if so directed by the Court of Session.

(8) A notice or order in respect of which an appeal lies to the sheriff under this Act (other than Part VIII) shall not have effect until either—

(a) the time for appealing has expired without an appeal being made, or

(b) in a case where an appeal is made, the appeal is determined or abandoned,

and no work shall be done or proceedings taken under such notice or order until it has effect.

Service

Occupier or tenant may be required to state interest

325.—(1) A local authority may, for the purpose of enabling them to serve—

(a) any order made by them under section 114 or section 115, or section 119; or

(b) any notice which they are by this Act authorised or required to serve,

require the occupier of any premises and any person who, either directly or indirectly, receives rent in respect of any premises to state in writing the nature of his own interest in the premises and the name and address of any other person known to him as having an interest in them whether as holder of a heritable security, lessee or otherwise.

(2) Any person who has been required by a local authority under subsection (1) to give them any information and either fails to do so or knowingly makes a false statement, shall be guilty of an offence and shall be liable on summary conviction to a fine not exceeding level 1 on the standard scale.

Service by description on certain persons whose identity is unknown and on a number of persons of one description

326.—(1) An order, notice or other document required or authorised to be served under this Act on any person as a person having control of premises may, if it is not practicable after reasonable enquiry to ascertain the name or address of that person, be served by addressing it to him by the description of "person having control of" the premises (naming them) to which it relates and by delivering it to some person on the premises or, if there is no person on the premises to whom it can be delivered, by affixing it, or a copy of it, to some conspicuous part of the premises.

(2) A document to be served on the person having control of premises, or on the person managing premises, or on the owner of premises under Parts IV, V, VI and VIII may be served on more than one person who comes within those descriptions.

Landlord's identity

Disclosure of landlord's identity

327.—(1) If the tenant of premises occupied as a house makes a written request for the landlord's name and address to any person who demands or to the last person who received rent payable under the tenancy or to any other person for the time being acting as agent for the landlord in relation to the tenancy, and that person fails without reasonable excuse to supply a written statement of the name and address within the period of 21 days beginning with the day on which he receives the tenant's request, that person shall be guilty of an offence and liable on summary conviction to a fine not exceeding level 4 on the standard scale.

(2) In any case where—

    (a) in response to a request under subsection (1), a tenant is supplied with the name and address of the landlord of the premises concerned; and

    (b) the landlord is a body corporate; and

    (c) the tenant makes a further written request to the landlord for information under this subsection,

the landlord shall, within the period of 21 days beginning with the day on which he receives the request under this subsection, supply to the tenant a written statement of the name and address of every director and the secretary of the landlord.

(3) Any reference in subsection (1) or subsection (2), to a person's address is a reference to his place of abode or his place of business or, in the case of a company, its registered office.

(4) A request under subsection (2) shall be deemed to be duly made to the landlord if it is made to an agent of the landlord or to a person who demands the rent of the premises concerned, and any such agent or person to whom such a request is made shall as soon as may be forward it to the landlord.

(5) A landlord who fails without reasonable excuse to comply with a request under subsection (2) within the period mentioned in that subsection and a person who fails without reasonable excuse to comply with any requirement imposed on him by subsection (4) shall be guilty of an offence and liable on summary conviction to a fine not exceeding level 4 on the standard scale.

(6) In this section—

    "landlord" means the immediate landlord and, in relation to premises occupied under a right conferred by an enactment, includes the person who, apart from that right, would be entitled to possession of the premises;

    "tenant" includes a sub-tenant and a tenant under a right conferred by an enactment.

Duty to inform tenant of assignation of landlord's interest

328.—(1) If the interest of the landlord under a tenancy of premises which consist of or include a house is assigned, the person to whom that interest is assigned (in this section referred to as "the new landlord") shall, within the appropriate period, give notice in writing to the tenant of the assignation and of the name and address of the new landlord.

(2) In subsection (1), "the appropriate period" means the period beginning on the date of the assignation in question and ending either two months after that date or, if it is later, on the first day after that date on which rent is payable under the tenancy.

(3) Subject to subsection (4), the reference in subsection (1) to the new landlord's address is a reference to his place of abode or his place of business or, if the new landlord is a company, its registered office.

(4) If trustees as such constitute the new landlord, it shall be a sufficient compliance with the obligation in subsection (1) to give the name of the new landlord to give a collective description of the trustees as the trustees of the trust in question, and where such a collective description is given—

    (a) the address of the new landlord for the purpose of that subsection may be given as the address from which the affairs of the trust are conducted; and

    (b) a change in the persons who are for the time being the trustees of the trust shall not be treated as an assignation of the interest of the landlord.

(5) If any person who is the new landlord under a tenancy falling within subsection (1) fails, without reasonable excuse, to give the notice required by that subsection, he shall be guilty of an offence and liable on summary conviction to a fine not exceeding level 4 on the standard scale.

(6) In this section, "tenancy" includes a sub-tenancy and a statutory tenancy, within the meaning of the Rent (Scotland) Act 1984 and "tenant" shall be construed accordingly.

(7) In this section, "assignation" means a conveyance or other transfer (other than in security), and any reference to the date of the assignation means the date on which the conveyance or other transfer was granted, delivered or otherwise made effective.

Powers of Secretary of State

Power of Secretary of State in event of failure of local authority to exercise powers

329.—(1) In any case where—

    (a) a complaint has been made to the Secretary of State as respects the district of any local authority, by any four or more local government electors of the area, that the local authority have failed to exercise any of their powers under this Act in any case where those powers ought to have been exercised; or

    (b) the Secretary of State is of opinion that an investigation should be made as to whether a local authority have so failed,

the Secretary of State may cause a public local inquiry to be held.

(2) If, after the inquiry has been held, the Secretary of State is satisfied that there has been such a failure on the part of the local authority, he may, after giving the authority an opportunity of making representations, make an order enabling him to exercise such of those powers as may be specified in the order.

(3) Any expenses incurred by the Secretary of State in exercising such powers shall be paid in the first instance out of moneys provided by Parliament, but the amount of those expenses as certified by the Secretary of State shall on demand be paid by the local authority to the Secretary of State and shall be recoverable as a debt due to the Crown.

(4) The payment of any such expenses shall, so far as the expenses are of a capital nature, be a purpose for which a local authority may borrow money.

(5) The Secretary of State may by order vest in and transfer to the local authority any property, debts or liabilities acquired or incurred by him in exercising the powers of the authority.

(6) If an order made under subsection (2) is revoked, the Secretary of State may, either by the revoking order or by a supplementary order, make such provision as appears to him desirable with respect to the transfer, vesting and discharge of any property, debts or liabilities acquired or incurred by the Secretary of State in exercising the powers and duties to which the order so revoked related.

Power of Secretary of State to prescribe forms, etc.

330.—(1) Subject to the provisions of this Act, the Secretary of State may by statutory instrument make regulations prescribing—

(a) the form of any notice, advertisement, statement or other document which is required or authorised to be used under, or for the purposes of, this Act;

(b) any other thing required or authorised to be prescribed under this Act.

(2) The forms so prescribed or forms as near as may be to those forms shall be used in all cases to which those forms apply.

Regulations: procedure

331. Subject to the provisions of this Act, regulations made by a statutory instrument under this Act shall be subject to annulment in pursuance of a resolution of either House of Parliament.

Secretary of State's power to dispense with advertisements and notices

332.—(1) The Secretary of State may dispense with the publication of advertisements or the service of notices required to be published or served by a local authority under this Act, if he is satisfied that there is reasonable cause for dispensing with the publication or service.

(2) Any such dispensation may be given by the Secretary of State either before or after the time at which the advertisement is required to be published or the notice is required to be served, and either unconditionally or upon such conditions as to the publication of other advertisements or the service of other notices or otherwise as the Secretary of State thinks fit, due care being taken by the Secretary of State to prevent the interests of any person being prejudiced by the dispensation.

Local inquiries

333. For the purposes of the execution of his powers and duties under this Act, the Secretary of State may cause such local inquiries to be held as he may think fit.

Miscellaneous

Power of heir of entail to sell land for housing purposes

334. Without prejudice to any powers, whether statutory or otherwise, already enjoyed by an heir of entail in possession of an entailed estate in Scotland to sell any part of such estate, any such heir in possession may, notwithstanding any prohibition or limitation in any deed of entail or in any Act of Parliament, sell any part or parts of such estate—

(a) to a local authority for any purpose for which a local authority may acquire land under this Act, or

(b) to a housing association for the purpose of the provision of houses, without its being necessary to obtain the consent of the next heir, and without any restrictions as to the extent of ground to be sold, excepting however, from the provisions of this section the subjects excepted in section 4 of the Entail (Scotland) Act 1914:

Provided that the price of land so sold shall, in accordance with the provisions of the Entail Acts, be invested for behoof of the heir of entail in possession and succeeding heirs of entail.

Crown rights

335. Nothing in this Act shall affect prejudicially any estate, right, power, privilege or exemption of the Crown, or authorise the use of or interference with any land (including tidal lands below high-water mark of ordinary spring tides) belonging to Her Majesty in right of the Crown or to any government department, without the consent of Her Majesty or the government department, as the case may be.

Limitation on liability of trustee etc. for expenses incurred by local authority

336.—(1) Where a local authority seek to recover expenses incurred by them under any enactment in respect of work done on a house from a person mentioned in subsection (2), that person's liability shall, if he proves the matters mentioned in subsection (3), be limited to the total amount of the funds, rents and other assets which he has, or has had, in his hands.

In this section "house" includes a building which contains a house, or a part of such a building.

(2) The person mentioned in subsection (1) is a person who receives the rent of the house as trustee, tutor, curator, factor or agent for or of some other person or as the liquidator of a company.

(3) The matters that person requires to prove are—
    (a) that he is a person mentioned in subsection (2); and
    (b) that he has not, and since the date of service on him of a demand for payment of the expenses has not had, in his hands on behalf of that other person or, in the case of a liquidator of a company, on behalf of the creditors or members of the company, sufficient funds, rents and other assets to pay those expenses in full.

(4) Nothing in this section affects any right of a local authority to recover the whole or any part of those expenses from any other person.

Fair wages

337. Every local authority that provides housing accommodation under this Act or any other enactment relating to housing, with or without financial assistance from the Secretary of State, shall secure the insertion in all contracts relating to such provision of a fair wages clause, complying with the requirements of any resolution of the House of Commons for the time being in force with respect to contracts of government departments.

Interpretation

338.—(1) In this Act, unless the context otherwise requires—
    "Act of 1966" means the Housing (Scotland) Act 1966;
    "Act of 1968" means the Housing (Financial Provisions) (Scotland) Act 1968;
    "Act of 1969" means the Housing (Scotland) Act 1969;
    "Act of 1972" means the Housing (Financial Provisions) (Scotland) Act 1972;
    "Act of 1974" means the Housing (Scotland) Act 1974;
    "Act of 1978" means the Housing (Financial Provisions) (Scotland) Act 1978;
    "Act of 1980" means the Tenants' Rights, Etc. (Scotland) Act 1980;
    "Act of 1985" means the Housing Act 1985;
    "Act of 1986" means the Housing (Scotland) Act 1986;
    "agricultural holding" means an agricultural holding within the meaning of the Agricultural Holdings (Scotland) Act 1949;
    "agriculture" means the use of land for agricultural or pastoral purposes, or for the purpose of poultry farming or market gardening, or as an orchard or woodlands, or for the purpose of afforestation, and "agricultural worker" shall be construed accordingly;

"apparatus" means sewers, drains, culverts, water-courses, mains, pipes, valves, tubes, cables, wires, transformers and other apparatus laid down or used for or in connection with the carrying, conveying or supplying to any premises of a supply of water, water for hydraulic power, gas or electricity, and standards and brackets carrying road lighting;

"bank" means—
    (a) an institution authorised under the Banking Act 1987, or
    (b) a company as to which the Secretary of State was satisfied immediately before the repeal of the Protection of Depositors Act 1963 that it ought to be treated as a banking company or discount company for the purposes of that Act;

"building regulations" means any statutory enactments, byelaws, rules and regulations or other provisions under whatever authority made, relating to the construction of new buildings and the laying out of and construction of new roads;

"building society" means a building society within the meaning of the Building Societies Act 1986;

"closing order" means a closing order made under sections 114 or 119;

"Corporation" means the Housing Corporation;

"croft" and "crofter" have the like meanings respectively as in the Crofters (Scotland) Acts 1955 and 1961;

"demolition order" has the meaning assigned to it by section 115;

"development corporation" means a development corporation established by an order made or having effect as if made under the New Towns (Scotland) Act 1968;

"disabled occupant" has the meaning assigned to it by section 236;

"disabled person" has the meaning assigned to it by section 236;

"Exchequer contribution" means a payment (other than a payment by way of advance or loan) which the Secretary of State is required or authorised by or under any Act relating to housing, to make for housing purposes;

"family" and any reference to membership thereof shall be construed in accordance with section 83;

"financial year", in relation to a local authority, has the same meaning as in section 96(5) of the Local Government (Scotland) Act 1973;

"flat" means a separate and self-contained set of premises, whether or not on the same floor and forming part of a building from some other part of which it is divided horizontally;

"friendly society" means a society registered under the Friendly Societies Act 1974 or earlier legislation;

"holding" has the like meaning as in the Small Landholders (Scotland) Acts 1886 to 1931;

"hostel" has the meaning assigned to it by section 2(5);

"house" (except in relation to Part XIV) includes any part of a building, being a part which is occupied or intended to be occupied as a separate dwelling, and, in particular, includes a flat, and includes also any yard, garden, out-houses and pertinents belonging to the house or usually enjoyed therewith and also includes any structure made available under section 1 of the Housing (Temporary Accommodation) Act 1944;

"housing action area" means a housing action area within the meaning of Part IV;

"housing association" has the same meaning as it has in the Housing Associations Act 1985;

"housing support grant" has the meaning assigned to it by section 191;

"improvement" has the meaning assigned to it by section 236(2);

"improvement grant" has the meaning assigned to it by section 236(1);

"insurance company" means an insurance company to which Part II of the Insurance Companies Act 1982 applies;

"land" includes any estate or interest in land;

"landholder" has the like meaning as in the Small Landholders (Scotland) Acts 1886 to 1931;

"Lands Tribunal" means the Lands Tribunal for Scotland;

"loan charges" means, in relation to any borrowed moneys, the sum required for the payment of interest on those moneys and for the repayment thereof either by instalments or by means of a sinking fund;

"local authority" means an islands council or a district council, and the district of a local authority means the islands area or the district, as the case may be;

"official representation" means, in the case of a local authority, a representation made to the authority by the proper officer of the local authority;

"open space" means any land laid out as a public garden or used for the purposes of public recreation, and any disused burial ground;

"order for possession" has the meaning assigned to it by section 115(1) of the Rent (Scotland) Act 1984;

"overspill agreement" has the same meaning as in section 9(1) of the Housing and Town Development (Scotland) Act 1957;

"owner" includes any person who under the Lands Clauses Acts would be enabled to sell and convey land to the promoters of an undertaking, but in Part XIII and sections 99 to 104, in relation to a house, means the person who is for the time being entitled to receive the rent of the house or who, if the house were let, would be so entitled and a tenant-at-will;

"prescribed" means prescribed by regulations made by the Secretary of State by statutory instrument;

"proper officer", in relation to any purpose of a local authority, means an officer appointed for that purpose by that authority;

"public undertakers" means any corporation, company, body or person carrying on a railway, canal, inland navigation, dock, harbour, tramway, gas, electricity, water or other public undertaking;

"registered housing association" means a housing association registered under the Housing Associations Act 1985;

"regular armed forces of the Crown" means the Royal Navy, the regular forces as defined by section 225 of the Army Act 1955, the regular air force as defined by section 223 of the Air Force Act 1955, Queen Alexandra's Royal Naval Nursing Service and the Women's Royal Naval Service;

"repairs grant" has the meaning assigned to it by section 248;

"road" has the same meaning as it has in the Roads (Scotland) Act 1984;

"secure tenancy" has the meaning assigned to it by section 44;

"sell" and "sale" include feu;

"a service charge" means any charge referred to in section 211;

"standard amenities" has the meaning assigned to it by section 244(5);

"statutory small tenant" has the like meaning as in the Small Landholders (Scotland) Acts 1886 to 1931;

"statutory tenant" has the same meaning as it has in section 3 of the Rent (Scotland) Act 1984;

"superior" includes the creditor in a ground annual;

"tenancy" in Parts IV and XIII includes a sub-tenancy, a statutory tenancy within the meaning of section 115(1) of the Rent (Scotland) Act 1984 and a contract to which Part VII of that Act applies and "tenant" shall be construed accordingly; and any reference to a tenancy of a house or to the tenant thereof shall be construed as including a reference to all the tenancies of that house or to all the tenants thereof as the case may be;

"tolerable standard" has the meaning assigned to it by section 86;

"water authority" has the meaning assigned to it by section 148 of the Local Government (Scotland) Act 1973;

"water development board" has the meaning assigned to it by section 109 of the Water (Scotland) Act 1980;

"year" means, in relation to a local authority, a financial year within the meaning of section 96(5) of the Local Government (Scotland) Act 1973 and, in relation to a development corporation, the Scottish Special Housing Association or a housing association, means a year ending on 31st March;

"the year 1986–87" means the year beginning in 1986 and ending in 1987, and so on.

(2) For the purposes of this Act—

(a) the person who for the time being is entitled to receive, or would, if the same were let, be entitled to receive, the rent of any premises, including a trustee, tutor, curator, factor or agent, shall be deemed to be the person having control of the premises; and

(b) a crofter or a landholder shall be deemed to be the person having control of any premises on his croft or holding in respect of which he would, on the termination of his tenancy, be entitled to compensation under the Crofters (Scotland) Acts 1955 and 1961 or, as the case may be, the Small Landholders (Scotland) Acts 1886 to 1931, as for an improvement.

(3) In this Act, any reference to the demolition of a building shall be deemed to include a reference to such reconstruction of the building as the local authority may approve; and where a building is so reconstructed any reference to selling, letting or appropriating the land, the building on which has been or will be demolished, shall, unless the context otherwise requires, be construed as a reference to selling, letting or appropriating the land and the reconstructed building.

Minor and consequential amendments, transitional provisions and repeals

339.—(1) This Act shall have effect subject to the transitional provisions and savings contained in Schedule 22.

(2) The enactments specified in Schedule 23 shall have effect subject to the amendments set out in that Schedule being minor amendments and amendments consequential on the provisions of this Act.

(3) The enactments specified in Schedule 24 are hereby repealed to the extent specified in the third column of that Schedule.

Citation, commencement and extent

340.—(1) This Act may be cited as the Housing (Scotland) Act 1987.

(2) This Act shall come into force at the end of the period of 3 months beginning with the day on which it is passed.

(3) This Act extends to Scotland only.

SCHEDULES

Section 10(4)   SCHEDULE 1

RULES AS TO ASSESSMENT OF COMPENSATION WHERE LAND PURCHASED COMPULSORILY IN CERTAIN CIRCUMSTANCES

1.—If the Lands Tribunal are satisfied that the rent of any premises was enhanced by reason of their being used for illegal purposes, the compensation shall, so far as it is based on rental, be based on the rental which would have been obtainable if the premises were occupied for legal purposes.

2.—If the Lands Tribunal are satisfied that the rent of any premises was higher than that generally obtained at the time for similar premises in the locality and that such enhanced rent was obtained by reason of the premises being overcrowded within the meaning of Part VII, the compensation shall, so far as it is based on rent, be based on the rent so generally obtained.

3.—The local authority may tender evidence as to the matters mentioned in paragraphs 1 or 2 although they have not taken any steps to remedy them.

4.—(1) The Lands Tribunal shall (except as provided in section 15(1) of the Land Compensation (Scotland) Act 1963) have regard to, and make an allowance in respect of, any increased value which, in their opinion, will be given to other premises of the same owner by the demolition by the local authority of any buildings.

5.—The Lands Tribunal shall embody in their award a statement showing separately whether compensation has been reduced by reference to the use of the premises for illegal purposes, to overcrowding, and to the considerations mentioned in paragraph 4 of this Schedule, and the amount (if any) by which compensation has been reduced by reference to each of those matters.

Section 44(4), (5)   SCHEDULE 2

TENANCIES WHICH ARE NOT SECURE TENANCIES

Premises occupied under contract of employment

1.—(1) A tenancy shall not be a secure tenancy if the tenant (or one of joint tenants) is an employee of the landlord or of any local authority or development corporation, and his contract of employment requires him to occupy the house for the better performance of his duties.

(2) In this paragraph "contract of employment" means a contract of service or of apprenticeship, whether express or implied, and (if it is express) whether it is oral or in writing.

Temporary letting to person seeking accommodation

2.—A tenancy shall not be a secure tenancy if the house was let by the landlord expressly on a temporary basis to a person moving into an area in order to take up employment there, and for the purpose of enabling him to seek accommodation in the area.

Temporary letting pending development

3.—A tenancy shall not be a secure tenancy if the house was let by the landlord to the tenant expressly on a temporary basis, pending development affecting the house.

In this paragraph "development" has the meaning assigned to it by section 19 of the Town and Country Planning (Scotland) Act 1972.

Temporary accommodation during works

4.—A tenancy shall not be a secure tenancy if the house is occupied by the tenant while works are being carried out on the house which he normally occupies as his home, and if he is entitled to return there after the works are completed—

(a) by agreement; or
(b) by virtue of an order of the sheriff under section 48(5).

Accommodation for homeless persons

5.—A tenancy shall not be a secure tenancy if the house is being let to the tenant expressly on a temporary basis, in the fulfilment of a duty imposed on a local authority by Part II.

Agricultural and business premises

6.—A tenancy shall not be a secure tenancy if the house—
   (a) is let together with agricultural land exceeding two acres in extent;
   (b) consists of or includes premises which are used as a shop or office for business, trade or professional purposes;
   (c) consists of or includes premises licensed for the sale of exciseable liquor; or
   (d) is let in conjunction with any purpose mentioned in sub-paragraph (b) or (c).

Police and fire authorities

7.—A tenancy shall not be a secure tenancy if the landlord is an authority or committee mentioned in—
   (a) section 61(2)(a)(viii) and the tenant—
      (i) is a constable of a police force, within the meaning of the Police (Scotland) Act 1967, who in pursuance of regulations under section 26 of that Act occupies the house without obligation to pay rent or rates; or
      (ii) in a case where head (i) above does not apply, is let the house expressly on a temporary basis pending its being required for the purposes of such a police force; or
   (b) section 61(2)(a)(ix) and the tenant—
      (i) is a member of a fire brigade, maintained in pursuance of the Fire Services Act 1947, who occupies the house in consequence of a condition in his contract of employment that he live in close proximity to a particular fire station; or
      (ii) in a case where head (i) above does not apply, is let the house expressly on a temporary basis pending its being required for the purposes of such a fire brigade.

Houses part of, or within curtilage of, certain other buildings

8.—(1) A tenancy shall not be a secure tenancy if the house forms part of, or is within the curtilage of, a building which mainly—
   (a) is held by the landlord for purposes other than the provision of housing accommodation; and
   (b) consists of accommodation other than housing accommodation.

Sections 48 and 51   SCHEDULE 3

GROUNDS FOR RECOVERY OF POSSESSION OF HOUSES LET UNDER SECURE TENANCIES

PART I

GROUNDS ON WHICH COURT MAY ORDER RECOVERY OF POSSESSION

1.—Rent lawfully due from the tenant has not been paid, or any other obligation of the tenancy has been broken.

2.—The tenant (or any one of joint tenants) or any person residing or lodging with him or any sub-tenant of his has been convicted of using the house or allowing it to be used for immoral or illegal purposes.

3.—The condition of the house or of any of the common parts has deteriorated owing to acts of waste by, or the neglect or default of, the tenant (or any one of joint tenants) or any person residing or lodging with him or any sub-tenant of his; and in the case of waste by, or the neglect or default of, a person lodging with a tenant or by a sub-tenant of his, the tenant has not, before the making of the order in question, taken such steps as he ought reasonably to have taken for the removal of the lodger or sub-tenant.

In this paragraph, "the common parts" means any part of a building containing the house and any other premises which the tenant is entitled under the terms of the tenancy to use in common with the occupiers of other houses.

4.—The condition of any furniture provided for use under the tenancy, or for use in any of the common parts (within the meaning given in paragraph 3), has deteriorated owing to ill-treatment by the tenant (or any one of joint tenants) or any person residing or lodging with him or any sub-tenant of his; and in the case of ill-treatment by a person lodging with a tenant or a sub-tenant of his the tenant has not, before the making of the order in question, taken such steps as he ought reasonably to have taken for the removal of the lodger or sub-tenant.

5.—The tenant and his spouse have been absent from the house without reasonable cause for a continuous period exceeding 6 months or have ceased to occupy the house as their principal home.

6.—The tenant is the person, or one of the persons, to whom the tenancy was granted and the landlord was induced to grant the tenancy by a false statement made knowingly or recklessly by the tenant.

7.—The tenant of the house (or any one of joint tenants) or any person residing or lodging with him or any sub-tenant of his has been guilty of conduct in or in the vicinity of the house which is a nuisance or annoyance and it is not reasonable in all the circumstances that the landlord should be required to make other accommodation available to him.

8.—The tenant of the house (or any one of joint tenants) or any person residing or lodging with him or any sub-tenant of his has been guilty of conduct in or in the vicinity of the house which is a nuisance or annoyance and in the opinion of the landlord it is appropriate in the circumstances to require the tenant to move to other accommodation.

9.—The house is overcrowded, within the meaning of section 135, in such circumstances as to render the occupier guilty of an offence.

10.—It is intended within a reasonable period of time to demolish, or carry out substantial work on, the building or a part of the building which comprises or includes the house, and such demolition or work cannot reasonably take place without the landlord obtaining possession of the house.

11.—The house has been designed or adapted for occupation by a person whose special needs require accommodation of the kind provided by the house and—

(a) there is no longer a person with such special needs occupying the house; and

(b) the landlord requires it for occupation (whether alone or with other members of his family) by a person who has such special needs.

12.—The house forms part of a group of houses which has been designed, or which has been provided with or located near facilities, for persons in need of special social support, and—

(a) there is no longer a person with such a need occupying the house; and

(b) the landlord requires it for occupation (whether alone or with other members of his family) by a person who has such a need.

13.—The landlord is a housing association which has as its object, or as one of its objects, the housing of persons who are in a special category by reason of age, infirmity, disability or social circumstances and the tenant (or one of joint tenants), having been granted a tenancy as a person falling into such a special category, has ceased to be in the special category, or for other reasons the accommodation in the house is no longer suitable for his needs, and the accommodation is required for someone who is in a special category.

14.—The interest of the landlord in the house is that of a lessee under a lease and that lease either—

(a) has terminated, or

(b) will terminate within a period of 6 months from the date of raising of proceedings for recovery of possession.

15.—(a) The landlord is an islands council; and

    (b) the house is—

        (i) held by the council for the purposes of its functions as education authority; and

        (ii) required for the accommodation of a person who is or will be employed by the council for those purposes; and

    (c) the council cannot reasonably provide a suitable alternative house for the accommodation referred to in sub-paragraph (b)(ii); and

    (d) the tenant (or any one of joint tenants) is, or at any time during the tenancy has been or, where the tenancy passed to the existing tenant under section 52, the previous tenant at any time during the tenancy was, employed by the council for the purposes of its functions as education authority and such employment has terminated or notice of termination has been given.

16.—The landlord wishes to transfer the secure tenancy of the house to—

(a) the tenant's spouse (or former spouse); or

(b) a person with whom the tenant has been living as husband and wife,

who has applied to the landlord for such transfer; and either the tenant or (as the case may be) the spouse, former spouse or person, no longer wishes to live together with the other in the house.

PART II

SUITABILITY OF ACCOMMODATION

1.—For the purposes of sections 48(3) and 51(3), accommodation is suitable if—

(a) it consists of premises which are to be let as a separate dwelling under a secure tenancy or under a protected tenancy within the meaning of the Rent (Scotland) Act 1984; and

(b) it is reasonably suitable to the needs of the tenant and his family.

2.—In determining whether accommodation is reasonably suitable to the needs of the tenant and his family, regard shall be had to—

(a) its proximity to the place of work (including attendance at an educational institution) of the tenant and of other members of his family, compared with his existing house;

(b) the extent of the accommodation required by the tenant and his family;

(c) the character of the accommodation offered compared to his existing house;

(d) the terms on which the accommodation is offered to the tenant compared with the terms of his existing tenancy;

(e) if any furniture was provided by the landlord for use under the existing tenancy, whether furniture is to be provided for use under the new tenancy which is of a comparable nature in relation to the needs of the tenant and his family;

(f) any special needs of the tenant or his family.

3.—If the landlord has made an offer in writing to the tenant of new accommodation which complies with paragraph 1(a) and which appears to it to be suitable, specifying the date when the accommodation will be available and the date (not being less than 14 days from the date of the offer) by which the offer must be accepted, the accommodation so offered shall be deemed to be suitable if—

(a) the landlord shows that the tenant accepted the offer within the time duly specified in the offer; or

(b) the landlord shows that the tenant did not so accept the offer, and the tenant does not satisfy the court that he acted reasonably in failing to accept the offer.

Section 55(6)   SCHEDULE 4

TERMS OF SECURE TENANCY RELATING TO SUBLETTING, ETC.

1.—A secure tenant who wishes to assign, sublet or otherwise give up to another person possession of the house which is the subject of the secure tenancy or any part thereof or take in a lodger shall serve on the landlord an application in writing for the landlord's consent, giving details of the proposed transaction, and in particular of any payment which has been or is to be received by the tenant in consideration of the transaction.

2.—In relation to an application under paragraph 1, the landlord may consent, or may refuse consent, provided that it is not refused unreasonably.

3.—(a) The landlord shall serve on the tenant notice in writing of consent or refusal, and in the case of refusal the reasons therefor, within one month of receipt of the application;

(b) where the landlord fails to serve a notice in accordance with paragraph (a) within the period therein mentioned, the landlord shall be deemed to have consented to the application.

4.—A tenant who is aggrieved by a refusal (other than a refusal on the grounds provided or in section 55(2)) may raise proceedings by summary application in the sheriff court of he district in which the house is situated.

5.—In proceedings under paragraph 4, the sheriff shall order the landlord to consent to he application unless it appears to him that the refusal is reasonable.

6.—In deciding whether a refusal is reasonable the sheriff shall have regard in particular to—

    (a) whether the consent would lead to overcrowding of the house in such circumstances as to render the occupier guilty of an offence under section 139; and

    (b) whether the landlord proposes to carry out works on the house or on the building of which it forms part so that the proposed works will affect the accommodation likely to be used by the sub-tenant or lodger who would reside in the house as a result of the consent.

Section 57(3)   SCHEDULE 5

TERMS OF SECURE TENANCY RELATING TO ALTERATIONS, ETC. TO HOUSE

1.—A secure tenant who wishes to carry out work shall serve on the landlord an application in writing for the landlord's consent, giving details of the work proposed to be carried out.

2.—In relation to an application under paragraph 1, the landlord may—

    (a) consent;

    (b) refuse consent, provided that it is not refused unreasonably; or

    (c) consent subject to such reasonable conditions as the landlord may impose.

3.—The landlord shall intimate consent or refusal, and any conditions imposed, and in the case of refusal the reasons therefor, to the tenant in writing within one month of receipt of the application.

4.—In the event that the landlord fails to make intimation in accordance with paragraph 3 within the period therein mentioned, the landlord shall be deemed to have consented to the application.

5.—A tenant who is aggrieved by a refusal, or by any condition imposed under paragraph 2(c), may raise proceedings by summary application in the sheriff court of the district in which the house is situated.

6.—In proceedings under paragraph 5, the sheriff shall order the landlord to consent to the application or, as the case may be, to withdraw the condition unless it appears to him that the refusal or condition is reasonable.

7.—In deciding whether a refusal or a condition is reasonable the sheriff shall have regard in particular to—

    (a) the safety of occupiers of the house or of any other premises;

    (b) any expenditure which the landlord is likely to incur as a result of the work;

    (c) whether the work is likely to reduce the value of the house or of any premises of which it forms part, or to make the house or such premises less suitable for letting or for sale; and

    (d) any effect which the work is likely to have on the extent of the accommodation provided by the house.

Section 77(3)   SCHEDULE 6

VESTING ORDER UNDER SECTION 77: MODIFICATION OF ENACTMENTS

The Town and Country Planning (Scotland) Act 1972 (c.52)

1.—Paragraphs 1(2), 6 to 13 and 16 to 39 of Schedule 24 only shall apply and in them any reference to a general vesting declaration shall be treated as a reference to an order under section 77.

2.—The references in paragraphs 6, 7 and 37 of that Schedule to the end of the period specified in a general vesting declaration shall be treated as references to the date on which such an order comes into force and the reference in paragraph 9 thereof to the acquiring authority having made a general vesting declaration shall be treated as a reference to such order having come into force.

3.—In paragraph 6 of that Schedule—

    (a) the reference to every person on whom, under section 17 of the Lands Clauses Consolidation (Scotland) Act 1845, the acquiring authority could have served a notice to treat, shall be treated as a reference to every person whose interest in the land to which such order relates is vested by the order in the landlord; and

    (b) sub-paragraph (a) shall be omitted.

4.—The reference in paragraph 20(2) of that Schedule to the date on which the notice required by paragraph 4 thereof is served on any person shall be treated as a reference to the date on which such an order comes into force.

5.—In paragraph 29 of that Schedule—
    (a) sub-paragraph (1)(a) shall be omitted; and
    (b) the reference in sub-paragraph (1)(b) to the date on which a person first had knowledge of the execution of the general vesting declaration shall be treated as a reference to the date on which such order came into force.

The Land Compensation (Scotland) Act 1963 (c.51)

6.—Any reference to the date of service of a notice to treat shall be treated as a reference to the date on which an order under section 77 comes into force.

7.—Section 25(2) shall be treated as if for the words "the authority proposing to acquire it have served a notice to treat in respect thereof, or an agreement has been made for the sale thereof to that authority" there were substituted the words "an order under section 77 of the Housing (Scotland) Act 1987 vesting the land in which the interest subsists in the landlord has come into force, or an agreement has been made for the sale of the interest to the landlord".

8.—In section 30—
    (a) subsection (2) shall be treated as if at the end of paragraph (c) there were added the words—
        ", or—
        (d) where an order has been made under section 77 of the Housing (Scotland) Act 1987 vesting the land in which the interest subsists in the landlord."; and
    (b) subsection (3) shall be treated as if in paragraph (a) the words "or (d)" were inserted after the words "subsection (2)(b)".

9.—Any reference to a notice to treat in section 45(2) shall be treated as a reference to an order under the said section 77.

10.—(1) In Schedule 2, paragraph 2(1)(a) shall be treated as if the words "or the coming into force of an order under section 77 of the Housing (Scotland) Act 1987 for the vesting of the land in the landlord" were inserted after the word "land".

Section 93   SCHEDULE 7

PART I

CONSENT TO DEMOLITION OF LISTED BUILDINGS IN HOUSING ACTION AREAS, ETC.

Buildings subject to compulsory purchase orders for demolition subsequently listed

1.—(1) In this paragraph, references to a compulsory purchase order are to a compulsory purchase order made under the provisions of Part IV in so far as the order relates to a building acquired for demolition under those provisions.

(2) Where a building to which a compulsory purchase order applies is (at any time after the making of the order) included in a list of buildings of special architectural or historic interest under section 52 of the Town and Country Planning (Scotland) Act 1972 or under any corresponding enactment repealed by that Act, the local authority making the order or its successor in the exercise of its functions relating to the order may, subject to sub-paragraph (3), apply to the Secretary of State (and only to him) under section 53 of the said Act of 1972 for consent to the demolition of the building.

(3) No such application may be made by virtue of sub-paragraph (2) after the expiry of the period of 3 months beginning with the date on which the building is included on the said list.

(4) The following provisions of this paragraph shall have effect where—
    (a) an application for consent has been made under the said section 53, by virtue of sub-paragraph (2), and has been refused, or
    (b) the period of 3 months mentioned in sub-paragraph (3) has expired without the authority having made such an application,
and in this paragraph "relevant date" means the date of the refusal or, as the case may be, of the expiry of the period of 3 months.

(5) If, at the relevant date—
    (a) the building has not vested in the authority, and

(b) no notice to treat has been served by the authority under section 17 of the Lands Clauses Consolidation (Scotland) Act 1845, in respect of any interest in the building,

the compulsory purchase order shall cease to have effect in relation to the building and, where applicable, the building shall cease to be comprised in a housing action area.

(6) Where a compulsory purchase order ceases to have effect, by virtue of sub-paragraph (5), in relation to a house which does not meet the tolerable standard, the authority concerned shall, in respect of the house, forthwith—

    (a) serve a notice under section 108 (power of local authority to secure repair of house in state of serious disrepair), or

    (b) make a closing order under Part VI,

whichever is appropriate.

(7) Where sub-paragraph (5) does not apply, the authority shall cease to be subject to the duty to demolish the building, and in relation to any interest in the building which at the relevant date has not vested in the authority the compulsory purchase order shall have effect as if—

    (a) in the case of a house, it had been made and confirmed under Part I, and

    (b) in any other case, it had been made and confirmed under Part VI of the Town and Country Planning (Scotland) Act 1972.

(8) If the building, or any interest in the building, was vested in the authority at the relevant date, it shall be treated—

    (a) in the case of a house, as appropriated to the purposes of Part I, and

    (b) in any other case, as appropriated to the purposes of Part VI of the said Act of 1972.

(9) As respects a building falling within sub-paragraph (2), where no notice to treat has, at the date on which the building is included in the list referred to in that sub-paragraph, been served under section 17 of the Lands Clauses Consolidation (Scotland) Act 1845, the authority shall not serve such a notice until after the relevant date.

Buildings acquired by agreement for demolition subsequently listed

2.—(1) Where Part IV applies to a building purchased by a local authority by agreement, and at any time the building is included in a list of buildings of special architectural or historic interest under section 52 of the Town and Country Planning (Scotland) Act 1972 or under any corresponding enactment repealed by that Act, the authority or its successor in the exercise of the powers conferred by Part IV may, subject to sub-paragraph (2), apply to the Secretary of State (and only to him) under the said section 53 for consent to the demolition of the building.

(2) No such application may be made by virtue of sub-paragraph (1) after the expiry of the period of 3 months beginning with the date on which the building is included on the said list.

(3) Where—

    (a) an application for consent has been made under the said section 53, by virtue of sub-paragraph (1), and has been refused, or

    (b) the period of 3 months mentioned in sub-paragraph (2) has expired without the authority having made such an application,

the authority shall cease to be subject to the duty imposed by Part IV to demolish the building, which shall be treated—

    (i) in the case of a house, as appropriated to the purposes of Part I of this Act, and

    (ii) in any other case, as appropriated to the purposes of Part VI of the Town and Country Planning (Scotland) Act 1972.

PART II

REHABILITATION ORDERS

Application and effect of rehabilitation orders

3.—(1) This Part of this Schedule applies to any house which—

    (a) is included in a clearance area under Part III of the Act of 1966, or

    (b) is included in a housing treatment area under Part I of the Act of 1969, where the resolution for the area provides for the demolition of the house,

being a house which—

    (i) has been purchased by agreement or compulsorily at any time before 2nd

December 1974 under section 38 of the Act of 1966 or section 7 of the Act of 1969 (provisions regarding acquisition of land in such areas), or

(ii) is subject to a compulsory purchase order which was made under the said section 38 or under the said section 7 (but not confirmed) before 2nd December 1974 and which, before 2nd March 1975, has been confirmed in accordance with Schedule 3 to the Act of 1966 or (as the case may be) in accordance with Schedule 1 to the Acquisition of Land (Authorisation Procedures) (Scotland) Act 1947 as applied by the said section 7, or

(iii) has been included in the area by virtue of section 41 of the Act of 1966 or section 9 of the Act of 1969 (land already belonging to the local authority).

(2) Where any house to which this Part of this Schedule applies in terms of sub-paragraph (1) does not comply with the full standard as defined in paragraph 12 and, in the opinion of the local authority, it is capable of being and ought to be improved to that standard, the authority may make and submit to the Secretary of State an order (in this Part of this Schedule referred to as a "rehabilitation order") in relation to the house.

(3) In addition to applying to any house to which this Part of this Schedule applies in terms of sub-paragraph (1), a rehabilitation order may, if the local authority think fit, be made to apply to any other relevant land, as defined in paragraph 12.

(4) On the date on which a rehabilitation order becomes operative, the local authority shall cease to be subject to any duty to demolish or secure the demolition of buildings on any land included in the order, imposed by Part III of the Act of 1966 or Part I of the Act of 1969.

(5) Where by virtue of sub-paragraph (4) a local authority are freed from the duty to demolish or secure the demolition of a house which does not comply with the full standard, the authority shall take such steps as are necessary—

(a) to bring the house up to the full standard, or

(b) where it is not vested in the authority, to ensure that it is brought up to that standard.

(6) A local authority may accept undertakings for the purpose of sub-paragraph (5)(b) from the owner of a house, or any other person who has or will have an interest in a house, concerning works to be carried out to bring it up to the full standard and the time within which they are to be carried out.

(7) Any reference in sub-paragraph (2), (5) or (6) to a house being improved or brought up to the full standard shall be construed as including a reference to a house, after integration with any other house to which this Part of this Schedule applies and which does not comply with the full standard, being improved or brought up to the full standard.

Miscellaneous provisions relative to rehabilitation orders

4.—Where the owner of a house to which this Part of this Schedule applies in terms of paragraph 3(1), and which does not comply with the full standard, requests the local authority to make a rehabilitation order in respect of the house, and the authority refuse to make the order, they shall give him in writing their reasons for so refusing.

5.—Where a local authority have made a rehabilitation order they shall not, until after the date on which the order becomes operative or on which confirmation of the order is refused—

(a) serve notice to treat, under section 17 of the Lands Clauses Consolidation (Scotland) Act 1845, in respect of any land included in a compulsory purchase order made and confirmed by virtue of section 38 of the Act of 1966 or section 7 of the Act of 1969 which includes notice land as defined in paragraph 12; or

(b) demolish, without the consent of the Secretary of State, any building on notice land.

6.—(1) Where—

(a) land included in a compulsory purchase order, made and confirmed by virtue of the said section 38 or the said section 7, is comprised in a rehabilitation order, and

(b) the rehabilitation order becomes operative in respect of that land, and

(c) no interest in the land has vested in the local authority before the date on which the rehabilitation order becomes operative, and

(d) neither the local authority nor a previous local authority entitled to serve a notice to treat in respect of any interest in the land under section 17 of the said Act of 1845 have done so before that date,

the compulsory purchase order shall cease to have effect in relation to that land on that date, and if the land is included in a clearance area or housing treatment area, it shall cease to be so included.

(2) On and after the date on which a rehabilitation order becomes operative, in a case where sub-paragraph (1) does not apply in relation to an area of land comprised in that

order, any compulsory purchase order relating to that land and confirmed by virtue of the said section 38 or the said section 7 shall have effect in relation to any interest in that land which at the said date was not vested in the authority—

  (a) in so far as it relates to a house, as if it had been made and confirmed under Part I of this Act, and

  (b) in so far as it relates to land other than a house, as if it had been made and confirmed under Part VI of the Town and Country Planning (Scotland) Act 1972.

(3) Where a rehabilitation order becomes operative in respect of an area of land and any interest in that land is vested in the local authority at the date when the order becomes operative—

  (a) any such interest in a house shall be treated as appropriated to the purposes of Part I of this Act, and

  (b) any such interest in land other than a house shall be treated as appropriated to the purposes of Part VI of the said Act of 1972.

7.—A rehabilitation order may be made and confirmed notwithstanding that the effect of the order in excluding any land from a clearance area or from a housing treatment area is to sever that area into two or more parts; and in any such case the provisions applicable to the area in Part III of the Act of 1966 or in Part I of the Act of 1969, relating to the effect of a compulsory purchase order when confirmed and to the proceedings to be taken after confirmation of such an order, shall apply as if those parts formed one clearance area or housing treatment area, as the case may be.

Procedure for making and confirming rehabilitation orders

8.—A rehabilitation order shall be made in the prescribed form and shall describe, by reference to a map—

  (a) the house to which, in terms of paragraph 3(1), it applies, and

  (b) the other land to which, in terms of paragraph 3(3), it applies.

9.—(1) Before submitting a rehabilitation order to the Secretary of State for confirmation, the local authority, except in so far as the Secretary of State directs otherwise—

  (a) shall publish in one or more newspapers circulating within their district a notice in the prescribed form stating that such an order has been made and describing the land to which it applies, and naming a place where a copy of the order and its accompanying map may be seen at all reasonable hours, and

  (b) shall serve on any such person as is specified in sub-paragraph (2) a notice in the prescribed form stating—

    (i) the effect of the rehabilitation order,

    (ii) that it is about to be submitted to the Secretary of State for confirmation, and

    (iii) the time within which and the manner in which objections to the order can be made.

(2) The persons mentioned in sub-paragraph (1)(b) are—

  (a) every person on whom notice was served of the making by virtue of section 38 of the Act of 1966 or section 7 of the Act of 1969 of any compulsory purchase order which, at the date of its confirmation, included any land subsequently comprised in the rehabilitation order;

  (b) every successor in title of such a person;

  (c) every owner, lessee and occupier of the relevant land other than a tenant for a month or a period less than a month;

  (d) creditors in heritable securities over relevant land, so far as it is reasonably practicable to ascertain such persons; and

  (e) every person on whom notice would have been required to be served under head (c) or (d) whose interest has been acquired under the said section 38 since the clearance area was declared to be such an area or (as the case may be) under the said section 7 since the housing treatment area was declared to be such an area.

(3) A notice under this paragraph shall be accompanied by a statement of the grounds on which the local authority are seeking confirmation of the rehabilitation order.

(4) A notice under this paragraph shall be served in accordance with section 5(3) of and paragraph 19 of Schedule 1 to the Acquisition of Land (Authorisation Procedure) (Scotland) Act 1947.

10.—(1) If no objection is duly made by any of the persons on whom notices are to be served under paragraph 9, or if all objections so made are withdrawn, the Secretary of State may confirm the order with or without modifications.

(2) If any objection duly made is not withdrawn, the Secretary of State, before confirming the order, shall cause a public local inquiry to be held or afford to any person by whom an

objection has been duly made and not withdrawn an opportunity of appearing before and being heard by a person appointed by the Secretary of State for the purpose.

(3) After considering any objection not withdrawn and the report of the person who held the inquiry or of the person appointed under sub-paragraph (2), the Secretary of State may confirm the order with or without modifications.

(4) The Secretary of State may require any person who has made an objection to state the grounds of the objection in writing, and may disregard the objection if he is satisfied that it relates exclusively to matters which can be dealt with by the tribunal by whom any compensation is to be assessed.

(5) The Secretary of State's power to modify a rehabilitation order includes power, subject to sub-paragraph (6), to extend it to any notice land.

(6) The Secretary of State shall not extend the application of a rehabilitation order to any land unless he has served on the following persons, namely—

(a) the local authority who made the rehabilitation order,

(b) every owner, lessee and occupier of that land, except a tenant for a month or a period less than a month, and

(c) so far as it is reasonably practicable to ascertain such persons, on the creditor in every heritable security over any such land,

a notice stating the effect of his proposals, and has afforded them an opportunity to make their views known.

11.—Paragraphs 6, 15 and 16 of Schedule 1 to the Acquisition of Land (Authorisation Procedure) (Scotland) Act 1947 (notification, challenge of validity and date of operation of orders) shall apply in relation to rehabilitation orders as if—

(a) any reference to a compulsory purchase order were a reference to a rehabilitation order and any reference to compulsory purchase were a reference to rehabilitation under this Part of this Schedule;

(b) any reference to the acquiring authority were a reference to the local authority;

(c) the reference in the said paragraph 6 to paragraph 3 of that Schedule were a reference to paragraph 9 of this Schedule;

(d) the reference in the said paragraph 15 to any such enactment as is mentioned in section 1(1) of that Act were a reference to this Part of this Schedule;

(e) the references in the said paragraph 15 to any requirement of that Act and to any requirement of that Schedule thereof were references to any requirement of this Part of this Schedule and of any provision of that Act (or that Schedule, as the case may be) applicable to the rehabilitation order;

(f) the references in the said paragraphs 15 and 16 to a certificate under Part III of that Schedule were deleted.

Interpretation of this Part of this Schedule

12.—In this Part of this Schedule, unless the context otherwise requires—

"clearance area" means a clearance area under Part III of the Housing (Scotland) Act 1966;

"full standard", in relation to a house, means the standard of a house which—

(a) meets the tolerable standard;

(b) is in a good state of repair (disregarding the state of internal decorative repair) having regard to the age, character and locality of the house; and

(c) is provided with all of the standard amenities;

"housing treatment area" means a housing treatment area under Part I of the Housing (Scotland) Act 1969;

"notice land" means land in relation to which a notice is to be served under paragraph 9;

"relevant land" means—

(a) land in the clearance area or housing treatment area (as the case may be), including land which has been included in that area by virtue of section 41 of the Act of 1966 or section 9 of the Act of 1969 (land already belonging to the local authority); or

(b) land surrounded by or adjoining that area, which the local authority or a previous local authority entitled to purchase the land under section 37 of the Act of 1966 or under section 6 of the Act of 1969 have determined to purchase (whether or not it has been so purchased).

PART III

APPLICATION OF ENACTMENTS RELATING TO COMPENSATION ON COMPULSORY PURCHASE, ETC.,
TO CASES UNDER PART I OF PART II OF THIS SCHEDULE

Compensation

13.—(1) Where, under Part I or II of this Schedule, a compulsory purchase order is to be treated as made under Part I of this Act or Part VI of the Town and Country Planning (Scotland) Act 1972, compensation for the compulsory acquisition of the land comprised in the compulsory purchase order is to be assessed in accordance with the provisions applying to a compulsory acquisition under Part I of this Act or, as the case may be, Part VI of the Act of 1972.

(2) Where, under Part I or II of this Schedule, land or any interest in land within any area is to be treated as appropriated by a local authority to the purposes of Part I of this Act, compensation for its compulsory acquisition shall (where it increases the amount) be assessed or re-assessed in accordance with the provisions applying to a compulsory acquisition under those Parts respectively.

(3) Where, under paragraph 2 of Part I of this Schedule, or under Part II, any interest in land acquired by a local authority by agreement (after the declaration of a housing action area which relates to that land) is to be treated as appropriate for the purposes of Part I of this Act—

(a) compensation shall (where sub-paragraph (2) would have increased the amount) be assessed and paid as if the acquisition were a compulsory acquisition, under Part I of this Act or Part II of Schedule 8 (as the case may be), to which the said sub-paragraph (2) applied; but

(b) there shall be deducted from the amount of compensation so payable any amount previously paid in respect of the acquisition of that interest by the authority.

(4) Where sub-paragraph (2) or (3) applies, the local authority shall serve on the person entitled to the compensation a notice in the prescribed form giving particulars of the amount of compensation payable in accordance with the provisions applying to a compulsory acquisition under Part I of this Act, and if the person served does not, within 21 days from service of the notice, accept the particulars, or if he disputes the amount stated, the question of disputed compensation shall be referred to the Lands Tribunal.

(5) The notice shall be served not later than 6 months after—

(a) the relevant date, as defined in paragraph 1(4) of this Schedule, or

(b) the date on which the rehabilitation order becomes operative for the purposes of Part II of this Schedule,

(as the case may be), and paragraph 19 of Schedule 1 to the Acquisition of Land (Authorisation Procedure) (Scotland) Act 1947 (service of notices) shall apply to the notice.

(6) Sub-paragraph (2) shall be left out of account in considering whether, under sections 117 and 118 of the Lands Clauses Consolidation (Scotland) Act 1845, compensation has been properly paid for the land; and accordingly sub-paragraph (2) shall not prevent an acquiring authority from remaining in undisputed possession of the land.

(7) Where sub-paragraph (2) makes an increase in compensation to be assessed in accordance with sections 56 to 60 and 63 of the said Act of 1845 (absent and untraced owners)—

(a) a notarial instrument executed under section 76 of that Act before the latest date for service of a notice under sub-paragraph (4) shall not be invalid because the increase in compensation has not been paid, and

(b) it shall be the duty of the local authority, not later than 6 months after the said date, to proceed under the said sections and pay the proper additional amount into the bank.

(8) Any sum payable by virtue of this paragraph shall carry interest at the rate prescribed under section 40 of the Land Compensation (Scotland) Act 1963 from the time of entry by the local authority on the land, or from vesting of the land or interest, whichever is the earlier, until payment.

(9) In this paragraph, references to an increase in compensation shall be read as if any payments under—

(a) section 49 of the Act of 1966, section 11 of the Act of 1969 or section 30 of the Act of 1974 or section 305 of this Act (payments in respect of well-maintained houses and payments to owner-occupiers),

(b) section 160 of the Act of 1966 or section 38 of the Land Compensation (Scotland) Act 1963 (allowances to persons displaced),

(c) sections 18 to 20 of the Act of 1969 or sections 308 to 311 of this Act (payments to

owner-occupiers and others in respect of houses not meeting the tolerable standard
purchased or demolished), and

(d) section 34 of the Land Compensation (Scotland) Act 1973 (disturbance payments for
persons without compensatable interests),

were, to the extent that they were made to the person in question, compensation in respect
of the compulsory purchase.

Extension of time limits for exercising powers under certain compulsory purchase orders

14.—In section 116 of the Lands Clauses Consolidation (Scotland) Act 1845 (time limits
for exercising powers under compulsory purchase orders) there shall be added at the end the
following paragraph—

"For the purposes of this section no account shall be taken of any period during
which an authority are, by virtue of Schedule 7 to the Housing (Scotland) Act 1987
(which relates to buildings in housing action areas) prevented from serving notice to
treat under section 17 of this Act.".

Section 95   SCHEDULE 8

PART I

HOUSING ACTION AREAS

Procedure after publication of draft resolution

1.—(1) The local authority shall have regard to any representations made to them by
virtue of section 94 and, within a period of 2 months from the expiry of the period of 2
months mentioned in section 94(7), shall—

(a) subject to the provisions of sub-paragraph (2), pass a final resolution confirming the
draft resolution, with or without modifications; or

(b) rescind the draft resolution.

(2) The power to make modifications by virtue of sub-paragraph (1)(a) shall not include
power to extend the area defined in the draft resolution.

(3) The local authority shall, as soon as may be—

(a) send a copy of the final resolution and a copy of the map to the Secretary of
State,

(b) publish in the manner required by section 94(5)(a) a notice that a final resolution
has been made, or as the case may be, that the draft resolution has been
rescinded and

(c) serve on such persons as were served with a notice in pursuance of section
94(5)(b), a notice stating the effect of any final resolution or, as the case may
be, stating that the draft resolution has been rescinded,

and the provisions of section 94(6) shall apply to the publication and service of a notice
under this paragraph as they apply to the publication and service of a notice under that
section.

(4) The provisions of section 92 shall apply to a final resolution as they apply to a draft
resolution.

2.—Any notice authorised or required to be sent to any owner, lessee or occupier by
virtue of section 94(5)(b) and paragraph 1(3)(c) may, if it is not practicable after reasonable
inquiry to ascertain the name of such owner, lessee or occupier, be served by addressing it
to him by the description of "owner", "lessee" or "occupier", as the case may be, identifying
the house to which it relates and by delivering it to some person in the house, or if there is
no person in the house to whom it can be delivered, by affixing it, or a copy of it, to some
conspicuous part of the house.

PART II

POWERS OF LOCAL AUTHORITY IN RELATION TO ACQUISITION OF LAND FOR HOUSING ACTION
AREAS

3.—(1) Subject to the provisions of sub-paragraph (2), where a local authority have
published and served, in accordance with the provisions of section 94, a notice of the passing
of a draft resolution made under section 89, 90 or 91 the local authority, from the date of

the said publication and service, shall have power to purchase land by agreement in the area to which the said draft resolution relates, in order themselves to undertake, or otherwise secure, the demolition, or improvement to the standard specified under section 90(3) or by virtue of section 91(3) (as the case may be), of the houses or buildings.

(2) Where under sub-paragraph (1) the local authority purchase a house identified in accordance with section 92(4)(c), they may also purchase any other part of the building so identified if in their opinion it is necessary to purchase such other part in order to integrate it with that house.

Land adjoining housing action area

4.—Where a local authority determine to acquire any land comprised in an area declared by them to be a housing action area, they may acquire also—
  (a) any land which is surrounded by the housing action area; and
  (b) any land adjoining the housing action area,
if the acquisition is reasonably necessary for the purpose of securing an area of convenient shape and dimensions or is reasonably necessary for the satisfactory development or use of the housing action area.

Further provisions relating to acquisition of land

5.—(1) In so far as a resolution passed under section 89 or 91 provides that some or all of the buildings in a housing action area should be demolished, the powers of acquiring land comprised in or surrounded by or adjoining such an area conferred on a local authority by Part IV and this Schedule shall not be restricted by the fact that buildings within that area have been demolished since the area was declared to be a housing action area.

(2) Land for the purposes of Part IV and this Schedule may be acquired by a local authority by agreement under section 70 of the Local Government (Scotland) Act 1973 (acquisition of land by agreement).

(3) Subject to the provisions of sub-paragraph (4), a local authority may be authorised by the Secretary of State to purchase land compulsorily for the same purposes as they may acquire land by agreement under paragraphs 3 and 4, and the Acquisition of Land (Authorisation Procedure) (Scotland) Act 1947 shall apply in relation to any such compulsory purchase as if this Act had been in force immediately before the commencement of that Act, but subject to the following modifications—
  (a) the compulsory purchase order shall not be in the form prescribed under paragraph 2 of Schedule 1 to that Act, but shall be in a form prescribed under this paragraph;
  (b) the notices referred to in paragraphs 3 and 6 of the said Schedule 1 shall not be in the form prescribed under those paragraphs, but shall be in a form prescribed under this paragraph;
  (c) the order shall show separately the houses in the housing action area which do not meet the tolerable standard and, as the case may be, that standard along with any other standard specified under section 90 or by virtue of section 91 and the land proposed to be purchased outside the area;
  (d) the order as confirmed by the Secretary of State shall not authorise the local authority to purchase any house on less favourable terms with respect to compensation than the terms on which the order would have authorised them to purchase the house if the order had been confirmed without modification;
  (e) if the Secretary of State is of opinion that any land included by a local authority in a housing action area ought not to have been so included, he shall on confirming the order so modify it as to exclude that land for all purposes from that area;
  (f) in section 1 of that Act, any reference to the said Schedule 1 shall be construed as a reference to that Schedule as modified by this sub-paragraph;
  (g) in Part IV of that Schedule any reference to that Act or that Schedule and any reference to any regulation made thereunder shall be construed respectively as a reference to that Act as modified by this sub-paragraph and as including a reference to any regulation made under this sub-paragraph;
  (h) section 3 of that Act (power to extinguish certain public rights of way over land acquired) shall be omitted.

(4) Where a local authority have published and served notice of a final resolution in accordance with the provisions of paragraph 1 declaring an area to be—
  (a) a housing action area for demolition, they shall submit any order authorising the compulsory purchase of land in the area to the Secretary of State within a period of 6 months from the date of the said publication and service.
  (b) a housing action area for improvement or for demolition and improvement, any such

order as aforesaid shall not be made by the local authority before the expiry of a period of 3 months and shall be submitted to the Secretary of State within a period of 9 months from the date of the said publication and service,

but the Secretary of State may in the circumstances of a particular case, allow such longer period for the periods of 6 months and 9 months mentioned respectively in paragraphs (a) and (b) as he thinks appropriate.

Land belonging to local authority

6.—(1) A local authority may include in a housing action area any land belonging to them which they might have included in such an area if the land had not belonged to them.

(2) Where any land belonging to a local authority is included in a housing action area, or where any land belonging to a local authority is surrounded by or adjoins a housing action area and might have been purchased by the authority under paragraph 4 had it not been previously acquired by them, the provisions of Part IV and this Schedule shall apply in relation to any such land as if it had been purchased compulsorily by the authority as being land comprised in the housing action area or, as the case may be, as being land surrounded by or adjoining the housing action area.

Local authority may take possession of land

7.—Section 11 (which provides that a local authority may take possession of land to be acquired by agreement or appropriated for the purposes of Part I) shall apply for the purposes of Part IV and this Schedule as it applies for the purposes of Part I.

Local authority may sell or lease land

8.—A local authority who have under Part IV or this Schedule purchased any land comprised in or surrounded by or adjoining a housing action area, may—

(a) where the land was purchased for the purpose of bringing the houses in the area up to the standard specified under section 90(3) or by virtue of section 91(3), sell or lease any such house to any person subject to the condition that that person will bring the house up to at least the appropriate standard and to any other restriction or condition that they may think fit; or

(b) in any other case, sell or lease the land subject to such restrictions and conditions, if any, as they think fit, or may, in accordance with section 73 of the Local Government (Scotland) Act 1973 (appropriation of land), appropriate the land for any purpose for which they are authorised to acquire land.

Extinction of rights of way servitudes, etc.

9.—(1) A local authority may, with the approval of the Secretary of State, by order extinguish any public right of way over any land purchased by them under Part IV or this Schedule or provide for the closing or diversion of any road in connection with the development of a housing action area.

(2) An order made by a local authority under sub-paragraph (1) shall be made in the prescribed form and be published in the prescribed manner, and, if any objection thereto is made to the Secretary of State before the expiry of 2 months from its publication, the Secretary of State shall not approve the order until he has caused a public local inquiry to be held into the matter.

(3) Where a local authority have resolved to purchase under Part IV or this Schedule land over which a public right of way exists, the authority may make and the Secretary of State may approve, in advance of the purchase, an order extinguishing that right as from the date on which the buildings on the land are vacated, or at the expiry of such period after that date as may be specified in the order or as the Secretary of State in approving the order may direct.

(4) Upon the completion by a local authority of the purchase by them of any land under Part IV or this Schedule, all private rights of way and all rights of laying down, erecting, continuing or maintaining any apparatus on, under or over that land, and all other rights or servitudes in or relating to that land, shall be extinguished, and any such apparatus shall vest in the authority; and any person who suffers loss by the extinction or vesting of any such right or apparatus as aforesaid shall be entitled to be paid by the authority compensation to be determined by the Lands Tribunal in accordance with the Land Compensation (Scotland) Act 1963:

Provided that this sub-paragraph shall not apply to any right vested in public undertakers of laying down, erecting, continuing or maintaining any apparatus or to any apparatus belonging to public undertakers, and shall have effect as respects other matters subject to any agreement which may be made between the local authority and the person in or to whom the right or apparatus in question is vested or belongs.

Provisions as to apparatus of public undertakers

10.—(1) Where the removal or alteration of apparatus belonging to public undertakers on, under or over land purchased by a local authority under Part IV or this Schedule or on, under or over a road running over or through or adjoining any such land is reasonably necessary for the purpose of enabling the authority to exercise any of the powers conferred upon them by that Part or this Schedule, the authority shall have power to execute works for the removal or alteration of the apparatus subject to and in accordance with the provisions of this paragraph.

(2) A local authority who intend to remove or alter any apparatus under the powers conferred by sub-paragraph (1) shall serve on the undertakers notice in writing of their intention, with particulars of the proposed works and of the manner in which they are to be executed and plans and sections thereof, and shall not commence any works until the expiry of a period of 28 days from the date of service of the notice, and the undertakers may within that period by notice in writing served on the authority—

(a) object to the execution of the works or any of them on the ground that they are not necessary for the purpose aforesaid; or

(b) state requirements to which in their opinion effect ought to be given as to the manner of, or the observance of conditions in, the execution of the works, as to the execution of other works for the protection of other apparatus belonging to the undertakers, or as to the execution of other works for the provision of substituted apparatus whether permanent or temporary;

and—

(i) if objection is so made to any works and not withdrawn, the local authority shall not execute the works unless they are determined by arbitration to be so necessary;

(ii) if any such requirement as aforesaid is so made and not withdrawn, the local authority shall give effect thereto unless it is determined by arbitration to be unreasonable.

(3) A local authority shall make to public undertakers reasonable compensation for any damage which is sustained by them by reason of the execution by the authority of any works under sub-paragraph (1) and which is not made good by the provision of substituted apparatus.

Any question as to the right of undertakers to recover compensation under this sub-paragraph or as to the amount thereof shall be determined by arbitration.

(4) Where the removal or alteration of apparatus belonging to public undertakers or the execution of works for the provision of substituted apparatus whether permanent or temporary is reasonably necessary for the purposes of their undertaking by reason of the stopping up, diversion or alteration of the level or width of a road by a local authority under powers exercisable by virtue of Part IV or this Schedule, such undertakers may, by notice in writing served on the authority, require them at the expense of the authority to remove or alter the apparatus or to execute the works, and, where any such requirement is so made and not withdrawn, the authority shall give effect thereto unless they serve notice in writing on the undertakers of their objection to the requirement within 28 days from the date of service of the notice upon them and the requirement is determined by arbitration to be unreasonable.

(5) At least 7 days before commencing any works which they are authorised or required under the provisions of this paragraph to execute, the local authority shall, except in case of emergency, serve on the undertakers notice in writing of their intention so to do, and the works shall be executed by the authority under the superintendence (at the expense of the authority) and to the reasonable satisfaction of the undertakers:

Provided that, if within 7 days from the date of service on them of notice under this sub-paragraph the undertakers so elect, they shall themselves execute the works in accordance with the reasonable directions and to the reasonable satisfaction of the local authority, and the reasonable costs thereof shall be repaid to the undertakers by the authority.

(6) Any difference arising between public undertakers and a local authority under sub-paragraph (5) and any matter which is by virtue of the provisions of this paragraph to be determined by arbitration shall—

(a) in the case of a question arising under sub-paragraph (3) be referred to and determined by the Lands Tribunal;

(b) in any other case be referred to and determined by an arbiter to be appointed, in default of agreement, by the Secretary of State.

(7) In this paragraph, references to the alteration of apparatus include references to diversion and to alterations of position or level.

Saving for telecommunication apparatus, etc.

11.—(1) Paragraph 23 of the telecommunications code (which provides a procedure for certain cases where works involve the alteration of telecommunication apparatus) shall apply to a local authority for the purposes of any works which they are authorised to execute under Part IV or this Schedule.

(2) Where in pursuance of an order under paragraph 9 a public right of way over land is extinguished or a road is closed or diverted, and, at the beginning of the day on which the order comes into operation, there is under, in, on, over, along or across the land or road any telecommunication apparatus kept installed for the purposes of a telecommunications code system, the operator of that system shall have the same powers in respect of that apparatus as if the order had not come into operation; but any person entitled to land over which the right of way subsisted shall be entitled to require the alteration of the apparatus.

(3) The proviso to sub-paragraph (4) of paragraph 9 shall have effect in relation to any right conferred by or in accordance with the telecommunications code on the operator of a telecommunications code system and to telecommunication apparatus kept installed for the purposes of any such system as it has effect in relation to rights vested in and apparatus belonging to statutory undertakers.

(4) Paragraph 1(2) of the telecommunications code (alteration of apparatus to include moving, removal or replacement of apparatus) shall apply for the purposes of the preceding provisions of this paragraph as it applies for the purposes of that code.

(5) Paragraph 21 of the telecommunications code (restriction on removal of tele-communication apparatus) shall apply in relation to any entitlement conferred by this paragraph to require the alteration, moving or replacement of any telecommunication apparatus as it applies in relation to an entitlement to require the removal of any such apparatus.

PART III

COMPENSATION IN RESPECT OF LAND ACQUIRED COMPULSORILY

12.—(1) Where land is purchased compulsorily by a local authority under Part IV or this Schedule, the compensation payable in respect thereof shall, subject to the following provisions of this paragraph, be assessed by the Lands Tribunal in accordance with the Land Compensation (Scotland) Act 1963.

(2) In the case of the compulsory acquisition of a house which either is specified in the compulsory purchase order as not meeting the tolerable standard, or is specified in an improvement order under section 88, such compensation shall not (except by virtue of paragraph 3 of Schedule 2 to the said Act of 1963) exceed the value, at the time when the valuation is made, of the site of the house as a cleared site available for development in accordance with the requirements of the building regulations for the time being in force in the district.

(3) The reference in sub-paragraph (2) to compensation is a reference to the compensation payable in respect of the purchase exclusive of any compensation for disturbance or for severance or for injurious affection.

(4) Schedule 1 shall have effect in relation to the compulsory purchase of land under sub-paragraph (1), but shall not have effect in relation to a house to which sub-paragraph (2) applies.

PART IV

ADJUSTMENT OF RELATIONS BETWEEN LESSORS AND LESSEES OF AGRICULTURAL HOLDINGS, ETC.

13.—(1) Section 8 of the Agricultural Holdings (Scotland) Act 1949 (increases of rent for improvements carried out by landlord) shall apply as if references in subsection (1) of that section to improvements carried out at the request of the tenant included references to improvements carried out in compliance with a notice of a final resolution under Part I of this Schedule:

Provided that where the tenant has contributed to the cost incurred by the landlord in carrying out the improvement, the increase in rent provided for by the said section 8 shall be reduced proportionately.

(2) Any works carried out in compliance with a notice of a final resolution under Part I of this Schedule shall be included among the improvements specified in paragraph 18 of Schedule 1 to the said Act of 1949 (tenant's right to compensation for erection, alteration or enlargement of buildings), but subject to the power conferred by section 79 of that Act to vary the said Schedule 1; and sections 51 and 52 of that Act (which make that right to compensation subject to certain conditions) shall not apply to any works carried out in compliance with such a notice:

Provided that where a person other than the tenant claiming compensation has contributed to the cost of carrying out the works in compliance with any such notice, compensation in respect of the works, as assessed under section 49 of the said Act of 1949, shall be reduced proportionately.

(3) Any works carried out in compliance with a notice of a final resolution under Part I of this Schedule shall—

    (a) if carried out on a croft, be permanent improvements on that croft and be deemed to be suitable to the croft for the purposes of section 14(1)(a) of the Crofters (Scotland) Act 1955 (crofter's right to compensation for improvements);

    (b) if carried out on a holding, be permanent improvements on that holding and be deemed to be suitable to the holding for the purposes of section 8(a) of the Crofters Holdings (Scotland) Act 1886 (landholder's right to compensation for improvements);

(4) In this paragraph, unless the context otherwise requires—

    "dwelling" means a building or part of a building occupied or intended to be occupied as a separate house;

    "tenant"—

        (a) has the same meaning as in section 115(1) of the Rent (Scotland) Act 1984 but does not include a tenant holding under a lease granted for a period of more than 21 years at a rent of less than two-thirds of the net annual value for rating purposes of the leased premises, or a heritable creditor in possession; and

        (b) includes, in relation to a dwelling, a person employed in agriculture (as defined in section 17 of the Agricultural Wages (Scotland) Act 1949) who occupies or resides in the dwelling as part of the terms of his employment,

    and "tenancy" shall be construed accordingly.

References in this paragraph to a tenant occupying a dwelling include, in the case of a tenant within head (b) of this definition, a tenant residing in the dwelling, and "occupation" and "occupied" and related expressions shall be construed accordingly; and in relation to a dwelling occupied by such a tenant "the person having control" of the dwelling means, in this paragraph, the employer or other person by whose authority the tenant occupies the dwelling.

Sections 109(5), 131(2), 164(4)   SCHEDULE 9

RECOVERY OF EXPENSES BY CHARGING ORDER

1.—Where under sections 108(3), 131(2) and 164(4) a local authority have themselves incurred expenses in relation to a house or building, they may make in favour of themselves an order (in this Schedule referred to as a "charging order") providing and declaring that the house or building is thereby charged and burdened with an annuity to pay the amount of the expenses.

2.—The annuity charged shall be such sum not exceeding such sum as may be prescribed, as the local authority may determine for every £100 of the said amount and so in proportion for any less sum, and shall commence from the date of the order and be payable for a term of 30 years to the local authority.

3.—A charging order shall be in such form as may be prescribed and shall be recorded in the General Register of Sasines, or registered in the Land Register, as the case may be.

4.—Every annuity constituting a charge by a charging order duly recorded in the General Register of Sasines or registered in the Land Register, as the case may be, shall be a charge on the premises specified in the order and shall have priority over—

    (a) all future burdens and incumbrances on the same premises, and

    (b) all existing burdens and incumbrances thereon except—

(i) feuduties, teinds, ground annuals, stipends and standard charges in lieu of stipends;

(ii) any charges created or arising under any provision of the Public Health (Scotland) Act 1897 or any Act amending that Act, or any local Act authorising a charge for recovery of expenses incurred by a local authority, or under this Schedule; and

(iii) any charge created under any Act authorising advances of public money.

5.—A charging order duly recorded in the General Register of Sasines or registered in the Land Register, as the case may be, shall be conclusive evidence that the charge specified therein has been duly created in respect of the premises specified in the order.

6.—Every annuity charged by a charging order may be recovered by the person for the time being entitled to it by the same means and in the like manner in all respects as if it were a feuduty.

7.—A charging order and all sums payable thereunder may be from time to time transferred in like manner as a bond and disposition in security and sums payable thereunder.

8.—Any owner of, or other person interested in, premises on which an annuity has been charged by any such charging order shall at any time be at liberty to redeem the annuity on payment to the local authority or other person entitled thereto of such sum as may be agreed upon or, in default of agreement, determined by the Secretary of State.

Section 113   SCHEDULE 10

LANDLORD'S REPAIRING OBLIGATIONS

Obligations to repair

1.—(1) This paragraph applies—

(a) to a contract entered into before 31st July 1923 for letting for human habitation a house at a rent not exceeding £16;

(b) to a contract entered into on or after 31st July 1923 for letting for human habitation a house at a rent not exceeding £26;

but shall not apply to a contract for the letting by a local authority of any house purchased or retained by the authority under section 121 or paragraph 5 of Schedule 8 for use for housing purposes.

(2) In any contract to which this paragraph applies there shall, notwithstanding any stipulation to the contrary, be implied a condition that the house is at the commencement of the tenancy, and an undertaking that the house will be kept by the landlord during the tenancy, in all respects reasonably fit for human habitation:

Provided that that condition and the undertaking shall not be implied when a house is let for a period of not less than 3 years upon the terms that it will be put by the lessee into a condition in all respects reasonably fit for human habitation, and the lease is not determinable at the option of either party before the expiration of 3 years.

(3) The landlord, or any person authorised by him in writing, may at reasonable times of the day, on giving 24 hours' notice in writing to the tenant or occupier, enter any premises in respect of which this paragraph applies for the purpose of viewing their state and condition.

(4) In determining for the purposes of this paragraph whether a house is fit for human habitation, regard shall be had to the extent, if any, to which by reason of disrepair or sanitary defects the house falls short of the provisions of any building regulations in operation in the district.

(5) In this paragraph—

(a) the expression "landlord" means any person who lets to a tenant for human habitation any house under any contract to which this paragraph applies, and includes his successors in title; and

(b) the expression "house" includes part of a house; and

(c) the expression "sanitary defects" includes lack of air space or of ventilation, darkness, dampness, absence of adequate and readily accessible water supply or of sanitary arrangements or of other conveniences, and inadequate paving or drainage of courts, yards or passages.

Application of paragraph 1 to houses occupied by agricultural workers otherwise than as tenants

2.—Notwithstanding any agreement to the contrary, where under any contract of employment of a workman employed in agriculture the provision of a house or part of a house for the occupation of the workman forms part of the remuneration of the workman, and the provisions of paragraph 1 are inapplicable by reason only of the house or part of the house not being let to the workman, there shall be implied as part of the contract of employment the like condition and undertaking as would be implied under those provisions if the house or part of the house were so let, and those provisions shall apply accordingly as if incorporated in this paragraph, with the substitution of "employer" for "landlord" and such other modifications as may be necessary:

Provided that this paragraph shall not affect the obligation of any person other than the employer to repair a house to which this section applies or any remedy for enforcing any such obligation.

Repairing obligations in short leases of houses

3.—(1) In any lease of a house, being a lease to which this paragraph applies, there shall be implied a provision that the lessor will—
  (a) keep in repair the structure and exterior of the house (including drains, gutters and external pipes); and
  (b) keep in repair and proper working order the installations in the house—
    (i) for the supply of water, gas and electricity, and for sanitation (including basins, sinks, baths and sanitary conveniences but not, except as aforesaid, fixtures, fittings and appliances for making use of the supply of water, gas or electricity), and
    (ii) for space heating or heating water;

and any provision that the lessee will repair the premises (including any that he will put in repair or deliver up in repair, or will paint, point or render the premises, or pay money in lieu of repairs by the lessee or on account of repairs by the lessor) shall be of no effect so far as it relates to any of the matters mentioned in paragraphs (a) and (b) of this paragraph.

(2) The provision implied by this paragraph (hereinafter referred to as "the implied repairs provision") shall not be construed as requiring the lessor—
  (a) to carry out any works or repairs for which the lessee is liable by virtue of his duty to use the premises in a proper manner, or would be so liable apart from any express undertaking on his part;
  (b) to rebuild or reinstate the premises in the case of destruction or damage by fire, or by tempest, flood or other inevitable accident; or
  (c) to keep in repair or maintain anything which the lessee is entitled to remove from the house;

and sub-paragraph (1) of this paragraph shall not avoid so much of any provision as imposes on the lessee any of the requirements mentioned in head (a) or head (c) of this sub-paragraph.

(3) In determining the standard of repair required by the implied repairs provision in relation to any house, regard shall be had to the age, character and prospective life of the house and the locality in which it is situated.

(4) In any lease in which the implied repairs provision is implied there shall also be implied a provision that the lessor, or any person authorised by him in writing, may at reasonable times of the day, on giving 24 hours' notice in writing to the occupier, enter the premises comprised in the lease for the purpose of viewing their condition and state of repair.

(5) In this paragraph and in paragraphs 4 and 5, unless the context otherwise requires, the following expressions have the meanings hereby assigned to them respectively, that is to say—
  (a) "lease" includes a sublease, and "lessor" and "lessee", in relation to a lease, include respectively any person for the time being holding the interest of lessor, and any person for the time being holding the interest of lessee, under the lease, and
  (b) "lease of a house" means a lease whereby a building or part of a building is let wholly or mainly as a private dwelling and "house", in relation to such a lease, means that building or part of a building.

Application of paragraph 3

4.—(1) Subject to the provisions of this paragraph, paragraph 3 applies to any lease of a house granted on or after 3rd July 1962 being a lease for a period of less than 7 years.
  (2) For the purpose of this paragraph a lease—
    (a) shall be treated as a lease for a period of less than 7 years if it is determinable at the option of the lessor before the expiration of 7 years from the commencement of the period of the lease, and

(b) shall be treated as a lease for a period of 7 years or more if it confers on the lessee an option for renewal for a period which, together with the original period, amounts to 7 years or more, and it is not determinable as mentioned in head (a) of this sub-paragraph.

(3) Where a lease (hereinafter referred to as "the new lease") of a house is granted—

    (a) to a person who, when or immediately before the new lease is granted, is or was the lessee of the house under another lease, or

    (b) to a person who was the lessee of the house under another lease which terminated at some time before the new lease is granted and who, between the termination of that other lease and the grant of the new lease, was continuously in possession of the house or entitled to the rents or profits thereof,

paragraph 3 shall not apply to the new lease unless the other lease, if granted on or after 3rd July 1962, was a lease to which that paragraph applies, or, if granted before the said date, would have been such a lease if it had been granted on or after that date.

(4) Paragraph 3 shall not apply to any lease of a house which is a tenancy of an agricultural holding.

(5) In the application of this paragraph to a lease for a period part of which falls before the date of the granting of the lease, that part shall be left out of account and the lease shall be treated as a lease for a period commencing with the date of the granting.

Restriction on contracting out

5.—(1) The sheriff may, on the application of either party to a lease, by order made with the consent of the other party concerned, authorise the inclusion in the lease, or in any agreement collateral to the lease, of provisions excluding or modifying in relation to the lease the provisions of paragraph 3 with respect to the repairing of obligations of the parties if it appears to him, having regard to the other terms and conditions of the lease and to all the circumstances of the case, that it is reasonable to do so, and any provision so authorised shall have effect accordingly.

(2) Subject to sub-paragraph (1) any provision, whether contained in a lease to which paragraph 3 applies or in any agreement collateral to such a lease, shall be void so far as it purports to exclude or limit the obligations of the lessor or the immunities of the lessee under that section, or to provide for an irritancy of the lease or impose on the lessee any penalty, disability or obligation, in the event of his enforcing or relying upon those obligations or immunities.

Sections 164(4), 184(2),
187(3), 189   SCHEDULE 11

Houses in Multiple Occupation: Control Orders

Part I

Management Schemes

1.—(1) A management scheme shall give particulars of all works which in the opinion of the local authority—

    (a) the local authority would have required to be carried out under the provisions of Part VIII (other than those relating to control orders), or under any other enactment relating to housing or public health, and

    (b) constitute works involving capital expenditure.

(2) A management scheme shall also—

    (a) include an estimate of the cost of carrying out the works of which particulars are given in the scheme; and

    (b) specify what is in the opinion of the local authority the highest number of individuals or households who should, having regard to the considerations set out in subsections (1) to (3) of section 161, live in the house having regard to its existing condition and to its future condition as the works progress which the authority carry out in the house; and

    (c) include an estimate of the balances which will from time to time accrue to the local authority out of the net amount of the rent and other payments received by the authority from persons occupying the house after deducting—

        (i) compensation payable by the authority under section 181 and section 183, and

(ii) all expenditure, other than expenditure of which particulars are given under subsection (2), incurred by the authority in respect of the house while the control order is in force, together with the appropriate establishment charges.

(3) In this Schedule, references to surpluses on revenue account as settled by the scheme are references to the amount included in the scheme by way of an estimate under sub-paragraph (2)(c), subject to any variation of the scheme made by the local authority under sub-paragraph (4), or made by the sheriff on an appeal or an application under the following provisions of this Schedule.

(4) The local authority may at any time vary the scheme in such a way as to increase the amount of the surpluses on revenue account as settled by the scheme for all or any periods (including past periods).

Recovery by local authority of capital expenditure

2.—(1) Account shall be kept by the local authority for the period during which a control order is in force showing—
(a) the surpluses on revenue account as settled by the management scheme, and
(b) the expenditure incurred by the authority in carrying out works of which particulars were given in the scheme.

(2) Balances shall be struck in the account at half-yearly intervals so as to ascertain the amount of expenditure under sub-paragraph (1)(b) which cannot be set off against the said surpluses on revenue account, and (except where the control order is revoked by the sheriff on an appeal against the control order and the account under this section is no longer needed) the final balance shall be struck at the date when the control order ceases to have effect.

(3) So far as, at the end of any half-yearly period, expenditure is not set off against the said surpluses on revenue account, the expenditure shall, for the purposes of this paragraph, carry interest at such reasonable rate as the local authority may determine until it is so set off or until a demand for such expenditure is served by local authority under section 109(1), as applied by sub-paragraph (6).

(4) So far as there is any sum out of the said surpluses on revenue account not required to meet any expenditure incurred by the local authority, it shall go to meet interest under sub-paragraph (3).

(5) Except where the control order is revoked by the sheriff on an appeal against the control order under the following provisions of this Schedule, on and after the time when the control order ceases to have effect the expenditure reasonably incurred by the local authority in carrying out works of which particulars were given in the scheme, together with interest as provided in this paragraph, shall, so far as not set off in accordance with this paragraph against the surpluses on revenue account as settled by the scheme, be recoverable from the dispossessed proprietor.

(6) Sections 108(6) (exercise of power of local authority to secure repair of house in state of serious disrepair without prejudice to other powers) and 109 (recovery by local authority of expenses) shall, subject to any necessary modifications, apply for the purpose of enabling the local authority to recover from the dispossessed proprietor any expenditure which, by virtue of sub-paragraph (5), is recoverable from him as they apply for the purpose of enabling a local authority to recover expenses incurred by them in executing works under sections 108(3) to (5) and 109(1).

(7) Sections 111 (appeals) and 112 (date of operation of notices, etc.) shall apply in relation to a demand by the local authority for the recovery of any such expenditure and to an order made by the local authority with respect to any such expenditure as they apply in relation to a demand for the recovery of expenses incurred by a local authority in executing works under section 108(3) to (5) and to an order made by a local authority with respect to an order made by a local authority with respect to any such expenses.

(8) The local authority may make a charging order in favour of themselves in respect of any such expenditure, and Schedule 9, shall, with any necessary modifications, apply to a charging order so made in like manner as it applies to a charging order made under that Schedule.

(9) Section 178(2) shall not apply so as to restrict the effect of any charging order made by virtue of sub-paragraph (8) to the part of the house to which a control order is applied.

(10) For the purposes of this paragraph, references to the provisions of a scheme include references to those provisions as varied under this Schedule and if when the control order ceases to have effect, proceedings under the following provisions of this Schedule are pending which may result in a variation of the scheme, those proceedings may be continued until finally determined; and if any expenditure which, by virtue of sub-paragraph (5), is

recoverable from the dispossessed proprietor is recovered from him before the final determination of those proceedings, the local authority shall be liable to account for any money so recovered which, having regard to the decision in the proceedings as finally determined, they ought not to have recovered.

PART II

APPEAL AND REVIEW

3.—(1) Within 6 weeks from the date on which a copy of the relevant scheme is served in accordance with section 184(1), any person having an estate or interest in the house may appeal to the sheriff against the scheme on all or any of the following grounds, that is to say—

(a) that having regard to the condition of the house and to the other circumstances, any of the works of which particulars are given in the scheme (whether already carried out or not) are unreasonable in character or extent, or are unnecessary;

(b) that any of the works do not involve expenditure which ought to be regarded as capital expenditure;

(c) that the number of individuals or households living in the house, as specified by the local authority in the scheme, is unreasonably low;

(d) that the estimate of the surpluses on revenue account in the scheme is unduly low on account of some assumptions, whether as to rents charged by the local authority or otherwise, made by the authority in arriving at the estimate as to matters, which are within the control of the authority.

(2) On an appeal under this paragraph the sheriff may, as he thinks fit, confirm or vary the scheme.

(3) If an appeal has been brought against the control order and the sheriff decides on the appeal to revoke the control order, the sheriff shall not proceed with any appeal against the scheme relating to that control order.

(4) Proceedings on an appeal against a scheme shall, so far as practicable, be combined with proceedings on any appeal against the control order to which the scheme relates.

4.—(1) Without prejudice to the right of appeal against a scheme conferred by paragraph 3, either the local authority or any person having an estate or interest in the house to which the scheme relates may at any time apply to the sheriff for a review of the estimate of the surpluses on revenue account in the scheme.

(2) On an application under this paragraph, the sheriff may, as he thinks fit, confirm or vary the scheme, but the sheriff shall not on such an application vary the scheme so as to affect the provisions thereof relating to the works.

(3) On the application under this paragraph the surpluses on revenue account as settled by the scheme may be varied for all or any periods including past periods, and the sheriff shall take into consideration whether in the period since the control order came into force the actual balances mentioned in paragraph 1(2)(c) have exceeded, or been less than, the surpluses on revenue account as settled by the scheme as for the time being in force, and shall also take into consideration whether there has been any change in circumstances such that the number of persons or households who should live in the house, or the net amount of the rents and other payments receivable by the local authority from persons occupying the house, ought to be greater or less than was originally estimated.

5.—(1) If a local authority refuse an application to revoke a control order under section 188(4) or do not within 42 days from the making of the application or within such further period as the applicant may in writing allow, inform the applicant of their decision on the application, the applicant may appeal to the sheriff, and the sheriff may revoke the control order:

Provided that, if an appeal has been brought under this paragraph then, except with the leave of the sheriff, another appeal shall not be so brought, whether by the same or a different appellant, in respect of the same control order until the expiry of a period of 6 months beginning with the final determination of the first-mentioned appeal.

(2) If on an appeal under this paragraph the local authority represent to the sheriff that revocation of the control order would unreasonably delay completion of any works of which particulars were given in the relevant scheme under Part VIII and which the authority have begun to carry out, the sheriff shall take the representations into account and may, if he thinks fit, revoke the control order as from the time when the works are completed.

(3) If an appellant under this paragraph has an estate or interest in the house which, apart from the rights conferred on the local authority by the provisions of Part VIII relating to

control orders, and apart from the rights of persons occupying any part of the house, would give him the right to possession of the house, and that estate or interest was, when the control order came into force, subject to a lease for a term of years which has subsequently expired, then, if that person satisfies the sheriff that he is in a position and intends, if the control order is revoked, to demolish or reconstruct the house or to carry out substantial work of construction on the site of the house, the sheriff shall revoke the control order.

(4) Where in a case falling under sub-paragraph (3), the sheriff is not satisfied as therein mentioned, but would be so satisfied if the date of revocation of the control order were a date later than the date of the hearing of the appeal, the sheriff shall, if the appellant so requires, make an order for the revocation of the control order on that later date.

(5) Where the sheriff on an appeal under sub-paragraph (1) decides to revoke a control order in respect of a house from the dispossessed proprietor of which any amount will be recoverable by virtue of Part VIII, the sheriff may make it a condition of the revocation of the control order that the appellant first pays off to the local authority that amount, or such part of that amount, as the sheriff may specify.

(6) Where the sheriff on an appeal under sub-paragraph (1) revokes a control order, he may authorise the local authority to create under section 179(2) interests which expire, or which the dispossessed proprietor can terminate, within 6 months from the time when the control order ceases to have effect being interests which, notwithstanding subsection (3) of that section, are for a fixed term exceeding one month, or are terminable by notice to quit (or an equivalent notice) of more than 4 weeks.

(7) Where a control order is revoked by the local authority under section 188(2), or by the sheriff on an appeal under sub-paragraph (1), the local authority shall as soon as practicable thereafter cause to be recorded in the General Register of Sasines or registered in the Land Register, as the case may be, the revocation order made by them or, as the case may be, a notice stating that the control has been revoked by the sheriff as aforesaid.

6.—(1) A sheriff who revokes a control order on appeal may authorise the local authority to create under section 179(2) interests which expire, or which the dispossessed proprietor can terminate, within 6 months from the time when the control order ceases to have effect, being interests which, notwithstanding subsection (3) of section 179, are for a fixed term exceeding one month, or are terminable by notice to quit (or an equivalent notice) of more than 4 weeks.

(2) The sheriff shall take into consideration whether the state or condition of the house is such that any action ought to be taken by the local authority under the provisions of Part VIII (other than those relating to control orders) and shall take all or any of the following steps accordingly, that is to say—

(a) approve the making of an order under section 157;

(b) approve the giving of a notice under section 160 or section 161 or section 162; or

(c) approve the giving of a direction under section 166;

and no appeal against any order or notice so approved shall lie under section 158 or section 163.

(3) In respect of the period from the coming into force of the control order until its revocation by the sheriff, the local authority shall, subject to this paragraph, be liable to pay to the dispossessed proprietor the balances which from time to time accrued to the authority out of the net amount of the rent and other payments received by the authority while the control order was in force from persons occupying the house after deducting—

(a) compensation payable by the local authority under section 181 and section 183, and

(b) all expenditure, other than capital expenditure, incurred by the local authority in respect of the house while the control order was in force, together with the appropriate establishment charges.

(4) If the sheriff is satisfied that the balances which the local authority are, under sub-paragraph (3), liable to pay to the dispossessed proprietor are unduly low for any reason within the control of the authority, having regard to the desirability of observing the standards of management contained in regulations made under section 156 and to the other standards which the authority ought to observe as to the number of persons living in the house and the rents which they ought to charge, the sheriff shall direct that, for the purposes of the authority's liability to the dispossessed proprietor under this paragraph, the balances under sub-paragraph (3) shall be deemed to be such greater sums as the sheriff may direct:

Provided that the sheriff shall not under this sub-paragraph give a direction which will afford to the dispossessed proprietor a sum greater than what he may, in the opinion of the sheriff, have lost by the making of the control order.

(5) If different persons are dispossessed proprietors in relation to different parts of the house, sums payable under this paragraph by the local authority shall be apportioned between them in the manner provided by section 183(5).

(6) For the purpose of enabling the local authority to recover capital expenditure incurred by them in carrying out works in the house in the period before the control order is revoked, the authority may on the hearing of the appeal apply to the sheriff for approval of those works on the ground that they were works which, if a control order had not been in force, the authority could have required some other person to carry out under the foregoing provisions of Part VIII (other than those relating to control orders), or under any other enactment relating to housing or public health, and that the carrying out of the works could not be postponed until after the determination of the appeal because the works were urgently required for the sake of the safety, welfare or health of the persons living in the house, or other persons.

(7) Any expenditure reasonably incurred by the local authority in carrying out works approved under sub-paragraph (6)—
  (a) may be deducted by the local authority out of the balances which the authority are, under sub-paragraph (3), liable to pay to the dispossessed proprietor;
  (b) so far as not so deducted, shall be recoverable from the dispossessed proprietor.

(8) Any expenditure recoverable by the local authority from the dispossessed proprietor by virtue of sub-paragraph (7)(b) shall carry interest at such reasonable rate as the local authority may determine from the date when the control order is revoked; and sub-paragraphs (6) to (8) of paragraph 2 shall, with any necessary modifications, apply for the purpose of enabling the authority to recover any such expenditure.

Powers of court to restrict recovery of possession

7.—(1) The provisions of this paragraph apply where—
  (a) a local authority have made an order under Part I of Schedule 1 to the Acquisition of Land (Authorisation Procedure) (Scotland) Act 1947, as applied to the acquisition of land under this Act (other than section 121) authorising the compulsory acquisition of a house which is let in lodgings or which is occupied by members of more than one family; and
  (b) any premises forming part of that house are at a time in the relevant period occupied by a person (in this paragraph referred to as "the former lessee") who was the lessee of those premises when the order was made or became the lessee thereof after the order was made, but who is no longer the lessee thereof.

(2) In this paragraph "the relevant period" means the period beginning with the making of that order and ending on the third anniversary of the date on which the order becomes operative or, if at a time before the expiration of the said period, the Secretary of State notifies the local authority that he declines to confirm the order, or the order is quashed by a court, the period beginning with the making of the order and ending with that time.

(3) Subject to the provisions of this paragraph, in proceedings in any court of competent jurisdiction instituted during the relevant period to enforce against the former lessee the right to recover possession of the premises the court may if it thinks fit—
  (a) suspend the execution of any decree of removing or warrant of ejection or other like order made in the proceedings for such period, not extending beyond the end of the period of three years beginning on the relevant date and subject to such conditions, if any, as the court thinks fit; and
  (b) from time to time vary the period of suspension (but not so as to enlarge that period beyond the end of the said period of 3 years, or terminate it), and vary the terms of the said decree, warrant or other like order in other respects.

(4) For the purposes of sub-paragraph (3), "the relevant date" means—
  (a) if the compulsory purchase order concerned has become operative before the date on which the court exercises its power under that sub-paragraph, the date on which the order became operative; and
  (b) in any other case the date on which the court exercises or, as the case may be, exercised its power under paragraph (a) of that sub-paragraph in relation to the decree of removing or warrant of ejection or other like order in question.

(5) If at any time the Secretary of State notifies the local authority that he declines to confirm the compulsory purchase order, or that order is quashed by a court, or, whether before or after that order has been submitted to the Secretary of State for confirmation, the authority decide not to proceed with it, it shall be the duty of the authority to notify the person entitled to the benefit of the decree of removing or warrant of ejection or other like order, and that person shall be entitled, on applying to the court, to obtain an order terminating the period of suspension, but subject to the exercise of such discretion in fixing the date on which possession is to be given as the court might exercise apart from this sub-paragraph if it were then making such a decree, warrant or other like order for the first time.

(6) Sub-paragraphs (3) to (5) shall not apply where the person entitled to possession of the premises is the local authority.

PART III

CONSEQUENCES OF CESSATION OF CONTROL ORDER

Transfer of landlord's interest in tenancies and agreements

8.—(1) On and after the date on which the control order ceases to have effect any lease, licence or agreement in which the local authority were substituted for any other party by virtue of section 180 shall have effect as if for the authority there were substituted in the lease, licence or agreement the original party or his successor in title.

(2) On and after the date on which the control order ceases to have effect any agreement in the nature of a lease or licence created by the local authority shall have effect as if the dispossessed proprietor were substituted in the agreement for the authority.

(3) If the dispossessed proprietor is a lessee, nothing in any superior lease shall impose any liability on the dispossessed proprietor or any superior lessee in respect of anything done in pursuance of the terms of an agreement in which the dispossessed proprietor is substituted for the local authority by virtue of this paragraph.

Cases where leases have been modified while control order was in force

9.—If under section 185 the sheriff modifies or determines a lease, the sheriff may include in the order modifying or determining the lease provisions for modifying the effect of paragraph 8 in relation to the lease.

Interpretation

10.—References in this Part of this Schedule to the control order ceasing to have effect are references to its ceasing to have effect whether on revocation or in any other circumstances.

PART IV

RECOVERY OF EXPENSES BY LOCAL AUTHORITY EXECUTING WORKS UNDER SECTION 164

11.—(1) Sections 108(6) (exercise of power of local authority to secure repair of house in state of serious disrepair without prejudice to other powers) and 109 (recovery by local authority of expenses) shall, subject to any necessary modifications, apply for the purpose of enabling a local authority to recover any expenses reasonably incurred by them in carrying out works under section 164 as they apply for the purpose of enabling a local authority to recover expenses incurred by them in executing works under section 108(3), but—

(a) the person from whom such expenses may be recovered shall be the person on whom the notice was served, and

(b) if that person was only properly served with the notice as trustee, tutor, curator, factor or agent for or of some other person, then the expenses may be recovered either from him or from that other person, or in part from him and in part from that other person.

(2) Sections 111 (Appeals) and 112 (Date of operation of notices etc.) shall apply in relation to a demand by a local authority for the recovery of such expenses and to an order made by a local authority with respect to any such expenses as they apply in relation to a demand for the recovery of expenses incurred by a local authority in executing works under section 108(3) and to an order made by a local authority with respect to any such expenses.

(3) Where a local authority have incurred such expenses, it shall be competent for them to make a charging order in favour of themselves in respect of such expenses; and Schedule 9 shall, with any necessary modifications, apply to a charging order so made in like manner as it applies to a charging order made under that Schedule.

(4) If a local authority apply to the sheriff and satisfy him—

(a) that any such expenses reasonably incurred by them (with the interest accrued due thereon) have not been, and are unlikely to be, recovered, and

(b) that some person is profiting by the execution of the works in respect of which the expenses were incurred to obtain rents or other payments which would not have been obtainable if those works had not been executed, the sheriff, if satisfied that that person has had proper notice of the application, may order him to make such payment or payments to the local authority as may appear to the sheriff to be just.

SCHEDULE 12

TERMINATION OF EXCHEQUER PAYMENTS TO LOCAL AUTHORITIES AND CERTAIN PERIODICAL PAYMENTS TO OTHER PERSONS

1.—(1) No payment shall be made—
    (a) for the year 1979–80 or any subsequent year to a local authority under any of the enactments specified in Part I of the Table in paragraph 2;
    (b) for the year 1978–79 or any subsequent year to—
        (i) the Scottish Special Housing Association under any of the enactments specified in Parts II or III of that Table;
        (ii) a development corporation under any of the enactments specified in Part II of that Table.

(2) The right of a local authority to receive any payment under any of the enactments specified in Part I of that Table or section 105 of the Housing (Scotland) Act 1950 shall be extinguished unless an application has been made for the payment before 31st March 1980 or such later date as the Secretary of State may in exceptional circumstances allow.

(3) Subject to the following provisions of this paragraph, where—
    (a) information given to the Secretary of State on any such application as is mentioned in sub-paragraph (2) for a payment includes any particulars which are, and are stated to be, based on an estimate; and
    (b) it appears to the Secretary of State—
        (i) that the estimate is reasonable; and
        (ii) that, assuming the estimate were correct, the information and other particulars given on the application are sufficient to enable him to determine the amount of the payment;
the Secretary of State may accept the estimate and make a payment accordingly.

(4) Any payment made in pursuance of sub-paragraph (3) so far as it is based on an estimate of the cost of land may be adjusted when the final cost of the land is ascertained.

(5) Where any payment is made in pursuance of sub-paragraph (3), the recipient shall not be entitled to question the amount of the payment on a ground which means that the estimate was incorrect.

(6) Where the Secretary of State is not satisfied that the estimate is reasonable, he may, if he thinks fit, accept the application and make a payment of such amount as appears to him reasonable.

(7) No housing association grant under Part II of the Housing Associations Act 1985 shall be paid to a local authority, the Association or a development corporation in respect of any project completed after 31st March 1979.

(8) No payment shall be made for the year 1979–80 or any subsequent year under—
    (a) section 27(1) of the Housing (Scotland) Act 1949, section 89(1) of the Housing (Scotland) Act 1950 or section 21(1) of the 1968 Act (exchequer contributions for hostels); or
    (b) section 33 of the Housing Act 1974 or section 55 of the Housing Associations Act 1985 (hostel deficit grants),
to a local authority, the Association or a development corporation.

2.—

Table

Part I

Payments to local authorities

Chapter	Act	Section
1968 c.31.	The Housing (Financial Provisions) (Scotland) Act 1968.	Section 13.
1969 c.34.	The Housing (Scotland) Act 1969.	Section 59(1) so far as the payments thereunder relate to land to which the housing revenue account relates.
1972 c.46.	The Housing (Financial Provisions) (Scotland) Act 1972.	Sections 2, 3 and 4.

Part II

Payments to the Scottish Special Housing Association and development corporations

Chapter	Act	Section
1968 c.31.	The Housing (Financial Provisions) (Scotland) Act 1968.	Section 13.
1969 c.34.	The Housing (Scotland) Act 1969.	Section 59(1).
1972 c.46.	The Housing (Financial Provisions) (Scotland) Act 1972.	Sections 8, 9 and 10.

Part III

Payments to the Scottish Special Housing Association

Chapter	Act	Section
1972 c.46.	The Housing (Financial Provisions) (Scotland) Act 1972.	Section 12.

Section 201(4)   SCHEDULE 13

ENACTMENTS SPECIFYING EXCHEQUER CONTRIBUTIONS

The Housing (Scotland) Act 1950.
The Housing (Scotland) Act 1962, Part I.
The Housing (Financial Provisions) (Scotland) Act 1968.
The Housing (Scotland) Act 1969, section 59.
The Housing (Scotland) Act 1974, Part I.
This Act, sections 254 and 255.

Section 201(5)   SCHEDULE 14

ENACTMENTS SPECIFYING EXCHEQUER CONTRIBUTIONS THAT MAY BE REDUCED, SUSPENDED OR DISCONTINUED

The Housing (Scotland) Act 1950, sections 105, 110 and 121.
The Housing (Scotland) Act 1962, sections 12(3) and 14.
The Housing (Financial Provisions) (Scotland) Act 1968, Part I, Part II (except sections 26 and 50) and section 58(4).
The Housing (Scotland) Act 1969, section 59.
The Housing (Financial Provisions) (Scotland) Act 1972, Part I.
The Housing (Scotland) Act 1974, Part I.
This Act, Part IX and sections 254 and 255.

Section 203   SCHEDULE 15

THE HOUSING REVENUE ACCOUNT

PART I

APPLICATION OF ACCOUNT

1.—(1) The houses, buildings and land specified for the purposes of section 203(1) (the housing revenue account) are—

(a) all houses and other buildings which have been provided after 12th February 1919 for the purpose of—
  (i) Part III of the Housing (Scotland) Act 1925, or
  (ii) any enactment relating to the provision of housing accommodation for the working classes repealed by that Act, or
  (iii) Part V of the Housing (Scotland) Act 1950, or
  (iv) Part VII of the Act of 1966, or
  (v) Part I of this Act;
(b) all land for which after that date has been acquired or appropriated for the purposes of any of the enactments mentioned or referred to in paragraph (a) including—
  (i) all land which is deemed to have been acquired under Part III of the said Act of 1925 by virtue of section 15(4) of the Housing (Scotland) Act 1935, and
  (ii) any structures on such land which were made available to a local authority under section 1 of the Housing (Temporary Accommodation) Act 1944;
(c) all dwellings provided or improved by the local authority in accordance with improvement proposals approved by the Secretary of State under—
  (i) section 2 of the Housing (Scotland) Act 1949, or
  (ii) section 105 of the said Act of 1950, or
  (iii) section 13 of the Act of 1968,
  and all land acquired or appropriated by the authority for the purpose of carrying out such proposals;
(d) all houses in housing action areas within the meaning of Part II of the Housing (Scotland) Act 1974 or Part IV of this Act which have been purchased by the local authority under Part II of the said Act of 1974 or Part IV of this Act for the purpose of bringing them or another house up to the standard specified under section 16(3) or by virtue of section 17(3) of the Housing (Scotland) Act 1974 or section 90(3) or 91(3) of this Act;
(e) all buildings provided or converted for use as lodging houses (that is to say houses not occupied as separate dwellings) or hostels as defined in section 138(4) of the Act of 1966 and section 2(5) of this Act or as parts of lodging houses or hostels.

(2) Where a house is for the time being vested in a local authority by reason of the default of any person in carrying out the terms of any arrangements under which assistance in respect of the provision, reconstruction or improvement of the house has been given under any enactment relating to housing, the house shall be deemed for the purposes of sub-paragraph (1) to be a house which has been provided by the authority under Part VII of the Act of 1966 or Part I of this Act.

(3) The houses and other property to which a local authority's housing revenue account relates shall include any property brought within the account before 27th August 1972—
(a) with the consent of the Secretary of State given under section 60(1)(f) of the Act of 1968, or
(b) by virtue of subsection (2) of the said section (house vesting in local authority on default of another person).

PART II

OPERATION OF ACCOUNT

Credits

2.—(1) For each year a local authority shall carry to the credit of the housing revenue account amounts equal to—
(a) the income receivable by the local authority from standard rents;
(b) any income receivable by the local authority for that year in respect of service charges, supplementary charges, feuduties and any other charges in respect of houses and other property to which the account relates;
(c) the housing support grant payable to the local authority for that year;
(d) any income receivable by the local authority for that year in respect of all such buildings as are referred to in paragraph 1(1)(e);
(e) any payments received by the local authority from another local authority in pursuance of any overspill agreement, being payments such as are mentioned in paragraph 3(f) of this Schedule;
(f) any contributions received by the local authority under section 101(1) of the Housing

Act 1964 or section 235, in so far as amounts equal to the expenditure towards which those contributions are made fall to be debited to the account;
  (g) income, and receipts in the nature of income, being income or receipts arising for that year from the investment or other use of money carried to the account;
  (h) any other income of any description, except a contribution out of the general fund kept under section 93 of the Local Government (Scotland) Act 1973, receivable by the local authority for that year, being income relating to expenditure falling to be debited to the account for that year;
  (i) such other income of the local authority as the Secretary of State may direct.

(2) Subject to sub-paragraph (3), where any house or other property to which the account relates has been sold or otherwise disposed of, an amount equal to any income of the local authority arising from the investment or other use of capital money received by the authority in respect of the transaction shall be carried to the credit of the account.

(3) Sub-paragraph (2) shall not apply—
  (a) where the Secretary of State otherwise directs as respects the whole or any part of such income, or
  (b) as respects income from capital money carried to a capital fund under paragraph 23 of Schedule 3 to the Local Government (Scotland) Act 1975.

(4) An amount equal to any income of the local authority arising from an investment or other use of borrowed moneys in respect of which the authority are required under paragraph 3 below to debit loan charges to the account shall be carried to the credit of the account.

(5) For any year, the local authority may, with the consent of the Secretary of State, carry to the credit of the account, in addition to the amounts required by the foregoing provisions of this Schedule, such further amounts, if any, as they think fit.

Debits

3.—Subject to paragraph 4 of this Schedule, for each year a local authority shall debit to the housing revenue account amounts equal to—
  (a) the loan charges which the local authority are liable to pay for that year in respect of money borrowed by a local authority for the purpose of—
    (i) the provision by them after 12th February 1919 of housing accommodation under the enactments referred to in paragraph 1(1)(a),
    (ii) the provision or improvement by them of dwellings in accordance with improvement proposals approved by the Secretary of State under section 2 of the Housing (Scotland) Act 1949 or under section 105 of the Housing (Scotland) Act 1950 or under section 13 of the Act of 1968,
    (iii) meeting expenditure on the repair of houses and other property to which the account relates,
    (iv) the improvement of amenities of residential areas under section 251 on land to which the account relates,
    (v) the alteration, enlargement or improvement under section 2(3) of any house:
    Provided that a local authority may, with the approval of the Secretary of State, debit to the account any payments, of which the amount and period over which they are payable have been approved by him, to meet outstanding capital debt in respect of any house which, being a house to which the account related—
    (a) was demolished after 27th July 1972; or
    (b) was disposed of after 25th May 1978;
  (b) the taxes, feuduties, rents and other charges which the local authority are liable to pay for that year in respect of houses and other property to which the account relates;
  (c) the expenditure incurred by the local authority for that year in respect of the repair, maintenance, supervision and management of houses and other property to which the account relates, other than the expenditure incurred by them in the administration of a rent rebate scheme;
  (d) the expenditure incurred by the local authority for that year in respect of all such buildings as are referred to in paragraph 1(1)(e);
  (e) the arrears of rent which have been written off in that year as irrecoverable, and the income receivable from any houses to which the account relates during any period in that year when they were not let;
  (f) any payments made by the local authority to another local authority or a development corporation in pursuance of any overspill agreement, being payments towards expenditure which, if it had been incurred by the first-mentioned authority, would have been debited by them to their housing revenue account in pursuance of this paragraph;

(g) such other expenditure incurred by the local authority as the Secretary of State directs shall be debited to the housing revenue account.

4.—A local authority shall not debit to the housing revenue account amounts equal to—

(a) expenditure on the provision of anything under section 3 or 5 (which relate respectively to the powers of a local authority to provide shops, etc., and laundry facilities) or the supply of anything under section 4 (which relates to the power of a local authority to provide furniture, etc.), or

(b) any part of expenditure attributable to site works and services of a house or houses or other property to which the housing revenue account relates which exceeds the expenditure required for the provision of the house or houses or other property:

Provided that nothing in sub-paragraph (a) shall apply to expenditure on the provision of—

(i) anything referred to in paragraphs (a) and (b) of section 211(1) in respect of which the local authority are required to make a service charge;

(ii) any garage, car-port or other car-parking facilities provided by the local authority under the terms of the tenancy of a house,

and the exclusion from the housing revenue account of expenditure on the supply or provision of anything under section 4 or 5 shall not extend to such expenditure when incurred in relation to a hostel or a lodging-house.

Supplemental

5.—(1) Any requirement of this Schedule as respects any amount to be debited or credited to the account may be met by taking in the first instance an estimate of the amount, and by making adjustments in the account for a later year when the amount is more accurately known or is finally ascertained.

6.—A local authority may, with the consent of the Secretary of State, exclude from the housing revenue account any of the items of income or expenditure mentioned in the foregoing provisions of this Schedule, or may with such consent include any items of income or expenditure not mentioned in those foregoing provisions.

7.—Where it appears to the Secretary of State that amounts in respect of any items of income or expenditure other than those mentioned in the foregoing provisions of this Schedule ought properly to be credited or debited to a housing revenue account, or that amounts in respect of any of the items of income and expenditure mentioned in the foregoing provisions of this Schedule which ought properly to have been credited or debited to the account have not been so credited or debited, or that any amounts have been improperly credited or debited to the account, he may, after consultation with the local authority, give directions for the appropriate credits or debits to be made or for the rectification of the account, as the case may require.

8.—The Secretary of State may direct that items of income or expenditure, either generally or of a specific category, shall be included in or excluded from the account.

9.—(1) If at any time a credit balance is shown in the housing revenue account, the whole or part of it may be made available for any purpose for which the general fund of the local authority maintained under section 93 of the Local Government (Scotland) Act 1973 may lawfully be applied.

(2) If for any year a deficit is shown in the said account, the local authority shall carry to the credit of the account a rate fund contribution of an amount equal to the deficit.

10.—References in this Schedule to houses and other property to which the housing revenue account of a local authority relates shall be construed as references to houses, buildings, land and dwellings in respect of which the authority are required by section 203 and Part I of this Schedule to keep the account.

Section 207(3)   SCHEDULE 16

The Slum Clearance Revenue Account

Credits

1.—For each year a local authority shall carry to the credit of the slum clearance revenue account amounts equal to—

(a) the income from the rents, feuduties and other charges in respect of houses and other property to which the account relates;

(b) any slum clearance subsidy payable to the local authority for that year;

(c) any income from the investment or other use of capital obtained from the disposal of houses and other property to which the account relates;

(d) any expenses incurred by the local authority in the demolition of a building to which the account relates which they have recovered from the owner of the building;

(e) such other income of the local authority as the Secretary of State may direct.

2.—Where for any year a deficit is shown in the account, the local authority shall carry to the credit of the account in respect of that year an amount equal to the amount of the deficit.

Debits

3.—For each year a local authority shall debit to the slum clearance revenue accounts amounts equal to—

(a) the loan charges which the local authority are liable to pay for that year referable to the amount of expenditure incurred by the local authority which falls within section 207(2);

(b) the taxes, feuduties, rents and other charges which the local authority are liable to pay for that year in respect of houses and other property to which the account relates;

(c) the expenditure incurred by the local authority for that year in respect of the repair, maintenance, supervision and management of houses and other property to which the account relates;

(d) the expenditure incurred by the local authority for that year in respect of the purchase, demolition, and clearance of sites of houses and other property to which the account relates where that expenditure is not met from capital;

(e) the arrears of rent which have been written off in that year as irrecoverable and the income receivable from any houses to which the account relates during any period in that year when they were not let;

(f) such other expenditure incurred by the local authority as the Secretary of State directs.

Supplemental

4.—Any surplus shown in a slum clearance revenue account at the end of a year shall be credited to the general fund kept under section 93 of the Local Government (Scotland) Act 1973.

5.—A local authority may, with the consent of the Secretary of State, exclude from the slum clearance revenue account any of the items of income or expenditure mentioned in the foregoing provisions of this Schedule, or may with such consent include any items of income or expenditure not mentioned in those foregoing provisions.

6.—The Secretary of State may direct that items of income or expenditure-either generally or of a specific category, shall be included in or excluded from the slum clearance revenue account.

Section 214(8)   SCHEDULE 17

CONDITIONS RELATING TO HOUSE LOANS

1.—The provisions of this Schedule shall have effect with respect to an advance under section 214.

2.—The advance, together with interest thereon, shall be secured by a heritable security.

3.—The amount of the principal of the advance shall not exceed the value of the subjects disponed or assigned in security, or as the case may be, the value which it is estimated the subjects disponed or assigned in security will bear when the construction, conversion, alteration, enlargement, repair or improvement has been carried out.

4.—The heritable security shall provide for repayment of the principal—

(a) by instalments (of equal or unequal amounts) beginning either on the date of the advance or at a later date, or

(b) at the end of a fixed period (with or without a provision allowing the local authority to extend that period) or on the happening of a specified event before the end of that period.

5.—It shall also provide for the payment of instalments of interest throughout the period beginning on the date of the advance and ending when the whole of the principal is repaid.

6.—In the event of any of the conditions subject to which the advance is made not being complied with, the balance for the time being unpaid shall become repayable on demand by the local authority.

7.—That balance may in any event be repaid at any term of Whitsunday or Martinmas by the debtor after one month's written notice of intention to repay has been given to the authority.

8.—Where the advance is for any of the purposes specified in paragraphs (b) to (d) of section 214(1) it may be made by instalments from time to time as the works of construction, conversion, alteration, enlargement, repair or improvement progress.

9.—The advance shall not be made except after a valuation duly made on behalf of the local authority.

10.—No advance shall be made unless the estate or interest in the lands proposed to be disponed or assigned in security is either ownership or a lease of which a period of not less than 10 years in excess of the period fixed for the repayment of the advance remains unexpired on the date on which the security is granted.

11.—In this Schedule, any reference, in relation to an advance, to a heritable security shall include a reference to such heritable security as may be agreed between the parties making and receiving the advance.

Section 244(6), (7) and (11)   **SCHEDULE 18**

STANDARD AMENITIES

PART I

LIST OF AMENITIES AND MAXIMUM ELIGIBLE AMOUNTS

Description of amenity	*Maximum eligible Amount*
Fixed bath or shower	£340
Hot and cold water supply at a fixed bath or shower	£430
Wash-hand basin	£130
Hot and cold water supply at a wash-hand basin	£230
Sink	£340
Hot and cold water supply at a sink	£290
Water closet	£515

PART II

LIMIT ON AMOUNT OF APPROVED EXPENSES FOR STANDARD AMENITIES

1.—Subject to paragraph 3, the total amount of approved expense for the provision of standard amenities in respect of any one application shall not exceed the sum of the amounts allowable under the following provisions of this Part of this Schedule.

2.—Subject to paragraph 4, for each of the standard amenities provided there shall be allowed an amount of approved expense not exceeding the maximum eligible amount specified for an amenity of that description in the second column of Part I of this Schedule or the amount substituted therefor under the following provisions of this Part of this Schedule.

3.—Subject to the provisions of section 242, the maximum eligible amounts specified in the second column of Part I of this Schedule may be exceeded by such amount as the local authority approve if the local authority are satisfied in any particular case that an increased estimate for the works is justifiable.

4.—An amount shall not be allowed for more than one amenity of the same description; and no amount shall be allowed for an amenity of any description if at the time the works were begun the house was provided with an amenity of that description, except where the works involved interference with or replacement of that amenity and the local authority are satisfied that it would not have been reasonably practicable to avoid the interference or replacement.

Section 246(5)   SCHEDULE 19

CONSEQUENCES OF BREACH OF CONDITIONS OF IMPROVEMENT GRANT

1.—Subject to paragraphs 4 and 5, the local authority shall forthwith demand the repayment to them by the owner for the time being of the house of the whole amount of any sums paid by the authority by way of improvement grant in respect of the expenses incurred for the purpose of the execution of those works together with interest thereon for the period from the date of payment of the grant, or where the grant was paid in instalments, from the date of payment of the final settlement of the balance by the authority to the date of repayment to the authority.

2.—If the local authority are satisfied that the breach of any condition is capable of being remedied, they may, with the consent of the Secretary of State and subject to such conditions (if any) as he may approve, direct that the operation of section 246 shall in relation to the breach be suspended for such period as appears to them to be necessary for enabling the breach to be remedied and if the breach is remedied within that period may direct that the said provisions shall not have effect in relation to the breach.

3.—If the local authority are satisfied that the breach although not capable of being remedied was not due to the act, default or connivance of the owner for the time being of the house, they may, with the like consent and subject to such conditions as mentioned in paragraph 2, direct that the said provisions shall not have effect in relation to the breach.

4.—Upon the satisfaction of a liability of an owner of a house to make payment under paragraph 1 above to a local authority observance with respect to the house of the conditions specified in section 246 shall cease to be required.

5.—On the application of the local authority, the sheriff within whose jurisdiction is situated any house with respect to which the conditions specified in section 246 are for the time being required to be observed may, whether or not any other relief is claimed, grant an interdict restraining a breach or apprehended breach in relation to the house of any of those conditions.

6.—(1) In any case where in pursuance of paragraph 4, observance of any conditions specified in section 246 ceases to be required with respect to a house the local authority shall so state in the notice mentioned in sub-paragraph (2) or the record mentioned in sub-paragraph (3).

(2) Where the applicant for the grant was not a tenant-at-will, or was a tenant-at-will who, since applying, has acquired his landlord's interest in the tenancy the local authority shall cause to be recorded in the General Register of Sasines or registered in the Land Register, as the case may be, a notice in the prescribed form.

(3) Where that applicant was, and continues to be, a tenant-at-will, the local authority shall keep a written record of the fact.

(4) The cost of such recording in the Register of Sasines or such registration in the Land Register shall be repaid to the authority by the owner of the house.

7.—In the event of a breach of any of the conditions specified in section 246 at a time when they are required to be observed with respect to a house it shall be competent for the local authority to make a charging order in favour of themselves for the amount that becomes payable to them by virtue of this Schedule in consequence of such a breach, and the provisions of Schedule 9 shall, subject to any necessary modifications, apply to a charging order so made in like manner as they apply to a charging order made under that Schedule.

8.—In this Schedule, "interest" means compound interest calculated at such reasonable rate as the local authority may determine and with yearly rests.

Section 275   SCHEDULE 20

ASSISTANCE BY WAY OF REPURCHASE

PART I

THE AGREEMENT TO REPURCHASE

The interest to be acquired

1.—In this Schedule, "the interest to be acquired" means the interest of the person entitled to assistance by way of repurchase, so far as subsisting in—
   (a) the defective dwelling, and

(b) any garage, outhouse, garden, yard and pertinents belonging to or usually enjoyed with the dwelling or a part of it.

Request for notice of proposed terms of acquisition

2.—A person who is entitled to assistance by way of repurchase may, within the period of three months beginning with the service of the notice of determination, or that period as extended, request the purchasing authority in writing to notify him of the proposed terms and conditions for their acquisition of the interest to be acquired.

Authority's notice of proposed terms

3.—The purchasing authority shall, within the period of three months beginning with the making of a request under paragraph 2, serve on the person so entitled a notice in writing specifying the proposed terms and conditions including those that are reasonably necessary to enable the authority to receive a good and marketable title and stating their opinion as to the value of the interest to be acquired.

Unreasonable terms

4.—Where an offer to purchase is served on the person so entitled and he wishes to sell but he considers that a term or condition contained in the offer to purchase is unreasonable, he may request the authority to strike out or vary the term or condition by serving on the authority, within one month after service of the offer to purchase, a notice in writing setting out his request; and if the authority agree they shall accordingly serve an amended offer to purchase within one month of service of the said notice setting out the request.

Appeal

5.—A person so entitled who is aggrieved by the refusal of an authority to agree to strike out or vary a term or condition or by their failure timeously to serve an amended offer to purchase may within one month of the refusal or failure apply by way of summary application to the sheriff for determination of the matter; and the sheriff may, as he thinks fit, uphold the term or condition or strike it out or vary it and where his determination results in a variation of the terms or conditions of the offer to purchase he shall order the authority to serve on the person entitled an amended offer to purchase within one month thereafter.

Notice of acceptance

6.—The person so entitled may at any time within the period of six months beginning with—
    (a) the service of the offer to purchase by the authority; or
    (b) the service of an amended offer to purchase under paragraph 4; or
    (c) the date of the determination of the sheriff;
serve a notice of acceptance on the authority.

Extensions

7.—The authority shall, if there are reasonable grounds for doing so, by notice in writing served on the person so entitled, extend (or further extend) the period within which—
    (a) under paragraph 2, he may request them to notify him of the terms and conditions proposed for their acquisition of the interest to be acquired;
    (b) under paragraph 4, he may request them to strike out or vary the term or condition;
    (c) under paragraph 5, he may apply to the sheriff for determination of a matter; or
    (d) under paragraph 6, he may serve a notice of acceptance on them;
whether or not the period has expired.

Interest acquired to be treated as if acquired under Part I

8.—An interest acquired by a local authority under this Part of this Schedule shall be treated as acquired under section 9.

PART II

PRICE PAYABLE AND VALUATION

The price

9.—(1) The price payable for the acquisition of an interest in pursuance of this Part is 95 per cent. of the value of the interest at the relevant time.

(2) In this Schedule, "the relevant time" means the time at which the notice under paragraph 3 (authority's notice of proposed terms of acquisition) is served on the person entitled to assistance.

The value

10.—(1) For the purposes of this Schedule, the value of an interest at the relevant time is the amount which, at that time, would be realised by a disposal of the interest on the open market by a willing seller to a person other than the purchasing authority on the following assumptions—

    (a) that none of the defective dwellings to which the designation in question relates is affected by the qualifying defect;

    (b) that no liability has arisen under the provisions in section 72;

    (c) that no obligation to acquire the interest arises under this Part; and

    (d) that (subject to the preceding paragraphs) the seller is selling with and subject to the rights and burdens with and subject to which the disposal is to be made.

(2) Where the value of an interest falls to be considered at a time later than the relevant time and there has been since the relevant time a material change in the circumstances affecting the value of the interest, the value at the relevant time shall be determined on the further assumption that the change had occurred before the relevant time.

(3) In determining the value of an interest no account shall be taken of any right to the grant of a tenancy under section 282 (former owner-occupier) or section 283 (former statutory tenant).

Determination of value

11.—(1) Any question arising under this Schedule as to the value of an interest in a defective dwelling shall be determined by the district valuer in accordance with this paragraph.

(2) The person entitled to assistance or the purchasing authority may require that value to be determined or redetermined by notice in writing served on the district valuer—

    (a) within the period beginning with the service on the person entitled to assistance of an offer to purchase under paragraph 3 (authority's notice of proposed terms of acquisition) and ending with the conclusion of missives; or

    (b) after the end of that period but before the parties enter into an agreement for the acquisition of the interest of the person so entitled, if there is a material change in the circumstances affecting the value of the interest.

(3) A person serving notice on the district valuer under this paragraph shall serve notice in writing of that fact on the other party.

(4) Before making a determination in pursuance of this paragraph, the district valuer shall consider any representation made to him, within four weeks of the service of the notice under this paragraph, by the person entitled to assistance or the purchasing authority.

Certain grant conditions cease to have effect

12.—Where the interest to be acquired is or includes a house in relation to which a grant has been made under Part XIII—

    (a) observance with respect to the house of any of the conditions specified in section 246 (conditions to be observed with respect to a house in respect of which a grant has been made) shall cease to be required with effect from the time of disposal of the interest and paragraph 6 of Schedule 19 (requirements as to records when observance of conditions ceases to be required) shall apply as it applies in the case there mentioned; and

    (b) the owner for the time being of the house shall not be liable to make in relation to the grant any payment under Schedule 19 (consequences of breach of conditions) unless the liability to do so arises from a demand made before the time of disposal of the interest.

Section 294   SCHEDULE 21

DWELLINGS INCLUDED IN MORE THAN ONE DESIGNATION

Introductory

1.—This Schedule applies in relation to a defective dwelling where the building that the dwelling consists of or includes falls within two or more designations under section 257 (designation by Secretary of State) or 287 (designation under local scheme).

Cases in which later designation to be disregarded

2.—Where a person is already eligible for assistance in respect of a defective dwelling at a time when another designation comes into operation, the later designation shall be disregarded if—

(a) he would not be eligible for assistance in respect of the dwelling by virtue of that designation, or

(b) he is by virtue of an earlier designation entitled to assistance by way of repurchase in respect of the dwelling.

In other cases any applicable designation may be relied on

3.—Where a person is eligible for assistance in respect of a defective dwelling and there are two or more applicable designations, this Part has effect in relation to the dwelling as if—

(a) references to the designation were to any applicable designation;

(b) references to the provision by virtue of which it is a defective dwelling were to any provision under which an applicable designation was made;

(c) references to the qualifying defect were to any qualifying defect described in an applicable designation;

(d) references to the period within which persons may seek assistance under this Part were to any period specified for that purpose in any applicable designation; and

(e) the reference in section 271(1)(c) (amount of reinstatement grant) to the maximum amount permitted to be taken into account for the purposes of that section were to the aggregate of the maximum amounts for each applicable designation.

Procedure to be followed where later designation comes into operation

4.—(1) The following provisions of this Schedule apply where—

(a) notice has been given to a person under section 264 (determination of eligibility) stating that he is in the opinion of the local authority eligible for assistance in respect of a defective dwelling, and

(b) after the notice has been given another designation comes into operation designating a class within which the building that consists of or includes the dwelling falls.

5.—(1) The local authority shall, as soon as reasonably practicable, give him notice in writing stating whether in their opinion the new designation falls to be disregarded in accordance with paragraph 2.

(2) If in their opinion it is to be disregarded the notice shall state the reasons for their view.

6.—(1) This paragraph applies where it appears to the authority that the new designation does not fall to be disregarded.

(2) They shall forthwith give him notice in writing—

(a) stating the effect of the new designation and of paragraph 3 (new designation may be relied on) and sub-paragraph (3) below (entitlement to be redetermined), and

(b) informing him that he has the right to make a claim under section 265(2) (claim that assistance by way of reinstatement grant is inappropriate in his case).

(3) They shall as soon as reasonably practicable—

(a) make a further determination under section 265(1) (determination of form of assistance to which person is entitled), taking account of the new designation, and

(b) give a further notice of determination in place of the previous notice;

and where the determination is that he is entitled to assistance by way of repurchase, the notice shall state the effect of paragraph 7 (cases where reinstatement work already begun or contracted for).

7.—(1) This paragraph applies where a person entitled to assistance by way of reinstatement grant is given a further notice of entitlement under paragraph 6 stating that he is entitled to assistance by way of repurchase; and "the reinstatement work" means the work stated in the previous notice or in a notice under section 272 (change of work required).

(2) Where in such a case—

(a) he satisfies the authority that he has, before the further notice was received, entered into a contract for the provision of services or materials for any of the reinstatement work, or

(b) any such work has been carried out before the further notice was received, and has been carried out to the satisfaction of the appropriate authority, the previous notice (and any notice under section 272 (change of work required)) continues to have effect for the purposes of reinstatement grant in relation to the reinstatement work or, in a case within paragraph (b), such of that work as has been carried out as mentioned in that paragraph, and the authority shall pay reinstatement grant accordingly.

(3) Where in a case within sub-paragraph (2) the reinstatement work is not completed but part of the work is carried out to the satisfaction of the appropriate authority within the period stated in the notice in question—

(a) the amount of reinstatement grant payable in respect of that part of the work shall be an amount equal to the maximum instalment of grant payable under section 273(2) (instalments not to exceed appropriate percentage of cost of work completed), and

(b) section 274 (repayment of grant in event of failure to complete work) does not apply in relation to reinstatement grant paid in respect of that part of the work.

Section 339   SCHEDULE 22

TRANSITIONAL PROVISIONS AND SAVINGS

PART I

TRANSITIONAL PROVISIONS

General

1.—The re-enactment of provisions in, and the consequent repeal of those provisions by this Act, does not affect the continuity of those provisions.

2.—In so far as—

(a) any requirement, prohibition, determination, order or regulation made by virtue of an enactment repealed by this Act, or

(b) any direction or notice given by virtue of such an enactment, or

(c) any proceedings begun by virtue of such an enactment, or

(d) anything done or having effect as if done,

could, if a corresponding enactment in this Act were in force at the relevant time, have been made, given, begun or done by virtue of the corresponding enactment, it shall, if effective immediately before the corresponding enactment comes into force, continue to have effect thereafter as if made, given, begun or done by virtue of that corresponding enactment.

3.—Where any enactment passed before this Act, or any instrument or document refers either expressly or by implication to an enactment repealed by this Act the reference shall (subject to its context) be construed as or as including a reference to the corresponding provision of this Act.

4.—Where any period of time specified in any enactment repealed by this Act is current at the commencement of this Act, this Act has effect as if its corresponding provision had been in force when that period began to run.

5.—(1) The general rule is that the provisions of this Act apply, in accordance with the foregoing paragraphs, to matters arising before the commencement of this Act as to matters arising after that commencement.

(2) The general rule has effect subject to any express provision to the contrary, either in this Schedule or in connection with the substantive provision in question.

(3) The general rule does not mean that the provisions of this Act apply to cases to which the corresponding repealed provisions did not apply by virtue of transitional provision made in connection with the commencement of the repealed provisions (such transitional provisions, if not specifically reproduced, are saved by paragraph 8).

(4) The general rule does not apply so far as a provision of this Act gives effect to an amendment made in pursuance of a recommendation of the Scottish Law Commission.

Persons holding office

6.—Any person who at the commencement of this Act is holding office or acting or serving under or by virtue of any enactment repealed by this Act or by the Act of 1966 shall continue to hold his office or to act or serve as if he had been appointed under this Act.

Security of tenure of tenants of regional councils, etc.

7.—Notwithstanding the repeal by this Act of section 16(2) and (3)(b) of the Tenants' Rights, Etc. (Scotland) Act 1980, those provisions shall continue to have effect for the

26–214

purposes of paragraph 4 of the Housing (Scotland) Act 1986 (Consequential, Transitional and Supplementary Provisions) Order 1986 (application of transitional provisions relating to secure tenant's right to written lease to tenants of regional councils, police authorities and fire authorities).

Part II

Savings

General saving for old transitional provisions

8.—The repeal by this Act of a provision relating to the coming into force of a provision it reproduces does not affect the operation of that provision, in so far as it is not specifically reproduced but remains capable of having effect, in relation to the corresponding provision of this Act.

General saving for old savings

9.—(1) The repeal by this Act of an enactment previously repealed subject to savings does not affect the continued operation of those savings.

(2) The repeal by this Act of a saving made on the previous repeal of an enactment does not affect the operation of the saving in so far as it is not specifically reproduced but remains capable of having effect.

Transfers under section 14 of the Housing (Homeless Persons) Act 1977

10.—(1) The repeal by this Act of section 14 of the Housing (Homeless Persons) Act 1977 (transfers of property and staff) does not affect the operation of any order previously made under that section.

(2) The transfer of an employee in pursuance of such an order shall be treated—

(a) for the purposes of section 94 of the Employment Protection (Consolidation) Act 1978 (redundancy payments) as occurring on a change in the ownership of a business;

(b) for the purposes of Schedule 13 to that Act (continuity of employment) as occurring on the transfer of an undertaking.

Use of existing forms, etc.

11.—Any document made, served or issued on or after this Act comes into force which contains a reference to an enactment repealed by this Act shall be construed, except so far as a contrary intention appears, as referring or, as the context may require, including a reference to the corresponding provision of this Act.

Secure tenant: reimbursement of cost of work done before 3rd October 1980

12.—The repeal of section 24(1) of the Tenants' Rights, Etc. (Scotland) Act 1980 does not affect the operation of that section in relation to works carried out before 3rd October 1980.

Contributions under sections 106 and 121 of the Housing (Scotland) Act 1950 (c.34) and section 14 of the Housing (Scotland) Act 1962 (c.28)

13.—Contributions remain payable by the Secretary of State under sections 106 and 121 of the Housing (Scotland) Act 1950 and section 14 of the Housing (Scotland) Act 1962 (contributions payable annually for periods of between 20 and 60 years).

Section 339   SCHEDULE 23

Minor and Consequential Amendments

General

1.—Any reference in any previous enactment to "standard amenities" as set out in section 39 of the Housing (Financial Provisions) (Scotland) Act 1968 or in section 7 of the Housing

(Scotland) Act 1974 is a reference to the standard amenities for the purposes of Part XIII as provided for in section 244.

2.—Any reference in any previous enactment to "tolerable standard" as defined in section 2 of the Housing (Scotland) Act 1969 or in section 14 of the Housing (Scotland) Act 1974 is a reference to the tolerable standard as defined in section 86.

The Crofters Holdings (Scotland) Act 1886 (c.29)

3.—In the Schedule, in paragraph 1A, for the words "Part II of the Housing (Scotland) Act 1974" substitute the words "Part I of Schedule 8 to the Housing (Scotland) Act 1987".

The Sheriff Courts (Scotland) Act 1907 (c.51)

4.—In the Sheriff Courts (Scotland) Act 1907, after section 38 there shall be inserted the following section—

    "Notice of termination in respect of dwelling-houses
    38A.—Any notice of termination of tenancy or notice of removal given under section 37 or 38 above in respect of a dwelling-house, on or after 2nd December 1974, shall be in writing and shall contain such information as may be prescribed by virtue of section 112 of the Rent (Scotland) Act 1984, and Rule 112 of Schedule 1 to this Act shall no longer apply to any such notice under section 37 above."

The Crofters (Scotland) Act 1955 (c.21)

5.—In Schedule 5, in paragraph 1A, for the words "Part II of the Housing (Scotland) Act 1974" substitute the words "Part I of Schedule 8 to the Housing (Scotland) Act 1987".

The Clean Air Act 1956 (c.52)

6.—(1) In section 12(3) (adaptation of fireplaces in private dwellings), in paragraph (b), for the words "27" and "1969" substitute the words "111" and "1987" respectively.

(2) In section 31(7) (application of Public Health Act 1936 etc.), in paragraph (a), for the words "2, 20 to 22, 161, 168 to 171, 197" and "1966" substitute the words "121 to 123, 131, 312 to 315 and 330" and "1987" respectively and for the words "section 14 of the Housing (Repairs and Rents) (Scotland) Act 1954" substitute the words "section 336 of the Housing (Scotland) Act 1987".

(3) In Schedule 3, in Part III (application of Scottish enactments), for the heading "Housing (Scotland) Act 1950" and following words substitute the words—

"Housing (Scotland) Act 1987

    Section 109 shall have effect as if the reference to section 108(3) included a reference to section 12 of this Act.
    Section 319 (Penalty) shall have effect as if subsection (1) included a reference to this Act and as if sub-paragraphs (b) and (c) were omitted."

The Coal Mining (Subsidence) Act 1957 (c.59)

7.—(1) In section 1(4) (duty of Board in respect of subsidence damage), in paragraph (b), for the words "Part III of the Housing (Scotland) Act 1950" and "subsection (2) of section thirty-six of the said Act of 1950" substitute the words "Part IV and VI of the Housing (Scotland) Act 1987"; and "paragraph 12(2) of Schedule 8 to the said Act of 1987"; and the words "and clearance" shall cease to have effect.

(2) In the proviso to section 1(4), in sub-paragraph (ii), for the words "1950" substitute the words "1987".

(3) In the First Schedule, in paragraph 2(1)(a) for the words "Part VII" and "1966" substitute the words "Part I" and "1987" respectively.

(4) In the First Schedule, in paragraph 5(3), in the proviso, for the words "1966" substitute the words "1987".

(5) In the Second Schedule, in paragraph 2(1), after the words "1950" insert the words "or under section 114 or 119 of the Housing (Scotland) Act 1987".

The Building (Scotland) Act 1959 (c.24)

8.—In the Sixth Schedule, in paragraph 4(b)(ii), for the words "1950" substitute the words "1987".

The Pipe-lines Act 1962 (c.58)

9.—In section 30(2), for the words "181", "1966" and "Part III" substitute the words "127", "1987" and "Part VI" respectively.

The Land Compensation (Scotland) Act 1963 (c.51)

10.—(1) In section 15(7), for paragraph (d) substitute the following paragraph—
"(d) paragraph 4 of Schedule 1 to the Housing (Scotland) Act 1987.".
(2) For Schedule 2 (acquisition of houses as being unfit for human habitation), substitute the following Schedule—

"SCHEDULE 2

ACQUISITION OF HOUSES WHICH DO NOT MEET THE TOLERABLE STANDARD

Acquisitions to which this Schedule applies

1.—(1) This Schedule applies to a compulsory acquisition of a description mentioned in sub-paragraph (2) where the land in question comprises a house which, in the opinion of the appropriate local authority does not meet the tolerable standard.
(2) The compulsory acquisitions referred to are—
(a) an acquisition under Part VI of the Town and Country Planning (Scotland) Act 1972, or
(b) an acquisition under section 13 of the Housing and Town Development (Scotland) Act 1957, or
(c) an acquisition in pursuance of Part IX of the Town and Country Planning (Scotland) Act 1972, or
(d) an acquisition of land within the area designated by an order under section 1 of the New Towns (Scotland) Act 1968 as the site of a new town, or
(e) an acquisition by a development corporation or a local roads authority or the Secretary of State under the New Towns (Scotland) Act 1968 or under any enactment as applied by any provision of that Act, or
(f) an acquisition by means of an order under section 141 of the Local Government, Planning and Land Act 1980 vesting land in an urban development corporation; or
(g) an acquisition by such a corporation under section 142 of that Act.

Procedure

2.—(1) The local authority may make and submit to the Secretary of State an order, in such form as may be prescribed by regulations made under section 330 of the Housing (Scotland) Act 1987, declaring that the house does not meet the tolerable standard and if—
(a) that order is confirmed by the Secretary of State, either before or concurrently with the confirmation of a compulsory purchase order for the acquisition of the land, or
(b) in a case where the acquisition is in pursuance of a notice to treat deemed to have been served in consequence of the service of a notice under section 170 of the Town and Country Planning (Scotland) Act 1972 or the provisions of that section as applied by or under any other enactment or in consequence of the service of a notice under section 11 of the New Towns (Scotland) Act 1968 or under section 182 of the Town and Country Planning (Scotland) Act 1972, the order is made before the date on which the notice to treat is deemed to have been served and is subsequently confirmed by the Secretary of State,
section 305 and paragraph 12(2) and (3) of Schedule 8 to the Housing (Scotland) Act 1987 (which relate respectively to payments in respect of certain well-maintained houses under Part XV and to compensation for compulsory acquisition under Part IV of the Housing (Scotland) Act 1987) shall apply as if the house had been purchased under Part IV as not meeting the tolerable standard, and as if any reference in that section and paragraph to the local authority were a reference to the acquiring authority.
(2) Before submitting to the Secretary of State an order under this paragraph, the local authority by whom the order was made shall serve on every owner, and (so far as it is reasonably practicable to ascertain such persons) on the superior of, and the holder of every heritable security over, the land or any part thereof, a notice in such form as may be prescribed as mentioned in the last preceding sub-paragraph, stating the effect

of the order and that it is about to be submitted to the Secretary of State for confirmation, and specifying the time within which, and the manner in which, objection thereto can be made.

(3) If no objection is duly made by any of the persons on whom notices are required to be served, or if all objections so made are withdrawn, the Secretary of State may, if he thinks fit, confirm the order; but in any other case he shall, before confirming the order, consider any objection not withdrawn, and shall, if either the person by whom the objection was made or the local authority so desires, afford to that person and the authority an opportunity of appearing before and being heard by a person appointed by the Secretary of State for the purpose.

(4) Section 86 of the Housing (Scotland) Act 1987 shall have effect in determining for the purposes of this paragraph whether a house meets the tolerable standard as it has effect in so determining for the purposes of that Act.

(5) In this paragraph "appropriate local authority" means a local authority who, in relation to the area in which the land in question is situated, are a local authority for the purposes of the provisions of Part IV of the Housing (Scotland) Act 1987 relating to housing action areas; and "owner," in relation to any land, includes any person who under the Lands Clauses Acts would be enabled to sell and convey the land to the promoters of an undertaking and includes also a lessee under a lease the unexpired period of which exceeds three years.

Amount of compensation

3.—(1) Where in relation to a compulsory acquisition, section 120(2) to (4) or paragraph 12(2) and (3) of Schedule 8 to the Housing (Scotland) Act 1987 (which relate respectively to the compensation to be paid on the compulsory acquisition of closed houses, and of houses not meeting the tolerable standard) apply (whether by virtue of that Act or of an order under paragraph 2 of this Schedule) and—

(a) the relevant land consists of or includes the whole or part of a house (in this paragraph referred to as "the relevant house") and, on the date of making of the compulsory purchase order in pursuance of which the acquisition is effected, the person then entitled to the relevant interest was, in right of that interest, in occupation of the relevant house or part thereof as a private dwelling, and

(b) that person either continues, on the date of service of the notice to treat, to be entitled to the relevant interest, or, if he has died before that date, continued to be entitled to that interest immediately before his death,

the following provisions of this paragraph shall apply in relation to the acquisition; and in those provisions "the dwelling" means so much of the relevant house as the said person occupied as aforesaid.

(2) Subject to the next following sub-paragraph, the amount of the compensation payable in respect of the acquisition of the relevant interest shall not in any event be less than the gross annual value of the dwelling.

(3) Where a payment falls to be made under section 304 or 305 of the Housing (Scotland) Act 1987 to the person entitled to the relevant interest, and that payment is attributable to the relevant house, any reference in the last preceding sub-paragraph to the amount of the compensation payable in respect of the acquisition of the relevant interest shall be construed as a reference to the aggregate of that amount and of the amount of the payment.

(4) For the purposes of this paragraph the gross annual value of the dwelling shall be determined as follows—

(a) if the dwelling constitutes the whole of the relevant house, the gross annual value of the dwelling shall be taken to be the value which, on the date of service of the notice to treat, is shown in the valuation roll then in force as the gross annual value of that house for rating purposes;

(b) if the dwelling is only part of the relevant house, an apportionment shall be made of the gross annual value of the relevant house for rating purposes, as shown in the valuation roll in force on the date of service of the notice to treat, and the gross annual value of the dwelling shall be taken to be the amount which, on such an apportionment, is properly attributable to the dwelling.

(5) Any reference in this paragraph to the compensation payable in respect of the acquisition of the relevant interest shall be construed as excluding so much (if any) of that compensation as is attributable to disturbance or to severance or injurious affection.

(6) Nothing in this paragraph shall affect the amount which is to be taken for the purposes of section 20 of this Act (which relates to the consideration payable for the

discharge of land from feu-duty and incumbrances) as the amount of the compensation payable in respect of the acquisition of the relevant interest.

(7) In the application of this paragraph to any lands and heritages whose net annual value is ascertained under subsection (8) of section 6 of the Valuation and Rating (Scotland) Act 1956 (and for which there is therefore no gross annual value shown in the variation roll)—

(a) in sub-paragraph (2) above, for the word 'gross' there shall be substituted the words '1.25 times the net'; and

(b) in sub-paragraph (4) above, for the word 'gross', wherever it occurs, there shall be substituted the word 'net'.

Interpretation

4.—This Schedule shall be construed as one with Parts IV and XV of the Housing (Scotland) Act 1987.".

The Local Government (Scotland) Act 1966 (c.51)

11.—In section 46(1) (general interpretation), in the definition of "housing revenue account", for the words "23 of the Housing (Financial Provisions) (Scotland) Act 1972", substitute the words "203 of the Housing (Scotland) Act 1987".

The National Loans Act 1968 (c.13)

12.—In Schedule 4, for the words "78" and "1950" substitute the words "231" and "1987" respectively.

The New Towns (Scotland) Act 1968 (c.16)

13.—(1) In section 6, subsection (6) shall cease to have effect.

(2) After section 38A of the New Towns (Scotland) Act 1968 (as inserted by section 4(2) of the Statutory Corporations (Financial Provisions) Act 1974) there shall be inserted the following section—

"Disposal of surplus funds of development corporations

38B.—(1) Where it appears to the Secretary of State, after consultation with the Treasury and the development corporation, that a development corporation have a surplus, whether on capital or on revenue account, after making allowance by way of transfer to reserve or otherwise for their future requirements, the development corporation shall, if the Secretary of State after such consultation as aforesaid so directs, pay to the Secretary of State such sum not exceeding the amount of that surplus as may be specified in the direction; and any sum received by the Secretary of State under this section shall, subject to subsection (3) of this section, be paid into the Consolidated Fund.

(2) The whole or part of any payment made to the Secretary of State by a development corporation under subsection (1) above shall, if the Secretary of State with the approval of the Treasury so determines, be treated as made by way of repayment of such part of the principal of advances under section 37(1) of this Act, and as made in respect of the repayments due at such times, as may be so determined.

(3) Any sum treated under subsection (2) above as a repayment of a loan shall be paid by the Secretary of State into the National Loans Fund."

The Clean Air Act 1968 (c.62)

14.—In section 8(7), for the words "193 and 194" substitute the words "329", and for the words "1966" substitute the words "1987".

The Post Office Act 1969 (c.48)

15.—In Schedule 4—

(a) in paragraph 83(1), for "II of the Housing (Scotland) Act 1974" substitute "IV of the Housing (Scotland) Act 1987";

(b) in paragraph 83(2), for "section 33 of the Housing (Scotland) Act 1974", substitute "paragraph 9 of Schedule 8 to the Housing (Scotland) Act 1987";

(c) in paragraph 83(3), for "33(4) of the Housing (Scotland) Act 1974" substitute "paragraph 9(4) of Schedule 8 to the Housing (Scotland) Act 1987";

(d) in paragraph 88(3), for "208 of the Housing (Scotland) Act 1966" substitute "section 338 of the Housing (Scotland) Act 1987".

The Local Authority Social Services Act 1970 (c.42)

16.—In Schedule 1, at the end insert in column 1 the words "Housing (Scotland) Act 1987 (c.26) Section 38(b)" and in column 2 the words "Co-operation in relation to homeless persons and persons threatened with homelessness.".

The Chronically Sick and Disabled Persons Act 1970 (c.44)

17.—In section 3(2), for the words "VII", "1966" and "137" substitute the words "I", "1987" and "1" respectively.

The Town and Country Planning (Scotland) Act 1972 (c.52)

18.—In section 186, for "section 26 of the Housing (Scotland) Act 1974" substitute "paragraph 5 of Schedule 8 to the Housing (Scotland) Act 1987" and for "section 29(2) and (3) of the Housing (Scotland) Act 1974", substitute "paragraph 12(2) and (3) of Schedule 8 to the Housing (Scotland) Act 1987".

The Land Compensation (Scotland) Act 1973 (c.56)

19.—(1) In section 27(1)(f), for the words "15(2) of the Tenants' Rights, Etc. (Scotland) Act 1980" and "2" substitute the words "48(2) of the Housing (Scotland) Act 1987" and "3" respectively.

(2) In section 27(7)—

(a) in paragraph (a), for the words "II", "1966", "14A of the Housing (Scotland) Act 1974" substitute the words "VI", "1987", "88 of that Act" respectively;

(b) in paragraph (b), for the words "56" substitute the words "125"; and omit the words "of 1966";

(c) in paragraph (c), for the words "15(4)(i)" substitute the words "117(2)(a)"; and omit the words "of 1966";

(d) in paragraph (d), for the words "II of the Housing (Scotland) Act 1974" substitute the words "I of Schedule 8 to that Act".

(3) In section 29(7AA), for the words "14 of the Tenants' Rights, Etc. (Scotland) Act 1980" and "2" substitute the words "47 and 48(2) of the Housing (Scotland) Act 1987" and "3" respectively.

(4) In section 34(2), for the words from "section 20" to the end substitute the words "section 121 and paragraph 12 of Schedule 8 to the Housing (Scotland) Act 1987 and "owner occupier's supplement" means a payment under sections 308 to 311 of that Act.".

(5) In section 36—

(a) in subsection (4)(b), after the words "1968" insert the words "or section 214 of the Housing (Scotland) Act 1987";

(b) in subsection (7), for the words "VII" and "1966" substitute the words "I" and "1987" respectively.

(6) In section 38(6), for the words "1974" and "14" substitute the words "1987" and "86".

(7) In section 39—

(a) in subsections 1(b) and 2(a), (b), for the words "VII" and "1966" substitute the words "I" and "1987" respectively;

(b) in subsection (6), for the words "(Financial Provisions) (Scotland) Act 1972" substitute the words "(Scotland) Act 1987".

(8) In section 53(3), for the words "114", "1966" and "VII" substitute the words "11", "1987" and "I" respectively.

(9) In section 69(1)—

(a) in paragraph (a), for the words "15 or 17 of the Housing (Scotland) Act 1974 or under section 16 of that Act" and "18(4)(c)" substitute the words "86, 89 and 91 of the Housing (Scotland) Act 1987" and "92(4)(c)";

(b) in paragraph (b), for the words "18(4)(a)" substitute the words "92(4)(a)".

(10) In section 69(3), for the words "II" and "1974" substitute the words "IV" and "1987".

(11) In section 80—

(a) in the definition of "housing association" for the words "section 208(1) of the Housing (Scotland) Act 1966" substitute the words "the Housing Associations Act 1985";

(b) in the definition of "registered", for the words from "in the register" to the end substitute the words "under the Housing Associations Act 1985".

The Local Government (Scotland) Act 1973 (c.65)

20.—(1) In section 130—
(a) in subsection (1), for the words "Acts 1966 to 1973" substitute the words "Act 1987";
(b) in subsection (2), for the words "VII" and "1966" substitute the words "I" and "1987".

(2) In section 131, subsection (2) shall cease to have effect.

(3) In section 236(2)(d), for the words "Acts 1966 to 1973" substitute the words "Act 1987".

(4) In Schedule 9, paragraph 73 shall cease to have effect.

(5) In Schedule 12, paragraphs 1, 2, 5, 6 to 19 and 21 to 24 shall cease to have effect.

Consumer Credit Act 1974 (c.37)

21.—In section 16(1)(ff), for the words "2 of the 1978 Act or section 31 of the 1980 Act" substitute the words "223 or 229 of the Housing (Scotland) Act 1987".

Land Tenure Reform (Scotland) Act 1974 (c.38)

22.—In section 8(7), for the words "Tenants' Rights, Etc. (Scotland) Act 1980" substitute the words "Housing (Scotland) Act 1987".

Local Government (Scotland) Act 1975 (c.30)

23.—(1) In Schedule 3—
(a) paragraph 27 shall cease to have effect;
(b) in paragraph 31, in the definition of "security" the words from "a local bond" to "enactment or" shall cease to have effect.

The National Health Service (Scotland) Act 1978 (c.29)

24.—In section 100(1)—
(a) in paragraph (a), for the words "1966" substitute the words "1987";
(b) for paragraph (b) substitute the following paragraphs—
"(b) the Scottish Special Housing Association;
(c) a Housing Association or Housing Trust within the meaning of the Housing Associations Act 1985.";
(c) in paragraph (c), for the word "(c)" substitute the word "(d)".

The Local Government, Planning and Land Act 1980 (c.65)

25.—(1) In section 152(1)(c), for the words "1 of the Homes Insulation Act 1978" substitute the words "252 of the Housing (Scotland) Act 1987";

(2) In section 153(1)(a), for the words "Housing (Scotland) Acts 1966 to 1978 and the Tenants' Rights, Etc. (Scotland) Act 1980" substitute the words "Housing Associations Act 1985 and the Housing (Scotland) Act 1987";

(3) In section 156(4), for the words "Parts I, II and III of the Tenants' Rights, Etc. (Scotland) Act 1980" substitute the words "Part III of the Housing (Scotland) Act 1987".

The Matrimonial Homes (Family Protection) (Scotland) Act 1981 (c.59)

26.—In section 13(11), for the words "the Tenants' Rights, Etc. (Scotland) Act 1980" substitute the words "Part III of the Housing (Scotland) Act 1987".

The Local Government and Planning (Scotland) Act 1982 (c.43)

27.—In section 24(2), for the words "32(1)(b) of the Housing (Financial Provisions) (Scotland) Act 1972" substitute the words "211(1)(b) of the Housing (Scotland) Act 1987".

The Civic Government (Scotland) Act 1982 (c.45)

28.—(1) In section 87(5), for the words "Part II of the Housing (Scotland) Act 1969" and "24(1) of the Housing (Scotland) Act 1969" substitute the words "Part V of the Housing (Scotland) Act 1987" and "108 of that Act" respectively.

(2) In section 108(2), for the words "2 to the Housing (Scotland) Act 1969" substitute the words "9 to the Housing (Scotland) Act 1987".

The Rent (Scotland) Act 1984 (c.58)

29.—(1) In section 5(5), for the words "5 of the Housing Rents and Subsidies (Scotland) Act 1975" substitute the words "22 of the Housing (Scotland) Act 1987".

(2) In section 6(8), for the words "208(1) of the Housing (Scotland) Act 1966" substitute the words "338 of the Housing (Scotland) Act 1987".

(3) In section 59, for the words "Subsections (1), (2) and (4) of section 62 of the Housing (Scotland) Act 1969" substitute the words "Sections 212 and 213 of the Housing (Scotland) Act 1987"; and the words from "except that" to the end shall cease to have effect.

(4) In section 63(4)—
    (a) in paragraph (f), for the words "5 of the Housing Rents and Subsidies (Scotland) Act 1975" substitute the words "22 of the Housing (Scotland) Act 1987";
    (b) in paragraph (g), the words from "or any" to the end shall cease to have effect.

(5) In section 66(1), for the words "23 of the Housing (Financial Provisions) (Scotland) Act 1972" substitute the words "203 of the Housing (Scotland) Act 1987".

(6) In section 101(2) and (3), for the words "4 to the Tenants' Rights, Etc. (Scotland) Act 1980" substitute the words "5 to the Housing (Scotland) Act 1987".

(7) In section 106—
    (a) in subsection (1), after the words "1974" insert the words "or Part XIII of the Housing (Scotland) Act 1987";
    (b) in subsection (2), after the words "1974" insert the words "or section 241(2) of the Act of 1987".
    (c) in subsection (5), for the words "39(1) of the said Act of 1968" and "2 of the Housing (Scotland) Act 1969" substitute the words "86 of the Act of 1987" and "240 of that Act" respectively.

(8) In Schedule 2, Part IV—
    (a) in paragraph 4, for the words "89" and "1966" substitute the words "135" and "1987" respectively;
    (b) in paragraph 6, for the words "VII" and "1966" substitute the words "I" and "1987".

The Housing Act 1985 (c.68)

30.—(1) In section 76—
    (a) in subsection (1)(a), for the words "5(1) of the Housing (Homeless Persons) Act 1977" substitute the words "33 and 34 of the Housing (Scotland) Act 1987";
    (b) in subsection 2, for the words "9(1) of the Housing (Homeless Persons) Act 1977" substitute the words "38 of the Act of 1987".

(2) In section 187, in the definition of "long tenancy", paragraph (b) shall cease to have effect.

(3) In section 458, in the definition of "the corresponding Scottish provisions" for the words from "the Home" to the end substitute the words "sections 222 to 228 of the Housing (Scotland) Act 1987".

(4) In Schedule 4, in paragraph 7(2)—
    (a) in the definition of "housing association", for the words "paragraph (e) of section 10(2) of the Tenants' Rights, Etc. (Scotland) Act 1980" and "11" substitute the words "section 61(2)(a)(vi) of the Housing (Scotland) Act 1987" and "45" respectively;
    (b) in the definition of "housing co-operative", for the words "5 of the Housing Rents and Subsidies (Scotland) Act 1975" substitute the words "22 of the said Act of 1987".

The Housing Associations Act 1985 (c.69)

31.—(1) In section 8(1), for the words "Part I of the Tenants' Rights, Etc. (Scotland) Act 1980" substitute the words "Part III of the Housing (Scotland) Act 1987".

(2) In section 10(2)(b), for the words "paragraphs 2 to 7 of Schedule 1 to the Tenants' Rights, Etc. (Scotland) Act 1980" substitute the words "paragraphs 1 to 8 of Schedule 2 to the Housing (Scotland) Act 1987".

(3) In section 39, in the definition of "secure tenancy" for the words "10 of the Tenants' Rights, Etc. (Scotland) Act 1980" substitute the words "44 of the Housing (Scotland) Act 1987".

(4) In section 44(1)(b), for the words "1 of the Tenants' Rights, Etc. (Scotland) Act 1980" substitute the words "65 of the Housing (Scotland) Act 1987".

(5) In section 45—

    (a) in subsection (2)(b), for the words "(11)(e) of section 1 of the Tenants' Rights, Etc. (Scotland) Act 1980" substitute the words "(4)(d) and (e) of section 61 of the Housing (Scotland) Act 1987";

    (b) in subsection (5), for the words "6 of the Tenants' Rights, Etc. (Scotland) Act 1980" substitute the words "72 of the Housing (Scotland) Act 1987".

(6) In section 52(1)(f), for the words "6 of the Tenants' Rights, Etc. (Scotland) Act 1980" substitute the words "72 of the Housing (Scotland) Act 1987".

(7) In section 59, at the end add the following subsection—

"(5) Sections 6, 15, 320 and 329 of the Housing (Scotland) Act 1987 (general provisions with respect to housing functions of local authorities etc.) apply in relation to this section and section 61, as they apply in relation to the provisions of that Act."

(8) In section 69A(b), for the words "5 of the Housing Rents and Subsidies (Scotland) Act 1975" substitute the words "22 of the Housing (Scotland) Act 1987".

(9) In section 88(5), for the words "175(2) of the Housing (Scotland) Act 1966" substitute the words "23 of the Housing (Scotland) Act 1987".

Airports Act 1986 (c.31)

32.—In Schedule 2, paragraph 4, for the words "56" and "1966" substitute the words "125" and "1987".

Section 339   SCHEDULE 24

REPEALS

Chapter	Short title	Extent of repeal
4 & 5 Geo. 5 c.31.	The Housing Act 1914.	The whole Act.
14 Geo. 6 c.34.	The Housing (Scotland) Act 1950.	The whole Act.
2 & 3 Eliz. 2 c.50.	The Housing (Repairs and Rents) (Scotland) Act 1954.	The whole Act.
7 & 8 Eliz. 2 c.33.	The House Purchase and Housing Act 1959.	The whole Act.
10 & 11 Eliz. 2 c.28.	The Housing (Scotland) Act 1962.	The whole Act.
1964 c.56.	The Housing Act 1964.	Section 101.
1966 c.49.	The Housing (Scotland) Act 1966.	The whole Act.
1967 c.20.	The Housing (Financial Provisions, Etc.) (Scotland) Act 1967.	The whole Act.
1968 c.16.	The New Towns (Scotland) Act 1968.	Section 6(6).
1968 c.31.	The Housing (Financial Provisions) (Scotland) Act 1968.	The whole Act, except sections 20, 67 and 71.
1969 c.34.	The Housing (Scotland) Act 1969.	The whole Act.
1970 c.44.	The Chronically Sick and Disabled Persons Act 1970.	Section 3(1), (2).
1971 c.76.	The Housing Act 1971.	The whole Act.
1972 c.46.	The Housing (Financial Provisions) (Scotland) Act 1972.	The whole Act, except sections 69, 78 and 81 and in Schedule 9, paragraph 31.
1973 c.5.	The Housing (Amendment) Act 1973.	The whole Act.

Chapter	Short title	Extent of repeal
1973 c.65.	The Local Government (Scotland) Act 1973.	Section 131(2), in Schedule 9, paragraph 73, in Schedule 12 paragraphs 1, 2, 5, 6 to 19 and 21 to 24.
1974 c.44.	The Housing Act 1974.	The whole Act, except sections 11, 18(2)–(6), 129, 130 and 131, Schedule 3 Part III, and Schedule 13 paragraphs 42 to 46.
1974 c.45.	The Housing (Scotland) Act 1974.	The whole Act.
1975 c.21.	The Criminal Procedure (Scotland) Act 1975.	In Schedules 7C and 7D, the entries relating to the Housing (Scotland) Act 1966.
1975 c.28.	The Housing Rents and Subsidies (Scotland) Act 1975.	The whole Act, except paragraphs 9 and 10 of Schedule 3.
1975 c.30.	The Local Government (Scotland) Act 1975.	In Schedule 3, paragraph 27; in paragraph 31 in the definition of "security" the words from "a local bond" to "enactment or".
1977 c.48.	The Housing (Homeless Persons) Act 1977.	The whole Act.
1978 c.14.	The Housing (Financial Provisions) (Scotland) Act 1978.	The whole Act, except paragraphs 12 to 14 and 39 of Schedule 2.
1978 c.27.	The Home Purchase Assistance and Housing Corporation Guarantee Act 1978.	The whole Act.
1978 c.48.	The Homes Insulation Act 1978.	The whole Act.
1979 c.33.	The Land Registration (Scotland) Act 1979.	In Schedule 2, paragraphs 5 and 6.
1980 c.51.	The Housing Act 1980.	The whole Act.
1980 c.52.	The Tenants' Rights, Etc. (Scotland) Act 1980.	Parts I to III and Part V except section 74; Part VI except section 86; Schedules A1 and 1 to 4.
1980 c.61.	The Tenants' Rights, Etc. (Scotland) Amendment Act 1980.	The whole Act.
1981 c.23.	The Local Government (Miscellaneous Provisions) (Scotland) Act 1981.	Sections 21 to 23, 34 and 35; in Schedule 2, paragraphs 11, 15, 35 and 36; in Schedule 3, paragraphs 8, 9, 10, 29 to 31 and 40 to 46.
1981 c.72.	The Housing (Amendment) (Scotland) Act 1981.	The whole Act.
1982 c.43.	The Local Government and Planning (Scotland) Act 1982.	Sections 51 to 55; in Schedule 3 paragraphs 29 to 33 and 39 to 40.
1982 c.45.	The Civil Government (Scotland) Act 1982.	In Schedule 3, paragraph 4.
1984 c.12.	The Telecommunications Act 1984.	In Schedule 4, paragraph 45.
1984 c.18.	The Tenants' Rights, Etc. (Scotland) Amendment Act 1984.	The whole Act.
1984 c.31.	Rating and Valuation Amendment (Scotland) Act 1984.	Section 8.
1984 c.50.	The Housing Defects Act 1984.	The whole Act.

Chapter	Short title	Extent of repeal
1984 c.58.	The Rent (Scotland) Act 1984.	In section 5(2)(b) and in section 63(4)(g), the words "or any authorised society within the meaning of the Housing Act 1914"; in section 59, the words from "except that" to the end.
1985 c.68.	The Housing Act 1985.	In section 187, in the definition of "long tenancy", paragraph (b).
1985 c.71.	The Housing (Consequential Provisions) Act 1985.	In Schedule 2, paragraphs 10, 16, 17, 37, 39, 40, 42 and 45.
1986 c.65.	The Housing (Scotland) Act 1986.	Sections 1 to 12 and 18 and 21, Schedule 1, Schedule 2, paragraph 2.
1986 c.63.	The Housing and Planning Act 1986.	Section 3; in Schedule 5, paragraphs 14 and 17.
1986 c.53.	The Building Societies Act 1986.	In Schedule 18, paragraph 12.

TABLE OF DERIVATIONS

1. The following abbreviations are used in this Table:

Acts of Parliament

1897	=	The Public Health (Scotland) Act 1897 c.38.
1914	=	The Housing Act 1914 c.31.
1950	=	The Housing (Scotland) Act 1950 c.34.
1954	=	The Housing (Repairs and Rents) (Scotland) Act 1954 c.50.
1959	=	The House Purchase and Housing Act 1959 c.33.
1962	=	The Housing (Scotland) Act 1962 c.28.
1964	=	The Housing Act 1964 c.56.
1966	=	The Housing (Scotland) Act 1966 c.49.
1967	=	The The Housing (Financial Provisions, Etc.) (Scotland) Act 1967 c.20.
1968	=	The Housing (Financial Provisions) (Scotland) Act 1968 c.31.
1969	=	The Housing (Scotland) Act 1969 c.34.
1970	=	The Housing (Amendment) (Scotland) Act 1970 c.5.
1971 (c.28)	=	The Rent (Scotland) Act 1971 c.28.
1971 (c.58)	=	The Sheriff Courts (Scotland) Act 1971 c.58.
1971	=	The Housing Act 1971 c.76.
1972	=	The Housing (Financial Provisions) (Scotland) Act 1972 c.46.
1972 (c.52)	=	The Town and Country Planning (Scotland) Act 1972 c.52.
1973	=	The Housing (Amendment) Act 1973 c.5.
1973 (c.56)	=	The Land Compensation (Scotland) Act 1973 c.56.
1973 (c.65)	=	The Local Government (Scotland) Act 1973 c.65.
1974 (c.39)	=	The Consumer Credit Act 1974 c.39.
1974 (c.44)	=	The Housing Act 1974 c.44.
1974	=	The Housing (Scotland) Act 1974 c.45.
1975 (c.21)	=	The Criminal Procedure (Scotland) Act 1975 c.21.
1975	=	The Housing Rents and Subsidies (Scotland) Act 1975 c.28.
1977	=	The Housing (Homeless Persons) Act 1977 c.48.
1978	=	The Housing (Financial Provisions) (Scotland) Act 1978 c.14.
1978 (c.27)	=	The Home Purchase Assistance and Housing Corporation Guarantee Act 1978 c.27.
1978 (c.48)	=	The Homes Insulation Act 1978 c.48.
1980 (c.51)	=	The Housing Act 1980 c.51.
1980	=	The Tenants' Rights, Etc. (Scotland) Act 1980 c.52.
1980 (c.61)	=	The Tenants' Rights, Etc. (Scotland) Amendment Act 1980 c.61.
1981 (c.23)	=	The Local Government (Miscellaneous Provisions) (Scotland) Act 1981 c.23.
1981	=	The Housing (Amendment) (Scotland) Act 1981 c.72.
1982 (c.24)	=	The Social Security and Housing Benefits Act 1982 c.24.
1982	=	The Local Government and Planning (Scotland) Act 1982 c.43.
1982 (c.45)	=	The Civic Government (Scotland) Act 1982 c.45.
1982 (c.48)	=	The Criminal Justice Act 1982 c.48.
1984 (c.12)	=	The Telecommunications Act 1984 c.12.
1984 (c.18)	=	The Tenants' Rights, Etc. (Scotland) Amendment Act 1984 c.18.
1984 (c.31)	=	The Rating and Valuation Amendment (Scotland) Act 1984 c.31.
1984	=	The Housing Defects Act 1984 c.50.
1984 (c.58)	=	The Rent (Scotland) Act 1984 c.58.
1985 (c.69)	=	The Housing Associations Act 1985 c.69.
1985	=	The Housing (Consequential Provisions) Act 1985 c.71.
1986 (c.53)	=	The Building Societies Act 1986 c.53.
1986 (c.63)	=	The Housing and Planning Act 1986 c.63.
1986	=	The Housing (Scotland) Act 1986 c.65.

Subordinate Legislation

S.I. 1983/271	=	The Housing (Improvement of Amenities of Residential Areas) (Scotland) Order 1983.
S.I. 1983/492	=	The Housing (Standard Amenities Approved Expense) (Scotland) Order 1983.

S.I. 1983/493   =   The Housing (Improvement or Repair Grants) (Approved Expenses Maxima) (Scotland) Regulations 1983.
S.I. 1983/1804   =   The Housing (Payments for Well-maintained Houses) (Scotland) Order 1983.

2. The Table does not show the effect of Transfer of Functions Orders.
3. The letter R followed by a number indicates that the provision gives effect to the Recommendation bearing that number in the Scottish Law Commission's Report on the Consolidation of the Housing Acts for Scotland (Cmnd. 104).
4. The entry "drafting" indicates a provision of a mechanical or editorial nature affecting the arrangement of the consolidation; for instance a provision introducing a Schedule.

Provision	Derivations
1(1)	1966 s.137; 1974 s.50(1), Sch. 3 para. 9; 1974 s.27(3)
(2)	1966 s.137; 1969 s.69(2), Sch. 6 para. 18; 1974 s.50(1), Sch. 3 para. 9
(3)	1966 s.137; 1969 s.69(2), (3), Sch. 6 para. 18, Sch. 7, 5
(4)	1970 (c.44) ss.3(1), (2)
2(1)	1966 s.138
(2)	1966 s.138(1)
(3)	1966 s.138(2)
(4)	1966 s.138(3); 1978 s.16(1), Sch. 2 Pt. I para. 1
(5)	1966 s.138(4); 1978 s.16(1), Sch. 2 Pt. I para. 1
3(1)–(3)	1966 s.139(1)
(4)	1966 s.139(2)
4(1)	1966 s.140(1)
(2)	1966 s.140(2); 1974 (c.39) s.192 Sch. 4 Pt. I para. 27
5(1)	1966 s.141(1)
(2)	1966 s.141(2)
(3)	1966 s.141(3); 1976 (c.66) Sch. 8
6(1)	1966 s.177(1); 1980 Sch. 5; 1981 (c.23) s.40 Sch. 3 para. 10; R.1
(2)	1966 s.177(2); 1980 Sch. 5
7	1966 s.147
8	1966 s.148
9(1)	1966 s.142
(2)	1966 s.142 proviso
10(1)	1966 s.143(1); 1974 s.50(1), Sch. 3 para. 10, Sch. 5
(2)	1966 s.143(2)
(3)	1966 s.143(3)
(4)	1966 s.143(4)
11	1966 s.144
12(1)	1966 s.145(1); 1978 s.16(1), Sch. 2 Pt. I para. 2(a); 1980 ss.8(3)(a), 8(4)
(2)	1966 s.145(2)
(3)	1966 s.145(3)
(4)	1966 s.145(4)
(5)	1966 s.145(5); 1980 Sch. 5
(6)	1966 s.145(8)
(7)	1966 s.145(6); 1972 s.79(1), Sch. 9 para. 7; 1978 s.16(1), Sch. 2 Pt. I para. 2
(8)	1966 s.145(6A), 1973 (c.65) s.237(2); 1980 ss.8(3)(c), 8(4)
(9)	1966 s.145(7); 1980 s.76(b)
(10)	1966 s.145(7) proviso; 1980 s.76(b)
(11)	1945 s.145(9)
13	1966 s.146; 1972 s.79(1), Sch. 9 para. 8
14(1)	1980 s.8(1); 1986 Sch. 1 para. 9
(2)	1980 s.8(1), (2)
15(1)	1966 s.178; R.1
(2)	1966 s.178 proviso
16	1966 s.179
17(1)	1966 s.149(1); 1972 Sch. 11, Pt. V; R.2
(2)	1966 s.149(2)

Provision	Derivations
18	1966 s.150(1); R.2
19(1)	1980 s.26(1); 1986 Sch. 1 para. 13
(2)	1980 s.26(2); 1986 Sch. 1 para. 13
(3)	1980 s.26(3); 1986 Sch. 1 para. 13
(4)	1980 s.26(4)
20(1)	1966 s.151(1), (2); 1969 s.69(2), Sch. 6 para. 19; 1977 s.6(2)
(2)	1980 s.26A; 1986 Sch. 1 para. 13; R.2
21(1)	1980 s.27(1); 1981 Sch. 3 para. 45
(2)	1980 s.27(1A); 1986 s.8
(3)	1980 s.27(1B); 1986 s.8
(4)	1980 s.27(2); 1981 (c.23) Sch. 3 para. 45
(5)	1980 s.27(2A); 1981 (c.23) Sch. 3 para. 45
(6)	1980 s.27(3); 1981 (c.23) Sch. 3 para. 45
22(1)	1975 s.5(1)
(2)	1975 s.5(2); 1980 s.81(a)
(3)	1975 s.5(3); 1980 s.81(b)
(4)	1975 s.5(4); 1985 Sch. 2 para. 27
(5)	1975 s.5(5)
23(1)	1966 s.175(1); 1972 Sch. 9 para. 10
(2)	1966 s.175(2); 1974 (c.44) Sch. 13 para. 14; 1985 Sch. 2 para. 10(2)
(3)	1966 s.175(3); 1974 (c.44) Sch. 13 para. 14
(4)	1966 s.175(4)
(5)	1966 s.175(5)
(6)	1959 s.59A; 1974 s.50(1) Sch. 3 para. 32; 1978 s.16(2) Sch. 3
Part II	
24(1)	1977 s.1(1); 1985 Sch. 2 para. 37
(2)	1977 s.1(1)
(3)	1977 s.1(2); 1986 s.21(2)
(4)	1977 s.1(3)
25(1)	1977 s.2(1)(2)
(2)	1977 s.2(3)
(3)	1977 s.2(3), 19(1)
(4)	1977 s.2(4)
26	1977 s.17(1)–(4)
27(1)–(3)	1977 s.18(1)–(3)
(4)	1975 s.15
28(1)	1977 s.3(1), (2)
(2)	1977 s.3(2), (3)
29	1977 s.3(4)
30(1)–(4)	1977 s.8(1)–(4)
(5)	1977 s.8(8), (9); R.3
31(1)	1977 s.4(1)
(2)	1977 s.4(5)
(3)	1977 s.4(2), (3)
(4)	1977 s.4(2)
32(1)	1977 s.4(1)
(2)	1977 s.4(4)
(3)	1977 s.4(2)
(4)	1977 s.4(6)
(5)	1977 s.4(7); 1986 s.21(3)
33(1)	1977 s.5(1); 1985 Sch. 2 para. 37
(2)	1977 s.5(1)
(3)	1977 s.5(11)
(4)	1977 s.5(7), (8)
(5)	1977 s.5(9)
(6)	1977 s.5(10)
34(1)	1977 s.5(6)
(2)	1977 s.5(3), (4), (5)
(3)	1977 s.8(5)
(4)	1977 s.8(8), (9); R.3
35(1)	1977 s.6(1)
(2)	1977 s.10

Provision	Derivations
36(1)	1977 s.7(1), (2)
(2)	1977 s.7(1), (3)
(3)	1977 s.7(4), (5)
(4)	1977 s.7(6), (7)
(5)	1977 s.7(8), (9), (10)
(6)	1977 s.8(6), (7)
(7)	1977 s.8(10), (11)
(8)	1977 s.7(1), (3) drafting
37	1977 s.12
38	1977 s.9(1)
39(1)	1977 s.13(1)
(2)	1977 s.13(2), (3)
(3)	1977 s.13(4)
(4)	1977 s.13(7)
(5)	1977 s.13(5), (6)
40(1)	1977 s.11(1)
(2)	1977 s.11(2), (3)
(3)	1977 s.11(4)
(4)	1977 s.11(5); 1975 (c.21) s.289F, s.289G, 457A
41	1977 s.16
42	1977 s.18A; 1985 Sch. 2 para. 37
43	1977 s.19(1); 1985 Sch. 2 para. 37
Part III	
44(1)	1980 s.10(1), (2)
(2)	1980 s.10(3)
(3)	1980 s.10(4)(a)
(4)	1980 s.10(4)(b); 1984 (c.18) s.5; 1986 Sch. 1 para. 10
(5)	1980 s.10(5)
(6)	1980 s.10(6)
45	1980 s.11(1)–(5); 1985 Sch. 2 para. 45(4); R.4
46(1)	1980 s.12(1)
(2)	1980 s.12(2)
47(1)	1980 s.14(1)
(2)	1980 s.14(2); 1981 (c.23) Sch. 3 para. 43
(3)	1980 s.14(3)
(4)	1980 s.14(4)
48(1)	1980 s.15(1); 1981 Sch. 3 para. 44; 1986 Sch. 1 para. 12(a)
(2)	1980 s.15(2); 1986 Sch. 1 para. 12(b)
(3)	1980 s.15(3); 1986 Sch. 1 para. 12(c)
(4)	1980 s.15(4)
(5)	1980 s.15(5); 1984 s.6
49(1)	1980 s.18(1)
(2)	1980 s.18(2)
(3)	1980 s.18(3)
(4)	1980 s.18(4)
50(1)	1980 s.19(1)
(2)	1980 s.19(2)
(3)	1980 s.19(3)
(4)	1980 s.19(4)
51(1)	1980 s.20(1)
(2)	1980 s.20(2)
(3)	1980 s.20(3)
52(1)	1980 s.13(1)
(2)	1980 s.13(2); 1986 Sch. 1 para. 11
(3)	1980 s.13(3)
(4)	1980 s.13(4)
(5)	1980 s.13(5)
(6)	1980 s.13(6)
(7)	1980 s.13(7)
53(1)	1980 s.16(1)
(2)	1980 s.16(3)
(3)	1980 s.16(6)

Provision	Derivations
54(1)	1980 s.17(1)
(2)	1980 s.17(2); 1984 (c.58) s.117(1) Sch. 8
(3)	1980 s.17(3)
(4)	1980 s.17(4)
(5)	1980 s.17(5)
(6)	1980 s.17(6)
55(1)	1980 s.21(1)
(2)	1980 s.21(2)
(3)	1980 s.21(3)
(4)	1980 s.21(4); 1984 (c.58) s.117(1) Sch. 8
(5)	1980 s.21(6)
(6)	1980 s.21(7)
56	1980 s.22(1), (2)
57	1980 s.23(1)–(3)
58	1980 s.24(1)–(3)
59	1980 s.25
60	1980 s.17A(1)–(4); 1984 s.7
61(1)	1980 s.1(1); 1982 c.43 Sch. 4
(2)	1980 s.1(3), 10(2), (11), (12); 1986 s.1(2) Sch. 1, para. 1(h)(iii) and (iv)
(3)	1980 s.9A; 1984 s.20
(4)	1980 s.1(11); 1986 Sch. 1, para. 1(f)
(5)	1980 s.1(2)
(6)	1980 s.1(4); 1986 Sch. 1, para. 1(b)
(7)	1986 Sch. 1, para. 1(g)
(8)	1980 s.1(11B); 1986 Sch. 1, para. 1(g)
(9)	1980 s.1(11C); 1986 Sch. 1, para. 1(g)
(10)	1980 s.1(12); 1984 ss.1, 2; 1986 Sch. 1, para. 1(h)
(11)	1980 s.1(10); 1984 (c.18) s.2, 8; 1984 (c.36) Sch. 3, para. 47; 1986 Sch. 1, para. 1(e)
62(1)	1980 s.1(5); 1986 Sch. 1, para. 1(c)
(2)	1980 s.1(5), (6)
(3)	1980 ss.1(5), 9A; 1984 s.1; 1984 c.50, s.20; 1986 s.2(1)(a) to (c); Sch. 1, para. 1(c); 1986 (c.63) s.3
(4)	1980 s.1(5A); 1986 Sch. 1, para. 1(d); 1986 s.2(1)(d)
(5)	1980 s.1(5B); 1986 (c.63) s.3
(6)	1980 s.1(5C); 1986 (c.63) s.3
(7)	1980 s.1(7); 1986 s.3
(8)	1980 s.1(7A); 1986 s.3
(9)	1980 s.1(8); 1986 s.3(2)
(10)	1980 s.1(9)
(11)	1986 s.3(4)
(12)	1986 s.3(4)
(13)	1986 s.3(5)
63(1)	1980 s.2(1)
(2)	1980 s.2(2); 1984 (c.18) s.4(2), 8(1)
64(1)	1980 s.4(1); 1982 s.53(2)(a)
(2)	1980 s.4(2)
(3)	1980 s.4(3); 1982 s.53(2)(b), Sch. 4
(4)	1980 s.4(4); 1980 (c.61) s.2(a)
(5)	1980 s.4(5)
(6)	1980 s.4(6)
(7)	1980 s.4(7); 1986 Sch. 1 para. 5(a)
(8)	1980 s.4(7A); 1986 Sch. 1 para. 5(b)
(9)	1980 s.4(8); 1980 (c.61) s.2(a)
65(1)	1980 s.2(3)
(2)	1980 s.2(4)
(3)	1980 s.2(5)
66(1)	1980 s.2(6); 1982 Sch. 3 para. 39; 1986 Sch. 1 para. 4
(2)	1980 s.2(7)
67(1)	1980 s.2(8), (11); 1981 (c.23) Sch. 3 para. 40; 1982 Sch. 3 para. 39; 1984 s.3, 4(2)

Provision	Derivations
67(2)	1980 s.2(9)
(3)	1980 s.2(11)
68	1980 s.3(1)–(4)
69(1)	1980 s.3A(1), (7); 1980 c.61 s.1(2)
(2)–(6)	1980 s.3A(2)–(6)
70	1980 s.3B(1)–(2); 1984 (c.18) s.4
71(1)	1980 s.7(2); 1982 s.55; Sch. 3 para. 40
(2)	1980 s.7(3); 1982 s.55(1)(b)
(3)	1980 s.7(4)
72(1)–(3)	1980 s.6(1)–(3); 1986 Sch. 1 para. 7
(4)	1981 Sch. 3 para. 42
(5)	1980 s.6(5); 1982 s.54
(6)	1980 s.6(5); 1986 Sch. 1 para. 7(c)
(7)	1980 s.6; 1986 Sch. 1 para. 7(d)
73	1980 s.6A; 1986 Sch. 1 para. (8)
74	1980 s.7(1)
75	1980 s.1(1A); 1982 s.53(1); 1986 Sch. 1 para. 1(a)
76	1980 s.1B; 1986 Sch. 1 para. 3
77(1)	1980 s.1A; 1981 (c.23) s.35(1)
(2)	1980 s.1A(2); 1981 (c.23) s.35(2); 1986 Sch. 1 para. 2
(3)	1980 s.1A(3); 1981 (c.23) s.35(3)
(4)	1980 s.1A(4); 1981 (c.23) s.35(4)
(5)	1980 s.1A(5); 1981 (c.23) s.35(5)
(6)	1980 s.1A(6); 1981 (c.23) s.35(6)
(7)	1980 s.1A(7); 1981 (c.23) s.35(7)
78	1980 s.4A; 1986 s.4
79	1980 s.9B; 1986 s.5
80	1980 s.25A; 1986 s.7
81	1980 s.9C; 1986 s.6
82	1980 s.82; 1980 (c.61) s.2(f); 1982 Sch. 3 para. 39(b); 1986 Sch. 1 para. 16
83	1980 s.82A; 1986 Sch. 1 para. 17
84	1980 s.83
Part IV	
85	1974 s.13(1)–(3)
86	1974 s.14(1)–(3)
87(1)	1966 s.180(1), (2); 1969 Sch. 6 para. 23; 1973 (c.65) Sch. 27 Part I para. 2
(2)	1966 s.180(5)
(3)	1966 s.180(6)
88(1)	1974 s.14A(1); 1978 s.10
(2)	1974 s.14A(1A); 1980 s.71
(3)	1974 s.14A(3); 1978 s.10
(4)	1974 s.14A(4); 1978 s.10
(5)	1974 s.14A(5); 1978 s.10
(6)	1974 s.14A(6); 1978 s.10
(7)	1974 s.14A(7); 1978 s.10
(8)	1974 s.14A(8); 1978 s.10
89(1)	1974 s.15(1)
(2)	1974 s.15(2); 1978 Sch. 2 para. 22
(3)	1974 s.15(3); 1978 Sch. 2 para. 22
90(1)	1974 s.16(1)
(2)	1974 s.16(2)
(3)	1974 s.16(3)
(4)	1974 s.16(4); 1978 Sch. 2 para. 23
91(1)	1974 s.17(1)
(2)	1974 s.17(2)
(3)	1974 s.17(3)
(4)	1974 s.17(4); 1978 Sch. 2 para. 24(a)
(5)	1974 s.17(5); 1978 Sch. 2 para. 24(b)
92	1974 s.18(1)–(4)
93	1974 (c.44) s.116A; 1975 Sch. 3 para. 16

Provision	Derivations
94	1974 s.19(1)–(7)
95(1)	1974 ss.20, 21
(2)	1974 ss.22, 23, 26, 28, 31–34, 36A
(3)	1974 s.29
(4)	1974 s.25; 1966 s.80, 87
96	1974 s.27(1)–(3)
97(1)	1974 s.35(1)
(2)	1974 s.35(2)
(3)	1974 s.35(3)
(4)	1974 s.35(4); 1975 (c.21) s.289E, 289G; 1982 (c.48) s.54
(5)	1974 s.35(5)
(6)	1974 s.35(6)
(7)	1974 s.35(7)
98	1974 s.36
99	1974 s.37(1)–(3)
100	1974 s.38(1), (2)
101	1974 s.39(1), (2)
102	1974 s.40; 1984 (c.58) Sch. 8 Pt. II
103	1974 s.41
104	1974 s.42
105(1)	1974 s.43(1); 1978 Sch. 2 para. 43
(2)	1974 s.43(2)
(3)	1974 s.43(3)
106	1974 s.44(1); 1978 Sch. 2 para. 26
107	1974 s.44A; 1978 Sch. 2 para. 27
Part V	
108(1)	1969 s.24(1)
(2)	1969 s.24(1); 1978 Sch. 2 para. 6(a) and (b)
(3)	1969 s.24(2); 1978 Sch. 2 para. 6(c)
(4)	1969 s.24(2)
(5)	1969 s.24(2)
(6)	1969 s.24(3)
(7)	1969 s.24(4)
(8)	1969 s.24(6); 1978 Sch. 2 para. 6(d)
109(1)	1969 s.25(1)
(2)	1969 s.25(1A); 1978 Sch. 2 para. 7
(3)	1969 s.25(2)
(4)	1969 s.25(3); 1973 (c.65) s.121; 1981 (c.23) Sch. 2 para. 15
(5)	1969 s.25(4)
110(1)	1969 s.26(1)
(2)	1969 s.26(1)
(3)	1969 s.26(2)
(4)	1969 s.26(3)
111(1)	1969 s.27(1)
(2)	1969 s.27(2)
112	1969 s.28
113	1969 ss.6–11
Part VI	
114(1)–(2)	1966 s.15(1); 1969 Sch. 6 para. 4(a); 1973 (c.65) Sch. 27 para. 2(1)
(3)	1966 s.17(1), (2); 1969 Sch. 6 para. 5
(4)	1966 s.17(2); 1969 Sch. 6 para. 5; 1980 s.84 Sch. 5
(5)	1966 s.17(3); 1980 s.84 Sch. 5
115	1966 s.15(2); 1969 Sch. 6 para. 4(b) and (c); 1973 (c.65) Sch. 27 Pt. I, para. 2(1)
116	1966 s.15(3); 1969 Sch. 6 para. 4(d)
117(1)–(3)	1966 s.15(4); 1969 Sch. 6 para. 4(d)
(4)	1966 s.15(5)
(5)	1966 s.15(6)
118(1)	1966 s.15(7)
(2)	1966 s.15(8)
119(1)	1966 s.18(1); 1969 Sch. 6 para. 6(a); 1972 (c.52) Sch. 21 Pt. II
(2)	1966 s.18(2); 1969 Sch. 6 para. 6(b); 1972 (c.52) Sch. 21 Pt. II

Provision	Derivations
119(3)	1966 s.18(3)
120(1)	1966 s.19(1); 1969 Sch. 6 para. 7(a)
(2)	1966 s.19(1A); 1969 Sch. 6 para. 7(b)
(3)	1966 s.19(2); 1969 Sch. 6 para. 7(c)
(4)	1966 s.19(3); 1969 Sch. 6 para. 7(d)
(5)	1966 s.19(4); 1969 Sch. 6 para. 7(d)
(6)	1966 s.19(6); 1969 Sch. 6 para. 7(e); 1974 Sch. 3 para. 5
121(1)–(2)	1966 s.20(1); 1969 Sch. 6 para. 8(a), Sch. 7
(3)	1966 s.20(2); 1969 Sch. 7
(4)	1966 s.20(3)
(5)	1966 s.20(4); 1969 Sch. 6 para. 8(b)
(6)	1966 s.20(5); 1969 Sch. 6 para. 8(c)
(7)	1966 s.20(6); 1969 Sch. 6 para. 8(c)
(8)	1966 s.20(8)
(9)	1966 s.20(9)
122(1)–(2)	1966 s.21; 1974 Sch. 3 para. 6; 1975 (c.21) s.289E; 1982 (c.48) s.54
123	1966 s.22(1)–(3)
124(1)	1966 s.23(1)
(2)	1966 s.23(2)
(3)	1966 s.23(3)
(4)	1966 s.23(4); 1974 Sch. 3 para. 7
125(1)	1966 s.56(1)
(2)	1966 s.56(2)
(3)	1966 s.56(3)
(4)	1966 s.56(4)
(5)	1966 s.56(5); 1975 (c.21) s.289G; 1982 (c.48) s.54
(6)	1966 s.56(6)
(7)	1966 s.56(7)
126(1)	1966 s.57(1)
(2)	1966 s.57(1)
(3)–(4)	1966 s.57(1)
(5)	1966 s.57(2)
(6)	1966 s.57(3)
127(1)	1966 s.181(1)
(2)–(3)	1966 s.181(2)
(4)–(5)	1966 s.181(3)
(6)	1966 s.181(4); 1975 (c.21) s.289E; 1982 (c.48) s.54
128	1966 s.182; 1969 Sch. 6 para. 24
129(1)	1966 s.26(1); 57(4); 1969 Sch. 7
(2)	1966 s.26(1)
(3)	1966 s.26(4)
130	1966 s.27; 1969 Sch. 7
131(1)–(2)	1966 s.30; 1969 Sch. 6 para. 12
(3)	1966 s.30(2); 1969 Sch. 7
132(1)	1966 s.31(1)
(2)	1966 s.31(2); 1969 Sch. 7
133	1966 s.33(1), (2)
134	1984 (c.12) Sch. 4 para. 45; 1986 (c.44) Sch. 7 para. 2(7)
Part VII	
135	1966 s.89(1); drafting
136(1)	1966 s.89(1)(a)
(2)	1966 ss.89(1)(a), 99
137(1)	1966 s.89(1)(b)
(2)	1966 ss.89(2), 99
(3)	1966 Sch. 5
(4)	1966 s.94(4)
(5)	1966 s.198
(6)	1966 s.94(5)
138(1)	1966 s.91(1)
(2)	1966 s.91(1)
(3)	1966 s.91(1); 1980 Sch. 5
(4)	1966 s.91(1)

Provision	Derivations
138(5)	1966 s.91(1)
(6)	1966 s.91(2); 1980 Sch. 5
(7)	1966 s.91(3)
139(1)	1966 s.90(1)
(2)	1966 ss.90(2), (3), 92(5), and 93(3)
(3)	1966 s.90(1); 1975 (c.21) s.289C, G; 1982 (c.48) s.54
140(1)	1966 s.90(2)
(2)	1966 s.90(2)(b)
141	1966 s.90(3)
142(1)	1966 s.92(1)
(2)	1966 s.92(1)
(3)	1966 s.92(2)
(4)	1966 s.92(3)
(5)	1966 s.92(3)
(6)	1966 s.92(4)
143(1)	1966 s.93(1)
(2)	1966 s.93(1), (2)
144(1)	1966 s.94(1)
(2)	1966 s.94(1); 1975 (c.21) s.289C, G; 1982 (c.48) s.54
(3)	1966 s.94(3)
145	1966 s.95(1)
146(1)	1966 s.88(1)
(2)	1966 s.88(1)
(3)	1966 s.88(1), (3)
(4)	1966 s.88(1)
(5)	1966 s.88(1)
(6)	1966 s.88(2)
147(1)	1966 s.96(2)
(2)	1966 s.96(2); 1975 (c.21) s.289C, G; 1982 (c.48) s.54
148(1)	1966 s.94(2)
(2)	1966 s.94(2)
149	1966 s.97
150	1966 s.96(1)
151	1966 s.99
Part VIII	
152(1)	1966 s.100(1)
(2)	1966 s.100(2)
(3)	1966 s.100(2); 1966 s.100(3)
(4)	1966 s.100(4)
(5)	1966 s.100(5)
153	1966 s.101(1)–(4); 1969 (c.19) s.10(1)
154	1966 s.101(4)
155(1)	1966 s.102(1)
(2)	1966 s.102(2); 1975 (c.21) s.289C, G; 1982 (c.48) s.54
156(1)	1966 s.103(1)
(2)	1966 s.103(2)
(3)	1966 s.103(3)
(4)	1966 s.103(4); 1975 (c.21) s.289C, G; 1982 (c.48) s.54
(5)	1966 s.103(5)
(6)	1966 s.103(5)
157(1)	1966 s.104(1)
(2)	1966 s.104(2)
(3)	1966 ss.104(3)
(4)	1966 s.104(3)
(5)	1966 s.104(6)
158(1)	1966 s.104(4)
(2)	1966 s.104(5)
(3)	1966 s.104(5)
(4)	1966 s.104(6)
159(1)	1966 s.104(7)
(2)	1966 s.104(7)
160(1)	1966 s.105(1)

Provision	Derivations
160(2)	1966 s.105(2)
(3)–(4)	1966 s.105(3)
(5)	1966 s.105(4)
161(1)	1966 s.106(1)
(2)	1966 s.106(2)
(3)	1966 s.106(1), (3)
(4)	1966 s.106(3)
(5)–(6)	1966 s.106(5) and (1)
(7)	1966 s.106(4)
(8)	1966 s.106(6)
162(1)	1966 s.107(1)
(2)	1966 s.107(1); 1982 s.52(2)
(3)	1966 s.107(2); 1973 (c.65) Sch. 12 para. 8
(4)	1966 s.107(3)
(5)	1966 s.107(4)
(6)	1966 s.107(5)
163(1)	1966 s.108(1)
(2)	1966 s.108(1)
(3)	1966 s.108(2)
(4)	1966 s.108(3)
(5)	1966 s.108(4)
164(1)	1966 s.109(1)
(2)	1966 s.109(1)
(3)	1966 s.109(2)
(4)	drafting, 1966 s.109(3)–(6)
165(1)	1966 s.110(1), (1A); 1975 (c.21) s.289C, G; 1982 (c.48) s.54
(2)	1966 s.110(1)
(3)	1966 s.110(2)
(4)	1966 s.110(3)
(5)	1966 s.110(4)
166(1)	1966 s.111(1)
(2)	1966 s.111(2)
(3)	1966 s.111(3)
(4)	1966 s.111(4); 1980 s.65(1)(e); S.I. 1980/1387
(5)	1966 s.111(5); 1980 s.65(1)(e); 1975 (c.21) s.289C, G; 1982 (c.48) s.54
167(1)	1966 s.112(1)
(2)	1966 s.112(2)
168	1966 s.112(5); 1980 s.65(1)(f); 1975 (c.21) s.289C, G; 1982 (c.48) s.54
169(1)	1966 s.112(3)
(2)	1966 s.112(3)
170	1966 s.112(4)
171(1)	1966 s.113(1)
(2)	1966 s.113(1), proviso (i)
(3)	1966 s.113(1), proviso (ii)
(4)	1966 s.113(2)
(5)	1966 s.113(3)
172(1)	1966 s.114(1)
(2)	1966 s.114(2)
(3)	1966 s.114(3)
(4)	1966 s.114(4); 1969 s.5; Sch. 6 para. 15; R.5
173	1966 s.115
174	1966 s.116
175	1966 s.117
176(1)–(2)	1966 s.192(2)
(3)	1966 s.192(3)
177	1966 s.119
178	1966 s.120(1)–(6)
179(1)	1966 s.121(1)
(2)	1966 s.121(2)
(3)	1966 s.121(3)

Provision	Derivations
179(4)	1966 s.121(4)
(5)	1966 s.121(5)
180(1)	1966 s.122(1)
(2)	1966 s.122(2)
(3)	1966 s.122(3)
(4)	1966 s.122(4); 1971 (c.28) Sch. 18 Pt. II; 1984 (c.58) Sch. 8 Pt. II
(5)	1966 s.122(5)
(6)	1966 s.122(6)
(7)	1966 s.122(7)
181(1)	1966 s.123(1)
(2)	1966 s.123(2)
(3)	1966 s.123(3); 1971 (c.28) Sch. 18 Pt. II; 1984 c.58 Sch. 8 Pt. II
(4)	1966 s.123(4)
(5)	1966 s.123(5)
(6)	1966 s.123(6)
182(1)	1966 s.124(1)
(2)	1966 s.124(2)
(3)	1966 s.124(3)
(4)	1966 s.124(4)
(5)	1966 s.124(5)
183(1)	1966 s.125(1)
(2)	1966 s.125(2)
(3)	1966 s.125(3)
(4)	1966 s.125(4)
(5)	1966 s.125(5)
(6)	1966 s.125(6); 1981 (c.23) s.40 Sch. 3 para. 8
184(1)	1966 s.126(1)
(2)	Drafting
(3)	1966 s.126(6)
185(1)	1966 s.128(1)
(2)	1966 s.128(2)
(3)	1966 s.128(3)
186(1)	1966 s.129(1)
(2)	1966 s.129(2)
(3)	1966 s.129(3)
(4)	1966 s.129(4)
(5)	1966 s.129(5)
(6)	1966 s.129(6)
187(1)	1966 s.130(1)
(2)	1966 s.130(2)
(3)	Drafting
188(1)	1966 s.133(1)
(2)	1966 s.133(2)
(3)	1966 s.133(3)
(4)	1966 s.133(4)
(5)	1966 s.133(10)
189	Drafting
190	1966 s.136(1)–(4)
Part IX	
191(1)	1978 s.1(1)
(2)	1978 s.1(2); 1981 (c.23) s.21(1)(a)(ii), (2)
(3)	1978 s.1(3)
(4)	1978 s.1(4)
(5)	1978 s.1(4A); 1981 (c.23) s.21(1)(b)
(6)	1978 s.1(4B); 1981 (c.23) s.21(1)(b)
(7)	1978 s.1(5)
(9)	1978 s.1(6)
(10)	1978 s.1(7); 1981 (c.23) s.21(1)(c)
192(1)	1978 s.2(1); 1981 (c.23) s.22
(2)	1978 s.2(1)
(3)	1978 s.2(2); 1981 (c.23) s.22
(4)	1978 s.2(3); 1981 (c.23) s.22

Provision	Derivations
192(5)	1978 s.2(4)
(6)	1978 s.2(5)
(7)	1978 s.2(7)
193	1978 s.3
194(1)	1978 s.4(1); 1986 s.18(1)
(2)	1978 s.4(2), (4); 1986 s.18(1)
(3)	1978 s.4(3)
195(1)–(5)	1978 s.4A(1)–(5); 1986 s.18(2)
196(1)	1968 s.25(1)
(1)(c)	1970 (c.5) s.1
(1)(f)	1978 Sch. 2 Pt. I para. 4
(1)(g)	1978 Sch. 2 Pt. I para. 4
(1)(g)(i)	1981 s.1(1)
(1)(g)(ii)	1968 s.25(1); 1970 (c.5) s.1; 1978 Sch. 2 para. 4; 1976 (c.11) s.1(1); 1981 s.1(1)
(2)	1968 s.25(2)
(3)	1968 s.25(3)
(4)	1985 (c.69) Sch. 2 para. 16(3)
(5)	1985 (c.69) Sch. 2 para. 16(3)
(6)	1968 s.25(5)
(7)	1968 s.25(6); 1972 Sch. 9 para. 16
197	1978 s.5; 1985 Sch. 2 para. 39(2)
198(1)	1978 s.6(1)
(2)	1978 s.6(2)
199	drafting; 1978 s.7; 1968 s.59; 1985 Sch. 2 para. 39(3)
200(1)	1972 s.7(2)
(2)	1972 s.7(4)
(3)	1972 s.7(5)
201(1)	1972 s.13(1)
(2)	1972 s.13(2)
(3)	1972 s.13(3)
(4)	1968 s.57(1)
(5)	1968 s.58(1)
202(1)	1968 s.58(1); 1972 s.73(a)
(2)	1968 s.58(1), (3)(aa)
(3)	1968 s.58(1)
(4)	1968 s.58(2)
(5)	1968 s.58(3); 1969 Sch. 6 para. 40; 1974 Sch. 3 para. 21; 1972 s.73(a); 1975 Sch. 3 para. 2
(6)	1968 s.58(4)
(7)	1968 s.58(5); 1972 Sch. 9 para. 20(a)(i)
Part X	
203(1)	1972 s.23(1); 1974 Sch. 3 para. 42; 1978 s.11(1)(a)
(2)	1972 s.23(4)
(3)	1972 s.23(5)
(4)	1972 s.23(3); 1978 s.11(1)(b)
(5)	1972 s.23(7)
(6)	1978 s.11(3)
(7)	1978 s.11(4); Interpretation Act 1978 s.14
204	1972 s.23A; 1984 (c.31) s.8
205	1972 s.24
206	1972 s.25
207	1972 s.26
208	1972 s.74
209	1972 s.75
Part XI	
210	1975 s.1(2)–(4)
211	1972 s.32(1), (2), (3)
212(1)	1969 s.62(1); 1975 Sch. 3 para. 3(1); R.2
(2)–(3)	1969 s.62(1), (3)
(4)	1969 s.62(5), (6); 1973 (c.65) Sch. 12 para. 22(a), (b); 1975 Sch. 3 para. 3(2)

Provision	Derivations
212(5)	1969 s.62(8); 1980 s.17(7)(c)
213	1969 s. 62(2), (3); 1975 (c.28) Sch. 3 para. 3(1)
Part XII	
214(1)–(2)	1968 s.49(1); 1974 s.45(2); 1980 ss.29, 84 Sch. 5
(3)	1968 s.49(1A); 1980 s.29
(4)	1968 s.49(2A); 1974 s.45(3)
(5)	1968 s.49(4)
(6)	1968 s.49(5); 1974 s.45(5)
(7)	1968 s.49(5); 1978 Sch. 2 Pt. 1 para. 5
(8)	drafting
215	1968 s.49(2); 1969 Sch. 6 para. 39
216(1)–(9)	1980 s.5(1)–(9); 1981 Sch. 3 para. 41; 1986 Sch. 1 para. 6
217(1)	1974 s.24(1)
(2)	1974 s.24(2)
(3)	1974 s.24(3)
(4)	1974 s.24(4)
(5)	1974 s.24(5)
(6)	1974 s.24(6); 1980 s.29(2)
(7)	1974 s.24(7)
(8)	1974 s.24(8)
(9)	1974 s.24(9)
218	1969 s.24A; 1978 s.9
219(1)	1980 s.30(1)
(2)	1980 s.30(2)
(3)	1980 s.30(3)
(4)	1980 s.30(4)
(5)	1980 s.30(5); 1986 Sch. 3
(6)	1980 s.30(6)
(7)	1980 s.30(7)
(8)	1980 s.30(10)
220	1980 s.30(8); 1986 Sch. 1 para. 15(b)
221	1980 s.30(9)
222(1)	1978 (c.27) s.1(1)
(2)	1978 (c.27) s.1(2)
(3)	1978 (c.27) s.1(2)
223(1)	1978 (c.27) s.1(4)
(2)	1978 (c.27) s.1(3), (5)
(3)	1978 (c.27) s.1(3)
(4)	1978 (c.27) s.1(5)
(5)	1978 (c.27) s.1(6)
(6)	1978 (c.27) s.2(7)
224(1)	1978 (c.27) Sch. 1 Pt. I; 1986 (c.53) Sch. 18
(2)	1978 (c.27) s.2(1)
(3)	1978 (c.27) s.2(7)
225(1)	1978 (c.27) Sch. 1 Pt. II
(2)	1978 (c.27) s.2(1)
(3)	1978 (c.27) s.2(7)
226(1)	1978 (c.27) s.2(2)
(2)	1978 (c.27) s.2(3)
(3)	1978 (c.27) s.2(4)
227(1)	1978 (c.27) ss.3(1), (3), (4), 4(2); 1986 (c.53) Sch. 18 para. 18
(2)	1978 s.2(5); 1985 (c.71) Sch. 2 para. 40(2)
228(1)–(3)	1984 s.28(1)–(3)
229(1)	1980 s.31(1); 1986 s.9
(2)	1980 s.31(2)
(3)	1980 s.31(3)
(4)	1980 s.31(4)
(5)	1980 s.31(5)
(6)	1980 s.31(5A); 1986 s.9
(7)	1980 s.31(5B); 1986 s.9
230(1)	1980 s.30(11)
(2)	1980 s.30(12)

Provision	Derivations
231	1968 s.52
232	1980 s.74
233(1)	1968 s.51(1)
(2)	1968 s.51(2)
(3)	1968 s.51(4)
234(1)–(3)	1972 s.71(1)–(3); R.2
(4)	1972 s.71; 1973 (c.56) s.34(7)
(5)	1966 s.160(3)
(6)	1966 s.160(4)
235	1964 s.101; 1966 s.212(5); 1973 (c.65) Sch. 12 para. 5
Part XIII	
236(1)	1974 s.1(1)
(2)	1974 s.1(3); 1978 Sch. 2 para. 16(a)
(3)	1974 s.1(4); 1978 Sch. 2 para. 16(b)
(4)	1974 s.1(3A); 1982 Sch. 3 para. 29
237	1974 s.2(2)
238	1974 s.2(1), 3(1)
239	1974 s.2(4)
240(1)	1974 s.2(3)(a); 1980 s.66(1); 1974 s.2(3)(b); 1980 s.66(1)
(2)	1974 s.3(2)(a); 1978 Sch. 2 Pt. I para. 17; 1974 s.3(2)(b); 1978 Sch. 2 Pt. I para. 17; 1974 s.3(2); 1978 Sch. 2 para. 17; 1980 s.67
(3)	1974 s.3(3), (5); 1980 s.67
(4)	1974 s.3(3A); 1980 s.67
(5)	1974 s.3(3B); 1980 s.67
(6)	1974 s.3(4); 1978 Sch. 2 Pt. I para. 17
241	1974 s.4; 1980 s.66(4)(a)
242(1)	1974 s.5(1); S.I. 1983/493
(2)	1974 s.5(2)
(3)	1974 s.5(3); 1980 s.68; S.I. 1983/493
(4)	1974 s.5(4)
(5)	1974 s.5(5); 1978 Sch. 2 para. 18(b); 1982 s.51
(6)	1974 s.5(6)
(7)	1974 s.48(3), 49(3); 1978 Sch. 2 para. 28; R.6(1)
(8)	1974 s.48(3), 49(3); 1978 Sch. 2 para. 28; R.6(1)
(9)	1974 s.48(3)
(10)	1974 s.5(1A), (3A)
243(1)	1974 s.6(1); Sch. 2 para. 40; 1982 Sch. 3
(2)	1974 s.6(2)
(3)	1974 s.6(3); 1981 Sch. 2 para. 35
244(1)	
(2)	1974 s.7(1A); Sch. 2 para. 19
(3)	1974 s.7(1AA); 1982 s.51
(4)	1974 s.7(1B); 1980 s.69
(5)	1974 s.7(2)
(6)	1974 s.7(3)
(7)	1974 s.7(4)
(8)	1974 s.7(5)
(9)	1974 s.7(6)
(10)	1974 s.7(7); 1980 s.66(2)
(11)	drafting
(12)	1974 s.48(3), s.49(3); 1978 Sch. 2 para. 28
(13)	1974 s.48(3)
(14)	1974 s.48(3), s.49(3)
245	1974 s.8(1); 1980 s.66(4)(c)
246(1)	1974 s.9(1)
(2)	1974 s.9(2)
(3)	1974 s.9(6); 1981 Sch. 3 para. 29
(4)	1974 s.9(7)
(5)	1974 s.9(8)
(6)	1974 s.9(9); 1978 Sch. 2 para. 20; 1979 (c.33) Sch. 2 para. 5; 1980 s.66(4)(d)(ii)
247	1974 s.10

Provision	Derivations
248(1)	1974 s.10A(1); 1978 s.8
(2)	1974 s.10A(2); 1980 s.70; 1981 Sch. 3 para. 30
(3)	1974 s.10A; 1980 s.66(4)(e); 1982 Sch. 3
(4)	1974 s.10A(4); S.I. 1983/493
(5)	1974 s.10A(5); 1982 Sch. 3 para. 31
(6)	1974 s.10A(6); 1982 (c.45) Sch. 3 para. 4
(7)–(9)	1974 s.49(3); 1978 Sch. 2 para. 28
(10)	1974 s.48(3)
249	1974 s.10B; 1982 (c.43) s.52; R.6(2)
250(1)–(4)	1974 s.11(1)–(4); 1978 Sch. 2 para. 41(a)
(5)	1974 s.2(3A); 1974 s.11(5); 1980 s.66(1)
(6)	1974 s.11(6); 1978 Sch. 2 para. 21(a), (b)
(7)	1974 s.11(7); 1980 Sch. 2 para. 41(b)
251(1)	1969 s.58(1); 1974 s.44(2)
(2)	1969 s.58(2)
252	1978 (c.48) s.1
253	1978 (c.48) s.1
254	1974 s.12; 1982 Sch. 3 para. 32
255(1)	1969 s.59(1); 1974 Sch. 3 para. 31(a)
(2)	1978 Sch. 3
(3)	1969 s.59(1A); 1974 Sch. 3 para. 31(b)
(4)	1969 s.59(2); 1974 Sch. 3 para. 31(c)
(5)	1969 s.59(3); 1980 s.32
(6)	1969 s.59(4); S.I. 1983/271
(7)	1969 s.59(5); S.I. 1983/271
(8)	1969 s.59(5A); 1974 (c.85) Sch. 3 para. 31(d); S.I. 1983/271
(9)	1969 s.59(6); 1974 Sch. 3 para. 31(e)
(10)	1969 s.59(7)
256	1968 s.53; 1974 Sch. 3 para. 20
Part XIV	
257(1)	1984 s.1(1)
(2)	1984 s.1(2)
(3)	1984 s.1(3)
(4)	1984 s.1(7)
(5)	1984 s.1(5)
(6)	1984 s.1(6)
258(1)	1984 s.1(4), (5)
(4)	1984 s.1(4), (5)
259(1)	1984 s.2(1)
(2)	1984 s.2(7)
(3)	1984 s.2(2)
(4)	1984 s.2(3)
260	1984 s.2(5)
261	1984 s.2(6), (8), 27(7)
262	1984 s.3(1)
263(1)	1984 s.3(8)
(2)	1984 s.3(9)
(3)	1984 s.3(9)
264(1)	1984 s.4(1)
(2)	1984 s.4(1)(a)
(3)	1984 s.4(1)(b)
265(1)	1984 s.3(2)
(2)	1984 s.3(3), (5)
(3)	1984 s.3(3)
266(1)	1984 s.3(4), (11)
(2)	1984 s.3(6)
(3)	1984 s.3(6)
(4)	1984 s.3(6)
267(1)	1984 s.3(7)
(2)	1984 s.4(6)
268(1)	1984 s.4(2)
(2)	1984 s.4(2)

Provision	Derivations
268(3)	1984 s.4(3)
(4)	1984 s.4(4)
(5)	1984 s.4(5)
269(1)	1984 s.5(1)
(2)	1984 s.5(2)
270(1)	1984 s.5(3)
(2)	1984 s.5(4)
(3)	1984 s.5(5)
(4)	1984 s.5(3)
271(1)	1984 Sch. 1 para. 1(1)
(2)	1984 Sch. 1 para. 1(2)
(3)	1984 Sch. 1 para. 1(3)
(4)	1984 Sch. 1 para. 2(1)
(5)	1984 Sch. 1 para. 2(2)
(6)	1984 s.24(1)(5)
272	1984 Sch. 1 para. 3
273(1)	1984 Sch. 1 para. 4(1)
(2)	1984 Sch. 1 para. 4(2)
(3)	1984 Sch. 1 para. 4(3)
274(1)	1984 Sch. 1 para. 5(1), (2)
(2)	1984 Sch. 1 para. 5(2)
275	1984 s.7; drafting
276(1)	1984 s.26(2)
(2)	1984 s.26(3), (4)
(3)	1984 s.26(5), (6)
(4)	1984 s.24(1)
277(1)	1984 s.9(1), (12)
(2)	1984 s.9(2)
(3)	1984 s.9(3)
(4)	1984 s.9(4)
278(1)	1984 s.8(1)
(2)	1984 s.8(2)
(3)	1984 s.8(3)(a)
(4)	1984 s.8(3)(b)
(5)	1984 s.8(3)(c)
(6)	1984 s.8(9)
279(1)	1984 s.8(4), 9(6)
(2)	1984 s.8(5), 9(7)
(3)	1984 s.8(6), 9(8)
(4)	1984 s.8(8), 9(10)
(5)	1984 s.8(7), 9(9)
280(1)	1984 s.11(1)
(2)	1984 s.11(2)
281(1)	1984 ss.9(5), 10(1), (10), 26(7), (8)
(2)	1984 s.10(10), (11)
282(1)	1984 ss.9(5), 10(1), (3), 26(7), (8)(a)
(2)	1984 ss.9(5), 10(3)
(3)	1984 ss.10(3), 26(7), (8)(b)
(4)	1984 ss.10(5), 26(8)(d)
283(1)	1984 ss.9(5), 10(1), (4), (11), 26(7)(b)
(2)	1984 s.10(5)
(3)	1984 s.10(9)
284(1)	1984 ss.10(1), (6), 26(8)(e), Sch. 3 paras. 1, 2
(2)	1984 s.10(6) Sch. 3 para. 3
285(1)	1984 ss.9(5)(b), 9(12)(d), 10(7), (12)(d), 26(8)(c), (f)
(2)	1984 s.10(8)
(3)	1984 s.10(8)
286	1984 s.10(1)(b), (2), Sch. 3 para. 1
287(1)	1984 s.12(1), (5)
(2)	1984 s.12(2)
(3)	1984 s.12(3)
(4)	1984 s.12(4)

Provision	Derivations
287(5)	1984 s.12(9)
(6)	1984 s.12(8)
288(1)	1984 s.12(5)
(2)	1984 s.12(5)
(3)	1984 s.12(5)
289(1)	1984 s.12(6)(a)
(2)	1984 s.12(6)(b)
(3)	1984 s.12(7)
290(1)	1984 s.14(1)
(2)	1984 s.14(1)
(3)	1984 s.14(2)
291(1)	1984 s.14(3)
(2)	1984 s.14(4), (8)
(3)	1984 s.14(5), (8)
(4)	1984 s.14(6)
(5)	1984 s.14(7)
292(1)	1984 s.16(1)
(2)	1984 s.16(2)
293(1)	1984 s.3(10)
(2)	1984 ss.8(10)(a), 9(11)
294	Drafting
295	1984 s.23
296(1)	1984 s.19(1)
(2)	1984 s.19(2)
(3)	1984 s.19(3)
(4)	1984 s.19(5)
(5)	1984 s.19(6)
(6)	1984 s.19(7), (8)
297(1)	1984 s.19(3)
(2)	1984 s.19(4), 24(1)
(3)	1984 s.19(3), (4)(c)
298(1)	1984 s.15(1)
(2)	1984 s.15(2)
299	1984 s.18
300(1)	1984 Sch. 4 para. 1
(2)	1984 Sch. 4 paras. 2(1)(a)(3)
(3)	1984 Sch. 4 para. 3(1)(a)(3)
(4)	1984 Sch. 4 para. 2(1)(b), 3(1)(b)
(5)	1984 Sch. 4 para. 2(2), 3(2)
(6)	1984 s.24(1)
301	1984 s.27(4)
302(1)	1984 s.27(2)
(2)	1984 s.27(2)
(3)	1984 s.27(3)
303	Drafting
Part XV	
304(1)	1966 s.25(1); 1969 Sch. 6 para. 11, Sch. 7; 1974 Sch. 3 para. 8
(2)	1966 s.25(2)
(3)	1966 s.25(3)
305(1)	1974 s.30(1); 1978 Sch. 2 para. 25(a)
(2)	1974 s.30(2)
(3)	1974 s.30(3); 1978 Sch. 2 para. 25(b)
(4)	1974 s.30(4); 1978 Sch. 2 para. 25(b)
306(1)	1969 s.21(1); 1974 Sch. 3 para. 30
(2)	1969 s.21(2); S.I. 1983/1804
(3)	1969 s.21(5)
(4)	1969 s.21(3)
(5)	1969 s.21(4); 1974 Sch. 3 para. 30
(6)	1969 s.21(5)
307	1969 s.23 R.7
308(1)	1969 s.18(1); 1974 Sch. 3 para. 26; 1978 Sch. 2 para. 30
(2)	1969 s.18(2)

Provision	Derivations
308(3)	1969 s.18(3)
309(1)	1967 s.18(1); 1969 Sch. 6 para. 32; 1974 Sch. 3 para. 15; 1978 Sch. 2 para. 30
(2)	1967 s.18(2); 1969 Sch. 6 para. 32
(3)	1967 s.18(3)
(4)	1967 s.18(5)
(5)	1967 s.18(6)
310	1969 s.19; 1974 Sch. 3 para. 27; 1978 Sch. 2 para. 31
311(1)	1969 s.20(1); 1974 Sch. 3 para. 28; 1978 Sch. 2 para. 32
(2)	1969 s.20(2); 1974 Sch. 3 para. 29
(3)	1969 s.20(3)
312	1966 s.161
Part XVI	
313(1)	1966 s.169(1)
(2)	1966 s.169(2)
(3)	1966 s.169(3)
(4)	1966 s.169(3)
(5)	1966 s.169(2); 1969 Sch. 6 para. 22
314	1966 s.170
315(1)	1966 s.171(1)
(2)	1966 s.171(1) proviso
(3)	1966 s.171(2)
(4)	1966 s.171(3)
(5)	1966 s.171(4)
(6)	1966 s.171(5)
316	1966 s.172; 1973 (c.65) s.237(2)
317(1)	1966 s.183; 1968 s.66; 1969 s.66; 1974 s.49(1)
(2)	1966 s.183(2)
(3)	1966 s.183(3)
318	1966 s.184; 1982 (c.48) s.54 Sch. 6 para. 22
319(1)	1966 ss.169(2), 185(1); 1969 Sch. 6 para. 26, Sch. 7
(2)	1966 s.185(2); 1980 s.65(1)(g); 1982 (c.48) s.54 Sch. 6 para. 23
320	1966 s.186; 1969 (c.19) s.10(1); 1982 (c.48) s.54
321(1)	1966 s.118(1); R.8
(2)	R.8
(3)	1966 s.118(2)
(4)	1966 s.118(2) proviso
322	1966 s.187
323	1966 s.188
324	1966 s.190(2)–(5); 1969 Sch. 6 para. 27; 1971 (c.58) s.35
325(1)	1966 s.192(4); 1969 Sch. 6 para. 28(1); 1974 Sch. 3 para. 13
(2)	1966 s.192(5); 1982 (c.48) s.54
326(1)	1966 s.192(6); 1969 Sch. 6 para. 28(b); 1974 Sch. 3 para. 13
(2)	1966 s.192(7); 1969 Sch. 6 para. 28(c); 1974 Sch. 3 para. 13
327	1974 (c.44) s.121
328	1974 (c.44) s.122
329(1)	1966 s.193(1)
(2)	1966 s.194(1)
(3)	1966 s.194(2)
(4)	1966 s.194(3)
(5)	1966 s.194(4)
(6)	1966 s.196(3)
330	1966 s.197; R.1
331	1966 s.198; 1974 s.48(4)
332	1966 s.199; R.1
333	1966 s.200; R.1
334	1966 s.203
335	1966 s.205
336(1)	1954 s.14(1)
(2)	1954 s.14(1)
(3)	1954 s.14(1)
(4)	1954 s.14(1)

Provision	Derivations
337	1966 s.204
338(1)	1966 ss.1 and 208(1); 1973 Sch. 12 para. 6; 1974 Sch. 13 para. 15
"development corporation"	1968 s.67(2);
"Exchequer contribution"	1968 s.67(2);
"financial year"	1968 s.67(2);
"house"	1966 s.208(1); 1972 s.78(1); R.9
"housing action area"	1974 s.49;
"housing association"	1974 s.49;
"improvement"	1974 s.49;
"improvement grant"	1974 s.49;
"land"	1972 s.78(1);
"loan charges"	1968 s.67(2);
"local authority"	1966 s.1; 1973 Sch. 12 para. 6;
"official representation"	1966 s.180(1); 1973 (c.65) Sch. 27 Part I para. 2;
"order for possession"	1974 s.49;
"overspill agreement"	1972 s.78(1);
"owner"	1966 s.208(1); 1974 s.49;
"prescribed"	1966 s.208(1); 1974 s.49; 1980 s.73; 1982 (c.43) Sch. 3 para. 33;
"proper officer"	drafting;
"public undertakers"	1973 (c.65), s.235(2);
"repair grants"	1974 s.49;
"a service charge"	1972 s.78(1);
"standard amenities"	1974 s.49;
"superior"	1966 s.208(1); 1974 Sch. 13 para. 15;
"tenancy"	1974 s.49;
"tolerable standard"	1974 s.49
"year"	1972 s.78(1);
"the year 1986–87"	1972 s.78(1)
(2)	1966 s.208(2)
(3)	1966 s.208(3)
339	Drafting
340	Drafting

SCHEDULES

Provision	Derivations
Sch. 1	1966 Sch. 4
Sch. 2	1980 Sch. 1; 1986 s.10, Sch. 1 para. 18
Sch. 3	
Part I	1980 Sch. 2 Pt. 1
para. 6	1986 Sch. 1 para. 19(b)
para. 10	1986 Sch. 1 para. 19(a)
para. 15	1984 (c.18) s.6
para. 16	1986 s.11
Part II	1980 Sch. 2 Pt. II
Sch. 4	1980 s.21(7), Sch. 3
Sch. 5	1980 s.23(3), Sch. 4
Sch. 6	1980 s.1A(3) Sch. A1; 1981 s.35(3)
Sch. 7	
Part I	
para. 1	1974 (c.44) Sch. 10A para. 1; 1975 (c.28) Sch. 3 para. 18; 1978 (c.14) Sch. 2 para. 15
(1)–(9)	para. 1(1)–(9)

Provision	Derivations
para. 2	para. 2(1)–(3)
Part II	
para. 3	para. 4; 1978 (c.14) Sch. 2 para. 15
(1)–(6)	para. 4(1)–(6)
(7)	para. 4(7); 1978 Sch. 2 para. 15
para. 4	para. 5
para. 5	para. 6
para. 6	para. 7(1)–(3)
para. 7	para. 8
para. 8	para. 9
para. 9	para. 10(1)–(4)
para. 10	para. 11(1)–(6)
para. 11	para. 12
para. 12	para. 13
Part III	
para. 13	para. 14(1)–(9)
para. 14	para. 15
Sch. 8	
Part I	
para. 1	1974 s.20(1)–(4)
para. 2	1974 s.21
Pt. II	
para. 3	1974 s.22(1), (2)
para. 4	1974 s.23
para. 5	1974 s.26(1)–(4)
para. 6	1974 s.28
para. 7	1974 s.31
para. 8	1974 s.32
para. 9	1974 s.33
para. 10	1974 s.34(1)–(7)
para. 11	1974 s.36A; 1984 (c.12) Sch. 4 para. 61
Pt. III	
para. 12(1), (3),	1974 s.29(1), (3), (4)
(4)	
(2)	1974 s.29(2); 1978 Sch. 2 para. 42(a) and (b)
Pt. IV	
para. 13(1)–(3)	1966 s.80; 1974 s.25
(4)	1966 s.87(1), (2); 1974 s.25(1)
Sch. 9	1969 Sch. 2
Sch. 10	
para. 1(1)	1966 s.6(1); 1969 Sch. 6 para. 3(a); 1974 Sch. 3 para. 4
(2)	1966 s.6(2)
(3)	1966 s.6(3)
(4)	1966 s.6(3A); 1969 Sch. 6 para. 3(b)
(5)	1966 s.6(4); 1969 Sch. 6 para. 3(c)
para. 2	1966 s.7(1)
para. 3	1966 s.8(1)–(5)
para. 4	1966 s.9(1)–(5)
para. 5	1966 s.10(1), (2)
Sch. 11	
Pt. I	
para. 1	1966 s.126(2)–(5)
para. 2	1966 s.127(1)–(8)
Pt. II	
para. 3	1966 s.131(1)–(4)
para. 4	1966 s.132(1)–(3)
para. 5(1)–(6)	1966 s.133(4)–(9)
(7)	1966 s.133(11)
para. 6(1)–(7)	1966 s.130(3)–(9)
(8)	1966 s.130(10); 1981 (c.23) Sch. 2 para. 11
para. 7(1)	1966 s.135(1)
(2)	1966 s.135(1); 1974 c.44 Sch. 13 para. 12

Provision	Derivations
para. 7(3)	1966 s.135(2); 1974 c.44 Sch. 13 para. 12
(4)	1966 s.135(2A); 1974 c.44 Sch. 13 para. 12
(5)	1966 s.135(3)
(6)	1966 s.135(4)
Pt. III	
para. 8	1966 Sch. 6 para. 1
para. 9	1966 Sch. 6 para. 3
para. 10	1966 Sch. 6 para. 4
Pt. IV	
para. 11	1966 s.109(3)–(6); 1969 Sch. 6 para. 14
Sch. 12	1978 s.7, Sch. 1
Sch. 13	1968 Sch. 5; 1969 Sch. 6 para. 45; 1974 Sch. 3 para. 24
Sch. 14	1968 Sch. 6; 1969 Sch. 6 para. 46; 1974 Sch. 3 para. 25
Sch. 15	
Pt. I	
para. 1(1)	1972 s.23(1)
(2)	1972 s.23(2)
(3)	1972 s.23(6)
Pt. II	
para. 2	1972 Sch. 4 para. 1; 1978 Sch. 2 Pt. II para. 37
para. 3	1972 Sch. 4 para. 2; 1978 Sch. 2 Pt. II para. 38; 1986 Sch. 2 para. 2
para. 4	1972 Sch. 4 para. 3
para. 5	1972 Sch. 4 para. 7
para. 6	1972 Sch. 4 para. 8
para. 7	1972 Sch. 4 para. 9
para. 8	1972 Sch. 4 para. 10
para. 9	1972 Sch. 4 para. 11; 1975 (c.28) Sch. 1 Pt. I para. 1(4); 1980 s.28(2)
para. 10	1972 Sch. 4 para. 12
Sch. 16	1972 Sch. 5
Sch. 17	1968 s.49(3); 1974 (c.45) s.45(4)
para. 3	R.10
Sch. 18	
Pt. I	1974 Sch. 1 Pt. I; S.I. 1983/492
Pt. II	1974 Sch. 1 Pt. II
Sch. 19	
para. 1	1974 Sch. 2 para. 1; 1981 (c.23) Sch. 3 para. 31(a)
para. 2	1974 Sch. 2 para. 2
para. 3	1974 Sch. 2 para. 4
para. 4	1974 Sch. 2 para. 5
para. 5	1974 Sch. 2 para. 6
para. 6	1974 Sch. 2 para. 7; 1978 Sch. 2 para. 29; 1981 Sch. 3 para. 31(b); S.I. 1980/1412
para. 7	1974 Sch. 2 para. 8
para. 8	1974 Sch. 2 para. 9; 1981 Sch. 2 para. 36
Sch. 20	
Pt. I	
para. 1	1984 s.7(1)
para. 2	1984 s.7(1)
para. 3	1984 s.7(2), (3)
para. 4	1984 s.7(4)
para. 5	1984 s.7(5)
para. 6	1984 s.7(6)
para. 7	1984 s.7(7)
para. 8	1984 s.7(8)
Pt. II	
para. 9	1984 Sch. 2 para. 1(1), (2)
para. 10(1)	1984 Sch. 2 para. 2(1), 2(a)–(c), (e), (3)
(2)	1984 Sch. 2 para. 2(2)(d)
(3)	1984 Sch. 2 para. 2(1)
para. 11(1)	1984 Sch. 2 para. 3(1)

Provision	Derivations
para. 11(2)	1984 Sch. 2 para. (8)*
(3)	1984 Sch. 2 para. 3(6)
(4)	1984 Sch. 2 para. 3(5)
para. 12	1984 Sch. 2 para. 5
Sch. 21	
para. 1	1984 s.13(1)–(4)
para. 2	1984 s.13(1)
para. 3	1984 s.13(2)
para. 4	1984 s.13(3), (4)(a)
para. 5	1984 s.13(3)
para. 6	1984 s.13(4)(b), (5), (6)
para. 7	1984 s.13(7), (8)
Sch. 22	
Pt. I	Drafting
para. 6	1966 s.212(3)
para. 7	S.I. 1986/2139
Pt. II	Drafting
Sch. 23	Drafting
para. 1	1974 Sch. 3 paras. 1, 2
para. 4	1974 Sch. 13 para. 1
para. 10	1969 Sch. 9; 1974 Sch. 3 para. 3; 1966 Sch. 9
para. 15	1974 Sch. 3 para. 33
para. 18	1974 Sch. 3 para. 47
Sch. 24	Drafting

* As printed in H.M.S.O.

FIRE SAFETY AND SAFETY OF PLACES OF SPORT ACT 1987*

(1987 c. 27)

ARRANGEMENT OF SECTIONS

PART I

FIRE SAFETY

PART II

SAFETY OF SPORTS GROUNDS

---

* Annotations by H. F. Baines, LL.B., Solicitor.

Schedules:
 Schedule 1—Fire precautions: special provision for certain premises.
 Schedule 2—Extension of application of Safety of Sports Grounds Act 1975 to
     sports grounds.
 Schedule 3—Indoor sports licences: consequential amendments.
 Schedule 4—Repeals.
 Schedule 5—Transitional and saving provisions.

An Act to amend the Fire Precautions Act 1971 and other enactments relating to fire precautions; to amend the Safety of Sports Grounds Act 1975 and make like provision as respects stands at sports grounds; to extend as respects indoor sports premises, and amend, the statutory provisions regulating entertainment licences; and for connected purposes. [15th May 1987]

PARLIAMENTARY DEBATES
 Hansard: H.L. Vol. 482, col. 936; Vol. 483, col. 130; Vol. 484, col. 137; Vol. 485, cols. 561, 878; Vol. 487, col. 482; H.C. Vol. 113, col. 813; Vol. 115, col. 889; Vol. 116, col. 239. The Bill was considered in Standing Committee D from April 9 to 24, 1987.

GENERAL NOTE
 In moving that the Bill be read a second time in the House of Commons (*Hansard*, H.C. Vol. 113, col. 813) the Parliamentary Under-Secretary of State for the Home Department (Mr. Douglas Hogg) described the purpose of the bill as follows: "to provide more effective protection from the dangers caused by fire and to ensure a higher standard of public safety at those sporting fixtures where a serious risk to public safety may exist."
 The Preamble describes the Act's purposes in more formal terms (see above).
 The Act has two distinct divisions. Pt. 1 deals with general fire safety and arises out of two consultative documents, issued in 1985 and 1986, based on proposals produced within the framework of the Central Fire Brigades Advisory Councils.
 Pts. 2, 3 and 4 arise out of the events of May 11, 1985, when 56 people lost their lives in a fire at the Valley Parade Ground, Bradford (the Bradford City F.C. Football Ground). Following that fire, the Committee of Inquiry into Crowd Safety and Control at Sports Grounds was set up, chaired by Popplewell J. The Inquiry's final report was published in January 1986, and those of its recommendations dealing with crowd safety were considered in the consultative document "*Fire Safety and Safety of Sports Venues.*"
 Pts. 2, 3, and 4 of the Act generally follow the conclusions of that document.

COMMENCEMENT
 This Act comes into force on such day as the Secretary of State may appoint (s.50(2)). At the date of writing (July 1, 1987) no Orders have been made pursuant to s.50(2).

EXTENT
Northern Ireland
 The Act does not extend to Northern Ireland (s.50(3)).

Scotland
 In Pt. 4, ss.42 and 43 do not extend to Scotland, and s.44 extends to Scotland only (s.50(3)(a)). In Pt. 5, ss.46 and 47 do not extend to Scotland, and s.48 extends to Scotland only (s.50(3)(b)).

Isles of Scilly
 Pts. 2 and 3 do not extend to the Isles of Scilly, except pursuant to an Order made by the Secretary of State under s.50(5) of this Act (s.50(4)). Such an Order may direct that Pts. 2 and 3 shall come into effect subject to such exceptions, adaptations and modifications as may be specified in the Order. Further, such an Order may contain such incidental and consequential provisions, including provisions conferring powers or imposing duties on the Council of the Isles of Scilly, as the Secretary of State thinks necessary (ss.50(5) and (6)). Such an Order shall further be subject to an annulment in pursuance of a resolution of either House of Parliament (s.50(7)). At the date of writing (July 1, 1987) no Orders have been made pursuant to s.50(5).

PART I

FIRE SAFETY

Exemption from requirement to have fire certificate

Power to exempt from requirement to have fire certificate

1.—(1) The Fire Precautions Act 1971 (in this Part referred to as "the principal Act") shall have effect with the following amendments.

(2) In section 1 (designated uses requiring cover by fire certificates)—

    (a) after subsection (3) there shall be inserted the following subsection—

        "(3A) An order under this section may, as respects any designated use, specify descriptions of premises which qualify for exemption by a fire authority under section 5A of this Act from the requirement for a fire certificate in respect of premises which are put to that use."; and

    (b) in subsection (4) (methods of description), after the words "subsection (3)" there shall be inserted the words "or (3A)", after the words "use for any purpose" there shall be inserted the words "or their situation, construction or arrangement", and for the words "that subsection" there shall be substituted the words "subsection (3) or (3A) above".

(3) In section 5(3) (duty of fire authority to inspect premises on application for fire certificate) after the words "duty of the fire authority" there shall be inserted the words "to consider whether or not, in the case of premises which qualify for exemption under section 5A of this Act, to grant exemption and, if they do not grant it, it shall be their duty".

(4) After section 5 there shall be inserted the following sections—

"Powers for fire authority to grant exemption in particular cases

5A.—(1) A fire authority may, if they think fit as regards any premises which appear to them to be premises qualifying for exemption under this section as respects any particular use, grant exemption from the requirement to have a fire certificate covering that use.

(2) Exemption under this section for any premises as respects any use of them may be granted by the fire authority, with or without the making of an application for the purpose,—

    (a) on the making of an application for a fire certificate with respect to the premises covering that use; or

    (b) at any time during the currency of a fire certificate with respect to the premises which covers that use.

(3) In deciding whether or not to grant exemption under this section for any premises the fire authority shall have regard to all the circumstances of the case and in particular to the degree of seriousness of the risk in case of fire to persons in the premises.

(4) For the purpose of making that decision the fire authority may—

    (a) require the applicant or, as the case may be, the occupier of the premises to give such information as they require about the premises and any matter connected with them; and

    (b) cause to be carried out an inspection of the relevant building.

(5) The fire authority shall not grant exemption under this section for any premises without causing an inspection to be carried out under subsection (4) above unless they have caused the premises to be inspected (under that or any other power) within the preceding twelve months.

(6) The effect of the grant of exemption under this section as respects any particular use of premises is that, during the currency of

the exemption, no fire certificate in respect of the premises is required to cover that use and accordingly—

(a) where the grant is made on an application for a fire certificate, the grant disposes of the application or of so much of it as relates to that use; and

(b) where the grant is made during the currency of a fire certificate, the certificate shall wholly or as respects that use cease to have effect.

(7) On granting an exemption under this section, the fire authority shall, by notice to the applicant for the fire certificate or the occupier of the premises, as the case may be, inform him that they have granted exemption as respects the particular use or uses of the premises specified in the notice and of the effect of the grant.

(8) A notice of the grant of exemption for any premises as respects a particular use of them may include a statement specifying the greatest number of persons of a description specified in the statement for the purposes of that use who, in the opinion of the fire authority, can safely be in the premises at any one time.

(9) Where a notice of the grant of exemption for any premises includes a statement under subsection (8) above, the fire authority may, by notice served on the occupier of the premises, direct that, as from a date specified in the notice, the statement—

(a) is cancelled; or

(b) is to have effect as varied by the notice;

and, on such a variation the statement shall be treated, so long as the variation remains in force, as if the variation were specified in it.

Withdrawal of exemptions under s.5A

5B.—(1) A fire authority who have granted an exemption under section 5A of this Act from the requirement to have a fire certificate covering any particular use of premises may, if they think fit, at any time, withdraw the exemption in accordance with subsections (2) to (4) below.

(2) In deciding whether or not to withdraw an exemption they have granted the fire authority shall have regard to all the circumstances of the case and in particular to the degree of seriousness of the risk in case of fire to persons in the premises.

(3) The fire authority may withdraw an exemption they have granted as respects any particular use of premises without exercising any of the powers of inspection or inquiry conferred by section 19 of this Act but they shall not withdraw the exemption without first giving notice to the occupier of the premises that they propose to withdraw it and the reasons for the proposal and giving him an opportunity of making representations on the matter.

(4) An exemption shall be withdrawn by serving a notice on the occupier of the premises to which the exemption relates stating that the exemption will cease to have effect as respects the particular use or uses of the premises specified in the notice on such date as is so specified, being a date not earlier than the end of the period of fourteen days beginning with the date on which service of the notice is effected.

(5) If premises cease to qualify for exemption under section 5A of this Act a fire authority who have granted an exemption under that section shall notify the occupier of the premises of the fact and date of the cessation of the exemption."

DEFINITIONS
"designated use": Fire Precautions Act 1971, s.1(1).
"fire authority": Fire Precautions Act 1971, s.43(1).
"fire certificate": Fire Precautions Act 1971, s.1(1).
"premises": Fire Precautions Act 1971, s.43(1).

GENERAL NOTE
Pt. 1 of this Act contains a number of detailed amendments to the Fire Precautions Act 1971.

The 1971 Act (largely) came into operation on March 20, 1972. Its stated purpose was to strengthen and rationalise the law relating to fire precautions in places of public entertainment and resort, and in certain kinds of residential premises.

The 1971 Act is applied to various classes of premises within its scope (according to the use to which they are put) largely by means of designating orders. The principal method of control is a requirement that a fire certificate (specifying means of escape from fire and firefighting and fire alarm systems) be obtained from the local fire-authority in respect of the designated classes of premises. It is an offence to use such premises without a fire certificate.

In moving that the Bill be read a second time in the House of Lords (*Hansard*, H.L. Vol. 483, col. 130) the Minister of State for the Home Office (The Earl of Caithness) commented on Clause (now section) 1, as follows:

"Clause 1 provides that a designation order may specify categories of premises which the fire authority may consider suitable for exemption. In the case of shops, for example, the designation order might specify those which consist of a ground floor only or of a ground floor and basement separated by a fire resisting barrier. The fire authority would be able to consider each case on its merits after either an inspection or a scrutiny of plans and other relevant documents and, where they thought it fit, grant exemption. In premises where certain quantities of highly flammable substances were stored the fire authority might decide against exemption even though the shop was of a layout and construction that brought it within the range of exemption. The intention is to allow for greater flexibility than is provided for by the present system of certification. In doing so, we must rely on the judgment of the fire authority.

Of course, flexibility must not be an excuse for inconsistency. I can reassure your Lordships that we intend to issue guidance to fire authorities about the way the criteria for exemption are to be applied to ensure fairness and consistency. The Fire Service Inspectorates will monitor the way fire authorities use their powers of exemption, and training will be provided at the Fire Service College.

We expect significant numbers of low risk factories, offices and shops to be exempted from the need to have a fire certificate. This will be of particular benefit to businesses. Premises which are exempted will be relieved of the obligations that certification carries, and this will also reduce the burden on fire authorities of keeping the certificate up to date. But that does not mean that safety will be put in jeopardy. The Government are, however, satisfied that essential fire safety standards will be maintained in these premises by the imposition and enforcement of the statutory duty to which I have already referred as regards means of escape and fire fighting equipment."

For the applicability of this Part of this Act, and the Fire Precautions Act 1971, to factory, office, railway or shop premises, see s.16 and Sched. 1 to this Act, (inserting a new Sched. 2 in the Fire Precautions Act 1971).

Subs. (2)
S.1 of the Fire Precautions Act 1971 lays down the uses of premises for which fire certificates are, or may be, made compulsory. In the original form of the 1971 Act, the main exemptions were factories, offices, shops and railway premises; premises appropriated to and used solely, or mainly, for religious worship; and ordinary private dwelling-houses.

The first such exemption was modified by the Fire Precautions (Factories, Offices, Shops and Railway Premises) Order 1976 (S.I. 1976 No. 2007), in respect of factories, etc., where more than 20 people are employed to work at any one time, or more than 10 are employed on any floor other than the ground floor.

Notwithstanding the exemption in favour of private dwelling-houses, there is a power (in s.3 of the 1971 Act) for a fire authority, after consultation with the local authority, to make fire certificates compulsory in respect of certain premises (for example, a multi-storey block of flats) considered to be especially at risk, after consultation with the local authority.

As to the exemption in favour of premises appropriated to, and used solely or mainly for, public religious worship, see s.13 of this Act.

By virtue of the definitions of "premises" and "building" in s.43(1) of the 1971 Act (" 'premises' means a building or part of a building': 'building' includes a temporary or movable building and also includes any permanent structure and any temporary structure other than a movable one."), the 1971 Act does not apply to activities which take place out-of-doors. In that regard, however, see s.17 of this Act.

Subs. (2) of this section empowers the Secretary of State to designate descriptions of premises to which the new ss.5A and 5B (inserted into the 1971 Act by subs. (4) of this section) will apply, and which thus are eligible to be exempted from the obligation to have a fire certificate. Any actual exemptions, however, are made by fire authorities themselves.

Exemption will not relieve the owner or occupier of the premises thus exempted from the duty to maintain standards of fire safety. Section 9A of the 1971 Act (as inserted by s.5 of this Act) requires exempted premises to comply with a duty to make provision for adequate means of escape and fire fighting equipment (see the General Note to s.5).

Exemptions, once granted, may be withdrawn at any time (after the fire authority has given not less than 14 days' notice in writing) (s.5B of the 1971 Act, as inserted by subs. (4) of this section).

Subs. (3)

S.5(3) of the 1971 Act provides that fire authorities must carry out inspections of any premises in respect of which an application for a fire certificate is made. The amendment to s.5(3) of the 1971 Act effected by this subsection means that fire authorities, following receipt of an application for a fire certificate, must first consider (in relation to qualifying premises) whether or not to grant an exemption. If they decide not to grant an exemption, they must then go on to consider whether or not to issue a fire certificate.

Exemption from requirement to have fire certificate: supplementary

2.—(1) After section 8 of the principal Act there shall be inserted the following section—

"Change of conditions affecting premises for which exemption has been granted

8A.—(1) If, during the currency of an exemption granted under section 5A of this Act for any premises, it is intended to carry out in relation to those premises any proposals to which this section applies, the occupier shall, before the carrying out of the proposals is begun, give notice of the proposals to the fire authority; and if the carrying out of the proposals is begun without such notice having been given, the occupier shall be guilty of an offence.

(2) This section applies to the following proposals, namely, any proposal—

    (a) to make—

        (i) an extension of, or structural alteration to, the premises which would affect the means of escape from the premises; or

        (ii) an alteration in the internal arrangement of the premises, or in the furniture or equipment with which the premises are provided, which would affect the means of escape from the premises; or

    (b) on the part of the occupier, to begin to keep explosive or highly flammable materials of any prescribed kind anywhere under, in or on the building which constitutes or comprises the premises in a quantity or aggregate quantity greater than the quantity prescribed for the purposes of this paragraph as the maximum in relation to materials of that kind; or

    (c) in a case where the notice of exemption under section 5A of this Act includes a statement under subsection (8) of that section, to make such a use of the premises as will involve there being in the premises at any one time a greater number of persons in relation to whom the statement applies than is specified or treated as specified in the statement.

(3) A person guilty of an offence under subsection (1) above shall be liable—

(a) on summary conviction, to a fine not exceeding the statutory maximum;

(b) on conviction on indictment, to a fine or to imprisonment for a term not exceeding two years, or both."

(2) In section 19(2) of the principal Act (premises within powers of inspection etc. of inspectors), after paragraph (a), there shall be inserted the following paragraph—

"(aa) any premises in respect of which there is in force an exemption under section 5A of this Act from the requirement for a fire certificate with respect to them;".

DEFINITIONS

"fire authority": Fire Precautions Act 1971, s.43(1).
"fire certificate": Fire Precautions Act 1971, s.1(1).
"inspector": Fire Precautions Act 1971, s.19(1).
"notice": Fire Precautions Act 1971, s.43(1).
"premises": Fire Precautions Act 1971, s.43(1).
"prescribed": Fire Precautions Act 1971, s.43(1).
"principal Act": s.1(1).
"statutory maximum": Criminal Justice Act 1982, s.74.

GENERAL NOTE

Subs. (1)

This subsection inserts a new section s.8A into the Fire Precautions Act 1971. S.8A, accordingly, requires occupiers to notify the fire authority of any material changes to premises exempted from the obligation to have a fire certificate, pursuant to the new ss.5A and 5B (inserted into the 1971 Act by s.1 of this Act, *ante*), to enable the fire authority to review the situation.

Occupier. The term is not defined. It is suggested that the occupier within the meaning of the 1971 Act is the person who runs the premises in question, and who regulates and controls any work that is done there; *cf. Cox* v. *Cutler & Sons, and Hampton Court Gas Co.* [1948] 1 All E.R. 665, C.A. It is suggested that that person may be a limited company; *cf.*, for example, *Smith* v. *Cammell Laird & Co.* [1940] A.C. 242. He may also be, for example, a receiver and manager appointed by a debenture holder; *cf. Meigh* v. *Wickenden* [1942] 2 K.B. 160.

Structural alteration. The term is not defined. The expression "structural alterations" has been defined by the Court of Appeal as "permanent alterations which affect the structure of the premises" (*cf. Bickmore* v. *Dimmer* [1903] 1 Ch. 158).

Conviction on indictment. See the Courts Act 1971, s.6(1). There is no limit on the amount of the fine which may be imposed on conviction on indictment, but the fine should be within the offender's ability to pay; *cf. R.* v. *Churchill (No. 2)* [1967] 1 All E.R. 215, C.C.A. (reversed on other grounds *sub nom. Churchill* v. *Walton* [1967] 1 All E.R. 497, H.L.).

Subs. (2)

S.19 of the Fire Precautions Act 1971 deals with the powers of "inspectors," namely persons appointed as such under s.18 of the 1971 Act, and inspectors or assistant inspectors appointed under the Fire Services Act 1947, s.24.

S.19(2) of the 1971 Act lists premises in respect of which an inspector's powers apply.

The amendment effected by subs. (2) of this section adds to such list of premises any premises in respect of which there is in force an exemption granted pursuant to s.5A of the 1971 Act (inserted by s.1(4) of this Act). Accordingly, albeit that such premises do not require to have a fire certificate, inspectors under the 1971 Act have the same powers in respect of such premises as they do in relation to premises which are required to have a fire certificate. For the detailed provisions as to such powers see the Fire Precautions Act 1971, s.19.

Charges for fire certification work

Charges for fire certification work

3. After the section 8A of the principal Act inserted by section 2 above there shall be inserted the following section—

"Charges for issue or amendment of fire certificates

8B.—(1) Where a fire authority—

(a) issue a fire certificate under section 5 of this Act, or

(b) except in a case falling within subsection (2) below, amend a fire certificate or, as an alternative to amendment, issue a new fire certificate, under section 8 of this Act,

the applicant for the certificate or, as the case may be, the occupier of the premises to which the amended or new certificate relates shall pay to the authority such fee as the authority determine.

(2) No fee shall be chargeable for the amendment of a fire certificate, or issue of a new fire certificate embodying amendments, under section 8(6) of this Act in a case where the amendment or amendments is or are made in consequence of the coming into force of regulations under section 12 of this Act.

(3) A fee charged by a fire authority under this section in connection with the issue of a fire certificate or the amendment of a, or issue of a new, fire certificate shall not exceed an amount which represents the cost to the authority of the work reasonably done by them for the purposes of the issue of the certificate or, as the case may be, the amendment of the certificate or issue of the new certificate, other than the cost of any inspection of the premises."

DEFINITIONS

"fire authority": Fire Precautions Act 1971, s.43(1).
"fire certificate": Fire Precautions Act 1971, s.1(1).
"premises": Fire Precautions Act 1971, s.43(1).
"prescribed": Fire Precautions Act 1971, s.43(1).
"principal Act": s.1(1).

GENERAL NOTE

The amendment to the 1971 Act effected by this section empowers fire authorities to make reasonable charges to recover the cost of work done by them in respect of certification (other than the cost of inspection). The fee to be charged shall be "such fee as the authority determine." Such charge, however, must not exceed the cost to the authority of the work done (other than the cost of inspection(s)).

No fee may be charged, however, where a fire certificate is amended, or a new fire certificate is issued, in consequence of regulations made under s.12 of the 1971 Act (subtitled "Power of Secretary of State to make regulations about fire precautions").

Means of escape and for fighting fire

Means of escape: scope of regulation

4.—(1) The following amendments of the principal Act with regard to means of escape from premises in case of fire shall have effect.

(2) In section 5 (applications for and issue of fire certificates), the following subsection shall be added at the end—

"(5) In this Act, "escape", in relation to premises, means escape from them to some place of safety beyond the building which constitutes or comprises the premises and any area enclosed by it or enclosed with it; and accordingly, for the purposes of any provision of this Act relating to means of escape, consideration may be given to, and conditions or requirements imposed as respects, any place or thing by means of which a person escapes from premises to a place of safety."

(3) In section 43(1) (interpretation), after the definition of "designated use", there shall be inserted the following—

"'escape' has the meaning assigned to it by section 5(5) of this Act and 'means of escape' is to be construed in accordance with that subsection;".

DEFINITIONS
   "fire certificate": Fire Precautions Act 1971, s.1(1).
   "premises": Fire Precautions Act 1971, s.43(1).
   "principal Act": s.1(1).

GENERAL NOTE
   Section 5 of the 1971 Act deals with applications for, and issue of, fire certificates. That
section requires, *inter alia*, that, before issuing a fire certificate, the fire authority should be
satisfied as to the following:
"(a) the means of escape in case of fire with which the premises are provided; and
   (b) the means (other than means for fighting fire) with which the relevant building is
       provided for securing that the means of escape with which the premises are provided
       can be safely and effectively used at all material times; and . . . " (Fire Precautions
       Act 1971, s.5(3)).
   The 1971 Act in its original form, however, does not contain any definition of "escape."
Such a definition is inserted in ss.5 and 43(1) ("interpretation") of the 1971 Act by this
section.
   The definition thus inserted means escape from the premises to some place of safety
beyond the building which comprises the premises, and beyond any area enclosed by or with
the premises (for example the actual playing pitch at a sports stadium).

General duty as to means of escape and for fighting fire

   5. For section 9A of the principal Act (duty to provide certain premises
with means of escape in case of fire) there shall be substituted the
following section—

   "Duty as to means of escape and for fighting fire
   9A.—(1) All premises to which this section applies shall be provided with—
       (a) such means of escape in case of fire, and
       (b) such means for fighting fire,
as may reasonably be required in the circumstances of the case.
   (2) The premises to which this section applies are premises which
are exempt from the requirement for a fire certificate by virtue of—
       (a) a provision made in an order under section 1 of this Act by
           virtue of subsection (3) of that section, or
       (b) the grant of exemption by a fire authority under section 5A of
           this Act.
   (3) In the event of a contravention of the duty imposed by subsection (1) above the occupier of the premises shall, except as provided
in subsection (4) below, be guilty of an offence and liable on summary
conviction to a fine not exceeding level 5 on the standard scale.
   (4) A person is not guilty of an offence under this section in respect
of any contravention of the duty imposed by subsection (1) above
which is the subject of an improvement notice under section 9D of
this Act."

DEFINITIONS
   "escape": Fire Precautions Act 1971, s.5(5).
   "fire authority": Fire Precautions Act 1971, s.43(1).
   "fire certificate": Fire Precautions Act 1971, s.1(1).
   "premises": Fire Precautions Act 1971, s.43(1).
   "principal Act": s.1(1).
   "standard scale": Criminal Justice Act 1982, s.75.

GENERAL NOTE
   S.9A of the Fire Precautions Act 1971 (sub-titled "Duty to provide certain premises with
means of escape in case of fire") was inserted into the 1971 Act by the Health and Safety at
Work etc. Act 1974, s.78(4). Under that section, "such means of escape in case of fire for
the persons employed to work therein as may reasonably be required" were to be provided

in respect of a relatively limited class of premises, which were outside the scope of the obligation to have a fire certificate.

The new s.9A provides that all premises which are exempt from the obligation to have a fire certificate either by virtue of s.1(3) or the 1971 Act, or an exemption granted pursuant to s.5A of the 1971 Act (as inserted by s.1(4) of this Act) shall nonetheless be provided with such means of escape in case of fire, and such means for fighting fire, "as may reasonably be required in the circumstances of the case." Failure to provide such means, except where the same are the subject of an improvement notice (as to which see the General Note to s.7 of this Act) is an offence.

Occupier. See the General Note to s.2(1).

Codes of practice

6. After the section 9A of the principal Act substituted by section 5 above there shall be inserted the following sections—

"**Codes of practice as to means of escape and for fighting fire**

9B.—(1) The Secretary of State may from time to time, after consultation with such persons or bodies of persons as appear to him requisite—

  (a) prepare and issue codes of practice for the purpose of providing practical guidance on how to comply with the duty imposed by section 9A of this Act; and

  (b) revise any such code by revoking, varying, amending or adding to the provisions of the code.

(2) A code prepared in pursuance of this section and any alterations proposed to be made on a revision of such a code shall be laid before both Houses of Parliament, and the Secretary of State shall not issue the code or revised code, as the case may be, until after the end of the period of 40 days beginning with the day on which the code or the proposed alterations were so laid.

(3) If, within the period mentioned in subsection (2) above, either House resolves that the code be not issued or the proposed alterations be not made, as the case may be, the Secretary of State shall not issue the code or revised code (but without prejudice to his power under that subsection to lay further codes or proposed alterations before Parliament).

(4) For the purposes of subsection (2) above—

  (a) where the code or proposed alterations are not laid before both Houses of Parliament on the same day, the later day shall be taken to be the day on which the code or the proposed alterations, as the case may be, were laid before both Houses, and

  (b) in reckoning any period of 40 days, no account shall be taken of any time during which Parliament is dissolved or prorogued or during which both Houses are adjourned for more than four days.

(5) In this Act references to a code of practice under this section are references to such a code as it has effect for the time being, with any revisions, under this section.

Legal effect of codes of practice

9C.—(1) A failure on the part of a person to observe any provision of a code of practice under section 9B of this Act shall not of itself render him liable to any criminal or civil proceedings.

(2) If, in any proceedings whether civil or criminal under this Act, it is alleged that there has been a contravention on the part of any person of the duty imposed by section 9A of this Act—

  (a) a failure to observe a provision of a code of practice under section 9B of this Act may be relied on as tending to establish liability, and

(b) compliance with such a code may be relied on as tending to negative liability."

DEFINITIONS
"escape": Fire Precautions Act 1971, s.5(5).
"principal Act": s.1(1).

GENERAL NOTE
By virtue of the amendments to the Fire Precautions Act 1971 effected by this section, the Secretary of State is empowered to issue codes of practice for the purpose of providing practical guidance as to how to comply with the duty imposed by s.9A of the 1971 Act (as inserted into the 1971 Act by s.5 of this Act).

Failure to comply with such a code does not, of itself, render a person liable to any civil or criminal proceedings but, in any such proceedings, a failure to observe a provision of a code of practice may be relied on as tending to establish liability, whereas compliance with a code of practice may be relied on as tending to negative liability.

Improvement notices

7.—(1) After the section 9C of the principal Act inserted by section 6 above there shall be inserted the following sections—

"Improvement notices

9D.—(1) Where a fire authority are of the opinion that the duty imposed by section 9A of this Act has been contravened in respect of any premises to which that section applies, they may serve on the occupier of those premises a notice (in this Act referred to as "an improvement notice") which—

(a) states they are of that opinion;

(b) specifies, by reference to a code of practice under section 9B of this Act if they think fit, what steps they consider are necessary to remedy that contravention; and

(c) requires the occupier to take steps to remedy that contravention within such period (ending not earlier than the period within which an appeal against the improvement notice can be brought under section 9E of this Act) as may be specified in the notice.

(2) Where an improvement notice has been served under subsection (1) above—

(a) the fire authority may withdraw that notice at any time before the end of the period specified in the notice; and

(b) if an appeal against the improvement notice is not pending, the fire authority may extend or further extend the period specified in the notice.

(3) Where any premises are premises to which section 9A of this Act applies and—

(a) the building which constitutes or comprises the premises is a building to which at the time of its erection building regulations imposing requirements as to means of escape in case of fire applied; and

(b) in connection with the erection of that building plans were, in accordance with building regulations, deposited with a local authority,

the fire authority shall not in pursuance of subsection (1) above serve an improvement notice requiring structural or other alterations relating to the means of escape from the premises unless the requirements of subsection (4) below are satisfied in relation to those premises.

(4) The requirements of this subsection are satisfied in relation to such premises as are mentioned in subsection (3) above if—

(a) regulations are in force under section 12 of this Act applying to the premises in relation to any use of them as respects which exemption under section 5A of this Act has been granted, being regulations which impose requirements as to means of escape in case of fire, and the fire authority are satisfied that alterations to the building which constitutes or comprises the premises are necessary to bring the premises into compliance with the regulations in respect of those requirements; or

(b) the fire authority are satisfied that the means of escape in case of fire with which the premises are provided are inadequate in relation to any such use of the premises by reason of matters or circumstances of which particulars were not required by or under the building regulations to be supplied to the local authority in connection with the deposit of plans.

(5) In this section "structural or other alterations relating to means of escape from the premises", in relation to any such premises as are mentioned in this section, means structural or other alterations directly connected with the provision of the premises with adequate means of escape in case of fire.

(6) Subsections (3) to (5) above extend to England and Wales only.

Rights of appeal against improvement notices

9E.—(1) A person on whom an improvement notice is served may, within twenty-one days from the date on which the improvement notice is served, appeal to the court.

(2) On an appeal under this section, the court may either cancel or affirm the notice, and, if it affirms it, may do so either in its original form or with such modifications as the court may in the circumstances think fit.

(3) Where an appeal is brought under this section against an improvement notice, the bringing of the appeal shall have the effect of suspending the operation of the notice until the appeal is finally disposed of or, if the appeal is withdrawn, until the withdrawal of the appeal.

Provision as to offences

9F.—(1) It is an offence for a person to contravene any requirement imposed by an improvement notice.

(2) Any person guilty of an offence under subsection (1) above shall be liable—

(a) on summary conviction, to a fine not exceeding the statutory maximum;

(b) on conviction on indictment, to a fine, or imprisonment for a term not exceeding two years, or both."

(2) In section 14(1) of the principal Act (exercise of certain powers of fire authority in Scotland where building standards regulations as to means of escape apply), for the words "or 8" there shall be substituted the words ", 8 or (in relation to premises to which section 9A applies) 9D(1) and (2)".

(3) In section 17(1) of the principal Act (duty of fire authorities to consult other authorities before requiring alterations to buildings), in paragraph (b), after the words "section 8(4) or (5)" there shall be inserted the words ", section 9D" and after the words "would have to be taken" there shall be inserted the words "or, in the case of a notice under section 9D, which must be taken".

(4) In section 48(4) of the Building Act 1984, (which modifies the effect of initial notices under that Act for the purposes of the exercise of powers

of a fire authority to require structural alterations where building regulations apply)—
   (a) after the words "For the purposes of" there shall be inserted the words "section 9D and"; and
   (b) in paragraph (b), after the words "the references in" there shall be inserted the words "subsection (4)(b) of section 9D and" and for the words "that section" there shall be substituted the words "section 13".

DEFINITIONS
   "building": Fire Precautions Act 1971, s.43(1).
   "building regulations": Building Act 1984, ss. 1 and 122.
   "escape": Fire Precautions Act 1971, s.5(5).
   "fire authority": Fire Precautions Act 1971, s.43(1).
   "local authority": Building Act 1984, s.126.
   "notice": Fire Precautions Act 1971, s.43(1).
   "premises": Fire Precautions Act 1971, s.43(1).
   "principal Act": s.1(1).
   "statutory maximum": Criminal Justice Act 1982, s.74.

GENERAL NOTE
   Where a fire authority is of the opinion that the duty imposed by s.9A of the 1971 Act (as inserted by s.5 of this Act) has been contravened, it may serve an "improvement notice" on the occupier of the premises specifying the steps necessary to remedy that contravention, and the period within which such steps should be taken. An improvement notice cannot be served in respect of a building in connection with the erection of which plans were deposited in accordance with building regulations unless the additional requirement set out in s.9D(4) are satisfied.
   By virtue of s.9E a person on whom an improvement notice is served may appeal to the court. The court may cancel or affirm the notice (if affirmed, or its original form or with such modifications as the court thinks fit). Where an appeal is brought, the operation of the notice is suspended until the appeal is withdrawn, or otherwise finally disposed of.
   It is an offence for any person to contravene any requirement imposed by an improvement notice.
   The maximum penalty on conviction for such an offence is greater than the maximum penalty on conviction of the offence of failing to comply with the duty imposed by s.9A of the 1971 Act (as inserted by s.5 of this Act).
   Conviction on indictment. See the General Note to s.2(1).
   Occupier. See the General Note to s.2(1).
   Structural or other alteration. See the General Note to s.2(1).

Subs. (3) of s.9D
   As to the building regulations and, in particular, building regulations imposing requirements as to means of escape in case of fire (in England and Wales), see the Building Act 1984; the Building Regulations 1985, (S.I. 1985 No. 1065), Sched. 1, Pt. B; Approved Document B issued in August 1985 pursuant to the Building Act 1984, s.6; and the document intituled "Mandatory rules for means of escape in case of fire" issued pursuant to the Building Act 1984, s.6 and the Building Regulations 1985, Sched. 1, para. B1 (issued July 1985).
   Subss. (3) to (5) of s.9D do *not* apply in Scotland.

Interim duties as to safety of premises

Duties as regards safety pending determination of applications for fire certificates

   8.—(1) The following amendments shall be made in section 5 (applications for fire certificates) and section 7 (offences) of the principal Act.
   (2) In section 5—
   (a) in subsection (2), after the words "fire authority", there shall be inserted the words "shall notify the applicant of his duties under subsection (2A) below and"; and

(b) after subsection (2) there shall be inserted the following subsection—

"(2A) Where an application is made for a fire certificate with respect to any premises it is the duty of the occupier to secure that, when the application is made and pending its disposal—

(a) the means of escape in case of fire with which the premises are provided can be safely and effectively used at all material times;

(b) the means for fighting fire with which the premises are provided are maintained in efficient working order; and

(c) any persons employed to work in the premises receive instruction or training in what to do in case of fire."

(3) In section 7, after subsection (3), there shall be inserted the following subsection—

"(3A) If, pending the disposal of an application for a fire certificate with respect to any premises, the premises are put to a designated use, then, if any requirement imposed by section 5(2A) of this Act is contravened by reason of anything done or not done to or in relation to any part of the relevant building, the occupier shall be guilty of an offence."

(4) In section 7, after subsection (5), there shall be inserted the following subsection—

"(5A) A person guilty of an offence under subsection (3A) above shall be liable, on summary conviction, to a fine not exceeding level 5 on the standard scale."

DEFINITIONS
"building": Fire Precautions Act 1971, s.43(1).
"designated use": Fire Precautions Act 1971, s.1(1).
"escape": Fire Precautions Act 1971, s.5(5).
"fire authority": Fire Precautions Act 1971, s.43(1).
"fire certificate": Fire Precautions Act 1971, s.1(1).
"premises": Fire Precautions Act 1971, s.43(1).
"principal Act": s.1(1).
"standard scale": Criminal Justice Act 1975, s.75.

GENERAL NOTE
This section, by virtue of the amendments effected to the Fire Precautions Act 1971, aims to fill the gap between the date when an application is submitted for a fire certificate and the date when such an application is finally disposed of. Accordingly, in that interim period, the *occupier* of the premises must ensure that: (i) the means of escape in case of fire with which the premises are provided can be safely and effectively used at all material times; (ii) the means for fighting fire are maintained in efficient working order; (iii) persons employed on the premises receive instruction or training as to what to do in case of fire.

There does not appear to be any sanction attached to a failure to comply with such duty, unless the premises are put to a *designated use* within that interim period. In that case, a failure to comply with the duties imposed by the new subs. 5(2A) constitutes an offence.

By virtue of subs. (2) of this section, which amends s.5(2) of the 1971 Act, the fire authority is required to notify the applicant of the duties imposed by the new s.5(2A).

Occupier. See the General Note to s.2(1).

Premises involving serious risk to persons

Special procedure in case of serious risk: prohibition notices

9.—(1) For section 10 of the principal Act (court's power to prohibit or restrict use of certain premises until excessive risk to persons in case of fire is reduced) there shall be substituted the following section—

"Special procedure in case of serious risk: prohibition notices

10.—(1) This section applies to—

(a) any premises which are being or are proposed to be put to a use (whether designated or not) which falls within at least one of the classes of use mentioned in section 1(2) of this Act, other than premises of the description given in section 2 of this Act; and

(b) any premises to which section 3 of this Act for the time being applies.

(2) If as regards any premises to which this section applies the fire authority are of the opinion that use of the premises involves or will involve a risk to persons on the premises in case of fire so serious that use of the premises ought to be prohibited or restricted, the authority may serve on the occupier of the premises a notice (in this Act referred to as "a prohibition notice").

(3) The matters relevant to the assessment by the fire authority, for the purposes of subsection (2) above, of the risk to persons in case of fire include anything affecting their escape from the premises in that event.

(4) A prohibition notice shall—

(a) state that the fire authority are of the opinion referred to in subsection (2) above;

(b) specify the matters which in their opinion give or, as the case may be, will give risk to that risk; and

(c) direct that the use to which the prohibition notice relates is prohibited or restricted to such extent as may be specified in the notice until the specified matters have been remedied.

(5) A prohibition notice may include directions as to the steps which will have to be taken to remedy the matters specified in the notice.

(6) A prohibition or restriction contained in a prohibition notice in pursuance of subsection (4)(c) above shall take effect immediately it is served if the authority are of the opinion, and so state in the notice, that the risk of serious personal injury is or, as the case may be, will be imminent, and in any other case shall take effect at the end of a period specified in the prohibition notice.

(7) Where a prohibition notice has been served under subsection (2) above the fire authority may withdraw the notice at any time."

(2) After the section 10 of the principal Act substituted by subsection (1) above there shall be inserted the following sections—

"Rights of appeal against prohibition notices

10A.—(1) A person on whom a prohibition notice is served may, within twenty-one days from the date on which the prohibition notice is served, appeal to the court.

(2) On an appeal under this section, the court may either cancel or affirm the notice, and, if it affirms it, may do so either in its original form or with such modifications as the court may in the circumstances think fit.

(3) Where an appeal is brought under this section against a prohibition notice, the bringing of the appeal shall not have the effect of suspending the operation of the notice, unless, on the application of the appellant, the court so directs (and then only from the giving of the direction).

Provision as to offences

10B.—(1) It shall be an offence for any person to contravene any prohibition or restriction imposed by a prohibition notice.

(2) In any proceedings for an offence under subsection (1) above where the person charged is a person other than the person on whom

the prohibition notice was served, it shall be a defence for that person to prove that he did not know and had no reason to believe the notice had been served.

(3) Any person guilty of an offence under subsection (1) above shall be liable—

(a) on summary conviction, to a fine not exceeding the statutory maximum;

(b) on conviction on indictment, to a fine, or imprisonment for a term not exceeding two years, or both."

(3) In section 43(1) of the principal Act (interpretation), after the definition of "prescribed" there shall be inserted the following definition—

""prohibition notice" has the meaning assigned by section 10(2) of this Act;".

DEFINITIONS

"court": Fire Precautions Act 1971, s.43(1).
"designated use": Fire Precautions Act 1971, s.1(1).
"fire authority": Fire Precautions Act 1971, s.43(1).
"premises": Fire Precautions Act 1971, s.43(1).
"principal Act": s.1(1).
"statutory maximum": Criminal Justice Act 1982, s.74.

GENERAL NOTE

Under the form of the Fire Precautions Act 1971, s.10, prior to the amendments effected by this section, the fire authority was empowered to apply to the courts for an order restricting or prohibiting the use of premises where there is a serious risk to persons in the event of fire.

The new s.10, substituted by this section into the Fire Precautions Act 1971, gives the fire authority the right to serve a "prohibition notice", restricting or prohibiting the use of premises until specified matters are remedied. Such a notice may come into force immediately it is served in the case of an imminent risk; otherwise it will come into effect at the end of a period, specified in the notice. The notice may specify the steps which should be taken to remedy the matters complained of. Such a notice, once served, may be withdrawn at any time.

By virtue of the new s.10A, inserted into the 1971 Act by subs. (2) of this section, a person on whom a prohibition notice is served has the right, within 21 days of its service, to appeal to the court. The court may confirm the notice (with or without modification), or may cancel it. The bringing of an appeal does *not* suspend the operation of the notice unless, on the application of the appellant, the court directs that it should be suspended. In those circumstances, the suspension takes effect from the date of the court's direction.

By virtue of s.10B, inserted into the 1971 Act by subs. (2) of this section, it is an offence for *any person* to contravene a prohibition or restriction imposed by a prohibition notice. A person other than the one on whom the notice was served does have a defence, however, if he can prove that he did not know, and had no reason to know, that the notice had been served.

For the purposes of the right of appeal, pursuant to the new s.10A, "the court" means, in England and Wales, the magistrates' court for the petty sessions area in which the premises are situated. In relation to premises in Scotland, "the court" means the sheriff within whose jurisdiction the premises are situated.

Subs. (1)

As to the service of notices under the Fire Precautions Act 1971, see s.38 ("service of documents") of that Act.

Occupier. See the General Note to s.2(1).

Opinion. See *Allcroft* v. *Lord Bishop of London* [1891] A.C. 666. It is suggested that the use of the expression: "if . . . the fire authority are of the opinion . . . " in s.10(2) of the Fire Precautions Act 1971 (as substituted by this subsection) makes the fire authority, acting in good faith, the sole judge of the matter in question (see, for example *Robinson* v. *Sunderland Corporation* [1899] 1 Q.B. 751, at pp.756, 757, *per* Channel J. and *Point of Ayr Collieries* v. *Lloyd-George* [1943] 2 All E.R. 546, C.A.). See, however, *Ross-Clunis* v.

Papadopoullos [1958] 2 All E.R. 23, P.C., which provides some authority for the proposition that a merely subjective test is insufficient.

Subs. (2)
   Within twenty-one days. The date of service of the notice is not to be included in calculating the period of twenty-one days (see, for example *Goldsmiths' Co.* v. *West Metropolitan Rail Co.* [1904] 1 K.B. 1 and *Re Figgis; Roberts* v. *Mclaren* [1968] 1 All E.R. 999).
   It shall be a defence . . . to prove. The burden of proof laid on the defendant is less onerous than that resting on the prosecutor as regards proving the offence. It may be discharged by satisfying the court of what the defendant is called on to prove "on the balance of probabilities" (see, for example, *R.* v. *Carr-Briant* [1943] 2 All E.R. 156 and *Rogers* v. *Cowley* [1962] 2 All E.R. 683, at p.687).
   Conviction on indictment. See the Crown Courts Act 1971, s.6(1) and the General Note to s.2(1) of this Act.

Inspections of premises

Inspections of premises

   10. Section 18 of the principal Act (enforcement) shall be amended—
   (a) by the insertion in subsection (1), after the word "inspectors", of the words "and cause premises to be inspected"; and
   (b) by the insertion, after subsection (2), of the following subsection—
       "(3) In performing the duty imposed by subsection (1) above so far as it requires premises in their areas to be inspected, fire authorities shall act in accordance with such guidance as the Secretary of State may give them."

DEFINITIONS
   "fire authorities": Fire Precautions Act 1971, s.43(1).
   "inspector": Fire Precautions Act 1971, s.19.
   "premises": Fire Precautions Act 1971, s.43(1).
   "principal Act": s.1(1).

GENERAL NOTE
   Under the Fire Precautions Act 1971, in its original form, there was no duty on fire authorities to reinspect premises which have been certificated—although, as a matter of practice, most fire authorities/brigades did carry out such reinspections.
   By virtue of the amendments to the 1971 Act effected by this section, fire authorities must henceforth inspect premises in accordance with such guidance as the Secretary of State may give.

Disclosure of information obtained in premises

   11. Section 21 of the principal Act (restriction on disclosure of information obtained in premises) shall be amended—
   (a) by the insertion, at the beginning, of the words "(1) Subject to subsection (2) below,"; and
   (b) by the insertion, at the end, of the following subsections—
       "(2) Nothing in subsection (1) above prohibits the disclosure of information to an enforcing authority within the meaning of the Health and Safety at Work etc. Act 1974 in order to enable that authority to discharge any function falling within its field of responsibility.
       (3) Section 18(7) of the Health and Safety at Work etc. Act 1974 (meaning in Part I of that Act of 'enforcing authority' and of such an authority's 'field of responsibility') shall apply for the purposes of this section as it applies for the purposes of that Part."

DEFINITIONS
"premises": Fire Precautions Act 1971, s.43(1).
"principal Act": s.1(1).

GENERAL NOTE
It is an offence under the Fire Precautions Act 1971, s.21, for any person to disclose any information obtained by him in any premises entered in pursuance of powers conferred by the 1971 Act, other than in the performance of his duty, or for the purposes of any legal proceedings.
The amendments to s.21 effected by this section further enable information to be disclosed to an "enforcing authority" within the meaning of the Health and Safety at Work etc. Act 1974, in order to enable that authority to discharge any function falling within its field of responsibility under that Act. See, generally, the Health and Safety at Work etc. Act 1974, s.18, and the Health and Safety (Enforcing Authority) Regulations 1977 (S.I. 1977 No. 746) (as amended by S.I. 1980 No.1744 and S.I. 1985 No. 1107).

Civil and other liability

Civil and other liability

12.—(1) After section 27 of the principal Act there shall be inserted the following section—

"Civil and other liability
27A. Except in so far as this Act otherwise expressly provides, and subject to section 18 of the Interpretation Act 1978 (offences under two or more laws), the provisions of this Act shall not be construed as—
(a) conferring a right of action in any civil proceedings (other than proceedings for the recovery of a fine) in respect of any contravention of a provision of this Act, of any regulations thereunder or of any fire certificate or notice issued or served thereunder by the fire authority; or
(b) affecting any requirement or restriction imposed by or under any other enactment whether contained in a public general Act or in a local or private Act; or
(c) derogating from any right of action or other remedy (whether civil or criminal) in proceedings instituted otherwise than under this Act."

(2) In consequence of subsection (1) above, section 43(2) of the principal Act shall be omitted.

DEFINITIONS
"fire authority": Fire Precautions Act 1971, s.43(1).
"fire certificate": Fire Precautions Act 1971, s.1(1).
"principal Act": s.1(1).

GENERAL NOTE
By virtue of the new s.27A, inserted into the Fire Precautions Act 1971 by this section, it is made clear that, except where expressly provided to the contrary, contravention of the 1971 Act or of any regulations made thereunder, or of any fire certificate or other notice issued or served by the fire authority, does not of itself give rise to civil liability.

Miscellaneous

Removal of exemption for premises used for public religious worship

13. Premises appropriated to, and used solely or mainly for, public religious worship shall cease to be exempt from the requirement for a fire certificate if put to a designated use and accordingly—
(a) in section 2 of the principal Act (exemptions), there shall be

omitted the words from "of any of the following" to "premises" where last occurring; and

(b) in section 12(1) (fire regulations), for the words "any description falling within any paragraph of" there shall be substituted the words "the description given in" and the words "other than paragraph (d)" shall be omitted.

DEFINITIONS

"designated use": Fire Precautions Act 1971, s.1(1).
"fire certificate": Fire Precautions Act 1971, s.43(1).
"premises": Fire Precautions Act 1971, s.43(1).
"principal Act": s.1(1).

GENERAL NOTE

Until the amendment effected by this section, premises "appropriated to, and used solely or mainly for, public religious worship" were exempt from the obligation to have a fire certificate, albeit that they might on occasion be put to a "designated use." By virtue of the amendments effected by this section, such exemption is removed.

As a consequence of the amendment effected by this section to the Fire Precautions Act 1971, s.2, the only general exemption from the requirement to have a fire certificate is in favour of "premises consisting of or comprised in a house which is occupied as a single private dwelling." In that context the words "private dwelling" refer to use as a dwelling of a private person, and a company is incapable of such use (see *G. E. Stevens (High Wycombe)* v. *High Wycombe Corporation* [1961] 2 All E.R. 738).

By virtue of the definition of "premises" in s.43(1) of the 1971 Act ("'premises' means a building or part of a building") the 1971 Act does not apply to activities which take place out of doors, or other than in a building or part of a building. In that regard, however, see s.17 of this Act, *post*.

A "building" for the purposes of the 1971 Act "includes a temporary or movable building and also includes any permanent structure and any temporary structure other than a movable one" (Fire Precautions Act 1971, s.43(1)). "Structure" is not defined in the 1971 Act. In *Hobday* v. *Nichol* [1944] 1 All E.R. 302, Humphreys J. said, "Structure, as I understand it, is anything which is constructed, and it involves the notion of something which is put together, consisting of a number of different things which are so put together or built together, constructed as to make one whole which is then called a structure." See also, for example, *Mills and Rockleys* v. *Leicester City Council* [1946] 1 All E.R. 424 and *London County Council* v. *Tann* [1954] 1 All E.R. 389.

Breaches of fire certificate requirements: restriction of defence

14. In section 7(4) of the principal Act (offence of contravening fire certificate requirements except where person charged does not know of his responsibility), after the words "Provided that a person" there shall be inserted the words "other than the occupier of the premises".

DEFINITIONS

"fire certificate": Fire Precautions Act 1971, s.43(1).
"premises": Fire Precautions Act 1971, s.43(1).
"principal Act": s.1(1).

GENERAL NOTE

Until the amendment effected by this section, the Fire Precautions Act 1971, s.7(4), provided that if, while a fire certificate is in force in any premises, any requirement imposed thereby is contravened, every "person responsible" (within the meaning of s.6(5) of the 1971 Act) is guilty of an offence, unless he can prove that his responsibility for contraventions of the requirement concerned had not been made known to him before the occurrence of the contravention in respect of which he is charged.

By virtue of the amendment to s.7(4) of the 1971 Act effected by this section, that defence is no longer available to the occupier of the premises concerned. The occupier is thus liable for contraventions of the requirements of fire certificates whether or not such potential liability has been made known to him.

Occupier. See the General Note to s.2(1).

Automatic means for fighting fire

15. In section 5(3)(c) (fire authority to be satisfied regarding means for fighting fire before issuing a fire certificate with respect to any premises) and section 6(1)(d) (contents of a fire certificate regarding means for fighting fire) of the principal Act the words from "for use" to "the building" shall be omitted.

DEFINITIONS
"building": Fire Precautions Act 1971, s.43(1).
"fire authority": Fire Precautions Act 1971, s.43(1).
"fire certificate": Fire Precautions Act 1971, s.1(1).
"premises": Fire Precautions Act 1971, s.43(1).
"principal Act": s.1(1).

GENERAL NOTE
One of the matters to be considered by the fire authority in considering an application for, and granting, a fire certificate, is the means provided for fighting fire. Before the amendments effected this section, ss.5(3)(c) and 6(1)(d) of the Fire Precautions Act 1971 referred to "the means of fighting fire (whether in the premises affecting the means of escape) with which the relevant building is provided *for use in the case of fire by persons in the building*" (author's italics). By virtue of this section, the words in italics are deleted.

Accordingly, before a fire certificate can be issued, the fire authority must be satisfied with all means provided for fighting fire—automatic as well as manual (for example, sprinkler systems). Fire certificates, similarly, are required to specify all means of fighting fire which should be provided—again, automatic as well as manual.

Special provision for certain premises

16.—(1) After section 28 of the principal Act there shall be inserted the following section—

"Special provision for factory, office, railway and shop premises

28A.—(1) This Act shall have effect in relation to premises of the descriptions specified in Part I of Schedule 2 to this Act subject to the modifications specified in Part II of that Schedule.

(2) The Secretary of State may by order vary the provisions of that Schedule by amending, omitting or adding to the descriptions of premises or the modifications for the time being specified in it if it appears to him to be necessary or expedient in connection with any provision made by health and safety regulations under section 15 of the Health and Safety at Work etc. Act 1974.

(3) The power to make an order under this section is exercisable by statutory instrument which shall be subject to annulment in pursuance of a resolution of either House of Parliament."

(2) After the Schedule to the principal Act, which shall become Schedule 1 to that Act, there shall be inserted as Schedule 2 to that Act the Schedule set out in Schedule 1 to this Act.

(3) In the principal Act—
  (a) in section 34 (modification of certain enactments relating to Scotland) for the words "the Schedule" there shall be substituted the words "Schedule 1"; and
  (b) in section 43(1) (definitions) in the definition of "the court" the words "and the Schedule thereto" shall cease to have effect.

DEFINITION
"principal Act": s.1(1).

GENERAL NOTE
By virtue of the Fire Precautions Act 1971, s.28A (inserted into the 1971 Act by this section), the Fire Precautions Act 1971 is made to apply, with certain modifications, to

factory, office, railway and shop premises. The modifications are set out in Sched. 1 to this Act, which is inserted as Sched. 2 to the 1971 Act.

For the meaning of "factory," see the Factories Act 1961, s.175.

For the meaning of "office premises," "shop premises" and "railway premises," see the Offices, Shops and Railway Premises Act 1963, s.1, subss. (2), (3) and (4) respectively. See also s.90(1) of that Act.

Premises which are deemed to form part of a mine for the purposes of the Mines and Quarries Act 1954 are excluded from the descriptions of "office premises", "shop premises" and "factory premises" (see the Fire Precautions Act 1971, Sched. 2, para. 2, as inserted by this section).

Extension of power to apply Act

17. Section 35 of the principal Act (power for Secretary of State to apply Act to vessels and movable structures) shall be amended by the insertion, at the end of paragraph (b), of the words "; and

(c) places of work in the open air of any prescribed description."

DEFINITIONS
"prescribed": Fire Precautions Act 1971, s.43(1).
"principal Act": s.1(1).

GENERAL NOTE
By virtue of the amendment to the Fire Precautions Act 1971 effected by this section, the Secretary of State is empowered to make regulations applying any of the provisions of the Fire Precautions Act 1971 to a place of work in the open air. "Prescribed" means prescribed by regulations made by the Secretary of State under the 1971 Act. At the date of writing (July 1, 1987) no such regulations had been made by the Secretary of State.

Application to Crown etc.

18.—(1) Section 40 of the principal Act (application of Act to Crown etc.) shall have effect with the following amendments.

(2) In subsection (1)(a) (provisions applying to premises occupied by the Crown) after "4" there shall be inserted "5(2A), 5A, 5B," and for the words "9A (except subsection (4))" there shall be substituted the words "9A (except subsections (3) and (4)), 9B and 9C".

(3) In subsection (1)(b) (provisions applying to premises owned but not occupied by the Crown), after "8" there shall be inserted "8A, 8B,", after "9A" there shall be inserted "9B, 9C, 9D, 9F," and after "10," there shall be inserted "10B,".

(4) After subsection (10A), there shall be inserted the following subsection—

"(10B) This Act shall apply to premises occupied by the National Radiological Protection Board as if they were premises occupied by the Crown."

DEFINITIONS
"premises": Fire Precautions Act 1971, s.43(1).
"principal Act": s.1(1).

GENERAL NOTE
The Crown is not bound by the provisions of any statute unless it is expressly or by necessary implication "named" therein (see, for example, *Bank voor Handel en Sheepvaart N.V.* v. *Administrator of Hungarian Property* [1954] 1 All E.R. 969, H.L.).

PART II

SAFETY OF SPORTS GROUNDS

GENERAL NOTE
The purpose of the Safety of Sports Grounds Act 1975, which came into operation on September 1, 1975, was to implement the main recommendations contained in the Report

of the Inquiry into Crowd Safety at Sports Grounds ("the Wheatley Report" 1972—Cmnd. 4952). The main mechanism under the 1975 Act for securing safety is the safety certificate. The 1975 Act empowers the Secretary of State to designate any sports stadium with spectator accommodation for over 10,000 people as requiring such a certificate. For the Act's purposes a "stadium" means a sports ground which is wholly or substantially surrounded by spectator accommodation. The 1975 Act provides for two kinds of certificate: a general safety certificate, which is the main continuing form of control, and a special safety certificate, which relates only to activities or occasions not covered by the general certificate. Certificates are required to contain terms as to entrances and exits; the means of escape in case of fire or other emergency; the number, situation and strength of crush barriers; and limitations on numbers to be admitted to the stadium or any part of it.

On May 11, 1985, 56 people lost their lives in a fire at the Valley Parade Ground, Bradford, the ground of Bradford City F.C. A Committee of Inquiry into Crowd Safety and Control at Sports Grounds, chaired by Popplewell J., was set up, and its final report ("The Popplewell Report") was published in January 1986. Those of the Popplewell Report's recommendations dealing with crowd safety were considered in the consultative document "Fire Safety and Safety at Sports Venues".

Parts 2, 3 and 4 of this Act generally follow the conclusions of that document.

In brief terms, the general regime of Parts 2, 3 and 4 of this Act are as follows:

Part 2

The Bradford fire demonstrated that the level of risk to spectators does not necessarily depend upon the type or particular layout of a sports ground. Thus the Act gives effect to the Popplewell Inquiry's conclusion that the distinction between a sports "ground" and a sports "stadium" should be removed. S.19 of this Act thus enables designation to be applied to all classes of sports ground. S.20 enables the 10,000 accommodation threshold for designation to be varied. Ss.19 and 20, between them, provide for a wider but more flexible application of designation, should the need arise. S.23 amends the procedure under the 1975 Act for local authorities to take action where there is a serious risk to spectators. In such circumstances, under the original form of the 1975 Act, a local authority could only apply to a magistrates' court for an order restricting or prohibiting the use of a ground, or part of it, until the risk is reduced to an acceptable level. By virtue of s.23, local authorities are empowered to issue a notice on those responsible for administering the ground restricting or prohibiting the admission of spectators until that risk is reduced. Under s.24 there is a right of appeal against such a notice, but the lodging of an appeal does not of itself have the effect of suspending the notice. Under s.25, local authorities are required to carry out inspections of designated sports grounds in accordance with guidance issued by the Secretary of State.

Part 3

Part 3 of the Act introduces a system of certification, similar in outline to that which applies to designated sports grounds, for stands at undesignated sports grounds where there is covered accommodation for 500 or more spectators.

Part 4

Part 4 of the Act provides for the licensing by local authorities of sports events held in indoor premises to which the public are invited as spectators. The Popplewell Report proposed that control should be exercised by designating indoor sports premises under the Fire Precautions Act 1971. The Act, however, seeks to increase control by amending the existing public entertainments legislation so as to apply to sporting events.

Application of Safety of Sports Grounds Act 1975 to all sports grounds

Application of Safety of Sports Grounds Act 1975 to all sports grounds

19.—(1) For the purpose of extending the provisions of the Safety of Sports Grounds Act 1975 (in this Part referred to as "the principal Act") which apply to sports stadia to other sports grounds and making a minor correction the amendments to the principal Act specified in Schedule 2 to this Act shall have effect.

(2) In consequence of those amendments the following other amendments of the principal Act shall be made, that is to say—

(a) for section 2(2) (obligatory terms of safety certificates) there shall be substituted the following subsection—

"(2) In so far as an order under section 15A below so requires as respects any class of sports ground, a safety certificate shall include such terms and conditions as may be provided for in the order.";

(b) section 15 (power of Secretary of State to extend the principal Act to other classes of sports grounds) shall cease to have effect;

(c) there shall be inserted as section 15A the following section—

"Power to modify Act for classes of grounds

15A.—(1) The Secretary of State may, as respects any specified class of sports ground, by order modify the provisions of this Act (except section 1(1) above) in their application to sports grounds of that class.

(2) An order under this section may—

(a) make different modifications in relation to different activities at the same class of ground; and

(b) include such supplementary and transitional provision as the Secretary of State thinks expedient."; and

(d) in section 18 (orders and regulations), after subsection (1), there shall be inserted the following subsection—

"(1A) Regulations under any provision of this Act may make different provision for different classes of sports ground."

DEFINITIONS

"principal Act": subs. 1(1).

"safety certificate": Safety of Sports Grounds Act 1975, ss.1(1) and 17(1).

"sports ground": Safety of Sports Grounds Act 1975, s.17(1).

"sports stadium": Safety of Sports Grounds Act 1975, s.17(1).

GENERAL NOTE

By virtue of the amendments effected by this section to the Safety of Sports Grounds Act 1975, designation may henceforward apply to all classes of sports ground, not merely "sports stadia". The Secretary of State may, however, modify the 1975 Act in its application to different classes of ground, and in its application to different activities at the same class of ground.

Regulations under this section. At the time of writing (July 1, 1987) no regulations had been made under this section.

Designation: spectator capacity

Designation of grounds: variation in qualifying spectator capacity

20. After section 1(1) of the principal Act (designation of sports grounds with spectator capacity of more than 10,000) there shall be inserted the following subsections—

"(1A) The Secretary of State may by order substitute, for the number for the time being specified in subsection (1) above, such other number as he considers appropriate; but no order made under this subsection shall affect the validity of any designation previously made.

(1B) An order under subsection (1A) above may make different substitutions for different classes of sports ground."

DEFINITIONS

"principal Act": s.19(1).

"spectator": Safety of Sports Grounds Act 1975, s.17(1).

"sports ground": Safety of Sports Grounds Act 1975, s.17(1).

GENERAL NOTE

By virtue of the amendments to the Safety of Sports Grounds Act 1975 effected by this section, the Secretary of State may vary the 10,000 accommodation threshold for designation, contained in s.1(1) of the 1975 Act. Different thresholds may be specified for different classes of sports ground.

Regulations under this section. At the time of writing (July 1, 1987) no regulations had been made under this section.

Safety certificates

Safety certificates: police presence

21. In section 2 of the principal Act (contents of safety certificates), after subsection (2), there shall be inserted the following subsection—

"(2A) No condition of a safety certificate shall require the provision of the services at the ground of any members of a police force unless the extent of the provision of their services is reserved for the determination of the chief officer of police of the force."

DEFINITIONS

"chief officer of police": Police Act 1964, s.62 and Sched. 8.
"principal Act": s.19(1).
"safety certificate": Safety of Sports Grounds Act 1975, s.1(1).

Safety certificates: appeals

22.—(1) Section 5 of the principal Act (appeals to Secretary of State against determinations etc. of local authority) shall have effect with the amendments specified in subsections (2) to (6) below.

(2) In subsections (1), (2) and (3) for the words "Secretary of State" wherever occurring, there shall be substituted the word "court".

(3) After subsection (3) there shall be inserted the following subsections—

"(3A) An appeal to the court under this section in England and Wales shall be by way of complaint for an order, the making of the complaint shall be deemed to be the bringing of the appeal and the Magistrates' Courts Act 1980 shall apply to the proceedings.

(3B) An appeal to the court under this section in Scotland shall be by summary application.

(3C) In England and Wales any of the following persons may appeal to the Crown Court against an order under this section, namely—

(a) the local authority; and
(b) any interested party.

(3D) In Scotland any of the following persons may appeal against an order made in an appeal under this section, namely—

(a) the local authority; and
(b) any interested party,

notwithstanding that that person was not party to the proceedings on the application."

(4) Subsection (4) shall be omitted.

(5) In subsection (5), for the words "subsections (3) and (4) above", there shall be substituted the words "this section".

(6) Subsections (6), (7) and (8) shall be omitted.

(7) In section 6(1) of the principal Act (power to make regulations) for paragraph (c) (appeals), there shall be substituted the following paragraph—

"(c) prescribe the time within which appeals under section 5 above are to be brought."

(8) In section 7 of the principal Act (supplementary provisions relating to determinations and appeals)—

(a) in subsection (1), for the words from "person" to the end of paragraph (b) there shall be substituted the words "applicant for a safety certificate, he shall be deemed to have withdrawn his application" and for the words after "section 6 above", there shall be substituted the words "an appeal against the authority's determination may be brought.";

(b) for subsection (2), there shall be substituted the following subsection—

"(2) Subsection (1) above shall not have effect if an appeal is brought before the expiry of the period there mentioned, but if the appeal is withdrawn or the court upholds the authority's determination, the appellant shall be deemed to have withdrawn his application on the date of the withdrawal of his appeal or of the court's determination.";

(c) in subsection (3), for the words "notice is given of an appeal" there shall be substituted the words "an appeal is brought", the words ", subject to subsection (4) below," shall be omitted and for the words "Secretary of State" there shall be substituted the word "court"; and

(d) subsections (4) and (5) shall be omitted.

DEFINITIONS
"interested party": Safety of Sports Grounds Act 1975, s.5(5).
"local authority": Safety of Sports Grounds Act 1975, s.17(1).
"principal Act": s.19(1).

GENERAL NOTE
This section, by virtue of the amendments effected to the Safety of Sports Grounds Act 1975, amends the procedure for appeals against determinations of local authorities in relation to safety certificates, including the refusal of a local authority to grant a special safety certificate or to amend or replace a safety certificate, and conditions included in or excluded from safety certificates. Under the 1975 Act, before the amendments effected by this section come into force, the procedure is by way of appeal. Once this section is brought into force, such appeals will be to the court; in England and Wales, by way of complaint for an order to the magistrates' court; in Scotland, by summary application to the court.

Grounds involving serious risk to spectators

Special procedure in case of serious risk: prohibition notices

23.—(1) For section 10 of the principal Act (emergency procedure by magistrates' court order), there shall be substituted the following section—

"Special procedure in case of serious risk: prohibition notices
10.—(1) If the local authority are of the opinion that the admission of spectators to a sports ground or any part of a sports ground involves or will involve a risk to them so serious that, until steps have been taken to reduce it to a reasonable level, admission of spectators to the ground or that part of the ground ought to be prohibited or restricted, the authority may serve a notice (in this Act referred to as a "prohibition notice") on such persons as are specified in subsection (6) below.

(2) A prohibition notice shall—

(a) state that the local authority are of that opinion;

(b) specify the matters which in their opinion give or, as the case may be, will give rise to that risk; and

(c) direct that no, or no more than a specified number of, spectators shall be admitted to, or to a specified part of, the sports ground until the specified matters have been remedied.

(3) A prohibition notice may prohibit or restrict the admission of spectators generally or on a specified occasion.

(4) A prohibition notice may include directions as to the steps which will have to be taken to reduce the risk to a reasonable level and these may require alterations or additions to the ground or things to be done or omitted which would contravene the terms or conditions of a safety certificate for the ground or for any stand at the ground.

(5) No prohibition notice shall include directions compliance with which would require the provision of the services at the sports ground of any members of a police force unless the chief officer of police of the force has consented to their inclusion and the extent of the provision of their services is reserved for his determination.

(6) A prohibition notice shall be served on the persons specified in the following paragraphs in the circumstances specified in those paragraphs, that is to say—

(a) if a general safety certificate is in operation for the ground, on the holder of it;

(b) if the prohibition or restriction applies to an occasion in respect of which a special safety certificate for the ground is in operation, on the holder of it;

(c) if no safety certificate is in operation for the ground, on the person who appears to the local authority to be responsible for the management of the ground;

(d) if the prohibition or restriction applies to an occasion and no safety certificate is in operation for the ground, on each person who appears to the local authority to be responsible for organising an activity at the ground on that occasion;

(e) if a general safety certificate is in operation for a stand at the ground, on the holder of it;

(f) if the prohibition or restriction applies to an occasion in respect of which a special safety certificate for a stand at the ground is in operation, on the holder of it;

but the validity of a prohibition notice served on any person under any of the foregoing provisions shall not be affected by a failure to serve another person required to be served with such a notice under those provisions.

(7) A prohibition or restriction contained in a prohibition notice shall take effect immediately it is served if the authority are of the opinion, and so state in the notice, that the risk to spectators is or, as the case may be, will be imminent, and in any other case shall take effect at the end of a period specified in the notice.

(8) A copy of any prohibition notice shall be sent by the local authority to each of the following, namely—

(a) the chief officer of police; and

(b) where the local authority is in Greater London or a metropolitan county, the fire authority, or, in any other case, the building authority.

(9) The local authority who have served a prohibition notice may, in any case where it appears appropriate to them to do so, amend the prohibition notice by notice served on the persons specified in subsection (6) above (subject to the saving in that subsection), and copies shall be sent to the officer and authorities specified in subsection (8) above.

(10) A notice under subsection (9) above amending a prohibition notice shall specify the date on which the amendment is to come into operation.

(11) Where a notice has been served under subsection (1) or (9) above the local authority may withdraw the notice at any time."

(2) In consequence of those amendments section 12 of the principal Act (offences) shall be amended as follows—

(a) in subsection (1)(d) (contravention of certificate terms), after the word "contravened" there shall be inserted the words "otherwise than in pursuance of a prohibition notice";

(b) in subsection (1)(e) (admission of spectators in contravention of section 10 order), for the words "an order" there shall be substituted the words "a prohibition notice"; and

(c) in subsection (4) (due diligence defence), for the word "order" there shall be substituted the words "prohibition notice".

(3) In section 17(1) (definitions)—

(a) after the definition of "qualified person" there shall be inserted the following—

" "prohibition notice" has the meaning assigned to it by section 10(1);", and

(b) in the definition of "safety certificate", after the word "certificate" there shall be inserted the words ", except with reference to a stand at a sports ground," and at the end there shall be inserted the words "and, where it refers to a stand, means a safety certificate (whether general or special) under Part III of the Fire Safety and Safety of Places of Sport Act 1987".

DEFINITIONS

"binding authority": Safety of Sports Grounds Act 1975, s.17(1).
"chief officer of police": Police Act 1964, s.62, Sched. 8.
"general safety certificate": Safety of Sports Grounds Act 1975, s.17(1).
"local authority": Safety of Sports Grounds Act 1975, s.17(1).
"principal Act": s.19(1).
"special safety certificate": Safety of Sports Grounds Act 1975, s.1(4).
"spectator": Safety of Sports Grounds Act 1975, s.17(1).
"sports ground": Safety of Sports Grounds Act 1975, s.17(1).

GENERAL NOTE

This section, by virtue of the amendments effected to the Safety of Sports Grounds Act 1975, amends the procedure under the 1975 Act for local authorities to take action where there is a serious risk to spectators. In such circumstances, under the 1975 Act before the above amendments take effect, the local authority may apply to a magistrates' court for an order restricting or prohibiting the use of a sports ground, or part of it, until the risk is reduced to a reasonable level.

By virtue of the amendments effected by this section, local authorities are empowered to issue a notice on those responsible for administering the ground restricting or prohibiting the entry of spectators until the risk is reduced.

In an appropriate case, such a notice may take effect immediately on being served.

A notice may specify the steps to be taken to remedy the matters complained of—and such steps may include matters which would otherwise contravene the terms or conditions of a safety certificate applying to the ground, or part thereof.

Fire authority. The expression is not defined in this Act, or in the Safety of Sports Grounds Act 1975, but *cf.* the Fire Services Act 1947, s.38(1), the Fire Precautions Act 1971, s.43(1), and the Local Government Act 1985, s.37, Sched. 11, paras. 2(1), (2).

Served. As to the service of documents, see the Safety of Sports Grounds Act 1975, s.14.

Prohibition notices: appeals

24. After section 10 of the principal Act there shall be inserted the following section—

"Appeals against prohibition notices

10A.—(1) Any person aggrieved by a prohibition notice may appeal to the court against the notice if he does so within such period as the Secretary of State may by regulations prescribe.

(2) Subsection (1) above applies to any amendment of a prohibition notice as it applies to the prohibition notice in its original form.

(3) An appeal to the court under this section in England and Wales shall be by way of complaint for an order, the making of the complaint shall be deemed to be the bringing of the appeal and the Magistrates' Courts Act 1980 shall apply to the proceedings.

(4) An appeal to the court under this section in Scotland shall be by summary application.

(5) On an appeal under subsection (1) above, the court may either cancel or affirm the notice or, in the case of an appeal against an amendment, annul or affirm the amendment and, if it affirms the notice or the notice as amended, as the case may be, may do so either in its original form or as amended, as the case may be, or with such modifications of the notice as the court may in the circumstances think fit.

(6) Where an appeal is brought under this section against a prohibition notice or an amendment of it, the bringing of the appeal shall not have the effect of suspending the operation of the notice or the notice as amended, as the case may be.

(7) In England and Wales any of the following persons may appeal to the Crown Court against an order under this section, namely—
  (a) any person aggrieved by the notice;
  (b) the local authority;
  (c) the chief officer of police; and
  (d) where the local authority is in Greater London or a metropolitan county, the fire authority, or, in any other case, the building authority.

(8) In Scotland any of the following persons may appeal against an order made in an appeal under this section, namely—
  (a) any person aggrieved by the notice;
  (b) the local authority;
  (c) the chief officer of police; and
  (d) the building authority;
notwithstanding that that person was not party to the proceedings on the application.

(9) The persons who are, for the purposes of this section, "aggrieved" by a prohibition notice are the persons on whom, in accordance with section 10(6) of this Act, the notice is required to be served."

DEFINITIONS
"building authority": Safety of Sports Grounds Act 1975, s.17(1).
"chief officer of police": Police Act 1964, s.62, Sched. 8.
"the court": Safety of Sports Grounds Act 1975, s.17(1).
"local authority": Safety of Sports Grounds Act 1975, s.17(1).
"prohibition notice": s.23 and Safety of Sports Grounds Act 1975, s.10.

GENERAL NOTE
By virtue of the new s.10A inserted into the Safety of Sports Grounds Act 1975 by this section, there is a right of appeal against the issue of a prohibition notice. The appeal may be brought by any person "aggrieved", that is, on whom the notice is required to be served pursuant to the Safety of Sports Grounds Act 1975, s.10(6) (apparently, whether or not the notice was actually served on them).

The bringing of an appeal does not, of itself, suspend the operation of a prohibition notice.

The appeal is to the magistrates' court for the petty sessions area in which the ground is situated (in England and Wales). In the case of Scotland, the appeal is to the sheriff within whose jurisdiction the ground is situated. On appeal, the notice or amendment may be cancelled or affirmed. If affirmed, that may be done with or without modification.

Fire authority. The expression is not defined in this Act or in the Safety of Sports Grounds Act 1975, but *cf.* the Fire Precautions Act 1971, s.43(1), and the Local Government Act 1985, s.37, Sched. 11, para. 2(1), (2).

May by regulations prescribe. At the time of writing (July 1, 1987) no regulations had been made under this section.

Enforcement: inspections and obstruction

Enforcement: inspections and offence of obstruction

25.—(1) After the section 10A of the principal Act inserted by section 24 above there shall be inserted the following section—

> **"Enforcement**
>
> **10B.**—(1) It shall be the duty of every local authority to enforce within their area the provisions of this Act and of regulations made under it and for that purpose to arrange for the periodical inspection of designated sports grounds; but nothing in this subsection shall be taken to authorise a local authority in Scotland to institute proceedings for an offence.
>
> (2) In performing the duty imposed by subsection (1) above so far as it requires designated sports grounds in their areas to be inspected, local authorities shall act in accordance with such guidance as the Secretary of State may give them.
>
> (3) For the purposes of subsection (1) above, "periodical" means at least once in every twelve months."

(2) In section 12(6)(d) of the principal Act (obstruction of person exercising powers of entry and inspection under that Act to constitute an offence), for the word "wilfully" there shall be substituted the word "intentionally".

DEFINITIONS
"designated": Safety of Sports Grounds Act 1975, s.1(4).
"local authority": Safety of Sports Grounds Act 1975, s.17(1).
"principal Act": s.19(1).
"sports ground": Safety of Sports Grounds Act 1975, s.17(1).

GENERAL NOTE
By virtue of the new s.10B inserted by this section into the Safety of Sports Grounds Act 1975, enforcement of the 1975 Act is made mandatory. Furthermore, designated sports grounds are to be inspected periodically by local authorities, at intervals of no more than 12 months.

In carrying out their duties under the new s.10B, local authorities are to act in accordance with guidance given by the Secretary of State.

Subs.(2)
The difference between "wilfully" and "intentionally" is not clear as an act is done wilfully if it is deliberate and intentional, not accidental or inadvertent, but so that the mind of the person who does the act goes with it (see, for example, *R.* v. *Senior* [1899] 1 Q.B. 253, *per* Lord Russell of Killowen, at pp.290 and 291).

PART III

SAFETY OF STANDS AT SPORTS GROUNDS

Safety certificates for stands at sports grounds

26.—(1) This Part applies in relation to a sports ground which—
 (a) provides covered accommodation in stands for spectators, and
 (b) is not a designated sports ground.

(2) A certificate under this Part (referred to as a "safety certificate") is required in respect of the use, at a sports ground in relation to which this Part applies, of each stand which provides covered accommodation for 500 or more spectators to view activities at the ground; but one certificate may be issued in respect of several such stands.

(3) The Secretary of State may by order amend subsection (2) above by substituting a smaller number for the number for the time being specified in it.

(4) The power to make an order under subsection (3) above is exercisable by statutory instrument which shall be subject to annulment in pursuance of a resolution of either House of Parliament.

(5) A stand in respect of the use of which a safety certificate under this Part is required is referred to in this Part as a "regulated stand".

(6) It shall be the function of the local authority to determine whether any, and if so, which of the stands at a sports ground in their area is a regulated stand, and to issue safety certificates.

(7) In determining whether any stand at a sports ground in their area is a regulated stand the local authority may apply any criteria which are appropriate for that purpose.

(8) In discharging their function of determination as respects the stands at sports grounds in their areas, local authorities shall act in accordance with such guidance as the Secretary of State may give them.

(9) A final determination of a local authority that a stand at a sports ground is a regulated stand shall be conclusive of the question subject only to an appeal under section 30 below.

(10) A safety certificate in respect of the use of a regulated stand at a sports ground may be either—

    (a) a certificate in respect of the use of the stand for viewing an activity or a number of activities specified in the certificate during an indefinite period commencing with a date so specified; or

    (b) a certificate in respect of the use of the stand for viewing an activity or a number of activities specified in the certificate on an occasion or series of occasions so specified;

and any reference in this Part to a safety certificate's being "for" a stand is a reference to its covering the use of the stand for viewing an activity or activities during an indefinite period or, as the case may be, on an occasion or occasions.

(11) In this Part—

    "final", in relation to a determination, is to be construed in accordance with section 28 below;

    "general safety certificate" means such a safety certificate for a stand as is mentioned in subsection (10)(a) above;

    "special safety certificate" means such a safety certificate for a stand as is mentioned in subsection (10)(b) above; and

    "stand", in relation to a sports ground, means an artificial structure (not merely temporary) which provides accommodation for spectators and is wholly or partly covered by a roof, and, in relation to the number of spectators in a stand provided with covered accommodation, "covered" means covered by the roof or other part of the structure which constitutes the stand.

DEFINITIONS

  "designated": s.41 and Safety of Sports Grounds Act 1975, s.1(4).
  "spectator": s.41.
  "sports ground": Safety of Sports Grounds Act 1975, s.17(1).

GENERAL NOTE

  Pt. 3 of this Act introduces a system of certification, similar in outline to that which applies to designated sports grounds under the Safety of Sports Grounds Act 1975, for stands at undesignated sports grounds where there is covered accommodation for 500 or more spectators.

There is provision, pursuant to subs. (3) for the threshold limit of 500 spectators to be varied by the Secretary of State. At the time of writing (July 1, 1987) no such variation had been made.

The task of determining whether a stand is a regulated stand falls to the appropriate local authority.

A safety certificate issued in respect of a regulated stand may be either a "general safety certificate", that is, a certificate for viewing one or more activities for an indefinite period, or may be a "special safety certificate", that is, a certificate granted in respect of one or more activities on one or more specified occasions.

This section is broadly analogous to the Safety of Sports Grounds Act 1975, s.1.

Contents of safety certificates for stands

27.—(1) A safety certificate for a regulated stand shall contain such terms and conditions as the local authority consider necessary or expedient to secure reasonable safety in the stand when it is in use for viewing the specified activity or activities at the ground, and the terms and conditions may be such as to involve alterations or additions to the stand or any installations in or serving the stand.

(2) In so far as an order under section 39 below so requires as respects any class of stand at sports grounds, a safety certificate shall include such terms and conditions as may be provided for in the order.

(3) No condition of a safety certificate shall require the provision of the services in or in the vicinity of the stand of any members of a police force unless the extent of the provision of their services is reserved for the determination of the chief officer of police of the force.

(4) Without prejudice to subsection (1) above, a safety certificate for a regulated stand may include a condition that the following records shall be kept—

(a) records of the number of spectators accommodated in covered accommodation in the stand; and

(b) records relating to the maintenance of safety in the stand.

(5) A general safety certificate shall contain or have attached to it a plan of the stand to which it applies and the area in the immediate vicinity of it, and the terms and conditions in the certificate or in any special safety certificate issued for the stand shall be framed, where appropriate, by reference to that plan.

(6) A safety certificate for a regulated stand at a sports ground may include different terms and conditions in relation to different activities taking place at the ground.

(7) Nothing in a safety certificate for a regulated stand at a sports ground shall derogate from any requirements imposed by regulations under section 6(2) of the Safety of Sports Grounds Act 1975.

DEFINITIONS
"chief officer of police": Police Act 1964, s.62, Sched. 8.
"general safety certificate": ss.26(10)(a), 26(11).
"local authority": s.41.
"regulated stand": ss.26(5), 41.
"safety": s.41.
"safety certificate": ss.26(2), 41.
"special safety certificate": ss.26(10)(b), 26(11).
"spectator": s.41.
"sports ground": s.41, and Safety of Sports Grounds Act 1975, s.17(1).
"stand": ss.26(11), 41.

GENERAL NOTE
This section is broadly analogous to the Safety of Sports Grounds Act 1975, s.2. The terms and conditions of a certificate for a stand will be decided by the local authority, which

will consult the building authority or fire authority, as appropriate, and the police. Conditions might well include matters such as fire protection; size, location and number of entrances and exits, including means of escape; and the means of maintaining those entrances or exits. A certificate may also contain terms limiting the number of spectators who may be admitted to a stand or part of a stand.

A certificate may include different terms and conditions in relation to different activities taking place at the ground.

As to the contravention of terms and conditions of safety certificates, see s.36 *post.*

Subs. (7)

At the time of writing (July 1, 1987) no regulations had been made under the Safety of Sports Grounds Act 1975, s.6(2).

Issue of certificates

28.—(1) For the purposes of this Part, the following persons qualify for the issue of a safety certificate for a regulated stand at a sports ground, that is to say—
  (a) the person who qualifies for the issue of a general safety certificate is the person who is responsible for the management of the ground; and
  (b) the person who qualifies for the issue of a special safety certificate for viewing an activity from the stand on any occasion is the person who is responsible for organising that activity.

(2) The local authority for an area shall, in respect of any stand at a sports ground in their area which appears to them to be a regulated stand, make a preliminary determination whether or not that stand is a regulated stand and, if they determine that it is, they shall serve a notice on the person who appears to them to qualify for the issue of a general safety certificate stating their determination and the effects of it.

(3) Subject to subsection (4) below, a preliminary determination that a stand at a sports ground is a regulated stand shall become final at the end of the period of two months beginning with the date of the notice of it.

(4) A local authority may revoke a determination of theirs that a stand at a sports ground is a regulated stand—
  (a) at any time before it becomes final, or
  (b) on considering an application for a general safety certificate for the stand, whether the determination has or has not become final.

(5) A local authority may, at any time before a determination of theirs that a stand at a sports ground is a regulated stand becomes final, withdraw the notice of it and serve a further notice under subsection (2) above on another person, but if they do so the period of two months at the end of which the determination becomes final shall be treated as beginning with the date of the further notice.

(6) If a local authority receive an application for a general safety certificate for a regulated stand at a sports ground in their area, it shall be their duty—
  (a) if they have not already done so, to determine whether the stand is a regulated stand and, if they determine that it is, to determine whether the applicant is the person who qualifies for the issue of the general safety certificate for it;
  (b) if they have made a determination that the stand is a regulated stand and do not decide to revoke it, to determine whether the applicant is the person who qualifies for the issue of the general safety certificate for it;
and a determination made under paragraph (a) above that a stand is a regulated stand i, when made, a final determination.

(7) If the local authority, on an application made under subsection (6) above in relation to a stand which they have determined or determine is

27–33

a regulated stand, determine that the applicant is the person who qualifies for the issue of the general safety certificate they shall (if no such certificate is in operation) issue to him such a certificate.

(8) If a local authority receive an application for a special safety certificate for a regulated stand at a sports ground in their area as respects which stand a general safety certificate is in operation, it shall be their duty to determine whether the applicant qualifies for the issue of a special safety certificate for it and, if they determine that he does, they may issue to him a special safety certificate.

(9) The local authority shall, if they determine that an applicant for a safety certificate does not qualify for the issue of the certificate, serve on him a notice stating their determination.

(10) The local authority shall send a copy of an application for a safety certificate for a regulated stand at a sports ground to the chief officer of police and where the local authority is in Greater London or a metropolitan county, the fire authority or, in any other case, the building authority for the area in which it is situated, and shall consult them about the terms and conditions to be included in the certificate.

(11) The local authority may, by notice, require an applicant for a safety certificate to furnish them within such reasonable time as they may specify in the notice with such information and such plans of the ground as they consider necessary for the purpose of discharging their functions in respect of the issue of safety certificates for the regulated stands at the ground.

(12) If an applicant for a safety certificate fails to comply with a requirement under subsection (11) above within the time specified by the local authority, or within such further time as they may allow, he shall be deemed to have withdrawn his application.

DEFINITIONS
  "building authority": s.41.
  "chief officer of police": Police Act 1964, s.62, Sched. 8.
  "final": ss.26(11), subs. (3).
  "general safety certificate": ss.26(10)(a), 26(11).
  "local authority": s.41.
  "regulated stand": ss.26(5), 41.
  "safety certificate": ss.26(2), 41.
  "special safety certificate": ss.26(10)(b), 26(11).
  "sports ground": s.41, and Safety of Sports Grounds Act 1975, s.17(1).
  "stand": ss.26(11), 41.

GENERAL NOTE
  This section is broadly analogous to the Safety of Sports Grounds Act 1975, s.5.
  The section thus deals with the persons who qualify for the issue of a safety certificate; the determination by the local authority as to whether stands at sports grounds in their area are regulated stands; and the issue of certificates.
  The responsibility for determining whether a stand is a regulated stand falls to the appropriate local authority. Thus, in relation to any stand which appears to be a regulated stand, the local authority must make a preliminary determination that a stand requires a safety certificate. That determination becomes final after no more than two months have elapsed, unless further information is brought to the local authority's attention leading them to conclude that a safety certificate is not required. Once a determination is final, those responsible for administering the stand, or stands, at the ground are notified. Thereafter it is an offence to admit spectators to that stand if no application for a safety certificate has been made or to contravene a term or condition of such a certificate, once issued—see s.36.
  Serve a notice. As to the service of documents under this Part, see s.38. "Notice" means "notice in writing" (s.41). For the meaning of "writing" see the Interpretation Act 1978, s.5, Sched. 1.
  Consult. On what constitutes consultation see, in particular, *Rollo* v. *Minister of Town and Country Planning* [1948] 1 All E.R. 13 and *Agricultural, Horticultural and Forestry Industry Training Board* v. *Aylesbury Mushrooms* [1972] 1 All E.R. 280.

Amendment, cancellation etc. of certificates

29.—(1) The local authority who have issued a safety certificate for a regulated stand at a sports ground—

(a) shall, if at any time it appears to them that the stand in respect of which it was issued is not or has ceased to be a regulated stand, revoke their previous determination and, by notice to its holder, cancel the certificate;

(b) may, in any case where it appears appropriate to them to do so, amend the certificate by notice to its holder; or

(c) may replace the certificate.

(2) A safety certificate may be cancelled, amended or replaced under subsection (1) above either on the application of the holder or without such an application.

(3) Section 27 above shall apply on the amendment or replacement of a safety certificate.

(4) A notice under subsection (1)(b) above amending a general safety certificate shall specify the date on which the amendment to which it relates is to come into operation, and the date so specified may be a date later than the date of issue of the notice.

(5) If the local authority receive an application for the transfer of a safety certificate for a regulated stand at a sports ground from the holder to some other person it shall be their duty to determine whether that person would, if he made an application for the purpose, qualify for the issue of the certificate; and if they determine that he would, they may transfer the certificate to him and shall in any case notify him of their determination.

(6) An application under subsection (5) above may be made either by the holder of the safety certificate or by the person to whom it is proposed that it should be transferred.

(7) The local authority shall send a copy of an application for the transfer of a safety certificate for a regulated stand at a sports ground to the chief officer of police and where the local authority is in Greater London or a metropolitan county the fire authority or, in any other case, · the building authority for the area in which it is situated.

(8) The local authority shall consult the chief officer of police and where the local authority is in Greater London or a metropolitan county, the fire authority or, in any other case, the building authority about any proposal to amend, replace or transfer a safety certificate.

(9) The holder of a safety certificate may surrender it to the local authority, and it shall thereupon cease to have effect.

(10) The local authority may cancel a safety certificate if the holder dies or (if a body corporate) is dissolved.

DEFINITIONS

"building authority": s.41.

"chief officer of police": Police Act 1964, s.62, Sched. 8.

"general safety certificate": ss.26(10)(a), 26(11).

"local authority": s.41.

"regulated stand": ss.26(5), 41.

"safety certificate": ss.26(2), 41.

"sports ground": s.41, and Safety of Sports Grounds Act 1975, s.17(1).

"stand": ss.26(11), 41.

GENERAL NOTE

This section is broadly analogous to the Safety of Sports Grounds Act 1975, s.4. The section provides for the amendment, cancellation, replacement, surrender or transfer of safety certificates. A safety certificate may be cancelled, amended or replaced on the application of the holder, or without any application at the local authority's behest. A procedure is set out for the transfer of certificates.

Fire authority. The term is not defined in this Part but *cf.* the Fire Services Act 1947, s.38(1); the Fire Precautions Act 1971, s.43(1) and the Local Government Act 1985, s.37 and Sched. 11, para. 2(1), (2).

Notice. This means "notice in writing" (s.41). As to what constitutes "writing", see the Interpretation Act 1978, s.5, Sched. 1.

Appeals

30.—(1) A person who has been served with a notice of a determination, which is or has become a final determination, of a local authority that any stand at a sports ground is a regulated stand may appeal against the determination to the court.

(2) Any person who, on an application for the issue or transfer to him of a safety certificate for a regulated stand at a sports ground, has been served with a notice of the determination of a local authority that he does not or, in the case of an application for a transfer, would not qualify for the issue of the certificate may appeal against the determination to the court.

(3) An applicant for a special safety certificate for a regulated stand at a sports ground may also appeal to the court against a refusal of his application on grounds other than a determination that he does not qualify for the issue of the certificate.

(4) An interested party may appeal to the court against—
    (a) the inclusion of anything in, or the omission of anything from, a safety certificate for a regulated stand at a sports ground; or
    (b) the refusal of the local authority to amend or replace a safety certificate for a regulated stand at a sports ground.

(5) Any appeal under this section shall be brought within the period prescribed under section 31 below.

(6) An appeal to the court under this section in England and Wales shall be by way of complaint for an order, the making of the complaint shall be deemed to be the bringing of the appeal and the Magistrates' Courts Act 1980 shall apply to the proceedings.

(7) An appeal to the court under this section in Scotland shall be by summary application.

(8) In this section "interested party", in relation to a safety certificate, includes—
    (a) the holder of the certificate;
    (b) any other person who is or may be concerned in ensuring compliance with the terms and conditions of the certificate;
    (c) the chief officer of police; and
    (d) where the local authority is in Greater London or a metropolitan county, the fire authority or, in any other case, the building authority.

(9) Subject to subsection (10) below, if a local authority serve on any applicant for a safety certificate a notice of a determination of theirs that he does not qualify for the issue of the certificate, he shall be deemed to have withdrawn his application on the expiry of the period within which an appeal must, by virtue of subsection (5) above, be brought.

(10) Subsection (9) above shall not have effect if an appeal is brought before the expiry of the period referred to in that subsection, but if the appeal is withdrawn or the court upholds the authority's determination, the appellant shall be deemed to have withdrawn his application on the date of the withdrawal of his appeal or of the court's order on the appeal.

(11) Where an appeal is brought against the inclusion of any term or condition in a safety certificate (whether it was included in the certificate originally or only on its amendment or replacement), the operation of that term or condition shall be suspended until the court has determined the appeal.

(12) In England and Wales any of the following persons may appeal to the Crown Court against an order under this section, namely—
(a) the local authority; and
(b) any interested party.
(13) In Scotland any of the following persons may appeal against an order under this section, namely—
(a) the local authority; and
(b) any interested party,
notwithstanding that that person was not party to the proceedings on the application.

DEFINITIONS
"building authority": s.41.
"chief officer of police": Police Act 1964, s.62, Sched. 8.
"court": s.41.
"final": ss.26(11), 28(3).
"local authority": s.41.
"regulated stand": ss.26(5), 41.
"safety certificate": ss.26(2), 41.
"special safety certificate": ss.26(10)(b), 26(11).
"sports ground": s.41, and Safety of Sports Grounds Act 1975, s.17(1).

GENERAL NOTE
This section is broadly analogous to the Safety of Sports Grounds Act 1975, s.5. The section provides for a right of appeal, *inter alia*, against final determination that a stand is required to have a safety certificate. It also provides for appeals against the terms and conditions of the certificate itself. As to the service of notices and other documents under this Part, see s.38.
The bringing of an appeal against the inclusion of any term or condition in a safety certificate suspends the operation of that term or condition until the court has determined the appeal.

Subs. (1)
Person. See the General Note to s.1.
Fire authority. The term is not defined in this Part but *cf.* the Fire Services Act 1947, s.38(1), the Fire Precautions Act 1971, s.45(1), and the Local Government Act 1985, s.37, and Sched. 11, para. 2(1), (2).
Notice. This means "notice in writing" (s.41). As to what constitutes "writing," see the Interpretation Act 1978, s.5, Sched. 1.

Regulations

31.—(1) The Secretary of State may by regulations—
(a) prescribe the procedure (subject to the provisions of this Part) for the issue, cancellation, amendment, replacement and transfer of safety certificates for regulated stands at sports grounds and the particulars to be given in applications for their issue, amendment, replacement or transfer;
(b) authorise local authorities to determine, subject to such limits or in accordance with such provisions as may be prescribed by the regulations, the fees (if any) to be charged in respect of applications for the issue, amendment, replacement or transfer of safety certificates or in respect of applications for the cancellation of safety certificates for stands which have ceased to be regulated stands; and
(c) prescribe the time within which appeals under section 30 above are to be brought.
(2) Regulations under this section may contain such incidental and supplementary provisions as the Secretary of State thinks expedient.

(3) The power to make regulations under this section is exercisable by statutory instrument which shall be subject to annulment in pursuance of a resolution of either House of Parliament.

(4) It shall be the duty of the Secretary of State, before making regulations under this section, to consult with such persons or bodies of persons as appear to him requisite.

DEFINITIONS
"local authority": s.41.
"regulated stands": ss.26(5), 41.
"safety certificate": ss.26(2), 41.
"stand": ss.26(11), 41.

GENERAL NOTE
This section is broadly analogous to the Safety of Sports Grounds Act 1975, s.6.
At the date of writing (July 1, 1987) no regulations had been made under this section.
Consult. On what constitutes consultation see, in particular, *Rollo* v. *Minister of Town and Country Planning* [1948] 1 All E.R. 13 and *Agricultural, Horticultural and Forestry Industry Training Board* v. *Aylesbury Mushrooms* [1972] 1 All E.R. 280.

Alterations and extensions

32.—(1) If while a general safety certificate for a regulated stand at a sports ground is in operation it is proposed to alter or extend the stand or its installations, and the alteration or extension is likely to affect the safety of persons in the stand, the holder of the certificate shall, before the carrying out of the proposals is begun, give notice of the proposals to the local authority.

(2) Subsection (1) above in particular requires notice when it is proposed to alter the entrances to or exits from a regulated stand at a sports ground (including any means of escape in case of fire or other emergency) or the means of access to any such entrances or exits.

DEFINITIONS
"general safety certificate": ss.26(10)(a), 26(11).
"regulated stand": ss.26(5), 41.
"sports ground": s. 41, and Safety of Sports Grounds Act 1975, s.17(1).
"stand": ss.26(11), 41.

GENERAL NOTE
This section is broadly analogous to the Safety of Sports Grounds Act 1975, s.8. The holder of a general safety certificate must give notice of any proposals to alter or extend a stand if such alteration or extension is likely to affect the safety of persons in the stand.
As to the service of notices under this Part, see s.38. "Notice" means "notice in writing" s.41. As to what constitutes "writing," see the Interpretation Act 1889, s.20.
As to offences in relation to this section, see s.36(7)(b).

Exclusion of other statutory requirements

33.—(1) While a general safety certificate is in force under this Part for a regulated stand at a sports ground, the following provisions shall not apply to the stand, that is to say—
   (a) section 37(1) of the Public Health Acts Amendment Act 1890 (platforms for public occasions);
   (b) any provision of the Fire Precautions Act 1971 or of a fire certificate issued under that Act in so far as it relates to any matter in relation to which requirements are imposed by the terms and conditions of the safety certificate;
   (c) section 89 of the Civic Government (Scotland) Act 1982 (which makes provision as to the safety of platforms, stands and similar structures) in so far as that section relates to any matter in relation

to which requirements are imposed by the terms and conditions of the safety certificate;

(d) sections 24 and 71 of the Building Act 1984 (exits, entrances etc. in the case of certain public and other buildings); and

(e) any provision of a local Act in so far as it relates to any matter in relation to which requirements are imposed by the terms and conditions of the safety certificate.

(2) Where an enactment provides for the licensing of premises of any class or description and the authority responsible for licences thereunder is required or authorised to impose terms, conditions or restrictions in connection with such licences, then, so long as there is in operation with respect to the premises a safety certificate under this Part covering the use of the premises by reason of which a licence under that enactment is required, any term, condition or restriction imposed with respect to those premises in connection with any licence under that enactment shall be of no effect in so far as it relates to any matter in relation to which requirements are imposed by the terms and conditions of the certificate under this Part.

(3) A person required by or under a local Act to do anything that would involve a contravention of the terms or conditions of a safety certificate under this Part shall not be treated as having contravened that Act if he fails to do it.

DEFINITIONS
"general safety certificate": ss.26(10)(a), s.26(11).
"regulated stand": ss.26(5), 41.
"safety certificate": ss.26(2), 41.
"sports ground": s.41, and Safety of Sports Grounds Act 1975, s.17(1).
"stand": ss.26(11), 41.

GENERAL NOTE
This section is broadly analogous to the Safety of Sports Grounds Act 1975, s.9.

Subs. (1)
As to the issue and contents of fire certificates, see the Fire Precautions Act 1971, ss. 5 and 6.

Subs. (2)
An example of this kind of enactment is the Licensing Act 1964, s.4(1), under which licensing justices may attach conditions to justices' on-licences.

Enforcement

34.—(1) It shall be the duty of every local authority to enforce within their area the provisions of this Part and for that purpose to arrange for the periodical inspection of sports grounds at which there are regulated stands, but nothing in this subsection shall be taken to authorise a local authority in Scotland to institute proceedings for an offence.

(2) In performing the duty imposed by subsection (1) above so far as it requires sports grounds in their areas to be inspected, local authorities shall act in accordance with such guidance as the Secretary of State may give them.

DEFINITIONS
"local authority": s.41.
"regulated stand": ss.26(5). 41.
"sports grounds": s.41, and Safety of Sports Grounds Act 1975, s.17(1).

GENERAL NOTE
This section is broadly analogous to the Safety of Sports Grounds Act 1975, s.10B (inserted into the 1975 Act by s.25(1) of this Act).

Periodical. This is not defined for the purposes of this Part, but *cf.* Safety of Sports Grounds Act 1975, s.10B(3).

Powers of entry and inspection

35. A person authorised by—
   (a) the local authority,
   (b) the chief officer of police, or
   (c) where the local authority is in Greater London or a metro-politan county, the fire authority or, in any other case, the building authority,
may, on production if so required of his authority, enter a sports ground at any reasonable time, and make such inspection of the stands and such inquiries relating to them as he considers necessary for the purposes of this Part, and in particular may examine records of the number of spectators accommodated, and the maintenance of safety, in the regulated stands at the ground, and take copies of such records.

DEFINITIONS
   "building authority": s.41.
   "chief officer of police": Police Act 1964, s.62, Sched. 8.
   "local authority": s.41.
   "regulated stand": ss.26(5), 41.
   "spectator": s.41.
   "sports ground": s.41, and Safety of Sports Grounds Act 1975, s.17(1).
   "stand": ss.26(11), 41.

GENERAL NOTE
   This section is broadly analogous to the Safety of Sports Grounds Act 1975, s.11.
   On production if so required. This does not mean that the right of entry can only be exercised if there is someone to whom the authority can be produced (see *Grove* v. *Eastern Gas Board* [1951] 2 All E.R. 1051, C.A.).
   Enter a sports ground. Note that this section does not authorise the entry of premises occupied by the Crown (see s.40(2)).
   Any reasonable time. What is a reasonable time is a question of fact. See, for example *Small* v. *Bickley* (1975) 32 L.T. 726 (Sunday afternoon).
   For offences in relation to this section, see s.36(7)(c).

Offences

36.—(1) Subject to subsections (2), (5) and (6) below, if—
   (a) spectators are admitted to a regulated stand at a sports ground on an occasion when no safety certificate which covers their use of the stand is in operation for it, or
   (b) any term or condition of a safety certificate for a regulated stand at a sports grounds is contravened,
any responsible person and, if a safety certificate is in operation, the holder of the certificate, shall be guilty of an offence.
   (2) No offence under subsection (1)(a) above is committed if—
   (a) the determination that the stand is a regulated stand is not a final one, or
   (b) an application has been made for a general safety certificate for the stand and has not been withdrawn or deemed to have been withdrawn.
   (3) In subsection (1) above "responsible person" means the person who is concerned in the management of the sports ground or of the regulated stand in question or in the organisation of any activity taking place at the ground at the time when an offence is alleged to have been committed.
   (4) A person guilty of an offence under subsection (1) above shall be liable—

(a) on summary conviction, to a fine not exceeding the statutory maximum; or

(b) on conviction on indictment, to a fine or to imprisonment for a term not exceeding two years or both.

(5) Where any person is charged with an offence under subsection (1) above it shall be a defence to prove—

(a) that the spectators were admitted or the contravention of the certificate in question took place without his consent; and

(b) that he took all reasonable precautions and exercised all due diligence to avoid the commission of such an offence by himself or any person under his control.

(6) Where any person is charged as a responsible person with an offence under subsection (1)(a) above it shall be a defence to prove that he did not know of the determination that the stand in relation to which the offence is alleged to have been committed is a regulated stand.

(7) Any person who—

(a) in purporting to carry out a requirement under section 28(11) above or for the purpose of procuring a safety certificate or the cancellation, amendment, replacement or transfer of a safety certificate, knowingly or recklessly makes a false statement or knowingly or recklessly produces, furnishes, signs or otherwise makes use of a document containing a false statement; or

(b) fails to give a notice required by section 32(1) above; or

(c) intentionally obstructs any person in the exercise of powers under section 35 above, or without reasonable excuse refuses, neglects or otherwise fails to answer any question asked by any person in the exercise of such powers,

shall be guilty of an offence and liable on summary conviction to a fine not exceeding level 5 on the standard scale.

(8) Where an offence under this Part which has been committed by a body corporate is proved to have been committed with the consent or connivance of, or to be attributable to any neglect on the part of, a director, manager, secretary or other similar officer of the body corporate, or any person who was purporting to act in that capacity, he, as well as the body corporate, shall be guilty of that offence and be liable to be proceeded against and punished accordingly.

(9) Where the affairs of a body corporate are managed by its members, subsection (8) above shall apply to the acts and defaults of a member in connection with his functions of management as if he were a director of the body corporate.

DEFINITIONS

"final": ss.26(11), 28(3).

"regulated stand": ss.26(5), 41.

"safety certificate": ss.26(2), 41.

"spectator": s.41.

"sports ground": s.41, and Safety of Sports Grounds Act 1975, s.17(1).

"stand": ss.26(11), 41.

"standard scale": Criminal Justice Act 1982, s.75.

"statutory maximum": Criminal Justice Act 1982, s.74.

GENERAL NOTE

This section is analogous to the Safety of Sports Grounds Act 1975, s.12.

Subs. (1)

No safety certificate which covers their use of the stand. See s.26(2).

Subs. (4)

Conviction on indictment. See General Note to s.2(1).

Subs. (5)

It shall be a defence to prove. The burden of proof laid on the defendant is less onerous than that resting on the prosecution, and may be discharged "on the balance of probabilities" (see *R.* v. *Carr-Briant* [1943] 2 All E.R. 156 and *R.* v. *Dunbar* [1957] 3 All E.R. 737).

Due diligence. Whether or not the defendant has exercised all due diligence is a question of fact, but on a Case stated the High Court will interfere if there was no evidence to support a finding on such point (see *R. C. Hammett* v. *Crabb* [1931] All E.R. Rep. 70).

Subs. (6)

Did not know. There is authority for the proposition that where a person deliberately refrains from making inquiries the result of which he might not care to have, that constitutes in law actual knowledge of the facts in question (see *Taylors' Central Garages (Exeter)* v. *Roper* (1951) J.P. 445, at pp. 449, 450, *per* Devlin J. and *Mallon* v. *Allon* [1963] 3 All E.R. 843 at p. 847). Mere neglect to ascertain what would have been found out by making reasonable inquiries is not tantamount to actual knowledge, however (see the above cases and *London Computation* v. *Seymour* [1944] 2 All E.R. 11).

Subs. (7)

Knowingly. See the note "did not know" under sub. (6).

Recklessly. See in particular, *Derry* v. *Peek* (1889) 14 App.Cas. 337 and *M.F.I. Warehouses* v. *Nattrass* [1973] 1 All E.R. 762.

False. A statement may be false because of what it omits although it is literally true (see *R.* v. *Lord Kylsant* [1931] All E.R. Rep. 179).

Obstructs. Obstruction need not involve physical violence (see *Borrow* v. *Howland* (1896) 74 L.T. 787). Anything which renders it more difficult for a person to carry out his duty may amount to obstruction (*Hinchliffe* v. *Sheldon* [1955] 3 All E.R. 406). Standing by and doing nothing does not amount to obstruction unless there is a legal duty to act (*Swallow* v. *London County Council* [1914–15] All E.R. Rep. 403). For obstruction to constitute an offence under this Part of the Act it must, of course, be intentional.

Civil and other liability

37. Except in so far as this Part otherwise expressly provides, and subject to section 18 of the Interpretation Act 1978 (offences under two or more laws), the provisions of this Part shall not be construed as—

   (a) conferring a right of action in any civil proceedings (other than proceedings for the recovery of a fine) in respect of any contravention of this Part or of any of the terms or conditions of a safety certificate thereunder; or

   (b) affecting any requirement or restriction imposed by or under any other enactment whether contained in a public general Act or in a local or private Act; or

   (c) derogating from any right of action or other remedy (whether civil or criminal) in proceedings instituted otherwise than under this Part.

DEFINITION

"safety certificate": ss.26(2), 41.

GENERAL NOTE

This section is broadly analogous to the Safety of Sports Grounds Act 1975, s.13. Thus, except where expressly provided to the contrary, contravention of any of the provisions of this Part of this Act, or any safety certificate, does not of itself give rise to civil liability.

Service of documents

38.—(1) Any notice or other document required or authorised by or by virtue of this Part to be served on any person may be served on him either by delivering it to him or by leaving it at his proper address or by sending it by post.

(2) Any notice or other document so required or authorised to be served on a body corporate or a firm shall be duly served if it is served on the secretary or clerk of that body or a partner of that firm.

(3) For the purposes of this section, and of section 7 of the Interpretation Act 1978 (service of documents) in its application to this section, the proper address of a person, in the case of a secretary or clerk of a body corporate shall be that of the registered or principal office of that body, in the case of a partner of a firm shall be that of the principal office of the firm, and in any other case shall be the last known address of the person to be served.

GENERAL NOTE
This section is broadly analogous to the Safety of Sports Grounds Act 1975, s.14.

Subs. (1)
May be served. The expression is permissive only. Where a notice is served in a different manner, and is received, that constitutes good service (*Sharpley* v. *Marley* [1942] 1 All E.R. 66, C.A. and *Stylo Shoes* v. *Prices Taylors* [1959] 3 All E.R. 901).
Sending it by post. See the Interpretation Act 1978, s.7, to the effect that service is deemed to be effected by properly addressing, prepaying and posting a letter containing the document. Unless the contrary is proved, service is effected at the time when that letter would be delivered in the ordinary course of post. "Properly addressing" is to be construed in the light of subs. (3).
Registered or principal office. As to a company's registered office, see the Companies Act 1985. A company's "principal office" is the place from where the company's business is managed and controlled as a whole (see, for example *Clokey* v. *London and North Western Railway Co.* [1905] 2 I.R. 251).
Last known address. Apparently the notice will be valid even if it is known that the addressee has left (*Re Follick, ex p. Trustee* (1907) 97 L.T. 645).

Power to modify Part for classes of stand

39.—(1) The Secretary of State may, as respects any specified class of stand at sports grounds, by order modify the provisions of this Part in their application to stands of that class.

(2) An order under this section may—
(a) make different modifications in relation to different activities taking place at sports grounds; and
(b) include such supplementary and transitional provision as the Secretary of State thinks expedient.

(3) The power to make an order under this section is exercisable by statutory instrument which shall be subject to annulment in pursuance of a resolution of either House of Parliament.

(4) It shall be the duty of the Secretary of State, before making an order under this section, to consult with such persons or bodies of persons as appear to him requisite.

DEFINITIONS
"sports ground": s.41 and Safety of Sports Grounds Act 1975, s.17(1).
"stand": ss.26(11), 41.

GENERAL NOTE
At the date of writing (July 1, 1987) no order had been made pursuant to this section.

Subs. (4)
Consult. As to what constitutes consultation, see in particular, *Rollo* v. *Minister of Town and Country Planning* [1948] 1 All E.R. 13 and *Agricultural, Horticultural and Forestry Industry Training Board* v. *Aylesbury Mushrooms* [1972] 1 All E.R. 280.

Application to Crown

40.—(1) Sections 26 to 29 above bind the Crown, but shall have effect, in relation to premises occupied by the Crown, with the substitution of a reference to the Secretary of State for any reference to the local authority.

(2) Nothing in this Part shall be taken to authorise the entry of premises occupied by the Crown.

DEFINITION
"local authority": s.41.

GENERAL NOTE
The Crown is not bound by the provisions of any statute unless it is expressly or by necessary implication "named" therein (see, for example, *Bank voor Handel en Sheepvaart N.V.* v. *Administrator of Hungarian Property* [1954] 1 All E.R. 969, H.L.)

Subs. (2)
Entry of premises. See s.35.

Interpretation

41. In this Part—
"building authority" means—
(a) in England outside Greater London and the metropolitan counties, or in Wales, the district council;
(b) in Scotland, the local authority within the meaning of the Building (Scotland) Act 1959;
"the court" means, in relation to a sports ground in England and Wales, a magistrates' court acting for the petty sessions area in which it is situated and, in relation to a sports ground in Scotland, the sheriff court within whose jurisdiction it is situated;
"general safety certificate" has the meaning assigned to it by section 26(11) above;
"local authority" means—
(a) in Greater London, the London borough council or the Common Council of the City of London;
(b) in England, in the metropolitan counties, the district council;
(c) in England outside Greater London and the metropolitan counties, or in Wales, the county council;
(d) in Scotland, the regional or islands council;
"means of access" includes means of access from a highway or, in Scotland, from a road;
"notice" means a notice in writing;
"safety" does not include safety from danger inherent in participation in a sporting or competitive activity;
"safety certificate" has the meaning assigned to it by section 26(2) above;
"special safety certificate" has the meaning assigned to it by section 26(11) above;
"spectator" means any person occupying accommodation provided in stands for spectators at a sports ground;
"sports ground" and "designated sports ground" have the same meaning as in the Safety of Sports Grounds Act 1975; and
"stand" has the meaning assigned to it by section 26(11) above; and
"regulated stand" has the meaning assigned to it by section 26(5) above.

GENERAL NOTE

Includes. This is a phrase of extension and not of restriction (*Mellows* v. *Law* [1923] 1 K.B. 522). It is not equivalent to "means" (*R.* v. *Hermann* (1879) 4 Q.B.D. 284). In the case of the word "means", the word defined is limited or confined to the definition (*Re Potts, ex p. Taylor* [1893] 1 Q.B. 648). Where the word "includes" is used it naturally signifies "includes in addition to its ordinary meaning" (see *Robinson* v. *Barton-Eccles Local Board* (1883) 8 App.Cas. 798 at p. 801, *per* Lord Selborne).

PART IV

INDOOR SPORTS LICENCES

Licensing in England and Wales

Licensing of indoor sports premises in London

42.—(1) In Schedule 12 to the London Government Act 1963 (licensing of certain public entertainments in London), after paragraph 3 there shall be inserted the following paragraphs—

"Indoor sports licences

3A.—(1) Subject to sub-paragraphs (2) and (3) below, no premises in a London borough or the City of London shall be used for any entertainment which consists of any sporting event to which the public are invited as spectators (a "sports entertainment") except under and in accordance with the terms of a licence granted under this paragraph by the Council.

(2) Sub-paragraph (1) above does not require a licence in respect of any occasion when the sporting event which constitutes the entertainment is not the principal purpose for which the premises are used on that occasion; but this provision does not apply in relation to a sports complex.

(3) Sub-paragraph (1) above does not apply to a sports entertainment held in a pleasure fair.

(4) The Council may grant to any applicant, and from time to time renew, a licence for the use of any premises specified in it for any sports entertainment on such terms and conditions and subject to such restrictions as may be so specified.

(5) Subject to the next following sub-paragraph and to paragraph 19(3) of this Schedule, a licence granted under this paragraph shall, unless previously cancelled under paragraph 8 or revoked under paragraph 10(4) of this Schedule, remain in force for one year or for such shorter period specified in the licence as the Council think fit.

(6) The Council may grant a licence under this paragraph in respect of such one or more particular occasions only as may be specified in the licence, and a licence granted by virtue of this sub-paragraph is hereafter in this Schedule referred to as an "occasional sports licence".

(7) Where a licence has been granted under this paragraph to any person the Council may if they think fit transfer that licence to any other person on the application of that other person or the holder of the licence.

(8) In this paragraph—
"premises" means any permanent or temporary building and any tent or inflatable structure and includes a part of a building where the building is a sports complex but does not include a part of any other building;
"sporting event" means any contest, exhibition or display of any sport;

"sports complex" means a building—
    (a) which provides accommodation and facilities for both those engaging in sport and spectators, and
    (b) the parts of which are so arranged that one or more sports can be engaged in simultaneously in different parts of the building; and
"sport" includes any game in which physical skill is the predominant factor and any form of physical recreation which is also engaged in for purposes of competition or display, except dancing (in any form).

3B.—(1) An applicant for the grant, renewal or transfer of a licence under paragraph 3A of this Schedule other than an occasional sports licence shall give to the Council, to the commissioner of police in whose district the premises to which the application relates are situated and to the fire authority not less than twenty-one days' notice of his intention to make the application.

(2) An applicant for the grant, renewal or transfer of an occasional sports licence shall give to the Council and the fire authority not less than fourteen days' notice of his intention to make the application.

3C. The person making an application for the grant, renewal or transfer of a licence under paragraph 3A of this Schedule shall on making the application pay to the Council such fee as the Council may fix."

(2) The consequential amendments of the said Schedule 12 specified in Schedule 3 to this Act shall also have effect.

DEFINITION
"London borough": London Government Act 1963, s.1.

GENERAL NOTE
Pt. 4 of this Act provides for the licensing by local authorities of sports events held in indoor premises to which the public are invited as spectators.

The *Popplewell Report* proposed that control should be exercised by designating indoor sports premises under the Fire Precautions Act 1971. The Act, however, seeks to increase control by amending the existing public entertainments legislation so as to apply to sporting events.

The London Government Act 1963, Sched. 12 provided for the licensing of public entertainments in Greater London on and after 1st April 1965. Prior to the amendments effected by this section, that Schedule related to the licensing of premises used for "public dancing or music or any other public entertainment of a like kind"; *ibid*, Sched. 12, para. 1(1). Such expression does not include sporting events, however. That lacuna is filled by the new para. 3A inserted into that Schedule by this section.

Note, however, that prior to the said amendments, boxing and wrestling entertainments were subject to licensing control pursuant to Sched. 12, para. 4. The said para. 4 is amended by Sched. 3, para. 3 to this Act.

The licensing system introduced in relation to sports entertainments is similar in detail to that already existing in relation to public entertainments.

On such terms and conditions. See the London Government Act 1963, Sched. 12, para. 9.

Think fit. Statutory powers are often conferred in subjective terms, the competent authority being entitled to act when it is "satisfied" or of the "opinion" that a certain state of affairs exists, or may act as it "thinks fit". The inherent jurisdiction of the courts to determine whether such powers have been exceeded is not readily ousted by the use of such language.

Not less that twenty-one days' notice. The words "not less than" indicate that twenty-one clear days must intervene between the day on which the notice is given and that on which the application is made (see, for example, *R. v. Turner* [1910] 1 K.B. 346 and *Re Hector Whaling* [1935] All E.R. Rep. 302).

Fire authority. See the London Government Act 1963, Sched. 12, para. 2(1).

Licensing of indoor sports premises outside London

43. In Schedule 1 to the Local Government (Miscellaneous Provisions) Act 1982 (licensing of certain public entertainments), for paragraph 2 (certain sports) there shall be substituted the following paragraph—

"2.—(1) Subject to sub-paragraphs (2) and (3) below, no premises shall be used for any entertainment which consists of any sporting event to which the public are invited as spectators (a "sports entertainment") except under and in accordance with the terms of a licence granted under this paragraph by the appropriate authority.

(2) Sub-paragraph (1) above does not require a licence in respect of any occasion when the sporting event which constitutes the entertainment is not the principal purpose for which the premises are used on that occasion; but this provision does not apply in relation to a sports complex.

(3) Sub-paragraph (1) above does not apply to a sports entertainment held in a pleasure fair.

(4) The appropriate authority may grant to any applicant, and from time to time renew, a licence for the use of any premises specified in it for any sports entertainment on such terms and conditions and subject to such restrictions as may be so specified.

(5) The appropriate authority may grant a licence under this paragraph in respect of such one or more particular occasions only as may be specified in the licence.

(6) In this paragraph—

"premises" means any permanent or temporary building and any tent or inflatable structure and includes a part of a building where the building is a sports complex but does not include a part of any other building;

"sporting event" means any contest, exhibition or display of any sport;

"sports complex" means a building—
  (a) which provides accommodation and facilities for both those engaging in sport and spectators, and
  (b) the parts of which are so arranged that one or more sports can be engaged in simultaneously in different parts of the building; and

"sport" includes any game in which physical skill is the predominant factor and any form of physical recreation which is also engaged in for purposes of competition or display, except dancing (in any form)."

GENERAL NOTE

This section provides, by means of the amendments made to the Local Government (Miscellaneous Provisions) Act 1982, for the licensing of indoor sports premises in England and Wales, outside London.

Licensing in Scotland

Licensing of indoor sports premises in Scotland

44.—(1) After section 41 of the Civic Government (Scotland) Act 1982 ("the 1982 Act") there shall be inserted the following section—

"Indoor sports entertainment licences

41A.—(1) Subject to subsection (2) below, a licence to be known as an "indoor sports entertainment licence" shall be required for the use of premises as a place of public sports entertainment.

(2) Subsection (1) above shall not apply to any occasion on which the entertainment of the public by the sport is not the principal

purpose for which the premises are used but this provision does not apply in relation to a sports complex.

(3) Without prejudice to paragraph 5 of Schedule 1 to this Act, a licensing authority may attach conditions to an indoor sports entertainment licence—

(a) restricting the use of the premises to a specified kind or specified kinds of public sports entertainment;

(b) limiting the number of persons to be admitted to the premises;

(c) fixing the days and times when the premises may be open for the purposes of public sports entertainment.

(4) In this section—

"premises" means any permanent or temporary building and any tent or inflatable structure and includes a part of a building where the building is a sports complex but does not include a part of any other building;

"public sports entertainment" means any sporting event to which the public are invited as spectators;

"sporting event" means any contest, exhibition or display of any sport;

"sports complex" means a building—

(a) which provides accommodation and facilities for both those engaging in sport and spectators; and

(b) the parts of which are so arranged that one or more sports can be engaged in simultaneously in different parts of the building; and

"sport" includes any game in which physical skill is the predominant factor and any form of physical recreation which is also engaged in for purposes of competition or display, except dancing (in any form).".

(2) On and after the date of coming into force of this section an application made (but not decided) before that date for the grant or renewal of a licence for the use of premises as a place of public entertainment shall, where the entertainment for which the premises are to be used will be a public sports entertainment as mentioned in section 41A of the 1982 Act, be treated for all purposes as an application for a grant or renewal (as the case may be) of a licence under the said section 41A.

(3) On and after the date of coming into force of this section a licence granted or renewed before that date for the use of premises as a place of public entertainment under section 41(2) of the 1982 Act shall, where the entertainment for which the premises are to be used will be a public sports entertainment as mentioned in section 41A of the 1982 Act, be deemed for all purposes to have been granted or renewed under the said section 41A.

(4) In section 9 of the 1982 Act (which makes provision for licensing authorities to resolve when licensing is to be required) in subsection (1) after the words "to 43" there shall be inserted the words "(except section 41A)".

(5) In section 41 of the 1982 Act (which makes provision for public entertainment licences) in subsection (2) after paragraph (a) there shall be inserted the following paragraph—

"(aa) premises in respect of which a licence is required under section 41A of this Act while such premises are being used for the purposes mentioned in that section;".

GENERAL NOTE

This section provides by means of the amendments made to the Civic Government (Scotland) Act 1982, for the licensing of indoor sports premises in Scotland.

PART V

MISCELLANEOUS AND GENERAL

Miscellaneous

Entertainment licences: removal of exemption

45. The Royal Albert Hall shall cease to be exempt from the requirement for a public entertainment licence under paragraph 1 of Schedule 12 to the London Government Act 1963.

GENERAL NOTE
The London Government Act 1963, Sched. 12, para. 1(6), exempts the following premises from the requirement for a public entertainment licence, namely:
—the Royal Albert Hall;
—the Theatre Royal, Drury Lane;
—the Royal Covent Garden Opera House;
—the Theatre Royal, Haymarket;
and any other entertainment lawfully held by virtue of letters patent or licence of the Crown. The Royal Albert Hall is deleted from such list by virtue of this section.

Entertainment licences: fees for variation

46. In Schedule 1 to the Local Government (Miscellaneous Provisions) Act 1982 (licensing of certain public entertainments), after paragraph 16, there shall be inserted the following paragraph—
    "16A. An applicant for the variation of the terms, conditions or restrictions on or subject to which an entertainments licence is held shall pay a reasonable fee determined by the appropriate authority."

GENERAL NOTE
This amendment to the Local Government (Miscellaneous Provisions) Act 1982 removes an anomaly whereby applicants for the variation of a public entertainments licence were not required to pay a fee.

Luminous tube signs: England and Wales

47. In section 10 of the Local Government (Miscellaneous Provisions) Act 1982 (luminous tube signs of certain voltage to have firemen's switches)—
    (a) in subsection (1), for the words "650 volts" there shall be substituted the words "the prescribed voltage"; and
    (b) after subsection (1), there shall be inserted the following subsections—
        "(1A) In subsection (1) above "the prescribed voltage" means 1000 volts A.C. or 1500 volts D.C. if measured between any two conductors or 600 volts A.C. or 900 volts D.C. if measured between any conductor and earth.
        (1B) The Secretary of State may, by order made by statutory instrument, substitute such different voltages for those for the time being specified in subsection (1A) above as appear to him to be appropriate for this purpose having regard to the current regulations of the Institution of Electrical Engineers."

Luminous tube signs: Scotland

48. In section 98 of the Civic Government (Scotland) Act 1982 (power of Secretary of State to make regulations for safe operation of electrical luminous tube signs) in subsection (2) for the words "normally exceeding 650 volts" there shall be substituted the words "of such description as may be specified in regulations made under subsection (1) above".

General

Repeals and transitional and saving provisions

49.—(1) Subject to subsection (2) below, the enactments mentioned in Schedule 4 to this Act are hereby repealed to the extent specified in the third column of that Schedule.

(2) The transitional and saving provisions contained in Schedule 5 to this Act shall have effect.

Short title, commencement and extent

50.—(1) This Act may be cited as the Fire Safety and Safety of Places of Sport Act 1987.

(2) This Act shall come into force on such day as the Secretary of State may appoint by order made by statutory instrument; and different days may be so appointed for different provisions or for different purposes.

(3) This Act does not extend to Northern Ireland and—

> (a) in Part IV, sections 42 and 43 extend to England and Wales only and section 44 extends to Scotland only; and
>
> (b) in Part V, sections 46 and 47 extend to England and Wales only and section 48 extends to Scotland only.

(4) Except as provided by an order under subsection (5) below, Parts II and III of this Act do not extend to the Isles of Scilly.

(5) The Secretary of State may by order direct that Parts II and III of this Act shall, subject to such exceptions, adaptations and modifications as may be specified in the order, extend to the Isles of Scilly.

(6) An order under subsection (5) above may contain such incidental and consequential provisions, including provisions conferring powers or imposing duties on the Council of the Isles of Scilly, as the Secretary of State thinks necessary.

(7) An order under subsection (5) above shall be subject to annulment in pursuance of a resolution of either House of Parliament.

SCHEDULES

Section 16   SCHEDULE 1

FIRE PRECAUTIONS: SPECIAL PROVISION FOR CERTAIN PREMISES

SCHEDULE TO BE INSERTED AS SCHEDULE 2 TO FIRE PRECAUTIONS ACT 1971

"SCHEDULE 2

SPECIAL PROVISION FOR CERTAIN PREMISES

PART I

THE PREMISES

1. Subject to paragraph 2 below, the following are the descriptions of premises in relation to which this Act is subject to the modifications specified in relation to them in Part II—

> (a) premises constituting, or forming part of, a factory within the meaning of the Factories Act 1961 and premises to which sections 123(1) and 124 of that Act (application to electrical stations and institutions) apply (in this Schedule referred to as "factory premises");
>
> (b) office premises within the meaning of the Offices, Shops and Railway Premises Act 1963, or premises deemed to be such premises for the purposes of that Act (in this Schedule referred to as "office premises");
>
> (c) railway premises within the meaning of that Act of 1963, or premises deemed to be

such premises for the purposes of that Act (in this Schedule referred to as "railway premises"); and

(d) shop premises within the meaning of that Act of 1963, or premises deemed to be such premises for the purposes of that Act (in this Schedule referred to as "shop premises").

2. Premises which are deemed to form part of a mine for the purposes of the Mines and Quarries Act 1954 are excluded from the descriptions of premises mentioned in sub-paragraphs (b) to (d) of paragraph 1 above.

PART II

THE MODIFICATIONS

3.—(1) This paragraph applies to premises in respect of which a fire certificate is required which are factory premises, office premises, railway premises or shop premises, and which—

(a) are held under a lease or an agreement for a lease or under a licence and consist of part of a building all parts of which are in the same ownership; or

(b) consist of part of a building in which different parts are owned by different persons.

(2) In relation to premises to which this paragraph applies this Act shall have effect with the following modifications.

(3) For the references to the occupier in sections 5(2A), 5A(4), 5A(6), 5A(8), 5B(3), 5B(4), 5B(5), 6(5), 7(1), 7(3A), 7(4), 8(2) (except paragraph (c) and the insertion made by sub-paragraph (5) below), 8(4), 8(5), 8(7), 8B(1), 9(5)(b), 9A(3), 9D(1) and 12(8)(b) there shall be substituted—

(a) in the case of premises falling within sub-paragraph (1)(a) above, references to the owner of the building;

(b) in the case of premises falling within sub-paragraph (1)(b) above, references to the persons who between them own the building.

(4) For the words "a fire certificate" where they occur in section 6(8) and where they first occur in section 7(6) there shall be substituted the words "a copy of the fire certificate" and in section 6(8) at the end of the subsection there shall be inserted the words "and the fire certificate shall be sent to the owner of the building or, as the case may be, the person who owns the part of the building of which the premises consist."

(5) In sections 8(2) and 8A(1) after the words "fire authority;" there shall be inserted the words "and the occupier shall, before the carrying out of the proposals is begun, furnish to the persons responsible for giving notice of the proposals to the fire authority any information in his possession which is relevant to those proposals;".

(6) In section 8A(1) for the references to the occupier (except the reference inserted by sub-paragraph (5) above) there shall be substituted—

(a) in the case of premises—

    (i) falling within sub-paragraph (1)(a) above; and

    (ii) in relation to which it is intended to carry out proposals falling within subsection (2)(a) or (c) of that section,

references to the owner of the building; and

(b) in the case of premises—

    (i) falling within sub-paragraph (1)(b) above; and

    (ii) in relation to which it is intended to carry out proposals falling within subsection (2)(a) or (c) of that section,

references to the persons who between them own the building.

(7) The expressions "owner of the building" and "the persons who between them own the building" do not include the Crown in the modifications made—

(a) by sub-paragraph (3) above of sections 7(1), 8(7), 9A(3) and of the word "occupier" in the third place where it occurs in section 8(2); and

(b) by sub-paragraph (6) above of the word "occupier" in the second place where it occurs in section 8A(1).

4. In section 6(1) as it has effect in relation to factory premises there shall be inserted after paragraph (e) the following paragraph—

"(f) particulars as to any explosive or highly flammable materials which may be stored or used in the premises,".

5. In section 8 as it has effect in relation to factory premises—

(a) for paragraph (c) of subsection (2) there shall be substituted the following paragraph—

27–51

"(c) the occupier of the premises proposes to begin to store or use explosive or highly flammable materials in the premises or materially to increase the extent of such storage or use,"; and

(b) in subsection (3) for the words from "keep explosive" to "that kind" there shall be substituted the words "store or use explosive or highly flammable materials in the premises or materially to increase the extent of such storage or use".

6. In section 8A as it has effect in relation to factory premises, for paragraph (b) of subsection (2) there shall be substituted the following paragraph—

"(b) on the part of the occupier of the premises to begin to store or use explosive or highly flammable materials in the premises or materially to increase the extent of such storage or use;".

7. Where a licence issued under the Explosives Act 1875 or the Petroleum (Consolidation) Act 1928 is in force with respect to factory premises, office premises, shop premises or railway premises, section 31 of this Act shall not have effect in relation to any term, condition or restriction imposed in connection with the issue, renewal, transfer or variation of such licence.

8. Where any premises ("the relevant premises")—

(a) are premises for which a fire certificate is required, premises for which a fire certificate is in force, premises to which section 9A of this Act applies or premises to which regulations under section 12 of this Act apply, and

(b) are factory premises, office premises, shop premises or railway premises,

section 28 shall apply to the premises or to any other premises comprised in the same building—

(i) with the substitution of the foregoing words (reading "this section" for "section 28") for subsection (1);

(ii) with the insertion, in subsection (2)(a), after "8(5)" of "9D(1)"; and

(iii) with the substitution, for subsection (2)(c) of the following—

"(c) in order to secure compliance with section 9A or a provision of regulations under section 12 of this Act;".

Section 19

SCHEDULE 2

EXTENSION OF APPLICATION OF SAFETY OF SPORTS GROUNDS ACT 1975 TO SPORTS GROUNDS

Section	Amendment
Section 1(1).	For the words "a stadium", substitute the words "a sports ground."
	For the words "any sports stadium", substitute the words "any sports ground".
Section 1(2).	For the word "stadium", wherever occurring, substitute the word "ground".
Section 1(3).	For the word "stadium", wherever occurring, substitute the words "sports ground".
Section 1(4).	For the words "'designated stadium'", substitute the words "'designated sports ground'".
	For the words "a stadium", substitute the words "a sports ground".
Section 2(1), (3) and (4).	For the word "stadium", wherever occurring, substitute the words "sports ground".
Section 3.	For the word "stadium", wherever occurring, substitute the words "sports ground".
Section 4(7).	For the word "stadium", substitute the words "sports ground".
Section 8.	For the word "stadium", wherever occurring, substitute the words "sports ground".
Section 9(1).	For the word "stadium", substitute the words "sports ground".
Section 9(1)(b).	For the words from "sections 168" to "relate", substitute "section 89 of the Civic Government (Scotland) Act 1982 (which makes provision as to the safety of platforms, stands and other structures), in so far as that section relates".
Section 12(1).	For the word "stadium", wherever occurring, substitute the words "sports ground".
Section 12(2).	Omit the words "stadium or other".
Section 17(1).	For the words "'designated stadium'", substitute the words "'designated sports ground'".
	Omit the definition of "sports stadium".

Section 42   SCHEDULE 3

INDOOR SPORTS LICENCES

CONSEQUENTIAL AMENDMENTS

Preliminary

1. In this Schedule references to paragraphs are references to paragraphs of Schedule 12 to the London Government Act 1963.

Amendments

Music and dancing licences

2. In paragraph 1, at the end, there shall be inserted the following subparagraph—
"(7) In this paragraph 'premises' includes any place."

Boxing and wrestling licences

3. In paragraph 4—
    (a) in sub-paragraph (1), after the words "which is provided" there shall be inserted the words "wholly or mainly in the open air" and the words "at the Royal Albert Hall" shall be omitted;
    (b) in sub-paragraph (5), for the words "'occasional sports licence'" there shall be substituted the words "'occasional outdoor boxing or wrestling licence'"; and
    (c) after sub-paragraph (6), there shall be inserted the following sub-paragraph—
"(7) In this paragraph 'premises' includes any place."
4. In paragraph 5(1) and (2), for the words "occasional sports licence" there shall be substituted the words "occasional outdoor boxing or wrestling licence".

Licences continued during applications

5. In paragraphs 6A and 6B, after the words "paragraph 1" there shall be inserted ", 3A".

Transmission and cancellation of licences

6. In paragraphs 7 and 8, after the words "paragraph 1" there shall be inserted ", 3A".

Power to impose general terms etc. by regulations

7. In paragraph 9(1), after the words "paragraph 1" there shall be inserted ", 3A".

Enforcement

8. In paragraph 10(1), (2)(a) and (4), after the words "paragraph 1" there shall be inserted ", 3A".
9. In paragraph 12(1) after the words "paragraph 1" there shall be inserted ", 3A" and, for the word "either", there shall be substituted the word "any".

Provisional grant of licences

10. In paragraph 17(1), after the words "paragraph 1" there shall be inserted ", 3A".

Variation of licences

11. In paragraph 18, after the words "paragraph 1" there shall be inserted ", 3A".

Appeals

12. In paragraph 19—
    (a) in sub-paragraphs (1)(a) and (3), after the words "paragraph 1" there shall be inserted ", 3A"; and
    (b) in sub-paragraph (4), after the words "paragraph 2(1)" there shall be inserted the words ", 3B(1)".

Meaning of "premises"

13. Paragraph 20 shall be omitted.

SCHEDULE 4

REPEALS

Chapter	Short title	Extent of repeal
1963 c.33.	London Government Act 1963.	In Schedule 12, in paragraph 1(6), the words "or the Royal Albert Hall", paragraph 4(1)(b) and paragraph 20.
1971 c.40.	Fire Precautions Act 1971.	In section 2, the words from "of any of the following" to "any premises" where last occurring.
		In section 5(3)(c), the words from "for use" to "the building".
		In section 6(1)(d), the words from "for use" to "the building".
		In section 12(1), the words "other than paragraph (d)".
		In section 43(1), in the definition of "the court", the words "and the Schedule thereto".
		Section 43(2).
1974 c.37.	Health and Safety at Work etc. Act 1974.	Section 78(4).
1975 c.52.	Safety of Sports Grounds Act 1975.	Section 5(4), (6), (7) and (8).
		In section 7, in subsection (3), the words ", subject to subsection (4) below," and subsections (4) and (5).
		In section 12(2), the words "stadium or other".
		Section 15.
		In section 17(1), the definition of "sports stadium".

SCHEDULE 5

TRANSITIONAL AND SAVING PROVISIONS

Preliminary

1. In this Schedule—
    "the 1963 Act" means the London Government Act 1963;
    "the 1971 Act" means the Fire Precautions Act 1971;
    "the 1975 Act" means the Safety of Sports Grounds Act 1975; and
    "the 1982 Act" means the Local Government (Miscellaneous Provisions) Act 1982.

Certain certificates deemed to be fire certificates

2. Where immediately before a fire certificate becomes required by or under the 1971 Act in respect of any premises a fire certificate issued or deemed to be issued under regulations made under the Health and Safety at Work etc. Act 1974 (a "1974 Act certificate") was in force in respect of those premises, the 1974 Act certificate shall continue in force and shall be deemed to be a fire certificate within the meaning of the 1971 Act validly issued with respect to the premises with respect to which it was issued and to cover the use or uses to which those premises were being put immediately before a fire certificate becomes required by or under the 1971 Act in respect of those premises; and, without prejudice to the generality of the foregoing, the 1974 Act certificate—
    (a) may be amended, replaced or revoked in accordance with the provisions of the 1971 Act; and
    (b) shall be treated as imposing in relation to the premises the like requirements as were previously imposed in relation to the premises.

Charges for fire certification work

3. Section 8B of the 1971 Act which is inserted by section 3 of this Act does not apply as respects an application for a fire certificate made before the said section 3 comes into force.

Fire safety: emergency orders

4. The substitution effected by section 9 of this Act of section 10 of the 1971 Act shall not affect any order of the court in force under that section when that substitution comes into force and any such order may be enforced, or an appeal made against it, accordingly.

Sports grounds: certain existing designations

5. Any designation of a sports ground made under section 1 of the 1975 Act by virtue of an order under section 15 of that Act and in force immediately before the repeal of section 15 by section 19 of this Act shall not be affected by the repeal but shall continue in force as if made under section 1 as amended by section 19 of (and Schedule 2 to) this Act.

Sports grounds certificates: appeals

6. The amendments effected by section 22 of this Act in section 5 of the 1975 Act shall not affect any appeal pending when those amendments come into force and any such appeal may be determined (with or without an inquiry and report thereon), and the decision on the appeal shall have effect, accordingly.

Sports grounds: emergency orders

7. The substitution effected by section 23 of this Act of section 10 of the 1975 Act shall not affect any order of the court in force under that section when that substitution comes into force and any such order may be enforced, modified or cancelled, or an appeal made against it, accordingly.

Entertainment licences for sports generally

8. Where the use of any premises for the purpose of an entertainment will, by virtue of the amendments effected by section 42 of this Act in the 1963 Act or by section 43 of this Act in the 1982 Act, require to be covered by a licence, then, if an application for a licence to cover their use for that entertainment has been made (and not withdrawn) when the amendments come into force, the use of the premises for that purpose shall continue to be lawful pending the disposal of the application.

9. The amendment of Schedule 1 to the 1982 Act effected by section 46 of this Act does not apply as respects an application made before that section comes into force.

Boxing or wrestling licences

10. Any licence under paragraph 4 of Schedule 12 to the 1963 Act covering the use of premises for a boxing or wrestling entertainment which was granted before the date of the coming into force of the amendments effected by section 42 of (and Schedule 3 to) this Act shall, if it relates to premises to which the paragraph 3A inserted by that section applies—

    (a) have effect as from that date as if granted under the paragraph 3A inserted by those amendments by the Council on and subject to terms, conditions and restrictions corresponding to those on and subject to which it was held immediately before that date; and

    (b) in the case of a licence granted or renewed for a specified period, remain in force, subject to paragraphs 8, 10(4) and 18 of the said Schedule 12, for so much of that period as falls on or after that date.

DEER ACT 1987

(1987 c. 28)

An Act to make it lawful for deer kept on deer farms in England and Wales to be killed during a close season.   [15th May 1987]

PARLIAMENTARY DEBATES

Hansard: H.C. Vol. 111, cols. 163, 562; Vol. 112, col. 664; H.L. Vol. 485, col. 1270, Vol. 487, cols. 85, 618.

Killing during close season of farmed deer to be lawful

1. In section 10 of the Deer Act 1963 (general exceptions), after subsection (2) there shall be inserted—
    "(2A) Where—
    (a) any person, by way of business, keeps deer on land enclosed by a deer-proof barrier for the production of meat or other foodstuffs or skins or other by-products, or as breeding stock; and
    (b) those deer are conspicuously marked in such a way as to identify them as deer kept by that person as mentioned in the preceding paragraph,
the killing of any of those deer by that person, or by any servant or agent of that person authorised by him for the purpose, shall not constitute an offence against section 1 of this Act.".

Short title, commencement and extent

2.—(1) This Act may be cited as the Deer Act 1987.
(2) This Act shall come into force at the end of the period of two months beginning with the day on which it is passed.
(3) This Act extends to England and Wales only.

AGRICULTURAL TRAINING BOARD ACT 1987

(1987 c. 29)

An Act to make further provision with respect to the functions of the Agricultural Training Board.   [15th May 1987]

PARLIAMENTARY DEBATES

Hansard: H.C. Vol. 107, col. 353, Vol. 108, cols. 1128, 1151; Vol. 113, col. 674; H.L. Vol. 486, cols. 448, 1556; Vol. 487, cols. 246; 618.

The Bill was considered in Standing Committee C on February 4, 1987.

Training in connection with activities outside the agricultural industry

1.—(1) After subsection (1)(*b*) of section 4 of the Agricultural Training Board Act 1982 (functions of the Board) there shall be inserted the following paragraph—

"(*bb*) shall provide or secure the provision of such courses and other facilities (which may include residential accommodation) for the purposes mentioned in section 5A(1) below as may be required, having regard to any courses or facilities otherwise available for those purposes;".

(2) After section 5 of that Act there shall be inserted the following section—

"**Training for the diversification of agricultural businesses and in amenity skills**

5A.—(1) The purposes for which the Board shall provide or secure the provision of courses and other facilities under section 4(1)(*bb*) above are—

(a) the training, in skills relevant to the carrying on of activities not comprised within the industry, of—

(i) persons who are or have been employed in the industry; or

(ii) members of the families of any such persons,

with a view to the diversification of the trades or businesses carried on by persons employed in the industry; and

(b) the training in amenity skills of persons who are not employed in the industry.

(2) In this section "amenity skills" means skills which are relevant to—

(a) the development, improvement, conservation or maintenance of land for sporting, recreational or environmental purposes; or

(b) the rearing or care of animals for any such purposes (excluding the training of animals for any such purposes);

and for the purposes of this definition "animals" includes birds and fish.

(3) Before providing or securing the provision of any courses or other facilities under section 4(1)(*bb*) above for the purpose mentioned in subsection (1)(*a*) above, the Board shall consult the Ministers.

(4) It shall be the duty of the Board so to conduct its affairs as to secure that such of its revenues as are derived from the exercise of functions under section 4(1)(*bb*) above become at the earliest possible date, and continue thereafter, at least sufficient to enable it to meet such of its expenditure as is incurred in connection with the exercise of those functions.".

(3) In section 7 of that Act (disclosure of information to the Board), after "section 4(1)(*a*)" there shall be inserted "or (*bb*)".

(4) In section 8(1A) of that Act (reports and accounts), the following paragraph shall be inserted before paragraph (*a*)—

"(*aa*) the exercise by it of functions under section 4(1)(*bb*) above;".

Short title, commencement and extent

2.—(1) This Act may be cited as the Agricultural Training Board Act 1987.

(2) This Act shall come into force at the end of the period of two months beginning with the day on which it is passed.

(3) This Act does not extend to Northern Ireland.

NORTHERN IRELAND (EMERGENCY PROVISIONS) ACT 1987*

(1987 c. 30)

ARRANGEMENT OF SECTIONS

PART I

PART II

PART III

PART IV

An Act to amend the Northern Ireland (Emergency Provisions) Act 1978; to confer certain rights on persons detained in police custody in

---

* Annotations by Professor K. Boyle, University College, Galway.

Northern Ireland under or by virtue of Part IV of the Prevention of Terrorism (Temporary Provisions) Act 1984; to regulate the provision of security services there; and for connected purposes.

[15th May 1987]

PARLIAMENTARY DEBATES

Hansard: H.C. Vol. 106, col. 778; Vol. 107, col. 1077; Vol. 114, col. 310; H.L. Vol. 486, col. 1205; Vol. 487, cols. 355, 634.

The Bill was considered in Standing Committee D from January 20 to March 3, 1987.

GENERAL NOTE

This Act amends The Northern Ireland (Emergency Provisions) Act 1978 (hereinafter the 1978 Act). The 1978 Act was a consolidation of several Acts dealing with emergency powers beginning with the Northern Ireland (Emergency Provisions) Act 1973. The 1973 Act was based on the recommendations of the *Report of the Commission to Consider Legal Procedures to deal with Terrorist Activities in Northern Ireland* (Cmnd. 5185). The Commission was chaired by Lord Diplock and the special criminal justice provisions and procedures introduced following his report have become known as the "Diplock Courts" or the "Diplock system".

The Diplock system, the chief feature of which is trial of a schedule of serious offences by a judge sitting without a jury, has been in existence for fourteen years. It has been twice reviewed by commissions of inquiry: in 1975 by Lord Gardiner (Cmnd. 5847) and 1984 by the late Sir George Baker (Cmnd. 9222). The 1987 Act is the legislative response to the Baker Report, although not all of his suggestions have been taken up.

The Secretary of State for Northern Ireland introducing the measure explained Government policy as one of fighting terrorism within the law:

"Our aim and ambition is that the laws under which the courts will operate are fair and must comply with international standards of human and civil rights. Against a background of terrorism and the difficulties that that causes the courts must diverge as little as possible from the ordinary law. It is vital to maintain the confidence of both communities in the institute of justice and we must do all that we can to ensure equal rights and remove grievances, if they are fairly demonstrated, thus further to isolate the mean of violence" (*Hansard*, H.C. Vol. 107, col. 1080).

The main developments since the Baker Report was published in 1984, have been the withdrawal of derogations under the European Convention on Human Rights and the International Covenant on Civil and Political Rights in respect of Northern Ireland, and the Anglo-Irish Agreement of November 15, 1985. In withdrawing notices of derogation, the Government essentially is stating that the special powers and provisions that now obtain in Northern Ireland do not violate minimum international standards, even where they deviate from established British criminal justice. Under the Anglo-Irish Agreement, the joint ministerial conference has regularly considered issues relating to criminal justice in Northern Ireland. It is known that the Irish Government has pressed for three-judge courts in preference to the single judge trial at the moment. However, this has not been accepted by the British Government. As a further general point, it may be noted that the Government did not drop the power to detain without trial (s.12 of the 1978 Act) although pressed by the Opposition to do so.

The 1987 Act is in four parts:

Part 1

This Part amends the rules governing bail and introduces novel powers to set time limits for preliminary stages of Diplock trials. The rules governing admissions and statements by accused persons are changed to include threats of violence as a ground for excluding an accused's admissions to the police and to confirm the existence of the judicial discretion to exclude. Additional offences are also created. Under s.13, the 1978 Act, as amended by this Act, will last a maximum five years. Thereafter, fresh legislation will be required if the powers are to be continued.

Part 2

Pt. 2 is concerned with the right of persons in police custody, following the Police and Criminal Evidence Act 1984, ss.56 and 58. It is the Government's intention to introduce by

Order in Council, codes of conduct equivalent to the Police and Criminal Evidence Act codes, and a non-statutory code for emergency powers (*Hansard*, H.C. Vol. 114, col. 391).

Part 3
This introduces a new system for control of bogus security guard services.

Part 4
This deals with expiry and repeal, and certain amendments, repeals, etc., of the 1978 Act.

Review of Emergency Provisions
The Government announced the appointment of Lord Colville of Culross to undertake a review of the Emergency Provisions Act 1978 as part of a commitment to review its operation each year. Lord Colville has already reviewed the Prevention of Terrorism (Emergency Provisions) Act 1984 and is engaged in a further review of that Act (*Hansard*, H.L. Vol. 487, col. 635).

Statistics
As recommended in the Baker report, the Government will publish quarterly and annual statistics concerning the operation of the Emergency Provisions Act. These are intended to provide the basis for the now annual renewal debate in Parliament. The statistics for 1986 were released in August 1987. Some notable features are: 17 per cent. only of total arrests under the 1978 Act led to subsequent charges (170 charges out of a total of 974 arrests—the R.U.C. made 903 of the arrests and the remaining 71 were arrested by the Army); in 1986, 596 defendants appeared before the Diplock Courts (698 in 1985), 567 were convicted; 528 of these defendants pleaded guilty and 67 not guilty (the percentage of defendants pleading not guilty who were acquitted was 43 per cent.); approximately £320,000 was paid in compensation for damage caused by security forces during searches or for the requisitioning of property.

DURATION
The 1978 Act as amended by this Act remains in force until March 21, 1988, when it will be renewable by order for 12 months. Thereafter, it will be subject to annual renewal for a period of five years when it will automatically lapse. These requirements harmonise the Northern Ireland Emergency Provisions Acts with the provisions governing renewal and expiry of the Prevention of Terrorism (Emergency Provisions) Act 1984.

COMMENCEMENT
The Act, except s.12 and Pt. 3 came into force on June 16, 1987 (see s.26).

ABBREVIATIONS
"1978 Act": Northern Ireland (Emergency Provisions) Act 1978.
PACE: Police and Criminal Evidence Act 1984.
PTA: Prevention of Terrorism (Emergency Provisions) Act 1984.

PART I

AMENDMENTS OF THE NORTHERN IRELAND (EMERGENCY PROVISIONS) ACT 1978

Limitation of power to grant bail in case of scheduled offences

1. The following section shall be substituted for section 2 of the Northern Ireland (Emergency Provisions) Act 1978 (in this Act referred to as "the 1978 Act")—

"Limitation of power to grant bail in case of scheduled offences

2.—(1) Subject to subsection (7) below, a person to whom this section applies shall not be admitted to bail except—
(a) by a judge of the High Court or the Court of Appeal; or
(b) by the judge of the court of trial, on adjourning the trial of a person charged with a scheduled offence.

(2) A judge may, in his discretion, admit to bail in pursuance of subsection (1) above a person to whom this section applies except where he is satisfied that there are substantial grounds for believing that that person, if released on bail (whether subject to conditions or not), would—

(a) fail to surrender to custody, or

(b) commit an offence while on bail, or

(c) interfere with any witness, or

(d) otherwise obstruct or attempt to obstruct the course of justice, whether in relation to himself or in relation to any other person,

or, if released subject to conditions, would fail to comply with all or any of those conditions.

(3) In exercising his discretion in accordance with subsection (2) above in relation to a person, a judge shall have regard to such of the following considerations as appear to him to be relevant, namely—

(a) the nature and seriousness of the offence with which the person is charged,

(b) the character, antecedents, associations and community ties of the person,

(c) the time which the person has already spent in custody and the time which he is likely to spend in custody if he is not admitted to bail, and

(d) the strength of the evidence of his having committed the offence,

as well as to any others which appear to be relevant.

(4) Without prejudice to any other power to impose conditions on admission to bail, a judge may impose such conditions on admitting a person to bail under this section as appear to him to be likely to result in that person's appearance at the time and place required, or to be necessary in the interests of justice or for the prevention of crime.

(5) This section applies, subject to subsection (6) below, to any person—

(a) who is charged with a scheduled offence; and

(b) who has attained the age of fourteen.

(6) This section does not apply to a person charged with a scheduled offence—

(a) which is being tried summarily, or

(b) which the Director of Public Prosecutions for Northern Ireland certifies is in his opinion suitable to be tried summarily.

(7) Subsection (1) above shall not preclude a resident magistrate from admitting to bail a person to whom this section applies if—

(a) the person is a serving member of any of Her Majesty's forces or a serving member of the Royal Ulster Constabulary or of the Royal Ulster Constabulary Reserve, and

(b) the resident magistrate is satisfied that suitable arrangements have been made for the person to be held in military or (as the case may be) police custody, and imposes a condition on admitting him to bail that he is to be held in such custody."

GENERAL NOTE

This section substitutes for s.2 of the 1978 Act. Its main effect is to change the onus on bail application in the case of scheduled offences from the defendant to the prosecution (subs. (2)) and to allow a member of the R.U.C. to be treated for purposes of bail like a serving soldier (subs. (7)). Bail for a scheduled offence which is to be tried on indictment continues to be available only through application to the superior courts (subs. (1)). The reversal of the onus follows a recommendation of the Baker Report (para. 81). The section does not create a presumption in favour of bail as in the Bail Act 1976. Bail is at the discretion of the judge. However, the considerations that should be taken into account by the judge in a bail application are spelled out (subs. (3)), again following the Baker Report (para. 81). The clause in s.2 of the 1978 Act providing for an appeal against a reference of bail is repealed. Sir George Baker considered this redundant (para. 82).

Maximum period of remand in custody in case of scheduled offences

2. The following section shall be inserted after section 3 of the 1978 Act—

> **"Maximum period of remand in custody in case of scheduled offences**
>   3A. Notwithstanding Article 47(2) and (3) of the Magistrates' Courts (Northern Ireland) Order 1981, the period for which a person charged with a scheduled offence may be remanded in custody by a magistrates' court shall be a period of not more than 28 days beginning with the day following that on which he is so remanded."

GENERAL NOTE
    Sir George Baker considered the practice in Northern Ireland of weekly remands in custody a waste of time and money (para. 84). In the case of scheduled offences, the magistrates' court may now remand for up to 28 days at a time; *cf.* Criminal Justice Act 1982, s.59 and Sched. 9. Some concern should be recorded over this provision. The controversy which has occasionally arisen over pre-trial delay could be refuelled by this new power. But see s.3 below.

Power of Secretary of State to set time limits in relation to preliminary proceedings for scheduled offences

3. The following section shall be inserted after section 5 of the 1978 Act—

> *"Time limits on preliminary proceedings*
>
> **Power of Secretary of State to set time limits in relation to preliminary proceedings for scheduled offences**
>   5A.—(1) The Secretary of State may by regulations make provision, with respect to any specified preliminary stage of proceedings for a scheduled offence, as to the maximum period—
>   (a) to be allowed to the prosecution to complete that stage;
>   (b) during which the accused may, while awaiting completion of that stage, be—
>   (i) in the custody of a magistrates' court; or
>   (ii) in the custody of the Crown Court,
>   in relation to that offence.
>   (2) The regulations may, in particular—
>   (a) provide for—
>   (i) the Magistrates' Courts (Northern Ireland) Order 1981,
>   (ii) section 2 above, or
>   (iii) any other enactment, or any rule of law, relating to bail,
>   to apply in relation to cases to which custody or overall time limits apply subject to such modifications as may be specified (being modifications which the Secretary of State considers necessary in consequence of any provision made by the regulations);
>   (b) provide for time limits imposed by the regulations to cease to have effect in cases where, after the institution of proceedings for a scheduled offence, the Attorney

30–5

General for Northern Ireland has certified that the offence in question is not to be treated as a scheduled offence;

(c) make such provision with respect to the procedure to be followed in criminal proceedings as the Secretary of State considers appropriate in consequence of any other provision of the regulations; and

(d) make such transitional provision in relation to proceedings instituted before the commencement of any provision of the regulations as the Secretary of State considers appropriate.

(3) Where separate counts of an indictment allege a scheduled offence and an offence which is not a scheduled offence, then (subject to, and in accordance with, the provisions of the regulations) the regulations shall have effect in relation to the latter offence as if it were a scheduled offence.

(4) The Crown Court may, at any time before the expiry of a time limit imposed by the regulations, extend, or further extend, that limit if it is satisfied—

(a) that there is good and sufficient cause for doing so; and

(b) that the prosecution has acted with all due expedition.

(5) Where, in relation to any proceedings for a relevant offence, an overall time limit has expired before the completion of the stage of the proceedings to which the limit applies, the accused shall be treated, for all purposes, as having been acquitted of that offence.

(6) Where—

(a) a person escapes from the custody of a magistrates' court or of the Crown Court before the expiry of a custody time limit which applies in his case; or

(b) a person who has been released on bail in consequence of the expiry of a custody time limit—

(i) fails to surrender himself into the custody of the court at the appointed time; or

(ii) is arrested by a constable in connection with any breach, or apprehended breach, of any condition of his bail,

the regulations shall, so far as they provide for any custody time limit in relation to the preliminary stage in question, be disregarded.

(7) Where—

(a) a person escapes from the custody of a magistrates' court or of the Crown Court; or

(b) a person who has been released on bail fails to surrender himself into the custody of the court at the appointed time,

the overall time limit which applies in his case in relation to the stage which the proceedings have reached at the time of the escape or, as the case may be, at the appointed time shall, so far as the relevant offence in question is concerned, cease to have effect.

(8) Where a person is convicted of a relevant offence in any proceedings, the exercise, in relation to any preliminary stage of those proceedings, of the power conferred by subsection (4) above shall not be called into question on any appeal against that conviction.

(9) In this section—

"custody of the Crown Court" includes custody to which a person is committed in pursuance of—

(a) Article 37 or 40(4) of the Magistrates' Courts (Northern Ireland) Order 1981 (magistrates' court committing accused for trial); or

(b) section 51(8) of the Judicature (Northern Ireland) Act

1978 (magistrates' court dealing with a person brought before it following his arrest in pursuance of a warrant issued by the Crown Court);

"custody of a magistrates' court" means custody to which a person is committed in pursuance of Article 47 or 49 of the Magistrates' Courts (Northern Ireland) Order 1981 (remand);

"custody time limit" means a time limit imposed by the regulations in pursuance of subsection (1)(b) above or, where any such limit has been extended by the Crown Court under subsection (4) above, the limit as so extended;

"preliminary stage", in relation to any proceedings, does not include any stage of the proceedings after the accused has been arraigned in the Crown Court or, in the case of a summary trial, the magistrates' court has begun to hear evidence for the prosecution at the trial;

"overall time limit" means a time limit imposed by the regulations in pursuance of subsection (1)(a) above or, where any such limit has been extended by the Crown Court under subsection (4) above, the limit as so extended;

"relevant offence" means—
   (a) a scheduled offence, or
   (b) an offence in relation to which the regulations have effect in accordance with subsection (3) above; and
"specified" means specified in the regulations.

(10) For the purposes of the application of any custody time limit in relation to a person who is in the custody of a magistrates' court or of the Crown Court—

(a) all periods during which he is in the custody of a magistrates' court in respect of the same offence shall be aggregated and treated as a single continuous period; and

(b) all periods during which he is in the custody of the Crown Court in respect of the same offence shall be aggregated and treated similarly."

DEFINITIONS
See subs. (9).

GENERAL NOTE
This section was added in Committee and derives from an amendment initially tabled by Mr. Mallon, S.D.L.P. It reproduces in the case of scheduled offences the provisions of the Prosecution of Offences Act 1985, s.22.

It is an enabling section, giving the Secretary of State power to impose statutory time limits relating to different phases of the preliminary trial and overall time limits prior to trial. The section is a response to the widespread concern felt over delays in the Diplock system, particularly with regard to defendants in custody.

When the regulations are made specifying time limits, then breach of any such time limit will result in an accused being bailed (subs. (2)). However, the time limits may be extended on application to the Crown Court (subs. (4)). Where an "overall time limit" has been breached, the accused shall be treated for all purposes as having been acquitted of that offence (subs. (5)).

The Minister emphasised that it was not immediately intended to introduce time limits, and there was as yet no clear view on the length of any such limit. The hope is that the current experiments on time limits in three police districts in England and Wales, will serve as a guide. The Minister said further:

"It is much too early to give any precise indications on time limits. We have to establish how long, on average, the various preliminary stages take and then decide what limits would maintain a degree of pressure on the system so that it operated without overdue delays, without creating unreasonable constraints on the system. . . . Any limits will certainly have to be longer than those applied in the pilot area of England and Wales" (*Hansard*, H.C. Vol. 114, col. 325).

Some statistics were disclosed in Parliament on delay. For the period January to June 1986, the average waiting time between remand and committal in scheduled cases was about 33 weeks, and between committal and trial 27 weeks; *i.e.* 60 weeks in all between initial remand and trial (*Hansard*, H.C. Vol. 114, col. 325).

Court for trial of scheduled offences

4. The following section shall be substituted for section 6 of the 1978 Act—

"Court for trial of scheduled offences

6.—(1) A trial on indictment of a scheduled offence shall be held only at the Crown Court sitting in Belfast, unless the Lord Chancellor after consultation with the Lord Chief Justice of Northern Ireland directs in any particular case that such a trial shall be held at the Crown Court sitting elsewhere.

(2) A person committed for trial for a scheduled offence, or for two or more offences at least one of which is a scheduled offence, shall be committed—

(a) to the Crown Court sitting in Belfast, or

(b) where the Lord Chancellor has given a direction under subsection (1) above with respect to the trial, to the Crown Court sitting at the place specified in the direction;

and section 48 of the Judicature (Northern Ireland) Act 1978 (committal for trial on indictment) shall have effect accordingly.

(3) Where—

(a) in accordance with subsection (2) above any person is committed for trial to the Crown Court sitting in Belfast, and

(b) a direction is subsequently given by the Lord Chancellor under subsection (1) above altering the place of trial,

that person shall be treated as having been committed for trial to the Crown Court sitting at the place specified in the direction."

GENERAL NOTE

This section enables trials of scheduled offences to be held other than at the Crown Court, Crumlin Road, Belfast. The Lord Chancellor in consultation with the Chief Justice may direct the trial or committal at another Crown Court. This flexibility of venue will be welcomed as of benefit to the family of an accused from other parts of Northern Ireland for whom a long trial in Belfast could involve considerable travel and expense.

Admissions by persons charged with scheduled offences

5. The following section shall be substituted for section 8 of the 1978 Act—

"Admissions by persons charged with scheduled offences

8.—(1) In any criminal proceedings for a scheduled offence, or for two or more offences at least one of which is a scheduled offence, a statement made by the accused may be given in evidence by the prosecution in so far as—

(a) it is relevant to any matter in issue in the proceedings, and

(b) it is not excluded by the court in pursuance of subsection (2) below or in the exercise of its discretion referred to in subsection (3) below (and has not been rendered inadmissible by virtue of such a direction as is mentioned in subsection (2)(iii) below).

(2) Where in any such proceedings—

(a) the prosecution proposes to give, or (as the case may be) has given, in evidence a statement made by the accused, and

(b) prima facie evidence is adduced that the accused was subject to torture, to inhuman or degrading treatment, or to any violence or threat of violence (whether or not amounting to torture), in order to induce him to make the statement,

then, unless the prosecution satisfies the court that the statement was not obtained by so subjecting the accused in the manner indicated by that evidence, the court shall do one of the following things, namely—

(i) in the case of a statement proposed to be given in evidence, exclude the statement;

(ii) in the case of a statement already received in evidence, continue the trial disregarding the statement; or

(iii) in either case, direct that the trial shall be restarted before a differently constituted court (before which the statement in question shall be inadmissible).

(3) It is hereby declared that, in the case of any statement made by the accused and not obtained by so subjecting him as mentioned in subsection (2)(b) above, the court in any such proceedings as are mentioned in subsection (1) above has a discretion to do one of the things mentioned in subsection (2)(i) to (iii) above if it appears to the court that it is appropriate to do so in order to avoid unfairness to the accused or otherwise in the interests of justice.

(4) This section does not apply to a summary trial."

GENERAL NOTE

It remains the case that most trials of scheduled offences involve reliance on admission or confession statements by the accused. This section which substitutes for s.8 of the 1978 Act is one of the most important in this amending Act. For an analysis of the original s.8, see the relevant annotations in *Current Law Statutes*, 1978, and the Baker Report (Chapter 5).

The substantive changes introduced to the former s.8 by this substituted section are:

(i) grounds for exclusion include not only confessions obtained by torture, inhuman or degrading treatment but confessions obtained as the result of "any violence or threat of violence (whether or not amounting to torture)" (subs. (2)(b)).

(ii) the spelling out of the judicial discretion to exclude statement evidence "if it appears to the court that it is appropriate to do so in order to avoid unfairness to the accused or otherwise in the interests of justice."

Both these changes derive from Sir George Baker's recommendations (para. 200). In effect, they are amendments to clarify the law, not to substantively change it. While Baker noted that Northern Ireland judges had occasionally expressed doubt as to whether the judicial discretion to exclude evidence survived s.8 of the 1978 Act, the courts have authoritatively determined that this discretion does exist (see *R. v. Corey* [1979] N.I. 49 (*per* Lord Lowry L.C.J.) and the detailed consideration of the question in *R. v. Dillon* [1984] N.I. 292, and *R. v. McBrien and Harmon* [1984] N.I. 28).

There was, however, some cause for concern over the issue of violence to an accused that did not constitute, or was considered not to constitute, the minimum standard of degrading treatment (see McGonigal L.J. in *R. v. McCormick* [1977] N.I. 111 and *R. v. O'Halloran* [1979] N.I.J.B., C.A.). The amendment now puts beyond doubt that any degree of violence, or the threat of such will result in exclusion. Issues may arise on the meaning of "threat" and "violence". Baker proposed *physical* violence. He was concerned that "verbal abuse" alleged to have taken place during interrogation would be taken as a threat of violence (para. 200). It is submitted that it may very well constitute a threat of violence.

The wording in s.5 of this Act should be compared with the Police and Criminal Evidence Act 1984, s.76. There can be little doubt that the PACE standards are more demanding. In other words, it remains the case that it will continue to be possible to admit confessions obtained by means which might be deemed improper by a court in England and Wales. Further, a different standard for scheduled offences and "ordinary" criminal offences will continue to co-exist in Northern Ireland. Indeed, the section does not apply to summary trial of scheduled offences, which continue to be governed by the common law voluntariness principles, now replaced for England and Wales by the PACE. It is to be noted that apart from the amendments discussed, the new s.5 involves a redrafting of the former s.8, and the two sections merit detailed comparison by practitioners.

Entry and search of premises for purpose of arresting terrorists

6. The following section shall be substituted for section 11 of the 1978 Act—

> **"Entry and search of premises for purpose of arresting terrorists**
>   **11.** For the purpose of arresting a person under section 12(1)(b) of the Prevention of Terrorism (Temporary Provisions) Act 1984 (arrest of persons suspected of being concerned in acts of terrorism) a constable may enter and search any premises or other place where that person is or where the constable has reasonable grounds for suspecting him to be."

GENERAL NOTE

A major change in the emergency provisions is legislated by this section. In effect, it abolishes the general arrest power in s.11 of the 1978 Act. The alternative arrest power—s.12 of the PTA—applicable throughout the U.K., will continue as the main R.U.C. power of arrest in connection with the violence in Northern Ireland.

S.11 of the 1978 Act had permitted arrest without warrant of any person suspected of "being a terrorist", and such a person could be detained for 72 hours. It had been introduced originally as a power preliminary to a decision to detain without trial, or internment. In practice, however, before and after internment was phased out in 1975, the R.U.C. used it as a power to detain for questioning. S.11 was of doubtful compatability with Art. 5 of the European Convention of Human Rights. There was no requirement that the arrest be based on reasonable grounds nor that a specific offence was in issue.

The Baker Report had drawn attention to the overlap between the PTA power and s.11. The result now is that the PTA power, which is based on *reasonable* suspicion of involvement, *inter alia*, in the commission, preparation, or instigation, of terrorist acts, replaces s.11. It may be noted that the period of arrest under the PTA, s.12, is 48 hours on the authority of the arresting officer, and the possible extension of this to a maximum of seven days requires the decision of the Secretary of State.

S.6, meanwhile, by substitution preserves the power of a constable to enter and search premises for the purpose of making an arrest of a suspected terrorist—which had been a feature of the old s.11 power of the 1978 Act.

In summary, the principal arrest power in connection with terrorism available in Northern Ireland is the arrest power in s.12 of the PTA. It is a significant safeguard that the use of the PTA power is based on reasonable suspicion, rather than subjective suspicion alone as in the now abolished s.11 of the 1978 Act. A similar requirement of reasonable suspicion is incorporated into a number of other arrest and search powers (see s.25 below).

Power to search for scanning receivers

7.—(1) Section 15 of the 1978 Act (power to search for munitions and radio transmitters) shall be amended as follows.

(2) The following subsection shall be inserted after subsection (4)—
> "(4A) The preceding provisions of this section shall have effect in relation to scanning receivers as they have effect in relation to transmitters."

(3) In subsection (5), after the definition of "munitions" there shall be inserted—
> ""scanning receiver" means—
>   (a) any apparatus for wireless telegraphy designed or adapted for the purpose of automatically monitoring selected frequencies, or automatically scanning a selected range of frequencies, so as to enable transmissions on any of those frequencies to be detected or intercepted; or
>   (b) part of any such apparatus;".

GENERAL NOTE

The new subsection here added to s.7 of the 1978 Act, adds scanning receivers to transmitters for purposes of the search powers of the security forces. The Secretary of State said:

"[the section] reveals . . . developments in the technology of terrorism over recent years. Very sophisticated scanning receivers are now available which can enable terrorists to monitor security force communications and can be used for the detonation of bombs by remote radio control. We are therefore including specialised receivers of that type in the list of items in respect of which the security forces are entitled to search dwellings and premises and stop and search vehicles." (*Hansard*, H.C. Vol. 107, col. 1083).

Power of Secretary of State to direct the closure etc. of roads

8. The following section shall be inserted after section 19 of the 1978 Act—

"Power of Secretary of State to direct the closure etc. of roads

19A.—(1) The Secretary of State may by order direct—

    (a) that any highway specified in the order shall either be wholly closed or be closed to such extent, or diverted in such manner, as may be so specified;

    (b) that any highway specified in the order, being a highway which has already been wholly or partly closed, or diverted, in the exercise or purported exercise of any power conferred by or under a relevant enactment, shall continue to be so closed or diverted by virtue of the order.

(2) Any person who, without lawful authority or reasonable excuse (the proof of which lies on him), interferes with—

    (a) works executed in connection with the closure or diversion of any highway specified in an order under this section (whether executed in pursuance of any such order or in pursuance of the exercise or purported exercise of any such power as is mentioned in subsection (1)(b) above), or

    (b) apparatus, equipment or any other thing used in pursuance of any such order in connection with the closure or diversion of any such highway,

shall be liable on summary conviction to imprisonment for a term not exceeding six months or to a fine not exceeding level 5 on the standard scale, or both.

(3) In this section "relevant enactment" means section 19(2) or (3) above, section 17(2) or (3) of the Northern Ireland (Emergency Provisions) Act 1973, or the Civil Authorities (Special Powers) Act (Northern Ireland) 1922.

(4) Nothing in this section shall prejudice the operation of section 19(2) or (3) above."

GENERAL NOTE

The purpose of this section is to rest the authority for road closures with the Secretary of State for Northern Ireland. The section empowers the Secretary of State to direct the closure of highways, and by order to confirm that existing closures are made under this section. The details are to be published in the *Belfast Gazette*.

The need for the section relates to doubts over the legal validity of some existing road closures. The Under-Secretary of State, Mr. Scott, emphasised that no change of policy was intended by the section.

The need for such powers arises from the land frontier with the Republic of Ireland. There are approximately 300 road crossings between the two jurisdictions. Approximately 100 of these are now closed either under the Civil Authority (Special Powers) Act 1922, or the 1978 Act (*Hansard*, H.C. Vol. 114, col. 315).

While the section does not specify that powers to close roads may only be exercised exceptionally, it will continue to be the practice that such a decision will only be taken on security considerations and because of the emergency (*Hansard*, H.C. Vol. 114, col. 313).

Additional offence relating to proscribed organisations

9. After paragraph (c) of section 21(1) of the 1978 Act (proscribed organisations) there shall be inserted "or

    (d) arranges or assists in the arrangement or management of, or addresses, any meeting of three or more persons (whether or not it is a meeting to which the public are admitted) knowing that the meeting—

        (i) is to support a proscribed organisation;

        (ii) is to further the activities of such an organisation; or

        (iii) is to be addressed by a person belonging or professing to belong to such an organisation,".

GENERAL NOTE

This additional offence added to s.21 of the 1978 Act is taken from the PTA. The equivalent offence in that Act does not extend to Northern Ireland. Sir George Baker recommended that it should be added to that Act (para. 408).

It is now an offence to organise or assist in the arrangement or management of a meeting or to address such a meeting knowing that it is held in support of a proscribed organisation, or is to be addressed by a member of a proscribed organisation. The meeting may be public or private but must be a meeting of three or more people.

Some concern has been expressed at the scope of this additional offence. The clause "to further the activities of such an organisation" is vague, and to outlaw participation in any meeting involving individuals from proscribed organisations may prevent legitimate efforts at dialogue, debate or exposure aimed at the prevention of terrorism. Clergymen, politicians (and governments) have on occasion met with paramilitary representatives. It would appear these meetings would be now unlawful and serious offences. It may be doubted if the abridgement of freedom of speech entailed by the offence is justified in terms of likely efficacy. On the other hand the target of the new offence is clear. It is open participation in rallies where representatives of proscribed organisations issue threats or justify previous acts of violence.

Extension of categories of persons about whom it is unlawful to collect information

10. In section 22(2) of the 1978 Act (unlawful collection etc. of information)—

    (a) at the end of paragraph (c) "and" shall be omitted; and

    (b) after paragraph (d) there shall be added "; and

        (e) any person who has at any time been a person falling within any of the preceding paragraphs."

GENERAL NOTE

S.22 of the 1978 Act makes it an offence, *inter alia*, to collect and communicate and possess information likely to be of use to terrorists about:

    (a) any constable or member of Her Majesty's forces;

    (b) any person holding judicial office;

    (c) any officer of any court;

    (d) any person employed in the prison service (s.22(1)).

Sir George Baker, rejected the claim that the section might involve media censorship and also accepted the view of the R.U.C. that the offence should be extended to include information about former members or officials, *i.e.* those who had retired or resigned. He also recommended that the offence should extend to Members of Parliament (para. 432).

The Government Bill had included all former and serving elected representatives in the offence but in a rare display of unity the Unionist and Nationalist representatives in Committee had argued against a higher level of protection being afforded to them not shared by their constituents. The Government accepted the point. Therefore, the offence in s.22 of the 1978 Act is added to only by the inclusion of former members or officials of the security forces, the judiciary and officers of the court.

Offences relating to behaviour and dress in public places

11.—(1) The following section shall be substituted for section 25 of the 1978 Act—

> **"Display of support in public for a proscribed organisation**
> 25. Any person who in a public place—
> (a) wears any item of dress; or
> (b) wears, carries or displays any article,
>
> in such a way or in such circumstances as to arouse reasonable apprehension that he is a member or supporter of a proscribed organisation, shall be liable—
> (i) on summary conviction, to imprisonment for a term not exceeding six months or to a fine not exceeding the statutory maximum, or both;
> (ii) on conviction on indictment to imprisonment for a term not exceeding one year or to a fine, or both."

(2) In section 26 of that Act (wearing of hoods etc. in public places), for the words from "a fine not exceeding" onwards there shall be substituted "a fine not exceeding the statutory maximum, or both, and on conviction on indictment to imprisonment for a term not exceeding one year or to a fine, or both."

(3) After sub-paragraph (c) of paragraph 19 of Schedule 4 to the 1978 Act (scheduled offences) there shall be inserted the following sub-paragraphs—

> "(ca) section 25;
> (cb) section 26;".

(4) Subsections (2) and (3) above shall not have effect in relation to an offence committed before the commencement of this section.

GENERAL NOTE

Subs. (1)

This offence concerns behaviour in a public place in a manner indicative of support for a proscribed organisation. The draft of the offence which substitutes for the existing offence in s.25 of the 1978 Act, is identical to the equivalent offence in Great Britain under the PTA. The offence was formerly a summary offence. It is now a hybrid offence.

Subs. (2)

The offence in s.26 of the 1975 Act (wearing a mask or hood in a public place) was a summary offence only and the maximum fine was £400. The offence is now hybrid. On summary conviction the maximum penalty is £1,000 (Magistrates Court Order 1976, art. 46(4)). The imprisonment term remains a maximum of six months. If tried on indictment the penalties are a fine or 12 months' imprisonment.

Subs. (3)

The offences contained in ss.25 and 26 (as substituted or amended by this section) are added to the list of scheduled offences by this subsection. This means that if tried on indictment they are governed by the provisions relating to trial and procedure in the Emergency Provisions Acts.

Subs. (4)

The changes in procedure or penalties relating to these offences are not to apply retrospectively (see *R. v. Deery* [1977] N.I. 164, C.A.).

Compensation

12.—(1) The following sections shall be substituted for section 28 of the 1978 Act—

> **"Compensation**
> 28.—(1) Where under this Act any real or personal property is taken, occupied, destroyed or damaged, or any other act is done

interfering with private rights of property, compensation shall, subject to the provisions of this section, be payable by the Secretary of State to any person who—

    (a) has an estate or interest in that property or (as the case may be) is entitled to those rights of property, and

    (b) suffers loss or damage as a result of the act.

(2) No compensation shall be payable under this section in respect of any act falling within subsection (1) above unless an application for such compensation is made to the Secretary of State, in such manner as he may specify, within—

    (a) the period of four months beginning with the relevant date; or

    (b) such longer period beginning with that date and not exceeding 12 months as—

        (i) the Secretary of State on a request being made to him in writing, or

        (ii) the county court on an appeal under subsection (4) below,

may in a particular case allow.

(3) In subsection (2) above "the relevant date", in relation to any such act as is there mentioned, means—

    (a) where the act was done before the date of the coming into force of section 12 of the Northern Ireland (Emergency Provisions) Act 1987, that date, and

    (b) in any other case, the date when the act was done.

(4) Where the Secretary of State refuses any request made to him for the purposes of subsection (2)(b) above, he shall serve a notice of his refusal on the person who made the request, and that person may, within the period of six weeks beginning with the date of service of the notice, appeal to the county court against that refusal.

(5) Where the Secretary of State has determined any application for compensation made in accordance with subsection (2) above, he shall serve on the applicant either—

    (a) a notice stating that he has decided to award the applicant compensation in pursuance of his application and specifying the amount of the award, or

    (b) a notice stating that he has decided to refuse the application;

and the applicant may within the period of six weeks beginning with the date of service of the notice appeal to the county court against the decision of the Secretary of State to pay the amount of compensation specified in the notice or (as the case may be) to refuse the application (and unless he so appeals within that period that decision shall become in all respects final and binding).

(6) Any notice served under subsection (4) or (5) above shall contain particulars of the right to make an appeal under that subsection and, in the case of a notice served under subsection (5), of the consequences of a failure to exercise that right.

(7) Where—

    (a) a person having a right to compensation under this section has made an application in accordance with subsection (2) above, and

    (b) by virtue of any assignment or operation of law that right has passed to any other person,

that other person (or, if he is subject to any legal disability, the person appearing to the Secretary of State to be entitled to act on his behalf) may be treated by the Secretary of State as the applicant for the purposes of any provision of this section.

(8) Where—

    (a) a person has a right to compensation in respect of any act falling within subsection (1) above, and

    (b) the act was done in connection with, or revealed evidence of the commission of—
        (i) a scheduled offence, or
        (ii) an offence under this Act (other than a scheduled offence), and
    (c) proceedings for that offence are brought against that person,
his right to such compensation shall not be enforceable at any time when any such proceedings have not been concluded, or if he is convicted of the offence.

Provisions supplementary to section 28

28A.—(1) The Lord Chief Justice of Northern Ireland after consultation with the Secretary of State may make rules as to—
    (a) the bringing of appeals under subsection (4) or (5) of section 28 above;
    (b) the hearing and determination of such appeals; and
    (c) any incidental or ancillary matters, including the awarding of costs in connection with such appeals;
and any such rules shall be statutory rules for the purposes of the Statutory Rules (Northern Ireland) Order 1979.

(2) Any notice required by section 28 above to be served on any person by the Secretary of State may—
    (a) if that person is an individual, be served on him—
        (i) by delivering it to him, or
        (ii) by sending it by post addressed to him at his usual or last-known place of residence or business, or
        (iii) by leaving it for him there;
    (b) if that person is a partnership, be served on the partnership—
        (i) by sending it by post to a partner, or to a person having the control or management of the partnership business, at the principal office of the partnership, or
        (ii) by addressing it to a partner or any such person and leaving it at that office;
    (c) if that person is a body corporate, be served on the body—
        (i) by sending it by post to the secretary or clerk of the body at its registered or principal office, or
        (ii) by addressing it to the secretary or clerk of the body and leaving it at that office; or
    (d) in any case, be served on that person's solicitor by delivering it to the solicitor, or by sending it by post to him at his office, or by leaving it for him there."

(2) Subsections (5) to (7) of section 28 of the 1978 Act, as amended by subsection (1) above, shall apply in relation to an application for compensation under that section made before the date of the coming into force of subsection (1) above and still outstanding on that date as they apply in relation to an application for compensation made in accordance with subsection (2) of that section, as so amended, but shall so apply as if any reference in those subsections to compensation under that section, as so amended, were a reference to compensation under that section, as originally enacted.

(3) For the purposes of subsection (2) above an application for compensation is still outstanding on the date mentioned in that subsection if, on that date, any question as to the compensation to which the application relates has still to be finally resolved and has not been referred to the county court or any arbitrator appointed by that court in accordance with subsections (2) and (3) of section 28 of the 1978 Act, as originally enacted.

DEFINITION
"relevant date": subs. (3).

COMMENCEMENT
This section is not in force, see s.26.

GENERAL NOTE
This section concerns the procedures and rules governing compensation where actions of the security forces interfere with property rights. The Baker Report recommended improvements (para. 108). The procedure is administrative by application to the Northern Ireland Office in the first instance with an appeal to the county court. A similar system operates for criminal injury compensation in Northern Ireland.

Subs. (2)
Time Limits. The normal period of application is *four months* after the act giving rise to the claim. But an extension up to 12 months, may be sought from the Secretary of State. In the case of a dispute over compensation reaching the county court, then the court may allow a longer period subject to the maximum of 12 months.

Subs. (3)
When the section comes into force, the date (the relevant date) from when the normal four-month period will run will be (a) for acts done before its coming into force, the date of it coming into force; (b) for acts committed after it comes into force, the four months period from the date of the act or incident giving rise to the claims.

Subs. (4)
Where the Secretary of State makes a ruling on an application for extension of time to claim compensation, or a determination on whether compensation is to be paid and in what amount, the applicant has six weeks from receipt of the decision to appeal to the county court. Failure to appeal within six weeks shall mean that the decision in question made by the Secretary of State shall be binding.

Subs. (8)
A claim for compensation cannot be maintained by an applicant who is charged and convicted of an offence under this Act, arising from the incident where he claims damage was done. For example, if during a search of a house, damage is done to flooring, then no compensation will be paid if the person is convicted of possession of any ammunition discovered in the search. However, that would not preclude another person, for example a spouse, or landlord who had an interest in the property maintaining a claim for compensation (*cf.* The Criminal Damage (Compensation) (N.I.) Order 1977, art. 10(3), and the Baker Report (para. 372)).

Supplementary Provisions
S.12 also adds a supplementary section to the 1978 Act—section 28A, which empowers the Lord Chief Justice to makes rules following consultation with the Secretary of State concerning the taking of appeals and serving notices arising from claims for compensation.

Expiry and eventual repeal of 1978 Act

13.—(1) Section 33 of the 1978 Act (commencement etc. of that Act) shall be amended as follows—
(2) In subsection (2), for "24th July 1978" there shall be substituted "21st March 1988".
(3) In subsection (3)(a) and (c), for "six" there shall be substituted "twelve".
(4) After subsection (8) there shall be added the following subsection—
"(9) This Act shall, by virtue of this subsection, be repealed as from the end of the period of five years beginning with the date of the passing of the Northern Ireland (Emergency Provisions) Act 1987."
(5) The amendment made by subsection (2) above does not affect any provision to which section 33(2) of the 1978 Act applies and which is not

in force at the commencement of this section, and accordingly that amendment shall not be taken—

    (a) to revive any such provision, or

    (b) to preclude the making of an order under section 33 with respect to any such provision.

(6) Where, immediately before the repeal of the 1978 Act takes effect under the provision inserted by subsection (4), a person is held in custody in a prison or other place by virtue of a direction under section 4 of that Act (holding in custody of young persons charged with scheduled offences), it shall be lawful for him to continue to be held in custody in that prison or place until arrangements can be made for him to be held in custody in accordance with the law then applicable to his case.

(7) Nothing in subsection (6) shall be taken to make lawful the holding in custody of any person who would, disregarding that subsection, be entitled to be released from custody.

(8) The repeal of the 1978 Act shall not affect the application of any provision of sections 6 to 9 of that Act to any trial on indictment where the indictment has been presented, or any summary trial which has started, before the repeal takes effect.

(9) It is hereby declared that the repeal of the 1978 Act shall not affect—

    (a) any committal of a person for trial in accordance with section 6 of that Act to the Crown Court sitting either in Belfast or elsewhere, or

    (b) any committal of a person for trial which, in accordance with that section, has taken effect as a committal for trial to the Crown Court sitting elsewhere than in Belfast,

in a case where the indictment has not been presented before the repeal takes effect.

(10) The repeal of the 1978 Act shall not affect the application of any provision of sections 28 and 28A of that Act in relation to any right to compensation under section 28 which arises before the date when the repeal takes effect.

GENERAL NOTE

The purpose of this section is to give effect to the recommendation in the Baker Report that the Northern Ireland Emergency Provisions legislation should be given a maximum life of five years subject to annual renewal, instead of an unlimited life subject to six months renewal by order as has pertained. The first renewal date will be March 22, 1988 to coincide with that of the PTA (which is subject to a maximum life of five years), thereby enabling Parliament to consider all current emergency measures together. This was a proposal of the Standing Advisory Commission on Human Rights in Northern Ireland. This section repeals or amends ancillary and transitional provisions relating to annual renewal and the expiry of the Act on June 16, 1992.

PART II

RIGHTS OF PERSONS DETAINED UNDER TERRORISM PROVISIONS IN POLICE CUSTODY

Right to have someone informed of detention under terrorism provisions

14.—(1) A person who is detained under the terrorism provisions and is being held in police custody shall be entitled, if he so requests, to have one friend or relative or other person who is known to him or is likely to take an interest in his welfare told that he is being detained under those provisions and where he is being held in police custody.

(2) A person shall be informed of the right conferred on him by subsection (1) as soon as practicable after he has become a person to whom that subsection applies.

(3) A request made by a person under subsection (1), and the time at which it is made, shall be recorded in writing.

(4) If a person makes such a request, it must be complied with as soon as is practicable except to the extent that any delay is permitted by this section.

(5) Any delay in complying with such a request is only permitted if—

    (a) it is authorised by an officer of at least the rank of superintendent; and

    (b) it does not extend beyond the end of the period referred to in subsection (6).

(6) That period is—

    (a) (except where paragraph (b) applies) the period of 48 hours beginning with the time when the detained person was first detained under the terrorism provisions;

    (b) where the detained person was, prior to the time when he was first so detained, being examined in accordance with any order under section 13 of the Prevention of Terrorism (Temporary Provisions) Act 1984, the period of 48 hours beginning with the time when he was first so examined.

(7) An officer may give an authorisation under subsection (5) orally or in writing but, if he gives it orally, he shall confirm it in writing as soon as is practicable.

(8) An officer may only authorise a delay in complying with a request under subsection (1) where he has reasonable grounds for believing that telling the person named in the request of the detention of the detained person—

    (a) will lead to interference with or harm to evidence connected with a scheduled offence or interference with or physical injury to any person; or

    (b) will lead to the alerting of any person suspected of having committed such an offence but not yet arrested for it; or

    (c) will hinder the recovery of any property obtained as a result of such an offence; or

    (d) will lead to interference with the gathering of information about the commission, preparation or instigation of acts of terrorism; or

    (e) by alerting any person, will make it more difficult—

        (i) to prevent an act of terrorism; or

        (ii) to secure the apprehension, prosecution or conviction of any person in connection with the commission, preparation or instigation of an act of terrorism.

(9) If any delay is authorised, then, as soon as is practicable—

    (a) the detained person shall be told the reason for authorising it; and

    (b) the reason shall be recorded in writing.

(10) Any authorisation under subsection (5) shall cease to have effect once the reason for giving it ceases to subsist.

(11) The right conferred by subsection (1) may be exercised by a person to whom that subsection applies on each occasion when he is transferred from one place to another; and this section applies to each subsequent occasion on which that right is so exercised as it applies to the first such occasion.

(12) Subsection (11) shall not be construed as prejudicing the operation of a request by a person to whom subsection (1) applies which was made, but not complied with, before he was transferred.

DEFINITION
"delay": see subss. (5), (6).

GENERAL NOTE

This section introduces Pt. 2 of the 1987 Act, which places on a statutory basis the rights of accused persons in police custody. Broadly the sections follow the Police and Criminal Evidence Act 1984, as it extends to arrests in Great Britain under the PTA.

An arrested person now has a right under this section to have someone informed of the detention and his or her whereabouts, "as soon as practicable" unless delay is justified on a ground set out in the section. The maximum period of delay in contacting a relative or other person is 48 hours. The section also enacts a statutory requirement to inform the person of the right to communicate with a relative (subs. (2)), and to be informed of any delay invoked and the reason (subs. (9)).

Although this section follows the PACE, s.56, as yet no accompanying Codes of Practice as accompany the statutory provisions of that Act, apply in Northern Ireland. However, codes relating to emergency powers are to be introduced. It may also be noted that delay for 48 hours maximum, is the maximum period of arrest under s.12 of the PTA before further authorisation of detention by the Secretary of State.

Right of access to legal advice

15.—(1) A person who is detained under the terrorism provisions and is being held in police custody shall be entitled, if he so requests, to consult a solicitor privately.

(2) A person shall be informed of the right conferred on him by subsection (1) as soon as practicable after he has become a person to whom that subsection applies.

(3) A request made by a person under subsection (1), and the time at which it is made, shall be recorded in writing unless it is made by him while at a court after being charged with an offence.

(4) If a person makes such a request, he must be permitted to consult a solicitor as soon as is practicable except to the extent that any delay is permitted by this section.

(5) Any delay in complying with a request under subsection (1) is only permitted if—

(a) it is authorised by an officer of at least the rank of superintendent; and

(b) it does not extend beyond the relevant time.

(6) In subsection (5) "the relevant time" means—

(a) where the request is the first request made by the detained person under subsection (1), the end of the period referred to in section 14(6); or

(b) where the request follows an earlier request made by the detained person under that subsection in pursuance of which he has consulted a solicitor, the end of the period of 48 hours beginning with the time when that consultation began.

(7) An officer may give an authorisation under subsection (5) orally or in writing but, if he gives it orally, he shall confirm it in writing as soon as is practicable.

(8) An officer may only authorise a delay in complying with a request under subsection (1) where he has reasonable grounds for believing that the exercise of the right conferred by that subsection at the time when the detained person desires to exercise it—

(a) will lead to interference with or harm to evidence connected with a scheduled offence or interference with or physical injury to any person; or

(b) will lead to the alerting of any person suspected of having committed such an offence but not yet arrested for it; or

(c) will hinder the recovery of any property obtained as a result of such an offence; or

   (d) will lead to interference with the gathering of information about the commission, preparation or instigation of acts of terrorism; or

   (e) by alerting any person, will make it more difficult—

      (i) to prevent an act of terrorism; or

     (ii) to secure the apprehension, prosecution or conviction of any person in connection with the commission, preparation or instigation of an act of terrorism.

(9) If any delay is authorised, then, as soon as is practicable—

   (a) the detained person shall be told the reason for authorising it; and

   (b) the reason shall be recorded in writing.

(10) If an officer of at least the rank of Assistant Chief Constable has reasonable grounds for believing that, unless he gives a direction under subsection (11), the exercise by a person of the right conferred by subsection (1) will have any of the consequences specified in subsection (8), he may give a direction under subsection (11).

(11) A direction under this subsection is a direction that a person desiring to exercise the right conferred by subsection (1) may only consult a solicitor in the sight and hearing of a qualified officer of the uniformed branch of the Royal Ulster Constabulary.

(12) An officer is qualified for the purposes of subsection (11) if—

   (a) he is of at least the rank of inspector; and

   (b) in the opinion of the officer giving the direction, he has no connection with the case.

(13) Any authorisation under subsection (5) or direction under subsection (11) shall cease to have effect once the reason for giving it ceases to subsist.

GENERAL NOTE

This section places on a statutory basis the right to access to a solicitor while detained in police custody under the PTA, s.12. There is a right equally to be informed of this right (subs. (2)). The right is exercisable "as soon as is practicable" subject to permitted delay of 48 hours (subs. 6), provided the authorised officer believes on reasonable grounds that one of the eventualities set out in subs. (8) may arise. Where delay in granting access to a solicitor is authorised by the specified senior police officer, the detained person is to be informed and to be told the reason.

Subs. (11)

Where access to a legal adviser is granted, a further direction may be given by a police officer of at least the rank of Assistant Chief Constable, that consultation with a solicitor may only take place within the sight and hearing of an R.U.C. officer, uniformed branch. Such a direction may be given if the directing officer believes that one of the consequences outlined in subs. (8) will occur if the legal right to consultation occurs in private.

The section follows s.58 of the Police and Criminal Evidence Act 1984. Both this section and the preceding s.14 are silent as to the consequences of the breach of rights created by their provisions. However, it is arguable that where a court is satisfied that the right to inform a relative or to allow access to a solicitor has been unjustifiably *denied* or *delayed*, then the court could exclude as evidence any admissions obtained while an accused was under interview in police custody. However, the proposed non-statutory code for the exercise of emergency powers may rule this out. The statutory codes under the PACE provide that breach is a disciplinary offence. For a discussion of these Codes, see Zander, *The Police and Criminal Evidence Act 1984* (1985).

Interpretation of Part II

   16.—(1) In this Part—

     "scheduled offence" and "terrorism" have the same meaning as in the 1978 Act; and

     "the terrorism provisions" means—

      (a) section 12 of the Prevention of Terrorism (Temporary Provisions) Act 1984 (powers of arrest and detention); and

(b) any provision conferring a power of detention and contained in an order under section 13 of that Act (control of entry and procedure for removal).

(2) A person is held in police custody for the purposes of this Part if he is detained at a police station or is detained elsewhere in the charge of a constable, except that a person who is at a court after being charged with an offence is not held in police custody for the purposes of section 14.

GENERAL NOTE

The terrorism provisions. It is to be recalled that following this Act, the arrest power—formerly s.11 of the 1978 Act—has been repealed, leaving s.12 of the PTA as the arrest power in connection with terrorism in Northern Ireland (see notes to s.6 above).

PART III

REGULATION OF THE PROVISION OF SECURITY SERVICES

GENERAL NOTE

Ss.17–27 are an attempt to stamp out the activities of paramilitary groups obtaining funds through offering private security guard services. For some years, there has been concern over extortion rackets surrounding the mushrooming of such private security services.

The scheme created by this part of the Act requires certification by the Secretary of State of any firm that offers such services for reward. Certificates will be denied or revoked if he is satisfied that the service will be operated for the benefit of a proscribed organisation or a front for a proscribed organisation. Certificates will be issued only to bona fide companies. This section makes it an offence to offer security services for reward without a certificate. Certificates will be issued for 12 months renewable. Certificates may be revoked. S.20 creates a duty to notify the Secretary of State of changes of personnel following the granting of a certificate. Offences under s.17 are added to the list of scheduled offences in the 1978 Act. S.21 creates an offence of payment for security services to someone who has not obtained a certificate.

COMMENCEMENT

Pt. 3 of the Act is not in force, see s.26.

Prohibition on provision of security services without a certificate

17.—(1) A person shall not provide, or offer to provide, security services for reward, unless he is, or is acting on behalf of, the holder of a certificate in force under this Part.

(2) A person shall not publish, or cause to be published, any advertisement for the provision of such services by a person who is not the holder of such a certificate.

(3) Any person who contravenes subsection (1) or (2) shall be guilty of an offence and liable—

(a) on summary conviction, to imprisonment for a term not exceeding six months, or to a fine not exceeding the statutory maximum, or to both;

(b) on conviction on indictment, to imprisonment for a term not exceeding five years, or to a fine, or to both.

(4) Where a person is charged with an offence under this section in respect of an advertisement, it shall be a defence for him to prove—

(a) that he is a person whose business it is to publish or arrange for the publication of advertisements; and

(b) that he received the advertisement for publication in the ordinary course of business; and

(c) that he had reasonable grounds for believing that the person advertised as the provider of the security services in question was the holder of a certificate in force under this Part.

(5) The following paragraph shall be inserted after paragraph 19C of Schedule 4 to the 1978 Act (scheduled offences)—

"Northern Ireland (Emergency Provisions) Act 1987

19D. Offences under section 17 of the Northern Ireland (Emergency Provisions) Act 1987 (provision of security services without a certificate)."

(6) In this Part "security services" means the services of one or more individuals as security guards (whether with or without any other services relating to the protection of property or persons).

Applications for certificates

18.—(1) An application for a certificate under this Part—
    (a) shall be made to the Secretary of State in such manner and form, and
    (b) shall be accompanied by such information concerning—
        (i) the applicant,
        (ii) any business carried on or proposed to be carried on by the applicant and involving the provision of security services for reward,
        (iii) any persons whom the applicant employs, or proposes to employ, as security guards,
        (iv) any partners or proposed partners of the applicant or (if the applicant is a partnership) the members, and any proposed members, of the partnership, and
        (v) if the applicant is a body corporate, the officers, and any proposed officers, of that body,
as the Secretary of State may specify.

(2) Any person who, in connection with any such application, knowingly or recklessly furnishes the Secretary of State with information which is false or misleading in a material respect shall be guilty of an offence and liable on summary conviction to imprisonment for a term not exceeding six months, or to a fine not exceeding level 5 on the standard scale, or to both.

(3) In this section and section 20—
    (a) "officer" includes a director, manager or secretary; and
    (b) any reference to the employment or proposed employment of any person or persons by an applicant for a certificate under this Part shall, in relation to an applicant who is, or is a member of, a partnership, be construed as a reference to the employment or proposed employment of any person or persons by the partnership or any of the partners.

(4) For the purposes of this section and section 20 a person in accordance with whose directions or instructions the directors of a body corporate are accustomed to act shall be treated as an officer of that body, except that a person shall not be so treated by reason only that the directors act on advice given by him in a professional capacity.

Issue, duration and revocation of certificates

19.—(1) Where an application for a certificate under this Part has been made to the Secretary of State in accordance with section 18, the Secretary of State may only refuse to issue such a certificate to the applicant in a case where he is satisfied that an organisation falling within subsection (8) would be likely to benefit from the issue of the certificate; and, if he does so, he shall notify the applicant of his refusal to issue such a certificate.

(2) A certificate under this Part shall come into force at the beginning of the day on which it is issued and, subject to subsection (3), shall expire at the end of the period of 12 months beginning with that day.

(3) Where the certificate is issued to a person who already holds a certificate in force under this Part, the new certificate shall expire at the end of the period of 12 months beginning with the day following that on which that person's current certificate expires.

(4) The Secretary of State may from time to time by order made by statutory instrument substitute for the period specified in each of subsections (2) and (3) such period exceeding 12 months as is specified in the order, and any such order shall be laid before Parliament after being made.

(5) Subject to subsection (6), the Secretary of State may revoke a certificate in force under this Part if he is satisfied that an organisation falling within subsection (8) would be likely to benefit from the certificate remaining in force.

(6) The Secretary of State shall not revoke a certificate under subsection (5) unless the holder of the certificate—

(a) has been notified of the Secretary of State's intention to revoke it, and

(b) has been given a reasonable opportunity of making representations to the Secretary of State.

(7) If the Secretary of State revokes a certificate under subsection (5), he shall forthwith notify the holder of the certificate of its revocation.

(8) An organisation falls within this subsection if—

(a) it is for the time being a proscribed organisation within the meaning of the 1978 Act, or

(b) it appears to the Secretary of State to be closely associated with an organisation which is for the time being such a proscribed organisation.

(9) In this section "benefit" means benefit whether directly or indirectly and whether financially or in any other way.

Duty to notify Secretary of State of changes of personnel

20.—(1) Where—

(a) an application has been made by any person under section 18, and

(b) that person proposes to employ a person as a security guard as from a relevant time, and

(c) information concerning the proposed employee was not furnished to the Secretary of State in pursuance of section 18(1)(b)(iii) at the time when the application was made,

the person who made the application shall, not later than 14 days before that relevant time, notify to the Secretary of State such information concerning the proposed employee as the Secretary of State may specify.

(2) Where an application has been made by any person under section 18, that person shall notify to the Secretary of State such information concerning any change to which this subsection applies as the Secretary of State may specify, and shall so notify any such information—

(a) not later than 14 days before the change occurs, or

(b) if that is not reasonably practicable, as soon as is reasonably practicable.

(3) Subsection (2) applies—

(a) in relation to an application made by a partnership or by a member of a partnership, to any change occurring at a relevant time in the members of the partnership, and

(b) in relation to an application made by a body corporate, to any change occurring at a relevant time in the officers of that body,

unless the change involves a person becoming a partner or officer and information relating to that change was furnished to the Secretary of State in pursuance of section 18(1)(b)(iv) or (v) at the time when the application was made.

(4) Any person who contravenes subsection (1) or (2) shall be guilty of an offence and liable on summary conviction to imprisonment for a term not exceeding six months, or to a fine not exceeding level 5 on the standard scale, or to both.

(5) In this section "relevant time", in relation to an application made under section 18, means a time when—

(a) the application has been neither granted nor refused by the Secretary of State; or

(b) a certificate issued in pursuance of the application is in force under this Part;

and subsections (3) and (4) of that section apply for the purposes of this section.

Payments in respect of the provision of security services

21.—(1) Any person who, in respect of the provision of security services, pays any sum of money to a person who is neither—

(a) the holder of a certificate in force under this Part, nor

(b) a person acting on behalf of the holder of such a certificate,

shall be guilty of an offence.

(2) A person guilty of an offence under subsection (1) shall be liable on summary conviction to imprisonment for a term not exceeding six months, or to a fine not exceeding level 5 on the standard scale, or to both.

(3) It shall be a defence for a person charged with an offence under subsection (1) to prove that, at the time when he paid the money in question, he had reasonable grounds for believing that the person to whom he paid it was, or was acting on behalf of, the holder of a certificate in force under this Part.

Liability of directors etc.

22.—(1) Where an offence under this Part which has been committed by a body corporate is proved to have been committed with the consent or connivance of, or to be attributable to any neglect on the part of, any director, manager, secretary or other similar officer of the body corporate, or any person purporting to act in any such capacity, he as well as the body corporate shall be guilty of that offence and be liable to be proceeded against and punished accordingly.

(2) Where the affairs of a body corporate are managed by its members, subsection (1) shall apply in relation to the acts and defaults of a member in connection with his functions of management as if he were a director of the body corporate.

Notifications

23.—(1) Any notification given under this Part shall be in writing.

(2) Any notification required by this Part to be given by any person to the Secretary of State may be sent to him by post.

(3) Any notification required by this Part to be given by the Secretary of State to any person may—

(a) if that person is an individual, be sent to him by post addressed to him at his usual or last-known place of residence or business;

(b) if that person is a partnership, be sent to a partner, or to a person having the control or management of the partnership business, at the principal office of the partnership; or

(c) if that person is a body corporate, be sent to the secretary or clerk of that body at its registered or principal office.

(4) This section is without prejudice to any other lawful method of giving a notification.

Expenses of Secretary of State

24. Any expenses incurred by the Secretary of State under this Part shall be paid out of money provided by Parliament.

PART IV

GENERAL

Minor and consequential amendments, repeals and revocation

25.—(1) The enactments mentioned in Schedule 1 shall have effect subject to the minor and consequential amendments there specified.

(2) The enactments mentioned in Part I of Schedule 2 are hereby repealed to the extent specified in the third column of that Schedule, and the enactment mentioned in Part II of that Schedule is hereby revoked to the extent so specified.

(3) Any order in force under section 33 of the 1978 Act at the commencement of section 13 of this Act is hereby revoked.

GENERAL NOTE

Subs. (1)

This section effects a large number of amendments termed minor or consequential to the 1978 Act which are gathered under Sched. 1. For convenience, the most significant of these are noted here. It is recommended that practitioners examine the schedule carefully because the range of amendments is considerable, as is their importance.

Arrest and search powers to be exercised on reasonable grounds

Police and army arrest powers (ss.13 and 14 of the 1978 Act), and search powers (s.15 of the 1978 Act) are now to be exercised only where there are *reasonable grounds* for arrest. Formerly these powers required only the genuine suspicion of the arrestor. These changes are significant because they enable the possibility of judicial challenge to allegations of arbitrary security force operations.

Power to stop and question

The power in s.18 of the Act has been a source of criticism over the years. The major complaint has been that soldiers have used the power to conduct "trawling" exercises in the Catholic community (see the Baker Report, para. 392). The amendment made is modest; the person stopped may only be questioned about *recent* incidents (a clarification suggested by the Baker Report, para. 384). However, the offence itself is made non-imprisonable. It is now subject to a fine.

Commencement, expiry, revival and eventual repeal of Act

26.—(1) This Act, except section 12 and Part III, shall come into force at the end of the period of one month beginning with the day on which it is passed, and section 12 and Part III shall come into force on such day as the Secretary of State may by order appoint.

(2) An order under subsection (1)—

(a) may appoint different days for different provisions, and

(b) shall be made by statutory instrument.

(3) The provisions of Parts II and III shall expire with 21st March 1988 unless continued in force by an order under subsection (4).

(4) The Secretary of State may provide by order made by statutory instrument—

    (a) that all or any of the provisions of Parts II and III which are for the time being in force (including any in force by virtue of an order under this subsection) shall continue in force for a period not exceeding 12 months from the coming into operation of the order;

    (b) that all or any of those provisions which are for the time being in force shall cease to be in force; or

    (c) that all or any of those provisions which are not for the time being in force shall come into force again and remain in force for a period not exceeding 12 months from the coming into operation of the order.

(5) No order under subsection (4) shall be made unless—

    (a) a draft of the order has been approved by resolution of each House of Parliament; or

    (b) it is declared in the order that it appears to the Secretary of State that by reason of urgency it is necessary to make the order without a draft having been so approved.

(6) Every order under subsection (4), except an order of which a draft has been so approved—

    (a) shall be laid before Parliament; and

    (b) unless approved by resolution of each House of Parliament before the end of the period of 40 days beginning with the date on which it was made, shall cease to have effect at the end of that period (but without prejudice to anything previously done or to the making of a new order).

In reckoning for the purposes of this subsection any period of 40 days, no account shall be taken of any period during which Parliament is dissolved or prorogued or during which both Houses are adjourned for more than four days.

(7) With the exception of section 13(6) to (10), this subsection and section 27, this Act shall, by virtue of this subsection, be repealed immediately after the repeal of the 1978 Act takes effect under section 33(9) of that Act (as amended by section 13(4) above).

GENERAL NOTE

The Act came into force on June 15, 1987, except s.12 (new compensation provisions) and Pt. 3.

The Act falls for renewal on March 21, 1988. It is intended to renew it thereafter annually subject as explained to a maximum life of five years (see s.13 above and annotations thereto).

Short title, construction and extent

27.—(1) This Act may be cited as the Northern Ireland (Emergency Provisions) Act 1987.

(2) In this Act "the 1978 Act" means the Northern Ireland (Emergency Provisions) Act 1978.

(3) This Act extends to Northern Ireland only.

SCHEDULES

SCHEDULE 1

MINOR AND CONSEQUENTIAL AMENDMENTS

NORTHERN IRELAND (EMERGENCY PROVISIONS) ACT 1978 (c.5)

1. In section 13 (constables' general power of arrest and seizure)—
    (a) in subsection (1), for "whom he suspects of committing, having committed or being" substitute "who he has reasonable grounds to suspect is committing, has committed or is";
    (b) in subsection (2), for "suspects him of being" substitute "has reasonable grounds for suspecting him to be"; and
    (c) in subsection (3), for "suspects" substitute "has reasonable grounds to suspect".
2. In section 14 (powers of arrest of members of Her Majesty's forces)—
    (a) in subsection (1), for "whom he suspects of committing, having committed or being" substitute "who he has reasonable grounds to suspect is committing, has committed or is"; and
    (b) in subsection (3), for paragraph (b) substitute the following paragraph—
        "(b) if there are reasonable grounds for suspecting that that person is a terrorist or has committed an offence involving the use or possession of an explosive substance or firearm, where there are reasonable grounds for suspecting him to be."
3. In section 15 (power to search for munitions and radio transmitters)—
    (a) in subsection (2), for "it is suspected" substitute "there are reasonable grounds for suspecting";
    (b) in subsection (3)(b), for "whom he suspects of having" substitute "who he has reasonable grounds to suspect has";
    (c) for subsection (4) substitute—
        "(4) Where a member of Her Majesty's forces or a constable is empowered by virtue of any provision of this Act to search any premises or other place or any person—
            (a) he may seize any munitions found in the course of the search (unless it appears to him that the munitions are being, have been and will be used only lawfully) and may retain and, if necessary, destroy them; and
            (b) he may seize any transmitter found in the course of the search (unless it appears to him that the transmitter has been, is being and is likely to be used only lawfully) and may retain it."; and
    (d) in subsection (5), in the definition of "transmitter", for "and includes" substitute "or".
4. In section 18 (power to stop and question)—
    (a) in subsection (1)(b), after "other" insert "recent"; and
    (b) in subsection (2), for the words from "imprisonment" onwards substitute "a fine not exceeding level 5 on the standard scale."
5. In section 31(1) (interpretation), omit the definition of "constable".
6. In section 32 (orders and regulations)—
    (a) in subsection (1), after "orders conferred by" insert "section 19A above and";
    (b) in subsection (3), for the words from the beginning to "Schedules)" substitute "Subject to subsection (5) below, no order or regulations under this Act";
    (c) in subsection (4), for the words from the beginning to "approved) shall" substitute "Subject to subsection (5) below, orders and regulations under this Act shall, if not so approved in draft,"; and
    (d) after that subsection add—
        "(5) Subsections (3) and (4) above do not apply to—
            (a) any order under section 19A above or under Schedule 1 or 3 to this Act; or
            (b) any regulations under section 5A above;
        but a statutory instrument containing any such regulations shall be subject to annulment in pursuance of a resolution of either House of Parliament."
7. In section 33 (commencement etc. of provisions of the 1978 Act)—
    (a) in subsection (5), at the end add "or (where the Lord Chancellor gives a

direction under that subsection with respect to the trial) to the Crown Court sitting at the place specified in the direction."; and

(b) for subsection (7) substitute—

"(7) It is hereby declared that the expiry or cesser of any provision of section 6 above shall not affect—

(a) any committal of a person for trial in accordance with that provision to the Crown Court sitting either in Belfast or elsewhere, or

(b) any committal of a person for trial which, in accordance with that provision, has taken effect as a committal for trial to the Crown Court sitting elsewhere than in Belfast,

in a case where the indictment has not been presented."

8.—(1) In Schedule 4 (scheduled offences), Part I (substantive offences) shall be amended as follows.

(2) In paragraph 12(f), at the end add ", subject also to note 2 below."

(3) In note 2, after paragraph (c) insert—

"(cc) section 20 of the Theft Act (Northern Ireland) 1969 (subject to note 5 below); or".

(4) In note 5—

(a) for "15 or 20" substitute "or 15"; and

(b) at the end add "; and the Attorney General for Northern Ireland shall not certify that an offence under section 20 of the said Act of 1969 is not to be treated as a scheduled offence in a case where it is charged that the offence was so committed."

JUDICATURE (NORTHERN IRELAND) ACT 1978 (c.23)

9. In Part II of Schedule 5 (minor and consequential amendments), in the entry relating to section 2(1)(a) of the Northern Ireland (Emergency Provisions) Act 1978, for "sections 2(1)(a) and" substitute "section".

Section 25(2)

SCHEDULE 2

REPEALS AND REVOCATION

PART I

REPEALS

Chapter	Short title	Extent of repeal
1978 c.5.	Northern Ireland (Emergency Provisions) Act 1978.	In section 22(2), the word "and" at the end of paragraph (c). In section 31(1), the definition of "constable".
1978 c.23.	Judicature (Northern Ireland) Act 1978.	In Part II of Schedule 5, the entries relating to sections 6 and 33(7) of the Northern Ireland (Emergency Provisions) Act 1978.

PART II

REVOCATION

Number	Title	Extent of revocation
S.I. 1981/1675 (N.I. 26).	Magistrates' Courts (Northern Ireland) Order 1981.	In Schedule 6, paragraph 49.

LANDLORD AND TENANT ACT 1987*

(1987 c. 31)

ARRANGEMENT OF SECTIONS

PART I

TENANTS' RIGHTS OF FIRST REFUSAL

Preliminary

PART II

APPOINTMENT OF MANAGERS BY THE COURT

PART III

COMPULSORY ACQUISITION BY TENANTS OF THEIR LANDLORD'S INTEREST

---

* Annotations by Stephen Tromans, M.A., Solicitor, and Delyth W. Williams, B.A., LL.B., M.C.D., M.R.T.P.I., Principal Lecturer and Course Director, Department of Surveying, Liverpool Polytechnic.

An Act to confer on tenants of flats rights with respect to the acquisition
   by them of their landlord's reversion; to make provision for the
   appointment of a manager at the instance of such tenants and for the
   variation of long leases held by such tenants; to make further provision
   with respect to service charges payable by tenants of flats and other
   dwellings; to make other provision with respect to such tenants; to
   make further provision with respect to the permissible purposes and
   objects of registered housing associations as regards the management
   of leasehold property; and for connected purposes.   [15th May 1987]

PARLIAMENTARY DEBATES
   Hansard: H.C. Vol. 111, col. 1050; Vol. 113, col. 769; Vol. 115, col. 594; H.L. Vol. 487,
cols. 291, 636.
   The Bill was considered in Standing Committee A from April 9 to 28, 1987.

GENERAL NOTE
   This Act implements the main recommendations of the Committee of Inquiry on the
management of privately owned blocks of flats, chaired by E. G. Nugee Q.C. ("The Nugee
Committee Report") and also contains certain other measures relating to the rights of
tenants of such flats and other dwellings. The main recommendations of the Nugee
Committee Report were recognised as having a geographical concentration.
   "The Bill is about 500,000 households, a high proportion of these in London and the
south-east. It is about households in privately owned flats. Many live in so-called mansion
blocks—sometimes that is a good term, and sometimes a bad term for the state in which
people live. The Bill applies also to the large number of purpose-built blocks of flats erected
between the wars and in the last 20 years, and to converted houses. About two-thirds of
these households are long leaseholders and the remaining third are Rent Act tenants" (Mr.
John Patten, March 30, 1987 *Hansard*, H.C. Vol. 113, col. 769). The main effect of the Act
is likely to be geographically concentrated in the London area and the south-east.
   The Nugee Committee Report marks the culmination of various reports and committee
investigations into the management of privately-owned blocks of flats. In January 1984 the
Law Commission reported on "Transfer of land—The Law of Positive and Restrictive
Covenants" (Law Com. No. 127). Adoption of the recommendations of that report are still
awaited but they represent a marked change from the existing law and might have made this
Act unneccessary. A working party of the Royal Institution of Chartered Surveyors published
a report (the James Report) on the management difficulties of privately-owned blocks of
flats and a copy of this report is annexed to the Nugee Committee Report. In addition, a
Building Societies Association report advocated the introduction of strata title in July 1984.
   The Act implements the main recommendations of the Nugee Committee Report but
without encompassing a major reform of the tenure system in England and Wales advocated
in some of the other reports.

The 1987 Act is divided into seven parts, namely
1. Pt. 1 deals with the tenants' rights of first refusal on a relevant disposal affecting premises containing two or more flats.
2. Pt. 2 deals with the appointment of managers by the court to assume responsibility for the management of the premises containing the flats where the landlord is in breach of any obligation as defined owed by him to the tenant under his tenancy.
3. Pt. 3 enables qualifying tenants of flats contained in any premises covered by Pt. 3 to acquire their landlord's interest in the premises without his consent by making application to the county court for an acquisition order.
4. Pt. 4 gives any party to a long lease of a flat the right to make an application to the county court for an order varying the terms of the lease.
5. The provisions contained in Pt. 5 make substantial amendments to the service charge provisions contained in ss.18–30 of the Landlord and Tenant Act 1985.
6. Pt. 6 extends a residential tenant's rights to information about his landlord's name and address and Pt. VI makes general provisions as to the operation of the 1987 Act.

COMMENCEMENT
The Act comes into force on a day to be appointed by the Secretary of State for the Environment who may appoint different days for different provisions or for different purposes. The Act also includes provision for the Secretary of State to make transitional, incidental, supplemental or consequential provisions by Order.

EXTENT
The Act does not extend to Scotland or Northern Ireland.

PART I

TENANTS' RIGHTS OF FIRST REFUSAL

GENERAL NOTE
Pt. 1 of the Act gives qualifying tenants a right of first refusal on a relevant disposal affecting premises which contains two or more flats held by qualifying tenants and the number of flats held by such tenants exceeds 50 per cent. of the total number of flats contained in the premises (s.1). In addition, the premises may consist of the whole or part of a building (s.1(2)(a), (b), (c)) but Pt. 1 does not apply to premises if (i) any part or parts of the premises are occupied or intended to be occupied other than for residential premises; and (ii) the internal floor area of those parts (taken together) exceeds 50 per cent. of the internal floor area of the premises (taken as a whole) with the internal floor area of the common parts to be disregarded. The definition of "landlord" for the purposes of Pt. 1 is contained in s.2 as being either (i) the immediate landlord of the qualifying tenants of the flats contained in the premises, or (ii) if any of the qualifying tenants is a statutory tenant, the person who would be entitled to possession of the flat in question were it not for the statutory tenancy. Where the landlord is himself a tenant there are provisions for the superior landlord to be the "landlord" (s.2(2)(a), (b)). A qualifying tenant is a tenant of a flat under a tenancy other than (i) a protected shorthold tenancy, or (ii) a tenancy to which the Landlord and Tenant Act 1954 Pt. 2 applies. In the case of a proposal to make a relevant disposal (s.4), the landlord must serve a notice on the tenant containing particulars of the principal terms of the disposal proposed. Such a notice constitutes an offer by the landlord to dispose of the property on those terms. If the requisite majority of the qualifying tenants accept the landlord's offer in writing, the landlord cannot dispose of the protected interest except to a person or persons nominated by the requisite majority of the qualifying tenants (s.6). The term "requisite majority" is defined as the qualifying tenants of those flats with more than 50 per cent. of the available votes (s.5(6)).
If an acceptance notice is not served on the landlord by the requisite majority of qualifying tenants of the constituent flats within the period specified in the landlord's notice, the landlord may (during the period of 12 months beginning with the end of that period) dispose of the protected interest to such a person as he thinks fit subject to certain conditions (s.7(1)(a), (b)). A majority of the qualifying tenants may also serve a counter-offer to the landlord's offer for the acquisition by them of such estate or interest in the property specified in the landlord's notice and the landlord may serve a notice accepting or rejecting the counter-offer (s.7(2)(a), (b)). Where the landlord serves a notice rejecting a counter-offer, such a notice may state that it constitutes a fresh offer by the landlord which can be accepted

31–4

by the requisite majority of the qualifying tenants of the constituent flats (s.8(1)(a)) but if not accepted within the period specified in the landlord's notice the landlord may (during the period of 12 months beginning with that period) dispose of any such estate or interest to such a person as he thinks fit.

S. 9 contains provisions for the withdrawal of either party from the transaction where, for example, the nominated person becomes aware that the requisite majority of qualifying tenants do not wish to proceed with the acquisition of the protected interest.

A landlord's offer notice ceases to have effect if the premises cease to be premises to which Pt. 1 of the Act applies and the landlord serves a notice on the qualifying tenants to that effect but if no such notice is served Pt. 1 continues to have effect on the disposal (s.10).

The provisions for the enforcement of rights against new landlords where the landlord did not serve a notice under s.5 or the disposal was made in contravention of ss.6–10 are contained in s.11 which also places a duty on the new landlord to furnish particulars of the disposal made in contravention of Pt. 1 of the Act. In the circumstances outlined in s.11, s.12 gives a right to qualifying tenants to compel the disposal by the new landlord of the estate or interest (which formed the original disposal) to them by way of a purchase notice. Any question arising in relation to any matters specified in a purchase notice is to be determined by a rent assessment committee sitting as a leasehold valuation tribunal (s.13).

S. 14 provides for the withdrawal of the nominated person from the transaction before a binding contract is entered into in pursuance of a purchase notice. The concluding sections of Pt. 1 provide for:

(a) the right of qualifying tenants to compel the grant of a new tenancy by a superior landlord if the landlord has disposed of the interest by the surrender to the head landlord (s.15);

(b) the enforcement of rights under s.11 or s.12 against subsequent purchasers (s.16);

(c) the termination of rights against a new landlord or subsequent purchaser (s.17);

(d) notices served by prospective purchasers to ensure that rights of first refusal do not apply (s.18).

Preliminary

Qualifying tenants to have rights of first refusal on disposals by landlord

1.—(1) A landlord shall not make a relevant disposal affecting any premises to which at the time of the disposal this Part applies unless—

(a) he has in accordance with section 5 previously served a notice under that section with respect to the disposal on the qualifying tenants of the flats contained in those premises (being a notice by virtue of which rights of first refusal are conferred on those tenants); and

(b) the disposal is made in accordance with the requirements of sections 6 to 10.

(2) Subject to subsections (3) and (4), this Part applies to premises if—

(a) they consist of the whole or part of a building; and

(b) they contain two or more flats held by qualifying tenants; and

(c) the number of flats held by such tenants exceeds 50 per cent. of the total number of flats contained in the premises.

(3) This Part does not apply to premises falling within subsection (2) if—

(a) any part or parts of the premises is or are occupied or intended to be occupied otherwise than for residential purposes; and

(b) the internal floor area of that part or those parts (taken together) exceeds 50 per cent. of the internal floor area of the premises (taken as a whole);

and for the purposes of this subsection the internal floor area of any common parts shall be disregarded.

(4) This Part also does not apply to any such premises at a time when the interest of the landlord in the premises is held by an exempt landlord or a resident landlord.

(5) The Secretary of State may by order substitute for the percentage for the time being specified in subsection (3)(b) such other percentage as is specified in the order.

DEFINITIONS
"exempt landlord": s.58(1).
"landlord": ss.2, 59(2).
"qualifying tenants": s.3.
"relevant disposal": s.4.
"resident landlord": ss.58(2), 60.

GENERAL NOTE
This section prohibits a landlord from making a relevant disposal unless he has served a notice under s.5 conferring the rights of first refusal on the tenants and the disposal is made in accordance with the requirements of ss. 6 to 10, which provide for:—
  (i) the acceptance of the landlord's offer (s.6);
  (ii) the rejection of the landlord's offer and the making of a counter-offer by the tenants (s.7);
  (iii) the making of a fresh offer by the landlord and provision for further negotiation between the parties (s.8);
  (iv) the withdrawal of either party from the transaction (s.9);
  (v) the lapse of the landlord's offer (s.10).

Subs. (2)
The premises must consist of the whole or part of a building and contain two or more flats held by qualifying tenants. The number of flats held by such tenants must exceed 50 per cent. of the total number of flats contained in the premises. For the provisions for calculating the 50 per cent. requirement see s.5(6).

Subs. (3)
There are no rights of first refusal where any part (or parts) are occupied (or intended to be occupied) for non-residential purposes and the internal floor area of that part (or parts) exceeds 50 per cent. of the internal floor area. In *Tandon* v. *Trustees of Spurgeon's Homes* [1982] A.C. 755, decided under the Leasehold Reform Act 1967 (as amended), it was found that that Act applied to premises where the non-residential use was up to 50 per cent. of the whole.

Subs. (4)
S.1 does not apply where the landlord is an exempt landlord or a resident landlord.

Landlords for the purposes of Part I

2.—(1) Subject to subsection (2), a person is for the purposes of this Part the landlord in relation to any premises consisting of the whole or part of a building if he is—
  (a) the immediate landlord of the qualifying tenants of the flats contained in those premises, or
  (b) where any of those tenants is a statutory tenant, the person who, apart from the statutory tenancy, would be entitled to possession of the flat in question.
(2) Where the person who is, in accordance with subsection (1), the landlord in relation to any such premises for the purposes of this Part ("the immediate landlord") is himself a tenant of those premises under a tenancy which is either—
  (a) a tenancy for a term of less than seven years, or
  (b) a tenancy for a longer term but terminable within the first seven years at the option of the person who is the landlord under that tenancy ("the superior landlord"),
the superior landlord shall also be regarded as the landlord in relation to those premises for the purposes of this Part and, if the superior landlord is himself a tenant of those premises under a tenancy falling within

paragraph (a) or (b) above, the person who is the landlord under that tenancy shall also be so regarded (and so on).

DEFINITIONS
"flat": s.60(1).
"qualifying tenants": s.3.
"statutory tenancy": s.60(1).

GENERAL NOTE
A landlord for the purposes of Pt. 1 is the immediate landlord of the qualifying tenants of the flats or, if any of the tenants are statutory tenants, the person who would be entitled to possession of the flat in question. If the immediate landlord is himself a tenant under a tenancy which is either a term for less than seven years or, for a longer term, subject to a break clause exercisable by the superior landlord within the first seven years, the superior landlord is also to be regarded as the landlord. The same rules apply to a chain of tenancies.

Qualifying tenants

3.—(1) Subject to the following provisions of this section, a person is for the purposes of this Part a qualifying tenant of a flat if he is the tenant of the flat under a tenancy other than—
  (a) a protected shorthold tenancy as defined in section 52 of the Housing Act 1980;
  (b) a tenancy to which Part II of the Landlord and Tenant Act 1954 (business tenancies) applies; or
  (c) a tenancy terminable on the cessation of his employment.
(2) A person is not to be regarded as being a qualifying tenant of any flat contained in any particular premises consisting of the whole or part of a building if—
  (a) he is the tenant of any such flat solely by reason of a tenancy under which the demised premises consist of or include—
      (i) the flat and one or more other flats, or
      (ii) the flat and any common parts of the building; or
  (b) he is the tenant of more than 50 per cent. of the total number of flats contained in those premises.
(3) For the purposes of subsection (2)(b) any tenant of a flat contained in the premises in question who is a body corporate shall be treated as the tenant of any other flat so contained and let to an associated company.
(4) A tenant of a flat whose landlord is a qualifying tenant of that flat is not to be regarded as being a qualifying tenant of that flat.

DEFINITIONS
"flat": s.60(1).
"tenancy": s.59(1).
"tenant": s.59(2).

GENERAL NOTE
The following are excluded from being a qualifying tenant if holding under (i) a protected shorthold tenancy under s.52 of the Housing Act 1980; (ii) a tenancy of business premises under the Landlord and Tenant Act 1954 Pt. 2; (iii) a service tenancy.

Subs. (2)
Pt. 1 of the Act does not apply in those cases stipulated in this subsection.

Subs. (3)
If a tenant of a flat falling within subs. (2) is a body corporate, it is to be treated as the tenant of any other flat in the premises let to an associated company so that the tenant is not to be treated as a qualifying tenant in such circumstances.

Relevant disposals

4.—(1) In this Part references to a relevant disposal affecting any premises to which this Part applies are references to the disposal by the landlord of any estate or interest (whether legal or equitable) in any such premises, including the disposal of any such estate or interest in any common parts of any such premises but excluding—

(a) the grant of any tenancy under which the demised premises consist of a single flat (whether with or without any appurtenant premises); and

(b) any of the disposals falling within subsection (2).

(2) The disposals referred to in subsection (1)(b) are—

(a) a disposal of—

(i) any interest of a beneficiary in settled land within the meaning of the Settled Land Act 1925,

(ii) any interest under a mortgage, or

(iii) any incorporeal hereditament;

(b) a disposal to a trustee in bankruptcy or to the liquidator of a company;

(c) a disposal in pursuance of an order made under section 24 or 24A of the Matrimonial Causes Act 1973 or section 2 of the Inheritance (Provision for Family and Dependants) Act 1975;

(d) a disposal in pursuance of a compulsory purchase order or in pursuance of an agreement entered into in circumstances where, but for the agreement, such an order would have been made or (as the case may be) carried into effect;

(e) a disposal by way of gift to a member of the landlord's family or to a charity;

(f) a disposal by one charity to another of an estate or interest in land which prior to the disposal is functional land of the first-mentioned charity and which is intended to be functional land of the other charity once the disposal is made;

(g) a disposal consisting of the transfer of an estate or interest held on trust for any person where the disposal is made in connection with the appointment of a new trustee or in connection with the discharge of any trustee;

(h) a disposal consisting of a transfer by two or more persons who are members of the same family either—

(i) to fewer of their number, or

(ii) to a different combination of members of the family (but one that includes at least one of the transferors);

(i) a disposal in pursuance of—

(i) any option or right of pre-emption binding on the landlord (whether granted before or after the commencement of this section), or

(ii) any other obligation binding on him and created before that commencement;

(j) a disposal consisting of the surrender of a tenancy in pursuance of any covenant, condition or agreement contained in it;

(k) a disposal to the Crown; and

(l) where the landlord is a body corporate, a disposal to an associated company.

(3) In this Part "disposal" means a disposal whether by the creation or the transfer of an estate or interest and—

(a) includes the surrender of a tenancy and the grant of an option or right of pre-emption, but

(b) excludes a disposal under the terms of a will or under the law relating to intestacy;

and references in this Part to the transferee in connection with a disposal shall be construed accordingly.

(4) In this section "appurtenant premises", in relation to any flat, means any yard, garden, outhouse or appurtenance (not being a common part of the building containing the flat) which belongs to, or is usually enjoyed with, the flat.

(5) A person is a member of another's family for the purposes of this section if—

(a) that person is the spouse of that other person, or the two of them live together as husband and wife, or

(b) that person is that other person's parent, grandparent, child, grandchild, brother, sister, uncle, aunt, nephew or niece.

(6) For the purposes of subsection (5)(b)—

(a) a relationship by marriage shall be treated as a relationship by blood,

(b) a relationship of the half-blood shall be treated as a relationship of the whole blood,

(c) the stepchild of a person shall be treated as his child, and

(d) an illegitimate child shall be treated as the legitimate child of his mother and reputed father.

DEFINITIONS
"common parts": s.60(1).
"flat": s.60(1).
"tenancy": s.59(1).

GENERAL NOTE
The relevant disposal falling within Pt. 1 of the Act is defined in this section to include the disposal by the landlord of any legal or equitable estate or interest in the premises or any of its common parts but excluding the grant of any tenancy where the demised premises consist of a single flat.

Subs. (2).
Paras. (a) to (l) contain the more detailed exclusions from the definition of relevant disposal so that such a disposal is outside the operation of the Act.

Subs. (3)
Disposal includes the surrender of a tenancy and the grant of an option or a right of pre-emption but does not include a disposal under the terms of a will or intestacy.

Notices conferring rights of first refusal

Requirement to serve notice conferring rights of first refusal

5.—(1) Where, in the case of any premises to which this Part applies, the landlord proposes to make a relevant disposal affecting the premises, he shall serve a notice under this section on the qualifying tenants of the flats contained in the premises.

(2) A notice under this section must—

(a) contain particulars of the principal terms of the disposal proposed by the landlord, including in particular—

(i) the property to which it relates and the estate or interest in that property proposed to be disposed of, and

(ii) the consideration required by the landlord for making the disposal;

(b) state that the notice constitutes an offer by the landlord to dispose of the property on those terms which may be accepted by the requisite majority of qualifying tenants of the constituent flats;

(c) specify a period within which that offer may be so accepted,

31–9

being a period of not less than two months which is to begin with the date of service of the notice; and

(d) specify a further period within which a person or persons may be nominated for the purposes of section 6, being a period of not less than two months which is to begin with the end of the period specified under paragraph (c).

(3) Where, as the result of a notice under this section being served on different tenants on different dates, the period specified in the notice under subsection (2)(c) would, apart from this subsection, end on different dates—

(a) the notice shall have effect in relation to all the qualifying tenants on whom it is served as if it provided for that period to end with the latest of those dates, and for the period specified in the notice under subsection (2)(d) to begin with the end of that period; and

(b) references in this Part to the period specified in the notice under subsection (2)(c) or (as the case may be) subsection (2)(d) shall be construed accordingly.

(4) Where a landlord has not served a notice under this section on all of the qualifying tenants on whom it was required to be served by virtue of subsection (1), he shall nevertheless be treated as having complied with that subsection if—

(a) he has served such a notice on not less than 90 per cent. of the qualifying tenants on whom it was so required to be served, or

(b) where the qualifying tenants on whom it was so required to be served number less than ten, he has served such a notice on all but one of them.

(5) Where a landlord proposes to effect a transaction that would involve both—

(a) a disposal of an estate or interest in the whole or part of a building constituting a relevant disposal affecting any premises to which this Part applies, and

(b) a disposal of an estate or interest in the whole or part of another building (whether or not constituting a relevant disposal affecting any premises to which this Part applies) or more than one such disposal,

the landlord shall, for the purpose of complying with this section in relation to any relevant disposal falling within paragraph (a) or (b) above, sever the transaction in such a way as to secure that, in the notice served by him under this section with respect to that disposal, the terms specified in pursuance of subsection (2)(a) are the terms on which he is willing to make that disposal.

(6) References in this Part to the requisite majority of qualifying tenants of the constituent flats are references to qualifying tenants of those flats with more than 50 per cent. of the available votes; and for the purposes of this subsection—

(a) the total number of available votes shall be determined as follows, namely—

(i) in a case where a notice has been served under this section, that number shall correspond to the total number of constituent flats let to qualifying tenants on the date when the period specified in that notice under subsection (2)(c) expires,

(ii) in a case where a notice is served under section 11 without a notice having been previously served under this section, that number shall correspond to the total number of constituent flats let to qualifying tenants on the date of service of the notice under section 11, and

(iii) in a case where a notice is served under section 12 or 15 without a notice having been previously served under this section

or under section 11, that number shall correspond to the total
number of constituent flats let to qualifying tenants on the date
of service of the notice under section 12 or 15; and

(b) there shall be one available vote in respect of each of the flats so
let on the date referred to in the relevant provision of paragraph
(a) which shall be attributed to the qualifying tenant to whom it is
let.

(7) Nothing in this Part shall be construed as requiring the persons
constituting the requisite majority of qualifying tenants in any one context
to be the same as the persons constituting any such majority in any other
context.

(8) For the purposes of—

(a) subsection (2) above and sections 6 to 10, and

(b) subsection (6) above so far as it has effect for the purposes of
those provisions,

a flat is a constituent flat if it is contained in the premises affected by the
relevant disposal with respect to which the notice was served under this
section; and for the purposes of sections 11 to 17, and subsection (6)
above so far as it has effect for the purposes of those sections, a flat is a
constituent flat if it is contained in the premises affected by the relevant
disposal referred to in section 11(1)(a).

DEFINITIONS
"flat": s.60(1).
"landlord": ss. 2, 59(2).
"qualifying tenants": s.3.
"relevant disposal": s.4.

GENERAL NOTE
In the case of a proposal to make a relevant disposal the landlord must serve a notice on
the tenant containing particulars of the principal terms of the proposed disposal and such a
notice constitutes an offer by the landlord to dispose of the premises on those terms. If the
requisite majority of the qualifying tenants accept the landlord's offer in writing, the landlord
cannot dispose of the protected interest except to a person or persons nominated by the
requisite majority of the qualifying tenants. See s.54 for provisions as to service of any
notice.

Subs. (2)

Para. (a)
Details of the property, the interest in the property and the consideration must be included
in the notice.

Para. (b)
The notice must state that it is an offer capable of acceptance by the requisite majority
(see note to subs. (6)).

Para. (c)
The notice must specify a period within which the offer may be accepted. Such a period
cannot be less than two months beginning with the date of service of the notice. In construing
the two and four months rule under the Landlord and Tenant Act 1954 Pt. 2 the Court of
Appeal, in Riley (E. J.) Investments v. Eurostile Holdings [1985] 1 W.L.R. 1139 held that
the corresponding date rule applied. See also Dodds v. Walker [1981] 1 W.L.R. 1027 (H.L.)
and Manorlike v. Le Vitas Travel Agency and Consultancy Services [1986] 1 All E.R. 573.

Para. (d)
The notice must also specify a further period within which a person(s) may be nominated
for the purposes of s.6. Such a period cannot be less than two months beginning after the
period in para. (c) has come to an end.

Subs. (4)
This a useful provision in that if the landlord has not served a notice on all the qualifying
tenants he is deemed to have complied with s.5(1) if he has served such a notice on not less

than 90 per cent. of the qualifying tenants (or on nine if there are less than 10 qualifying tenants).

Subs. (6)

This defines the requisite majority of qualifying tenants as being those tenants with more than 50 per cent. of the available votes. The total number of votes corresponds to the number of constituent flats let to qualifying tenants on either (i) the date of expiry of the period under s.5(2)(c); or (ii) the date of service of a notice under s.11; or (iii) on the date of the service of a notice under s.12 or s.15.

Each constitutent flat has one vote.

Acceptance of landlord's offer

6.—(1) Where—
  (a) the landlord has, in accordance with the provisions of section 5, served an offer notice on the qualifying tenants of the constituent flats, and
  (b) within the period specified in that notice under section 5(2)(c), a notice is served on him by the requisite majority of qualifying tenants of the constituent flats informing him that the persons by whom it is served accept the offer contained in his notice,
the landlord shall not during the relevant period dispose of the protected interest except to a person or persons nominated for the purposes of this section by the requisite majority of qualifying tenants of the constituent flats.

(2) In subsection (1) "the relevant period" means—
  (a) in every case, the period beginning with the date of service of the acceptance notice and ending with the end of the period specified in the offer notice under section 5(2)(d), and
  (b) if any person is nominated for the purposes of this section within that period, an additional period of three months beginning with the end of the period so specified.

(3) If no person has been nominated for the purposes of this section during the period so specified, the landlord may, during the period of 12 months beginning with the end of that period, dispose of the protected interest to such person as he thinks fit, but subject to the following restrictions, namely—
  (a) that the consideration required by him for the disposal must not be less than that specified in the offer notice, and
  (b) that the other terms on which the disposal is made must, so far as relating to any matters covered by the terms specified in the offer notice, correspond to those terms.

(4) It is hereby declared that the entitlement of a landlord, by virtue of subsection (3) or any other corresponding provision of this Part, to dispose of a particular estate or interest in any property during a specified period of 12 months extends only to a disposal of that estate or interest in the property, and accordingly the requirements of section 1(1) must be satisfied with respect to any other disposal by him affecting that property and made during that period of 12 months (unless the disposal is not a relevant disposal affecting any premises to which at the time of the disposal this Part applies).

(5) A person nominated for the purposes of this section by the requisite majority of qualifying tenants of the constituent flats may only be replaced by another person so nominated if he has (for any reason) ceased to be able to act as a person so nominated.

(6) Where two or more persons have been so nominated and any of them ceases to act as such a person without being replaced in accordance with subsection (5), any remaining person or persons so nominated shall be entitled to continue to act in his or their capacity as such.

(7) Where subsection (1) above applies to the landlord, and he is precluded by virtue of any covenant, condition or other obligation from disposing of the protected interest to the nominated person unless the consent of some other person is obtained, then, subject to subsection (8)—

    (a) he shall use his best endeavours to secure that the consent of that person to that disposal is given, and

    (b) if it appears to him that that person is obliged not to withhold his consent unreasonably but has nevertheless so withheld it, he shall institute proceedings for a declaration to that effect.

(8) Subsection (7) shall not apply once a notice is served by or on the landlord in accordance with any provision of section 9 or 10.

(9) In this Part—

    "acceptance notice" means a notice served on the landlord in pursuance of subsection (1)(b);

    "offer notice" means a notice served under section 5; and

    "the protected interest" means (subject to section 9(9)) any such estate or interest in any property as is specified in an offer notice in pursuance of section 5(2)(a).

DEFINITIONS
  "flat": s.. 60(1).
  "landlord": ss.2, 59(2).
  "qualifying tenants": s.3.
  "relevant disposal": s.4.
  "requisite majority": s.5(6).

GENERAL NOTE
  If an offer notice has been served by the landlord and accepted by the requisite majority of the qualifying tenants of the constituent flats the landlord cannot dispose of the protected interest during the relevant period except to a person or persons nominated. See s.54 for provisions as to service of any notice.

Subs. (2)
  The relevant period is defined by reference to the date of the service of the acceptance notice and ending with the period specified in s.5(2)(d). If a person(s) is nominated there is an additional period of three months beginning with the end of the period specified in s.5(2)(d).

Subs. (3)
  If no person is nominated, the landlord may dispose of the protected interest to such person as he thinks fit during the 12 months beginning with the end of any period specified under subs. (2).

Subs. (7)
  If a landlord is precluded from disposing of the protected interest to the nominated person by reason of any covenant, condition or obligation he must use his best endeavours to secure that consent and to institute proceedings if such consent has been unreasonably withheld. See the tests laid down in International Drilling Fluids v. Louisville Investments (Uxbridge) [1986] 1 E.G.L.R. 39 for unreasonably withholding consent.

Rejection of landlord's offer: counter-offer by tenants

  7.—(1) Where—

    (a) a landlord has, in accordance with section 5, served an offer notice on the qualifying tenants of the constituent flats, and

    (b) an acceptance notice is not served on the landlord by the requisite majority of qualifying tenants of the constituent flats within the period specified in the offer notice under section 5(2)(c), and

    (c) paragraph (b) of subsection (2) below does not apply,

the landlord may, during the period of 12 months beginning with the end of that period, dispose of the protected interest to such person as he thinks fit, but subject to the restrictions mentioned in section 6(3)(a) and (b).

(2) Where—
  (a) a landlord has served an offer notice as mentioned in subsection (1)(a), and
  (b) within the period specified in the offer notice under section 5(2)(c), a notice is served on the landlord by the requisite majority of qualifying tenants of the constituent flats stating that the persons by whom it is served are making him a counter-offer for the acquisition by them of such estate or interest in the property specified in the offer notice under section 5(2)(a) as is specified in their notice,

the landlord shall serve on such person as is specified in that notice in pursuance of subsection (3)(b) a notice which either accepts the counter-offer or rejects it.

(3) Any notice making a counter-offer in accordance with subsection (2)(b) must specify—
  (a) the terms (including those relating to the consideration payable) on which the counter-offer is made; and
  (b) the name and address of a person on whom any notice by the landlord under subsection (2) is to be served.

(4) If the landlord serves a notice under subsection (2) above accepting the counter-offer, section 6(1) and the other provisions of section 6 shall apply to him as if an acceptance notice had been served on him as mentioned in section 6(1)(b), except that—
  (a) any reference to the protected interest shall be read as a reference to any such estate or interest as is specified in the notice making the counter-offer in accordance with subsection (2)(b) above;
  (b) any reference in section 6(3) to the offer notice shall be read as a reference to the notice making the counter-offer; and
  (c) where the landlord's notice is served under subsection (2) above after the end of the period specified under section 5(2)(c), section 6(2) and (3) shall have effect as if the period specified under section 5(2)(d) began with the date of service of the landlord's notice.

(5) If the landlord serves a notice under subsection (2) above rejecting the counter-offer, then, unless it is a notice falling within section 8(1), subsection (1) above shall apply to him as if no such notice as is mentioned in subsection (2)(b) above had been served on him (except that where he serves his notice under subsection (2) above after the end of the period specified under section 5(2)(c), subsection (1) above shall have effect as if the period of 12 months there mentioned began with the date of service of that notice).

DEFINITIONS
  "acceptance notice": s.6(9).
  "flat": s.60(1).
  "landlord": ss.2, 59(2).
  "offer notice": s.6(9).
  "qualifying tenants": s.3.
  "protected interest": s.6(9).
  "requisite majority": s.5(6).

GENERAL NOTE
If an acceptance notice is not served on the landlord by the requisite majority of qualifying tenants of the constituent flats within the period specified in the landlord's notice the landlord may (during the period of 12 months beginning with the end of that period) dispose of the protected interest to such person as he thinks fit. A majority of the qualifying tenants

may also serve a counter-offer to the landlord's offer (within the period specified in the landlord's offer) to which the landlord may serve a notice accepting or rejecting it. See s.54 for provisions as to service of any notice.

Subs. (3)

This specifies the contents of a counter-offer in accordance with subs. (2)(b).

Subs. (4)

This makes provision for the amendment of the provisions of s.6 where the landlord serves a notice accepting the counter-offer under subs. (2) above.

Fresh offer by landlord: further negotiations between parties

8.—(1) This section applies where the landlord serves a notice under subsection (2) of section 7 rejecting a counter-offer but the notice—

    (a) states that it constitutes a fresh offer by the landlord to dispose of an estate or interest in the property specified in the offer notice under section 5(2)(a) which may be accepted by the requisite majority of qualifying tenants of the constituent flats;

    (b) contains particulars of the estate or interest in that property which he proposes to dispose of, the consideration required by him for the disposal and the other principal terms of the disposal; and

    (c) specifies a period within which the offer may be accepted as mentioned in paragraph (a) above.

(2) If, within the period specified in the landlord's notice under subsection (1)(c) above, a notice is served on the landlord by the requisite majority of qualifying tenants of the constituent flats informing him that the persons by whom it is served accept the offer contained in the landlord's notice, section 6(1) and the other provisions of section 6 shall apply to the landlord as if an acceptance notice had been served on him as mentioned in section 6(1)(b), except that—

    (a) any reference to the protected interest shall be read as a reference to any such estate or interest as is specified in the landlord's notice in pursuance of subsection (1)(b) above; and

    (b) any reference in section 6(3) to the offer notice shall be read as a reference to the landlord's notice under subsection (1) above; and

    (c) where the notice served on the landlord in pursuance of this subsection is served after the end of the period specified under section 5(2)(c), section 6(2) and (3) shall have effect as if the period specified under section 5(2)(d) began with the date of service of that notice.

(3) If, within the period specified in the landlord's notice under subsection (1)(c) above, no notice is served on the landlord as mentioned in subsection (2) above and subsection (4) below does not apply, the landlord may, during the period of 12 months beginning with the end of that period dispose of any such estate or interest as is specified in the landlord's notice under subsection (1)(b) above to such person as he thinks fit, but subject to the following restrictions, namely—

    (a) that the consideration required by him for the disposal must not be less than that specified in his notice under subsection (1), and

    (b) that the other terms on which the disposal is made must, so far as relating to any matters covered by the terms specified in that notice, correspond to those terms.

(4) If, within the period so specified in the landlord's notice, a notice is served on him by the requisite majority of qualifying tenants of the constituent flats stating that the persons by whom it is served are making him a further counter-offer for the acquisition by them of such estate or interest in the property specified in the offer notice under section 5(2)(a) as is specified in their notice, the provisions of subsections (2) to (5) of

section 7 and the provisions of this section (including this subsection) shall apply, with any necessary modifications, in relation to any such notice as they apply in relation to a notice served as mentioned in subsection (2)(b) of section 7.

DEFINITIONS
"flat": s.60(1).
"landlord": ss.2, 59(2).
"qualifying tenants": s.3.
"protected interest": s.6(a).
"requisite majority": s.5(6).

GENERAL NOTE
If a landlord serves a notice rejecting a counter-offer such a notice may state that it constitutes a fresh offer by the landlord which can be accepted by the requisite majority of the qualifying tenants of the constituent flats but (if not accepted in the period specified in the landlord's notice) the landlord may (during the period of 12 months beginning with that period) dispose of any such estate or interest to such person as he thinks fit. See s.54 for provisions as to service of any notice.

Subs. (3)
If no notice is served on the landlord accepting the landlord's fresh offer he may, during the period of 12 months beginning with the end of the period, dispose of any estate or interest specified in the notice subject to the conditions in subs. (3)(a), (b).

Subs. (4)
This enables the requisite majority of the qualifying tenants of the constituent flats to make a further counter-offer but only within the period specified in the landlord's notice.

Withdrawal of either party from transaction

9.—(1) Where—

(a) section 6(1) applies to a landlord by virtue of any provision of sections 6 to 8, and

(b) any person has been nominated for the purposes of section 6 by the requisite majority of qualifying tenants of the constituent flats within the period specified by the landlord in his offer notice under section 5(2)(d) (taking into account any postponement of the commencement of that period effected by any of the preceding provisions of this Part), and

(c) the nominated person serves a notice on the landlord indicating an intention no longer to proceed with the acquisition of the protected interest,

the landlord may, during the period of 12 months beginning with the date of service of the nominated person's notice, dispose of the protected interest to such person as he thinks fit, but subject to the restrictions mentioned in subsection (2).

(2) The restrictions referred to in subsection (1) are—

(a) that the consideration required by him for the disposal must not be less than the amount which has been agreed to by the parties (subject to contract) for the disposal of the protected interest, and

(b) that the other terms on which the disposal is made must correspond to those so agreed to by the parties in relation to the disposal.

(3) If at any time the nominated person becomes aware that the number of the qualifying tenants of the constituent flats desiring to proceed with the acquisition of the protected interest is less than the requisite majority of qualifying tenants of those flats, he shall forthwith serve on the landlord such a notice as is mentioned in subsection (1)(c).

(4) Where—
   (a) paragraphs (a) and (b) of subsection (1) apply, and
   (b) the landlord serves a notice on the nominated person indicating an intention no longer to proceed with the disposal of the protected interest,
the landlord shall not be entitled to dispose of that interest in accordance with that subsection but the notice shall have the consequences set out in subsection (5) or (6) (as the case may be).

(5) If any notice served in pursuance of subsection (1), (3) or (4) above is served not later than the end of the first four weeks of the period referred to in subsection (1)(b) above, the party serving it shall not be liable for any costs incurred by the other party in connection with the disposal.

(6) If any such notice is served after the end of those four weeks, the party on whom it is served may recover from the other party any costs reasonably incurred by the first-mentioned party in connection with the disposal between the end of those four weeks and the time when that notice is served on him.

(7) For the purposes of this section the parties are—
   (a) the landlord, and
   (b) the qualifying tenants who served the acceptance notice or other notice accepting an offer by the landlord, or (as the case may be) the notice making the counter-offer which was accepted by the landlord, together with the nominated person,
and any liability of those tenants and the nominated person which arises under this section shall be a joint and several liability.

(8) Nothing in this section applies where a binding contract for the disposal of the protected interest has been entered into by the landlord and the nominated person.

(9) In this section and section 10—
   "the nominated person" means the person or persons for the time being nominated for the purposes of section 6 by the requisite majority of qualifying tenants of the constituent flats; and
   "the protected interest" means—
   (a) except where section 6(1) applies to the landlord by virtue of section 7(4) or 8(2), the protected interest as defined by section 6(9); and
   (b) where section 6(1) applies to the landlord by virtue of section 7(4) or 8(2), any such estate or interest as is mentioned in section 7(4)(a) or (as the case may be) in section 8(2)(a).

DEFINITIONS
   "flat": s.60(1).
   "landlord": ss.2, 59(2).
   "protected interest": s.6(9).
   "qualifying tenants": s.3.
   "requisite majority": s.5(6).

GENERAL NOTE
Where a person has been nominated by the requisite majority of the qualifying tenants that person may serve a notice on the landlord indicating an intention no longer to proceed with the acquisition of the protected interest. See s.54 as to provisions for the service of any notice.

Subs. (1)
This provides the power for the landlord to dispose of the protected interest within the stipulated period subject to certain restrictions (see note on subs. (2) *post*).

Subs. (2)
This subsection provides for the restrictions on the disposal allowed by virtue of subs. (1).

Subs. (3)
The nominated person is under a duty to serve a notice on the landlord on becoming aware that the number of qualifying tenants desiring to proceed with the acquisition of the protected interest is less than the requisite majority defined in s.5(6).

Subs. (4)
The landlord may also serve a notice on the nominated person indicating an intention no longer to proceed with the disposal of the protected interest in which case the landlord is not entitled to dispose of that interest. Such a notice has the consequence outlined in either subss. (5) or (6).

Subs. (8)
Neither party can withdraw where a binding contract for the disposal of the protected interest has been entered into between the landlord and the nominated person.

Lapse of landlord's offer

10.—(1) If, at any time after a landlord has served an offer notice with respect to any relevant disposal affecting any premises to which this Part applies, those premises cease to be premises to which this Part applies, the landlord may serve a notice on the qualifying tenants of the constituent flats stating—
    (a) that the premises have ceased to be premises to which this Part applies, and
    (b) that the offer notice, and anything done in pursuance of it, is to be treated as not having been served or done;
and, on the service of any such notice, the provisions of this Part shall cease to have effect in relation to that disposal.
    (2) Subsection (4) of section 5 shall apply to a notice under subsection (1) above as it applies to a notice under that section, but as if the references to the qualifying tenants on whom such a notice is required to be served by virtue of subsection (1) of that section were references to the qualifying tenants mentioned in subsection (1) above.
    (3) In a case where a landlord is entitled to serve a notice under subsection (1) above but does not do so, this Part shall continue to have effect in relation to the disposal in question as if the premises in question were still premises to which this Part applies.
    (4) Where—
        (a) in the case of a landlord to whom section 6(7) applies—
            (i) the landlord has discharged any duty imposed on him by that provision, and
            (ii) any such consent as is there mentioned has been withheld, and
            (iii) no such declaration as is there mentioned has been made, or
        (b) the period specified in section 6(2)(b) has expired without any binding contract having been entered into between the landlord and the nominated person,
and the landlord serves a notice on the nominated person stating that paragraph (a) or (b) above applies, the landlord may, during the period of 12 months beginning with the end of the period specified in section 6(2)(b), dispose of the protected interest to such person as he thinks fit, but subject to the restrictions mentioned in section 9(2).
    References in this subsection to section 6(2)(b) include references to that provision as it has effect by virtue of section 7(4)(c) or 8(2)(c).
    (5) Where any such notice is served in a case to which paragraph (b) of subsection (4) applies, the landlord may recover from the other party any costs reasonably incurred by him in connection with the disposal to the nominated person between the end of the first four weeks of the

period referred to in section 9(1)(b) and the time when that notice is
served by him; and section 9(7) shall apply for the purposes of this section
as it applies for the purposes of section 9.

(6) Where any binding contract with respect to the disposal of the
protected interest has been entered into between the landlord and
the nominated person but it has been lawfully rescinded by the landlord,
the landlord may, during the period of 12 months beginning with the date
of the rescission of the contract, dispose of that interest to such person
(and on such terms) as he thinks fit.

(7) Section 9(9) applies for the purposes of this section.

DEFINITIONS
 "flat": s.60(1).
 "landlord": ss.2, 59(2).
 "nominated person": s.9(9).
 "protected interest": s.6(9).
 "qualifying tenants": s.3.
 "requisite majority": s.5.

GENERAL NOTE
 A landlord's offer notice ceases to have effect if the premises ceases to be premises to
which Pt. 1 of the Act applies and the landlord serves a notice on the qualifying tenants to
that effect but if no such notice is served the provisions of Pt. 1 continue to have effect on
the disposal. See s.54 as to provisions for the service of any notice.

Subs. (4)
 If any consent was required for the disposal of the protected interest and such consent has
been withheld (and no declaration been made in proceedings) or the period specified in
s.6(2)(b) has expired without a binding contract being entered into, the landlord may dispose
of the protected interest subject to the restrictions in s.9(2). See also the note to s.6(7).

Enforcement by tenants of rights against new landlords

**Duty of new landlord to furnish particulars of disposal made in contra-
vention of Part I**

11.—(1) Where—
 (a) a landlord has made a relevant disposal affecting any premises
   to which at the time of the disposal this Part applied ("the
   original disposal"), and
 (b) either no notice was served by the landlord under section 5
   with respect to that disposal or it was made in contravention of
   any provision of sections 6 to 10, and
 (c) those premises are still premises to which this Part applies,
the requisite majority of qualifying tenants of the constituent flats may,
before the end of the period specified in subsection (2) below, serve a
notice on the transferee under the original disposal requiring him to
furnish a person (whose name and address are specified for the purpose
in the notice) with particulars of the terms on which the original disposal
was made (including those relating to the consideration payable) and the
date on which it was made; and in the following provisions of this Part the
transferee under that disposal is referred to as "the new landlord".

(2) The period referred to in subsection (1) is the period of two months
beginning with the date by which—
 (a) notices under section 3 of the Landlord and Tenant Act 1985 (in
   this Act referred to as "the 1985 Act") relating to the original
   disposal, or
 (b) documents of any other description indicating that the original
   disposal has taken place,

have been served on the requisite majority of qualifying tenants of the constituent flats.

(3) Any person served with a notice in accordance with subsection (1) shall comply with the notice within the period of one month beginning with the date on which it is served on him.

DEFINITIONS
  "landlord": ss.2, 59(2).
  "protected interest": ss. 6(9), 9(9).
  "qualifying tenants": s.3.

GENERAL NOTE
  This section contains provisions for the enforcement of rights against a new landlord where the landlord did not serve a notice under s.5 or the disposal was made in contravention of ss.6–10 of the Act. See s.54 for the provisions as to service of any notice.

Right of qualifying tenants to compel sale etc. by new landlord

12.—(1) Where—
  (a) paragraphs (a) and (b) of section 11(1) apply to a relevant disposal affecting any premises to which at the time of the disposal this Part applied (other than a disposal consisting of such a surrender as is mentioned in section 15(1)(b)), and
  (b) those premises are still premises to which this Part applies,
the requisite majority of qualifying tenants of the constituent flats may, before the end of the period specified in subsection (2), serve a notice ("a purchase notice") on the new landlord requiring him (except as provided by the following provisions of this Part) to dispose of the estate or interest that was the subject-matter of the original disposal, on the terms on which it was made (including those relating to the consideration payable), to a person or persons nominated for the purposes of this section by any such majority of qualifying tenants of those flats.
  (2) The period referred to in subsection (1) is—
  (a) in a case where a notice has been served on the new landlord under section 11(1), the period of three months beginning with the date on which a notice is served by him under section 11(3); and
  (b) in any other case, the period of three months beginning with the date mentioned in section 11(2).
  (3) A purchase notice—
  (a) shall, where the estate or interest that was the subject-matter of the original disposal related to any property in addition to the premises to which this Part applied at the time of the disposal—
      (i) require the new landlord to dispose of that estate or interest only so far as relating to those premises, and
      (ii) require him to do so on the terms referred to in subsection (1) subject to such modifications as are necessary or expedient in the circumstances;
  (b) may, instead of specifying the estate or interest to be disposed of or any particular terms on which the disposal is to be made by the new landlord (whether doing so expressly or by reference to the original disposal), provide for that estate or interest, or (as the case may be) for any such terms, to be determined by a rent assessment committee in accordance with section 13.
  (4) Where the property which the new landlord is required to dispose of in pursuance of the purchase notice has at any time since the original disposal become subject to any charge or other incumbrance, then, unless the court by order directs otherwise—

(a) in the case of a charge to secure the payment of money or the performance of any other obligation by the new landlord or any other person, the instrument by virtue of which the property is disposed of by the new landlord to the person or persons nominated for the purposes of this section shall (subject to the provisions of Part I of Schedule 1) operate to discharge the property from that charge; and

(b) in the case of any other incumbrance, the property shall be so disposed of subject to the incumbrance but with a reduction in the consideration payable to the new landlord corresponding to the amount by which the existence of the incumbrance reduces the value of the property.

(5) Subsection (4)(a) and Part I of Schedule 1 shall apply, with any necessary modifications, to mortgages and liens as they apply to charges; but nothing in those provisions shall apply to a rentcharge.

(6) Where the property referred to in subsection (4) has at any time since the original disposal increased in monetary value owing to any change in circumstances (other than a change in the value of money), the amount of the consideration payable to the new landlord for the disposal by him of the property in pursuance of the purchase notice shall be the amount that might reasonably have been obtained on a corresponding disposal made on the open market at the time of the original disposal if the change in circumstances had already taken place.

(7) The person or persons initially nominated for the purposes of this section shall be so nominated in the purchase notice; and any such person may only be replaced by another person so nominated by the requisite majority of qualifying tenants of the constituent flats if he has (for any reason) ceased to be able to act as a person so nominated.

(8) Where two or more persons have been so nominated and any of them ceases to act as such a person without being replaced in accordance with subsection (7), any remaining person or persons so nominated shall be entitled to continue to act in his or their capacity as such.

(9) Where, in the exercise of its power to award costs, the court or the Lands Tribunal makes, in connection with any proceedings arising under or by virtue of this Part, an award of costs against the person or persons so nominated, the liability for those costs shall be the joint and several liability of that person or those persons together with the qualifying tenants by whom the relevant purchase notice was served.

DEFINITIONS
 "flat": s.60(1).
 "landlord": ss.2, 59(2).
 "qualifying tenants": s.3.
 "rent assessment committee": s.60(1).
 "requisite majority": s.5(6).

GENERAL NOTE
 In the circumstances outlined in s.11, the section gives a right to qualifying tenants to compel the disposal by the new landlord of the estate or interest (which formed the original disposal) to them by way of a purchase notice on the terms on which such a disposal was made. See s.54 as to the provisions for the service of any notice.

Subs. (2)
 The notice must be served by the requisite majority of the qualifying tenants before the end of the period being either (i) a period of three months beginning with the date on which a notice has been served by the new landlord under s.11(3); or (ii) a period of three months beginning with the date prescribed in s.11(2).

Subs. (3)

This subsection prescribes the scope of a purchase notice and such a notice may either (i) specify the estate or interest to be disposed of or any particular terms on which the disposal is to be made by the new landlord; or (ii) provide for that estate or interest or any such terms to be determined by a rent assessment committee.

Subs. (6)

Provisions where the property has increased in monetary value since the disposal (owing to any change in circumstances) are contained in this subsection. A change in the value of money is not a relevant circumstance.

Determination by rent assessment committees of questions relating to purchase notices

13.—(1) A rent assessment committee shall have jurisdiction to hear and determine—
  (a) any question arising in relation to any matters specified in a purchase notice (whether relating to the nature of the estate or interest, or the identity of the property, to be disposed of or relating to any other terms on which the disposal by the new landlord is to be made); and
  (b) any question arising for determination in consequence of a provision in a purchase notice such as is mentioned in section 12(3)(b).

(2) An application to a rent assessment committee under this section must be in such form, and contain such particulars, as the Secretary of State may by regulations prescribe.

(3) On any application under this section the interests of the persons by whom a purchase notice has been served shall be represented by the nominated person, and accordingly the parties to any such application shall not include those persons.

(4) Any costs incurred by a party to an application under this section in connection with the application shall be borne by that party.

(5) A rent assessment committee shall, when constituted for the purpose of hearing and determining any question falling within subsection (1) above, be known as a leasehold valuation tribunal, and paragraphs 1 to 3 and 7 of Schedule 22 to the Housing Act 1980 (provisions relating to leasehold valuation tribunals) shall accordingly apply to any such committee when so constituted.

(6) In this section and sections 14, 16 and 17 "the nominated person" means (subject to section 15(5)) the person or persons for the time being nominated for the purposes of section 12 by the requisite majority of qualifying tenants of the constituent flats.

DEFINITION
"rent assessment committee": s.60(1).

GENERAL NOTE
Any question arising in relation to any matters specified in a purchase notice is to be determined by a rent assessment committee sitting as a leasehold valuation tribunal. This means that the provisions contained in the Rent Act 1977 relating to the constitution and working of a rent assessment committee are as supplemented by paras. 1–3, 7 of Sched. 22 to the Housing Act 1980.

Subs. (4)

Each party to an application before a leasehold valuation tribunal pursuant to this section is to bear its own costs.

Withdrawal of nominated person from transaction

14.—(1) Where, at any time before a binding contract is entered into in pursuance of a purchase notice, the nominated person serves a notice on the new landlord indicating an intention no longer to proceed with the disposal required by the purchase notice, the new landlord may recover from that person any costs reasonably incurred by him in connection with that disposal down to the time when the notice is served on him under this subsection.

(2) If, at any such time as is mentioned in subsection (1) above, the nominated person becomes aware that the number of qualifying tenants of the constituent flats desiring to proceed with the disposal required by the purchase notice is less than the requisite majority of those tenants, he shall forthwith serve on the new landlord a notice indicating such an intention as is mentioned in subsection (1), and that subsection shall apply accordingly.

(3) If a notice is served under this section at a time when any proceedings arising under or by virtue of this Part are pending before the court or the Lands Tribunal, the liability of the nominated person for any costs incurred by the new landlord as mentioned in subsection (1) above shall be such as may be determined by the court or (as the case may be) by the Tribunal.

(4) By virtue of section 13(4) the costs that may be recovered by the new landlord under the preceding provisions of this section do not include any costs incurred by him in connection with an application to a rent assessment committee.

(5) Any liability for costs to which a nominated person becomes subject by virtue of this section shall be such a joint and several liability as is mentioned in section 12(9).

(6) Section 13(6) applies for the purposes of this section.

DEFINITIONS
   "landlord": ss.2, 59(2).
   "purchase notice": s.9.
   "qualifying tenants": s.3.

GENERAL NOTE
   If the nominated person serves a notice on the new landlord indicating an intention no longer to proceed with the disposal required by the purchase notice, the new landlord may recover from the nominated person any costs reasonably incurred by him subject to certain reservations. See s.54 for the provisions as to the service of any notice.

Right of qualifying tenants to compel grant of new tenancy by superior landlord

15.—(1) Where—
   (a) paragraphs (a) and (b) of section 11(1) apply to a relevant disposal affecting any premises to which at the time of the disposal this Part applied, and
   (b) the disposal consisted of the surrender by the landlord of a tenancy held by him ("the relevant tenancy"), and
   (c) those premises are still premises to which this Part applies,
the requisite majority of qualifying tenants of the constituent flats may, before the end of the period specified in section 12(2), serve a notice on the new landlord requiring him (except as provided by the following provisions of this Part) to grant a new tenancy of the premises subject to the relevant tenancy, on the terms referred to in subsection (2) below and expiring on the date on which that tenancy would have expired, to a person or persons nominated for the purposes of this section by any such majority of qualifying tenants of those flats.

(2) Those terms are—
   (a) the terms of the relevant tenancy; and
   (b) if the new landlord paid any amount to the landlord as

consideration for the surrender by him of that tenancy, that any such amount is paid to the new landlord by the person or persons so nominated.

(3) A notice under this section—

(a) shall, where the premises subject to the relevant tenancy included premises other than those to which this Part applied at the time of the original disposal—

(i) require the new landlord to grant a new tenancy only of the premises to which this Part so applied, and

(ii) require him to do so on the terms referred to in subsection (2) subject to such modifications as are necessary or expedient in the circumstances;

(b) may, instead of specifying the premises to be demised under the new tenancy or any particular terms on which that tenancy is to be granted by the new landlord (whether doing so expressly or by reference to the relevant tenancy), provide for those premises, or (as the case may be) for any such terms, to be determined by a rent assessment committee in accordance with section 13 (as applied by subsection (4) below).

(4) The following provisions, namely—

section 12(7) to (9),

sections 13 and 14, and

sections 16 and 17,

shall apply in relation to a notice under this section as they apply in relation to a purchase notice (whether referred to as such or as a notice served under section 12(1)) but subject to the modifications specified in subsection (5) below.

(5) Those modifications are as follows—

(a) any reference to the purposes of section 12 shall be read as a reference to the purposes of this section;

(b) the reference in section 13(1)(b) to section 12(3)(b) shall be read as a reference to subsection (3)(b) above;

(c) the references in section 16 to the estate or interest that was the subject-matter of the original disposal shall be read as a reference to the estate or interest which, prior to the surrender of the relevant tenancy, constituted the reversion immediately expectant on it; and

(d) the references in sections 16 and 17 to sections 12 to 14 shall be read as references to sections 12(7) to (9), 13 and 14 (as applied by subsection (4) above) and this section.

DEFINITIONS

"flat": s.60(1).
"landlord": ss.2, 59(2).
"qualifying tenants": s.3.
"requisite majority": s.5(6).

GENERAL NOTE

This section provides for the right of the qualifying tenants to compel the grant of a new tenancy by a superior landlord if the landlord has disposed of the interest (without complying with ss.5 or 6–10 of the Act) by the surrender of the interest to the head landlord. The notice must be served before the end of the period specified in s.12(2). The provisions as to the service of any notice are contained in s.54. The tenancy is to be granted to a person or persons nominated by the requisite majority of the qualifying tenants.

Enforcement by tenants of rights against subsequent purchasers

Right of qualifying tenants to compel sale etc. by subsequent purchaser

16.—(1) Where, at the time when a notice is served under section 11(1) or 12(1) on the new landlord, he no longer holds the estate or interest that was the subject-matter of the original disposal, then—

  (a) in the case of a notice served under section 11(1), the new landlord shall, within the period specified in section 11(3)—

    (i) furnish such person as is specified in the notice with the information that he is required to furnish by virtue of it, and

    (ii) serve on that person a notice informing him of the name and address of the person to whom the new landlord disposed of that estate or interest ("the subsequent purchaser"), and

    (iii) serve on the subsequent purchaser a copy of the notice under section 11(1) and of the information furnished by him under sub-paragraph (i) above;

  (b) in the case of a notice served under section 12(1), the new landlord shall forthwith—

    (i) forward the notice to the subsequent purchaser, and

    (ii) serve on the nominated person such a notice as is mentioned in paragraph (a)(ii) above.

(2) If the new landlord serves a notice in accordance with subsection (1)(a)(ii) or (b)(ii) above, sections 12 to 14 shall, instead of applying to the new landlord, apply to the subsequent purchaser as if he were the transferee under the original disposal.

(3) Subsections (1) and (2) above shall have effect, with any necessary modifications, in a case where, instead of disposing of the whole of the estate or interest referred to in subsection (1) to another person, the new landlord has disposed of it in part or in parts to one or more other persons and accordingly sections 12 to 14 shall—

  (a) in relation to any part of that estate or interest retained by the new landlord, apply to the new landlord, and

  (b) in relation to any part of that estate or interest disposed of to any other person, apply to that other person instead as if he were (as respects that part) the transferee under the original disposal.

(4) Subsection (1) shall not apply in a case where the premises affected by the original disposal have ceased to be premises to which this Part applies.

(5) Section 13(6) applies for the purposes of this section.

DEFINITION
  "landlord": ss.2, 59(2).

GENERAL NOTE
  This section provides for the enforcement of rights under ss.11 and 12 against a subsequent purchaser, namely the person referred to in the Act as the "new landlord". See the General Notes to ss.11 and 12 (*ante*). See s.54 for the provisions as to the service of any notice.

Termination of rights against new landlords etc.

Termination of rights against new landlord or subsequent purchaser

17.—(1) If, at any time after a notice has been served under section 11(1) or 12(1), the premises affected by the original disposal cease to be premises to which this Part applies, the new landlord may serve a notice on the qualifying tenants of the constituent flats stating—

  (a) that the premises have ceased to be premises to which this Part applies, and

  (b) that any notice served on him under section 11(1) or 12(1), and anything done in pursuance of it, is to be treated as not having been served or done.

(2) Subsection (4) of section 5 shall apply to a notice under subsection (1) above as it applies to a notice under that section, but as if the references to the qualifying tenants on whom such a notice is required to be served by virtue of subsection (1) of that section were references to the qualifying tenants mentioned in subsection (1) above.

(3) Where a period of three months beginning with the date of service of a purchase notice on the new landlord has expired—

  (a) without any binding contract having been entered into between the new landlord and the nominated person, and

  (b) without there having been made any application in connection with the purchase notice to the court or to a rent assessment committee under section 13,

the new landlord may serve on the nominated person a notice containing such a statement as is mentioned in subsection (1)(b) above.

(4) Where—

  (a) any such application as is mentioned in paragraph (b) of subsection (3) was made within the period of three months referred to in that subsection, but

  (b) a period of two months, beginning with the date of the determination of that application has expired, and

  (c) no binding contract has been entered into between the new landlord and the nominated person, and

  (d) no other such application as is mentioned in subsection (3)(b) is pending,

the new landlord may serve on the nominated person a notice containing such a statement as is mentioned in subsection (1)(b).

(5) Where the new landlord serves a notice in accordance with subsection (1), (3) or (5), this Part shall cease to have effect in relation to him in connection with the original disposal.

(6) In a case where a new landlord is entitled to serve a notice under subsection (1) above but does not do so, this Part shall continue to have effect in relation to him in connection with the original disposal as if the premises in question were still premises to which this Part applies.

(7) References in this section to the new landlord shall be read as including references to any other person to whom sections 12 to 14 apply by virtue of section 16(2) or (3).

(8) Section 13(6) applies for the purposes of this section.

DEFINITIONS
  "flat": s.60(1).
  "landlord": ss.2, 59(2).
  "qualifying tenants": s.3.

GENERAL NOTE
  If at any time after a notice has been served under s.11(1) or s.12(1) the premises cease to be premises to which the Act applies, the new landlord may serve a notice on the qualifying tenants stating that the premises have ceased to be premises to which the Act applies and that any notice served in pursuance of either section is to be treated as not having been served. See s.54 for the provisions as to service of any notice.

Subs. (3)
  This subsection provides for the circumstance where a period of three months beginning with the date of service of the purchase notice on the new landlord has elapsed and no binding contract has been entered into between the nominated person and the new landlord nor a reference to a rent assessment committee made. In such a case the new landlord may serve a notice to the effect that any notice served on him under either s.11 or s.12 is to be treated as not having been served.

Notices served by prospective purchasers

Notices served by prospective purchasers to ensure that rights of first refusal do not arise

18.—(1) Where—

 (a) any disposal of an estate or interest in any premises consisting of the whole or part of a building is proposed to be made by a landlord, and

 (b) it appears to the person who would be the transferee under that disposal ("the purchaser") that any such disposal would, or might, be a relevant disposal affecting premises to which this Part applies,

the purchaser may serve notices under this subsection on the tenants of the flats contained in the premises referred to in paragraph (a) ("the flats affected").

 (2) Any notice under subsection (1) shall—

 (a) inform the person on whom it is served of the general nature of the principal terms of the proposed disposal, including in particular—

  (i) the property to which it would relate and the estate or interest in that property proposed to be disposed of by the landlord, and

  (ii) the consideration required by him for making the disposal;

 (b) invite that person to serve a notice on the purchaser stating—

  (i) whether the landlord has served on him, or on any predecessor in title of his, a notice under section 5 with respect to the disposal, and

  (ii) if the landlord has not so served any such notice, whether he is aware of any reason why he is not entitled to be served with any such notice by the landlord, and

  (iii) if he is not so aware, whether he would wish to avail himself of the right of first refusal conferred by any such notice if it were served; and

 (c) inform that person of the effect of the following provisions of this section.

 (3) Where the purchaser has served notices under subsection (1) on at least 80 per cent. of the tenants of the flats affected and—

 (a) not more than 50 per cent. of the tenants on whom those notices have been served by the purchaser have served notices on him in pursuance of subsection (2)(b) by the end of the period of 28 days beginning with the date on which the last of them was served by him with a notice under this section, or

 (b) more than 50 per cent. of the tenants on whom those notices have been served by the purchaser have served notices on him in pursuance of subsection (2)(b) but the notices in each case indicate that the tenant serving it either—

  (i) does not regard himself as being entitled to be served by the landlord with a notice under section 5 with respect to the disposal, or

  (ii) would not wish to avail himself of the right of first refusal conferred by such a notice if it were served,

the premises affected by the disposal shall, in relation to the disposal, be treated for the purposes of this Part as premises to which this Part does not apply.

 (4) For the purposes of subsection (3) each of the flats affected shall be regarded as having one tenant, who shall count towards any of the

percentages specified in that subsection whether he is a qualifying tenant of the flat or not.

DEFINITIONS
"flat": s.60(1).
"landlord": ss.2, 59(2).
"relevant disposal": s.4.

GENERAL NOTE
Where a landlord proposes to make a disposal and it appears to the purchaser that such a disposal would be a relevant disposal for the purposes of Pt. 1 of the Act, the purchaser may serve notices on the tenants of the flats informing them of the general nature of the principal terms of the proposed disposal and inviting each tenant to state whether (i) the landlord has served a notice on him under s.5, and (ii) if not, whether he is aware of any reason why he is not entitled to be served and (iii) if he is not aware, whether he would wish to avail himself of the right of first refusal if any such notice were served. A prospective purchaser may thus be able to ensure that rights of first refusal do not apply to the premises of which he is the prospective purchaser.

Subs. (3)
This subsection provides for the calculation of the number of tenants wishing (and able) to avail themselves of the right of first refusal. If the stipulated limits are not obtained the premises affected by the disposal are treated as premises to which Pt. 1 does not apply.

Supplementary

Enforcement of obligations under Part I

19.—(1) The court may, on the application of any person interested, make an order requiring any person who has made default in complying with any duty imposed on him by any provision of this Part to make good the default within such time as is specified in the order.

(2) An application shall not be made under subsection (1) unless—
> (a) a notice has been previously served on the person in question requiring him to make good the default, and
> (b) more than 14 days have elapsed since the date of service of that notice without his having done so.

(3) The restriction imposed by section 1(1) may be enforced by an injunction granted by the court.

Construction of Part I and power of Secretary of State to prescribe modifications

20.—(1) In this Part—
> "acceptance notice" means a notice served on a landlord in pursuance of section 6(1)(b);
> "associated company", in relation to a body corporate, means another body corporate which is (within the meaning of section 736 of the Companies Act 1985) that body's holding company, a subsidiary of that body or another subsidiary of that body's holding company;
> "constituent flat" shall be construed in accordance with section 5(8);
> "disposal" has the meaning given by section 4(3), and references to the acquisition of an estate or interest shall be construed accordingly;
> "landlord", in relation to any premises, shall be construed in accordance with section 2;
> "the new landlord" means any such transferee under a relevant disposal as is mentioned in section 11(1);
> "offer notice" means a notice served by a landlord under section 5;

"the original disposal" means the relevant disposal referred to in section 11(1);

"the protected interest" means (subject to section 9(9)) any such estate or interest in any property as is specified in an offer notice in pursuance of section 5(2)(a);

"purchase notice" means a notice served on a new landlord in pursuance of section 12(1);

"qualifying tenant", in relation to a flat, shall be construed in accordance with section 3;

"relevant disposal" shall be construed in accordance with section 4;

"the requisite majority", in relation to qualifying tenants, shall be construed in accordance with section 5(6) and (7);

"transferee", in relation to a disposal, shall be construed in accordance with section 4(3).

(2) In this Part—

(a) any reference to an offer or counter-offer is a reference to an offer or counter-offer made subject to contract, and

(b) any reference to the acceptance of an offer or counter-offer is a reference to its acceptance subject to contract.

(3) Any reference in this Part to a tenant of a particular description shall be construed, in relation to any time when the interest under his tenancy has ceased to be vested in him, as a reference to the person who is for the time being the successor in title to that interest.

(4) The Secretary of State may by regulations make such modifications of any of the provisions of sections 5 to 18 as he considers appropriate, and any such regulations may contain such incidental, supplemental or transitional provisions as he considers appropriate in connection with the regulations.

(5) In subsection (4) "modifications" includes additions, omissions and alterations.

PART II

APPOINTMENT OF MANAGERS BY THE COURT

GENERAL NOTE

Pt. 2 deals with the appointment of managers by the court to assume responsibility for the management of the premises containing the flats where the landlord is in breach of any obligation owed by him to the tenant under his tenancy and relating to the management of the premises in question or any part of them (or, in the case of an obligation dependent on notice, would be in breach of any such obligation but for the fact that it has not been reasonably practicable for the tenant to give him the appropriate notice). In addition, for the court to make an order appointing a manager it must be satisfied that the circumstances by virtue of which the landlord is (or would be) in breach of any such obligation are likely to continue and it would be just and convenient for the order to be made.

Pt. 2 brings together the law on the appointment of managers of property by the court and simplifies the power of the court under s.37 of the Supreme Court Act 1981 to "appoint a receiver [where] it appears to the court to be just and convenient to do so" and the case law which had developed (see the decisions in *Hart* v. *Emelkirk* [1983] 1 W.L.R. 1289 and *Daiches* v. *Bluelake Investments* [1985] 2 E.G.L.R. 67 where a receiver was appointed but in *Parker* v. *Camden London Borough Council; Newman* v. *Camden London Borough Council* (1985) 17 H.L.R. 380 the Court of Appeal refused the tenant's applications for the appointment of a receiver).

Under s.21 a tenant of a flat contained in any premises to which Pt. 2 applies can apply to the court for an order appointing a manager to act in relation to those premises. Pt. 2 applies to premises consisting of the whole or part of a building if the building or part contains two or more flats (s.21(2)) but it does not apply to the premises where the tenant is a tenant holding a tenancy under the Landlord and Tenant Act 1954, Pt. 2.

S.22 requires a preliminary notice by the tenant on the landlord before an application for an order can be made and, where the matters complained of are capable of being remedied by the landlord, it must require the landlord (within such reasonable period as is specified in the notice) to take such steps for the purpose of remedying them as are specified. The court may, however, dispense with the requirement to serve such a notice.

The conditions for the making of the application for the appointment of a manager are outlined in s.23, namely in a case where a notice has been served under s.22 the period specified for compliance has expired without the landlord having taken the steps he was required to take under the notice or it may be that the requirement for compliance was not applicable in the circumstances of the case. There are also provisions applicable where the requirement to serve a notice has been dispensed with by an order of the court.

The court may appoint a manager to carry out such functions in connection with the management of the premises or such functions of a receiver as it thinks fit. The court can only make an order where it is satisfied that the landlord either is in breach of any obligation owed by him to the tenant under his tenancy and relating to the management of the premises in question or (if notice is required) would be in breach but for the fact it had not been reasonably practicable for the tenant to give him the appropriate notice or where it is satisfied that other circumstances exist which make it just and convenient for the order to be made (s.24(2)(a), (b)). Pt. 2 also makes provision for the court to order remuneration to be paid to the manager by the landlord or the tenants of the premises or both. The order appointing a manager is registrable under the Land Charges Act 1972 and the Land Registration Act 1925.

The importance of the provision for the appointment of a manager by the court is highlighted by the fact that one of the conditions for the making of an *acquisition order* under Pt. 3 of the Act is that the appointment of a manager under Pt. 2 of the Act would not be an adequate remedy in the circumstances or that, for a period of three years up to the date of the application, there was in force an appointment of a manager under Pt. 2.

Tenant's right to apply to court for appointment of manager

21.—(1) The tenant of a flat contained in any premises to which this Part applies may, subject to the following provisions of this Part, apply to the court for an order under section 24 appointing a manager to act in relation to those premises.

(2) Subject to subsection (3), this Part applies to premises consisting of the whole or part of a building if the building or part contains two or more flats.

(3) This Part does not apply to any such premises at a time when—

    (a) the interest of the landlord in the premises is held by an exempt landlord or a resident landlord, or

    (b) the premises are included within the functional land of any charity.

(4) An application for an order under section 24 may be made—

    (a) jointly by tenants of two or more flats if they are each entitled to make such an application by virtue of this section, and

    (b) in respect of two or more premises to which this Part applies; and, in relation to any such joint application as is mentioned in paragraph (a), references in this Part to a single tenant shall be construed accordingly.

(5) Where the tenancy of a flat contained in any such premises is held by joint tenants, an application for an order under section 24 in respect of those premises may be made by any one or more of those tenants.

(6) An application to the court for it to exercise in relation to any premises any jurisdiction existing apart from this Act to appoint a receiver or manager shall not be made by a tenant (in his capacity as such) in any circumstances in which an application could be made by him for an order under section 24 appointing a manager to act in relation to those premises.

(7) References in this Part to a tenant do not include references to a tenant under a tenancy to which Part II of the Landlord and Tenant Act 1954 applies.

DEFINITIONS
  "charity": s.60.
  "court": s.60.

"exempt landlord": ss.58(1), 60.
"flat": s.60.
"functional land": s.60.
"landlord": ss.59(2), 60.
"resident landlord": ss.58(2), 60.
"tenancy": ss.59(1), 60.
"tenant": s.59(2).

GENERAL NOTE

This section creates a statutory remedy for tenants of flats: subject to various qualifications it allows the tenant of a flat to apply to court for an order appointing a manager to carry out management and receivership functions in relation to the premises of which the flat forms part.

Jurisdiction to appoint a receiver exists also by virtue of the Supreme Court Act 1981, s.37(1) in all cases where it appears just and convenient to do so. This jurisdiction has been considered in relation to flats in a number of decisions (see *Hart* v. *Emelkirk* [1983] 1 W.L.R. 1289; *Daiches* v. *Bluelake Investments* [1985] 2 E.G.L.R. 67; *Clayhope Properties* v. *Evans* [1986] 1 W.L.R. 1223; *Parker* v. *Camden London Borough Council* [1986] Ch. 162; *Evans* v. *Clayhope Properties* [1987] 1 W.L.R. 225). However, in cases where the statutory remedy under s.21 is available, a tenant may not in his capacity as tenant apply under the Supreme Court jurisdiction (or indeed any inherent jurisdiction) (see s.21(6)).

The new procedure can be seen as differing in two main ways from its earlier counterpart. First, the procedure for obtaining the appointment of a manager is formalised, in that the tenant must first give the landlord notice of his intention to seek the order and the grounds on which it will be sought, thereby giving the landlord an opportunity to rectify the problems complained of. Secondly, the jurisdiction under s.21 is to be exercised by county courts (see s.52). The Nugee Committee suggested that the jurisdiction under s.37 of the Supreme Court Act was exercisable only by the High Court (para. 7.2.17). However, it seems clear that county courts could, prior to the 1987 Act, exercise the jurisdiction of appointing a receiver and manager (see County Courts Act 1984, ss.38 and 39, and County Court Rules 1981, Ord. 32). Now, however, the jurisdiction is entirely that of the county courts (subject to limited exceptions), irrespective of the rateable value of the relevant premises.

The application may be made by a single tenant, or by a number of tenants jointly (subs. (1) and (4(a)). There is no provision for an application to be made by a representative residents' association.

It should be noted that the application need not be made in respect of the whole building; it can be made in respect of part of a building containing two or more flats. Furthermore, an application may be made in respect of two or more premises (subs. (4)(b)), so that tenants of different buildings owned by the same landlord and suffering similar problems could join in making an application.

Where a tenancy is vested in joint tenants, any one or more of them may make the application (subs. (5)). As to the exclusion of tenants under tenancies to which Pt. 2 of the Landlord and Tenant Act 1954 applies (subs. (7)), this is likely to have two main consequences. First, it may exclude a tenant who sublets flats as a business yet retains sufficient control and presence to have occupation for the purposes of the 1954 Act (see *Lee Verhulst Investments* v. *Harwood Trust* [1973] 1 Q.B. 204; *William Boyer & Sons* v. *Adams* (1975) 32 P. & C.R. 89; *Groveside Properties* v. *Westminster Medical School* (1984) 47 P. & C.R. 507; *Linden* v. *Department of Health and Social Security* [1986] 1 W.L.R. 164; and *cf. Bagettes* v. *G.P. Estates* [1956] Ch. 290 and *Trans-Britannia Properties* v. *Darby Properties* [1986] 1 E.G.L.R. 151). Secondly, it may exclude a tenant who uses the flat for business purposes to such a degree that he may be said to occupy it for the purposes of a business (see *Cheryl Investments* v. *Saldanha; Royal Life Saving Society* v. *Page* [1978] 1 W.L.R. 1329; *Simmonds* v. *Egyed* [1985] C.L.Y. 1908).

Preliminary notice by tenant

22.—(1) Before an application for an order under section 24 is made in respect of any premises to which this Part applies by a tenant of a flat contained in those premises, a notice under this section must (subject to subsection (3)) be served on the landlord by the tenant.

(2) A notice under this section must—

    (a) specify the tenant's name, the address of his flat and an address in England and Wales (which may be the address of his flat) at which the landlord may serve notices, including notices in proceedings, on him in connection with this Part;

(b) state that the tenant intends to make an application for an order under section 24 to be made by the court in respect of such premises to which this Part applies as are specified in the notice, but (if paragraph (d) is applicable) that he will not do so if the landlord complies with the requirement specified in pursuance of that paragraph;

(c) specify the grounds on which the court would be asked to make such an order and the matters that would be relied on by the tenant for the purpose of establishing those grounds;

(d) where those matters are capable of being remedied by the landlord, require the landlord, within such reasonable period as is specified in the notice, to take such steps for the purpose of remedying them as are so specified; and

(e) contain such information (if any) as the Secretary of State may by regulations prescribe.

(3) The court may (whether on the hearing of an application for an order under section 24 or not) by order dispense with the requirement to serve a notice under this section in a case where it is satisfied that it would not be reasonably practicable to serve such a notice on the landlord, but the court may, when doing so, direct that such other notices are served, or such other steps are taken, as it thinks fit.

(4) In a case where—

(a) a notice under this section has been served on the landlord, and

(b) his interest in the premises specified in pursuance of subsection (2)(b) is subject to a mortgage,

the landlord shall, as soon as is reasonably practicable after receiving the notice, serve on the mortgagee a copy of the notice.

DEFINITIONS
"court": s.60.
"flat": s.60.
"landlord": ss.59(2), 60.
"mortgage": s.60.
"notices in proceedings": s.60.
"tenant": s.59(2).

GENERAL NOTE
This section contains the requirement that the tenant serve a preliminary notice on the landlord before making an application for the appointment of a manager. The court has a wide power to dispense with service of the notice where it is satisfied that service would not be reasonably practicable. One difficulty is of course the landlord who cannot be found, but the tenant should note the weapons at his disposal in such a case (see Landlord and Tenant Act 1985, ss.1–7; 1987 Act, Pt. 6).

It is important to note the information to be contained in the notice. The idea behind the recommendation of the Nugee Committee was that the procedure should follow the lines of s.146 notices under the Law of Property Act 1925, in that "the landlord should be notified of the precise breach of covenant he is alleged to have committed, and should have an opportunity to put matters right before the application is made to the court." (para. 7.2.16)

The requirements are:—

(a) the notice should give the tenant's name (or in the case of a joint application, all their names), the address of his or their flat(s), and an address in England and Wales for service;

(b) the notice should state that the tenant intends to apply for an order under the Act, but if the matters complained of are remediable it should also state that no application will be made if the landlord complies with the notice by remedying the matters complained of. The premises in respect of which the order is to be sought must be specified;

(c) the grounds upon which the order is to be sought and the matters that will be relied on to establish those grounds must be specified. This requirement must clearly be read in conjunction with s.24(2), which states the grounds upon which an order may be made. Given the obvious similarity with s.146 notice, it seems likely that a court would require the notice to be such as to enable the landlord to understand with reasonable certainty what he is required to do (see *Fox* v. *Jolly* [1916] 1 A.C. 1; *Fletcher* v. *Nokes* [1897] 1 Ch. 271; *Re Serle* [1898] 1 Ch. 652);

(d) where the matters specified are capable of being remedied the landlord should be required to do so by taking steps specified in the notice within a reasonable period (also specified). The distinction between remediable and irremediable breaches, familiar in the context of s.146 notices, is relevant here. The distinction between a remediable and irremediable breach does not lie in whether the covenant broken is positive or negative (though breach of a positive covenant will usually be remediable), nor in whether the breach is a once-and-for-all or a continuing breach, but in whether the harm done by the breach is for practical purposes capable of being retrieved within a reasonable time (*Expert Clothing Service and Sales* v. *Hillgate House* [1986] Ch. 340, at 355, 358). It seems likely that most sins which a landlord will commit which may justify a management order will be of a remediable nature—for example, failing to repair, appoint staff, and so on. However, it is possible to envisage cases where the breach may be irremediable, for example: failing to carry out work pursuant to an obligation to do so within a specified time (*Stephens* v. *Junior Army and Navy Stores* [1914] 2 Ch. 516); failure to lay out insurance moneys on rebuilding within a reasonable time (*Farimani* v. *Gates* (1984) 271 E.G. 887); and possibly failing to exercise control over the activities of other tenants so that the premises have become disreputable (*cf.*, for example, *Rugby School Governors* v. *Tannahill* [1935] 1 K.B. 87; *Egerton* v. *Esplanade Hotels London* [1947] 2 All E.R. 88; *British Petroleum Pension Trust* v. *Behrendt* [1985] 2 E.G.L.R. 97). Possibly also it might be argued that the landlord's conduct is irremediable where it has resulted in a total breakdown of trust and confidence between the landlord and the tenants, for example where the landlord has been guilty of deliberate misappropriation of service charge funds. The notice must specify what is required by way of remedy, which a s.146 notice need not. It seems unlikely that this would require the tenants to give detailed specifications or instructions as to how, for example, repairs are to be carried out. Clearly, much will depend on the type of matter complained of. The same is true of the requirement that a reasonable period be specified for steps to be taken to remedy those matters capable of being remedied. Where the tenants complain of a number of different matters which will require differing periods to be remedied, it may be prudent to serve separate notices specifying different periods (see *Wykes* v. *Davies* [1975] Q.B. 843—a case under the Agricultural Holdings legislation).

(e) the notice must contain such further information as the Secretary of State may by regulations prescribe.

Application to court for appointment of manager

23.—(1) No application for an order under section 24 shall be made to the court unless—

(a) in a case where a notice has been served under section 22, either—

(i) the period specified in pursuance of paragraph (d) of subsection (2) of that section has expired without the landlord having taken the steps that he was required to take in pursuance of that provision, or

(ii) that paragraph was not applicable in the circumstances of the case; or

(b) in a case where the requirement to serve such a notice has been dispensed with by an order under subsection (3) of that section, either—

(i) any notices required to be served, and any other steps required to be taken, by virtue of the order have been served or (as the case may be) taken, or

      (ii) no direction was given by the court when making the order.

(2) Rules of court shall make provision—

    (a) for requiring notice of an application for an order under section 24 in respect of any premises to be served on such descriptions of persons as may be specified in the rules; and

    (b) for enabling persons served with any such notice to be joined as parties to the proceedings.

DEFINITIONS
"court": s.60.
"landlord": ss.59(2), 60.

GENERAL NOTE
Under this section, no application may be made for an order appointing a manager unless either:

    (i) the period specified in the s.22 notice has elapsed without the landlord having complied with the notice, *or*

    (ii) the matters complained of in the notice were irremediable (see General Note to s.22), *or*

    (iii) the requirement of notice was dispensed with by an order of the court, *or*

    (iv) any requirements of the court have been complied with pursuant to such an order.

Subs. (2) requires rules of court to be made to deal with third parties.

Appointment of manager by the court

24.—(1) The court may, on an application for an order under this section, by order (whether interlocutory or final) appoint a manager to carry out in relation to any premises to which this Part applies—

    (a) such functions in connection with the management of the premises, or

    (b) such functions of a receiver,

or both, as the court thinks fit.

(2) The court may only make an order under this section in the following circumstances, namely—

    (a) where the court is satisfied—

        (i) that the landlord either is in breach of any obligation owed by him to the tenant under his tenancy and relating to the management of the premises in question or any part of them or (in the case of an obligation dependent on notice) would be in breach of any such obligation but for the fact that it has not been reasonably practicable for the tenant to give him the appropriate notice, and

        (ii) that the circumstances by virtue of which he is (or would be) in breach of any such obligation are likely to continue, and

        (iii) that it is just and convenient to make the order in all the circumstances of the case; or

    (b) where the court is satisfied that other circumstances exist which make it just and convenient for the order to be made.

(3) The premises in respect of which an order is made under this section may, if the court thinks fit, be either more or less extensive than the premises specified in the application on which the order is made.

(4) An order under this section may make provision with respect to—

    (a) such matters relating to the exercise by the manager of his functions under the order, and

    (b) such incidental or ancillary matters,

as the court thinks fit; and, on any subsequent application made for the purpose by the manager, the court may give him directions with respect to any such matters.

(5) Without prejudice to the generality of subsection (4), an order under this section may provide—

(a) for rights and liabilities arising under contracts to which the manager is not a party to become rights and liabilities of the manager;

(b) for the manager to be entitled to prosecute claims in respect of causes of action (whether contractual or tortious) accruing before or after the date of his appointment;

(c) for remuneration to be paid to the manager by the landlord, or by the tenants of the premises in respect of which the order is made or by all or any of those persons;

(d) for the manager's functions to be exercisable by him (subject to subsection (9)) either during a specified period or without limit of time.

(6) Any such order may be granted subject to such conditions as the court thinks fit, and in particular its operation may be suspended on terms fixed by the court.

(7) In a case where an application for an order under this section was preceded by the service of a notice under section 22, the court may, if it thinks fit, make such an order notwithstanding—

(a) that any period specified in the notice in pursuance of subsection (2)(d) of that section was not a reasonable period, or

(b) that the notice failed in any other respect to comply with any requirement contained in subsection (2) of that section or in any regulations applying to the notice under section 54(3).

(8) The Land Charges Act 1972 and the Land Registration Act 1925 shall apply in relation to an order made under this section as they apply in relation to an order appointing a receiver or sequestrator of land.

(9) The court may, on the application of any person interested, vary or discharge (whether conditionally or unconditionally) an order made under this section; and if the order has been protected by an entry registered under the Land Charges Act 1972 or the Land Registration Act 1925, the court may by order direct that the entry shall be cancelled.

(10) An order made under this section shall not be discharged by the court by reason only that, by virtue of section 21(3), the premises in respect of which the order was made have ceased to be premises to which this Part applies.

(11) References in this section to the management of any premises include references to the repair, maintenance or insurance of those premises.

DEFINITIONS
    "court": s.60.
    "landlord": ss.59(2), 60.
    "tenancy": ss.59(1), 60.
    "tenant": s.59(2).

GENERAL NOTE
    S.24 confers upon the court power to make an order appointing a manager to carry out such functions in connection with the management of the premises or such functions of a receiver as the court thinks fit. The order may be interlocutory or final (subs. (1)), suspended on terms fixed by the court (subs. (2)), and may relate to premises either more or less extensive than those in respect of which the application was made (subs. (3)).

Pre-conditions of appointment
    An order may only be made where the court is satisfied either:
    (a) (i) that the landlord is in breach of any obligation owed by him to the tenant under his tenancy and relating to the management of the premises or part of them (or

in the case of an obligation dependent upon notice would be in breach but for the fact that it has not been possible to give the requisite notice), *and*

(ii) the circumstances by virtue of which he is in breach of any such obligation are likely to continue, *and*

(iii) it is just and convenient to make the order in all the circumstances of the case; *or*

(b) other circumstances exist which make it just and convenient for the order to be made.

Condition (a)(i) depends upon some breach of an obligation *under the tenancy*. This clearly covers express obligations such as repairs, maintenance, the provision of services, etc. In relation to such breaches it should be noted that lack of funds to carry out the necessary functions will not excuse the landlord's breach (see, *e.g. Francis* v. *Cowcliffe* (1977) 33 P. & C.R. 368; *Peninsular Maritime* v. *Padseal* (1981) 259 E.G. 860). Also, it should not necessarily be assumed that payment of service charges by the tenant is a condition precedent to the landlord's liability. On the words of the lease this may be so, but clear wording will be needed to produce that result (see *Yorkbrook Investments* v. *Batten* [1985] 2 E.G.L.R. 100). Nor will the landlord be excused where performance of his obligations becomes difficult, perhaps because of heating installations and the like becoming antiquated and unreliable (*Yorkbrook Investments* v. *Batten, supra*) or because of the difficulty of recruiting suitable staff (*cf. Posner* v. *Scott-Lewis* [1986] 3 W.L.R. 531). However, no doubt such matters might go to the question of whether it is just and convenient to appoint a receiver. Landlords' obligations to provide services are sometimes qualified by stating that the landlord is obliged merely to use "best endeavours" or "reasonable endeavours" (or some similar phrase) to provide the service. Here it may be a difficult question as to whether the landlord is in breach (see *UBH (Mechanical Services)* v. *Standard Life Assurance Co., The Times*, November 13, 1986; also *Terrell* v. *Mabie Todd and Co.* [1952] 2 T.L.R. 547; *Pips (Leisure) Productions* v. *Walton* (1982) 43 P. & C.R. 415; *I.B.M. United Kingdom* v. *Rockware Glass Ltd.* [1980] F.S.R. 335). The obligation must relate to the management of the premises, which includes (but is not confined to) the repair, maintenance and insurance of the premises (subs. (11)). As well as express obligations under the tenancy, the section seems capable of applying to those obligations implied as terms of the tenancy by statute, for example those as to fitness for habitation and repair by ss.8 and 11 of the Landlord and Tenant Act 1985. Similarly, where the tenancy requires the landlord to provide services, the implied terms as to reasonable care and skill and provision within a reasonable time in ss.13 and 14 of the Supply of Goods and Services Act 1982 would seem to meet the description of obligations owed "under" the tenancy. However, the condition seems not to extend to obligations arising outside the tenancy (such as in negligence or under the Defective Premises Act 1972) unless "under his tenancy" can be equated with "in his capacity as tenant". That part of the condition dealing with obligations dependent upon notice seems aimed at landlords' repairing covenants, where the condition is implied that the landlord must be given notice of disrepair before any obligation arises (see, *e.g. Makin* v. *Watkinson* (1870) L.R. 6 Ex. 24; *Torrens* v. *Walker* [1906] 2 Ch. 166; *O'Brien* v. *Robinson* [1973] A.C. 912; *McGreal* v. *Wake* (1984) 13 H.L.R. 107, C.A.).

On condition (a)(ii), it should be noted that what must appear likely to continue is not the breach itself, but the circumstances by virtue of which the landlord stands in breach.

Condition (a)(iii) echoes the wording of s.37(1) of the Supreme Court Act 1981 and confers a wide jurisdiction to grant or withhold relief. In *Parker* v. *Camden L.B.C.* [1986] Ch. 162, Sir John Donaldson M.R. described the s.37 jurisdiction in the following terms:

". . .the jurisdiction, as a jurisdiction, is quite general and, in terms, unlimited. Nevertheless it has to be exercised judicially and with due regard to authorities which are binding on this court."

The underlying basis of the jurisdiction as so far asserted in relation to receivers of flats seems to rest upon the enforcement of the landlord's obligations and the tenants' rights and also upon the need to preserve property (see *Hart* v. *Emelkirk* [1983] 1 W.L.R. 1289 and also Kerr, *The Law and Practice of Receivers* (16th ed., 1983), p.5, and Picarda, *The Law Relating to Receivers and Managers* (1984), p.211). No doubt these grounds will continue to be of importance. One circumstance where it seems likely that the remedy may be refused is where it cannot be shown to be necessary, for example where adequate alternative relief is available—the principles relating to the grant of injunctive relief may be of relevance here (see *Cummins* v. *Perkins* [1899] 1 Ch. 16 at 19, 20). Nor would it seem that a receiver will be appointed in circumstances such as would be impracticable or would lead to overlap between the functions of the receiver and landlord. For example, in *Parker* v. *Camden L.B.C. (supra)* Browne-Wilkinson L.J. stated that it would be impracticable to appoint a receiver simply of a heating installation within a building. One particularly significant problem may occur where insufficient funds will be available from service charges or otherwise to enable the receiver and manager to perform the necessary functions. A salutary example is *Evans* v. *Clayhope Properties* [1987] 1 W.L.R. 225, where the rents and other moneys the receiver was appointed to receive proved incapable of meeting even the expenses of management. Refusing an order that the landlord meet the receiver's remuneration, Vinelott J. said (at pages 230–231):

"The position is a most unfortunate one. It may serve as a reminder of the limitations inherent in the power of the court to appoint a receiver. A receiver should not take office unless he is satisfied that the assets of which he is appointed a receiver will be adequate to meet his remuneration, or that he has an enforceable indemnity by a party to the litigation capable of meeting his remuneration. Moreover, although the appointment of a receiver in order, indirectly, to ensure that property is kept in repair in accordance with covenants to repair entered into by a landlord, is a valuable extension of the power of the court to appoint a receiver for the preservation of property in cases where urgent repairs are necessary, where the landlord is plainly in breach of a covenant to repair and where the income of the property will enable the receiver to remedy the want of repair (in particular where, as in *Hart* v. *Emelkirk* [1983] 1 W.L.R. 1289, a service charge capable of being recovered by the landlord, and capable of being vested in the receiver can be imposed in advance of the carrying out of work of repair to meet their eventual cost) the appointment of a receiver in a case where the income including any service charge, or any other property or money which can be put under the control of the receiver, is patently inadequate to meet the cost of repair, is likely to prove ineffective and may even frustrate the carrying out of repairs that the landlord is willing to carry out."

Alternative condition (b) (other circumstances making it just and convenient to make the order) may be very useful where the landlord cannot be shown positively to be in breach of any obligation as to management yet still can be said to be failing to manage the premises properly.

Terms of order and functions of manager

An order under s.24 may make provision as to the functions of the manager and incidental or ancillary matters (subs. (4)). A further list of specific matters for which the order may provide is given in subs. (5); of particular note is that the order may provide for remuneration to be paid to the manager by the landlord or by the tenants, which may go some way to surmounting the difficulties encountered in *Evans* v. *Clayhope Properties (supra)*. Also, the order may be granted subject to such conditions as the court thinks fit (subs. (6)).

An example of an order appointing a receiver and manager under the Supreme Court Act jurisdiction is set out in the report of *Clayhope Properties* v. *Evans* [1986] 1 W.L.R. 1223. In essence the function of the manager is to receive the rents, profits and other moneys payable under the terms of the relevant leases and to apply them in managing the premises in accordance with the rights and obligations of the landlord and tenants. Depending upon the circumstances it may also be desirable to give the receiver power to receive and similarly apply any local authority grants payable in respect of the premises, to charge the premises, and to grant leases of any unlet flats. However, it should be noted that on general principles it is not usual practice to insert an express power of leasing in an order appointing a receiver (see Kerr, *op. cit.*, p.171; Picarda, *op. cit.*, p. 293). The usual procedure is to apply to the judge in chambers for authority to grant a specific lease. However, it seems that there is power to give a general authority to create leases within proper limits, and where it is envisaged that the manager will need to do so it would seem sensible for the order appointing him to contain the requisite directions, given that he is appointed for the specific purpose of managing property intended for leasing. Care is also required over borrowing by the manager: if service charge moneys are only forthcoming in arrear, he may need to borrow, for which he will require the leave of the court. As to the manager's powers of borrowing, see Kerr, *op. cit.*, pp.176, 222; Picarda, *op. cit.*, p.301. As to whether interest on sums borrowed may be recovered from the tenants, the onus lies on the landlord to show that such sums fall within the true construction of the service charge provisions (see *Boldmark* v. *Cohen* (1986) 130 S.J. 356, C.A.). The order will also make provision for progress reports and the submission of accounts by the receiver (see Kerr, *op. cit.*, Chap. 11; Picarda, *op. cit.*, Chap. 32; also C.C.R., Ord. 32, r.3, and R.S.C., Ord. 30).

Choice of manager and security

The court will no doubt wish to be satisfied before making an order appointing a manager that the person proposed is a fit and proper person so to act (see generally Kerr, *op. cit.*, Chap. 4; Picarda, *op. cit.*, Chap. 4). Certain persons are statutorily disqualified from so acting, but the general principle is simply that the appointee should not be an interested party (*Re Lloyd* (1879) 12 Ch.D. 447). Even then, the court may waive this principle. The court should also be satisfied that the appointee can, consistently with his professional duties, spare sufficient time for the duties of his office (*Wynne* v. *Lord Newborough* (1808) 15 Ves. 283). The person should also of course possess the requisite skill and experience to perform the duties to be laid upon him. In the case of a manager appointed under the Act to manage residential property it would seem that in most cases a chartered surveyor will be the most suitable type of professional.

A receiver or manager will usually be required to provide security to account for and properly apply the assets he receives. In *Hart* v. *Emelkirk (supra)* Goulding J. saw no reason to depart from this usual practice when ordering the appointment of a receiver of residential flats. On security, see generally Kerr, *op. cit.*, p.109; Picarda, *op. cit.*, Chap. 30. In the county court security is required unless the court orders otherwise (C.C.R., Ord. 32, r.2) and the amount of the security is settled by the registrar (C.C.R., Ord. 50, r.9). For the provisions in the High Court, see R.S.C., Ord. 30, r.2.

The County Court rules as to matters such as the remuneration of receivers, receivers' accounts, default of receivers and directions to receivers are the same as those of the Supreme Court, to be found in R.S.C., Ord. 30 (see C.C.R., Ord. 30, r.3).

Subs. (7)

This provision confers a further dispensing power on the court in relation to notices required under s.22 (see also s.22(3)).

Subs. (8)

It is provided that the Land Charges Act 1972 and the Land Registration Act 1925 shall apply in relation to an order appointing a manager under the section as they apply in relation to an order appointing a receiver or sequestrator of land. This gives statutory force to the decision of the Court of Appeal in *Clayhope Properties* v. *Evans (supra)*. Thus in the case of unregistered land the order may be registered in the register of writs and orders under s.6 of the Land Charges Act 1972, and for registered land, protected by lodging a caution (Land Registration Act 1925, ss.54 and 59(1) and (5)).

Part III

Compulsory Acquisition by Tenants of their Landlord's Interest

GENERAL NOTE

Pt. 3 of the Act enables qualifying tenants of flats contained in any premises covered by Pt. 3 to acquire their landlord's interest in the premises without his consent by making application to the court for an acquisition order (s.25). This right is applicable where the landlord has failed to discharge his obligations relating to the repair, maintenance, insurance or management of the premises and either the appointment of a manager under Pt. 2 of the Act would not be an adequate remedy or such a manager has been appointed for three years preceding the date of application. There are complex provisions for the premises to satisify in order to fall within the provisions, namely, they must consist of the whole or part of a building and contain two or more flats held by tenants of the landlord who are qualifying tenants and, in addition:

(a) where the premises contain less than four flats, that all of the flats are let by the landlord on long leases; or

(b) where the premises contain more than three but less than 10 flats, that all, or all but one, of the flats are so let; or

(c) where the premises contain 10 or more flats, that at least 90 per cent. of the flats are so let.

There is an exclusion for non-residential use similar to that found in Pt. 2 so that the provisions do not apply if any part of parts of the premises is or are occupied or intended to be occupied otherwise than for residential purposes and the internal floor area of that part or parts (taken together) exceeds 50 per cent. of the internal floor area of the premises taken as a whole disregarding the internal floor area of the common parts. To qualify, a tenant must hold under a long lease and the tenancy must not be one to which the Landlord and Tenant Act 1954, Pt. 2 applies. A person is not a qualifying tenant if he is the tenant of a flat solely by reason of a long lease under which the demised premises consist of or include a flat and one or more other flats, or a flat and any common parts of the building. If the tenant's landlord is a qualifying tenant the tenant cannot be.

The procedure for compulsory acquisition by the tenants commences with the service of a preliminary notice by the requisite majority of the tenants on the landlord. In this context the requisite majority means more than 50 per cent. of the qualifying tenants. The requirements for the preliminary notice by the tenants are contained in s.27(2)(a)–(e). In particular, the notice must specify the grounds on which the court would be asked to make the acquisition order and the matters relied upon by the tenants for establishing those grounds. The notice must also require the landlord (where those matters are capable of being remedied by him) to take such steps to remedy the matters as are specified. No application to the court for an acquisition order can be made unless a preliminary notice has been served by the tenants and either the period specified for compliance with the remedial requirements has expired without compliance or such a requirement was not applicable or the requirement to serve such a notice was dispensed with by an order of the court (s.28(2)(a), (b)).

The conditions for the making of an acquisition order are delineated in s.29 which stipulates that the court may make an order where it is satisfied that:

(a) the premises are premises to which Pt. 3 applies both at the date of service of the s.27 notice and at the time when the application is made and they have not ceased to be such premises since the date of such application; and *either*

(b) (i) the landlord either is in breach of any obligation owed by him to the applicants under their leases and relating to the repair, maintenance, insurance or management of the premises (or any part of them) or (where any such obligation is dependent on notice) would have been in breach of any such obligation but it has not been reasonably practicable for the tenant to give the appropriate notice, and

  (ii) the circumstances by virtue of which he is (or would be) in breach of any such obligation are likely to continue, and

  (iii) the appointment of a manager under Pt. 2 of the Act in relation to those premises would not be an adequate remedy,

  or

(c) both at the date when the application was made and throughout the period of three years immediately preceding that date a manager had been appointed under Pt. 2 of the Act in relation to the premises in question; and

(d) the court considers it appropriate to make the order in the circumstances of the case.

An acquisition order made by the court shall provide for the nominated person to be entitled to acquire the landlord's interest in the premises specified in the order on such terms as may be determined by agreement between the parties or, in default of agreement, by a rent assessment committee. The terms of acquisition (other than consideration) are to be on the basis of what appears to the rent assessment committee to be fair and reasonable. The price to be paid is to be on the basis of the amount which the landlord's interest in the premises might be expected to realise if sold on the open market by a willing seller on the appropriate terms (*i.e.* those determined by agreement or, in default, by the rent assessment committee) and on the assumption that none of the tenants of the landlord of any premises comprised in those premises was buying or seeking to buy that interest (s.31(2), (3)).

Pt. 3 also contains provisions for:

(a) the discharge of existing mortgages except where it has been agreed between the qualifying tenants or the nominated person and the landlord (or the court is satisfied) that the landlord's interest should be acquired subject to the charge (s.32 and Sched. 1 of the Act);

(b) the making of an acquisition order where the landlord cannot be found and in such a case the amount to be paid into court shall be certified by a surveyor selected by the President of the Lands Tribunal;

(c) the discharge of the acquisition order and the withdrawal by the tenants (s.34).

Compulsory acquisition of landlord's interest by qualifying tenants

25.—(1) This Part has effect for the purpose of enabling qualifying tenants of flats contained in any premises to which this Part applies to make an application to the court for an order providing for a person nominated by them to acquire their landlord's interest in the premises without his consent; and any such order is referred to in this Part as "an acquisition order".

(2) Subject to subsections (4) and (5), this Part applies to premises if—

    (a) they consist of the whole or part of a building; and

    (b) they contain two or more flats held by tenants of the landlord who are qualifying tenants; and

    (c) the appropriate requirement specified in subsection (3) is satisfied with respect to them.

    (3) For the purposes of subsection (2)(c) the appropriate requirement is—

    (a) where the premises contain less than four flats, that all of the flats are let by the landlord on long leases;

    (b) where the premises contain more than three but less than ten flats, that all, or all but one, of the flats are so let; and

    (c) where the premises contain ten or more flats, that at least 90 per cent. of the flats are so let.

    (4) This Part does not apply to premises falling within subsection (2) if—

    (a) any part or parts of the premises is or are occupied or intended to be occupied otherwise than for residential purposes; and

    (b) the internal floor area of that part or those parts (taken together) exceeds 50 per cent. of the internal floor area of the premises (taken as a whole);

and for the purposes of this subsection the internal floor area of any common parts shall be disregarded.

    (5) This Part also does not apply to any such premises at a time when—

    (a) the interest of the landlord in the premises is held by an exempt landlord or a resident landlord, or

    (b) the premises are included within the functional land of any charity.

    (6) The Secretary of State may by order substitute for the percentage for the time being specified in subsection (4)(b) such other percentage as is specified in the order.

DEFINITIONS

    "charity": s.60.
    "common parts": s.60.
    "court": s.60.
    "exempt landlord": ss.58(1), 60.
    "flat": s.60.
    "functional land": s.60.
    "landlord": ss.59(2), 60.
    "long lease": ss.59(3), 60.
    "resident landlord": ss.58(2), 60.
    "tenant": s.59(2).

GENERAL NOTE

    This section states to which premises Pt. 3 of the Act applies. The premises must consist of the whole or part of a building containing at least two flats held by qualifying tenants. Further, a specified number or proportion of the flats within the premises must be let on long leases, depending upon the total number of flats (subs. (3)). Also the premises are excluded if more than 50 per cent. of the internal floor area (excluding common parts) is occupied for non-residential purposes. This may give rise to contentious questions of floor-space measurement methods.

    Where some parts of a building are used for non-residential purposes or are let on short leases, the choice of the part of the building to count as the premises for the purpose of the Pt. 3 application may be an important tactical consideration. However, the tenants' advisers should bear in mind s.29(5), which will prevent any acquisition order being made where the landlord's interest in larger premises of which the application premises form part is not reasonably capable of being severed. What this means is not entirely clear, though presumably severance may be difficult where the part of the building to be acquired shares essential parts of facilities with the part to be retained. No express power is given for the acquisition order to include or create easements of way, support, and so on; but see the General Notes to ss.29(4) and 30.

Qualifying tenants

26.—(1) Subject to subsections (2) and (3), a person is a qualifying tenant of a flat for the purposes of this Part if he is the tenant of the flat under a long lease other than one constituting a tenancy to which Part II of the Landlord and Tenant Act 1954 applies.

(2) A person is not to be regarded as being a qualifying tenant of a flat contained in any particular premises consisting of the whole or part of a building if he is the tenant of the flat solely by reason of a long lease under which the demised premises consist of or include—

(a) the flat and one or more other flats, or

(b) the flat and any common parts of the building.

(3) A tenant of a flat under a long lease whose landlord is a qualifying tenant of that flat is not to be regarded as being a qualifying tenant of that flat.

DEFINITIONS
   "common parts": s.60.
   "flat": s.60.
   "landlord": ss.59(2), 60.
   "long lease": ss.59(3), 60.
   "tenancy": ss.59(1), 60.
   "tenant": s.59(2).

GENERAL NOTE
   This section defines "qualifying tenant". The tenant must be the tenant of a flat under a long lease, other than one falling within Pt. 2 of the Landlord and Tenant Act 1954—as to which see General Note to s.21. A tenant will not qualify if his lease includes one or more other flats or any common parts of the building. Where a qualifying tenant sublets a flat, the tenant rather than the sub-tenant will be regarded as the qualifying tenant in relation to that flat.

Preliminary notice by tenants

27.—(1) Before an application for an acquisition order is made in respect of any premises to which this Part applies, a notice under this section must (subject to subsection (3)) be served on the landlord by qualifying tenants of the flats contained in the premises who, at the date when it is served, constitute the requisite majority of such tenants.

(2) A notice under this section must—

(a) specify the names of the qualifying tenants by whom it is served, the addresses of their flats and the name and the address in England and Wales of a person on whom the landlord may serve notices (including notices in proceedings) in connection with this Part instead of serving them on those tenants;

(b) state that those tenants intend to make an application for an acquisition order to be made by the court in respect of such premises to which this Part applies as are specified in the notice, but (if paragraph (d) is applicable) that they will not do so if the landlord complies with the requirement specified in pursuance of that paragraph;

(c) specify the grounds on which the court would be asked to make such an order and the matters that would be relied on by the tenants for the purpose of establishing those grounds;

(d) where those matters are capable of being remedied by the landlord, require the landlord, within such reasonable period as is specified in the notice, to take such steps for the purpose of remedying them as are so specified; and

31–41

(e) contain such information (if any) as the Secretary of State may by regulations prescribe.

(3) The court may by order dispense with the requirement to serve a notice under this section in a case where it is satisfied that it would not be reasonably practicable to serve such a notice on the landlord, but the court may, when doing so, direct that such other notices are served, or such other steps are taken, as it thinks fit.

(4) Any reference in this Part to the requisite majority of qualifying tenants of the flats contained in any premises is a reference to qualifying tenants of the flats so contained with more than 50 per cent. of the available votes; and for the purposes of this subsection—

(a) the total number of available votes shall correspond to the total number of those flats for the time being let to qualifying tenants; and

(b) there shall be one available vote in respect of each of the flats so let which shall be attributed to the qualifying tenant to whom it is let.

(5) Nothing in this Part shall be construed as requiring the persons constituting any such majority in any one context to be the same as the persons constituting any such majority in any other context.

DEFINITIONS
"court": s.60.
"flat": s.60.
"landlord": ss.59(2), 60.
"notices in proceedings": s.60.
"tenant": s.59(2).

GENERAL NOTE
This section provides for notice to be served on the landlord before an application for an acquisition order can be made. The notice must specify the matters required by subs. (2) (as to which see the General Note to s.22 in relation to paras. (c) and (d)). The notice must also be served by the requisite majority of qualifying tenants as defined in subs. (4): each flat has one vote and the majority required is more than 50 per cent. of the available votes. No guidance is given as to how to treat joint tenants of a flat who differ over how the single vote available to them should be allocated.

Applications for acquisition orders

28.—(1) An application for an acquisition order in respect of any premises to which this Part applies must be made by qualifying tenants of the flats contained in the premises who, at the date when it is made, constitute the requisite majority of such tenants.

(2) No such application shall be made to the court unless—

(a) in a case where a notice has been served under section 27, either—

    (i) the period specified in pursuance of paragraph (d) of subsection (2) of that section has expired without the landlord having taken the steps that he was required to take in pursuance of that provision, or

    (ii) that paragraph was not applicable in the circumstances of the case; or

(b) in a case where the requirement to serve such a notice has been dispensed with by an order under subsection (3) of that section, either—

    (i) any notices required to be served, and any other steps required to be taken, by virtue of the order have been served or (as the case may be) taken, or

    (ii) no direction was given by the court when making the order.

(3) An application for an acquisition order may, subject to the preceding provisions of this Part, be made in respect of two or more premises to which this Part applies.

(4) Rules of court shall make provision—

(a) for requiring notice of an application for an acquisition order in respect of any premises to be served on such descriptions of persons as may be specified in the rules; and

(b) for enabling persons served with any such notice to be joined as parties to the proceedings.

(5) The Land Charges Act 1972 and the Land Registration Act 1925 shall apply in relation to an application for an acquisition order as they apply in relation to other pending land actions.

(6) The persons applying for an acquisition order in respect of any premises to which this Part applies shall be treated for the purposes of section 57 of the Land Registration Act 1925 (inhibitions) as persons interested in relation to any registered land containing the whole or part of those premises.

DEFINITIONS
"court": s.60.
"flat": s.60.
"landlord": ss.59(2), 60.
"tenant": s.59(2).

GENERAL NOTE
This section provides that an application for an acquisition order may be made by the requisite majority of qualifying tenants at the date of the application. Changes in the identity of some or all of the tenants may have occurred since the s.27 notice was served, but provided that the requisite majority was attained on each occasion this would seem immaterial.

As to subs. (2), see General Note to s.23.

Subss. (5) and (6)
Subs. (5) makes clear that an application for an acquisition order is a pending land action for the purposes of the Land Charges Act 1972 and Land Registration Act 1925. Accordingly, the application is registrable under the Land Charges Act, s.5, and in the case of registered land may be protected by lodging a caution (Land Registration Act 1925, s.59(1), (2)). There seems little doubt that even without this provision an application for an acquisition order would be a pending land action as "relating to land" within the meaning given to that phrase by the courts (see *e.g. Whittingham* v. *Whittingham* [1979] Fam. 19; *Greenhi Builders* v. *Allen* [1979] 1 W.L.R. 156; *Selim* v. *Bickenhall Engineering* [1981] 1 W.L.R. 1318; *Regan & Blackburn* v. *Rodgers* [1985] 1 W.L.R. 870). However, subs. (5) avoids the argument being taken and to that extent is welcome.

Subs.(6) provides a further, and more drastic, means of protection in the case of registered land. The applicants for an acquisition order may apply under s.57 of the Land Registration Act for the entry of an inhibition preventing registration of any dealing with the land.

Conditions for making acquisition orders

29.—(1) The court may, on an application for an acquisition order, make such an order in respect of any premises if—

(a) the court is satisfied—

(i) that those premises were, at the date of service on the landlord of the notice (if any) under section 27 and on the date when the application was made, premises to which this Part applies, and

(ii) that they have not ceased to be such premises since the date when the application was made, and

(b) either of the conditions specified in subsections (2) and (3) is fulfilled with respect to those premises, and

(c) the court considers it appropriate to make the order in the circumstances of the case.

(2) The first of the conditions referred to in subsection (1)(b) is that the court is satisfied—

   (a) that the landlord either is in breach of any obligation owed by him to the applicants under their leases and relating to the repair, maintenance, insurance or management of the premises in question, or any part of them, or (in the case of an obligation dependent on notice) would be in breach of any such obligation but for the fact that it has not been reasonably practicable for the tenant to give him the appropriate notice, and

   (b) that the circumstances by virtue of which he is (or would be) in breach of any such obligation are likely to continue, and

   (c) that the appointment of a manager under Part II to act in relation to those premises would not be an adequate remedy.

(3) The second of those conditions is that, both at the date when the application was made and throughout the period of three years immediately preceding that date, there was in force an appointment under Part II of a person to act as manager in relation to the premises in question.

(4) An acquisition order may, if the court thinks fit—

   (a) include any yard, garden, outhouse or appurtenance belonging to, or usually enjoyed with, the premises specified in the application on which the order is made;

   (b) exclude any part of the premises so specified.

(5) Where—

   (a) the premises in respect of which an application for an acquisition order is made consist of part only of more extensive premises in which the landlord has an interest, and

   (b) it appears to the court that the landlord's interest in the latter premises is not reasonably capable of being severed, either in the manner contemplated by the application or in any manner authorised by virtue of subsection (4)(b),

then, notwithstanding that paragraphs (a) and (b) of subsection (1) apply, the court shall not make an acquisition order on the application.

(6) In a case where an application for an acquisition order was preceded by the service of a notice under section 27, the court may, if it thinks fit, make such an order notwithstanding—

   (a) that any period specified in the notice in pursuance of subsection (2)(d) of that section was not a reasonable period, or

   (b) that the notice failed in any other respect to comply with any requirement contained in subsection (2) of that section or in any regulations applying to the notice under section 54(3).

(7) Where any premises are premises to which this Part applies at the time when an application for an acquisition order is made in respect of them, then, for the purposes of this section and the following provisions of this Part, they shall not cease to be such premises by reason only that—

   (a) the interest of the landlord in them subsequently becomes held by an exempt landlord or a resident landlord, or

   (b) they subsequently become included within the functional land of any charity.

DEFINITIONS
  "charity": s.60.
  "court": s.60.
  "exempt landlord": ss.58(1), 60.
  "functional land": s.60.
  "landlord": ss.59(2), 60.

"lease": ss.59(1), 60.
"resident landlord": ss.58(2), 60.

GENERAL NOTE
    This section states the conditions on which an acquisition order may be made. The court
must be satisfied that:
(i)   the premises fulfilled the requirements of s.25 when the s.27 notice was served and
      the application was made and have not ceased to do so (note here however subs.
      (7)), *and*
(ii) it is appropriate to make the order in the circumstances, *and*
(iii) *either*
      the circumstances justifying the appointment of a manager under s.24 (except the
      requirement that it be just and convenient to do so) are present but that the
      appointment of a manager would not be an adequate remedy. Thus the remedy might
      be appropriate where the landlord is not performing his obligations, but the income
      available to a receiver would not be sufficient to justify the appointment (see General
      Note to s.24, and in particular, *Evans* v. *Clayhope Properties* [1987] 1 W.L.R. 225),
      or
      an appointment of a person acting as a manager under Pt. 2 of the Act has been in
      force in relation to the premises throughout the previous three years. The service of
      a s.27 preliminary notice of intention to seek an acquisition order gives the landlord
      the opportunity to assure the court that he can and will fulfil his obligations henceforth
      and thereby obtain a discharge of the management order under s.24(9). If he fails to
      do so he will be vulnerable to an acquisition order once the three-year period is past.

Subs. (4), para. (a)
    See General Note to "dwelling" in s.60 as to "appurtenance". Given the lack of any
express provisions as to easements and other ancillary rights on an acquisition order (see
General Note to s.30), it may be asked whether "appurtenance" could be used in its original
and strict sense to comprehend incorporeal hereditaments. It seems that in certain cases the
word may be competent to pass incorporeal hereditaments (see *Trim* v. *Sturminster Rural
District Council* [1938] 2 K.B. 508 at 515–516; *Methuen-Campbell* v. *Walters* [1979] Q.B. 525
at 535). However, here the word follows "yard, garden, outhouse" and it would seem likely
that it is therefore to be construed in the more modern sense of corporeal hereditaments
within the relevant curtilage.

Content of acquisition orders

    30.—(1) Where an acquisition order is made by the court, the order
shall (except in a case falling within section 33(1)) provide for the
nominated person to be entitled to acquire the landlord's interest in the
premises specified in the order on such terms as may be determined—
    (a) by agreement between the landlord and the qualifying tenants in
        whose favour the order is made, or
    (b) in default of agreement, by a rent assessment committee under
        section 31.
    (2) An acquisition order may be granted subject to such conditions as
the court thinks fit, and in particular its operation may be suspended on
terms fixed by the court.
    (3) References in this Part, in relation to an acquisition order, to the
nominated person are references to such person or persons as may be
nominated for the purposes of this Part by the persons applying for the
order.
    (4) Those persons must secure that the nominated person is joined as
a party to the application, and no further nomination of a person for the
purposes of this Part shall be made by them after the order is made
(whether in addition to, or in substitution for, the existing nominated
person) except with the approval of the court.
    (5) Where the landlord is, by virtue of any covenant, condition or other
obligation, precluded from disposing of his interest in the premises in
respect of which an acquisition order has been made unless the consent of
some other person is obtained—

(a) he shall use his best endeavours to secure that the consent of that person to that disposal is obtained and, if it appears to him that that person is obliged not to withhold his consent unreasonably but has nevertheless so withheld it, shall institute proceedings for a declaration to that effect; but

(b) If—

    (i) the landlord has discharged any duty imposed on him by paragraph (a), and

    (ii) the consent of that person has been withheld, and

    (iii) no such declaration has been made,

the order shall cease to have effect.

(6) The Land Charges Act 1972 and the Land Registration Act 1925 shall apply in relation to an acquisition order as they apply in relation to an order affecting land made by the court for the purpose of enforcing a judgment or recognisance.

DEFINITIONS
"court": s.60.
"landlord": ss.59(2), 60.
"rent assessment committee": s.60.
"tenant": s.59(2).

GENERAL NOTE
An acquisition order will provide for the landlord's interest to be acquired by a person nominated by the tenants applying for the order. The order must specify the premises to be acquired. The terms of acquisition are to be determined either by agreement or in default of agreement by a rent assessment committee.

Subs. (5)
This provision deals with the situation (most likely where the landlord's interest is leasehold) where the consent of a third party is required for disposal of the landlord's interest. The landlord must use his best endeavours to secure that the consent to the disposal is obtained. It has been said that best endeavours

". . . are something less than efforts which go beyond the bounds of reason, but are considerably more than casual and intermittent activities. There must at least be the doing of all that reasonable persons reasonably could do in the circumstances." (*Pips (Leisure) Productions* v. *Walton* (1980) 43 P. & C.R. 415 at 420, *per* Sir Robert Megarry V.-C.)

(See also *Terrell* v. *Mabie Todd and Co.* (1952) 2 T.L.R. 574; *I.B.M. United Kingdom* v. *Rockware Glass* [1980] F.S.R. 335; *Alghussein Establishment* v. *Eton College, The Times,* February 16, 1987; [1986] L.S.Gaz., June 25, 1992 (M.D. Varcoe-Cocks)).

If it appears that the third party is under an obligation not to withhold his consent unreasonably and is in fact unreasonably withholding his consent, the landlord must institute proceedings for declaratory relief to that effect. The obligation as to reasonableness may be expressed, or in the case of a leasehold covenant against disposition without the superior landlord's consent, the covenant is subject to a statutory proviso that consent shall not be unreasonably withhheld: Landlord and Tenant Act 1927, s.19(1)(*a*). A considerable body of case law exists as to the reasonableness of refusal, but the underlying principles are comprehensively summarised in the judgment of Balcombe L.J. in *International Drilling Fluids* v. *Louisville Investments (Uxbridge)* [1986] Ch. 513 at 519–521. The principles are as follows:

(1) the purpose of a qualified covenant against assignment is to protect the landlord from having his premises used or occupied in an undesirable way, or by an undesirable tenant or assignee;

(2) therefore, a landlord is not entitled to refuse consent on grounds which have nothing whatever to do with the relationship of landlord and tenant in regard to the subject-matter of the lease. Put slightly differently, this means that the landlord may not object on grounds extraneous to the intention of the parties when the covenant was granted and accepted, so as to gain some "uncovenanted advantage";

(3) the onus of proving that consent has been unreasonably withheld is on the tenant;

(4) it is not necessary for the landlord to prove that the conclusions which led him to

refuse consent were justified, if they were conclusions which might be reached by a reasonable man in the circumstances;

(5) it may be reasonable to refuse consent on the ground of the purpose for which the proposed assignee intends to use the premises, even if that purpose is not expressly forbidden by the lease;

(6) while a landlord need usually consider only his own relevant interests in deciding whether to refuse consent, there may be cases where a refusal of consent will cause disproportionate harm to the tenant compared with the resulting benefit to the landlord. In such cases refusal may be unreasonable;

(7) subject to these propositions, the reasonableness or otherwise of refusal is in each case a question of fact, dependent upon all the circumstances.

If the landlord fulfils his statutory obligations and fails to obtain either consent or a declaration that consent is being unreasonably withheld, the order ceases to have effect. The same is presumably true if the landlord sought the third party's consent and was unable to take the matter further because of the lack of any obligation not to unreasonably withhold consent; for example where there was an absolute prohibition on disposal.

Subs. (6)

The effect of this provision is that an acquisition order may be registered in the register of writs and orders affecting land under the Land Charges Act 1972, s.6, and, in the case of registered land, may be protected by lodging a caution (Land Registration Act 1925, s.59(1), (3)). It may also be protected by way of notice (see Land Registration Act, s.49(1) as amended by Sched. 4 of the 1987 Act).

Premises comprised in the order and ancillary rights

S.30 provides that the premises to be acquired are to be specified in the order (see also s.29(4) and General Note thereto). It may be noted that there are no detailed provisions dealing with easements and other ancillary rights on the acquisition. Since the acquisition order may comprise part only of a building this question may be an important one, and it is instructive to compare s.10 of the Leasehold Reform Act 1967 which makes thorough and detailed provision for ancillary rights on enfranchisement under that Act. In the case of the 1987 Act it appears that such matters are left simply to be settled by agreement, or in default by a rent assessment committee on the basis of what is "fair and reasonable" (s.31(1)).

Determination of terms by rent assessment committees

31.—(1) A rent assessment committee shall have jurisdiction to determine the terms on which the landlord's interest in the premises specified in an acquisition order may be acquired by the nominated person to the extent that those terms have not been determined by agreement between the landlord and either—

(a) the qualifying tenants in whose favour the order was made, or

(b) the nominated person;

and (subject to subsection (2)) such a committee shall determine any such terms on the basis of what appears to them to be fair and reasonable.

(2) Where an application is made under this section for such a committee to determine the consideration payable for the acquisition of a landlord's interest in any premises, the committee shall do so by determining an amount equal to the amount which, in their opinion, that interest might be expected to realise if sold on the open market by a willing seller on the appropriate terms and on the assumption that none of the tenants of the landlord of any premises comprised in those premises was buying or seeking to buy that interest.

(3) In subsection (2) "the appropriate terms" means all of the terms to which the acquisition of the landlord's interest in pursuance of the order is to be subject (whether determined by agreement as mentioned in subsection (1) or on an application under this section) apart from those relating to the consideration payable.

(4) On any application under this section the interests of the qualifying tenants in whose favour the acquisition order was made shall be repre-

sented by the nominated person, and accordingly the parties to any such application shall not include those tenants.

(5) Subsections (2), (4) and (5) of section 13 shall apply for the purposes of this section as they apply for the purposes of that section, but as if the reference in subsection (5) to subsection (1) of that section were a reference to subsection (1) of this section.

(6) Nothing in this section shall be construed as authorising a rent assessment committee to determine any terms dealing with matters in relation to which provision is made by section 32 or 33.

DEFINITIONS
"landlord": ss.59(2), 60.
"rent assessment committee": s.60.
"tenant": s.59(2).

GENERAL NOTE
Under this section rent assessment committees are given very wide jurisdiction to determine the terms on which the landlord's interest is to be acquired pursuant to an acquisition order in cases where agreement cannot be reached between the landlord and the tenant or the nominated person representing them. All terms except the consideration are simply to be fixed on the basis of what appears to the committee to be fair and reasonable. The consideration payable is to be based on the other terms agreed or determined and the expected open market price by a willing seller on the assumption that none of the tenants was buying or seeking to buy the relevant interest. In other words, the landlord's interest is assumed to be sold subject to the existing leases, but ignoring the fact or possibility that any of the tenants is willing to purchase that interest (which might of course otherwise have an inflating effect on the price which could be commanded). It might be difficult to find adequate comparables for the valuation exercise contemplated by this section, especially in the case of a building in a poor state of repair and maintenance and subject to a number of long leases at low rents. A variety of valuation approaches seem likely to evolve to meet these problems, and as in the case of the rather more complex exercise under s.9(1) of the Leasehold Reform Act 1967, which also includes the open market and willing seller concepts, the courts seem likely to incline to the view that there is no single "correct" approach (see *Rees and Rees* v. *Scott* (1969) R. & V.R. 610).

The assumption of an "open market" transaction was discussed in the context of a commercial rent review clause by the Court of Appeal in *Dennis & Robinson* v. *Kiossis Establishment* (1987) 282 E.G. 857. There it was held to import the assumptions that the transaction contemplated will take place in the context of a market and by willing parties. This remains so even if in actual fact the market is weak or non-existent. However, though a market must be assumed, the court held that the strength of the market can be taken into account in deciding what a willing purchaser/lessee would be willing to pay: "It is essentially a matter for the valuer to inquire into and determine the strength of the market" (p.859, *per* Fox L.J.). Again, "The strength of the market and the . . . value of premises in the market are matters for the valuer's discretion based on his own knowledge and experience of the value of such premises" (p.862, *per* Dillon L.J.).

Discharge of existing mortgages

32.—(1) Where the landlord's interest in any premises is acquired in pursuance of an acquisition order, the instrument by virtue of which it is so acquired shall (subject to subsection (2) and Part II of Schedule 1) operate to discharge the premises from any charge on that interest to secure the payment of money or the performance of any other obligation by the landlord or any other person.

(2) Subsection (1) does not apply to any such charge if—
    (a) it has been agreed between the landlord and either—
        (i) the qualifying tenants in whose favour the order was made, or
        (ii) the nominated person,
        that the landlord's interest should be acquired subject to the charge, or
    (b) the court is satisfied, whether on the application for the order

or on an application made by the person entitled to the benefit of the charge, that in the exceptional circumstances of the case it would be fair and reasonable that the landlord's interest should be so acquired, and orders accordingly.

(3) This section and Part II of Schedule 1 shall apply, with any necessary modifications, to mortgages and liens as they apply to charges; but nothing in those provisions shall apply to a rentcharge.

DEFINITIONS
"court": s.60.
"landlord": ss.59(2), 60.
"mortgage": s.60.
"tenant": s.59(2).

GENERAL NOTE
This section, together with Sched. 1, Pt. 2, provides for the discharge of charges, mortgages and liens (but not rentcharges) affecting the interest of the landlord acquired under the Act. The section does not operate to discharge the incumbrance where the court so orders or where it is agreed that the interest shall be acquired subject to the charge, which will no doubt be reflected in the consideration agreed or assessed under s.31.
See also the General Note to Sched. 1.

Acquisition order where landlord cannot be found

33.—(1) Where an acquisition order is made by the court in a case where the landlord cannot be found, or his identity cannot be ascertained, the order shall provide for the landlord's interest in the premises specified in the order to vest in the nominated person on the following terms, namely—

(a) such terms as to payment as are specified in subsection (2), and

(b) such other terms as the court thinks fit, being terms which, in the opinion of the court, correspond so far as possible to those on which the interest might be expected to be transferred if it were being transferred by the landlord.

(2) The terms as to payment referred to in subsection (1)(a) are terms requiring the payment into court of—

(a) such amount as a surveyor selected by the President of the Lands Tribunal may certify to be in his opinion the amount which the landlord's interest might be expected to realise if sold as mentioned in section 31(2); and

(b) any amounts or estimated amounts remaining due to the landlord from any tenants of his of any premises comprised in the premises in respect of which the order is made, being amounts or estimated amounts determined by the court as being due from those persons under the terms of their leases.

(3) Where any amount or amounts required by virtue of subsection (2) to be paid into court are so paid, the landlord's interest shall, by virtue of this section, vest in the nominated person in accordance with the order.

DEFINITIONS
"court": s.60.
"landlord": ss.59(2), 60.
"lease": ss.59(1), 60.
"tenant": s.59(2).

GENERAL NOTE
This section makes provision for cases where the landlord's identity or whereabouts cannot be ascertained. The terms on which the landlord's interest is to vest in the nominated person are fixed by the court rather than by a rent assessment committee, and payment of the consideration is made into court, the amount being fixed on the same basis as under

s.31, but by a surveyor certified by the President of the Lands Tribunal rather than a rent assessment committee. As well as the consideration, any amounts or estimated amounts due to the landlord from the tenants of the premises under the terms of their leases are to be paid into court.

Discharge of acquisition order and withdrawal by tenants

34.—(1) If, on an application by a landlord in respect of whose interest an acquisition order has been made, the court is satisfied—

(a) that the nominated person has had a reasonable time within which to effect the acquisition of that interest in pursuance of the order but has not done so, or

(b) that the number of qualifying tenants of flats contained in the premises in question who desire to proceed with the acquisition of the landlord's interest is less than the requisite majority of qualifying tenants of the flats contained in those premises, or

(c) that the premises in question have ceased to be premises to which this Part applies,

the court may discharge the order.

(2) Where—

(a) a notice is served on the landlord by the qualifying tenants by whom a notice has been served under section 27 or (as the case may be) by whom an application has been made for an acquisition order, or by the person nominated for the purposes of this Part by any such tenants, and

(b) the notice indicates an intention no longer to proceed with the acquisition of the landlord's interest in the premises in question,

the landlord may (except in a case where subsection (4) applies) recover under this subsection any costs reasonably incurred by him in connection with the disposal by him of that interest down to the time when the notice is served; and, if the notice is served after the making of an acquisition order, that order shall cease to have effect.

(3) If (whether before or after the making of an acquisition order) the nominated person becomes aware—

(a) that the number of qualifying tenants of flats contained in the premises in question who desire to proceed with the acquisition of the landlord's interest is less than the requisite majority of qualifying tenants of the flats contained in those premises, or

(b) that those premises have ceased to be premises to which this Part applies,

he shall forthwith serve on the landlord a notice indicating an intention no longer to proceed with the acquisition of that interest, and subsection (2) shall apply accordingly.

(4) If, at any time when any proceedings taken under or by virtue of this Part are pending before the court or the Lands Tribunal—

(a) such a notice as is mentioned in subsection (2) or (3) is served on the landlord, or

(b) the nominated person indicates that he is no longer willing to act in the matter and nobody is nominated for the purposes of this Part in his place, or

(c) the number of qualifying tenants of flats contained in the premises in question who desire to proceed with the acquisition of the landlord's interest falls below the requisite majority of qualifying tenants of the flats contained in those premises, or

(d) those premises cease to be premises to which this Part applies,

or if the court discharges an acquisition order under subsection (1), the landlord may recover such costs incurred by him in connection with the disposal by him of his interest in those premises as the court or (as the case may be) the Tribunal may determine.

(5) The costs that may be recovered by the landlord under subsection (2) or (4) include costs incurred by him in connection with any proceedings under this Part (other than proceedings before a rent assessment committee).

(6) Any liability for costs arising under this section shall be the joint and several liability of the following persons, namely—

(a) where the liability arises before the making of an application for an acquisition order, the tenants by whom a notice was served under section 27, or

(b) where the liability arises after the making of such an application, the tenants by whom the application was made,

together with (in either case) any person nominated by those tenants for the purposes of this Part.

(7) In relation to any time when a tenant falling within paragraph (a) or (b) of subsection (6) has ceased to have vested in him the interest under his lease, that paragraph shall be construed as applying instead to the person who is for the time being the successor in title to that interest.

(8) Nothing in this section shall be construed as authorising the court to discharge an acquisition order where the landlord's interest has already been acquired in pursuance of the order.

(9) If—

(a) an acquisition order is discharged, or ceases to have effect, by virtue of any provision of this Part, and

(b) the order has been protected by an entry registered under the Land Charges Act 1972 or the Land Registration Act 1925,

the court may by order direct that that entry shall be cancelled.

DEFINITIONS
"court": s.60.
"flat": s.60.
"landlord": ss.59(2), 60.
"rent assessment committee": s.60.
"tenant": s.59(2).

GENERAL NOTE
This section contains a number of provisions dealing with the position where acquisition proceedings become abortive.

Subs. (1) allows a landlord against whom an order has been made to apply for its discharge on the basis of delay by the nominated person, or where the number of tenants wishing to proceed with the acquisition has fallen below the requisite majority, or where the premises have ceased to be premises to which Pt. 3 of the Act applies (as to which see s.29(7)). However, it is too late to seek discharge of an order once the landlord's interest has actually been acquired (subs. (8)).

Subs. (2) allows the landlord to recover any costs reasonably incurred by him in a case where qualifying tenants or the nominated person indicate that they no longer intend to proceed with the acquisition; it is also provided that if the intention is notified after an acquisition order has been made, then the order ceases to have effect.

Subs. (3) obliges the nominated person to serve notice on the landlord indicating that he intends no longer to proceed if at any time he becomes aware that the requisite majority of tenants no longer wish to proceed, or that Pt. 3 does not apply to the premises. The provisions of subs. (2) as to costs and cessation of any order then apply.

If a notice of intention not to proceed is served whilst proceedings are pending under Pt. 3 before a court or the Lands Tribunal, or the proceedings otherwise become abortive as mentioned in subs. (4), then the costs to be recovered by the landlord are to be determined by the court or Tribunal. If an order is discharged or ceases to have effect after the proceedings are completed, then the landlord may recover his costs in those proceedings under subs. (2) provided they were reasonably incurred. No costs may be recovered in respect of proceedings before a rent assessment committee.

Liability for the costs mentioned in the preceding subsections falls upon those tenants who served the preliminary s.27 notice or (if the matter got as far as making an application for acquisition) the tenants who made the application, and also upon the nominated person.

Where tenancies have changed hands since the making of the application or the service of the notice, it is the successors in title who are liable. Liability is joint and several. Finally, provision is made by subs. (9) for cancellation of any entry upon the relevant registers where an acquisition order is discharged or ceases to have effect.

PART IV

VARIATION OF LEASES

GENERAL NOTE

Variation of the terms of long leases

In some circumstances a long lease of a flat may be "defective" in that it fails to make satisfactory provision with respect to one or more of the following:

(a) the repair or maintenance of the flat in question or the building containing the flat or any land or building which is let to the tenant under the lease (or in respect of which rights are conferred on him under it);

(b) the insurance of the flat or any such building or land;

(c) the repair or maintenance of any installations reasonably necessary to ensure that occupiers of the flat enjoy a reasonable standard of accommodation;

(d) the provision and maintenance of any services which are reasonably necessary to ensure that occupiers of the flat enjoy a reasonable standard of accommodation;

(e) the recovery by one party to the lease from another party to it of expenditure incurred or to be incurred by him (or on his behalf) for the benefit of that other party (or a number of persons who include that other party);

(f) the computation of a service charge payable under the lease.

Pt. 4, in s.35, provides that *any party* to a long lease can make an application to the court for an order varying the lease where that lease fails to make satisfactory provision for the matters outlined in (a)–(f) (above). The provisions do not apply where the demised premises consist of or include the flat and one or more other flats or the flat and any common parts of the building containing the flat. Neither do the provisions apply to a long lease if it constitutes a tenancy to which the Landlord and Tenant Act 1954, Pt. 2, applies (other than an assured tenancy). Where an application is made under s.35 by any party to a lease any other party to the lease may make an application to the court asking it (in the event of its deciding to make any variation of the lease under the original application) to make an order which effects a corresponding variation of each of other leases specified in the application (s.36). In addition, application may be made to the court in respect of two or more leases for an order varying each of those leases on the ground that the variation cannot be satisfactorily achieved unless all leases are varied to the same effect (s.37).

The powers of the court to make an order varying a lease or leases are detailed in s.38. The court may make an order varying the lease if the grounds on which the application was made are established to the satisfaction of the court (s.38(1)) and, similarly, may make an order varying each of the leases under s.36 and s.37. The variation specified in an order under s.35 or s.36 can be either the variation specified in the relevant application or such other variation as the court thinks fit (s.38(4)). The court cannot make an order affecting a variation in the lease if that variation would be likely substantially to prejudice any respondent to the application or any person who is not a party to the application and that an award of monetary compensation would not afford adequate compensation or that for any other reason it would not be reasonable to order the variation (s.38(6)). There are also specific restrictions for the variation of the provisions in a lease with regard to insurance in s.38(7). Under s.39 a court order to vary a lease binds third parties whether or not that party has been a party to the proceedings and a third party for these purposes includes any predecessors in title of the parties.

S.40 provides that any party to a long lease of a *dwelling* (other than a flat) may make an application to vary the lease on the grounds that the lease fails to make satisfactory provision with respect to any matters relating to the insurance of the dwelling (including the recovery of the costs of such insurance).

Applications relating to flats

Application by party to lease for variation of lease

35.—(1) Any party to a long lease of a flat may make an application to the court for an order varying the lease in such manner as is specified in the application.

(2) The grounds on which any such application may be made are that the lease fails to make satisfactory provision with respect to one or more of the following matters, namely—

   (a) the repair or maintenance of—
       (i) the flat in question, or
      (ii) the building containing the flat, or
    (iii) any land or building which is let to the tenant under the lease or in respect of which rights are conferred on him under it;
   (b) the insurance of the flat or of any such building or land as is mentioned in paragraph (a)(ii) or (iii);
   (c) the repair or maintenance of any installations (whether they are in the same building as the flat or not) which are reasonably necessary to ensure that occupiers of the flat enjoy a reasonable standard of accommodation;
   (d) the provision or maintenance of any services which are reasonably necessary to ensure that occupiers of the flat enjoy a reasonable standard of accommodation (whether they are services connected with any such installations or not, and whether they are services provided for the benefit of those occupiers or services provided for the benefit of the occupiers of a number of flats including that flat);
   (e) the recovery by one party to the lease from another party to it of expenditure incurred or to be incurred by him, or on his behalf, for the benefit of that other party or of a number of persons who include that other party;
   (f) the computation of a service charge payable under the lease.

(3) For the purposes of subsection (2)(c) and (d) the factors for determining, in relation to the occupiers of a flat, what is a reasonable standard of accommodation may include—

   (a) factors relating to the safety and security of the flat and its occupiers and of any common parts of the building containing the flat; and
   (b) other factors relating to the condition of any such common parts.

(4) For the purposes of subsection (2)(f) a lease fails to make satisfactory provision with respect to the computation of a service charge payable under it if—

   (a) it provides for any such charge to be a proportion of expenditure incurred, or to be incurred, by or on behalf of the landlord or a superior landlord; and
   (b) other tenants of the landlord are also liable under their leases to pay by way of service charges proportions of any such expenditure; and
   (c) the aggregate of the amounts that would, in any particular case, be payable by reference to the proportions referred to in paragraphs (a) and (b) would exceed the whole of any such expenditure.

(5) Rules of court shall make provision—

   (a) for requiring notice of any application under this Part to be served by the person making the application, and by any respondent to the application, on any person who the applicant, or (as the case may be) the respondent, knows or has reason to believe is likely to be affected by any variation specified in the application, and
   (b) for enabling persons served with any such notice to be joined in parties to the proceedings.

(6) For the purposes of this Part a long lease shall not be regarded as a long lease of a flat if the demised premises consist of or include—

   (a) the flat and one or more other flats, or
   (b) the flat and any common parts of the building containing the flat.

(7) This Part does not apply to a long lease of a flat if it constitutes a tenancy to which Part II of the Landlord and Tenant Act 1954 applies

(other than an assured tenancy as defined in section 56(1) of the Housing Act 1980).

(8) In this section "service charge" has the meaning given by section 18(1) of the 1985 Act.

DEFINITIONS
"common parts": s.60.
"court": s.60.
"flat": s.60.
"landlord": ss.59(2), 60.
"lease": ss.59(1), 60.
"long lease": ss.59(3), 60.
"tenant": s.59(2).

GENERAL NOTE

This section provides that any party to a long lease of a flat may apply to court for an order varying the lease, and states the grounds on which the application may be made.

The lease must be a long lease, must not include within the demise any other flat or any common parts of the building, and must not constitute a tenancy within Pt. 2 of the Landlord and Tenant Act 1954 (other than an assured tenancy). As to this last requirement, see General Note to s.21(7). Assured tenancies (*i.e* those granted by approved bodies in accordance with s.56 of the Housing Act 1980) can fall within the provisions of Pt. 4 (subs. (7)), and it should be noted that Pt. 4 provides for no exceptions such as resident landlords, charities, exempt public sector landlords, and so on: though of course one is unlikely to encounter long leases granted by local authorities or similar bodies.

The application may be made on the ground that the lease fails to make satisfactory provision with regard to one or more of the matters specified in subs. (2). The Act is silent as to how the lack of satisfactory provision may have originated, and this would appear to be immaterial. The lease may be defectively drafted, or may lean too far in the landlord's favour, or may have been drafted many years ago so that it fails to reflect modern requirements. In any event, Pt. 4 of the Act may provide a remedy.

The matters specified in subs. (2) are as follows:

(a) the repair and maintenance of the flat, the building containing the flat, or any other land or building included in the lease or in respect of which the tenant enjoys rights under his lease (for example a garage forming part of the demise, or service media or means of access over which the tenant has an easement). An extreme case might be where the lease contains no obligation on the landlord to keep the structure of the building in repair. A more difficult question could arise where a building proves to be inherently defective, since a repairing obligation will not extend to rectifying an inherent defect which has not given rise to disrepair (see, *e.g., Post Office* v. *Aquarius Properties* (1987) 281 E.G. 798 (where weak areas of concrete made the basement of a commercial building prone to flooding but caused no damage); *Quick* v. *Taff-Ely Borough Council* [1986] Q.B. 809 (where badly-designed window frames caused condensation but no disrepair); *Stent* v. *Monmouth District Council* (1987) 282 E.G. 705 (where a defectively designed door which let in water was held not *per se* to constitute disrepair, but had as a result become rotten and distorted and thereby out of repair)). S.35 raises the question of whether tenants afflicted by badly designed windows which cause condensation or by a poor and inefficient heating system could apply for their leases to be amended so as to require the landlord to rectify these inherent defects. The problem is that grounds (a) and (c) of subs. (2) both speak of "repair or maintenance" of the building or of installations, and it seems highly questionable whether, on the strength of the cases mentioned above, such defects would fall within those words. The phraseology might also exclude any redress in the case of defects where the work required is so considerable that it constitutes renewal rather than repair (see, *e.g., Ravenseft Properties* v. *Davstone Holdings* [1980] Q.B. 12; *Hilliard Property Co.* v. *Nicholas Clarke Investments* (1984) 269 E.G. 1257; *Smedley* v. *Chumley & Hawkes* (1982) 44 P. & C.R. 50; *Elmcroft Developments* v. *Tankersley-Sawyer* (1984) 270 E.G. 140; *Elite Investments* v. *T.I. Bainbridge Silencers* [1986] 2 E.G.L.R. 43; *Mullaney* v. *Maybourne Grange (Croydon) Management Co.* [1986] 1 E.G.L.R. 70). The problem is that if the lease provides that the landlord is to repair, but the works which are badly needed go beyond repair as defined in these cases, it is difficult to argue that the lease fails to make satisfactory provision with regard to repair: the work which is not provided for does not fall within "repair", "maintenance" or the provision of services as set out in subs. (2);

(b) the insurance of the flat, building or other land as mentioned in (a). This covers cases where the landlord is not obliged to insure, or where the insured risks specified in the lease are inadequate. It does not appear to cover the situation where the lease fails to provide for other forms of insurance, such as insurance against loss of rent where the premises are destroyed or damaged. It seems unclear whether the words "with respect to . . . the insurance of . . . the flat" would cover the situation where the lease provides for insurance cover to be maintained but fails to provide adequately for important related matters, such as outlay of insurance moneys on reinstatement or the destination of such moneys if reinstatement is not to take place. These may be questions of real importance: see *Re King* [1963] 1 Ch. 459; *Beacon Carpets* v. *Kirby* [1985] Q.B. 755;

(c) the repair or maintenance of any installations which are reasonably necessary to ensure that occupiers of the flat enjoy a reasonable standard of accommodation. Obvious examples are installations for heating space and water, lighting of common parts, and refuse disposal facilities. The same problems as mentioned in (a) could arise where the installation is inherently defective or requires complete replacement. The concept of "reasonable standard of accommodation" seems capable of giving rise to endless dispute. Will the standard of accommodation which may be expected vary according to the type or location of the building? Or according to the rent or premium paid by the tenant? The installations necessary to provide an elderly retired couple with "a reasonable standard of accommodation" may be very different from those required by a family with young children. Is the standard to be judged by the needs of the actual tenants or on an objective basis of the possible range of reasonable occupants? The wording of condition (c) perhaps suggests the latter approach. However, turning to subs. (3), which specifies some relevant factors in determining what is reasonable accommodation, this speaks of determination "in relation to *the* occupiers of a flat", which seems to suggest a more subjective approach. Of course the ground for the application is that the lease does not deal with the maintenance and repair of existing installations, and not that it fails to require their provision if they are non-existent;

(d) the provision or maintenance of any services which are reasonably necessary to ensure that occupiers of the flat enjoy a reasonable standard of accommodation. This will cover the situation where the lease makes no provision for the service at all (*cf.* the situation with regard to non-existent "installations" under (c)). Similar controversy to that discussed in relation to (c) can be foreseen over what is a reasonable standard of accommodation. Another difficulty is what is meant by "services". In the Rent Act 1977 in connection with restricted contracts, "services" are defined as including "attendance, the provision of heating or lighting, the supply of hot water and any other privilege or facility connected with the occupancy of a dwelling, other than a privilege or facility requisite for the purposes of access, cold water supply or sanitary accommodation" (s.19(8)). However, clearly this definition should not be taken as limiting the meaning of the expression in the 1987 Act. Subs. (3) states that the services may include matters relating to the safety and security of the flat and common parts and to the condition of common parts. Thus services could clearly include the cleaning and lighting of common parts and the provision of security staff. S.35 appears to draw a distinction between "installations" (para.(c)) and "services" (para. (d)). Presumably "installations" connotes physical apparatus, whereas "services" might be taken as relating to a facility provided, or the measures taken to provide that facility. For example, in relation to heating, the boilers, pipes and radiators would be "installations". The heat and hot water transmitted to the flats would be a service, and the steps taken to fuel and maintain the installations would also be services. The problem mentioned in (c) above where the boiler needs replacing entirely might be met by relying on para. (d) and considering whether the lease makes adequate provision for the service of heating. The problem might then be resolved by (if necessary) varying the lease to require the provision of heating to a specific standard; if the old boiler is incapable of meeting that standard then it will have to be replaced if the landlord is not to be in breach of his obligations. Similarly, in relation to the lighting of stairs and other common parts, a distinction may be drawn between the physical installations (wiring, light fittings and bulbs), the services to keep them in operation (such as changing the bulbs, switching them on and off, etc.) and the overall service of the provision of adequate illumination. Some services may be provided independently of any installation, for example cleaning and the collection of residents' refuse. However, difficult borderline cases might arise. Take the case of residents of a block who are concerned about security and who wish the landlord to install new door and window locks and an answerphone system at the main entrance. Certainly these items could be said to be necessary or desirable to afford a reasonable standard of accommodation (see subs. (3)), but are they simply "installations" or could they also be regarded as "services"? The answerphone could be seen as a service, falling into the same category as lighting, but it seems strained to suggest that a stronger lock is a "service". If so, then the lease could be amended to require the provision of an answerphone, but provided the existing locks are properly maintained and in a state of repair, it would be difficult to require their replacement. But could the provision of "adequate security measures" for the block as a whole be taken as a composite service, requiring, where necessary, the replacement of inadequate security apparatus?

Other examples of this type of problem suggest themselves. Could the provision of a play area and play apparatus for children be regarded as a service? If so, it might certainly be regarded as reasonably necessary to give children and their parents living in an upstairs flat a reasonable standard of accommodation. Is the provision of sufficient parking spaces for occupants and their visitors a service? What of the provision of facilities for drying washing?

(e) the recovery of expenditure incurred by one party to the lease for the benefit of the other. This of course allows the landlord to rectify defective service charge provisions which are not sufficiently comprehensive to allow the recovery of all items of expenditure;

(f) the computation of a service charge payable under the lease. This would seem to cover both the means by which the total service charge for the block is calculated and the way in which it is apportioned between the flats. Particularly vulnerable to challenge is the method under which some landlords attempt to cover management expenses by specifying percentages of total expenditure for each flat which together amount to more than 100 per cent. (subs. (4)). As to "service charge" (subs. (8)), see the General Note to s.42.

Application by respondent for variation of other leases

36.—(1) Where an application ("the original application") is made under section 35 by any party to a lease, any other party to the lease may make an application to the court asking it, in the event of its deciding to make an order effecting any variation of the lease in pursuance of the original application, to make an order which effects a corresponding variation of each of such one or more other leases as are specified in the application.

(2) Any lease so specified—

(a) must be a long lease of a flat under which the landlord is the same person as the landlord under the lease specified in the original application; but

(b) need not be a lease of a flat which is in the same building as the flat let under that lease, nor a lease drafted in terms identical to those of that lease.

(3) The grounds on which an application may be made under this section are—

(a) that each of the leases specified in the application fails to make satisfactory provision with respect to the matter or matters specified in the original application; and

(b) that, if any variation is effected in pursuance of the original application, it would be in the interests of the person making the application under this section, or in the interests of the other persons who are parties to the leases specified in that application, to have all of the leases in question (that is to say, the ones specified in that application together with the one specified in the original application) varied to the same effect.

DEFINITIONS
  "court": s.60.
  "flat": s.60.
  "landlord": ss.59(2), 60.
  "lease": ss.59(1), 60.
  "long lease": ss.59(3), 60.

GENERAL NOTE
  This section allows the respondent to an application for the variation of a lease to apply for an order effecting corresponding variations to other long leases of flats with the same landlord. The other flat or flats need not be in the same building, nor their leases be drafted in identical terms.

Application by majority of parties for variation of leases

37.—(1) Subject to the following provisions of this section, an application may be made to the court in respect of two or more leases for an order varying each of those leases in such manner as is specified in the application.

(2) Those leases must be long leases of flats under which the landlord is the same person, but they need not be leases of flats which are in the same building, nor leases which are drafted in identical terms.

(3) The grounds on which an application may be made under this section are that the object to be achieved by the variation cannot be satisfactorily achieved unless all the leases are varied to the same effect.

(4) An application under this section in respect of any leases may be made by the landlord or any of the tenants under the leases.

(5) Any such application shall only be made if—

  (a) in a case where the application is in respect of less than nine leases, all, or all but one, of the parties concerned consent to it; or

  (b) in a case where the application is in respect of more than eight leases, it is not opposed for any reason by more than 10 per cent. of the total number of the parties concerned and at least 75 per cent. of that number consent to it.

(6) For the purposes of subsection (5)—

  (a) in the case of each lease in respect of which the application is made, the tenant under the lease shall constitute one of the parties concerned (so that in determining the total number of the parties concerned a person who is the tenant under a number of such leases shall be regarded as constituting a corresponding number of the parties concerned); and

  (b) the landlord shall also constitute one of the parties concerned.

DEFINITIONS
  "court": s.60.
  "flat": s.60.
  "landlord": ss.59(2), 60.
  "lease": ss.59(1), 60.
  "long lease": ss.59(3), 60.
  "tenant": s.59(2).

GENERAL NOTE
  This section allows for applications for the variation of two or more leases with a common landlord. The leases need not be of flats in the same building nor be drafted in identical

terms. The essential point is that consistent variation to all the leases is necessary in order to achieve the object of variation. This will be of most significance in the case of variations relating to common parts and services and to service charges; the service charge provisions in relation to a whole block will only effectively recast if all the leases adopt a consistent approach. Thus the section may be used to make common improvements to a number of leases drafted in defective terms, or to bring into line a number of leases with inconsistent provisions.

The application may be made by the landlord or by any tenant, subject to the provisions of subs. (5). If the application relates to eight leases or less, all parties (including the landlord as one party) or all except one party, must consent to it. Thus in a block of six flats, a multiple variation application can be made if the landlord and any five of the tenants agree to it, or if all the tenants agree to it, or if the landlord and all the tenants agree. If the application relates to nine or more leases, at least 75 per cent. of the parties must consent, and it must not be opposed by more than 10 per cent. Thus, in a block of nine flats, there will be 10 parties involved, including the landlord. At least eight of them must consent to the application and not more than one must oppose it. If eight of the tenants favour variation and the landlord opposes it, the attitude of the ninth tenant will be crucial. If his attitude is neutral, the application may be made, his consent not being necessary to attain the 75 per cent. majority. But if he actively opposes the variation, no application may be made.

Orders varying leases

Orders by the court varying leases

38.—(1) If, on an application under section 35, the grounds on which the application was made are established to the satisfaction of the court, the court may (subject to subsections (6) and (7)) make an order varying the lease specified in the application in such manner as is specified in the order.

(2) If—
    (a) an application under section 36 was made in connection with that application, and
    (b) the grounds set out in subsection (3) of that section are established to the satisfaction of the court with respect to the leases specified in the application under section 36,
the court may (subject to subsections (6) and (7)) also make an order varying each of those leases in such manner as is specified in the order.

(3) If, on an application under section 37, the grounds set out in subsection (3) of that section are established to the satisfaction of the court with respect to the leases specified in the application, the court may (subject to subsections (6) and (7)) make an order varying each of those leases in such manner as is specified in the order.

(4) The variation specified in an order under subsection (1) or (2) may be either the variation specified in the relevant application under section 35 or 36 or such other variation as the court thinks fit.

(5) If the grounds referred to in subsection (2) or (3) (as the case may be) are established to the satisfaction of the court with respect to some but not all of the leases specified in the application, the power to make an order under that subsection shall extend to those leases only.

(6) The court shall not make an order under this section effecting any variation of a lease if it appears to the court—
    (a) that the variation would be likely substantially to prejudice—
        (i) any respondent to the application, or
        (ii) any person who is not a party to the application,
    and that an award under subsection (10) would not afford him adequate compensation, or
    (b) that for any other reason it would not be reasonable in the circumstances for the variation to be effected.

(7) The court shall not, on an application relating to the provision to be made by a lease with respect to insurance, make an order under this section effecting any variation of the lease—

(a) which terminates any existing right of the landlord under its terms to nominate an insurer for insurance purposes; or

(b) which requires the landlord to nominate a number of insurers from which the tenant would be entitled to select an insurer for those purposes; or

(c) which, in a case where the lease requires the tenant to effect insurance with a specified insurer, requires the tenant to effect insurance otherwise than with another specified insurer.

(8) The court may, instead of making an order varying a lease in such manner as is specified in the order, make an order directing the parties to the lease to vary it in such manner as is so specified; and accordingly any reference in this Part (however expressed) to an order which effects any variation of a lease or to any variation effected by an order shall include a reference to an order which directs the parties to a lease to effect a variation of it or (as the case may be) a reference to any variation effected in pursuance of such an order.

(9) The court may by order direct that a memorandum of any variation of a lease effected by an order under this section shall be endorsed on such documents as are specified in the order.

(10) Where the court makes an order under this section varying a lease the court may, if it thinks fit, make an order providing for any party to the lease to pay, to any other party to the lease or to any other person, compensation in respect of any loss or disadvantage that the court considers he is likely to suffer as a result of the variation.

DEFINITIONS
  "court": s.60.
  "lease": ss.59(1), 60.
  "tenant": s.59(2).

GENERAL NOTE
  This section confers upon the court the power to make an order varying a lease or leases upon being satisfied that the grounds of the application are made out. The order can be for the variation of a single lease (with consequent amendments to other leases under s.36 where appropriate) or for the variation of a number of leases under s.37. If the grounds for variation are not made out for all the leases, only those in which they are established may be varied. The court is not confined to the variation specified in the application, but may make such variation as it thinks fit (subs. (4)). The court may itself make the variation by order (subs. (1)), or may make an order directing the parties themselves to vary the lease (subs. (8)).
  An order may be made requiring the payment of compensation by any party to the lease to any other party to the lease (or indeed any other person), if it appears that the person is likely to suffer any loss or disadvantage as a result of the variation (subs. (10)). If substantial prejudice is likely and such an award would not afford adequate compensation, the court must not make a variation order (subs. (6)(a)). Similarly, an order must not be made if it appears to the court that for any other reason it would not be reasonable to effect the variation (subs. (6)(b)).
  A number of possible variations relating to insurance are specifically precluded by subs. (7), with the underlying principle that the landlord must remain free to nominate the insurer.
  Given the wide terms of the discretion and the uncertainties as to the grounds of variation, mentioned in connection with s.35, it is hard to differ from the appraisal of Lord Coleraine that:

  "This matter will be green fields for some years, and I fear that for some considerable time to come there will be a flood of expensive litigation, with appeals." (*Hansard*, H.L. Vol. 487, col. 642, May 13, 1987.)

Effect of orders varying leases: applications by third parties

  39.—(1) Any variation effected by an order under section 38 shall be binding not only on the parties to the lease for the time being but also on other persons (including any predecessors in title of those parties), whether or not they were parties to the proceedings in which the order was made or were served with a notice by virtue of section 35(5).

(2) Without prejudice to the generality of subsection (1), any variation effected by any such order shall be binding on any surety who has guaranteed the performance of any obligation varied by the order; and the surety shall accordingly be taken to have guaranteed the performance of that obligation as so varied.

(3) Where any such order has been made and a person was, by virtue of section 35(5), required to be served with a notice relating to the proceedings in which it was made, but he was not so served, he may—

(a) bring an action for damages for breach of statutory duty against the person by whom any such notice was so required to be served in respect of that person's failure to serve it;

(b) apply to the court for the cancellation or modification of the variation in question.

(4) The court may, on an application under subsection (3)(b) with respect to any variation of a lease—

(a) by order cancel that variation or modify it in such manner as is specified in the order, or

(b) make such an order as is mentioned in section 38(10) in favour of the person making the application,

as it thinks fit.

(5) Where a variation is cancelled or modified under paragraph (a) of subsection (4)—

(a) the cancellation or modification shall take effect as from the date of the making of the order under that paragraph or as from such later date as may be specified in the order, and

(b) the court may by order direct that a memorandum of the cancellation or modification shall be endorsed on such documents as are specified in the order;

and, in a case where a variation is so modified, subsections (1) and (2) above shall, as from the date when the modification takes effect, apply to the variation as modified.

DEFINITIONS
"court": s.60.
"lease": ss.59(1), 60.

GENERAL NOTE
This section contains a number of supplementary provisions relating to variation orders. An order is binding not only upon the parties to the lease but also upon their predecessors in title and other persons (subs. (1)). However, any person required by rules of court to be served with notice of an application for a variation order and who was not so notified is given a remedy by way of action for breach of statutory duty and may apply for the variation to be cancelled or modified (subs. (3)). A general power of cancellation and modification is also given (subs. (4)).

It is expressly provided by subs. (2) that a variation effected under the Act is binding on any surety to the lease, who is then taken to have guaranteed the performance of the obligation thus varied. This is necessary since the usual rule is that a variation in the terms of the lease made without the surety's concurrence will discharge him from his obligations, even if the change was not such as to be prejudicial to him (see *Holme* v. *Brunskill* (1878) 3 Q.B.D. 495; *Selous Street Properties* v. *Oronel Fabrics* [1984] 270 E.G. 643 and 743).

Applications relating to dwellings other than flats

Application for variation of insurance provisions of lease of dwelling other than a flat

40.—(1) Any party to a long lease of a dwelling may make an application to the court for an order varying the lease, in such manner as is specified in the application, on the grounds that the lease fails to make satisfactory provision with respect to any matter relating to the insurance of the dwelling, including the recovery of the costs of such insurance.

(2) Sections 36 and 38 shall apply to an application under subsection (1) subject to the modifications specified in subsection (3).

(3) Those modifications are as follows—

    (a) in section 36—

        (i) in subsection (1), the reference to section 35 shall be read as a reference to subsection (1) above, and

        (ii) in subsection (2), any reference to a flat shall be read as a reference to a dwelling; and

    (b) in section 38—

        (i) any reference to an application under section 35 shall be read as a reference to an application under subsection (1) above, and

        (ii) any reference to an application under section 36 shall be read as a reference to an application under section 36 as applied by subsection (2) above.

(4) For the purposes of this section a long lease shall not be regarded as a long lease of a dwelling if the demised premises consist of or include the dwelling and one or more other dwellings; and this section does not apply to a long lease of a dwelling if it constitutes a tenancy to which Part II of the Landlord and Tenant Act 1954 applies (other than an assured tenancy as defined in section 56(1) of the Housing Act 1980).

(5) In this section "dwelling" means a dwelling other than a flat.

DEFINITIONS
"court": s.60.
"dwelling": s.60.
"flat": s.60.
"lease": ss.59(1), 60.
"long lease": ss.59(3), 60.
"tenancy": ss.59(1), 60.

GENERAL NOTE
This section provides for the variation of long leases of dwellings other than flats in relation to insurance. The relevant ground for variation is that the lease fails to make satisfactory provision with respect to any matter relating to the insurance of the dwelling, including recovery of the costs of the insurance. The words "any matters relating to" are significantly broader in scope than the words relating to the insurance of flats in s.35(2)(b), and could well be read as extending to matters such as reinstatement and the division of insurance moneys (see the General Note to s.35).

There is no provision for a joint application relating to a number of dwellings, though a respondent to an application can make use of s.36 to apply for the variation of other leases should the application be granted. The provisions of s.38 as to orders apply, and the effect of s.38(7) should be particularly carefully noted.

Subs. (4)
As to Pt. 2 of the Landlord and Tenant Act 1954, see the General Notes to s.21(7) and to s.35.

PART V

MANAGEMENT OF LEASEHOLD PROPERTY

GENERAL NOTE

Amendments to the service charge provisions
The provisions contained in Pt. 5 make substantial amendments to the service charge provisions contained in ss.18–30 of the Landlord and Tenant Act 1985 by extending the

provisions of the 1985 Act (which relate to flats) to other residential dwellings (s.41 and Sched. 2). S.41 and Sched. 2 amend the service charge provisions in the 1985 Act and also substitute new sections into that Act. The *main* changes thus introduced are:

(a) Ss.18–30 of the 1985 Act are extended to other residential dwellings (s.41) so that the provisions relating to variable service charges are extended to all dwellings (not only flats) (Sched. 1, para. 1).

(b) A new s.20 is substituted for s.20 of the 1985 Act and extends the application of s.20 to any works the costs of which the tenant may be required to contribute to under the terms of the lease and not just works to a particular building. Additional requirements of consultation are placed on the landlord where the premises have a recognised tenants' association (s.41 and Sched. 1, para. 3).

(c) A new s.20B is inserted into the 1985 Act which provides that a tenant is not liable to pay any service charges relating to costs incurred more than 18 months before the demand for payment unless the tenant had been notified within the period of 18 months beginning with the date when the costs were incurred that he would subsequently be required to contribute to their payment (s.41 and Sched. 1, para. 4).

(d) The provisions of s.21 of the 1985 Act relating to a request for a summary of relevant costs are amended with specific items being stipulated as having to be summarised (s.41 and Sched. 1, para. 5).

(e) If the tenants of two or more dwellings may be required under the terms of their leases to contribute to the same costs by payment of service charges any sums paid to the payee by the contributing tenants shall be held by the payee in a trust fund (s.42).

Pt. 5 also contains other important changes to the existing provisions relating to the management of residential leasehold property. A new s.30A and Sched. is added to the 1985 Act by s.43 and Sched. 3 to the Act conferring detailed rights on tenants where a service charge is payable by the tenant of a dwelling which consists of or includes an amount payable directly or indirectly for insurance.

The tenant covered by s.30A, can, *inter alia*, (i) request a summary of the insurance cover from the landlord; (ii) request to inspect the insurance policy, etc.; (iii) challenge (in the county court) the landlord's choice of insurers where the tenancy of the dwelling requires the tenant to insure the dwelling with an insurer nominated by the landlord.

A new s.30B is added to the 1985 Act by s.44 of the Act which gives recognised tenants' associations a right to serve a notice on the landlord requesting him to consult the association on matters relating to the appointment or employment by him of a managing agent for the relevant premises.

S.45 of the Act amends s.4 of the Housing Associations Act 1985 so as to extend the permissible objects of registered housing associations to the management of houses held on leases or blocks of flats.

Service charges

Amendments relating to service charges

41.—(1) Sections 18 to 30 of the 1985 Act (regulation of service charges payable by tenants) shall have effect subject to the amendments specified in Schedule 2 (which include amendments—

(a) extending the provisions of those sections to dwellings other than flats, and

(b) introducing certain additional limitations on service charges).

(2) Sections 45 to 51 of the Housing Act 1985 (which are, so far as relating to dwellings let on long leases, superseded by sections 18 to 30 of the 1985 Act as amended by Schedule 2) shall cease to have effect in relation to dwellings so let.

DEFINITIONS
"dwelling": s.60.
"flat": s.60.
"long lease": ss.59(3), 60.
"the 1985 Act": s.60.

GENERAL NOTE
This section amends that part of the Landlord and Tenant Act 1985 dealing with the regulation of service charges. The provisions are extended to dwellings other than flats and

some additional protection is conferred. The detail of the amendments is discussed in the General Note to Sched. 2. The amendments render the part of the Housing Act 1985 dealing with dwellings let on long leases otiose, and that part of the Act accordingly ceases to have effect in relation to such lettings.

Service charge contributions to be held in trust

42.—(1) This section applies where the tenants of two or more dwellings may be required under the terms of their leases to contribute to the same costs by the payment of service charges; and in this section—
"the contributing tenants" means those tenants;
"the payee" means the landlord or other person to whom any such charges are payable by those tenants under the terms of their leases;
"relevant service charges" means any such charges;
"service charge" has the meaning given by section 18(1) of the 1985 Act, except that it does not include a service charge payable by the tenant of a dwelling the rent of which is registered under Part IV of the Rent Act 1977, unless the amount registered is, in pursuance of section 71(4) of that Act, entered as a variable amount;
"tenant" does not include a tenant of an exempt landlord; and
"trust fund" means the fund, or (as the case may be) any of the funds, mentioned in subsection (2) below.

(2) Any sums paid to the payee by the contributing tenants by way of relevant service charges, and any investments representing those sums, shall (together with any income accruing thereon) be held by the payee either as a single fund or, if he thinks fit, in two or more separate funds.

(3) The payee shall hold any trust fund—
(a) on trust to defray costs incurred in connection with the matters for which the relevant service charges were payable (whether incurred by himself or by any other person), and
(b) subject to that, on trust for the persons who are the contributing tenants for the time being.

(4) Subject to subsections (6) to (8), the contributing tenants shall be treated as entitled by virtue of subsection (3)(b) to such shares in the residue of any such fund as are proportionate to their respective liabilities to pay relevant service charges.

(5) If the Secretary of State by order so provides, any sums standing to the credit of any trust fund may, instead of being invested in any other manner authorised by law, be invested in such manner as may be specified in the order; and any such order may contain such incidental, supplemental or transitional provisions as the Secretary of State considers appropriate in connection with the order.

(6) On the termination of the lease of a contributing tenant the tenant shall not be entitled to any part of any trust fund, and (except where subsection (7) applies) any part of any such fund which is attributable to relevant service charges paid under the lease shall accordingly continue to be held on the trusts referred to in subsection (3).

(7) If after the termination of any such lease there are no longer any contributing tenants, any trust fund shall be dissolved as at the date of the termination of the lease, and any assets comprised in the fund immediately before its dissolution shall—
(a) if the payee is the landlord, be retained by him for his own use and benefit, and
(b) in any other case, be transferred to the landlord by the payee.

(8) Subsections (4), (6) and (7) shall have effect in relation to a contributing tenant subject to any express terms of his lease which relate to the distribution, either before or (as the case may be) at the termination

of the lease, of amounts attributable to relevant service charges paid under its terms (whether the lease was granted before or after the commencement of this section).

(9) Subject to subsection (8), the provisions of this section shall prevail over the terms of any express or implied trust created by a lease so far as inconsistent with those provisions, other than an express trust so created before the commencement of this section.

DEFINITIONS
"dwelling": s.60.
"exempt landlord": ss.58(1), 60.
"landlord": ss.59(2), 60.
"lease": ss.59(1), 60.
"the 1985 Act": s.60.
"tenant": s.59(2).

GENERAL NOTE
This section follows from the Nugee Committee's consideration of the problems of service charges and sinking funds. Two related problems arise—to whom do such funds belong and how are they taxed? This section attempts to address itself to both these problems.

The section applies where the tenants of two or more dwellings may be required under the terms of their leases to contribute to the same costs by the payment of service charges. Thus the section is not confined to service charges in flats. "Service charges" are defined by reference to s.18 of the Landlord and Tenant Act 1985. The relevant definition is as follows (as amended by s.41 and Sched. 2 of the 1987 Act):

> "service charge" means an amount payable by a tenant of a [dwelling] as part of or in addition to the rent—
>> (a) which is payable, directly or indirectly, for services, repairs, maintenance or insurance or the landlord's costs of management, and
>> (b) the whole or part of which varies or may vary according to the relevant costs.

"Costs" are defined as including overheads (s.18(3)) and "relevant costs" as "the costs or estimated costs incurred or to be incurred by or on behalf of the landlord, or a superior landlord, in connection with the matters for which the service charge is payable" (s.18(2)). The obligation to pay must derive from the lease: thus the terms of the lease must be the starting point (see *Embassy Court Residents' Association* v. *Lipman* (1984) 271 E.G. 545; *Boldmark* v. *Cohen* [1986] 1 E.G.L.R. 47; *Rapid Results College* v. *Angell* [1986] 1 E.G.L.R. 53; *Mullaney* v. *Maybourne Grange (Croydon) Management Co.* [1986] 1 E.G.L.R. 70). However, it is irrelevant whether the charge is levied as rent or otherwise. For the purposes of this of this Part of the Act the definition of "service charge" excludes sums payable by tenants where a fair rent has been registered under Pt. 4 of the Rent Act 1977, unless the service charge element is reflected in a variable rent registered under s.71(4) of the Rent Act.

Funds held on trust
Subss. (2) and (3) provide that sums paid by way of service charges (whether to the landlord or to some other person, such as a management company) are to be held by the payee on trust, together with any investments representing those sums and any interest accruing. The trust fund is to be held primarily to defray the relevant costs and, subject to that, on trust for the contributing tenants for the time being. This trust prevails over any express or implied trust created by a lease so far as it is inconsistent, other than an express trust created before the commencment of the section (subs. (9)). As to trusts arising by implication, see *Re Chelsea Cloisters* (1980) 41 P. & C.R. 98 and *Frobisher (Second Investments)* v. *Kiloran Trust Co.* [1980] 1 W.L.R. 425. The advantage of a trust is that it protects the fund from creditors in the event of the payee's insolvency. Further, it gives the beneficiaries the ability to trace funds in the event of misappropriation and provides a remedy under trust law against the trustee for breach of trust.

The ordinary rules of trust investment will apply to the funds, but power is reserved to the Secretary of State to make provision by order for other means of investment. Though some service charge funds are held in the long term as sinking funds for major repairs and similar contingencies, others will only be held on a short term basis and so the ordinary investment rules would be inappropriate. The payee may hold moneys in two or more separate funds if he thinks fit (subs. (2)).

Shares in fund

Subs. (4) provides that the contributing tenants shall be entitled to shares in the residue of the trust in proportion to their respective liabilities to pay relevant service charges. The subsection must be read subject to the specific provisions dealing with the termination of leases and the dissolution of funds (subss. (6) and (7)) and also the express terms of the lease (subs. (8)).

Entitlement is determined according to liability to pay rather than actual payment, and "contributing tenant" is defined in similar terms. Thus (sensibly enough) a tenant taking an assignment of a lease will become entitled to a share in the trust fund, and (more surprisingly) a tenant who has failed to meet his obligations to contribute will nonetheless be entitled to a share in the fund proportionate to what he should have contributed.

Termination of lease

By subs. (6), where a lease is terminated (as by forfeiture, surrender, effluxion of time or otherwise), the tenant is not entitled to any part of the fund. However, it is possible for a lease to make express provision for repayment of a proportion of the fund in such circumstances (subs. (8)).

Dissolution of trust fund

Where the termination of a lease or leases means that there are no longer any contributing tenants, the trust fund is dissolved, and the landlord is entitled absolutely to any remaining assets: subs. (7). Again, the lease may make express provision to the contrary.

Other problems

There are a number of other problems not expressly covered by the section. There is no express obligation on a landlord to transfer the trust fund to the purchaser upon a sale of the reversion. No perpetuity period is specified for the trust. No provision is made for what is to happen where the leases remain in existence but the fund cannot be applied for its primary purpose; *e.g.* where the building is destroyed and not reinstated. Presumably, if the primary trust stated in subs. (3)(a) failed, the contributing tenants for the time being as the beneficiaries could together, under the rule in *Saunders* v. *Vautier* (1841) 1 Beav. 115, put an end to the trust and distribute the assets between them. What is to be done if the tenants cannot agree on this course is less clear, though there is no reason why the lease should not provide for this eventuality.

Taxation

The tax implications of sinking funds are extremely complex and are capable of many permutations and erratic results. For useful summaries, see the Nugee Report, Annex 4; [1986] L.S.Gaz. April 9, 1057; [1986] L.S.Gaz. July 9, 2153 (R.W. Maas); [1982] 3 *Property Law Bulletin* 13 (P. C. Soares). S.42 was said to have been drafted with a careful eye on the tax consequences (see *Hansard*, H.C. Vol. 115, col. 595). However, it is in no sense the "coherent and comprehensive tax code" advocated by the Nugee Committee (para. 7.4.8). The main advantage of holding sinking funds on trust is that the money paid no longer constitutes taxable income in the hands of the landlord under Schedule A or D. Instead it will be taxable as trust income, which is likely to avoid some anomalies. However, where payments are made to a trust the position is far from being free of doubt. How the payment is taxable will depend on its character in the hands of the trustees as recipients, and it is not clear whether the payments are of a capital or income nature and, if income, under which Schedule or Case (if any) they are taxable (see M. Gammie, *Land Taxation* (1986), para. B2.042). Income from interest on the trust fund will be liable to tax at the basic rate and also (presumably) to the surcharge on trust income under the Finance Act 1973, s.16. The most advantageous situation may be for the contributions to be paid not to the landlord but to a management company owned by the tenants for the time being—here the principle of mutuality will mean that the company will incur no tax liability on the contributions (see M. Gammie, *op. cit.*, para. B2.062 and *Styles* v. *New York Life Insurance Company* (1889) 2 T.C. 460).

As well as the problems of income tax, service charge contributions may also require consideration of capital allowances and value added tax.

Insurance
Rights of tenants with respect to insurance

43.—(1) The following section shall be inserted after section 30 of the 1985 Act—

"Insurance

Rights of tenants with respect to insurance
    30A. The Schedule to this Act (which confers on tenants certain rights with respect to the insurance of their dwellings) shall have effect."

(2) Schedule 3 to this Act shall be added to the 1985 Act as the Schedule to that Act.

DEFINITION
"the 1985 Act": s.60.

GENERAL NOTE
    This section adds a new section and Schedule to the Landlord and Tenant Act 1985. Tenants of dwellings are given additional rights in relation to service charges which include amounts payable in respect of insurance. The details of the provisions is discussed in the General Note to Sched. 3.

Managing agents

Recognised tenants' associations to be consulted about managing agents
    44. The following section shall be inserted in the 1985 Act after the section 30A inserted by section 43—

"Managing agents

Recognised tenants' associations to be consulted about managing agents
    30B.—(1) A recognised tenants' association may at any time serve a notice on the landlord requesting him to consult the association in accordance with this section on matters relating to the appointment or employment by him of a managing agent for any relevant premises.
    (2) Where, at the time when any such notice is served by a recognised tenants' association, the landlord does not employ any managing agent for any relevant premises, the landlord shall, before appointing such a managing agent, serve on the association a notice specifying—
    (a) the name of the proposed managing agent;
    (b) the landlord's obligations to the tenants represented by the association which it is proposed that the managing agent should be required to discharge on his behalf; and
    (c) a period of not less than one month beginning with the date of service of the notice within which the association may make observations on the proposed appointment.
    (3) Where, at the time when a notice is served under subsection (1) by a recognised tenants' association, the landlord employs a managing agent for any relevant premises, the landlord shall, within the period of one month beginning with the date of service of that notice, serve on the association a notice specifying—
    (a) the landlord's obligations to the tenants represented by the association which the managing agent is required to discharge on his behalf; and
    (b) a reasonable period within which the association may make observations on the manner in which the managing agent has been discharging those obligations, and on the desirability of his continuing to discharge them.
    (4) Subject to subsection (5), a landlord who has been served with a notice by an association under subsection (1) shall, so long as he employs a managing agent for any relevant premises—
    (a) serve on that association at least once in every five years a notice specifying—

(i) any change occurring since the date of the last notice served by him on the association under this section in the obligations which the managing agent has been required to discharge on his behalf; and

(ii) a reasonable period within which the association may make observations on the manner in which the managing agent has discharged those obligations since that date, and on the desirability of his continuing to discharge them;

(b) serve on that association, whenever he proposes to appoint any new managing agent for any relevant premises, a notice specifying the matters mentioned in paragraphs (a) to (c) of subsection (2).

(5) A landlord shall not, by virtue of a notice served by an association under subsection (1), be required to serve on the association a notice under subsection (4)(a) or (b) if the association subsequently serves on the landlord a notice withdrawing its request under subsection (1) to be consulted by him.

(6) Where—

(a) a recognised tenants' association has served a notice under subsection (1) with respect to any relevant premises, and

(b) the interest of the landlord in those premises becomes vested in a new landlord,

that notice shall cease to have effect with respect to those premises (without prejudice to the service by the association on the new landlord of a fresh notice under that subsection with respect to those premises).

(7) Any notice served by a landlord under this section shall specify the name and the address in the United Kingdom of the person to whom any observations made in pursuance of the notice are to be sent; and the landlord shall have regard to any such observations that are received by that person within the period specified in the notice.

(8) In this section—

"landlord", in relation to a recognised tenants' association, means the immediate landlord of the tenants represented by the association or a person who has a right to enforce payment of service charges payable by any of those tenants;

"managing agent", in relation to any relevant premises, means an agent of the landlord appointed to discharge any of the landlord's obligations to the tenants represented by the recognised tenants' association in question which relate to the management by him of those premises; and

"tenant" includes a statutory tenant;

and for the purposes of this section any premises (whether a building or not) are relevant premises in relation to a recognised tenants' association if any of the tenants represented by the association may be required under the terms of their leases to contribute by the payment of service charges to costs relating to those premises."

DEFINITION
"the 1985 Act": s.60.

GENERAL NOTE
The new s.30B inserted into the Landlord and Tenant Act 1985 gives recognised tenants' associations (defined in s.29 of the 1985 Act) rights of consultation on matters relating to the appointment or employment of managing agents.

The section applies to any premises where any of the tenants represented by the association may be required by the terms of their leases to contribute to the costs of the premises by way of service charge (see General Note to s.42 for the definition of "service charge").

The association may serve notice on the landlord requesting consultation in accordance with the section.

The landlord shall then:

(i) before appointing a managing agent serve notice on the association specifying the name of the proposed agent and the obligations which the agent is to discharge on the landlord's behalf (subs. (2)). A period of not less than one month beginning with the date of service should be specified within which the association may make observations on the proposed appointment. (For the meaning of "month" see *Dodds* v. *Walker* [1981] 1 W.L.R. 1027; *Riley (E.J.) Investments* v. *Eurostile Holdings* [1985] 1 W.L.R. 1139; *Manor-Like* v. *Le Vitas Travel Agency and Consultancy Services* [1986] 1 E.G.L.R. 79—applying the "corresponding date" rule);

(ii) where a managing agent is already employed, within one month (see above) serve on the association a notice specifying the landlord's obligations which the agent is required to discharge and also a reasonable period within which the association may make observations as to the agent's performance and the desirability of retaining him (subs. (3));

(iii) so long as an agent continues to be employed, serve at least once every five years a notice specifying any changes in the obligations performed by the agent and a reasonable period for the association's observations (subs. (4)(a));

(iv) when a new agent is to be appointed, serve notice specifying the matters at (i) above (subs. (4)(b)).

If observations are received within the specified period, the landlord is to "have regard" to them (s.44(7)). In practice, unless the landlord chooses to explain his decisions in a reasoned fashion, it would appear to be very difficult to demonstrate that he had failed to have regard to the observations.

Management by registered housing associations

Extension of permissible objects of registered housing associations as regards the management of leasehold property

45.—(1) Section 4 of the Housing Associations Act 1985 (eligibility for registration) shall be amended as follows.

(2) In subsection (3) (permissible additional purposes or objects), after the paragraph (dd) inserted by section 19 of the Housing and Planning Act 1986 there shall be inserted—

"(ddd) managing houses which are held on leases (not being houses falling within subsection (2)(a) or (b)) or blocks of flats;".

(3) After that subsection there shall be inserted—

"(4) In subsection (3)(ddd) "block of flats" means a building—

(a) containing two or more flats which are held on leases or other lettings; and

(b) occupied or intended to be occupied wholly or mainly for residential purposes."

(4) The amendments made by this section shall not extend to Scotland.

GENERAL NOTE

This section makes amendments to the statutory conditions of eligibility for registration with the Housing Corporation. To the list of the permissible additional purposes or objects contained in s.4(3) of the Housing Associations Act 1985 is added the management of houses or blocks of flats. For this purpose a new definition of "block of flats" is given. It must be a building containing at least two flats held on leases, and the building must be occupied or intended to be occupied wholly or mainly for residential purposes: borderline cases may arise in the case of flats over shop premises, in which case it will no doubt be relevant to consider the respective floor areas (*cf. Tandon* v. *Trustees of Spurgeons Homes* [1982] A.C. 755). The management of houses falling within s.4(2)(a) or (b) of the 1985 Act is excluded, since the management of such premises is already among the objects for which the association must be established in order to be eligible for registration under s.4.

PART VI

INFORMATION TO BE FURNISHED TO TENANTS

GENERAL NOTE

Pt. 6 extends a residential tenant's rights to information about his landlord's name and address. S.47 provides that where any written demand for rent (or other sums payable to the landlord under the terms of the tenancy) is given to a tenant such a demand must contain the name and address of the landlord (or, if that address is not in England and Wales, an address at which notices may be served on the landlord by the tenant). If such a demand does not contain the prescribed information, any part of the amount demanded which consists of a service charge shall be treated as not being due until such information is furnished.

A landlord of residential premises is under a duty to furnish the tenant with an address in England and Wales at which notices may be served on him by the tenant (s.48). If the landlord does not comply with this duty any rent or service charge otherwise due from the tenant to the landlord shall be treated as not being due until the duty is complied with.

S.49 amends s.196 of the Law of Property Act 1925 so as to enable a tenant to serve a notice on his landlord at an address provided in accordance with ss.47 or 48.

S.50 inserts ss.3A and 3B into the 1985 Act which provide that the former landlord will remain liable to his former tenant for any breach of covenant, condition or agreement under the tenancy until such time as he notifies the tenant in writing of the assignment and the name and address of the new landlord or the new landlord does so himself. A new s.112C is inserted into the Land Registration Act 1925 providing for a tenant of residential premises to have the right to inspect the Land Register to ascertain the landlord's name and address.

Application of Part VI, etc.

46.—(1) This Part applies to premises which consist of or include a dwelling and are not held under a tenancy to which Part II of the Landlord and Tenant Act 1954 applies.

(2) In this Part "service charge" has the meaning given by section 18(1) of the 1985 Act.

DEFINITIONS
    "dwelling": s.60.
    "tenancy": ss.59(1), 60.

GENERAL NOTE

Subs. (1) states the scope of Pt. 6 of the Act. As to the Landlord and Tenant Act 1954, Pt. 2, see the General Note to s.21(7).

Subs. (2). As to "service charge," see the General Note to s.42.

Landlord's name and address to be contained in demands for rent etc.

47.—(1) Where any written demand is given to a tenant of premises to which this Part applies, the demand must contain the following information, namely—

   (a) the name and address of the landlord, and
   (b) if that address is not in England and Wales, an address in England and Wales at which notices (including notices in proceedings) may be served on the landlord by the tenant.

(2) Where—

   (a) a tenant of any such premises is given such a demand, but
   (b) it does not contain any information required to be contained in it by virtue of subsection (1),

then (subject to subsection (3)) any part of the amount demanded which consists of a service charge ("the relevant amount") shall be treated for all purposes as not being due from the tenant to the landlord at any time before that information is furnished by the landlord by notice given to the tenant.

(3) The relevant amount shall not be so treated in relation to any time when, by virtue of an order of any court, there is in force an appointment of a receiver or manager whose functions include the receiving of service charges from the tenant.

(4) In this section "demand" means a demand for rent or other sums payable to the landlord under the terms of the tenancy.

DEFINITIONS
 "court": s.60.
 "landlord": ss.59(2), 60.
 "tenant": s.59(2).

GENERAL NOTE
 This section introduces a new requirement for the landlord of residential premises. Any written demand for rent or other sums payable under the terms of the tenancy must contain the landlord's name and address, and an address for service if the landlord's address is not in England and Wales. Failure to give this information renders any part of the amount demanded *consisting of a service charge* irrecoverable until the information is furnished. The right to recover rent and other sums than service charges is, by inference, not affected (for the meaning of "service charge," see s.46(2) and the General Note to s.42).

Notification by landlord of address for service of notices

48.—(1) A landlord of premises to which this Part applies shall by notice furnish the tenant with an address in England and Wales at which notices (including notices in proceedings) may be served on him by the tenant.

(2) Where a landlord of any such premises fails to comply with subsection (1), any rent or service charge otherwise due from the tenant to the landlord shall (subject to subsection (3)) be treated for all purposes as not being due from the tenant to the landlord at any time before the landlord does comply with that subsection.

(3) Any such rent or service charge shall not be so treated in relation to any time when, by virtue of an order of any court, there is in force an appointment of a receiver or manager whose functions include the receiving of rent or (as the case may be) service charges from the tenant.

DEFINITIONS
 "landlord": ss.59(2), 60.
 "notices in proceedings": s.60.
 "tenant": s.59(2).

GENERAL NOTE
 The landlord of residential premises is by this section required to notify the tenant of an address for service in England and Wales. Failure to do so renders any rent or service charge otherwise due irrecoverable until the landlord complies with the section; nor can the landlord use the failure to pay such sums as a basis for forfeiture or possession proceedings, since the sum is deemed not to be due "for all purposes."

Extension of circumstances in which notices are sufficiently served

49. In section 196 of the Law of Property Act 1925 (regulations respecting notices), any reference in subsection (3) or (4) to the last-known place of abode or business of the person to be served shall have effect, in its application to a notice to be served by a tenant on a landlord of premises to which this Part applies, as if that reference included a reference to—
   (a) the address last furnished to the tenant by the landlord in accordance with section 48, or
   (b) if no address has been so furnished in accordance with section 48,

the address last furnished to the tenant by the landlord in accordance with section 47.

DEFINITIONS
"landlord": ss.59(2), 60.
"tenant": s.59(2).

GENERAL NOTE

This section amends s.196 of the Law of Property Act 1925 so that notices served at addresses furnished under s.48 or (if no address has been furnished under s.48) s.47 are sufficiently served. This is in addition to, and not in substitution for, the other modes of service recognised by the section: *i.e.* if the landlord's "last-known place of abode or business" is different to the s.48 address, it seems that service at either would be good—but service at the s.48 address will obviously be safer as precluding argument as to what was in fact the last known place of abode or business (see *Price* v. *West London Building Society* [1964] 1 W.L.R. 616).

Continuation of former landlord's liability to tenant where no notice of assignment

50. In section 3 of the 1985 Act (duty to inform tenant of assignment of landlord's interest) the following subsections shall be inserted after subsection (3)—

"(3A) The person who was the landlord under the tenancy immediately before the assignment ("the old landlord") shall be liable to the tenant in respect of any breach of any covenant, condition or agreement under the tenancy occurring before the end of the relevant period in like manner as if the interest assigned were still vested in him; and where the new landlord is also liable to the tenant in respect of any such breach occurring within that period, he and the old landlord shall be jointly and severally liable in respect of it.

(3B) In subsection (3A) "the relevant period" means the period beginning with the date of the assignment and ending with the date when—

(a) notice in writing of the assignment, and of the new landlord's name and address, is given to the tenant by the new landlord (whether in accordance with subsection (1) or not), or

(b) notice in writing of the assignment, and of the new landlord's name and last-known address, is given to the tenant by the old landlord.

whichever happens first."

DEFINITIONS
"1985 Act": s.60.
"landlord": s.59(2).
"tenant": s.59(2).

GENERAL NOTE

This section supplements and strengthens the duty imposed on a landlord of a dwelling by s.3 of the Landlord and Tenant Act 1985 to give notice of the assignment and of his name and address after taking an assignment of the reversion. Two new subsections, (3A) and (3B), provide that the assignor of the reversion remains liable to the tenant for breaches of covenant or contract under the tenancy as though the reversion were still vested in him. His liability is joint and several with that of the new landlord. The old landlord's liability continues until either the new landlord gives notice of the assignment and of his name and address, or the old landlord gives the notice. Even then the old landlord remains liable for breaches committed between the assignment and the date on which notice was given. Since the new landlord is not obliged to give the notice until the next rent day following the assignment or for two months, whichever is longer, the assigning landlord would be wise to safeguard his position by giving notice and the relevant information to the tenant immediately he assigns.

Right of tenant to search proprietorship register for landlord's name and address

51.—(1) In section 112(1) of the Land Registration Act 1925 (inspection of register and other documents at Land Registry), for "sections 112A and 112AA" there shall be substituted "sections 112A, 112AA and 112C".

(2) The following section shall be inserted after section 112B of that Act—

"Right of residential tenant to search for landlord's name and address
112C.—(1) For the purpose of enabling him to ascertain the name and address of his landlord, the tenant of premises to which this section applies shall (subject to subsection (3)) have a right, on payment of a fee and in accordance with the prescribed procedure, to inspect and make copies of, and take extracts from, any part of any register kept in the custody of the registrar which contains the name and address of the proprietor of any registered land containing those premises.

(2) This section applies to premises which consist of or include a dwelling and are not held under a tenancy to which Part II of the Landlord and Tenant Act 1954 (business tenancies) applies.

(3) The registrar may refuse to allow a tenant to exercise his right of inspection under subsection (1) above in relation to any registered land if he has reason to believe that the proprietor of that land is not the landlord of the tenant.

(4) In this section—

"dwelling" means a building or part of a building occupied or intended to be occupied as a separate dwelling, together with any yard, garden, outhouses and appurtenances belonging to it or usually enjoyed with it;

"landlord" means the immediate landlord or, in relation to a statutory tenant, the person who, apart from the statutory tenancy, would be entitled to possession of the premises subject to the tenancy;

"statutory tenancy" and "statutory tenant" mean a statutory tenancy or statutory tenant within the meaning of the Rent Act 1977 or the Rent (Agriculture) Act 1976; and

"tenant" includes a statutory tenant."

GENERAL NOTE

A new section, 112C, is inserted into the Land Registration Act 1925. The new section constitutes a further and limited exception to the general principle that the register may only be inspected with the registered proprietor's authority. A tenant of a dwelling (defined as in s. 60) may inspect the register for the purpose of ascertaining the name and address of his landlord, subject to payment of a fee and in accordance with the prescribed procedure. As to conditions of inspection, see Land Registration Rules 1925, S.I. 1925 No. 1093, r.291. The relevant part of the register will usually be the proprietorship register, which contains the name, address and description of the registered proprietor. Every registered proprietor must furnish to the registrar a place of address in the United Kingdom (Land Registration Act 1925 s.79(1)) and any person may if he wishes have up to three addresses entered in the register, including if he thinks fit the address of his solicitor (Ruoff & Roper, *Registered Conveyancing* (5th ed., 1986), pages 22–23). Unfortunately, there is of course no guarantee that the addresses stated are current, since a proprietor is under no obligation to notify the registrar of changes of address.

By subs. (3) the registrar may refuse inspection if he has reason to believe that the proprietor of the land is not the landlord of the tenant.

PART VII

GENERAL

GENERAL NOTE
Pt. 7 of the Act provides, *inter alia*, for
  (a) the county court to have jurisdiction to deal with any question arising out of the operation of Pts. 1 to 4 of the Act, except those to be dealt with by a rent assessment committee, and any question under ss.42, 46–48 (s.52);
  (b) any power of the Secretary of State to make an order or regulations under the Act is to be exercisable by statutory instrument (s.53);
  (c) s.54 makes provision for the service of any notice required or authorised to be served under the Act.

Jurisdiction of county courts

52.—(1) A county court shall have jurisdiction to hear and determine any question arising under any provision to which this section applies (other than a question falling within the jurisdiction of a rent assessment committee by virtue of section 13(1) or 31(1)).

(2) This section applies to—
  (a) any provision of Parts I to IV;
  (b) any provision of section 42; and
  (c) any provision of sections 46 to 48.

(3) Where any proceedings under any provision to which this section applies are being taken in a county court, the county court shall have jurisdiction to hear and determine any other proceedings joined with those proceedings, notwithstanding that the other proceedings would, apart from this subsection, be outside the court's jurisdiction.

(4) If a person takes any proceedings under any such provision in the High Court he shall not be entitled to recover any more costs of those proceedings than those to which he would have been entitled if the proceedings had been taken in a county court; and in any such case the taxing master shall have the same power of directing on what county court scale costs are to be allowed, and of allowing any item of costs, as the judge would have had if the proceedings had been taken in a county court.

(5) Subsection (4) shall not apply where the purpose of taking the proceedings in the High Court was to enable them to be joined with any proceedings already pending before that court (not being proceedings taken under any provision to which this section applies).

DEFINITION
"rent assessment committee": s.60.

GENERAL NOTE
This section confers jurisdiction on county courts to hear and determine questions arising under Pts. 1–4 of the Act, s.42 (trusts of service charge contributions) and ss. 46–48 (information to be given to tenants). Questions falling within the jurisdiction of rent assessment committees under ss.13(1) and 31(1) are excluded from the county court jurisdiction. Thus questions as to the rateable value of the relevant premises are irrelevant to jurisdiction. Furthermore, a county court also has jurisdiction in any proceedings joined with proceedings to which the section applies (s.52(3)), *e.g.* a claim for damages or an application for a mandatory injunction or specific performance.

Subs. (4) provides that a person taking proceedings under the Act in the High Court in a case where a county court has jurisdiction shall be entitled only to county court costs. Subs. (5) provides that this limitation on costs does not apply where the purpose of taking the proceedings in the High Court was to enable them to be joined with proceedings already pending before the High Court. Presumably this is a transitional provision aimed at proceedings pending when the Act comes into force. Otherwise the objective of channelling proceedings under the Act into the county courts could easily be circumvented by first issuing proceedings for damages or other relief in the High Court and then joining the proceedings under the Act, especially in view of the extended county court jurisdiction under subs. (3), mentioned above.

Regulations and orders

53.—(1) Any power of the Secretary of State to make an order or regulations under this Act shall be exercisable by statutory instrument and may be exercised so as to make different provision for different cases, including different provision for different areas.

(2) A statutory instrument containing—

(a) an order made under section 1(5), 25(6), 42(5) or 55, or

(b) any regulations made under section 13(2) (including any made under that provision as it applies for the purposes of section 31) or under section 20(4),

shall be subject to annulment in pursuance of a resolution of either House of Parliament.

GENERAL NOTE

This section provides that the power of the Secretary of State to make orders or regulations under the Act is exercisable by statutory instrument. Orders and regulations made under specified provisions are subject to annulment by resolution of either House.

Notices

54.—(1) Any notice required or authorised to be served under this Act—

(a) shall be in writing; and

(b) may be sent by post.

(2) Any notice purporting to be a notice served under any provision of Part I or III by the requisite majority of any qualifying tenants (as defined for the purposes of that provision) shall specify the names of all of the persons by whom it is served and the addresses of the flats of which they are qualifying tenants.

(3) The Secretary of State may by regulations prescribe—

(a) the form of any notices required or authorised to be served under or in pursuance of any provision of Parts I to III, and

(b) the particulars which any such notices must contain (whether in addition to, or in substitution for, any particulars required by virtue of the provision in question).

(4) Subsection (3)(b) shall not be construed as authorising the Secretary of State to make regulations under subsection (3) varying either of the periods specified in section 5(2)(which accordingly can only be varied by regulations under section 20(4)).

DEFINITION

"flats": s.60.

GENERAL NOTE

Notices under the Act must be in writing and may be served by post. The Secretary of State may make regulations prescribing the form and particulars of such notices. Where regulations as to form are made, a court may be willing to overlook a departure from the proper form provided the intention underlying the notice is clear in substance and that the notice does not seriously mislead the recipient (cf. *Lewis* v. *M.T.C. (Cars)* [1975] 1 W.L.R. 457; *Philipson-Stow* v. *Trevor Square* (1980) 257 E.G. 1262; *Morris* v. *Patel* (1986) 281 E.G. 419; *Barclays Bank* v. *Ascott* [1961] 1 W.L.R. 717; *Morrow* v. *Nadeem* [1986] 1 W.L.R. 1381).

Service by post is permitted rather than mandatory. It would seem prudent to use the recorded delivery service (Recorded Delivery Service Act 1962; and see *Chiswell* v. *Griffon Land & Estates Ltd.* [1975] 1 W.L.R. 1181 and *Italica Holdings S.A.* v. *Bayadea* [1985] 1 E.G.L.R. 70).

Application to Isles of Scilly

55. This Act shall apply to the Isles of Scilly subject to such exceptions, adaptations and modifications as the Secretary of State may by order direct.

Crown land

56.—(1) This Act shall apply to a tenancy from the Crown if there has ceased to be a Crown interest in the land subject to it.

(2) A variation of any such tenancy effected by or in pursuance of an order under section 38 shall not, however, be treated as binding on the Crown, as a predecessor in title under the tenancy, by virtue of section 39(1).

(3) Where there exists a Crown interest in any land subject to a tenancy from the Crown and the person holding that tenancy is himself the landlord under any other tenancy whose subject-matter comprises the whole or part of that land, this Act shall apply to that other tenancy, and to any derivative sub-tenancy, notwithstanding the existence of that interest.

(4) For the purposes of this section "tenancy from the Crown" means a tenancy of land in which there is, or has during the subsistence of the tenancy been, a Crown interest superior to the tenancy, and "Crown interest" means—

(a) an interest comprised in the Crown Estate;
(b) an interest belonging to Her Majesty in right of the Duchy of Lancaster;
(c) an interest belonging to the Duchy of Cornwall;
(d) any other interest belonging to a government department or held on behalf of Her Majesty for the purposes of a government department.

GENERAL NOTE

This section makes provision as to Crown Land. The Act will not bind the Crown (see *Ministry of Agriculture, Fisheries and Food* v. *Jenkins* [1963] 2 Q.B. 317). However, the Act applies to tenancies originally granted by the Crown, or where a Crown interest is superior to the tenancy has existed, provided the Crown interest in the land has ceased (subs. (1)). Further, the Act applies to tenancies and derivative sub-tenancies where the landlord himself holds under a tenancy from the Crown, notwithstanding the subsisting Crown interest in the land (subs. (3)).

Financial provision

57. There shall be paid out of money provided by Parliament any increase attributable to this Act in the sums payable out of money so provided under any other Act.

Exempt landlords and resident landlords

58.—(1) In this Act "exempt landlord" means a landlord who is one of the following bodies, namely—

(a) a district, county or London borough council, the Common Council of the City of London, the Council of the Isles of Scilly, the Inner London Education Authority, or a joint authority established by Part IV of the Local Government Act 1985;
(b) the Commission for the New Towns or a development corporation established by an order made (or having effect as if made) under the New Towns Act 1981;
(c) an urban development corporation within the meaning of Part XVI of the Local Government, Planning and Land Act 1980;
(d) the Development Board for Rural Wales;

(e) the Housing Corporation;

(f) a housing trust (as defined in section 6 of the Housing Act 1985) which is a charity;

(g) a registered housing association, or an unregistered housing association which is a fully mutual housing association, within the meaning of the Housing Associations Act 1958; or

(h) an authority established under section 10 of the Local Government Act 1985 (joint arrangements for waste disposal functions).

(2) For the purposes of this Act the landlord of any premises consisting of the whole or part of a building is a resident landlord of those premises at any time if—

(a) the premises are not, and do not form part of, a purpose-built block of flats; and

(b) at that time the landlord occupies a flat contained in the premises as his only or principal residence; and

(c) he has so occupied such a flat throughout a period of not less than 12 months ending with that time.

(3) In subsection (2) "purpose-built block of flats" means a building which contained as constructed, and contains, two or more flats.

GENERAL NOTE
Subs. (1)
This subsection defines the bodies which are exempt landlords for the purposes of the Act. Pts. 1, 2 and 3 of the Act do not apply to premises with an exempt landlord (ss.1(4), 21(3)(a) and 25(5)(a)). In *Parker* v. *Camden London Borough Council* [1986] Ch. 162 the Court of Appeal held that it would be improper to appoint a manager to assume duties and responsibilities placed upon a public body (in that case a local authority) by Parliament (see *Gardner* v. *London, Chatham and Dover Railway Co. (No. 1)* (1867) L.R. 2 Ch.App. 201). This principle may continue to be of importance, since it will remain open to a tenant of an exempt landlord to seek appointment of a receiver and manager under s.17 of the Supreme Court Act 1981 (see General Note to s.21).

Subs. (2)
This subsection defines the term "resident landlord." Pts. 1, 2 and 3 do not apply in the case of a resident landlord (ss. 1(4), 21(3)(a) and 25(5)(a)). In order to be a resident landlord, the landlord must occupy a flat contained in the relevant premises as his only or principal residence, and must have occupied "such a flat" (*semble*, not necessarily the same one) throughout the previous 12 months. Further, the premises in question must not be, or form part of, a purpose-built block of flats (see subs. (3), below). The question of occupation as an only or principal residence seems capable of throwing up many problems similar to those encountered under provisions in the Rent Act 1977 and the Leasehold Reform Act 1967 imposing analogous requirements. Possible examples include the landlord who does not occupy the whole of his or her flat but who sub-lets part (*Berkeley* v. *Papadoyannis* [1954] 2 Q.B. 149; *Herbert* v. *Byrne* [1964] 1 W.L.R. 519; *Regalian Securities* v. *Ramsden* [1981] 1 W.L.R. 611; *Harris* v. *Swick Securities* [1969] 1 W.L.R. 1604) and the landlord who does not reside personally but who claims to occupy the flat through a member of his family or other agent (*Brown* v. *Draper* [1944] K.B.309; *Old Gate Estates* v. *Alexander* [1950] 1 K.B. 311; *Wabe* v. *Taylor* [1952] 2 Q.B. 735 and cf. *Robson* v. *Headland* (1948) 64 T.L.R. 596; *Vaughan* v. *Vaughan* [1953] 1 Q.B. 762; *Thompson* v. *Ward* [1953] 2 Q.B. 153; *Heath Estates* v. *Burchell* (1979) 251 E.G. 1173). The question of residence is likely to be treated as one of fact and degree. Under both the Rent Act and the Leasehold Reform Act it is clear that it is possible to occupy premises during a period of physical absence from them, if it can be shown that there is an intention to return, though the longer the period of absence the more difficult this will be to demonstrate. Relevant authorities include: *Poland* v. *Earl Cadogan* [1980] 3 All E.R. 544; *Brown* v. *Brash* [1948] 2 K.B. 247; *Gofor Investments* v. *Roberts* (1975) 29 P. & C.R. 366; *Atyeo* v. *Fardoe* (1978) 37 P. & C.R. 494; *Richards* v. *Green* (1983) 268 E.G. 443; *Duke* v. *Porter* (1987) 19 H.L.R. 1. However, in making use of these decisions, it is important to have regard to the actual words used in the statute, as the concepts of occupation and residence may bear different shades of emphasis according to their statutory context (see *Poland* v. *Earl Cadogan* [1980] 3 All E.R 544 at 548). A related question can arise in the case of the landlord with two or more homes. It is possible to occupy two dwelling houses as residences, dividing one's time between the two (*Hampstead*

Way Investments v. *Lewis-Weare* [1985] 1 W.L.R. 164). However, for the purposes of the subsection the landlord must not only occupy the flat as a residence, but as "his only or principal residence." Which of two residences is the "principal residence" is a potentially very difficult question of fact, analogous to the question under the Leasehold Reform Act 1967 as to which is the "main residence" (as to which, see *Byrne* v. *Rowbotham* (1969) 210 E.G. 823; *Fowell* v. *Radford* (1970) 21 P. & C.R. 99; *Baron* v. *Philips* (1978) 38 P. & C.R. 91).

Subs. (3)

This subsection defines "purpose-built block of flats." The expression appears in a similar context in the Rent Act 1977, where it receives a substantially identical definition (Rent Act 1977, Sched. 2, para. 4). The building must have contained, as originally constructed, at least two flats. Thus a single dwelling house subsequently divided into flats would not be a purpose-built block of flats (see generally *Barnes* v. *Gorsuch* (1982) 43 P. & C.R. 294). Nor, *a fortiori*, would a building originally constructed for a non-residential purpose, such as a mill or warehouse, and subsequently converted into flats.

Meaning of "lease", "long lease" and related expressions

59.—(1) In this Act "lease" and "tenancy" have the same meaning; and both expressions include—

(a) a sub-lease or sub-tenancy, and

(b) an agreement for a lease or tenancy (or for a sub-lease or sub-tenancy).

(2) The expressions "landlord" and "tenant", and references to letting, to the grant of a lease or to covenants or the terms of a lease shall be construed accordingly.

(3) In this Act "long lease" means—

(a) a lease granted for a term certain exceeding 21 years, whether or not it is (or may become) terminable before the end of that term by notice given by the tenant or by re-entry or forfeiture;

(b) a lease for a term fixed by law under a grant with a covenant or obligation for perpetual renewal, other than a lease by sub-demise from one which is not a long lease; or

(c) a lease granted in pursuance of Part V of the Housing Act 1985 (the right to buy).

GENERAL NOTE
Subs. (3)

This subsection defines "long lease". The definition is similar to that of "long tenancy" in the Leasehold Reform Act 1967, s.3, though there are some important differences. In determining whether a lease was granted for "a term certain exceeding 21 years" the term will be taken as running from the date of execution of the lease, not from any earlier date on which the term is expressed to commence (*Roberts* v. *Church Commissioners for England* [1972] 1 Q.B. 278). In considering s.3 of the 1967 Act the Court of Appeal held in *Eton College* v. *Bard* [1983] 3 W.L.R. 231 that the word "certain" makes it clear that a tenancy from year to year is not within the definition and that in calculating the length of the term any option to take a lease for a further term is to be disregarded. The fact that a lease is or may become terminable before the end of its term "by notice given by the tenant or by re-entry or forfeiture" does not prevent it being a long lease (s.59(3)(a)). This wording differs significantly from that employed in the Leasehold Reform Act and considered in *Eton College* v. *Bard*—"by notice given by *or to* the tenant or by re-entry, forfeiture *or otherwise*." In that case, the Court of Appeal held that "terminable" was capable of bearing both a transitive and an intransitive meaning and that consequently the words "or otherwise" could apply to a lease expressed to terminate upon ceasing to be vested in a member of a specified tenants' association. However, the words "or otherwise" do not appear in the 1987 Act, and therefore a lease of the type under consideration in *Eton College* v. *Bard* would not seem to qualify as a long lease under the Act.

General interpretation

60.—(1) In this Act—

"the 1985 Act" means the Landlord and Tenant Act 1985;

"charity" means a charity within the meaning of the Charities Act 1960, and "charitable purposes", in relation to a charity, means charitable purposes whether of that charity or of that charity and other charities;

"common parts", in relation to any building or part of a building, includes the structure and exterior of that building or part and any common facilities within it;

"the court" means the High Court or a county court;

"dwelling" means a building or part of a building occupied or intended to be occupied as a separate dwelling, together with any yard, garden, outhouses and appurtenances belonging to it or usually enjoyed with it;

"exempt landlord" has the meaning given by section 58(1);

"flat" means a separate set of premises, whether or not on the same floor, which—

(a) forms part of a building, and

(b) is divided horizontally from some other part of that building, and

(c) is constructed or adapted for use for the purposes of a dwelling;

"functional land", in relation to a charity, means land occupied by the charity, or by trustees for it, and wholly or mainly used for charitable purposes;

"landlord" (except for the purposes of Part I) means the immediate landlord or, in relation to a statutory tenant, the person who, apart from the statutory tenancy, would be entitled to possession of the premises subject to the tenancy;

"lease" and related expressions shall be construed in accordance with section 59(1) and (2);

"long lease" has the meaning given by section 59(3);

"mortgage" includes any charge or lien, and references to a mortgagee shall be construed accordingly;

"notices in proceedings" means notices or other documents served in, or in connection with, any legal proceedings;

"rent assessment committee" means a rent assessment committee constituted under Schedule 10 to the Rent Act 1977;

"resident landlord" shall be construed in accordance with section 58(2);

"statutory tenancy" and "statutory tenant" mean a statutory tenancy or statutory tenant within the meaning of the Rent Act 1977 or the Rent (Agriculture) Act 1976;

"tenancy" includes a statutory tenancy.

(2) In this Act (except in Part IV) any reference to a tenancy to which Part II of the Landlord and Tenant Act 1954 applies includes a reference to an assured tenancy (as defined in section 56(1) of the Housing Act 1980).

GENERAL NOTE
Common parts.

As to what constitutes "the structure and exterior", see *Hopwood* v. *Cannock Chase D.C.* [1975] 1 W.L.R. 373; *Brown* v. *Liverpool Corporation* [1969] 3 All E.R. 1345; *Camden Hill Towers* v. *Gardner* [1977] Q.B. 823; *Douglas-Scott* v. *Scorgie* [1984] 1 W.L.R. 716—but note that (a) one is considering what is the structure and exterior of the building or part of the building, *not* the flat within the building; (b) the "common parts" are merely said to include, not be limited to, the structure and exterior. The common parts are also said to include any common facilities within the building, and thus would include, for example, entrance halls, stairs and lifts, rubbish chutes, common drains, conduits and other service media, and communal heating equipment. It seems less clear whether parts of the building which are not put to any communal use, such as a cellar or roof void, could be regarded as common parts. Nor would common facilities outside the building (such as a garden, parking areas, or rubbish disposal facilities) seem to be "common parts", unless they can be regarded as part of the structure and exterior of the building.

Dwelling

The building or part of building must be occupied or be intended to be occupied as a separate dwelling. There seems to be no requirement that it was originally let as a separate dwelling (*cf.* Rent Act 1977 s.1 and *Wolfe* v. *Hogan* [1949] 1 K.B. 194 and *Pulleng* v. *Curran* (1982) 44 P. & C.R. 58). What matters is how the premises are occupied or how they are intended to be occupied; not how they were let. However, some of the Rent Act authorities on what constitutes "a separate dwelling" may be of use. A letting comprising a number of units of habitation will not constitute a separate dwelling (*Horford Investments* v. *Lambert* [1976] Ch. 39; *St. Catherine's College* v. *Dorling* [1980] 1 W.L.R. 66). Nor, it would appear, will a dwelling be "separate" if essential living accommodation is shared—this may be relevant in the case of sub-division of a larger building. See *Cole* v. *Harris* [1945] K.B. 474; *Neale* v. *Del Soto* [1964] K.B. 144; *Goodrich* v. *Paisner* [1957] A.C. 65. Premises where the occupant carries on only a small part of the usual activities of daily life may also be incapable of being regarded as a dwelling (see *Wright* v. *Howell* (1947) 92 S.J. 26; *Curl* v. *Angelo* [1948] 2 All E.R. 189). However, in the case of a tenant who occupies a number of rooms held under separate lease, which together make up his living accommodation, it would seem possible to aggregate the rooms (provided they are within the same building) as "part of a building" occupied as a separate dwelling. The fact that attention is focused upon occupation as opposed to letting avoids the difficulties encountered under the Rent Act in cases such as *Kavanagh* v. *Lyroudias* (1983) 269 E.G. 629 and *Hampstead Way Investments* v. *Lewis-Weare* [1985] 1 W.L.R. 164.

"Dwelling" includes any yard, garden, outhouses or appurtenances belonging to the dwelling or usually enjoyed with it. The meaning of "appurtenances" is obscure, since the word can be used in many senses. However, it appears likely that it would be construed in the same sense as that adopted by the Court of Appeal in *Methuen-Campbell* v. *Walters* [1979] Q.B. 525, as including land falling within the curtilage of the dwelling. In that case Buckley L.J. considered what that meant in practice, and concluded that the question is whether the land or items under consideration can reasonably be regarded as constituting one messuage or parcel of land, or an integral whole: ancillary buildings such as garages may therefore be regarded as "appurtenances". See also the General Note to s.38 of the Landlord and Tenant Act 1985, annotated by Andrew Arden and Siobhan McGrath.

Flat

The definition of a "flat" is a centrally important one: the most important rights conferred by the Act apply only to tenants of flats. Essentially there are four ingredients:—

  (i) a separate set of premises, whether or not on the same floor. The words "separate set" would seem to connote premises forming a distinct unit. In the vast majority of cases the flats in mansion blocks at which the Act was aimed there is unlikely to be any difficulty. However, it is easy to foresee that difficulties might arise over premises which are not entirely self contained, or where the rooms making up the flat are not physically contiguous (though they need not be on the same floor). In the first case it might be argued that the premises are not "separate", and in the second that they are not a single set (*quare* whether one room could of itself be regarded as a "set of premises", as "set" would seem to suggest a number of entities which belong together).

 (ii) the set of premises must form part of a building. This would seem straightforward enough, but what of a flat which includes a room or rooms in an adjacent building?

(iii) the set of premises must be divided horizontally from some other part of that building.

 (iv) the set of premises must be constructed or adapted for use for the purposes of a dwelling. The flat need not have been purpose-built originally; it may have been adapted as such subsequently. The purposes for which it is constructed or adapted must be those of a dwelling: see the definition of "dwelling" above. It may be noted that, whereas the essence of the definition of a dwelling is occupation as such, the essence of the definition of a flat is construction or adaptation as a dwelling. (Compare the definition of "flat" in s.30 of the Landlord and Tenant Act 1985, which is in the same terms but goes on to add "and is occupied wholly or mainly as a private dwelling.") Thus, somewhat curiously, it would seem that a flat can be such even if not a dwelling in the sense of being occupied as a dwelling, provided it was constructed or adapted for such occupation. But occupation for the purposes of a business such as to bring the premises within the scope of the Landlord and Tenant Act 1954 Pt. 2

may preclude the application of certain parts of the Act (see ss.3(1)(b), 21(7), 26(1), 35(7) and 46(1)).

Consequential amendments and repeals

61.—(1) The enactments mentioned in Schedule 4 shall have effect subject to the amendments there specified (being amendments consequential on the preceding provisions of this Act).

(2) The enactments mentioned in Schedule 5 are hereby repealed to the extent specified in the third column of that Schedule.

Short title, commencement and extent

62.—(1) This Act may be cited as the Landlord and Tenant Act 1987.

(2) This Act shall come into force on such day as the Secretary of State may by order appoint.

(3) An order under subsection (2)—

   (a) may appoint different days for different provisions or for different purposes; and

   (b) may make such transitional, incidental, supplemental or consequential provision or saving as the Secretary of State considers necessary or expedient in connection with the coming into force of any provision of this Act or the operation of any enactment which is repealed or amended by a provision of this Act during any period when the repeal or amendment is not wholly in force.

(4) This Act extends to England and Wales only.

SCHEDULES

Sections 12 and 32   SCHEDULE 1

DISCHARGE OF MORTGAGES ETC.: SUPPLEMENTARY PROVISIONS

PART I

DISCHARGE IN PURSUANCE OF PURCHASE NOTICES

Construction

1. In this Part of this Schedule—

   "the consideration payable" means the consideration payable to the new landlord for the disposal by him of the property referred to in section 12(4);

   "the new landlord" has the same meaning as in section 12, and accordingly includes any person to whom that section applies by virtue of section 16(2) or (3); and

   "the nominated person" means the person or persons nominated as mentioned in section 12(1).

Duty of nominated person to redeem mortgages

2.—(1) Where in accordance with section 12(4)(a) an instrument will operate to discharge any property from a charge to secure the payment of money, it shall be the duty of the nominated person to apply the consideration payable, in the first instance, in or towards the redemption of any such charge (and, if there are more than one, then according to their priorities).

(2) Where sub-paragraph (1) applies to any charge or charges, then if (and only if) the consideration payable is applied by the nominated person in accordance with that sub-paragraph or paid into court by him in accordance with paragraph 4, the instrument in question shall operate as mentioned in sub-paragraph (1) notwithstanding that the consideration payable is insufficient to enable the charge or charges to be redeemed in its or their entirety.

(3) Subject to sub-paragraph (4), sub-paragraph (1) shall not apply to a charge which is a debenture holders' charge, that is to say, a charge (whether a floating charge or not) in favour of the holders of a series of debentures issued by a company or other body of persons, or in favour of trustees for such debenture holders; and any such charge shall be disregarded in determining priorities for the purposes of sub-paragraph (1).

(4) Sub-paragraph (3) above shall not have effect in relation to a charge in favour of trustees for debenture holders which at the date of the instrument by virtue of which the property is disposed of by the new landlord is (as regards that property) a specific and not a floating charge.

Determination of amounts due in respect of mortgages

3.—(1) For the purpose of determining the amount payable in respect of any charge under paragraph 2(1), a person entitled to the benefit of a charge to which that provision applies shall not be permitted to exercise any right to consolidate that charge with a separate charge on other property.

(2) For the purpose of discharging any property from a charge to which paragraph 2(1) applies, a person may be required to accept three months or any longer notice of the intention to pay the whole or part of the principal secured by the charge, together with interest to the date of payment, notwithstanding that the terms of the security make other provision or no provision as to the time and manner of payment; but he shall be entitled, if he so requires, to receive such additional payment as is reasonable in the circumstances in respect of the costs of re-investment or other incidental costs and expenses and in respect of any reduction in the rate of interest obtainable on re-investment.

Payments into court

4.—(1) Where under section 12(4)(a) any property is to be discharged from a charge and, in accordance with paragraph 2(1), a person is or may be entitled in respect of the charge to receive the whole or part of the consideration payable, then if—

(a) for any reason difficulty arises in ascertaining how much is payable in respect of the charge, or

(b) for any reason mentioned in sub-paragraph (2) below difficulty arises in making a payment in respect of the charge,

the nominated person may pay into court on account of the consideration payable the amount, if known, of the payment to be made in respect of the charge or, if that amount is not known, the whole of that consideration or such lesser amount as the nominated person thinks right in order to provide for that payment.

(2) Payment may be made into court in accordance with sub-paragraph (1)(b) where the difficulty arises for any of the following reasons, namely—

(a) because a person who is or may be entitled to receive payment cannot be found or ascertained;

(b) because any such person refuses or fails to make out a title, or to accept payment and give a proper discharge, or to take any steps reasonably required of him to enable the sum payable to be ascertained and paid; or

(c) because a tender of the sum payable cannot, by reason of complications in the title to it or the want of two or more trustees or for other reasons, be effected, or not without incurring or involving unreasonable cost or delay.

(3) Without prejudice to sub-paragraph (1)(a), the whole or part of the consideration payable shall be paid into court by the nominated person if, before execution of the instrument referred to in paragraph 2(1), notice is given to him—

(a) that the new landlord or a person entitled to the benefit of a charge on the property in question requires him to do so for the purpose of protecting the rights of persons so entitled, or for reasons related to the bankruptcy or winding up of the new landlord, or

(b) that steps have been taken to enforce any charge on the new landlord's interest in that property by the bringing of proceedings in any court, or by the appointment of a receiver or otherwise;

and where payment into court is to be made by reason only of a notice under this sub-paragraph, and the notice is given with reference to proceedings in a court specified in the notice other than a county court, payment shall be made into the court so specified.

Savings

5.—(1) Where any property is discharged by section 12(4)(a) from a charge (without the obligations secured by the charge being satisfied by the receipt of the whole or part of the consideration payable), the discharge of that property from the charge shall not prejudice any right or remedy for the enforcement of those obligations against other property comprised in the same or any other security, nor prejudice any personal liability as principal or otherwise of the new landlord or any other person.

(2) Nothing in this Schedule shall be construed as preventing a person from joining in the instrument referred to in paragraph 2(1) for the purpose of discharging the property in question from any charge without payment or for a lesser payment than that to which he would otherwise be entitled; and, if he does so, the persons to whom the consideration payable ought to be paid shall be determined accordingly.

PART II

DISCHARGE IN PURSUANCE OF ACQUISITION ORDERS

Construction

6. In this Part of this Schedule—
"the consideration payable" means the consideration payable for the acquisition of the landlord's interest referred to in section 32(1); and
"the nominated person" means the person or persons nominated for the purposes of Part III by the persons who applied for the acquisition order in question.

Duty of nominated person to redeem mortgages

7.—(1) Where in accordance with section 32(1) an instrument will operate to discharge any premises from a charge to secure the payment of money, it shall be the duty of the nominated person to apply the consideration payable, in the first instance, in or towards the redemption of any such charge (and, if there are more than one, then according to their priorities).

(2) Where sub-paragraph (1) applies to any charge or charges, then if (and only if) the consideration payable is applied by the nominated person in accordance with that sub-paragraph or paid into court by him in accordance with paragraph 9, the instrument in question shall operate as mentioned in sub-paragraph (1) notwithstanding that the consideration payable is insufficient to enable the charge or charges to be redeemed in its or their entirety.

(3) Subject to sub-paragraph (4), sub-paragraph (1) shall not apply to a charge which is a debenture holders' charge within the meaning of paragraph 2(3) in Part I of this Schedule; and any such charge shall be disregarded in determining priorities for the purposes of sub-paragraph (1).

(4) Sub-paragraph (3) above shall not have effect in relation to a charge in favour of trustees for debenture holders which at the date of the instrument by virtue of which the landlord's interest in the premises in question is acquired is (as regards those premises) a specific and not a floating charge.

Determination of amounts due in respect of mortgages

8.—(1) For the purpose of determining the amount payable in respect of any charge under paragraph 7(1), a person entitled to the benefit of a charge to which that provision applies shall not be permitted to exercise any right to consolidate that charge with a separate charge on other property.

(2) For the purpose of discharging any premises from a charge to which paragraph 7(1) applies, a person may be required to accept three months or any longer notice of the intention to pay the whole or part of the principal secured by the charge, together with interest to the date of payment, notwithstanding that the terms of the security make other provision or no provision as to the time and manner of payment; but he shall be entitled, if he so requires, to receive such additional payment as is reasonable in the circumstances in respect of the costs of re-investment or other incidental costs and expenses and in respect of any reduction in the rate of interest obtainable on re-investment.

Payments into court

9.—(1) Where under section 32 any premises are to be discharged from a charge and, in accordance with paragraph 7(1), a person is or may be entitled in respect of the charge to receive the whole or part of the consideration payable, then if—
(a) for any reason difficulty arises in ascertaining how much is payable in respect of the charge, or

(b) for any reason mentioned in sub-paragraph (2) below difficulty arises in making a payment in respect of the charge,
the nominated person may pay into court on account of the consideration payable the amount, if known, of the payment to be made in respect of the charge or, if that amount is not known, the whole of that consideration or such lesser amount as the nominated person thinks right in order to provide for that payment.

(2) Payment may be made into court in accordance with sub-paragraph (1)(b) where the difficulty arises for any of the following reasons, namely—

(a) because a person who is or may be entitled to receive payment cannot be found or ascertained;

(b) because any such person refuses or fails to make out a title, or to accept payment and give a proper discharge, or to take any steps reasonably required of him to enable the sum payable to be ascertained and paid; or

(c) because a tender of the sum payable cannot, by reason of complications in the title to it or the want of two or more trustees or for other reasons, be effected, or not without incurring or involving unreasonable cost or delay.

(3) Without prejudice to sub-paragraph (1)(a), the whole or part of the consideration payable shall be paid into court by the nominated person if, before execution of the instrument referred to in paragraph 7(1), notice is given to him—

(a) that the landlord or a person entitled to the benefit of a charge on the premises in question requires him to do so for the purpose of protecting the rights of persons so entitled, or for reasons related to the bankruptcy or winding up of the landlord, or

(b) that steps have been taken to enforce any charge on the landlord's interest in those premises by the bringing of proceedings in any court, or by the appointment of a receiver or otherwise;

and where payment into court is to be made by reason only of a notice under this sub-paragraph, and the notice is given with reference to proceedings in a court specified in the notice other than a county court, payment shall be made into the court so specified.

Savings

10.—(1) Where any premises are discharged by section 32 from a charge (without the obligations secured by the charge being satisfied by the receipt of the whole or part of the consideration payable), the discharge of those premises from the charge shall not prejudice any right or remedy for the enforcement of those obligations against other property comprised in the same or any other security, nor prejudice any personal liability as principal or otherwise of the landlord or any other person.

(2) Nothing in this Schedule shall be construed as preventing a person from joining in the instrument referred to in paragraph 7(1) for the purpose of discharging the premises in question from any charge without payment or for a lesser payment than that to which he would otherwise be entitled; and, if he does so, the persons to whom the consideration payable ought to be paid shall be determined accordingly.

GENERAL NOTE

Sched. 1 contains supplementary provisions relating to the discharge of mortgages. Pt. I deals with disposals by a new landlord pursuant to a purchase notice served by tenants under s.12; s.14(4)(a) provides that the disposal operates to discharge any charge to which the property has become subject since the disposal to the new landlord for securing the payment of money or the performance of any other obligation. Pt. 2 deals with the acquisition of a landlord's interest under Pt. 3 or the Act; s.32(1) provides for the discharge of any charge on the landlord's interest to secure the payment of money or the performance of any other obligation.

Both parts of the Schedule follow the same scheme:—

(1) It is the duty of the nominated person acquiring the interest of the new landlord or the landlord to apply the consideration payable for the acquisition in or towards the redemption of relevant charges according to their priorities. This has the effect of discharging the property from the charges, even if the consideration is insufficient to redeem the charges entirely; this does not however prejudice the right of the chargee to enforce the charge against any other property comprised in the same security or to proceed against the landlord or new landlord on the basis of their personal liability. The provisions do not apply to a debenture holders' charge as defined in sub-paras. 2(3) and (4) of the Schedule; *i.e.* a charge in favour of the holders of a series of debentures issued by a company or other body of persons, or in favour of trustees for them, except where the charge is in favour of trustees and at the date of acquisition is a specific (rather than floating) charge in relation to the relevant property.

(2) In determining the amounts due in respect of each charge, any right of consolidation is excluded. Further, the chargee may be required to accept as little as three months' notice of intention to repay the moneys secured by the charge, regardless of the provisions of the charge as to repayment. However, the chargee may require the payment of reasonable costs of re-investment, including any reduction in the rate of interest available on re-investment.

(3) In the case of difficulty in redeeming a charge for various specified reasons the nominated person may pay the moneys into court. Also in certain circumstances payment into court is compulsory. Payment into court has the effect of discharging the charge as mentioned above.

Section 41   SCHEDULE 2

AMENDMENTS RELATING TO SERVICE CHARGES

Meaning of "service charge" and "relevant costs"

1. In section 18(1) of the 1985 Act, for "flat" substitute "dwelling".

Limitation of service charges: reasonableness

2. In section 19 of the 1985 Act—
   (a) in subsection (3), for "flat" substitute "dwelling"; and
   (b) after subsection (4) add—
       "(5) If a person takes any proceedings in the High Court in pursuance of any of the provisions of this Act relating to service charges and he could have taken those proceedings in the county court, he shall not be entitled to recover any costs."

Limitation of service charges: estimates and consultation

3. The following section shall be substituted for section 20 of the 1985 Act—
   "20.—(1) Where relevant costs incurred on the carrying out of any qualifying works exceed the limit specified in subsection (3), the excess shall not be taken into account in determining the amount of a service charge unless the relevant requirements have been either—
   (a) complied with, or
   (b) dispensed with by the court in accordance with subsection (9);
   and the amount payable shall be limited accordingly.
   (2) In subsection (1) "qualifying works", in relation to a service charge, means works (whether on a building or on any other premises) to the costs of which the tenant by whom the service charge is payable may be required under the terms of his lease to contribute by the payment of such a charge.
   (3) The limit is whichever is the greater of—
   (a) £25, or such other amount as may be prescribed by order of the Secretary of State, multiplied by the number of dwellings let to the tenants concerned; or
   (b) £500, or such other amount as may be so prescribed.
   (4) The relevant requirements in relation to such of the tenants concerned as are not represented by a recognised tenants' association are—
   (a) At least two estimates for the works shall be obtained, one of them from a person wholly unconnected with the landlord.
   (b) A notice accompanied by a copy of the estimates shall be given to each of those tenants or shall be displayed in one or more places where it is likely to come to the notice of all those tenants.
   (c) The notice shall describe the works to be carried out and invite observations on them and on the estimates and shall state the name and the address in the United Kingdom of the person to whom the observations may be sent and the date by which they are to be received.
   (d) The date stated in the notice shall not be earlier than one month after the date on which the notice is given or displayed as required by paragraph (b).
   (e) The landlord shall have regard to any observations received in pursuance of the notice; and unless the works are urgently required they shall not be begun earlier than the date specified in the notice.

(5) The relevant requirements in relation to such of the tenants concerned as are represented by a recognised tenants' association are—

(a) The landlord shall give to the secretary of the association a notice containing a detailed specification of the works in question and specifying a reasonable period within which the association may propose to the landlord the names of one or more persons from whom estimates for the works should in its view be obtained by the landlord.

(b) At least two estimates for the works shall be obtained, one of them from a person wholly unconnected with the landlord.

(c) A copy of each of the estimates shall be given to the secretary of the association.

(d) A notice shall be given to each of the tenants concerned represented by the association, which shall

(i) describe briefly the works to be carried out,

(ii) summarise the estimates,

(iii) inform the tenant that he has a right to inspect and take copies of a detailed specification of the works to be carried out and of the estimates,

(iv) invite observations on those works and on the estimates, and

(v) specify the name and the address in the United Kingdom of the person to whom the observations may be sent and the date by which they are to be received.

(e) The date stated in the notice shall not be earlier than one month after the date on which the notice is given as required by paragraph (d).

(f) If any tenant to whom the notice is given so requests, the landlord shall afford him reasonable facilities for inspecting a detailed specification of the works to be carried out and the estimates, free of charge, and for taking copies of them on payment of such reasonable charge as the landlord may determine.

(g) The landlord shall have regard to any observations received in pursuance of the notice and, unless the works are urgently required, they shall not be begun earlier than the date specified in the notice.

(6) Paragraphs (d)(ii) and (iii) and (f) of subsection (5) shall not apply to any estimate of which a copy is enclosed with the notice given in pursuance of paragraph (d).

(7) The requirement imposed on the landlord by subsection (5)(f) to make any facilities available to a person free of charge shall not be construed as precluding the landlord from treating as part of his costs of management any costs incurred by him in connection with making those facilities so available.

(8) In this section "the tenants concerned" means all the landlord's tenants who may be required under the terms of their leases to contribute to the costs of the works in question by the payment of service charges.

(9) In proceedings relating to a service charge the court may, if satisfied that the landlord acted reasonably, dispense with all or any of the relevant requirements.

(10) An order under this section—

(a) may make different provision with respect to different cases or descriptions of case, including different provision for different areas, and

(b) shall be made by statutory instrument which shall be subject to annulment in pursuance of a resolution of either House of Parliament."

Additional limitations on service charges

4. The following sections shall be inserted in the 1985 Act after the section 20A inserted by paragraph 9 of Schedule 5 to the Housing and Planning Act 1986—

"Limitation of service charges: time limit on making demands

20B.—(1) If any of the relevant costs taken into account in determining the amount of any service charge were incurred more than 18 months before a demand for payment of the service charge is served on the tenant, then (subject to subsection (2)), the tenant shall not be liable to pay so much of the service charge as reflects the costs so incurred.

(2) Subsection (1) shall not apply if, within the period of 18 months beginning with the date when the relevant costs in question were incurred, the tenant was notified in writing that those costs had been incurred and that he would subsequently be required under the terms of his lease to contribute to them by the payment of a service charge.

Limitation of service charges: costs of court proceedings

20C.—(1) A tenant may make an application to the appropriate court for an order that all or any of the costs incurred, or to be incurred, by the landlord in connection with any proceedings are not to be regarded as relevant costs to be taken into account in determining the amount of any service charge payable by the tenant or any other person or persons specified in the application; and the court may make such order on the application as it considers just and equitable in the circumstances.

(2) In subsection (1) "the appropriate court" means—

    (a) if the application is made in the course of the proceedings in question, the court before which the proceedings are taking place; and

    (b) if the application is made after those proceedings are concluded, a county court."

Request for summary of relevant costs

5.—(1) Section 21 of the 1985 Act shall be amended as follows.

(2) In subsection (2), for the words from "there is" to "and the tenant" substitute "the tenant is represented by a recognised tenants' association and he".

(3) In subsection (5), for the words from "how they are or will be" onwards substitute "how they have been or will be reflected in demands for service charges and, in addition, shall summarise each of the following items, namely—

    (a) any of the costs in respect of which no demand for payment was received by the landlord within the period referred to in subsection (1)(a) or (b),

    (b) any of the costs in respect of which—

        (i) a demand for payment was so received, but

        (ii) no payment was made by the landlord within that period, and

    (c) any of the costs in respect of which—

        (i) a demand for payment was so received, and

        (ii) payment was made by the landlord within that period,

and specify the aggregate of any amounts received by the landlord down to the end of that period on account of service charges in respect of relevant dwellings and still standing to the credit of the tenants of those dwellings at the end of that period.

(5A) In subsection (5) "relevant dwelling" means a dwelling whose tenant is either—

    (a) the person by or with the consent of whom the request was made, or

    (b) a person whose obligations under the terms of his lease as regards contributing to relevant costs relate to the same costs as the corresponding obligations of the person mentioned in paragraph (a) above relate to."

(4) In subsection (6)—

    (a) for the words from the beginning to "another building" substitute "If the service charges in relation to which the costs are relevant costs as mentioned in subsection (1) are payable by the tenants of more than four dwellings"; and

    (b) for "requirement" substitute "requirements".

Request to inspect supporting accounts etc.

6. In section 22 of the 1985 Act, after subsection (4) add—

"(5) The landlord shall—

    (a) where such facilities are for the inspection of any documents, make them so available free of charge;

    (b) where such facilities are for the taking of copies or extracts, be entitled to make them so available on payment of such reasonable charge as he may determine.

(6) The requirement imposed on the landlord by subsection (5)(a) to make any facilities available to a person free of charge shall not be construed as precluding the landlord from treating as part of his costs of management any costs incurred by him in connection with making those facilities so available."

Effect of assignment on request

7. In section 24 of the 1985 Act, for "flat" substitute "dwelling".

Exception where rent is registered and not entered as variable

8. In section 27 of the 1985 Act, for "flat" substitute "dwelling".

Meaning of "qualified accountant"

9.—(1) Section 28 of the 1985 Act shall be amended as follows.

(2) In subsection (4)—

(a) in paragraph (b), for "or employee" substitute ", employee or partner"; and

(b) after paragraph (c) add—

"(d) an agent of the landlord who is a managing agent for any premises to which any of the costs covered by the summary in question relate;

(e) an employee or partner of any such agent."

(3) After subsection (5) insert—

"(5A) For the purposes of subsection (4)(d) a person is a managing agent for any premises to which any costs relate if he has been appointed to discharge any of the landlord's obligations relating to the management by him of the premises and owed to the tenants who may be required under the terms of their leases to contribute to those costs by the payment of service charges."

Meaning of "recognised tenants' association"

10.—(1) Section 29 of the 1985 Act shall be amended as follows.

(2) In subsection (1), for "tenants of flats in a building" substitute "qualifying tenants (whether with or without other tenants)".

(3) In subsection (4), for "the building is situated" substitute "the dwellings let to the qualifying tenants are situated, and for the purposes of this section a number of tenants are qualifying tenants if each of them may be required under the terms of his lease to contribute to the same costs by the payment of a service charge."

(4) For subsection (5) substitute—

"(5) The Secretary of State may by regulations specify—

(a) the procedure which is to be followed in connection with an application for, or for the cancellation of, a certificate under subsection (1)(b);

(b) the matters to which regard is to be had in giving or cancelling such a certificate;

(c) the duration of such a certificate; and

(d) any circumstances in which a certificate is not to be given under subsection (1)(b)."

Definitions

11. In section 30—

(a) omit the definition of "flat"; and

(b) in the definition of "tenant", for "flat" substitute "dwelling".

GENERAL NOTE

This Schedule makes amendments to the provisions of the Landlord and Tenant Act 1985 dealing with service charges. The provisions are extended to apply to dwellings and not just flats. It is also provided that a person taking High Court proceedings in pursuance of the Act's provisions on service charges where the proceedings would have been taken in the county court shall not be entitled to recover *any* costs, *i.e.* it is not merely a case of restricting costs to the county court scale.

S.20 of the 1985 Act is amended to draw a distinction between tenants represented by a recognised tenants' association and those not so represented. In the case of unrepresented tenants the requirements before the landlord may begin with works covered by the section remain the same: the landlord must obtain at least two estimates for the work, at least one from a person wholly unconnected to the landlord; a copy of the estimates must be notified to the tenants and displayed (though it need no longer be displayed in the building so long as it is likely to come to the notice of all tenants); the notice must describe the works proposed and invite observations within a period of not less than one month. For such tenants as are represented by a tenants' association, the landlord must:

(i) give the secretary of the association a detailed specification of the proposed work and give a reasonable period within which the association may put to the landlord names or persons from whom in its view estimates should be obtained;

(ii) obtain at least two estimates, one from a wholly unconnected person;

(iii) give a copy of the estimates to the secretary of the association;

(iv) give to each tenant represented by the association a notice describing briefly the works, summarising the estimates, informing the tenant that he has the right to inspect and take copies of the detailed specification and estimates, (alternatively, the landlord may simply enclose a copy of the estimate), inviting observations on the work and estimates, and specifying a name and address in the United Kingdom to whom observations may be sent and a date (not earlier than one month) by which they are to be received;

(v) afford to any tenant who so requests reasonable facilities for free inspection of the specification and estimates, and for taking copies of them on payment of such reasonable charge as the landlord determines. The landlord may treat the cost of making the facilities available as part of his management costs;

(vi) have regard to any observations received in pursuance of the notice;

(vii) not begin the works earlier than the date specified in the notice unless they are "urgently required." As before, a court may dispense with the relevant requirements if satisfied that the landlord acted reasonably, *e.g.* in the case of work urgently required for safety reasons.

Additional limitations on service charges

A new s.20B introduced into the 1985 Act provides that a tenant shall not be liable to pay service charge costs incurred more than 18 months before a demand for payment is served on the tenant. The landlord may only recover such costs if within the 18 months from when the costs were incurred he notified the tenant in writing that the costs had been incurred and that he would subsequently be required to contribute to them.

A new s.20C allows a tenant to apply to court for an order that all or part of costs incurred by the landlord in any court proceedings are not to be regarded as relevant costs in determining the amount of the service charge.

Request for summary of relevant costs.

S.21 of the 1985 Act (which allows a tenant to obtain written details of service charge costs) is amended. The most significant change is to subs. (5). In addition to setting out the costs in a way showing how they are or will be reflected in demands for service charges, the landlord must now break down the costs into those in respect of which (i) no demand for payment was received by the landlord within the relevant period; (ii) a demand for payment was received but no payment was made by the landlord; and (iii) a demand for payment was received and payment was made. The landlord must also state the total amount received on account of service charges and still standing to the credit of the tenants.

Inspection of supporting accounts

A new subs. 22(5) is inserted relating to the inspection and copying of supporting accounts by tenants or the secretary of a recognised tenants' association. Facilities for inspection must be provided by the landlord free of charge (though any cost to the landlord can be treated as management costs) and facilities for the taking of copies or extracts may be made subject to the payment of such reasonable charges as the landlord may determine.

Qualified accountant

Extensions are made to the persons disqualified from acting as a qualified accountant to certify summaries of costs under s.21. A partner of the landlord is disqualified, as is the landlord's managing agent in relation to the premises to which the costs relate and any employee or partner of such agent.

Section 43(2)   SCHEDULE 3

RIGHTS OF TENANTS WITH RESPECT TO INSURANCE

Construction

1. In this Schedule—

"landlord", in relation to a tenant by whom a service charge is payable which includes an amount payable directly or indirectly for insurance, includes any person who has a right to enforce payment of that service charge;

"relevant policy", in relation to a dwelling, means any policy of insurance under which the dwelling is insured (being, in the case of a flat, a policy covering the building containing it); and

"tenant" includes a statutory tenant.

Request for summary of insurance cover

2.—(1) Where a service charge is payable by the tenant of a dwelling which consists of or includes an amount payable directly or indirectly for insurance, the tenant may require the landlord in writing to supply him with a written summary of the insurance for the time being effected in relation to the dwelling.

(2) If the tenant is represented by a recognised tenants' association and he consents, the request may be made by the secretary of the association instead of by the tenant and may then be for the supply of the summary to the secretary.

(3) A request is duly served on the landlord if it is served on—

(a) an agent of the landlord named as such in the rent book or similar document, or

(b) the person who receives the rent on behalf of the landlord;

and a person on whom a request is so served shall forward it as soon as may be to the landlord.

(4) The landlord shall, within one month of the request, comply with it by supplying to the tenant or the secretary of the recognised tenants' association (as the case may require) such a summary as is mentioned in sub-paragraph (1), which shall include—

(a) the insured amount or amounts under any relevant policy, and

(b) the name of the insurer under any such policy, and

(c) the risks in respect of which the dwelling or (as the case may be) the building containing it is insured under any such policy.

(5) In sub-paragraph (4)(a) "the insured amount or amounts", in relation to a relevant policy, means—

(a) in the case of a dwelling other than a flat, the amount for which the dwelling is insured under the policy; and

(b) in the case of a flat, the amount for which the building containing it is insured under the policy and, if specified in the policy, the amount for which the flat is insured under it.

(6) The landlord shall be taken to have complied with the request if, within the period mentioned in sub-paragraph (4), he instead supplies to the tenant or the secretary (as the case may require) a copy of every relevant policy.

(7) In a case where two or more buildings are insured under any relevant policy, the summary or copy supplied under sub-paragraph (4) or (6) so far as relating to that policy need only be of such parts of the policy as relate—

(a) to the dwelling, and

(b) if the dwelling is a flat, to the building containing it.

Request to inspect insurance policy etc.

3.—(1) This paragraph applies where a tenant, or the secretary of a recognised tenants' association, has obtained either—

(a) such a summary as is referred to in paragraph 2(1), or

(b) a copy of any relevant policy or of any such parts of any relevant policy as relate to the premises referred to in paragraph 2(7)(a) or (b),

whether in pursuance of paragraph 2 or otherwise.

(2) The tenant, or the secretary with the consent of the tenant, may within six months of obtaining any such summary or copy as is mentioned in sub-paragraph (1)(a) or (b) require the landlord in writing to afford him reasonable facilities—

(a) for inspecting any relevant policy,

(b) for inspecting any accounts, receipts or other documents which provide evidence of payment of any premiums due under any such policy in respect of the period of insurance which is current when the request is made and the period of insurance immediately preceding that period, and

(c) for taking copies of or extracts from any of the documents referred to in paragraphs (a) and (b).

(3) Any reference in this paragraph to a relevant policy includes a reference to a policy of insurance under which the dwelling in question was insured for the period of insurance immediately preceding that current when the request is made under this paragraph (being, in the case of a flat, a policy covering the building containing it).

(4) Subsections (3) to (6) of section 22 shall have effect in relation to a request made under this paragraph as they have effect in relation to a request made under that section.

Request relating to insurance effected by superior landlord

4.—(1) If a request is made under paragraph 2 in a case where a superior landlord has effected, in whole or in part, the insurance of the dwelling in question and the landlord to whom the request is made is not in possession of the relevant information—

(a) he shall in turn make a written request for the relevant information to the person who is his landlord (and so on, if that person is not himself the superior landlord),

(b) the superior landlord shall comply with that request within a reasonable time, and

(c) the immediate landlord shall then comply with the tenant's or secretary's request in the manner provided by sub-paragraphs (4) to (7) of paragraph 2 within the time allowed by that paragraph or such further time, if any, as is reasonable in the circumstances.

(2) If, in a case where a superior landlord has effected, in whole or in part, the insurance of the dwelling in question, a request under paragraph 3 relates to any policy or insurance effected by the superior landlord—

(a) the landlord to whom the request is made shall forthwith inform the tenant or secretary of that fact and of the name and address of the superior landlord, and

(b) that paragraph shall then apply to the superior landlord in relation to that policy as it applies to the immediate landlord.

Effect of assignment on request

5. The assignment of a tenancy does not affect the validity of a request made under paragraph 2, 3 or 4 before the assignment; but a person is not obliged to provide a summary or make facilities available more than once for the same dwelling and for the same period.

Failure to comply with paragraph 2, 3 or 4 an offence

6.—(1) It is a summary offence for a person to fail, without reasonable excuse, to perform a duty imposed on him by or by virtue of paragraph 2, 3 or 4.

(2) A person committing such an offence is liable on conviction to a fine not exceeding level 4 on the standard scale.

Tenant's right to notify insurers of possible claim

7.—(1) This paragraph applies to any dwelling in respect of which the tenant pays to the landlord a service charge consisting of or including an amount payable directly or indirectly for insurance.

(2) Where—

(a) it appears to the tenant of any such dwelling that damage has been caused—
(i) to the dwelling; or
(ii) if the dwelling is a flat, to the dwelling or to any other part of the building containing it,
in respect of which a claim could be made under the terms of a policy of insurance, and

(b) it is a term of that policy that the person insured under the policy should give notice of any claim under it to the insurer within a specified period,

the tenant may, within that specified period, serve on the insurer a notice in writing stating that it appears to him that damage has been caused as mentioned in paragraph (a) and describing briefly the nature of the damage.

(3) Where—

(a) any such notice is served on an insurer by a tenant in relation to any such damage, and

(b) the specified period referred to in sub-paragraph (2)(b) would expire earlier than the period of six months beginning with the date on which the notice is served,

the policy in question shall have effect as regards any claim subsequently made in respect of that damage by the person insured under the policy as if for the specified period there were substituted that period of six months.

(4) Where the tenancy of a dwelling to which this paragraph applies is held by joint tenants, a single notice under this paragraph may be given by any one or more of those tenants.

(5) The Secretary of State may by regulations prescribe the form of notices under this paragraph and the particulars which such notices must contain.

(6) Any such regulations—

(a) may make different provision with respect to different cases or descriptions of case, including different provision for different areas, and

(b) shall be made by statutory instrument.

Right to challenge landlord's choice of insurers

8.—(1) This paragraph applies a tenancy of a dwelling which requires the tenant to insure the dwelling with an insurer nominated by the landlord.

(2) Where, on an application made by the tenant under any such tenancy, the court is satisfied—

(a) that the insurance which is available from the nominated insurer for insuring the tenant's dwelling is unsatisfactory in any respect, or

(b) that the premiums payable in respect of any such insurance are excessive,

the court may make either an order requiring the landlord to nominate such other insurer as is specified in the order or an order requiring him to nominate another insurer who satisfies such requirements in relation to the insurance of the dwelling as are specified in the order.

(3) A county court shall have jurisdiction to hear and determine any application under this paragraph.

Exception for tenants of certain public authorities

9.—(1) Paragraphs 2 to 8 do not apply to a tenant of—
    a local authority,
    a new town corporation, or
    the Development Board for Rural Wales,
unless the tenancy is a long tenancy, in which case paragraphs 2 to 5 and 7 and 8 apply but paragraph 6 does not.

(2) Subsections (2) and (3) of section 26 shall apply for the purposes of sub-paragraph (1) as they apply for the purposes of subsection (1) of that section.

GENERAL NOTE

Sched. 3 (which becomes the Schedule to the 1985 Act) confers rights upon tenants in relation to insurance cover. Where the landlord is to insure by the terms of the lease, the lease will often merely require insurance with a "reputable" office. In *Bandar Property Holdings* v. *J. S. Darwen (Successors)* [1968] 2 All E.R. 305 it was held that there was no obligation on the landlord to "shop around" for economic insurance; but a query how far this may have been affected by *Finchbourne* v. *Rodrigues* [1976] 3 All E.R. 581.

Under Sched. 3, the tenant of a dwelling where the service charge includes insurance costs may require the landlord in writing to provide a written summary of the current insurance effected in relation to the dwelling (or in the case of a flat, the whole building containing it). Alternatively, the request may come from the secretary of a recognised tenants' association representing the tenant. Within a month the landlord must supply a summary including the insured amount, the name of the insurer and the risks insured. Alternatively the landlord may simply supply a copy of the relevant policy. The tenant or association secretary may then within six months require the landlord to allow inspection of the policy and any account, receipts or documents providing evidence of the payment of premiums, and facilities for taking copies of or extracts from these documents.

Provision is made for obtaining information from a superior landlord who effects the insurance. Failure to comply with relevant requests is a summary offence. Provision is also made for the case where the insurance policy requires notification of a possible claim within a specified period. The tenant may serve written notice on the insurer where it appears that damage to the dwelling or building has occurred, describing briefly the nature of the damage. The notice must be given within the period specified in the policy, except where that period is less than six months, in which case the period stated in the policy shall be taken to be six months. It should be noted that the Schedule does not give the tenant the right to make a claim under the policy or to compel the landlord to do so or lay out the insurance moneys on reinstatement; thus as well as the Schedule, the tenant will need to be aware of any rights under the terms of the lease, under the Fires Prevention (Metropolis) Act 1774, and under the decision in *Mumford Hotels* v. *Wheler* [1964] 1 Ch. 117.

Provision is also made for the situation where the tenant is required to insure with an insurer nominated by the landlord. The tenant may apply to a county court, and if the court is satisfied that the insurance available from the nominated insurer is unsatisfactory in any respect or that the premiums payable are excessive the court may order the landlord to nominate another insurer. Though it seems galling to the tenant, it would not seem to justify interference merely because the landlord nominates an insurer who will pay him commission (unless of course that insurer's terms are unsatisfactory or premium excessive).

The Schedule does not apply to tenants of local authorities, new town corporations, or the Development Board for Rural Wales. If a tenant from such bodies holds under a long tenancy (defined in s.26(2) of the 1985 Act), the Schedule applies, but failure of the landlord to comply with requests under the Schedule is not an offence.

Section 61(1)   SCHEDULE 4

CONSEQUENTIAL AMENDMENTS

LAND REGISTRATION ACT 1925 (c.21)

1. In section 49(1) (rules to provide for notices of other rights, interests and claims), at the end add—

"(h) acquisition orders (within the meaning of Part III of the Landlord and Tenant Act 1987) which in the case of unregistered land may be protected by registration under the Land Charges Act 1972 and which, notwithstanding section 59 of this Act, it may be deemed expedient to protect by notice instead of by caution."

2. In section 64 (certificates to be produced and noted on dealings), at the end add—

"(6) Subsection (1) above shall also not require the production of the land certificate when a person applies for—

(a) the registration of a notice of any variation of a lease effected by or in pursuance of an order under section 38 of the Landlord and Tenant Act 1987 (orders by the court varying leases), including any variation as modified by an order under section 39(4) of that Act (effect of orders varying leases: applications by third parties), or

(b) the cancellation of any such notice where a variation is cancelled or modified by an order under section 39(4) of that Act."

LOCAL GOVERNMENT ACT 1985 (c.51)

3. In Schedule 13 (provisions with respect to residuary bodies)—

(a) in paragraph 24—

(i) omit "and" in the second place where it occurs, and

(ii) at the end add ", and

paragraph 9(1) of the Schedule."; and

(b) at the end add—

"25. A residuary body shall be included among the bodies specified in section 58(1) of the Landlord and Tenant Act 1987."

HOUSING ACT 1985 (c.68)

4. In section 45 (disposals in relation to which ss.46 to 51 apply, etc.)—

(a) in subsection (1), for paragraphs (a) to (c) substitute—

"(a) the freehold of a house has been conveyed by a public sector authority; and

(b) the conveyance enabled the vendor to recover from the purchaser a service charge."; and

(b) in subsection (2), omit the words from "(a) the" to "; and (b)".

5. Omit section 49 (information held by superior landlord).

6. In section 50(1) (offences), omit "or 49".

HOUSING ASSOCIATIONS ACT 1985 (c.69)

7. In section 107(3) (extent), for "section 4(3)(g)" substitute "section 4(3)(ddd) and (g) and (4)".

GENERAL NOTE

The most important point to note here is that the Land Registration Act 1925 is amended to allow an acquisition order under Pt. 3 of the Act to be protected by registration of notice. For the effect of such protection, see ss.48 and 49 of the 1925 Act. For protection by way of caution, and for the position in relation to unregistered land, see the General Note to s.29(6).

Also, s.64 of the 1925 Act is qualified to allow notice of a variation of a lease under s.38 of the 1987 Act to be registered without the necessity of production of the land certificate.

SCHEDULE 5

REPEALS

Chapter	Short title	Extent of repeal
1985 c.51.	Local Government Act 1985.	In paragraph 24 of Schedule 13, the word "and" in the second place where it occurs.
1985 c.68.	Housing Act 1985.	In section 45(2), the words from "(a) the" to "; and (b)".
		Section 49.
		In section 50(1), the words "or 49".
1985 c.70.	Landlord and Tenant Act 1985.	In section 30, the definition of "flat".

CROSSBOWS ACT 1987

(1987 c. 32)

An Act to create offences relating to the sale and letting on hire of crossbows to, and the purchase, hiring and possession of crossbows by, persons under the age of seventeen; and for connected purposes.

[15th May 1987]

PARLIAMENTARY DEBATES
  Hansard: H.C. Vol. 107, col. 353; Vol. 109, cols. 590, 619; Vol. 113, col. 709; H.L. Vol. 486, cols. 448, 1668; Vol. 487, col. 662.
  The Bill was considered in Standing Committee C on February 25, 1987.

Sale and letting on hire

1. A person who sells or lets on hire a crossbow or a part of a crossbow to a person under the age of seventeen is guilty of an offence, unless he believes him to be seventeen years of age or older and has reasonable ground for the belief.

Purchase and hiring

2. A person under the age of seventeen who buys or hires a crossbow or a part of a crossbow is guilty of an offence.

Possession

3. A person under the age of seventeen who has with him—
    (a) a crossbow which is capable of discharging a missile, or
    (b) parts of a crossbow which together (and without any other parts) can be assembled to form a crossbow capable of discharging a missile,
is guilty of an offence, unless he is under the supervision of a person who is twenty-one years of age or older.

Powers of search and seizure etc.

4.—(1) If a constable suspects with reasonable cause that a person is committing or has committed an offence under section 3, the constable may—
    (a) search that person for a crossbow or part of a crossbow;
    (b) search any vehicle, or anything in or on a vehicle, in or on which the constable suspects with reasonable cause there is a crossbow, or part of a crossbow, connected with the offence.

(2) A constable may detain a person or vehicle for the purpose of a search under subsection (1).

(3) A constable may seize and retain for the purpose of proceedings for an offence under this Act anything discovered by him in the course of a search under subsection (1) which appears to him to be a crossbow or part of a crossbow.

(4) For the purpose of exercising the powers conferred by this section a constable may enter any land other than a dwelling-house.

Exception

5. This Act does not apply to crossbows with a draw weight of less than 1·4 kilograms.

Punishments

6.—(1) A person guilty of an offence under section 1 shall be liable, on summary conviction, to imprisonment for a term not exceeding six months, to a fine not exceeding level 5 on the standard scale, or to both.

(2) A person guilty of an offence under section 2 or 3 shall be liable, on summary conviction, to a fine not exceeding level 3 on the standard scale.

(3) The court by which a person is convicted of an offence under this Act may make such order as it thinks fit as to the forfeiture or disposal of any crossbow or part of a crossbow in respect of which the offence was committed.

Corresponding provision for Northern Ireland

7. An Order in Council under paragraph 1(1)(b) of Schedule 1 to the Northern Ireland Act 1974 (legislation for Northern Ireland in the interim period) which contains a statement that it is made only for purposes corresponding to the purposes of this Act—

(a) shall not be subject to paragraph 1(4) and (5) of that Schedule (affirmative resolution of both Houses of Parliament), but

(b) shall be subject to annulment in pursuance of a resolution of either House of Parliament.

Short title, commencement and extent

8.—(1) This Act may be cited as the Crossbows Act 1987.

(2) Sections 1 to 6 shall come into force at the end of the period of two months beginning with the day on which this Act is passed.

(3) Sections 1 to 6 shall not extend to Northern Ireland.

AIDS (CONTROL) ACT 1987

(1987 c. 33)

An Act to make provision in relation to Acquired Immune Deficiency
Syndrome and Human Immunodeficiency Virus.   [15th May 1987]

PARLIAMENTARY DEBATES
Hansard: H.C. Vol. 107, col. 354; Vol. 108, col. 1168; Vol. 110, col. 286; Vol. 113, col.
679; H.L. Vol. 486, cols. 448, 1564; Vol. 487, col. 662.
The Bill was considered in Standing Committee C on February 11, 1987.

Periodical reports on matters relating to AIDS and HIV

1.—(1) Reports shall be made in accordance with this section—
  (a) to each Regional Health Authority by the District Health Authority
       for each district in the region; and
  (b) to the Secretary of State by—
       (i)   each Regional Health Authority;
       (ii) each District Health Authority in Wales; and
       (iii) each Health Board in Scotland.
 (2) The reports made by a District Health Authority and a Health
Board shall contain the information specified in the Schedule to this Act
and such other relevant information as the Secretary of State may direct;
and the reports made by a Regional Health Authority shall contain the
information supplied to it in the reports of the District Health Authorities
in the region.
 (3) The reports made by a Regional Health Authority, District Health
Authority or Health Board shall be published by the Authority or Board
by which they are made and the information contained in the reports
made by District Health Authorities in Wales shall be published by the
Secretary of State.
 (4) The reports shall be in such form and shall be made at such times
or intervals and relate to such periods as the Secretary of State may direct
but those periods shall not be more than twelve months and the first
reports shall be made and published not later than the end of 1988.
 (5) The Secretary of State may by order made by statutory
instrument—
  (a) make provision for requiring any special health authority specified
       in the order to make reports to him under this section and for that
       purpose modify the Schedule to this Act in its application to that
       authority;
  (b) amend the Schedule to this Act.
 (6) The Schedule to this Act may be modified or amended under
subsection (5) above either by altering or deleting any of the matters for
the time being specified in it or by specifying additional relevant
information.
 (7) An order under subsection (5) above shall be subject to annulment
in pursuance of a resolution of either House of Parliament.
 (8) Directions and orders under this section may make different provision for different cases and directions under subsection (4) above may
require reports in respect of periods falling wholly or partly before the
coming into force of this Act.
 (9) In this section "Regional Health Authority", "District Health
Authority" and "special health authority" have the same meaning as in
the National Health Service Act 1977, "Health Board" has the same
meaning as in the National Health Service (Scotland) Act 1978 and
"relevant information" means information relating to, or to any matter
connected with, AIDS or HIV.

Power to make corresponding provision for Northern Ireland

2. An Order in Council under paragraph 1(1)(b) of Schedule 1 to the Northern Ireland Act 1974 (legislation for Northern Ireland in the interim period) which states that it is made only for purposes corresponding to those of this Act—

(a) shall not be subject to paragraph 1(4) and (5) of that Schedule (affirmative resolution of both Houses of Parliament); but

(b) shall be subject to annulment in pursuance of a resolution of either House.

Expenses

3. There shall be paid out of money provided by Parliament any increase attributable to this Act in the sums so payable under any other enactment.

Short title, interpretation and extent

4.—(1) This Act may be cited as the AIDS (Control) Act 1987.

(2) In this Act "AIDS" means Acquired Immune Deficiency Syndrome and "HIV" means Human Immunodeficiency Virus.

(3) Except for section 2, this Act does not extend to Northern Ireland.

Section 1   SCHEDULE

CONTENTS OF REPORTS

1. The number of persons known to the Authority or Board to be persons with AIDS at the end of the period to which the report relates ("the reporting period") having been diagnosed as such—

(a) in that period; and

(b) up to the end of that period,

by facilities or services provided by the Authority or Board.

2. The number of persons known to the Authority or Board to have been diagnosed as persons with AIDS by such facilities or services in the reporting period or a previous reporting period and to have died—

(a) in the reporting period; and

(b) up to the end of the reporting period.

3. Where the number to be reported under any of the foregoing provisions is between one and nine (inclusive) the report shall state only that the number is less than ten.

4. Particulars of the facilities and services provided by the Authority or Board, or known to it to have been provided in its district or area by others, in the reporting period for testing for, and preventing the spread of, AIDS and HIV and for treating, counselling and caring for persons with AIDS or infected with HIV.

5. The number of persons employed by the Authority or Board wholly or mainly in providing in the reporting period such facilities and services as are mentioned in paragraph 4 above.

6. An estimate of the facilities and services which the Authority or Board will provide in the twelve months following the reporting period for the purposes mentioned in paragraph 4 above.

7. Particulars of action taken by the Authority or Board, or known to it to have been taken in its district or area by others, in the reporting period to educate the public in relation to AIDS and HIV and to provide training for testing for AIDS and HIV and for the treatment, counselling and care of persons with AIDS or infected with HIV.

MOTOR CYCLE NOISE ACT 1987

(1987 c. 34)

An Act to prohibit the supply of motor cycle exhaust systems and silencers likely to result in the emission of excessive noise; and for connected purposes.   [15th May 1987]

PARLIAMENTARY DEBATES
  Hansard: H.C. Vol. 107, col. 357; Vol. 109, col. 1290; Vol. 110, cols. 706, 719; Vol. 114, col. 910; H.L. Vol. 486, col. 1421; Vol. 487, col. 702.
  The Bill was considered in Standing Committee C on March 11, 1987.

Prohibition of supply of exhaust systems etc. not complying with prescribed requirements

1.—(1) Subject to subsections (3) and (4) below, no person shall, in the course of carrying on a business, supply or offer or agree to supply or expose or have in his possession for the purpose of supplying—
  (a) an exhaust system for a motor cycle; or
  (b) a silencer, or any component other than a silencer or fixing, for such a system,
unless the system, silencer or component complies with such requirements as may be prescribed by regulations made by the Secretary of State and, as respects such a system or silencer, the requirements of the regulations as to packaging, labelling and the provision of accompanying instructions are complied with.

(2) The regulations made by the Secretary of State for the purposes of this section shall be such as he considers necessary for preventing the supply of exhaust systems, silencers and components which are likely to result in motor cycles to which they are fitted emitting excessive noise; and those regulations may—
  (a) prescribe requirements by reference to any British Standard Specification, any regulations made under section 40 of the Road Traffic Act 1972, any Community instrument or any other instrument issued by an international authority; and
  (b) make different provision for different cases.

(3) Exemptions from this section or any requirements imposed under it may be conferred by regulations made by the Secretary of State or, in the case of an exemption applying to a particular person, by a notice in writing given by him to that person.

(4) Subsection (1) above does not apply in any case in which the person in question reasonably believes that the exhaust system, silencer or component will not be used in the United Kingdom.

(5) Before making any regulations under this section the Secretary of State shall consult such representative organisations as he thinks fit.

(6) The power to make regulations under this section shall be exercisable by statutory instrument subject to annulment in pursuance of a resolution of either House of Parliament.

(7) The Schedule to this Act shall have effect with respect to contraventions of this section and the enforcement of its provisions.

Short title, interpretation, commencement and extent

2.—(1) This Act may be cited as the Motor Cycle Noise Act 1987.

(2) In this Act references to a motor cycle include references to a moped and a motor scooter and references to supply include references to gratuitous supply.

(3) This Act shall come into force on such day as may be appointed by the Secretary of State by an order made by statutory instrument; and different days may be appointed for different provisions or different purposes.

(4) This Act does not extend to Northern Ireland.

Section 1(7) SCHEDULE

OFFENCES AND ENFORCEMENT

Offences

1.—(1) Any person who contravenes section 1 of this Act shall be guilty of an offence and liable on summary conviction to imprisonment for a term not exceeding three months or to a fine not exceeding the fifth level on the standard scale.

(2) Where the commission by any person of such an offence is due to the act or default of some other person the other person shall be guilty of the offence and may be charged with and convicted of the offence whether or not proceedings are taken against the first-mentioned person.

(3) It shall be a defence to a charge of committing an offence under this paragraph that the accused took all reasonable steps and exercised all due diligence to avoid committing the offence.

2.—(1) Where an offence under paragraph 1 above which has been committed by a body corporate is proved to have been committed with the consent or connivance of, or to be attributable to any neglect on the part of, a director, manager, secretary or other similar officer of the body corporate or any person who was purporting to act in any such capacity, he as well as the body corporate shall be guilty of that offence and shall be liable to be proceeded against and punished accordingly.

(2) Where the affairs of a body corporate are managed by its members sub-paragraph (1) above shall apply in relation to the acts and defaults of a member in connection with his functions of management as if he were a director of the body corporate.

Enforcement

3. It shall be the duty of each weights and measures authority to enforce this Act within its area.

4.—(1) Schedule 2 to the Consumer Safety Act 1978 (which confers power to enter premises and seize goods) shall have effect in relation to a weights and measures authority exercising its functions under this Act as it has effect in relation to an enforcement authority within the meaning of that Schedule.

(2) In its application by virtue of this paragraph that Schedule shall have effect as if the provisions of section 1 of this Act were relevant provisions.

5. Nothing in the preceding provisions of this Schedule authorises a weights and measures authority to institute proceedings in Scotland for an offence.

PROTECTION OF ANIMALS (PENALTIES) ACT 1987

(1987 c. 35)

An Act to amend the Protection of Animals Act 1911 to increase the penalties for offences against animals under section 1(1).

[15th May 1987]

PARLIAMENTARY DEBATES
  Hansard: H.C. Vol. 107, col. 1483; Vol. 108, col. 1196; Vol. 114, col. 895; H.L. Vol. 486, col. 1421; Vol. 487, col. 706.
  The Bill was considered in Standing Committee C on February 18, 1987.

Amendment of Protection of Animals Act

1.—(1) In section 1(1) of the Protection of Animals Act 1911 (offences of cruelty to animals), for the words from "shall be liable" onwards substitute "shall be liable on summary conviction to imprisonment for a term not exceeding six months or to a fine not exceeding level 5 on the standard scale, or both".

(2) The above amendment does not apply in relation to offences committed before the commencement of this Act.

Short title, repeals, commencement and extent

2.—(1) This Act may be cited as the Protection of Animals (Penalties) Act 1987.

(2) The following enactments are repealed—
(a) the Protection of Animals Act (1911) Amendment Act 1912;
(b) in Schedule 6 to the Criminal Law Act 1977, the entry relating to the Protection of Animals Act 1911.

(3) This Act shall come into force at the end of the period of two months beginning with the day on which it is passed.

(4) This Act does not extend to Scotland or Northern Ireland.

1987 c. 35

PROTECTION OF ANIMALS (PENALTIES) ACT 1987

An Act to amend the Protection of Animals Act 1911 so as to increase the penalties for cruelty to animals; and for connection therewith.

[15th May 1987]

Short title, etc.

Repeal: 50 & 51 Geo. 5, c. 152, s. 10(1)...

Amendment of Protection of Animals Act

1.—(1) In section 1(1) of the Protection of Animals Act...

Short title, repeals, commencement and extent.

3.—(1) This Act may be cited as the Protection of Animals (Penalties) Act 1987.

(2) The following enactments are repealed—

(a) the Protection of Animals Act, 1911; Amendment Act 1912...

(4) This Act extends to the whole of Great Britain only.

PRESCRIPTION (SCOTLAND) ACT 1987

(1987 c. 36)

An Act to amend Part I of the Prescription and Limitation (Scotland) Act 1973; and for connected purposes.   [15th May 1987]

PARLIAMENTARY DEBATES
  Hansard: H.C. Vol. 112, col. 299; Vol. 113, col. 1398; Vol. 114, col. 958; H.L. Vol. 486, col. 1421; Vol. 487, col. 708.

Definition of "relevant claim"

1.—(1) In section 9 of the Prescription and Limitation (Scotland) Act 1973 (which defines "relevant claim" for certain purposes), after paragraph (c) of subsection (1) there shall be inserted the following—
    "or
    (d) by the presentation of, or the concurring in, a petition for the winding up of a company or by the submission of a claim in a liquidation in accordance with rules made under section 411 of the Insolvency Act 1986;".

(2) In paragraph (b) of the said subsection (1) the words "(or those sections as applied by section 613 of the Companies Act 1985)" shall be omitted.

(3) The said section 9 as amended by subsection (1) above shall have effect as regards any claim (whenever submitted) in a liquidation in respect of which the winding up commenced on or after 29 December 1986.

Short title and extent

2.—(1) This Act may be cited as the Prescription (Scotland) Act 1987.
(2) This Act extends to Scotland only.

ACCESS TO PERSONAL FILES ACT 1987*

(1987 c. 37)

An Act to provide access for individuals to information relating to themselves maintained by certain authorities and to allow individuals to obtain copies of, and require amendment of, such information.

[15th May 1987]

PARLIAMENTARY DEBATES

Hansard: H.C. Vol. 107, col. 354; Vol. 110, col. 1167; Vol. 114, col. 944; H.L. Vol. 486, col. 1421; Vol. 487, cols. 398, 710.

The Bill was considered in Standing Committee C on March 25 and April 1, 1987.

INTRODUCTION AND GENERAL NOTE

This is another Act to add to the access to information statutes which we have seen introduced since 1984. The legislation falls under a freedom of information rubric—with exempt categories—such as the Local Government (Access to Information) Act 1985 (see *Current Law* Statutes 1985, Vol. 2, c.43) and the Health Service Joint Consultative Committees (Access to Information) Act 1986.

The converse rubric is a "privacy"—although such a term in the present context is a misnomer—protection law allowing access by individuals to personal information, with exemptions, stored upon them by individuals or institutions within the terms of the statute. The Data Protection Act 1984 (DPA) allowing access by data subjects (on whom information is kept) to personal data (which is computerised or processed automatically) held by data users in both the public and private sectors is the major example of legislation under the latter rubric. That Act was passed to ratify and incorporate the European Convention on Data Protection (1981) into British law. If this had not been incorporated the transnational flow of computerised personal information into Great Britain could have been prohibited by signatory countries. Unlike the Privacy legislation of the U.S.A. and Canada and the Australian Freedom of Information Act, to name a few common law countries, the DPA does not apply to manual, *e.g.* paper, files.

The proponents of the present Act were not slow to point out the inconsistencies in similar authorities holding identical information, where one would be under a duty to disclose because it was covered by the DPA and not exempt, while in the other case it was not open to inspection because it was in manual form. Also, according to David Waddington M.P., Minister of State at the Home Office: "Many manual files are far more detailed and complex, and contain more by way of comment and opinion, than do computerised files" (*Hansard* H.C. Vol. 110, col. 1172). He cited figures of 75 million personal social security files; 3.75 million Immigration Department files "many over a foot thick"; other figures included files on 8.7 million current schoolchildren; 11 million council house tenants; 1 million social work records, etc. The National Computing Centre had advised: "This business of serious confidential records is terribly worrying, so if the information is extremely serious, my advice is to take it off the computer and put it back on a manual record where it is not covered [by the DPA]" (H.C. Vol. 110, col. 1183). On the other hand many multi-nationals had moved to a "completely paperless environment" (I.B.M. was cited as an example, *Hansard* H.C. Vol. 110, col. 1214). Whatever the position, the proponents wanted legislation to cover manual files.

The current Act was introduced by Mr. Archy Kirkwood M.P., who had received considerable assistance from the Freedom of Information Campaign. The Bill originally covered manual files relating to: health records; educational records (including those maintained by "any school, college, polytechnic, university, or any other educational establishment as defined in the Education Act 1944, s.77" and education authorities); housing records; benefit or other records (*eiusdem generis*); social services and welfare records; employment records held by *any* employer; bank, building society and credit records (*cf.* Consumer Credit Act 1974, s.158) and immigration records. The debates and the Campaign for Freedom of Information literature are punctuated by examples of numerous cases where personal information of the above kind had been inaccurate, misleading, erroneous and, potentially or actually, extremely damaging to innocent victims. Shortly after the introduction of the Bill, ITV's *World In Action* broadcast a programme

---

* Annotations by Patrick Birkinshaw: Barrister, Lecturer, Law School, Hull University.

about the Economic League's use of personal information on prospective employees which employers may obtain from the League to be advised of the political leanings of potential employees. This trade had brought about a "black-list" of those "not suitable" to employ, it was alleged, which in some cases had spread to their relatives.

Where such personal information was in the hands of an "employer" or other specified holder, it could have been examined by the individual concerned under the Bill. Applications were generally to be in writing. The remedies available under the Bill included amendment of inaccurate or irrelevant information and written reasons for refusing amendment, records of *ex parte* communications in writing (not orally) were to form part of the record, and compensation for damage suffered as a consequence of inaccurate or irrelevant information. A defence was provided that the record holder had taken such care "as in all the circumstances was reasonably required to ensure the accuracy and relevance of the information." Giving access in accordance with the terms of the Bill would not "constitute publication nor affect any privilege for the purposes of the law relating to defamation nor be a breach of confidence", *i.e.* to a third party provider. Parties seeking access who had been denied in whole or in part, or whose request had not been dealt with within the time limits, had been deferred or who sought compensation could apply to the High Court, county court, or in Scotland the Court of Session or Sheriff's court. The court could make a variety of orders. The Bill described those entitled to apply for access, especially their duly authorised representatives (*N.B.* Disabled Persons (Services, Consultation and Representation) Act 1986, s.1) or parents and guardians if the individual is under 16, though there were safeguards to protect confidentiality between the record holder and the individual (*cf. Gillick* v. *West Norfolk and Wisbech Area Health Authority and the D.H.S.S.* [1985] 3 All E.R. 402 (H.L.)) or where disclosure would expose the individual to a risk of serious physical or mental harm. A maximum charge for access was to be provided. Records within the kinds of classes covered by the Act compiled prior to the Act coming into effect would be accessible where they were referred to in any part of a record to which access was available and were "reasonably required to render that record intelligible". Exemptions protected against disclosure which would:

— affect the privacy of another individual who could be identified from that information unless s/he consented;
— reveal the identity of an individual who had provided information to the record holder (*D.* v. *N.S.P.C.C.* [1978] A.C. 171) unless s/he consented;
— expose another person to the risk of serious physical or mental harm;
— reveal information held for the purpose of preventing or detecting crime or apprehending or prosecuting offenders or assessing or collecting any tax or duty in any case where to do so would prejudice that purpose (for the latter duty *cf.: Alfred Crompton Amusement Machines* v. *Commissioners of Customs and Excise (No. 2)* [1973] 2 All E.R. 1169 (H.L.); and *N.B. Norwich Pharmacal Co.* v. *Commissioners of Customs and Excise* [1973] 2 All E.R. 943 (H.L.));
— jeopardise national security (though presumably the *ipse dixit* of a Minister that national security was involved would not be sufficient (some evidence would be necessary to support such, given *in camera* if necessary, *see Council of Civil Service Unions* v. *Minister for the Civil Service* [1985] A.C. 374; *R.* v. *Secretary of State for the Home Department, ex p. Ruddock* [1987] 2 All E.R. 518); or
— interfere with legal professional privilege.

Where it appeared to the record-holder on the advice of a "suitably qualified practitioner" (as defined) that access would expose the applicant to (i) distress or; (ii) serious physical or mental harm, safeguards existed. For (i) the record-holder could require that the record be inspected in the presence of a person nominated by the practitioner before being supplied with copies. For (ii) access could be deferred for a period of not more than six months except that another similarly qualified medical practitioner named by the applicant may, at the applicant's request, receive the file within one month, disclosing to the applicant "so much of the record as he or she deems fit" within six months of the application.

The Bill met with opposition from those representing the interests of small businesses, and from trade associations. The Building Societies Association called it "anti-competitive". A host of organisations representing the interests of information holders supported the Bill including many health bodies. The British Medical Association was against, though feeling was mixed. Many housing, education, social services and some health authorities operated voluntary access schemes. Mr. Austin Mitchell M.P., did not believe that the "Government, or any other body, should want surreptitiously to quash the Bill at the last minute, because they have not dared to show opposition by putting the argument clearly here, and having it discussed openly" (*Hansard,* H.C. Vol. 110, col. 1198).

The Bill was not quashed. It was eviscerated! To prevent the Bill falling before the dissolution of Parliament for the 1987 General Election, the proponents accepted a Government draft. This only applied to housing and social services' authorities (for current social services practice and the relevant circular, see *infra*, note to Sched. 1, para. 1). An undertaking was given that education would be covered by regulations made under the Education Act 1980, s.27—none had been made in seven years. All other classes of record holder were dropped. All the details of the Bill as described above were elided. Instead the Secretary of State "may by regulations make such provisions as he considers appropriate" providing for access by individuals to "accessible personal information" and for the "erasure" or "rectification" of inaccurate records containing such personal information of which they are (or are treated as) the subjects. The details of the procedures and provisions are to be drafted in the regulations which are to be statutory instruments approved by the *affirmative resolution procedure*. The details of the Bill as described above will give an idea of the sorts of areas to be covered, even if the precise scope eventually differs. Comparison will be interesting.

Consultation shall take place with such authorities, or bodies representing authorities as the Secretary of State thinks appropriate. The regulations may, *inter alia,* authorise authorities to charge fees not exceeding the prescribed maximum. There is a firm undertaking that regulations will be passed. But this could not be an absolute guarantee. Periods from 12 months to the end of the following year after Royal Assent were variously put forward as the time scale for their presentation which should be expected: "unless consultation disclosed problems likely to delay the timetable. We made it plain that we accepted an obligation to make regulations" (Mr. Waddington M.P., Standing Committee C, first sitting March 25, 1987). The Minister of State at the Home Office undertook to enter into talks with the medical professions at an early stage with a view to achieving substantive and timely progress in opening up medical records still further on a non-statutory basis (Standing Committee C, col. 60).

The Access to Personal Files Regulations will, when (if?) approved, extend access to housing and social services records. Education records may be otherwise provided for, *supra*. However, other elements of the DPA are not likely to be extended to the present Act, *e.g.* registration of record holders or the appointment of a Registrar. The act only provides for possible access to a limited amount of personal information; it does not seek to regulate the use to which information can be put or the method by which it can be collected. It is unlikely that subjects will be able to add to or insist that information be removed if not inaccurate. It should be noted that irrelevant information is no longer specifically referred to. Nor is there any duty in the statute to ensure that information collected relates directly to an operating programme or activity of the authority nor that information is kept up to date, and is accurate and as complete as possible. Nor is there a requirement that it shall be used only for the purpose for which it was collected. It is hoped that regulations will attend to these matters. It is a pusillanimous Act and is meagre by the standards of the Privacy Acts of the United States or Canada for instance, both of which have been subject to serious criticism and appraisal by the respective legislatures in those countries recently (see, *e.g. Open and Shut: Enhancing the Right to Know and the Right to Privacy,* Standing Committee on Justice and Solicitor General (March 1987, Ottawa)). The notable fact about data (manual and computerised) protection legislation is its failure to define "privacy". If privacy can be defined as "the claim of individuals, groups or institutions to determine for themselves when, how, and to what extent information about them is to be communicated to others" absenting good reasons for invading such, we have a long way to go in Great Britain.

Where personal information is held by "holders" of a kind not specified by the Act and where their possession of information is not otherwise prohibited by the law, *e.g.* Official Secrets Act 1911, s.2, it will be well to remember that the possibility of a breach of confidence, trespass or wrongful interference with personalty (documents) under the Torts (Interference with Goods) Act 1977 may have occurred in the manner in which the information was obtained. In the absence of a breach of confidence, or breach of copyright or patent or such protection over intellectual property, British law does not provide for the protection of personal information *per se* unless an action, for, *e.g.* defamation, can be maintained. Further, the dealing with inaccurate information which causes harm—financial or physical/emotional—could on the facts amount to negligence as well as being defamatory. The proximity of the holder to the subject ought to be sufficient to satisfy a duty of care situation—in spite of recent attempts to limit the range of victims (*cf. Lawton* v. *B.O.C. Transhield* [1987] 2 All E.R. 608—duty between referee and job applicant).

Discovery may be applied for to obtain the "offending" or relevant documents, but in the nature of the action such a claim is likely to appear speculative unless the allegations are itemised, and may meet with little sympathy at the interlocutory stage before pleadings, *e.g.*

for an interim injunction (*see* R.S.C., Ord. 24, r.1(1)); *cf. Gaskin* v. *Liverpool City Council* [1980] 1 W.L.R. 1549) unless the applicant can satisfy the court on application that they are necessary to dispose fairly of the case and not to substantiate a suspicion (*R.H.M. Foods* v. *Bovril* [1982] 1 All E.R. 673 (C.A.)—a case concerning property rights of the plaintiff). *Anton Piller* orders may be invoked where there is a risk of destruction or interference with essential evidence (*Anton Piller K.G.* v. *Manufacturing Processes* [1976] Ch. 55). Specificity will be required. However, judges may be less sympathetic to bodies which peddle in personal information for profit than to statutory bodies collecting information in the exercise of their public duties and powers and where confidentiality is often required (*cf. Campbell* v. *Tameside M.B.C.* [1982] 2 All E.R. 791 (C.A.), though here a claim for immunity was unsuccessfully entered by the defendant and it was a personal injuries case). For pre-trial disclosure of expert medical reports in cases alleging professional negligence, see *Naylor* v. *Preston Area Health Authority* [1987] 2 All E.R. 353 and R.S.C., Ord. 38, r.38).

A final point takes us back to our introductory theme. This Act is not a freedom of information act, but an act allowing individuals access to a limited range of information about themselves. The relationship between the two themes which run in tandem was nicely expressed by Conservative M.P., Mr. Steve Norris in supporting the original Bill (*Hansard*, H.C. Vol. 110, col. 1172).

ABBREVIATIONS
    DPA: Data Protection Act 1984.
    LG(AI)A: Local Government (Access to Information) Act 1985.

Obligation to give access etc.

1.—(1) Subject to the provisions of this Act and regulations under section 3, any authority keeping records containing personal information which is accessible personal information for the purposes of this Act shall have such obligations as regards access to, and the accuracy of, that information as are imposed by the regulations.

(2) Where an individual is, or would but for any exemption be, entitled under section 21 of the Data Protection Act 1984 to be supplied with information constituting personal data of which he is the subject no obligation arises under this Act to give him access to that information.

(3) Section 106(5) of the Housing Act 1985 (duty of landlord authority to give access to certain information) shall not apply in respect of any information recorded by a landlord authority in respect of which the authority is under an obligation to give access under this Act.

(4) Section 27(3) of the Tenants' Rights, etc. (Scotland) Act 1980 (entitlement of applicant for housing to inspect certain records) shall not apply in respect of any information recorded by a body mentioned in subsection (1) of that section in respect of which the body is under an obligation to give access under this Act.

(5) The obligation to give access to information under this Act applies, subject to any exemptions or restrictions prescribed in the regulations, notwithstanding any enactment or rule of law prohibiting or restricting the disclosure, or authorising the withholding, of information.

DEFINITIONS
    "accessible personal information": s.2(3).
    "authority": Sched. 1 (for England and Wales); Sched. 2 (for Scotland).
    "personal information": s.2(2).

GENERAL NOTE
    As explained above, obligations upon authorities covered by this Act, health and social services, are to be provided for by regulations. The LG(AI)A provided for general access to local authority meetings and documents but exempted personal information even to the individual subjects.

Subs. (1)
    Personal information means information which relates to a living individual who can be identified from that information (or from that information and other information in the

possession of the authority keeping the record). It includes an expression of opinion. It does not include an indication of the intentions of the authority with respect to that individual. This will cause some difficulty where an expression of opinion is a ground for proposing a particular course of action. Identity may be by general description and not simply by name. It is to be hoped that authorities will be under a duty to provide an accurate and suitable index for a subject's inspection, especially to locate "other information" by cross reference. The spectre of the hidden file behind the public file was raised in the debates, and it was acknowledged that there was little that could be done to eradicate such a practice if there was a determination to utilise it.

Accessible personal information is that held by a relevant authority (housing and social services) on a record held for purposes as specified in Scheds. 1 and 2 with respect to those authorities.

For information recorded before the commencement date, see the General Note to s.2 and the note on s.2(4) *infra.*

Subs. (2)
   The DPA, s.21 creates the right of access for subjects *vis-à-vis* data holders. Where a right is created under s.21 to computerised data no right obtains under the current Act.

Subs. (3)
   Under the Housing Act 1985, s.106(5) (originally Housing Act 1980, s.44(6)) information about an applicant for housing on himself or his family *which he had provided,* was to be made available for his inspection. This right is to be subsumed under the present Act and claimed under Access legislation, not the Housing Act.

Subs. (4)
   This section allowed an applicant for housing to a body covered by the 1980 Act to have access to information provided by him in connection with his application. As with subs. (3) *supra,* the present Act subsumes that right.

Subs. (5)
   The rights under the current Act and regulations prevail against any other statutory prohibitions or restrictions on the disclosure of information. The most obvious statute is the Official Secrets Act 1911, especially s.2. This covers what may be loosely termed "Crown information". Police information is such and may be relevant in social services cases. Rights under the present Act will therefore override the prohibitions, etc., in the 1911 Act unless these are re-incorporated in "any exemptions or restrictions prescribed in the regulations". It is unlikely that this would be done wholesale but specific exemptions, *e.g.* investigation of crime, will doubtless be introduced.

Definition of accessible personal information

   2.—(1) The following provisions apply for the interpretation of this Act.

   (2) "Personal information" means information which relates to a living individual who can be identified from that information (or from that and other information in the possession of the authority keeping the record) including any expression of opinion about the individual but not any indication of the intentions of the authority with respect to that individual.

   (3) Subject to subsection (4) below, information is "accessible personal information" for the purposes of this Act if it is held in a record kept by an authority specified in the Table in Schedule 1 to this Act or, as respects Scotland, Schedule 2 to this Act and is information of a description specified in that Table in relation to that authority; and any obligation to give access to information is an obligation to give access to the individual who is the subject of it or is, under that Schedule, to be treated as such.

   (4) As respects any regulations under section 3, information is not accessible personal information if recorded before the commencement date of the regulations or the first commencement date of regulations imposing a corresponding obligation except to the extent that access to it is required to make intelligible information recorded on or after that date.

GENERAL NOTE

The definitional issues have been examined, *supra* (s.1(1)). However, under s.2(4) information is not "accessible personal information" if recorded *before* the commencement date of the regulations or the first commencement date of regulations imposing an obligation to allow access. But if access to "prior information" is required to make intelligible information recorded on or after that date, it will, to that extent, be accessible. The most obvious, but not exclusive, case is where there is a reference in "accessible personal information" to other records. Again, an index would be essential in many cases where information is not filed in one folder or receptacle.

Subs. (3)
See Sched. 1, para. 1, *infra.*

Subs. (4)
Supra.

Access regulations

3.—(1) The Secretary of State may by regulations make such provision as he considers appropriate for securing access by individuals to accessible personal information of which they are (or are treated as) the subjects and the rectification or erasure of inaccurate records containing such information.

(2) Regulations under this section may, in particular, for those purposes—

(a) impose obligations on the authorities keeping records containing such information to give access to the information in the prescribed manner;

(b) impose obligations on the authorities keeping records containing such information to rectify or make erasures in records containing inaccurate information;

(c) provide for exemptions from or impose restrictions on access to information or the rectification or erasure of inaccurate records;

(d) regulate the procedure for obtaining access to information or the rectification or erasure of inaccurate records;

(e) provide for decisions taken by authorities to be reconsidered or reviewed;

(f) authorise authorities to charge fees not exceeding the prescribed maximum; and

(g) make incidental and supplementary provision including provision defining the corresponding obligation for the purposes of section 2(4).

(3) Regulations under this section may make different provision for different descriptions of information, different authorities or other different circumstances.

(4) The Secretary of State shall, before making regulations under this section, consult such authorities or bodies representing authorities as he thinks appropriate.

(5) The power to make regulations under this section is exercisable by statutory instrument but no regulations under this section shall be made unless a draft of the regulations has been laid before and approved by a resolution of each House of Parliament.

(6) In this section "prescribed" means prescribed in regulations under it.

GENERAL NOTE

Subs. (1)

The proponents attempted to substitute the word "shall" for "may", thereby imposing, it was hoped, a mandatory duty. "May" prevailed, so the provision is empowering. As to the undertaking to make the regulations, see *supra* under the Introduction.

Subs. (2)

This specifies that the regulations may impose an obligation to:
—allow access in the prescribed manner;
—rectify or make erasures in records containing inaccurate information;
—provide for exemptions or restrictions on access or rectification or erasure;
—provide for decisions taken by authorities to be reconsidered or reviewed;
—authorise the charging of fees not in excess of a prescribed maximum;
—regulations for incidental and supplementary provision including the definition of the corresponding obligation for the purposes of s.2(4), *supra*.

Para. (c)

Under the DPA, s.29, health and social service records may be exempted from access, or access may be modified by an order under that section. Lengthy discussions have taken place between the Government and interests within the medical and social services fields. The D.H.S.S. published circulars on *Subject Access to Personal Health Information* seeking the views of health authorities, community health councils and family practitioner committees on the question of subject access. The Circulars pointed out that whatever provisions applied to computerised information would be expected to apply *de facto* to manual information. The general consensus was that a clinician would make the decision on what medical information was accessible, subject to independent review by another clinician and ultimate resort to the courts or Registrar. An order under the DPA on this matter is apparently pending.

Paras. (d), (e)

Access provision was spelt out in detail in the original Bill and it included a right to be "supplied with an explanation, which if the applicant so requests shall be in writing, or any abbreviations or symbols in such records which are not otherwise intelligible".

Para. (e) provides for reconsideration and review procedures to be made.

It is a standard feature of U.S. and Canadian provisions on access that there is a higher *de novo* review internally. In some cases, *e.g.* social service records, or medical records on a housing file there will be a need for expert reconsideration.

Subs. (3)

This subsection provides scope for tailoring provisions to suit particular kinds of information, different kinds of authorities or "other different circumstances".

Subs. (4)

The Secretary of State shall (that connotes a mandatory duty) consult with bodies representing authorities and authorities as he thinks fit before making regulations. He has a discretion as to whom is appropriate or "fit", reviewable on the limited grounds spelt out in *Associated Provincial Picture Houses* v. *Wednesbury Corp.* [1948] 1 K.B. 223, *per* Lord Greene M.R. as supplemented/explained by Lord Diplock's test of "irrationality" in *Council of Civil Service Unions* v. *Minister for Civil Service* [1984] 3 All E.R. 935 (H.L.). Once considered "fit" to be consulted, a mandatory duty to consult will usually obtain. What constitutes "consultation" has been discussed in *Rollo* v. *Minister of Town and Country Planning* [1948] 1 All E.R. 13; *Port Louis Corp.* v. *Att.-Gen. of Mauritius* [1965] A.C. 1111; see also *Agricultural, Horticultural and Forestry Industry Training Board* v. *Aylesbury Mushrooms* [1972] 1 W.L.R. 190.

A recent discussion of "consultation" by a Secretary of State with organisations representative of authorities is in *R.* v. *Secretary of State for Social Services, ex p. Association of Metropolitan Authorities* [1986] 1 All E.R. 164. On the facts, the length of time allowed for consultation was insufficient, and a declaration was granted to that effect. However, certiorari quashing the regulations was refused as the regulations had come into effect and were being administered by local authorities. There is a nice mix of conceptual confusions in the judge's ruling for the classically trained administrative lawyer but it must be remembered that relief under R.S.C., Ord. 53 is discretionary.

Subs. (5)

Regulations are to be made by statutory instrument having been approved *affirmatively* by both Houses in draft.

Financial provisions

4. There shall be paid out of money provided by Parliament any increase attributable to this Act in the sums payable out of moneys so provided under any other enactment.

GENERAL NOTE

Provision is made for payment out of the Exchequer of any increase attributable to the current Act "in the sums payable out of moneys so provided under any other enactment."

Short title and extent

5.—(1) This Act may be cited as the Access to Personal Files Act 1987.

(2) This Act does not extend to Northern Ireland.

GENERAL NOTE

Subs. (2)

This Act does not extend to Northern Ireland but an assurance was given in Standing Committee C, col. 59 (April 1, 1987) that the Act would be extended by way of Order in Council.

SCHEDULES

Section 2(3)   SCHEDULE 1

ACCESSIBLE PERSONAL INFORMATION: ENGLAND AND WALES

1. The following is the Table referred to in section 2(3).

TABLE OF AUTHORITIES AND INFORMATION

The authorities	*The accessible information*
Housing Act local authority.	Personal information held for any purpose of the authority's tenancies.
Local social services authority.	Personal information held for any purpose of the authority's social services functions.

Interpretation

2.—(1) The following provisions apply for the interpretation of the Table in paragraph 1 above.

(2) Any authority which, by virtue of section 4(e) of the Housing Act 1985, is a local authority for the purpose of any provision of that Act is a "Housing Act local authority" for the purposes of this Act and so is any residuary body established under section 57 of the Local Government Act 1985.

(3) Personal information contained in records kept by a Housing Act local authority is "held for any purpose of the authority's tenancies" if it is held for any purpose of the relationship of landlord and tenant of a dwelling which subsists, has subsisted or may subsist between the authority and any individual who is, has been or, as the case may be, has applied to be, a tenant of the authority; and, for the purposes of this Act, information about any member of the individual's family held for any purpose of that relationship or potential relationship shall be treated as information of which he is the subject and accessible by him accordingly.

(4) Any authority which, by virtue of section 1 or 12 of the Local Authority Social Services Act 1970, is or is treated as a local authority for the purposes of that Act is a "local social services authority" for the purposes of this Act; and personal information contained in records kept by such an authority is "held for any purpose of the authority's social services functions" if it is held for the purpose of any past, current or proposed exercise of such a function in any case.

(5) Any expression used in this Schedule and in Part II of the Housing Act 1985 or the Local Authority Social Services Act 1970 has the same meaning as in that Act.

GENERAL NOTE

Para. (1)

One question which springs to mind is the status of the private organisations that might take over the administration of publicly owned estates under the Government's plans as outlined in the Queen's Speech of June 25, 1987. It is to be hoped that they will be included as being under the duties of access provided by regulations. Sched. 2 for Scotland contains a specific reference to a Scottish Special Housing Association. There is no reference to housing associations in Sched. 1.

Regulations for education records are to be made under the Education Act 1980, s.27(1)(*d*), the Minister assured. S.27(7) of that Act refers to schools maintained by an L.E.A., any "special school not so maintained", *quaere* those that opt out of L.E.A. control under the Government's proposals in the Queen's Speech, *supra,* and basically further education establishments funded or financed by an L.E.A. or in receipt of grants under the Education Act 1944, s.100(1)(*b*). It is *not* as wide as the institutions covered in the original Bill (*supra,* Introduction).

Local social services authority. Since 1983, social services authorities have operated under a D.H.S.S. circular LAC(83)14 concerning "Disclosure of Information To Clients." The Circular provides guidance under the Local Authority Social Services Act 1970, s.7 which social service authorities "shall" act under (see Birkinshaw *Open Government, Freedom of Information and Local Government*, Local Government Legal Society Trust (1986), for details). It is likely that this detailed Circular will continue until the regulations are operative.

Section 2(3)   SCHEDULE 2

ACCESSIBLE PERSONAL INFORMATION: SCOTLAND

1. The following is the Table referred to in section 2(3).

TABLE OF AUTHORITIES AND INFORMATION

The authorities	*The accessible information*
Local authority. Development corporation. Scottish Special Housing Association.	Personal information held for any purpose of any of the authority's the corporation's or, as the case may be, the Association's tenancies.
Social work authority.	Personal information held for any purpose of the authority's functions under the Social Work (Scotland) Act 1968 and the enactments referred to in section 2(2) of that Act.

Interpretation

2.—(1) The following provisions apply for the interpretation of the Table in paragraph 1 above.

(2) "Local authority" means a regional, islands or district council, a joint board or joint committee of two or more of those councils or any trust under the control of such a council and "development corporation" has the same meaning as in the New Towns (Scotland) Act 1968.

(3) Personal information contained in records kept by a local authority, a development corporation or the Scottish Special Housing Association is held for any purpose of any of their tenancies if it is held for any purpose of the relationship of landlord and tenant of a dwelling-house which subsists, has subsisted or may subsist between the authority, corporation or, as the case may be, Association and any individual who is, has been or, as the case may be, has applied to be a tenant of theirs; and, for the purposes of this Act, information about any member of the individual's family held for any purpose of that relationship or potential relationship shall be treated as information of which he is the subject and accessible by him accordingly.

(4) "Social work authority" means a local authority for the purposes of the Social Work (Scotland) Act 1968 and personal information contained in records kept by such an authority is held for any purpose of their functions if it is held for the purpose of any past, current or proposed exercise of such a function in any case.

CRIMINAL JUSTICE ACT 1987*

(1987 c. 38)

An Act to make further provision for the investigation of and trials for fraud; and for connected purposes.   [15th May 1987]

PRELIMINARY NOTE

The Criminal Justice Act 1987 received the Royal Assent on 15 May 1987. The purpose of the Act is to reform the law relating to fraud trials following the Report of the Roskill Committee on Fraud Trials (HMSO, 1986). Although the Committee's most controversial recommendation, that in some instances of complex fraud the trial should take place not before a judge and jury but rather before a fraud trials tribunal comprising a judge and two members with financial expertise, was rejected by the government, many of its other proposals on fraud trials are incorporated. The recommendations of the Roskill report are discussed in the commentary on the sections which follow, as appropriate. The wider reforms

---

* Annotations by Ian Leigh, LL.M., Solicitor, Lecturer in Law, Newcastle upon Tyne Polytechnic.

proposed by the Roskill report so as to allow greater use of documentary evidence in criminal trials will have to await further legislation.

The Act began life as a far-reaching Bill described as the centrepiece of the government's legislative programme for 1986–87. As originally published it covered not only fraud trials but also evidence, jury trials, sentencing, confiscation, compensation, the distribution of court business and extradition. However it was severely truncated when, to make way for an impending dissolution of Parliament and a general election, all the provisions except those relating to fraud trials were dropped at the Committee stage in the House of Lords. Although the Bill enjoyed a full Committee stage in the House of Commons without the guillotine, the Committee and Report stages in the House of Lords and the Commons' consideration of the Lords' amendments took place in a flurry of legislative activity with the government trying to secure the passage of as many Bills as possible in the available time. Nevertheless the House of Lords did secure some notable amendments, in relation to the Serious Fraud Office's powers of questioning (s.2), the disclosure of the defence case at preparatory hearings (s.9(5)) and the sanctions available against departures from the disclosed case (s.10).

S.1 establishes a Serious Fraud Office presided over by a Director under the superintendence of the Attorney-General to investigate and prosecute serious or complex frauds. S.2 gives the Director wide-ranging powers of investigation backed by criminal liability as a sanction for non-cooperation. S.3 deals with disclosure of information to and by the Serious Fraud Office. Ss.4–11 create procedures aimed at simplifying the conduct of fraud trials. By virtue of ss.4–6 a case involving alleged fraud may be transferred to the Crown Court without the need for committal proceedings if a notice of transfer is issued. Ss.7–11 provide for Preparatory Hearings before the judge sitting alone to be held at the commencement of fraud trials on indictment so as to simplify the issues going to the jury. S.12 allows the offence of conspiracy to defraud to be charged although the accused's alleged conduct may amount to other substantive offences or conspiracies to commit them. S.13 deals with the bringing into force of the Act in Northern Ireland. S.14 deals with financial provision. S.15 makes minor and consequential amendments. S.16 provides for commencement.

ABBREVIATION
"the Roskill report": The Report of the Roskill Committee on Fraud Trials (HMSO, 1986).

COMMENCEMENT
With the exception of ss.13 and 16–18, the Act comes into force on a day to be appointed by orders made by the Secretary of State under s.16. The Criminal Justice Act 1987 (Commencement No. 1) Order 1987 (S.I. 1987 No. 1061) brings into force ss.1, 12 and 14 and Sched. 1 with effect from July 20, 1987. S.1 and Sched. 1 come into force for the purposes only of the appointment of the Director of the Serious Fraud Office and the doing of such other things as may be necessary or expedient for the establishment of the Office.

EXTENT
The whole Act applies to England and Wales (s.17(1)). The Serious Fraud Office provisions (ss.1–3 and Sched. 1) apply to Northern Ireland (s.17(3)).

The powers of the Serious Fraud Office to obtain information (s.2) and reporting restrictions on preparatory hearings and applications to dismiss (s.11) apply to Scotland (s.17(2)).

PARLIAMENTARY DEBATES
Hansard: H.C. Vol. 105, col. 112; Vol. 106, col. 465; Vol. 113, cols. 912, 1120; Vol. 116, col. 426; H.L. Vol. 486, cols. 857, 1266; Vol. 487, col. 575.

The Bill was considered in Standing Committee F from December 11 to March 17, 1987.

PART I

FRAUD

Serious Fraud Office

The Serious Fraud Office

1.—(1) A Serious Fraud Office shall be constituted for England and Wales and Northern Ireland.

(2) The Attorney General shall appoint a person to be the Director of the Serious Fraud Office (referred to in this Part of this Act as "the Director"), and he shall discharge his functions under the superintendence of the Attorney General.

(3) The Director may investigate any suspected offence which appears to him on reasonable grounds to involve serious or complex fraud.

(4) The Director may, if he thinks fit, conduct any such investigation in conjunction either with the police or with any other person who is, in the opinion of the Director, a proper person to be concerned in it.

(5) The Director may—
(a) institute and have the conduct of any criminal proceedings which appear to him to relate to such fraud; and
(b) take over the conduct of any such proceedings at any stage.

(6) The Director shall discharge such other functions in relation to fraud as may from time to time be assigned to him by the Attorney General.

(7) The Director may designate for the purposes of subsection (5) above any member of the Serious Fraud Office who is—
(a) a barrister in England and Wales or Northern Ireland;
(b) a solicitor of the Supreme Court; or
(c) a solicitor of the Supreme Court of Judicature of Northern Ireland.

(8) Any member so designated shall, without prejudice to any functions which may have been assigned to him in his capacity as a member of that Office, have all the powers of the Director as to the institution and conduct of proceedings but shall exercise those powers under the direction of the Director.

(9) Any member so designated who is a barrister in England and Wales or a solicitor of the Supreme Court shall have, in any court, the rights of audience enjoyed by solicitors holding practising certificates and shall have such additional rights of audience in the Crown Court in England and Wales as may be given by virtue of subsection (11) below.

(10) The reference in subsection (9) above to rights of audience enjoyed in any court by solicitors includes a reference to rights enjoyed in the Crown Court by virtue of any direction given by the Lord Chancellor under section 83 of the Supreme Court Act 1981.

(11) For the purpose of giving members so designated who are barristers in England and Wales or solicitors of the Supreme Court additional rights of audience in the Crown Court in England and Wales, the Lord Chancellor may give any such direction as respects such members as he could give under the said section 83.

(12) Any member so designated who is a barrister in Northern Ireland or a solicitor of the Supreme Court of Judicature of Northern Ireland shall have—
(a) in any court the rights of audience enjoyed by solicitors of the Supreme Court of Judicature of Northern Ireland and, in the Crown Court in Northern Ireland, such additional rights of audience as may be given by virtue of subsection (14) below; and
(b) in the Crown Court in Northern Ireland, the rights of audience enjoyed by barristers employed by the Director of Public Prosecutions for Northern Ireland.

(13) Subject to subsection (14) below, the reference in subsection (12)(a) above to rights of audience enjoyed by solicitors of the Supreme Court of Judicature of Northern Ireland is a reference to such rights enjoyed in the Crown Court in Northern Ireland as restricted by any direction given by the Lord Chief Justice of Northern Ireland under section 50 of the Judicature (Northern Ireland) Act 1978.

(14) For the purpose of giving any member so designated who is a barrister in Northern Ireland or a solicitor of the Supreme Court of

Judicature of Northern Ireland additional rights of audience in the Crown Court in Northern Ireland, the Lord Chief Justice of Northern Ireland may direct that any direction given by him under the said section 50 shall not apply to such members.

(15) Schedule 1 to this Act shall have effect.

(16) For the purposes of this section (including that Schedule) references to the conduct of any proceedings include references to the proceedings being discontinued and to the taking of any steps (including the bringing of appeals and making of representations in respect of applications for bail) which may be taken in relation to them.

(17) In the application of this section (including that Schedule) to Northern Ireland references to the Attorney General are to be construed as references to him in his capacity as Attorney General for Northern Ireland.

DEFINITIONS

"Crown Court": Interpretation Act 1978, Sched. 1.
"England and Wales": Interpretation Act 1978, Sched. 1.

GENERAL NOTE

This section establishes a Serious Fraud Office under a Director appointed by and answerable to the Attorney-General. The powers of the Director and his staff are laid down in s.2 and in Sched. 1. The Roskill Committee had suggested that the government should consider creating an independent office to investigate and prosecute serious fraud which would bring together accountants, lawyers and policemen. The Serious Fraud Office is the government's response, modelled upon the Metropolitan Police's acclaimed Fraud Investigation Group. It is envisaged that it will have a staff of around 125 and deal with 50–100 cases each year. Its jurisdiction extends to Northern Ireland but not to Scotland (although the powers given by s.2 are exercisable there) (s.17).

Some concern was expressed in Parliament at the combining of the investigatory and prosecution roles in the one office. This appears to run directly counter to their separation in the case of other criminal offences by the creation of the Crown Prosecution Service in the Prosecution of Offences Act 1985, following the recommendations of the Royal Commission on Criminal Procedure (Cmnd. 8092 (1981) and see the White Paper, *An Independent Prosecution Service for England and Wales,* Cmnd. 9074 (1983)). The government argued, however, that the special and complex nature of some frauds made continuity of investigation and prosecution desirable. In similar vein the Roskill report had suggested that there should be early involvement of prosecuting counsel in fraud cases so as to establish at which points further evidence was needed in order to bring a successful prosecution (paras. 2.68–69).

Subs. (2)

The Director is appointed by and acts "under the superintendence" of the Attorney-General, the senior Law Officer. The Attorney-General's position in relation to the Director is equivalent to his relationship with the Director of Public Prosecutions where other offences are concerned (see Prosecution of Offences Act 1985, s.3(1)). The Director of the Serious Fraud Office is thus accountable directly, and not through the D.P.P., to the Attorney who in turn is accountable to the House of Commons for the Director's actions. Sched. 1, para. 3 provides that the Director of the Serious Fraud Office is to make an annual report to the Attorney-General, who is to lay it before Parliament. Opposition attempts to amend the Bill so as to give the supervisory role to the Lord Chancellor in place of the Attorney-General in the light of disquiet over the latter's role in the Westland affair and the Wright (MI5 memoirs) case, failed.

Under Sched. 1 the Attorney-General has various powers in relation to the conduct of proceedings by the Serious Fraud Office: these include powers to make regulations requiring justices of the peace and chief police officers to provide information (paras. 6 and 7 respectively). The Attorney-General also has power under para. 8 to make regulations prescribing scales of fees for counsel, remuneration for interpreters and recompense for witnesses in connection with proceedings brought by the Serious Fraud Office.

Subs. (3)

Serious or complex fraud. These words are not defined in the Act, with the effect that the Serious Fraud Office has a wide discretion as to which cases it chooses to investigate;

however, the powers are only exercisable on reasonable grounds. The requirement of reasonableness was introduced at the Committee stage in the House of Lords so as to harmonise with similar limitations on the powers to obtain information under s.2.

Some indication of the types of case which may be considered to involve serious or compiex fraud may be gleaned from the Home Office guidelines (H.O. Circular 16/1985, reproduced as Appendix H to the Roskill report) which previously advised the police on which types of case should be reported to the Fraud Investigation Group. These were (in cases of suitable complexity and importance) fraud upon government departments or local authorities, those involving large-scale corruption or large shipping or currency offences, frauds discovered during investigations by Inspectors under the Companies Acts, frauds upon the governments of other countries, those with an international dimension, or involving nationalised industries, by persons connected with Lloyds, the Stock Exchange or other Commodity Exchanges and those involving well-known public figures.

Subs. (4)

Where the Serious Fraud Office commences or takes over proceedings it will in effect take the place of the Crown Prosecution Service. By virtue of Sched. 1, para. 4 the Director of the Serious Fraud Office is not prevented from taking any step (such as the institution of proceedings) which would otherwise require the consent of the Director of Public Prosecutions or another; see also subs. (16).

Subss. (5)–(14)

These subsections allow the Director to designate barristers and solicitors who are members of the Serious Fraud Office to conduct proceedings. Subss. (9)–(11) give rights of audience to qualified members of the Serious Fraud Office identical to those enjoyed by Crown Prosecutors (see the Prosecution of Offences Act 1985, s.4). Subss. (12)–(14) make similar provision in Northern Ireland.

Director's investigation powers

2.—(1) The powers of the Director under this section shall be exercisable, but only for the purposes of an investigation under section 1 above, in any case in which it appears to him that there is good reason to do so for the purpose of investigating the affairs, or any aspect of the affairs, of any person.

(2) The Director may by notice in writing require the person whose affairs are to be investigated ("the person under investigation") or any other person whom he has reason to believe has relevant information to attend before the Director at a specified time and place and answer questions or otherwise furnish information with respect to any matter relevant to the investigation.

(3) The Director may by notice in writing require the person under investigation or any other person to produce at a specified time and place any specified documents which appear to the Director to relate to any matter relevant to the investigation or any documents of a specified class which appear to him so to relate; and—

  (a) if any such documents are produced, the Director may—

     (i) take copies or extracts from them;

     (ii) require the person producing them to provide an explanation of any of them;

  (b) if any such documents are not produced, the Director may require the person who was required to produce them to state, to the best of his knowledge and belief, where they are.

(4) Where, on information on oath laid by a member of the Serious Fraud Office, a justice of the peace is satisfied, in relation to any documents, that there are reasonable grounds for believing—

  (a) that—

     (i) a person has failed to comply with an obligation under this section to produce them;

     (ii) it is not practicable to serve a notice under subsection (3) above in relation to them; or

        (iii) the service of such a notice in relation to them might seriously prejudice the investigation; and

    (b) that they are on premises specified in the information,

he may issue such a warrant as is mentioned in subsection (5) below.

(5) The warrant referred to above is a warrant authorising any constable—

    (a) to enter (using such force as is reasonably necessary for the purpose) and search the premises, and

    (b) to take possession of any documents appearing to be documents of the description specified in the information or to take in relation to any documents so appearing any other steps which may appear to be necessary for preserving them and preventing interference with them.

(6) Unless it is not practicable in the circumstances, a constable executing a warrant issued under subsection (4) above shall be accompanied by an appropriate person.

(7) In subsection (6) above "appropriate person" means—

    (a) a member of the Serious Fraud Office; or

    (b) some person who is not a member of that Office but whom the Director has authorised to accompany the constable.

(8) A statement by a person in response to a requirement imposed by virtue of this section may only be used in evidence against him—

    (a) on a prosecution for an offence under subsection (14) below; or

    (b) on a prosecution for some other offence where in giving evidence he makes a statement inconsistent with it.

(9) A person shall not under this section be required to disclose any information or produce any document which he would be entitled to refuse to disclose or produce on grounds of legal professional privilege in proceedings in the High Court, except that a lawyer may be required to furnish the name and address of his client.

(10) A person shall not under this section be required to disclose information or produce a document in respect of which he owes an obligation of confidence by virtue of carrying on any banking business unless—

    (a) the person to whom the obligation of confidence is owed consents to the disclosure or production; or

    (b) the Director has authorised the making of the requirement or, if it is impracticable for him to act personally, a member of the Serious Fraud Office designated by him for the purposes of this subsection has done so.

(11) Without prejudice to the power of the Director to assign functions to members of the Serious Fraud Office, the Director may authorise any competent investigator (other than a constable) who is not a member of that Office to exercise on his behalf all or any of the powers conferred by this section, but no such authority shall be granted except for the purpose of investigating the affairs, or any aspect of the affairs, of a person specified in the authority.

(12) No person shall be bound to comply with any requirement imposed by a person exercising powers by virtue of any authority granted under subsection (11) above unless he has, if required to do so, produced evidence of his authority.

(13) Any person who without reasonable excuse fails to comply with a requirement imposed on him under this section shall be guilty of an offence and liable on summary conviction to imprisonment for a term not exceeding six months or to a fine not exceeding level 5 on the standard scale or to both.

(14) A person who, in purported compliance with a requirement under this section—

(a) makes a statement which he knows to be false or misleading in a material particular; or

(b) recklessly makes a statement which is false or misleading in a material particular,

shall be guilty of an offence.

(15) A person guilty of an offence under subsection (14) above shall—

(a) on conviction on indictment, be liable to imprisonment for a term not exceeding two years or to a fine or to both; and

(b) on summary conviction, be liable to imprisonment for a term not exceeding six months or to a fine not exceeding the statutory maximum, or to both.

(16) Where any person—

(a) knows or suspects that an investigation by the police or the Serious Fraud Office into serious or complex fraud is being or is likely to be carried out; and

(b) falsifies, conceals, destroys or otherwise disposes of, or causes or permits the falsification, concealment, destruction or disposal of documents which he knows or suspects are or would be relevant to such an investigation,

he shall be guilty of an offence unless he proves that he had no intention of concealing the facts disclosed by the documents from persons carrying out such an investigation.

(17) A person guilty of an offence under subsection (16) above shall—

(a) on conviction on indictment, be liable to imprisonment for a term not exceeding 7 years or to a fine or to both; and

(b) on summary conviction, be liable to imprisonment for a term not exceeding 6 months or to a fine not exceeding the statutory maximum or to both.

(18) In this section, "documents" includes information recorded in any form and, in relation to information recorded otherwise than in legible form, references to its production include references to producing a copy of the information in legible form.

(19) In the application of this section to Scotland, the reference to a justice of the peace is to be construed as a reference to the sheriff; and in the application of this section to Northern Ireland, subsection (4) above shall have effect as if for the references to information there were substituted references to a complaint.

DEFINITIONS
"appropriate person": subs. (7).
"the Director": s.1(2).
"documents": subs. (18).
"level 5 of the standard scale": Criminal Justice Act 1982, ss.37 and 75.
"the person under investigation": subs. (2).
"the statutory maximum": Criminal Justice Act 1982, s.74.

GENERAL NOTE
This section contains the Serious Fraud Office's investigatory powers. It is modelled on similar powers given to inspectors of the Department of Trade and Industry by the Companies Act 1985 and the Financial Services Act 1986. However in some respects s.2 goes further since it applies to "any person" and the investigating officer may require questions to be answered. The powers granted by the section may be exercised not only by members of the Serious Fraud Office authorised by the Director but also any "competent investigator" from outside who is designated for the particular investigation (subs. (11)). Although the powers granted by the section are very wide, the use to which information obtained may be put is limited so far as court proceedings are concerned by subs. (8) and in relation to disclosure to others by s.3.

Nothing in s.2 prevents the Serious Fraud Office obtaining information voluntarily rather than in reliance on the coercive powers granted to it. Indeed one advantage from the Office's point of view of obtaining information wherever possible on the basis of co-operation (no doubt encouraged by the fact that the powers are in reserve) is that there will then be no limitations on the use which can be made of the information obtained. In particular, a confession voluntarily given will be allowed to be adduced as evidence-in-chief by the prosecution, provided it complies with ss.76 and 78 of the Police and Criminal Evidence Act 1984.

Subs. (1)

The circumstances in which the powers of investigation granted by the section could be used were the subject of great concern in Parliament. After much debate the government agreed to introduce the limitation "but only for the purposes of an investigation under section 1"—that is an investigation into "any suspected offence which appears to him on reasonable grounds to involve complex or serious fraud" (s.1(3)). The powers granted by s.2 may be used not only against suspected fraudsters but against "any person"—in other words potential witnesses also. Indeed in view of the nature of complex fraud, it will often be uncertain until an advanced stage in the investigation whether a particular person who is being questioned is a possible suspect or an innocent witness.

Subss. (2), (3)

These subsections contain very wide powers to require information, to demand answers to questions and to compel the production of documents. There is no exception made to allow a person under investigation to decline to answer questions on the grounds that to do so might incriminate him. However a statement so obtained may not be used directly in relation to the offence under investigation except as a prior inconsistent statement (subs. (8)). Documents which are legally privileged will be exempt from production by virtue of subs. (9). Likewise bankers may only be required to breach an obligation of confidence in the circumstances specified in subs. (10).

Failure to comply with a notice in writing under these subsections may result in the issue of a magistrates' warrant under subs. (4) and, if it is without reasonable excuse, will amount to an offence under subs. (13). There are further offences of knowingly or recklessly making a false or misleading statement (subs. (14)) and of falsifying, concealing or destroying documents relevant to an investigation (subs. (15)).

A requirement under subs. (3) to produce documents may include a requirement to produce a computer printout or a transcript of a recorded conversation by virtue of the definition of "documents" contained in subs. (18). If documents produced require interpretation in order to make them comprehensible to the investigator, this also may be required to be given under subs. (3).

Subs. (4)

Justice of the peace. In Scotland, the Sheriff, see subs. (19).

On information. In Northern Ireland, on complaint, see subs. (19).

A warrant may be issued to search for and seize documents not only where the justice of the peace is satisfied (on reasonable grounds) that there has been a failure to comply with a written notice, but also where a notice cannot be served because of grounds in paras. (ii) and (iii). The section does not specify what might make it impracticable to comply with a notice but presumably it might cover the situation of the occupier of premises who is unavailable, in which case reasonable force may be used to effect an entry (subs. (5)(a)). Serious prejudice to an investigation is not defined in para. (iii) but arguably it might occur if there were good reason to believe that documents would be destroyed or interfered with if prior notice were given. It is noticeable that neither this subsection nor those which follow provide protection for what would be "excluded material" or "special procedure material" (except information held by bankers to the extent of subs. (10)) under the Police and Criminal Evidence Act 1984, ss.8–14 and Sched. 1.

Subss. (5)–(7)

The execution of warrants by police constables is subject in all cases to the requirements of the Police and Criminal Evidence Act 1984, ss.15 and 16. These subsections act as an addition to those provisions. Similarly the powers of seizure must be read in conjunction with ss.19–22 of the 1984 Act. A constable executing a warrant under subs. (5) may, in addition to searching for and seizing documents, take steps to preserve them. Presumably intended are steps short of seizure where, for instance, the volume of documents prevents their immediate removal. A constable executing a warrant must, if practicable, be accompanied by a member of the Serious Fraud Office or some other person authorised by the Director. The reason is that specialist financial knowledge will often be required to identify the documents or the class of documents to which the warrant is applicable.

Subs. (8)

The only situations in which evidence of a statement given by a defendant under subs. (2) may be used against him are on a prosecution for making a false or misleading statement or where it is put to him in cross-examination or adduced in rebuttal as a prior inconsistent statement (for procedure see the Criminal Procedure Act 1865, ss.4 and 5). In the latter case the statement is not capable of founding a finding of fact but only goes to the credit of the witness (*R.* v. *Golder* [1960] 1 W.L.R. 1169).

Subs. (9)

Legal professional privilege. I.e. communications between a lawyer and his client for the purpose of giving advice and communications between a client or his legal adviser and third parties in contemplation or furtherance of proceedings, provided that use for the purpose of litigation is the dominant purpose of the communication, *cf.* Police and Criminal Evidence Act 1984, s.8(1)(d) and s.10.

A lawyer may only be required to furnish the name and address of his client. The subsection overrides the normal rules that a solicitor may be required to divulge the identity of his client on order of the court and is under a duty not to disclose his client's address unless properly called on to do so or by order of the court (see *The Professional Conduct of Solicitors* (1986), para. 10.05, and *Pascall* v. *Galanski* [1969] 3 All E.R. 1090, *Ramsbottom* v. *Senior* (1869) L.R. 8 Eq. 575 and *Arnott, ex p. Chief Official Receiver* 60 L.T. 109).

Subs. (10)

This subsection limits the circumstances in which bankers may be required to disclose information. The requirement that the Director must personally authorise the request is a comparatively weak safeguard when compared to the general rule that a court order is required to gain access to bank records (see s.7 of the Bankers' Books Evidence Act 1879, *R.* v. *Grossman* (1981) 71 Cr.App.R. 302 and *Williams* v. *Summerfield* [1972] 2 Q.B. 513).

Subs. (13)

Without reasonable excuse. The Court of Appeal held in *Re an Inquiry under the Company Securities (Insider Dealing) Act 1985, The Times,* May 7, 1987 that a journalist who refused to disclose his source did not have a reasonable excuse under the similar offence of refusing to give information, contained in the Financial Service Act 1986, s.178.

Disclosure of information

3.—(1) Where any information subject to an obligation of secrecy under the Taxes Management Act 1970 has been disclosed by the Commissioners of Inland Revenue or an officer of those Commissioners to any member of the Serious Fraud Office for the purposes of any prosecution of an offence relating to inland revenue, that information may be disclosed by any member of the Serious Fraud Office—

  (a) for the purposes of any prosecution of which that Office has the conduct;

  (b) to any member of the Crown Prosecution Service for the purposes of any prosecution of an offence relating to inland revenue; and

  (c) to the Director of Public Prosecutions for Northern Ireland for the purposes of any prosecution of an offence relating to inland revenue,

but not otherwise.

  (2) Where the Serious Fraud Office has the conduct of any prosecution of an offence which does not relate to inland revenue, the court may not prevent the prosecution from relying on any evidence under section 78 of the Police and Criminal Evidence Act 1984 (discretion to exclude unfair evidence) by reason only of the fact that the information concerned was disclosed by the Commissioners of Inland Revenue or an officer of those

Commissioners for the purposes of any prosecution of an offence relating to inland revenue.

(3) Where any information is subject to an obligation of secrecy imposed by or under any enactment other than an enactment contained in the Taxes Management Act 1970, the obligation shall not have effect to prohibit the disclosure of that information to any person in his capacity as a member of the Serious Fraud Office but any information disclosed by virtue of this subsection may only be disclosed by a member of the Serious Fraud Office for the purposes of any prosecution in England and Wales, Northern Ireland or elsewhere and may only be disclosed by such a member if he is designated by the Director for the purposes of this subsection.

(4) Without prejudice to his power to enter into agreements apart from this subsection, the Director may enter into a written agreement for the supply of information to or by him subject, in either case, to an obligation not to disclose the information concerned otherwise than for a specified purpose.

(5) Subject to subsections (1) and (3) above and to any provision of an agreement for the supply of information which restricts the disclosure of the information supplied, information obtained by any person in his capacity as a member of the Serious Fraud Office may be disclosed by any member of that Office designated by the Director for the purposes of this subsection—

  (a) to any government department or Northern Ireland department or other authority or body discharging its functions on behalf of the Crown (including the Crown in right of Her Majesty's Government in Northern Ireland);

  (b) to any competent authority;

  (c) for the purposes of any prosecution in England and Wales, Northern Ireland or elsewhere; and

  (d) for the purposes of assisting any public or other authority for the time being designated for the purposes of this paragraph by an order made by the Secretary of State to discharge any functions which are specified in the order.

(6) The following are competent authorities for the purposes of subsection (5) above—

  (a) an inspector appointed under Part XIV of the Companies Act 1985 or Part XV of the Companies (Northern Ireland) Order 1986;

  (b) an Official Receiver;

  (c) the Accountant in Bankruptcy;

  (d) an Official Assignee;

  (e) a person appointed to carry out an investigation under section 55 of the Building Societies Act 1986;

  (f) a body administering a compensation scheme under section 54 of the Financial Services Act 1986;

  (g) an inspector appointed under section 94 of that Act;

  (h) a person exercising powers by virtue of section 106 of that Act;

  (i) an inspector appointed under section 177 of that Act or any corresponding enactment having effect in Northern Ireland;

  (j) an inspector appointed under section 38 of the Banking Act 1987;

  (k) a person exercising powers by virtue of section 44(2) of the Insurance Companies Act 1982;

  (l) any body having supervisory, regulatory or disciplinary functions in relation to any profession or any area of commercial activity; and

  (m) any person or body having, under the law of any country or territory outside the United Kingdom, functions corresponding to any of the functions of any person or body mentioned in any of the foregoing paragraphs.

(7) An order under subsection (5)(d) above may impose conditions subject to which, and otherwise restrict the circumstances in which, information may be disclosed under that paragraph.

DEFINITIONS
"competent authority": subs. (5).
"England and Wales": Interpretation Act 1978, Sched. 1.

GENERAL NOTE
This section deals with the circumstances in which the Serious Fraud Office may lawfully obtain and disclose different categories of confidential information. Essentially the section establishes four categories of confidential information:
  1. Information supplied by the Inland Revenue (governed by subss. (1) and (2));
  2. Information under other (*i.e.* non-revenue) statutory obligations of secrecy (subs. (3));
  3. Information supplied subject to an agreement under subs. (4); and
  4. Other information obtained by the Serious Fraud Office (subss. (5)–(7)).

The section does not purport to deal with the consequences of improper disclosure beyond the authorised terms. Although no specific offence is created by this Act, it is probable that any such disclosure would amount to a criminal offence under the Official Secrets Act 1911, s.2(1). A person receiving such information could also be guilty of an offence under s.2(2) of the same Act. Civil remedies may also flow from improper disclosure in the form of an action for breach of confidence, unless the disclosure is in the public interest. In addition, agreements entered into by the Serious Fraud Office under subs. (4) will be enforceable on normal contractual principles. Where subs. (2) does not apply it may also be possible to argue that information improperly obtained outside the permitted breaches of confidence under the section should be excluded in any criminal proceedings in exercise of the court's discretion under the Police and Criminal Evidence Act 1984, s.78.

Subss. (1), (2)
  Obligation of secrecy under the Taxes Management Act 1970. As to the extent of such obligations see Taxes Management Act 1970, s.6 and Sched. 1.
  Information supplied to the Serious Fraud Office by the Inland Revenue is subject to a more restricted regime than other categories of information mentioned above. The effect of subs. (1) is that revenue offences may be prosecuted either by the Inland Revenue, the Crown Prosecution Service or the Serious Fraud Office (and in Northern Ireland, the D.P.P. for Northern Ireland). These subsections allow the Serious Fraud Office to use confidential information disclosed by the Commissioners of Inland Revenue to it for the prosecution of a revenue offence in investigating and prosecuting other categories of offence and to pass it on to the Crown Prosecution Service, but only for prosecuting revenue offences.
  The intention behind subs. (2) is to allow information to be used by the Serious Fraud Office where the fraud is believed, at least initially, to partially involve a revenue offence. It does not permit the Inland Revenue to disclose information to the Serious Fraud Office where no revenue offence is suspected in the first place. The potential importance of information obtained from the Inland Revenue was attested in Committee by the Minister of State:
  "It is difficult to imagine several very large frauds taking place without there also being a fraud on the Revenue. Just as Al Capone was finally brought to justice as a result of revenue offences, it is inevitable that anyone who obtains a large sum of money unlawfully must also inevitably transgress against the Revenue." (H.C. Standing Committee F, January 20, 1987, col. 142.)
  Paradoxically, if a fraudster does declare his unlawful income for tax purposes no revenue offence is committed and the Inland Revenue would not be entitled under the section to inform the Serious Fraud Office.
  The Inland Revenue cannot be compelled to give information—the subsections are permissive rather than mandatory.

Subs. (3)
  By or under any enactment. Examples of such obligations of secrecy overridden under this subsection would include the Race Relations Act 1976, s.52 and the Police and Criminal Evidence Act 1984, s.98.

Note that both this subsection and subs. (5) allow disclosure to authorities in other countries in some instances.

Subs. (4)

It was made clear in Committee that the government had in mind that this section would be useful not only for entering into agreements with individuals but also for long-term agreements between the Serious Fraud Office and large financial institutions or fraud agencies in other countries.

Subs. (5)

There is no express limitation under this subsection on the use which may be made by the receiving body under paras. (a) (b) or (d) (but see also subs. (7)). Information disclosed for the purposes of prosecution under (c) may be used in prosecutions unconnected with fraud.

Competent authority. Subs. (6) specifies thirteen categories. By far the widest is that in subs. (6)(l) which would permit disclosure of information, for instance, to the Law Society about the activities of a solicitor. Regulatory bodies such as self-regulating organisations under the Financial Services Act 1986 would also be included.

Transfer of cases to Crown Court

Notices of transfer and designated authorities

4.—(1) If—

    (a) a person has been charged with an indictable offence; and

    (b) in the opinion of an authority designated by subsection (2) below or of one of such an authority's officers acting on the authority's behalf the evidence of the offence charged—

        (i) would be sufficient for the person charged to be committed for trial; and

        (ii) reveals a case of fraud of such seriousness and complexity that it is appropriate that the management of the case should without delay be taken over by the Crown Court; and

    (c) before the magistrates' court in whose jurisdiction the offence has been charged begins to inquire into the case as examining justices the authority or one of the authority's officers acting on the authority's behalf gives the court a notice (in this Act referred to as a "notice of transfer") certifying that opinion,

the functions of the magistrates' court shall cease in relation to the case, except as provided by section 5(3) and (8) below and by section 28(7A) of the Legal Aid Act 1974.

(2) The authorities mentioned in subsection (1) above (in this Act referred to as "designated authorities") are—

    (a) the Director of Public Prosecutions;

    (b) the Director of the Serious Fraud Office;

    (c) the Commissioners of Inland Revenue;

    (d) the Commissioners of Customs and Excise; and

    (e) the Secretary of State.

(3) A designated authority's decision to give notice of transfer shall not be subject to appeal or liable to be questioned in any court.

DEFINITIONS

"Crown Court": Interpretation Act 1978, Sched. 1.

"designated authorities": subs. (2).

"magistrates' court": Interpretation Act, Sched. 1; Magistrates' Courts Act 1980, s.148.

GENERAL NOTE

Together with ss.5 and 6 this section establishes a mechanism for by-passing committal proceedings in the magistrates' court in alleged indictable offences involving fraud, where one of the subs. (2) authorities is satisfied that the pre-conditions in subs. (1) are met. The procedure (styled "a notice of transfer") will be available in cases of serious and complex fraud whether the Serious Fraud Office intervenes or not.

In 1981 the Royal Commission on Criminal Procedure (Cmnd. 8092) recommended that committal proceedings for all categories of criminal offences be abolished and replaced by the possibility of an application to discharge in the Crown Court, where a defendant claimed that there was insufficient evidence to go to trial. Pending action on this proposal (which it endorsed in relation to fraud), the Roskill report proposed as a more immediate method for avoiding potentially cumbersome and protracted committal hearings in complex fraud cases, the transfer of some cases direct to the Crown Court (Roskill report, paras. 4.43–46). This recommendation forms the basis of the "notice of transfer" procedure.

Subs. (1)

A notice of transfer may be served at any time between the defendant being charged and the commencement of normal committal proceedings. The circumstances prescribed by para. (b) are more limited than those envisaged in the Roskill report (which proposed that transfer should take place whenever the prosecution thought it appropriate). However since the Act contains no definition of serious or complex fraud and subs. (3) attempts to exclude judicial review (see comment below), there is a fair degree of discretion as to when the procedure may be invoked.

Sufficient for the person charged to be committed for trial. Presumably the test is the same as that to be applied by examining justices, namely whether there is a prima facie case upon which a reasonable jury could convict.

Subs. (3)

This subsection purports to exclude judicial review of the designated authority's decision to serve a notice of transfer. The Roskill report (para. 4.39) concluded that judicial review or interlocutory appeals should not be allowed because they would provide an opportunity to delay the proceedings and undermine the purpose of the new procedure. A defendant who wishes to challenge the strength of the evidence against him before trial will be able to do so under s.6. However, it is arguable that the Act also leaves open some possibility of judicial review in the case of the designated authority making an error as to jurisdiction, since ouster clauses of this kind have on occasion been held to be inapplicable in such cases (see *Anisminic* v. *Foreign Compensation Commission* [1969] 2 A.C. 147, *Pearlman* v. *Harrow School Governors* [1979] Q.B. 56 and *Re a Company* [1981] A.C. 374). It is noticeable that the subsection does not attempt to exclude review of the contents of the transfer notice under s.5, only the decision to serve it.

Notices of transfer—procedure

5.—(1) A notice of transfer shall specify the proposed place of trial and in selecting that place the designated authority shall have regard to the considerations to which section 7 of the Magistrates' Courts Act 1980 requires a magistrates' court committing a person for trial to have regard when selecting the place at which he is to be tried.

(2) A notice of transfer shall specify the charge or charges to which it relates and include or be accompanied by such additional matter as regulations under subsection (9) below may require.

(3) If a magistrates' court has remanded a person to whom a notice of transfer relates in custody, it shall have power, subject to section 4 of the Bail Act 1976 and regulations under section 22 of the Prosecution of Offences Act 1985—

(a) to order that he shall be safely kept in custody until delivered in due course of law; or

(b) to release him on bail in accordance with the Bail Act 1976, that is to say, by directing him to appear before the Crown Court for trial;

and where his release on bail is conditional on his providing one or more surety or sureties and, in accordance with section 8(3) of the Bail Act 1976, the court fixes the amount in which the surety is to be bound with a view to his entering into his recognizance subsequently in accordance with subsections (4) and (5) or (6) of that section, the court shall in the meantime make an order such as is mentioned in paragraph (a) of this subsection.

(4) If the conditions specified in subsection (5) below are satisfied, a court may exercise the powers conferred by subsection (3) above without the person charged being brought before it in any case in which by virtue of section 128(3A) of the Magistrates' Courts Act 1980 it would have power further to remand him on an adjournment such as is mentioned in that subsection.

(5) The conditions mentioned in subsection (4) above are—

 (a) that the person charged has given his written consent to the powers conferred by subsection (3) above being exercised without his being brought before the court; and

 (b) that the court is satisfied that, when he gave his consent, he knew that the notice of transfer had been issued.

(6) Where notice of transfer is given after the person charged has been remanded on bail to appear before examining justices on an appointed day, the requirement that he shall so appear shall cease on the giving of the notice, unless the notice states that it is to continue.

(7) Where the requirement that a person charged shall appear before examining justices ceases by virtue of subsection (6) above, it shall be his duty to appear before the Crown Court at the place specified by the notice of transfer as the proposed place of trial or at any place substituted for it by a direction under section 76 of the Supreme Court Act 1981.

(8) For the purposes of the Criminal Procedure (Attendance of Witnesses) Act 1965—

 (a) any magistrates' court for the petty sessions area for which the court from which a case was transferred sits shall be treated as examining magistrates; and

 (b) a person whose written statement is tendered in evidence for the purposes of the notice of transfer shall be treated as a person who has been examined by the court.

(9) The Attorney General—

 (a) shall by regulations make provision requiring the giving of a copy of a notice of transfer, together with a statement of the evidence on which any charge to which it relates is based—

  (i) to the person charged; and

  (ii) to the Crown Court sitting at the proposed place of trial; and

 (b) may by regulations make such further provision in relation to notices of transfer, including provision as to the duties of a designated authority in relation to such notices, as appears to him to be appropriate.

(10) The power to make regulations conferred by subsection (9) above shall be exercisable by statutory instrument subject to annulment in pursuance of a resolution of either House of Parliament.

(11) Any such regulations may make different provision with respect to different cases or classes of case.

DEFINITIONS
 "magistrates' court": Interpretation Act 1978, Sched. 1; Magistrates' Courts Act 1980, s.148.
 "notice of transfer": s.4(1).

GENERAL NOTE
 This section deals with the contents of notices of transfer and with incidental matters involved in the transfer of the case from the magistrates' court to the Crown Court. The Attorney-General is given the duty of making regulations which will deal with service of notices, disclosure of evidence and the contents of notices by virtue of subs. (9). Subss. (1) and (2) provide that the notice of transfer shall specify the proposed place of trial and

specify the charges to which it relates. The effect of a notice of transfer is that the magistrates' functions cease in respect of the defendant (s.4(1)). However the court retains jurisdiction by virtue of subss. (3)–(5) to deal with the question of bail for a defendant remanded in custody. Where, however, the court has already granted bail prior to the issue of the notice of transfer, the effect of subss. (6) and (7) is that the defendant's duty to answer to bail to the magistrates' court is superseded by an obligation to appear at the Crown Court trial.

Subs. (1)

The factors contained in s.7 of the Magistrates' Courts Act 1980 which must be considered in selecting the place of trial are the convenience of the defence, prosecution and witnesses, the expediting of the trial and any directions given by the Lord Chief Justice under s.75 of the Supreme Court Act 1981.

Subss. (3)–(5)

Subs. (3) preserves the jurisdiction of the magistrates' court which formerly remanded a defendant in custody to further remand him or release him on bail notwithstanding a notice of transfer. Subss. (4) and (5) allow the court to remand such a defendant in his absence where it would have had power to do so if no notice of transfer had been issued and he has given consent in the knowledge that a notice of transfer had been issued. The point about the defendant's knowledge is an important one because the issue of the notice of transfer will amount to a change of circumstances entitling the defendant to a fresh hearing of a full bail application under the rule in *R.* v. *Nottingham Justices, ex p. Davies* [1981] Q.B. 38.

Subs. (8)

The effect of this subs. is that the magistrates' court from which the case is transferred must make either full or conditional witness orders in relation to persons whose written statements are served with the notice of transfer in compliance with regulations made under subs. (9).

Dismissal of transferred charge

6.—(1) Where notice of transfer has been given, the person charged may at any time before he is arraigned apply orally or in writing to the Crown Court for the charge to be dismissed on the ground that the evidence which has been disclosed would not be sufficient for a jury properly to convict him of it.

(2) Subject to subsection (4) below, oral evidence may be given on the hearing of such an application only with leave of the judge.

(3) The judge shall grant such leave only if it appears to him, having regard to any matters stated in the application for leave, that the interests of justice require him to do so.

(4) The judge may order a person who has made a written statement which it is proposed to adduce in evidence to supplement that statement by oral evidence.

(5) If—

(a) the judge makes an order under subsection (4) above; and

(b) the written statement is submitted to the court,

the statement shall not be admitted as evidence unless

(i) the person who made it gives oral evidence; or

(ii) the judge gives leave for it to be admitted without his doing so.

(6) In deciding whether to grant an application under this section the judge shall have regard—

(a) to the evidence tendered by the prosecution;

(b) to any written or oral statement tendered by the defence in support of the application; and

(c) to any oral evidence on behalf of the prosecution or the defence given under this section.

(7) A discharge under this section shall have the same effect as a refusal by examining magistrates to commit for trial, except that no further

proceedings may thereafter be brought on the charge except by means of the preferment of a voluntary bill of indictment.

DEFINITIONS
"Crown Court": Interpretation Act 1978, Sched. 1.
"notice of transfer": s.4(1).

GENERAL NOTE
This section allows a defendant whose case is subject to a notice of transfer a similar opportunity to challenge the prosecution case prior to trial to that which he would have had at a committal hearing in the magistrates' court. However there are some noticeable differences between an application to dismiss made to the Crown Court under this section and committal proceedings:
1. There is no right to the equivalent of a "full" (that is with consideration of the evidence) committal hearing. Oral evidence may only be adduced on application to dismiss with the leave of the judge, either to supplement a written statement under subs. (4) or if the judge is of the view that the interests of justice require it. Thus the defence cannot require the prosecution to call witnesses whose testimony is relied upon nor can they call witnesses themselves as of right. This contrasts with the rule in committal proceedings that evidence may only be tendered in the form of statements under s.102 of the Magistrates' Courts Act 1980 if all parties consent.
2. The procedure does not appear to allow for the opportunity of a submission of no case to answer which the defence possess at the close of the prosecution's evidence in a full committal hearing (Magistrates' Courts Rules 1981, r.7(6)).
3. Magistrates have the possibility of committing for the trial of an indictable offence other than that with which the defendant was charged, even though there is insufficient evidence to commit for the offence charged. There is no express equivalent power for the judge who dismisses a charge under this section to substitute a different charge. It could probably be achieved by amending the indictment so as to include a fresh count (*cf. R.* v. *Johal* [1973] Q.B. 475). In any event, by virtue of subs. (7), the prosecution would not be prevented from proceeding from another alleged indictable offence and serving a fresh notice of transfer or, perhaps, preferring a voluntary bill of indictment.

Subs. (1)
The subsection does not prescribe a form for an application to dismiss save to establish that it may be orally or in writing. It may also be made at a preparatory hearing (s.9(3)). The judge is obliged to consider the matters listed in subs. (6).
Not sufficient for a jury to properly convict. In *R.* v. *Galbraith* [1981] 2 All E.R. 1060 the Court of Appeal considered the requisite standard in the context of the judge's role on a submission of no case to answer in the course of a trial. It held that if the weakness of the evidence derives from the view taken of the reliability of a particular witness, the judge should nevertheless allow the case to be tried by the jury. The same test would seem to be applicable to this subsection.

Subs. (2)
The Roskill report (paras. 4.48–4.50) envisaged that oral evidence at the application to dismiss stage would be rare, otherwise the main advantage of the notice of transfer procedure—to avoid unacceptable delays caused by protracted committal hearings—would be lost. It took the view that the right to cross-examine prosecution witnesses ought to be limited to those cases where the defendant stated in advance his reasons for wishing to do so (possibly supported by an affidavit stating why he believed the witness to be untruthful or unreliable). The subsection as drafted leaves a wider discretion with the judge but he must be satisfied that the interests of justice require leave to be granted (subs. (3)). The Roskill report suggested: "If it is clear to the judge that the defence are in effect pursuing a fishing expedition and are seeking a virtual dress rehearsal of the trial, the judge would refuse." (Para. 4.50.)

Subs. (7)
The effect of a refusal by examining magistrates to commit for trial is that it does not act as an acquittal and the prosecution are not subsequently prevented from proceeding with fresh charges either for the same offence or other offences (*R.* v. *Manchester City Stipendiary Magistrate, ex p. Snelson* [1977] 1 W.L.R. 791). This is subject, however, to the High Court's

power to prevent second committal proceedings as an abuse of the process of the court (*R. v. Horsham Justices, ex p. Reeves* (1981) 75 Cr.App.R. 236). The subsection modifies the principle in relation to a dismissal so as to prevent further charges for the same offence unless brought by the preferment of a voluntary bill of indictment.

Preparatory hearings

Power to order preparatory hearing

7.—(1) Where it appears to a judge of the Crown Court that the evidence on an indictment reveals a case of fraud of such seriousness and complexity that substantial benefits are likely to accrue from a hearing (in this Act referred to as a "preparatory hearing") before the jury are sworn, for the purpose of—

(a) identifying issues which are likely to be material to the verdict of the jury;

(b) assisting their comprehension of any such issues;

(c) expediting the proceedings before the jury; or

(d) assisting the judge's management of the trial,

he may order that such a hearing shall be held.

(2) A judge may make an order under subsection (1) above on the application either of the prosecution or of the person indicted or, if the indictment charges a number of persons, any of them, or of his own motion.

(3) If a judge orders a preparatory hearing, he may also order the prosecution to prepare and serve any documents that appear to him to be relevant and whose service could be ordered at the preparatory hearing by virtue of this Part of this Act or Crown Court Rules.

(4) Where—

(a) a judge has made an order under subsection (3) above; and

(b) the prosecution have complied with it,

the judge may order the person indicted or, if the indictment charges a number of persons, any of them to prepare and serve any documents that appear to him to be relevant and whose service could be so ordered at the preparatory hearing.

(5) An order under this section may specify the time within which it is to be complied with, but Crown Court Rules may make provision as to the minimum or maximum time that may be specified for compliance.

DEFINITION
"preparatory hearing": subs. (1).

GENERAL NOTE
A large part of the Roskill report was taken up with proposals for preparatory hearings in trials involving complex or serious fraud, which formed the basis for ss.7–9. The use of preparatory hearings is not limited to cases in which the Serious Fraud Office is involved. They may be ordered on the application of the prosecution or the defence (or any of the defendants in a multi-defendant case) or on the judge's own motion. The perceived advantages of preparatory hearings are those which appear in para. (1)(b) as the grounds on which such a hearing may be ordered. The effectiveness of preparatory hearings in simplifying the task of the jury is likely to receive close scrutiny, since the government stayed its hand on legislating on Roskill's more controversial proposal of replacing jury trial in some complex frauds with trial before a Fraud Trials Tribunal in order to see whether less drastic reforms would be successful.

The Act sets out in detail the powers which may be exercised at a preparatory hearing in s.9. However, *this* section also provides that orders for the service of documents may be made prior to the commencement of the trial. The structure of subss. (3)–(5) will in effect allow for orders to be made for something akin to an exchange of pleadings at a civil trial.

Although the timetable below is not written into the Act, the Roskill report gave it as an indication of the pre-trial stages:

"Before the first preparatory hearing
  (1) Prosecuting counsel to draft the indictment.
  (2) Trial judge to be nominated at an early stage.
  (3) Date of preparatory hearing to be fixed.
  (4) Service by prosecution of any remaining witness statements and documentary exhibits on the court and on the defence.
  (5) Prosecution to prepare and serve on the court and on the defence:
      (a) a case statement
      (b) schedules and summaries of contents of documentary evidence as appropriate.
  (6) Prosecution to prepare charts and glossaries of terms.
  (7) Prosecution to serve a schedule of facts which defence should be asked to admit.
  (8) Prosecution to serve a schedule of documents and defence to be asked to admit or deny authenticity and whether they intend to challenge the admissibility of the documents on any ground and if so to state them.
  (9) If the case has been brought to the Crown Court by way of a transfer certificate, the defendant would have the right to apply for discharge at an early stage.
  (10) Defence to agree appropriate schedules and summaries of documentary evidence served on them by prosecution.
  (11) Defence to disclose a written outline of their case following the receipt of prosecution's case statement.
  (12) Defence to serve on prosecution a counter-notice to (7) stating which facts are admitted and which are not, with reasons.
  (13) Defence to serve on prosecution a counter-notice to (8) and to admit or deny the authenticity of documents and to state, where relevant, grounds for challenging the admissibility of documents.
  (14) Defence to prepare a case statement, if desired.
At the first preparatory hearing:
  (15) Judge to ensure that all the above steps have been carried out, where appropriate, and, in any case where they have not, to give the appropriate orders and directions to the parties.
  (16) Points of law going to the root of the case or relating to the admissibility of evidence intended to be raised at the trial should be dealt with.
  (17) Judge to consider the need for further hearings.
  (18) Date of the trial to be fixed at this stage, if possible, or at a further preparatory hearing.
At further preparatory hearings (as required):
  (19) All outstanding matters to be dealt with." (Roskill report, para. 6.104.)
A timetable of this kind could be ordered under ss.7–9 but is not prescribed.
More detail may be put onto the bare bones of s.7 by Crown Court Rules.

Subs. (3)

Since the preparatory hearing will take place at the commencement of the trial but in the absence of the jury (s.8), it is probable that extensive use will be made of the powers under this subsection to order the preparation and service of documents in advance of the preparatory hearing. The orders made will no doubt resemble those made at pre-trial reviews in civil litigation. The documents which may be so required are those listed in s.9(4).

Subs. (4)

Where the two preconditions described in paras. (a) and (b) are met, the defence may be required to serve any of the documents which could be ordered under s.9(5) at a preparatory hearing. According to the phraseology of the subsection the power to make the order against the defence only arises if the prosecution has complied with an order under subs. (3). Contingent orders appear to be *ultra vires*.

Commencement of trial and arraignment

8.—(1) If a judge orders a preparatory hearing, the trial shall begin with that hearing.

(2) Arraignment shall accordingly take place at the start of the preparatory hearing.

DEFINITION
  "preparatory hearing": s.7(1).

GENERAL NOTE

The Roskill report (paras. 6.12–6.26) highlighted several factors which tended to make the existing voluntary system of pre-trial reviews in complicated criminal cases ineffective: an unwillingness to regard the procedure as important, changes of counsel or the judge between the pre-trial review and the trial, inadequate preparation (caused partly by the system of remuneration of the Bar) and the lack of sanctions attaching to undertakings given at pre-trial reviews. In *R. v. Hutchinson* [1985] Crim.L.R. 730 the Court of Appeal held that admissions made at an informal pre-trial review might not be used in evidence at trial without the consent of the party on whose behalf they were made.

To overcome these difficulties the Roskill report proposed a pre-trial review as "a preparatory part of (*not preparatory to*) the trial." This was seen to have two consequences. First, it would underline the importance of having the same counsel and judge throughout the trial and for the essential preparatory work to be done before the preparatory hearing, so as to get the maximum benefit from it. Whether s.8 will achieve this without corresponding changes in the professional conduct rules of the Bar and in the method of remuneration so as to encourage early preparatory work has been doubted by one commentator (Zander, [1985] Crim.L.R. 423, 428–429). Secondly, it would mean that the steps taken at the preparatory hearing could be referred to at the trial itself, thus remedying the defect identified in *Hutchinson*. Consequently, if, during the trial, a defendant retracts an admission made on his behalf at the preparatory hearing, it may be put to him in cross-examination (s.10).

In the normal course of a criminal trial on indictment, after arraignment the jury is sworn. However by virtue of s.7(1) the preparatory hearing takes place before the jury is sworn. Since the preparatory hearing may well be adjourned repeatedly (see s.9(2)), the trial may in effect continue for a substantial period in the absence of the jury. Although arraignment at this stage appears therefore to be mainly symbolic, it will also have some consequential effects. This will be the appropriate point at which to apply to amend or quash the indictment, to raise a plea of *autrefois convict* or *autrefois acquit* or to argue unfitness to plead.

The preparatory hearing

9.—(1) At the preparatory hearing the judge may exercise any of the powers specified in this section.

(2) The judge may adjourn a preparatory hearing from time to time.

(3) He may determine—

    (a) an application under section 6 above;

    (b) any question as to the admissibility of evidence; and

    (c) any other question of law relating to the case.

(4) He may order the prosecution—

    (a) to supply the court and the defendant or, if there is more than one, each of them with a statement (a "case statement") of the following—

        (i) the principal facts of the prosecution case;

        (ii) the witnesses who will speak to those facts;

        (iii) any exhibits relevant to those facts;

        (iv) any proposition of law on which the prosecution proposes to rely; and

        (v) the consequences in relation to any of the counts in the indictment that appear to the prosecution to flow from the matters stated in pursuance of sub-paragraphs (i) to (iv) above;

    (b) to prepare their evidence and other explanatory material in such a form as appears to him to be likely to aid comprehension by the jury and to supply it in that form to the court and to the defendant or, if there is more than one, to each of them;

    (c) to give the court and the defendant or, if there is more than one, each of them notice of documents the truth of the contents of which ought in the prosecution's view to be admitted and of any other matters which in their view ought to be agreed;

    (d) to make any amendments of any case statement supplied in pursuance of an order under paragraph (a) above that appear to the court to be appropriate, having regard to objections made by the defendant or, if there is more than one, by any of them.

(5) Where—

    (a) a judge has ordered the prosecution to supply a case statement; and

    (b) the prosecution have complied with the order,

he may order the defendant or, if there is more than one, each of them—

    (i) to give the court and the prosecution a statement in writing setting out in general terms the nature of his defence and indicating the principal matters on which he takes issue with the prosecution;

    (ii) to give the court and the prosecution notice of any objections that he has to the case statement;

    (iii) to inform the court and the prosecution of any point of law (including a point as to the admissibility of evidence) which he wishes to take, and any authority on which he intends to rely for that purpose;

    (iv) to give the court and the prosecution a notice stating the extent to which he agrees with the prosecution as to documents and other matters to which a notice under subsection (4)(c) above relates and the reason for any disagreement.

(6) Crown Court Rules may provide that except to the extent that disclosure is required—

    (a) by section 11 of the Criminal Justice Act 1967 (alibi); or

    (b) by rules under section 81 of the Police and Criminal Evidence Act 1984 (expert evidence),

a summary required by virtue of subsection (5) above need not disclose who will give evidence.

(7) A judge making an order under subsection (5) above shall warn the defendant or, if there is more than one, all of them of the possible consequence under section 10(1) below of not complying with it.

(8) If it appears to a judge that reasons given in pursuance of subsection (5)(iv) above are inadequate, he shall so inform the person giving them, and may require him to give further or better reasons.

(9) An order under this section may specify the time within which any specified requirement contained in it is to be complied with, but Crown Court Rules may make provision as to the minimum or maximum time that may be specified for compliance.

(10) An order or ruling made at or for the purposes of a preparatory hearing shall have effect during the trial, unless it appears to the judge, on application made to him during the trial, that the interests of justice require him to vary or discharge it.

(11) An appeal shall lie to the Court of Appeal from any order or ruling of a judge under subsection (3)(b) or (c) above, but only with the leave of the judge or of the Court of Appeal.

(12) Subject to rules of court made under section 53(1) of the Supreme Court Act 1981 (power by rules to distribute business of Court of Appeal between its civil and criminal divisions), the jurisdiction of the Court of Appeal under subsection (11) above shall be exercised by the criminal division of the court; and the reference in that subsection to the Court of Appeal shall be construed as a reference to that division.

(13) The judge may continue a preparatory hearing notwithstanding that leave to appeal has been granted under subsection (11) above, but no jury shall be sworn until after the appeal has been determined or abandoned.

(14) On the termination of the hearing of an appeal, the Court of Appeal may confirm, reverse or vary the decision appealed against.

DEFINITION

"preparatory hearing": s.7(1).

GENERAL NOTE

This section contains the kernel of the powers to make orders at a preparatory hearing and governs appeals from those orders (subss. (11)–(14)). At the preparatory hearing the judge may deal with any question of law or evidence or an application to dismiss under s.6(1), in addition to making any procedural orders for the preparation and service of documents (subs. (3)). It is envisaged that the crucial documents will be the prosecution case statement ordered under subs. (4)(a) and the defence objections in reply under subs. (5). The proposal that the judge should be able to order the defence to disclose its case under subs. (5) aroused considerable hostility from professional groups during the passage of the Bill.

In effect subss. (4)–(8) allow for the equivalent of civil pleadings and notices to admit documents and to admit facts to be provided. The judge has a discretion to order further and better particulars in the case of the prosecution under subs. (4)(d) and in the case of the defence under subs. (8).

The Roskill report laid stress upon how a jury's comprehension of a case could be greatly enhanced by effective non-traditional means of presenting evidence (especially financial data) such as the use of glossaries, flow charts and even computer graphics on in-court visual display units (paras. 6.63–66 and see also the research studies published with the Roskill report on the comprehension of jurors: A Report of Four Research Studies carried out for the Roskill Committee, HMSO 1986). The power to order such forms of presentation of evidence appears in subs. (4)(b).

Throughout the section the power of the court to make orders is expressed to be exercisable against defendants themselves rather than against their representatives. This form of words was adopted to avoid the professional ethical difficulty which would otherwise face counsel who was instructed by his client not to comply with an order under the section.

An order against the defence under subs. (5) can only be made where the prosecution has already disclosed its case in accordance with a prior order. The sanction against either side for non-compliance with an order requiring disclosure is that it may attract adverse comment under s.10; no doubt also costs sanctions could be employed in appropriate cases. The judge is under a duty by virtue of subs. (7) to warn the defence (but not the prosecution) of the possible adverse consequences of non-compliance.

The principles in the Act will be given substance by Crown Court Rules made under subss. (6) and (9).

Subs. (3)

Questions on the admissibility of evidence and other questions of law determined by the judge under this subsection are appealable under subs. (11). If the defendant wishes to apply to have the case dismissed, s.6(1) requires the application to be made before arraignment. Where the application is taking place at a preparatory hearing this requirement is difficult to reconcile with s.8(2) which provides that the hearing is to commence with arraignment. The safest way to reconcile the provisions in practice would be for the defendant to give notice of the intention to apply before arraignment even though the application is not heard until afterwards.

Subs. (5)

This subs. broadly follows a recommendation in the Roskill report (para. 6.75). The power to order the defence to disclose its case at a preparatory hearing attracted more controversy than any other part of the Act as it stands. The main ground of opposition voiced by professional groups was that the subsection abrogated the defendant's right of silence by requiring him to reveal his case before the prosecution had proved its. The wording which now appears was the result of a compromise reached at the Committee stage in the House of Lords (*Hansard,* H.L. Vol. 487, cols. 586–589). It enables disclosure by the defence to be ordered in a form which is considerably less precise than that originally proposed. Hence the reference to "a statement in writing in general terms". The defence will be able to keep in reserve the question of which witnesses they wish to call by virtue of rules made under subs. (6). A further safeguard exists in s.10 which prevents the prosecution or co-defendants referring before the jury to matters contained in a statement supplied under this subsection without first obtaining either the leave of the judge or consent.

Subs. (6)

Crown Court Rules may allow the defendant to keep the element of surprise, unless notice is required under the existing provisions in the cases of an alibi or an expert witness. The rules may also prescribe minimum and maximum time limits for compliance with orders made under this section (subs. (9)).

Subs. (10)

Orders made at preparatory hearings may be varied.

Subss. (11)–(14)

The provisions allowing appeal against orders at preparatory hearings have been constructed with two objectives: to allow appeals on interlocutory points to be dealt with without awaiting the outcome of the trial, but to limit the scope for repeated interruption of the preparatory hearing. The second objective is achieved by making the refusal of an application to dismiss unappealable, by making appeals subject to leave (subs. (10)) and by allowing the judge to continue the preparatory hearing (but not to proceed to swearing in the jury) while the appeal is outstanding (subs. (12)). Sched. 2, paras. 4 and 5 deal with the issue of bail pending an appeal against an order made at a preparatory hearing and para. 8 of the same schedule provides for legal aid to be available both for the application to seek leave and the appeal itself.

Provisions relating to later stages of trial

10.—(1) Where there has been a preparatory hearing, any party may depart from the case which he disclosed at the hearing but, in the event of such a departure or of failure to comply with a requirement imposed at the hearing, the judge or, with the leave of the judge, any other party may make such comment as appears to him to be appropriate and the jury may draw such inference as appears proper.

(2) In deciding whether to give leave the judge shall have regard in all cases—

    (a) to the extent of any departure from a case indicated at the preparatory hearing; and

    (b) to whether there was any justification for it.

(3) Except as provided by this section no part—

    (a) of a statement supplied under section 9(5) above; or

    (b) of any other information relating to the case for the defendant or, if there is more than one, the case for any of them, which was given at the preparatory hearing,

may be disclosed at a stage in the trial after the jury have been sworn without the consent of the person who supplied or gave it.

Definition

"preparatory hearing": s.7(1).

General Note

Although subs. (1) affirms the right to depart from the case disclosed at the preparatory hearing, the real significance of this section lies in the possible sanctions which it specifies for such a departure. These are in effect the teeth which the Roskill report recommended (paras. 6.76–82) were necessary in order to make the system of preparatory hearings bite. Read as a whole, the section prevents disclosure of any part of the defence case disclosed at the preparatory hearing unless there has been a departure from it and the judge gives leave (subs. (1)) or the defence consent. Comment may only be made on any departure by the prosecution or defence from their cases disclosed at the preparatory hearing by or with the leave of the judge. The section operates as an additional safeguard to the judge's discretion to exclude evidence at common law and under s.78 of the Police and Criminal Evidence Act 1984.

Subs. (1)

The subsection gives the judge and, with his leave, the prosecution, defence and co-defendants the right to comment on departures from the case disclosed at the preparatory hearings or on non-compliance with any orders made then. In deciding whether to give leave the judge must have regard to the extent of the departure and whether there was any justification (subs. (2)), but seemingly this does not apply expressly when he himself is deciding whether to comment.

Such comment as appears to him appropriate. Curiously the wording appears to be subjective, *i.e.* the person to whom the comment must seem appropriate is the one commenting, not necessarily the judge.

Adverse comment by a defendant or his representative upon a departure or non-disclosure by the prosecution may result in loss of the defendant's immunity from cross-examination about his previous convictions if it amounts to casting imputations on the character of the prosecutor or of a prosecution witness (Criminal Evidence Act 1898, s.1(f)(ii)). Similar adverse comment on departures from the case of a co-defendant would *not* result in a similar loss of immunity under s.1(f)(iii) of the same Act, unless the defendant himself gave evidence against the co-defendant.

The jury may draw such inference as appears to be proper. This form of words was introduced by way of amendment at the Committee Stage in the House of Lords (*Hansard*, H.L. Vol. 487, cols. 591–595) to limit the type of inference a jury may make on the basis of a departure from a case statement or defence reply or because of non-compliance with an order made under s.9(4). It is similar to that used in the Police and Criminal Evidence Act 1984, s.62, which allows a jury to draw inferences from a refusal to supply an intimate sample. The intention was to prevent a jury reaching a verdict of guilty *solely* because of such a departure or non-compliance. The subsection thus affords a possible ground of appeal under the Criminal Appeal Act 1968, s.2(1) in respect of inferences which a jury could not properly make.

Subs. (3)

This subsection affords some protection to the defendant required to reveal "in general terms the nature of his defence" under s.9(5). The fear was expressed in Parliament that without such a limitation, the prosecution case would become more of an exercise in anticipating and discrediting the defence than an exposition of the evidence against the defendant.

Except as provided by this section. The requirement for consent is overridden if the judge grants leave under subs. (1).

Reporting restrictions

Restrictions on reporting applications for dismissal and preparatory hearings

11.—(1) Except as provided by this section, it shall not be lawful to publish in Great Britain a written report, or to broadcast or include in a cable programme in Great Britain a report—

(a) of an application under section 6(1) above; or

(b) of a preparatory hearing,

containing any matter other than that permitted by this section.

(2) The Crown Court shall, on an application for the purpose with respect to any such application or hearing by the accused or one of the accused, as the case may be, order that subsection (1) above shall not apply to reports of the application or hearing.

(3) Where in the case of two or more accused one of them objects to the making of an order under subsection (2) above, the court shall make the order if, and only if, it is satisfied, after hearing the representations of the accused, that it is in the interests of justice to do so.

(4) An order under subsection (2) above shall not apply to reports of proceedings under subsection (3) above, but any decisions of the court to make or not to make such an order may be contained in reports published, broadcast or included in a cable programme before the time authorised by subsection (5) below.

(5) It shall not be unlawful under this section to publish, broadcast or include in a cable programme a report of an application under section 6(1) above containing any matter other than that permitted by subsection (8) below where the application is successful.

(6) Where—

(a) two or more persons were jointly charged; and

(b) applications under section 6(1) above are made by more than one of them,

subsection (5) above shall have effect as if for the words "the application is" there were substituted the words "all the applications are".

(7) It shall not be unlawful under this section to publish, broadcast or include in a cable programme a report of an unsuccessful application or a preparatory hearing at the conclusion of the trial of the person charged, or of the last of the persons charged to be tried.

(8) The following matters may be contained in a report published, broadcast or included in a cable programme without an order under subsection (2) above before the time authorised by subsections (5) and (6) above, that is to say—

(a) the identity of the court and the name of the judge;

(b) the names, ages, home addresses and occupations of the accused and witnesses;

(c) any relevant business information;

(d) the offence or offences, or a summary of them, with which the accused is or are charged;

(e) the names of counsel and solicitors engaged in the proceedings;

(f) where the proceedings are adjourned, the date and place to which they are adjourned;

(g) any arrangements as to bail;

(h) whether legal aid was granted to the accused or any of the accused.

(9) The following is relevant business information for the purposes of subsection (8) above—

(a) any address used by the accused for carrying on a business on his own account;

(b) the name of any business which he was carrying on on his own account at any relevant time;

(c) the name of any firm in which he was a partner at any relevant time or by which he was engaged at any such time;

(d) the address of any such firm;

(e) the name of any company of which he was a director at any relevant time or by which he was otherwise engaged at any such time;

(f) the address of the registered or principal office of any such company; and

(g) any working address of the accused in his capacity as a person engaged by any such company.

(10) The addresses that may be published or broadcast or included in a cable programme under subsection (8) above are addresses—

(a) at any relevant time; and

(b) at the time of their publication, broadcast or inclusion in a cable programme.

(11) In this section—

"engaged" means engaged under a contract of service or a contract for services, and

"relevant time" means a time when events giving rise to the charges to which the proceedings relate occurred.

(12) If a report is published, broadcast or included in a cable programme in contravention of this section, the following persons, that is to say

(a) in the case of a publication of a written report as part of a newspaper or periodical, any proprietor, editor or publisher of the newspaper or periodical;

(b) in the case of a publication of a written report otherwise than as part of a newspaper or periodical, the person who publishes it;

(c) in the case of a broadcast of a report, any body corporate which transmits or provides the programme in which the report is broadcast and any person having functions in relation to the programme corresponding to those of the editor of a newspaper or periodical;

(d) in the case of an inclusion of a report in a cable programme, any body corporate which sends or provides the programme and any person having functions in relation to the programme corresponding to those of an editor of a newspaper,

shall be liable on summary conviction to a fine not exceeding level 5 on the standard scale.

(13) Proceedings for an offence under this section shall not, in England and Wales, be instituted otherwise than by or with the consent of the Attorney General.

(14) Subsection (1) above shall be in addition to, and not in derogation from, the provisions of any other enactment with respect to the publication of reports of court proceedings.

(15) In this section—

"broadcast" means broadcast by wireless telegraphy sounds or visual images intended for general reception;

"cable programme" means a programme included in a cable programme service;

"publish", in relation to a report, means publish the report, either by itself or as part of a newspaper or periodical, for distribution to the public.

DEFINITIONS

"broadcast": subs. (15).

"cable programme": subs. (15).

"Crown Court": Interpretation Act 1978, Sched. 1.

"engaged": subs. (11).

"England and Wales": Interpretation Act 1978, Sched. 1.

"level 5 on the standard scale": Criminal Justice Act 1982, ss.37 and 75.

"preparatory hearing": s.7(1).

"publish": subs. (15).

"relevant business information": subs. (9).

"relevant time": subs. (11).

GENERAL NOTE

The effect of the section is to impose reporting restrictions on preparatory hearings and on applications to dismiss under s.6(1) in similar terms to those which apply to committal proceedings (Magistrates' Courts Act 1980, s.8). The section makes it an offence for details other than those specified in subs. (8) to be published prior to an application to dismiss succeeding (subs. (5)) or the conclusion of the case (subs. (7)). A prosecution for a contravention of the section may only be commenced with the consent of the Attorney-General (subs. (13)).

Subss. (2)–(4)

Reporting restrictions must be lifted if the defendant applies to the court. In a case involving two or more defendants the restrictions must be lifted if any of them applies, unless any of the others objects, in which case the court must decide whether it is in the interests of justice to do so. Where the defendants are in dispute as to whether restrictions should be lifted each has a right to be heard by the court under subs. (3). Restrictions continue to apply to a hearing to determine the issue of whether they should be lifted, but the outcome of the application may be reported (subs. (4)). The drafting of subs. (4) would appear to have the somewhat curious effect that even where, in a multi-defendant case, the court decides to lift restrictions in the interests of justice, the argument in court preceeding the decision cannot be reported until the restrictions would have ceased to apply if not lifted.

Subss. (5), (6)

Reporting restrictions cease to apply to applications to dismiss if the application is successful or, in the case of more than one defendant making such an application, all of them succeed. Thus if one co-defendant fails in an application to dismiss, the successful applications of the remainder may not be reported until the conclusion of the case against him, because to do so might prejudice the jury which is to try him. However the drafting of subs. (6) leaves an undersirable lacuna in that in a case where two or more defendants are jointly charged, reporting restrictions will be lifted in relation to successful s.6(1) applications by one or more defendants (provided all who apply to have their cases dismissed succeed), notwithstanding that there are outstanding charges against those who did not apply which may be prejudiced. It is anomalous that a defendant will be able to secure the continuation of a blanket reporting restriction against all his co-defendants if he (unsuccessfully) applies to have the case against him dismissed but not otherwise. (A possible means of avoiding this outcome is suggested in the note on subs. (14) below.) The fact that restrictions are lifted so as to allow the reporting of a successful application to dismiss will not, however, affect their application to the remaining aspects of the preparatory hearing of the cases of any defendants which are still outstanding.

Subs. (7)

Restrictions on reporting preparatory hearings are lifted at the conclusion of the trial of the defendant or of the last person charged with him.

Subs. (8)

This section contains a list of the details which may be published while restrictions continue to apply to preparatory hearings or to applications to dismiss.

Subs. (9)

By virtue of subss. (10) and (11) details of the addresses permitted to be published include not only addresses at the time of publication but also those at the time of the events giving rise to the prosecution.

Subs. (12)

This subsection places the liability for any failure to observe reporting restrictions under the section on the editorial staff and publishers. Reporters are not liable.

Subs. (14)

The most likely other source of reporting restrictions in a fraud case is the Contempt of Court Act 1981, s.4(2), which allows a court to make an order that reports of proceedings be postponed if immediate reporting would entail a substantial risk to the administration of justice either in the proceedings concerned or in other or pending proceedings. In *R.* v. *Horsham Justices, ex p. Farquharson* [1982] Q.B. 762 it was held that s.4(2) could be used by examining justices to prevent the lifting of reporting restrictions on committal proceedings. This subsection appears to allow a similar use of s.4(2) of the 1981 Act in relation to applications to dismiss under s.6(1) and preparatory hearings. This may be especially useful where it is desired partially to lift restrictions (a possibility not envisaged by subss. (2) and (3)) or to avoid the possibility of prejudice to a defendant whose co-defendants have successfully applied to have the cases against them dismissed (see note on subss. (5) and (6) above).

Conspiracy to defraud

Charges of and penalty for conspiracy to defraud

    12.—(1) If—

        (a) a person agrees with any other person or persons that a course of conduct shall be pursued; and

        (b) that course of conduct will necessarily amount to or involve the commission of any offence or offences by one or more of

the parties to the agreement if the agreement is carried out in accordance with their intentions,
the fact that it will do so shall not preclude a charge of conspiracy to defraud being brought against any of them in respect of the agreement.

(2) In section 5(2) of the Criminal Law Act 1977, the words from "and" to the end are hereby repealed.

(3) A person guilty of conspiracy to defraud is liable on conviction on indictment to imprisonment for a term not exceeding 10 years or a fine or both.

GENERAL NOTE

This section has two purposes. Subs. (1) reverses the decision in *R.* v. *Ayres* [1984] 1 All E.R. 619 that conspiracy to defraud could only be charged where the agreement was one which, if carried into effect, would not amount to the commission of a substantive offence by any of the conspirators. Subs. (3) limits the penalty for the offence, which was formerly at large.

Subs. (1)

The background to this subsection lies in the reform of the law of conspiracy effected by the Criminal Law Act 1977 following the Law Commission's Report on Conspiracy and Criminal Law Reform (Law Com. No. 76). Although the 1977 Act provided generally that conspiracy could only be charged where the course of conduct, if pursued, would amount to a criminal offence (Criminal Law Act 1977, s.1), it nevertheless preserved the common law offence of conspiracy to defraud (see s.5(2) of the 1977 Act). The reason for the survival of the offence was that the Law Commission had concluded that its abolition would leave unacceptable gaps in the law, in view of the fact that there is no substantive offence of fraud *per se* in English law (see Law Com. 76, paras. 1.14–1.16 and Law Commission Working Paper No. 56, Conspiracy to Defraud). The Law Commission conceived the retention of the offence to be a stop-gap pending the creation of a new general offence of fraud. This is still awaited. The effectiveness of the offence as a stop-gap was severely curtailed as a result of the decision in *R.* v. *Ayres* (see General Note).

Following *Ayres,* if the conspiracy would entail the commission of any substantive offence (however minor) by any of the defendants, it had to be charged as a conspiracy to commit the substantive offence under s.1(1) of the 1977 Act and not as conspiracy to defraud. Often the lesser offence would fail adequately to reflect the gravity of the accused's conduct because it simply focussed upon some incidental ingredient. This difficulty is amply demonstrated in the string of cases which followed *Ayres* (see *R.* v. *Cox and Mead, The Times,* December 6, 1984, *R.* v. *Tonner* [1985] 1 W.L.R. 344, *R.* v. *Lloyd* [1985] 3 W.L.R. 30, *R.* v. *Hollinshead* [1985] 3 W.L.R. 159, *R.* v. *Cooke* [1985] Crim.L.R. 215 and *R.* v. *Grant, The Times,* December 24, 1985). Although the Roskill report considered briefly the possibility that *Ayres* should be reversed by legislation, it recommended that the issue be considered further by an appropriate law reform agency.

Accordingly the Criminal Law Revision Committee (C.L.R.C.) was asked to consider whether the restrictions on the use of a charge of conspiracy to defraud resulting from *Ayres* and subsequent cases "could be removed without causing injustice to defendants." The C.L.R.C. duly recommended in its Eighteenth Report (Conspiracy to Defraud, Cmnd. 9873 (1986)) that legislation be introduced to return the law to its pre-1977 position (see *Scott* v. *Commissioner of Police for the Metropolis* [1975] A.C. 819) so that conspiracy to defraud could be charged notwithstanding that conspiracy to commit another offence could also be charged. This is the effect of subs. (1) and it incidentally required the amendment of s.5(2) of the Criminal Law Act 1977 in subs. (2). The subsection follows the form of the draft clause appended to the C.L.R.C.'s Report.

The C.L.R.C. recognised that this course of action would inevitably revive a wide overlap between conspiracy to defraud and conduct falling within s.1(1) of the Criminal Law Act 1977, but suggested that any possible injustice to defendants from the oppressive use of conspiracy to defraud charges could be avoided by the issue of guidelines to the Crown Prosecution Service on which charge to prefer in particular kinds of case. The D.P.P. has a statutory responsibility to issue a Code for the guidance of Crown Prosecutors under s.10 of the Prosecution of Offences Act 1985. The Minister of State indicated that guidelines would be included on the use of conspiracy to defraud charges (H.C. Standing Committee F, January 27, 1987, col. 288). Technically the Code under s.10 of the 1985 Act is made for the guidance of the Crown Prosecution Service only, however the C.L.R.C. understood that its guidelines would be commended to other authorities likely to prosecute conspiracy to defraud, such as the Inland Revenue, the Customs and Excise and the Serious Fraud Office.

There is an additional safeguard against the inappropriate use of the charge in the trial judge's inherent jurisdiction to control the proceedings.

Subs. (3)
Generally speaking conspiracy now carries the same maximum penalty as the relevant substantive offence (Criminal Law Act 1977, s.3). However, in the case of conspiracy to defraud the penalty was left at large by the 1977 Act, since there was no relevant substantive offence. Subs. (3) imposes a limit. The maximum term of imprisonment available for theft (10 years) was thought to be analogous, despite the C.L.R.C.'s opinion that in those instances where it would be appropriate to use the charge, 10 years would be insufficient.

PART II

GENERAL AND SUPPLEMENTARY

Northern Ireland

13.—(1) An Order in Council under paragraph 1(1)(b) of Schedule 1 to the Northern Ireland Act 1974 (legislation for Northern Ireland in the interim period) which contains a statement that it operates only so as to make for Northern Ireland provision corresponding to any provision of this Act to which this section applies—
  (a) shall not be subject to paragraph 1(4) and (5) of that Schedule (affirmative resolution of both Houses of Parliament); but
  (b) shall be subject to annulment in pursuance of a resolution of either House.

(2) The provisions of this Act to which this section applies are sections 4 to 12.

Financial provision

14. There shall be paid out of money provided by Parliament—
  (a) any expenses incurred under this Act by a Minister of the Crown; and
  (b) any increase attributable to the provisions of this Act in the sums payable out of such money under any other Act.

Minor and consequential amendments

15. The enactments mentioned in Schedule 2 to this Act shall have effect with the amendments there specified (being minor amendments and amendments consequential on the foregoing provisions of this Act).

Commencement

16.—(1) Subject to subsection (3) below, this Act shall come into force on such day as the Secretary of State may by order made by statutory instrument appoint; and different days may be appointed in pursuance of this subsection for different provisions or different purposes of the same provision.

(2) An order under subsection (1) above may make such transitional provision as appears to the Secretary of State to be necessary or expedient in connection with any provision thereby brought into force.

(3) The following provisions shall come into force on the day this Act is passed—
        section 13;
        this section;
        sections 17 and 18.

Extent

17.—(1) Subject to the following provisions of this section, this Act extends to England and Wales only.

(2) The following provisions extend also to Scotland—

    section 2;

    section 11;

    section 16;

    this section; and

    section 18.

(3) The following provisions extend also to Northern Ireland—

    section 1 (including Schedule 1) and sections 2 and 3;

    section 16;

    this section; and

    section 18.

(4) Section 13 above extends to Northern Ireland only.

(5) The extent of any amendment of an enactment in Schedule 2 to this Act is the same as that of the enactment amended.

(6) Her Majesty may by Order in Council direct that section 2 above shall extend, subject to such modifications as may be specified in the Order, to any of the Channel Islands.

(7) In subsection (6) above "modifications" includes additions, omissions and amendments.

Citation

18. This Act may be cited as the Criminal Justice Act 1987.

SCHEDULES

SCHEDULE 1

THE SERIOUS FRAUD OFFICE

General

1. There shall be paid to the Director of the Serious Fraud Office such remuneration as the Attorney General may, with the approval of the Treasury, determine.

2. The Director shall appoint such staff for the Serious Fraud Office as, with the approval of the Treasury as to numbers, remuneration and other terms and conditions of service, he considers necessary for the discharge of his functions.

3.—(1) As soon as practicable after 4th April in any year the Director shall make to the Attorney General a report on the discharge of his functions during the year ending with that date.

(2) The Attorney General shall lay before Parliament a copy of every report received by him under sub-paragraph (1) above and shall cause every such report to be published.

Procedure

4.—(1) Where any enactment (whenever passed) prohibits the taking of any step—

    (a) except by the Director of Public Prosecutions or except by him or another; or

    (b) without the consent of the Director of Public Prosecutions or without his consent or the consent of another,

it shall not prohibit the taking of any such step by the Director of the Serious Fraud Office.

(2) In this paragraph references to the Director of Public Prosecutions include references to the Director of Public Prosecutions for Northern Ireland.

5.—(1) Where the Director has the conduct of any criminal proceedings in England and Wales, the Director of Public Prosecutions shall not in relation to those proceedings be subject to any duty by virtue of section 3(2) of the Prosecution of Offences Act 1985.

(2) Where the Director has the conduct of any criminal proceedings in Northern Ireland, the Director of Public Prosecutions for Northern Ireland shall not in relation to those

proceedings be required to exercise any function under Article 5 of the Prosecution of Offences (Northern Ireland) Order 1972.

6.—(1) Where the Director or any member of the Serious Fraud Office designated for the purposes of section 1(4) above ("designated official") gives notice to any justice of the peace that he has instituted, or is conducting, any criminal proceedings in England and Wales, the justice shall—

(a) at the prescribed time and in the prescribed manner; or

(b) in a particular case, at the time and in the manner directed by the Attorney General; send him every recognizance, information, certificate, deposition, document and thing connected with those proceedings which the justice is required by law to deliver to the appropriate officer of the Crown Court.

(2) Where the Director or any designated official gives notice that he has instituted, or is conducting, any criminal proceedings in Northern Ireland—

(a) to a resident magistrate or a justice of the peace in Northern Ireland;

(b) to a clerk of petty sessions in Northern Ireland,

the person to whom the notice is given shall—

(i) at the prescribed time and in the prescribed manner; or

(ii) in a particular case, at the time and in the manner directed by the Attorney General, send him every recognizance, complaint, certificate, deposition, document and thing connected with those proceedings which that person is required by law to deliver to the appropriate officer of the Crown Court.

(3) The Attorney General may make regulations for the purpose of supplementing this paragraph; and in this paragraph "prescribed" means prescribed by the regulations.

(4) The Director or, as the case may be, designated official shall—

(a) subject to the regulations, cause anything which is sent to him under this paragraph to be delivered to the appropriate officer of the Crown Court; and

(b) be under the same obligation (on the same payment) to deliver to an applicant copies of anything so sent as that officer.

7.—(1) The Attorney General may make regulations requiring the chief officer of any police force to which the regulations are expressed to apply to give to the Director information with respect to every offence of a kind prescribed by the regulations which is alleged to have been committed in his area and in respect of which it appears to him that there is a prima facie case for proceedings.

(2) The regulations may also require every such chief officer to give to the Director such information as the Director may require with respect to such cases or classes of case as he may from time to time specify.

8.—(1) The Attorney General may, with the approval of the Treasury, by regulations make such provision as he considers appropriate in relation to—

(a) the fees of counsel briefed to appear on behalf of the Serious Fraud Office in any criminal proceedings; and

(b) the costs and expenses of witnesses attending to give evidence at the instance of the Serious Fraud Office and, subject to sub-paragraph (2) below, to any other person who in the opinion of that Office necessarily attends for the purpose of the case otherwise than to give evidence.

(2) The power conferred on the Attorney General by sub-paragraph (1)(b) above only relates to the costs and expenses of an interpreter if he is required because of the lack of English of a person attending to give evidence at the instance of the Serious Fraud Office.

(3) The regulations may, in particular—

(a) prescribe scales or rates of fees, costs or expenses; and

(b) specify conditions for the payment of fees, costs or expenses.

(4) Regulations made under sub-paragraph (1)(b) above may provide that scales or rates of costs and expenses shall be determined by the Attorney General with the consent of the Treasury.

9.—(1) Any power to make regulations under this Schedule shall be exercisable by statutory instrument subject to annulment in pursuance of a resolution of either House of Parliament.

(2) Any such regulations may make different provision with respect to different cases or classes of case.

Section 15   SCHEDULE 2

MINOR AND CONSEQUENTIAL AMENDMENTS

Administration of Justice (Miscellaneous Provisions) Act 1933 (c.36)

1.—(1) The following paragraph shall be inserted after paragraph (a) of subsection (2) of section 2 of the Administration of Justice (Miscellaneous Provisions) Act 1933 (procedures for indictment of offenders)—

"(aa) the offence is specified in a notice of transfer under section 4 of the Criminal Justice Act 1987 (serious and complex fraud); or".

(2) The following paragraph shall be inserted after paragraph (i) of the proviso to that subsection—

"(iA) in a case to which paragraph (aa) above applies, the bill of indictment may include, either in substitution for or in addition to any count charging an offence specified in the notice of transfer, any counts founded on evidence set out in the statement of evidence that was included in or accompanied that notice, in pursuance of regulations under section 5(9) of the Criminal Justice Act 1987, being counts which may lawfully be joined in the same indictment;".

Criminal Justice Act 1967 (c.80)

2. At the end of section 11(8) of the Criminal Justice Act 1967 (by virtue of which the period for giving notice of an alibi is 7 days from the end of the proceedings before the examining justices) there shall be added the words "or, where a notice of transfer has been given under section 4 of the Criminal Justice Act 1987, of the giving of that notice".

Criminal Appeal Act 1968 (c.19)

3. At the end of subsection (1) of section 33 of the Criminal Appeal Act 1968 (right of appeal to House of Lords) there shall be added the words "or section 9 (preparatory hearings) of the Criminal Justice Act 1987".

4. In section 36 of that Act (bail on appeal by defendant) after the word "Lords," there shall be inserted the words "other than a person appealing or applying for leave to appeal from a decision on an appeal under section 9(11) of the Criminal Justice Act 1987 (appeals against orders or rulings at preparatory hearings),".

5. In section 38 of that Act (presence of defendant at hearing) after the word "who" there shall be inserted the words "has been convicted of an offence and".

Prosecution of Offences (Northern Ireland) Order 1972 (S.I., 1972, No. 538 N.I. 1.)

6. In Article 5(3) of the Prosecution of Offences (Northern Ireland) Order 1972 (which makes provision, amongst other things, for the functions of the Director of Public Prosecutions in Northern Ireland in relation to the conduct of criminal proceedings) after the word "Director" there shall be inserted the words ", subject to any provision contained in the Criminal Justice Act 1987".

Legal Aid Act 1974 (c.4)

7. The following subsection shall be inserted after section 28(7) of the Legal Aid Act 1974—

"(7A) Where a notice of transfer is given under section 4 of the Criminal Justice Act 1987, the magistrates' court in whose jurisdiction the offence was charged or the Crown Court may order that the person charged shall be given legal aid for the purpose of the trial.".

8. The following subsection shall be inserted after section 28(8) of that Act—

"(8A) The Crown Court or the criminal division of the Court of Appeal may order that a person shall be given legal aid for the purpose—

(a) of an application for leave to appeal under section 9(11) of the Criminal Justice Act 1987 (appeals against orders or rulings at preparatory hearings); or

(b) of an appeal under that subsection.".

9. The following subsection shall be inserted after section 3(8) of the Bail Act 1976—

"(8A) Where a notice of transfer is given under section 4 of the Criminal Justice Act 1987, subsection (8) above shall have effect in relation to a person in relation to whose case the notice is given as if he had been committed on bail to the Crown Court for trial.".

Supreme Court Act 1981 (c.54)

10. In section 76 of the Supreme Court Act 1981 (alteration by Crown Court of place of trial)—

(a) in subsection (1), after the word "or", in the second place where it occurs, there shall be inserted the words "by substituting some other place for the place specified in a notice under section 4 of the Criminal Justice Act 1987 (notices of transfer from magistrates' court to Crown Court) or by varying";

(b) after subsection (2), there shall be inserted the following subsection—

"(2A) Where a preparatory hearing has been ordered under section 7 of the Criminal Justice Act 1987, directions altering the place of trial may be given under subsection (1) at any time before the jury are sworn"; and

(c) in subsection (3), for the word "or", in the second place where it occurs, there shall be substituted the words "as specified in a notice under section 4 of the Criminal Justice Act 1987 or as fixed".

11. In section 77(1) of that Act (by virtue of which Crown Court Rules are required to prescribe the minimum and maximum period which may elapse between a person's committal for trial and the beginning of the trial) after the word "trial", in the first place where it occurs, there shall be inserted the words "or the giving of a notice of transfer under section 4 of the Criminal Justice Act 1987".

12. In section 81(1)(a) of that Act (power of Crown Court to grant bail to any person committed in custody for appearance before the Crown Court) after the word "Court" there shall be inserted the words "or in relation to whose case a notice of transfer has been given under section 4 of the Criminal Justice Act 1987".

Prosecution of Offences Act 1985 (c.23)

13. In section 3(2) of the Prosecution of Offences Act 1985 (which makes provision, amongst other things, for the duties of the Director of Public Prosecutions in relation to the conduct of criminal proceedings) after the word "Director" there shall be inserted the words ", subject to any provisions contained in the Criminal Justice Act 1987".

14. The following paragraph shall be inserted after paragraph (a) of section 16(2) of that Act (defendant's costs order)—

"(aa) a notice of transfer is given under section 4 of the Criminal Justice Act 1987 but a person in relation to whose case it is given is not tried on a charge to which it relates; or".

15. The following subsection shall be inserted after section 16(4) of that Act—

"(4A) The court may also make a defendant's costs order in favour of the accused on an appeal under section 9(11) of the Criminal Justice Act 1987 (appeals against orders or rulings at preparatory hearings).".

16. At the end of subsection (2)(b) of section 18 of that Act (award of costs against accused) there shall be added "or

(c) an appeal or application for leave to appeal under section 9(11) of the Criminal Justice Act 1987;".

PARLIAMENTARY AND HEALTH SERVICE COMMISSIONERS ACT 1987*

(1987 c. 39)

ARRANGEMENT OF SECTIONS

SECT.
1. Extension of the jurisdiction of the Parliamentary Commissioner.
2. Removal of a Commissioner on grounds of incapacity for medical reasons.
3. Delegation of Parliamentary Commissioner's functions to officers.
4. Consultation and disclosure of information.
5. Reports by Health Service Commissioners: further provision.
6. Appointment of acting Commissioners.
7. Extension of time limit for reference of complaint to Health Service Commissioner for England or Wales.
8. Time limits in relation to references to Health Service Commissioner for Scotland.
9. Financial provision.
10. Citation, repeals, commencement and extent.

SCHEDULES:
Schedule 1—Schedule substituted for Schedule 2 to the 1967 Act.
Schedule 2—Enactments repealed.

An Act to make further provision in relation to the Parliamentary Commissioner for Administration and the Health Service Commissioners for England, Wales and Scotland, to provide for the appointment of persons for a limited period to act as the Parliamentary Commissioner or as a Health Service Commissioner, to extend the period within which complaints may be referred to the Health Service Commissioner for England or Wales by a body subject to investigation and to make fresh provision in relation to references of complaints to the Health Service Commissioner for Scotland.   [15th May 1987]

GENERAL NOTE

This Act implements the undertaking given by the Government in the White Paper, Observations by the Government on the Fourth Report from the Select Committee on the Parliamentary Commissioner for Administration, "Non-Departmental Public Bodies", 1983–84, Cmnd. 9563 (1985).

The main purpose, contained in s.1, is to extend the jurisdiction of the Parliamentary Commissioner for Administration to allow him to investigate the actions of certain non-departmental public bodies or quangos, specified in Sched. 1.

The range of bodies included in the Act largely follows that of the White Paper, although there are also some additions.

The Act also introduces, in the remaining sections, a number of more minor amendments to the legislation governing the operation of the Parliamentary and Health Service Commissioners.

Sched. 1 substitutes a new Sched. 2 to the Parliamentary Commissioner Act 1967, containing the extended list of departments and bodies subject to investigation.

Sched. 2 contains the enactments repealed.

ABBREVIATIONS

In the annotations the following abbreviations are used:

Select Committee: The Select Committee on the Parliamentary Commissioner for Administration.

H.C.619: Fourth Report from the Select Committee on the Parliamentary Commissioner for Administration, "Non-Departmental Public Bodies", Session 1983–84 H.C.619.

---

* Annotations by Colin Crawford, LL.M., Lecturer in Law, University of Manchester.

White Paper: Observations by the Government of the Fourth Report from the Select Committee on the Parliamentary Commissioner for Administration, "Non-Departmental Public Bodies", 1983–84, Cmnd. 9563 (1985).

PARLIAMENTARY DEBATES
   Hansard: H.C. Vol. 107, col. 679; Vol. 109, col. 1056; Vol. 112, col. 204; Vol. 116, col. 438; H.L. Vol. 485, col. 1126; Vol. 486, cols. 140, 964; Vol. 487, cols. 299, 606.
   The Bill was considered by Standing Committee E on February 17 to 19, 1987.

Extension of the jurisdiction of the Parliamentary Commissioner

1.—(1) The following section shall be substituted for section 4 of the Parliamentary Commissioner Act 1967 ("the 1967 Act")—

"Departments etc. subject to investigation
   4.—(1) Subject to the provisions of this section and to the notes contained in Schedule 2 to this Act, this Act applies to the government departments, corporations and unincorporated bodies listed in that Schedule; and references in this Act to an authority to which this Act applies are references to any such corporation or body.
   (2) Her Majesty may by Order in Council amend Schedule 2 to this Act by the alteration of any entry or note, the removal of any entry or note or the insertion of any additional entry or note.
   (3) An Order in Council may only insert an entry if—
      (a) it relates—
         (i) to a government department; or
         (ii) to a corporation or body whose functions are exercised on behalf of the Crown; or
      (b) it relates to a corporation or body—
         (i) which is established by virtue of Her Majesty's prerogative or by an Act of Parliament or an Order in Council or order made under an Act of Parliament or which is established in any other way by a Minister of the Crown in his capacity as a Minister or by a government department;
         (ii) at least half of whose revenues derive directly from money provided by Parliament, a levy authorised by an enactment, a fee or charge of any other description so authorised or more than one of those sources; and
         (iii) which is wholly or partly constituted by appointment made by Her Majesty or a Minister of the Crown or government department.
   (4) No entry shall be made in respect of a corporation or body whose sole activity is, or whose main activities are, included among the activities specified in subsection (5) below.
   (5) The activities mentioned in subsection (4) above are—
      (a) the provision of education, or the provision of training otherwise than under the Industrial Training Act 1982;
      (b) the development of curricula, the conduct of examinations or the validation of educational courses;
      (c) the control of entry to any profession or the regulation of the conduct of members of any profession;
      (d) the investigation of complaints by members of the public regarding the actions of any person or body, or the supervision or review of such investigations or of steps taken following them.
   (6) No entry shall be made in respect of a corporation or body operating in an exclusively or predominantly commercial manner or

a corporation carrying on under national ownership an industry or undertaking or part of an industry or undertaking.

(7) Any statutory instrument made by virtue of this section shall be subject to annulment in pursuance of a resolution of either House of Parliament.

(8) In this Act—

> (a) any reference to a government department to which this Act applies includes a reference to any of the Ministers or officers of such a department; and
>
> (b) any reference to an authority to which this Act applies includes a reference to any members or officers of such an authority.".

(2) The Schedule set out in Schedule 1 to this Act shall be substituted for Schedule 2 to the 1967 Act.

(3) The 1967 Act shall be further amended as follows—

> (a) in section 13(2) (application to Northern Ireland)—
>
>> (i) after the word "authority", in the first place where it occurs, there shall be inserted the words "or body"; and
>>
>> (ii) for the words "or authority", in the first place where they occur, there shall be substituted the words "authority or body";
>
> (b) in section 14(3) (complaints in respect of matters which arose before commencement) for the words "which arose before the commencement of this Act" there shall be substituted the words "whenever arising"; and
>
> (c) in paragraph 10(1) of Schedule 3 (matters not subject to investigation) for the words "listed in Schedule 2 to this Act" there shall be substituted the words "to which this Act applies".

GENERAL NOTE

The Select Committee on the Parliamentary Commissioner for Administration began an inquiry into the possible extension of jurisdiction of the Parliamentary Commissioner in the session 1979–80, but had delayed making a final report until the Government had completed its review of the nature and number of non-departmental public bodies (see Report of Non-Departmental Public Bodies, Cmnd. 7797, (1980)).

The Committee saw the subjection of quangos to possible investigation by the Commissioner as one of principle. That principle was to make such bodies as accountable as possible, but the Committee made it clear that it would be inappropriate for all these bodies to be included in the Commissioner's jurisdiction.

The criteria for exclusion employed by the Committee were as follows. First, those quangos which could be regarded as advisory were excluded on the ground that any action taken in the light of unsound advice was the responsibility of the Minister. Second, those which could be seen as a tribunal were excluded as being supervised already by the Council on Tribunals. This left those that could be regarded as executive or administrative but, again, it was not thought that all which fell into this category were appropriate for inclusion. The other groups of quangos to be excluded were therefore within this category. These were:

> (i) professional bodies or those involved in examinations or the dissemination of knowledge, on the ground that their administrative activities do not affect the man in the street;
>
> (ii) charities, on the ground that they are subject to the supervision of the Charities Commission;
>
> (iii) levy funded bodies already in existence, because these were not subject to audit by the Comptroller and Auditor General and therefore no Parliamentary oversight; and
>
> (iv) the nationalised industries on the ground that, although their complaints investigating mechanisms may be in need of reform, no evidence on this had been sought by the Committee.

The Committee, however, thought that other "commercial" quangos, such as development agencies and the Civil Aviation Authority should be included.

In addition it was considered that the functions of the Commission for New Towns and the New Town Development Corporations, other than housing and development which were already included, should be made subject to the jurisdiction of the Commissioners for Local Administration.

In the light of these criteria, a list of bodies considered appropriate was included as the Appendix to H.C.619.

The response of the Government, in the White Paper, was to note that the Select Committee had not shown evidence of significant maladministration by any of the bodies recommended for inclusion. Nevertheless, the case in principle for extending the jurisdiction of the Parliamentary Commissioner for Administration (PCA) to the actions of certain non-departmental bodies was accepted, although the range of bodies considered appropriate was different from that suggested by the Select Committee.

While accepting that advisory bodies and tribunals should be excluded, the Government limited the inclusion to bodies which

"(a) have executive or administrative functions which directly affect individual citizens or groups of citizens (including companies) and which would be within the PCA's jurisdiction if carried out by a government department; and

(b) are subject to some degree of ultimate Ministerial accountability to Parliament, in that they are dependent for their financing and continued existence on Government policy (even if legislation would be needed to abolish them)." (White Paper, para. 3).

The Government, however, did not accept the restriction suggested by the Select Committee that charities and levy funded bodies should be excluded *per se* but, instead, considered that they should be treated on their merits in the light of the general criteria.

The Government did not accept that other non-departmental public bodies which are "exclusively or predominantly commercial in character" should be included in the widened jurisdiction.

In regard to the Commission for New Towns, the New Town Development Corporations, and the Urban Development Corporations, the Government suggested that the functions of these bodies, other than housing and development which were already included in the jurisdiction of the Commissioners for Local Administration, should be within the jurisdiction of the Parliamentary Commissioner for Administration.

The list of those considered appropriate was included as Appendix B, and those suggested by the Select Committee, but which were excluded by the Government, as Appendix C to the White Paper.

The range of bodies included in the Act largely follows that of the White Paper, although there are also significant additions.

Subs. (1)

This subsection replaces s.4 of the Parliamentary Commissioner Act 1967, and it provides for the extension of jurisdiction to cover certain non-departmental public bodies specified in Sched. 1 to the 1987 Act. It also allows for the Schedule to be amended by Order in Council according to the criteral laid down in this subsection. The Order in Council is subject to negative resolution of either House.

The criteria utilised for the bodies to be included in the new Schedule follow largely those proposed in the White Paper, although they are open to interpretation. Thus, despite pressure in Parliament during the course of the debates, the Monopolies and Mergers Commission and the Boundary Commission are not included because they are deemed to be advisory only, and the Criminal Injuries Board and Civil Aviation Authority are deemed to be tribunals.

The Schedule does, however, include some which were not included in the list suggested in the White Paper, including:

—the Co-operative Development Agency;

—the Data Protection Registrar;

—the Equal Opportunities Commission and the Commission for Racial Equality, which were not considered to be caught by the "watchdog" exclusion under the new subs.(5)(d);

—the Horserace Betting Levy Board;

—Medical Practices Committees;

—the Central Council for Education and Training in Social Work; and

—the Industry Training Boards.

The criteria in the new subs. (3), for inclusion in the future, restricts the inclusion to bodies more than half of whose running costs comes from money provided by Parliament or funds raised under legislative authority. While this could be the subject of argument based on different accounting conventions, it must be noted that although a body may qualify under these criteria, there is no duty placed on the Government to include it.

The criteria for exclusion are laid down in the new subss. (5) and (6). Again, these are open to interpretation, but examples of their effect are as follows:

subs. (5)(a)	excludes educational establishments;
subs. (5)(b)	excludes the Council for National Academic Awards;
subs. (5)(c)	excludes the UK Central Council for Nursery and Midwifery;
subs. (5)(d)	excludes the Police Complaints Authority;
subs. (6)	excludes the nationalised industries, the Scottish and Welsh Development Agencies, and the commercial side of the Civil Aviation Authority.

Subs. (3)

This subsection contains drafting amendments consequential on the changes introduced by subs. (1).

Removal of a Commissioner on grounds of incapacity for medical reasons

2.—(1) Section 1 of the 1967 Act and section 90 of the National Health Service (Scotland) Act 1978 ("the 1978 Act") (which deal with the appointment of, and tenure of office by, respectively, the Parliamentary Commissioner and the Health Service Commissioner for Scotland) shall be amended as follows—

(a) in subsection (2), for the words "subsection (3)" there shall be substituted the words "subsections (3) and (3A)"; and

(b) after subsection (3), there shall be inserted the following subsection—

"(3A) Her Majesty may declare the office of Commissioner to have been vacated if satisfied that the person appointed to be the Commissioner is incapable for medical reasons—

(a) of performing the duties of his office; and

(b) of requesting to be relieved of it.".

(2) Section 106 of the National Health Service Act 1977 ("the 1977 Act") (appointment of, and tenure of office by, the Health Service Commissioner for England and the Health Service Commissioner for Wales) shall be amended as follows—

(a) in subsection (2), for the words "subsection (3)" there shall be substituted the words "subsections (3) and (3A)"; and

(b) after subsection (3), there shall be inserted the following subsection—

"(3A) Her Majesty may declare the office of Health Service Commissioner for England or Health Service Commissioner for Wales to have been vacated if satisfied that the person appointed to be the Commissioner is incapable for medical reasons—

(a) of performing the duties of his office; and

(b) of requesting to be relieved of it.".

DEFINITION

"the 1967 Act": s.1(1).

GENERAL NOTE

This section enables the removal of a commissioner who is incapable of carrying out the duties of the office, but is so severely incapacitated as to be unable to offer his resignation. The existing legislation provided no mechanism for such an eventuality, other than removal after addresses by both Houses of Parliament, which the Minister of State suggested was insensitive and inappropriate. It was stated that this provision was included as a purely precautionary measure to avoid considerable difficulties for the work of the ombudsmen.

Delegation of Parliamentary Commissioner's functions to officers

3. At the end of section 3(2) of the 1967 Act (which provides that any function of the Commissioner under the Act may be performed by any officer of the Commissioner authorised for that purpose by the Commissioner) there shall be added the words "or may be performed by any officer so authorised—

(a) of the Health Service Commissioner for England;
(b) of the Health Service Commissioner for Scotland; or
(c) of the Health Service Commissioner for Wales".

DEFINITION
"the 1967 Act": s.1(1).

GENERAL NOTE
This section enables the Parliamentary Commissioner for Administration to delegate authority to the staff of the Health Service Commissioners. This mirrors the existing provisions, in s.108 of the National Health Service Act 1977 and s.92 of the National Health Service (Scotland) Act 1978, by which the Health Service Commissioner can delegate authority to the staff of other commissioners. This was designed to allow the most effective use of the total staff, particularly for joint investigations.

Consultation and disclosure of information

4.—(1) In section 11 of the 1967 Act (provision for secrecy of information), the following subsection shall be inserted after subsection (2)—
"(2A) Where the Commissioner also holds office as a Health Service Commissioner and a person initiates a complaint to him in his capacity as such a Commissioner which relates partly to a matter with respect to which that person has previously initiated a complaint under this Act, or subsequently initiates such a complaint, information obtained by the Commissioner or his officers in the course of or for the purposes of investigating the complaint under this Act may be disclosed for the purposes of his carrying out his functions in relation to the other complaint.".
(2) The following section shall be inserted after that section—

"Consultations between Parliamentary Commissioner and Health Service Commissioners
11A.—(1) Where, at any stage in the course of conducting an investigation under this Act, the Commissioner forms the opinion that the complaint relates partly to a matter within the jurisdiction of the Health Service Commissioner for England, Wales or Scotland, he shall—
(a) unless he also holds office as that Commissioner, consult about the complaint with him; and
(b) if he considers it necessary, inform the person initiating the complaint under this Act of the steps necessary to initiate a complaint under Part V of the National Health Service Act 1977 (Health Service Commissioner for England and for Wales) or, as the case may be, Part VI of the National Health Service (Scotland) Act 1978 (Health Service Commissioner for Scotland).
(2) Where by virtue of subsection (1) above the Commissioner consults with the Health Service Commissioner in relation to a complaint under this Act, he may consult him about any matter relating to the complaint, including—
(a) the conduct of any investigation into the complaint; and
(b) the form, content and publication of any report of the results of such an investigation.
(3) Nothing in section 11(2) of this Act shall apply in relation to the disclosure of information by the Commissioner or any of his officers in the course of consultations held in accordance with this section.".
(3) In section 118 of the 1977 Act (consultations between Health Service Commissioners and Local Commissioners)—
(a) the following subsection shall be inserted after subsection (1)—

"(1A) Where, at any stage in the course of conducting an investigation under this Part of this Act, the Commissioner conducting the investigation forms the opinion that the complaint relates partly to a matter which could be the subject of an investigation under the Parliamentary Commissioner Act 1967, he shall—

   (a) unless he also holds office as the Parliamentary Commissioner, consult about the complaint with the Parliamentary Commissioner; and

   (b) if he considers it necessary, inform the person initiating the complaint under this Part of this Act of the steps necessary to initiate a complaint under the Parliamentary Commissioner Act 1967.

(1B) Where, at any stage in the course of conducting an investigation under this Part of this Act, the Commissioner conducting the investigation forms the opinion that the complaint relates partly to a matter within the jurisdiction of another Health Service Commissioner (whether under this Part of this Act or under Part VI of the National Health Service (Scotland) Act 1978), he shall—

   (a) unless he also holds office as that other Health Service Commissioner; consult about the complaint with him; and

   (b) if he considers it necessary, inform the person initiating the complaint under this Part of this Act of the steps necessary to initiate a complaint to the other Health Service Commissioner."; and

   (c) in subsection (2), for the words from the beginning to "any", in the first place where it occurs, there shall be substituted the words "Where a Commissioner consults with another Commissioner in accordance with this section, the consultations may extend to".

(4) In Schedule 13 to that Act (provisions as to investigations by Health Service Commissioner for England and for Wales), the following paragraph shall be inserted after paragraph 16—

"16A.—(1) Where the Commissioner also holds office as a relevant commissioner and a person initiates a complaint to him in his capacity as such a commissioner which relates partly to a matter with respect to which that person has previously initiated a complaint to him in his capacity as the Commissioner, or subsequently initiates such a complaint, information obtained by the Commissioner or his officers in the course of or for the purposes of the investigation under Part V of this Act may be disclosed for the purposes of his carrying out his functions in relation to the other complaint.

(2) In this paragraph "relevant commissioner"—

   (a) in relation to the Health Service Commissioner for England, means the Parliamentary Commissioner, the Health Service Commissioner for Wales and the Health Service Commissioner for Scotland; and

   (b) in relation to the Health Service Commissioner for Wales, means the Parliamentary Commissioner, the Health Service Commissioner for England and the Health Service Commissioner for Scotland.".

(5) The following section shall be inserted after section 95 of the National Health Service (Scotland) Act 1978—

"Consulting other Commissioners

95A.—(1) Where, at any stage in the course of conducting an investigation under this Part, the Commissioner forms the opinion that the complaint relates partly to a matter which could be the subject of an investigation under—

(a) the Parliamentary Commissioner Act 1967; or

(b) Part V of the National Health Service Act 1977,

he shall, if he considers it necessary, inform the person initiating the complaint of the steps necessary to initiate a complaint under the Parliamentary Commissioner Act 1967 or, as the case may be, Part V of the National Health Service Act 1977.

(2) In the circumstances described in subsection (1), the Commissioner shall consult the Parliamentary Commissioner or the Health Service Commissioner for England or for Wales, as appropriate, about the complaint (unless he also holds office as that other Commissioner) and such consultation may extend to any matter relating to the complaint, including—

(a) the conduct of any investigation into the complaint; and

(b) the form, content and publication of any report of the results of such an investigation;

and the application by section 95 of section 11(2) of the Parliamentary Commissioner Act 1967 shall not extend to the disclosure of information by the Commissioner or any of his officers in the course of such consultations.

(3) Where the Commissioner also holds office as any of the other Commissioners mentioned in subsection (2) and a person initiates a complaint to him in his capacity as such other Commissioner which relates partly to a matter with respect to which that person has previously initiated a complaint to him under this Part, or subsequently initiates such a complaint, information obtained by him or his officers in the course of or for the purposes of the investigation under this Part may be disclosed for the purposes of his carrying out his functions as such other Commissioner in relation to that person's complaint.".

DEFINITIONS

"the 1967 Act": s.1(1).

"the 1977 Act": s.2(2).

GENERAL NOTE

This section enables consultation and exchange of information between the Parliamentary Commissioner for Administration and the Health Service Commissioners. At present, these posts are held by the same person, and the Government stated that they had no intention of changing this allocation. The new provision is intended to provide a "prudent procedure" only.

Subss. (1), (5)

These subsections provide for information received in one capacity to be used in relation to a matter dealt with under another office, where the different offices are held by the same person.

Subss. (2), (3), (4)

These subsections provide for consultation and exchange of information between commissioners where the offices are held by different persons. The three subsections deal respectively with the Parliamentary Commissioner, the Health Service Commissioners for England and Wales, and the Health Service Commissioner for Scotland. Where a commissioner receives a complaint that seems to involve the responsibility of another commissioner, then he should consult that commissioner and if necessary inform the complainant of the possibility of making a second linked complaint.

Reports by Health Service Commissioner: further provision

5.—(1) In section 119(1) of the 1977 Act (which lists the persons to whom a Health Service Commissioner for England or Wales is required to send a report of the results of his investigation of a complaint) and section 96(1) of the 1978 Act (corresponding provision in relation to the Commissioner for Scotland), the following paragraph shall be inserted after paragraph (a)—

"(aa) to any member of the House of Commons who, to the Commissioner's knowledge, assisted in the making of the complaint (or if he is no longer a member to such other member as the Commissioner thinks appropriate),".

(2) In section 119(2) of the 1977 Act (Commissioner's duty, where he decides not to investigate a complaint, to send a statement of the reasons for his decision to the complainant and the body concerned) after "complaint" there shall be inserted "and to any such member of the House of Commons as is mentioned in subsection (1)(aa) above".

(3) In section 96(3) of the 1978 Act (corresponding provision in relation to the Commissioner for Scotland), for the word "and," in the second place where it occurs, there shall be substituted the word "to".

DEFINITIONS
  "the 1977 Act": s.2(2).
  "the 1978 Act": s.2(1).

GENERAL NOTE
  This section authorises the Health Service Commissioner to send copies of his reports to Members of Parliament who have been associated with the complaint. Previously the Commissioner had felt unable to do this because he had taken a cautious approach to the question of whether the reports would be privileged if disclosed in this way.

Appointment of acting Commissioners

6.—(1) The following section shall be inserted after section 3 of the 1967 Act—

"Appointment of acting Commissioner

3A.—(1) Where the office of Commissioner becomes vacant, Her Majesty may, pending the appointment of a new Commissioner, appoint a person under this section to act as the Commissioner at any time during the period of twelve months beginning with the date on which the vacancy arose.

(2) A person appointed under this section shall hold office during Her Majesty's pleasure and, subject to that, shall hold office—

(a) until the appointment of a new Commissioner or the expiry of the period of twelve months beginning with the date on which the vacancy arose, whichever occurs first; and

(b) in other respects, in accordance with the terms and conditions of his appointment which shall be such as the Treasury may determine.

(3) A person appointed under this section shall, while he holds office, be treated for all purposes, except those of section 2 of this Act, as the Commissioner.

(4) Any salary, pension or other benefit payable by virtue of this section shall be charged on and issued out of the Consolidated Fund."

(2) The following section shall be inserted after section 108 of the 1977 Act—

"Appointment of acting Commissioners

108A.—(1) Where the office of Health Service Commissioner for England or Health Service Commissioner for Wales becomes vacant, Her Majesty may, pending the appointment of a new Commissioner, appoint a person under this section to act as the Commissioner at any time during the period of twelve months beginning with the date on which the vacancy arose.

(2) A person appointed under this section shall hold office during Her Majesty's pleasure and, subject to that, shall hold office—

(a) until the appointment of a new Commissioner or the expiry of the period of twelve months beginning with the date on which the vacancy arose, whichever occurs first; and

(b) in other respects, in accordance with the terms and conditions of his appointment which shall be such as the Secretary of State may, with the approval of the Treasury, determine.

(3) A person appointed under this section shall, while he holds office, be treated for all purposes, except those of section 107 above, as the Commissioner.

(4) Any salary, pension or other benefit payable by virtue of this section shall be charged on and issued out of the Consolidated Fund.

(5) A person who is a member of a relevant body (within the meaning of section 109 below) shall not be appointed under this section; and a person so appointed shall not, during his appointment, become a member of a relevant body.".

(3) The following section shall be inserted after section 92 of the 1978 Act—

"Appointment of acting Commissioner

92A.—(1) Where the office of Commissioner becomes vacant, Her Majesty may, pending the appointment of a new Commissioner, appoint a person under this section to act as the Commissioner at any time during the period of twelve months beginning with the date on which the vacancy arose.

(2) A person appointed under this section shall hold office during Her Majesty's pleasure and, subject to that, shall hold office—

(a) until the appointment of a new Commissioner or the expiry of the period of twelve months beginning with the date on which the vacancy arose, whichever occurs first; and

(b) in other respects, in accordance with the terms and conditions of his appointment which shall be such as the Secretary of State may, with the approval of the Treasury, determine.

(3) A person appointed under this section shall, while he holds office, be treated for all purposes, except those of section 91, as the Commissioner.

(4) Any salary, pension or other benefit payable by virtue of this section shall be charged on and issued out of the Consolidated Fund.

(5) A person appointed under this section shall not, during his appointment, be a member of a body subject to investigation or any management committee thereof.".

DEFINITIONS
"the 1967 Act": s.1(1).
"the 1977 Act": s.2(2).
"the 1978 Act": s.2(1).

GENERAL NOTE
This section allows for the appointment of an acting commissioner for a period of up to 12 months, in the event of one of the offices becoming unexpectedly vacant. It was again stated that this provision was included as a purely precautionary measure, to avoid considerable difficulties for the work of the ombudsmen during the time it would take to appoint a permanent commissioner.

Extension of time limit for reference of complaint to Health Service Commissioner for England or Wales

7. In section 117(b) of the 1977 Act (which limits the time within which a relevant body (as defined in section 109 of that Act), may refer a

complaint against it to the Health Service Commissioner to three months),
for the word "three" there shall be substituted the word "twelve".

DEFINITION
   "the 1977 Act": s.2(2).

GENERAL NOTE
   This section extends to 12 months the period within which a health authority in England
and Wales may itself refer a complaint to the Health Service Commissioner. It was
considered that the three month time limit caused problems in practice, and that the 12
month period which already operated under the Scottish legislation was to be preferred.

Time limits in relation to references to Health Service Commissioner for Scotland

8. For section 94(5) of the 1978 Act (which allows a body subject to
investigation to refer a complaint to the Commissioner), there shall be
substituted the following—

   "(5) Notwithstanding the foregoing provisions of this section, a
   body subject to investigation—
      (a) may itself (excluding its officers) refer to the Commissioner a
          complaint that a person has, in consequence of a failure or
          maladministration for which the body is responsible, sustained
          such injustice or hardship as is mentioned in section 93(2)
          above if the complaint—
             (i) is made in writing to that body by that person, or by a
                 person authorised by virtue of subsection (2) above to
                 make the complaint to the Commissioner on his behalf,
                 and
            (ii) is so made not later than one year from the day mentioned
                 in subsection (3) above, or within such other period as
                 the Commissioner considers appropriate in any particular
                 case, but
      (b) shall not be entitled to refer a complaint in pursuance of
          paragraph (a) above after the expiry of twelve months begin-
          ning with the day on which the body received the complaint;
   and a complaint referred to the Commissioner in pursuance of this
   subsection shall, subject to section 93(6) above, be deemed to be duly
   made to him under this Part.".

DEFINITION
   "the 1968 Act": s.2(1).

GENERAL NOTE
   This section clarifies the operation of the existing 12 month time limit within which a
health authority in Scotland may itself refer a complaint to the Health Service Commissioner.
Previously, the National Health Service (Scotland) Act 1978 did not specify clearly from
when the 12 month period started.

Financial provision

9. There shall be paid out of money provided by Parliament any
increase attributable to the provisions of this Act in the sums payable out
of such money under any other Act.

Citation, repeals, commencement and extent

10.—(1) This Act may be cited as the Parliamentary and Health Service
Commissioners Act 1987.

   (2) The enactments mentioned in Schedule 2 to this Act are repealed
to the extent specified in the third column of that Schedule.

(3) This Act shall come into force at the end of the period of two months beginning with the date on which it is passed.

(4) For the purposes of subsection (3) of section 6 of the 1967 Act any time elapsing between the date of the passing and the date of the commencement of this Act (but not any time before the first of those dates) shall be disregarded in relation to a complaint against a corporation or body first listed in Schedule 2 to the 1967 Act on the commencement of this Act.

(5) This Act only extends to Northern Ireland so far as it relates to the 1967 Act and to the repeal of any enactment amending that Act.

DEFINITION
"the 1967 Act": s.1(1).

GENERAL NOTE
Subs. (2)
This subsection repeals those statutory provisions which had already made certain non-departmental bodies subject to the jurisdiction of the Parliamentary Commissioner for Administration, but which are now included, by Sched. 1, within the new Sched. 2 to the Parliamentary Commissioner Act 1967.

Subs. (3)
The Act received the Royal Assent on May 15, 1987.

Subs. (4)
This subsection provides that the two month period, between the passing and coming into effect of the Act, shall not exclude any complaints made in regard to matters which came to the attention of the complainant within 12 months prior to the passing of the Act.

SCHEDULES

Section 1   SCHEDULE 1

SCHEDULE SUBSTITUTED FOR SCHEDULE 2 TO THE 1967 ACT

SCHEDULE 2

DEPARTMENTS ETC. SUBJECT TO INVESTIGATION

Advisory, Conciliation and Arbitration Service.
Agricultural wages committee.
Ministry of Agriculture, Fisheries and Food.
Arts Council of Great Britain.
British Council.
British Library Board.
Building Societies Commission.
Certification Officer.
Charity Commission.
Civil Service Commission.
Co-operative Development Agency.
Countryside Commission.
Countryside Commission for Scotland.
Crafts Council.
Crofters Commission.
Crown Estate Office.
Customs and Excise.
Data Protection Registrar.
Ministry of Defence.
Development Commission.
Department of Education and Science.
Central Bureau for Educational Visits and Exchanges.

Department of Employment.
Department of Energy.
Department of the Environment.
Equal Opportunities Commission.
Export Credits Guarantee Department.
Office of the Director General of Fair Trading.
British Film Institute.
Foreign and Commonwealth Office.
Forestry Commission.
Registry of Friendly Societies.
Office of the Director General of Gas Supply.
Health and Safety Commission.
Health and Safety Executive.
Department of Health and Social Security.
Highlands and Islands Development Board.
Historic Buildings and Monuments Commission for England.
Home Office.
Horserace Betting Levy Board.
Housing Corporation.
Central Office of Information.
Inland Revenue.
Intervention Board for Agricultural Produce.
Land Registry.
The following general lighthouse authorities—
    (a) the Corporation of the Trinity House of Deptford Strond;
    (b) the Commissioners of Northern Lighthouses.

The Lord Chancellor's Department.
Lord President of the Council's Office.
Management and Personnel Office.
Manpower Services Commission.
Medical Practices Committee.
Scottish Medical Practices Committee.
Museums and Galleries Commission.
National Debt Office.
Trustees of the National Heritage Memorial Fund.
Department for National Savings.
Nature Conservancy Council.
Commission for the New Towns.
Development corporations for new towns.
Northern Ireland Court Service.
Northern Ireland Office.
Ordnance Survey.
Office of Population Censuses and Surveys.
Registrar of Public Lending Right.
Public Record Office.
Scottish Record Office.
Commission for Racial Equality.
Red Deer Commission.
Department of the Registers of Scotland.
General Register Office, Scotland.
Agricultural and Food Research Council.
Economic and Social Research Council.
Medical Research Council.
Natural Environment Research Council.
Science and Engineering Research Council.
Residuary Bodies.
Royal Mint.
Scottish Courts Administration.
Scottish Office.
Council for Small Industries in Rural Areas.
Central Council for Education and Training in Social Work.
Sports Council.
Scottish Sports Council.

Sports Council for Wales.
Stationery Office.
Office of the Director General of Telecommunications.
English Tourist Board.
Scottish Tourist Board.
Wales Tourist Board.
Board of Trade.
Department of Trade and Industry.
Agricultural Training Board.
Clothing and Allied Products Industry Training Board.
Construction Industry Training Board.
Engineering Industry Training Board.
Hotel and Catering Industry Training Board.
Plastics Processing Industry Training Board.
Road Transport Industry Training Board.
Department of Transport.
Treasury.
Treasury Solicitor.
Urban development corporations.
Development Board for Rural Wales.
Welsh Office.

NOTES

1. The reference to the Ministry of Defence includes the Defence Council, the Admiralty Board, the Army Board and the Air Force Board.

2. The reference to the Registry of Friendly Societies includes the Central Office, the Office of the Assistant Registrar of Friendly Societies for Scotland and the Office of the Chief Registrar and the Industrial Assurance Commissioner.

3. In the case of the Corporation of the Trinity House of Deptford Strond an investigation under this Act may only be conducted in respect of action in connection with their functions as a general lighthouse authority.

4. The reference to the Lord Chancellor's Department includes the department of the Accountant General of the Supreme Court and the department of the Public Trustee (whether or not either office is held by the Permanent Secretary to the Lord Chancellor).

5. The reference to the Lord President of the Council's Office includes the Office of Arts and Libraries but does not include the Privy Council Office.

6. The references to the Management and Personnel Office and the Treasury do not include the Cabinet Office, but subject to that include the subordinate departments of the Management and Personnel Office and of the Treasury and the office of any Minister whose expenses are defrayed out of moneys provided by Parliament for service of the Management and Personnel Office or the Treasury.

7. In the case of the Commission for the New Towns, a development corporation for a new town or the Development Board for Rural Wales, no investigation shall be conducted under this Act in respect of any action in connection with functions in relation to housing.

8. The reference to the Treasury Solicitor does not include a reference to Her Majesty's Procurator General.

9. In the case of an urban development corporation no investigation under this Act shall be conducted in respect of any action in connection with functions in relation to town and country planning.

10. In relation to any function exercised on behalf of the Crown by a department or authority to which this Act applies which was previously exercisable on behalf of the Crown by a department or authority to which this Act does not apply, the reference to the department or authority to which this Act applies includes a reference to the other department or authority if the other department or authority—

(a) ceased to exercise the function before the commencement of this Act; or

(b) where it exercised the function after the commencement of this Act, only did so when it was a department or authority to which this Act applied.

SCHEDULE 2

ENACTMENTS REPEALED

Chapter	Short title	Extent of repeal
1969 c.48.	The Post Office Act 1969.	Section 93(3).
1973 c.50.	The Employment and Training Act 1973.	In Schedule 3, paragraph 9.
1974 c.37.	The Health and Safety at Work etc. Act 1974.	In Schedule 9, paragraph 3.
1984 c.12.	The Telecommunications Act 1984.	In Schedule 1, paragraph 4.
1985 c.51.	The Local Government Act 1985.	In Schedule 13, paragraph 11.
1986 c.44.	The Gas Act 1986.	In Schedule 1, paragraph 6.
1986 c.53.	The Building Societies Act 1986.	In Schedule 1, paragraph 13.
1986 c.57.	The Public Trustee and Administration of Funds Act 1986.	In the Schedule, paragraph 4.

REGISTERED ESTABLISHMENTS (SCOTLAND) ACT 1987

(1987 c. 40)

An Act to make further provision as to the registration of establishments under the Social Work (Scotland) Act 1968 and the Nursing Homes Registration (Scotland) Act 1938; and for connected purposes.

[15th May 1987]

PARLIAMENTARY DEBATES
   Hansard: H.C. Vol. 110, cols. 475, 1232; Vol. 112, col. 1212; Vol. 116, col. 447; H.L. Vol. 486, cols. 70, 1083; Vol. 487, cols. 319, 618.
   The Bill was considered in the Second Scottish Standing Committee on March 18, 1987.

Definition of "establishments"

1.—(1) For subsection (1) of section 61 of the Social Work (Scotland) Act 1968 (in this Act referred to as "the 1968 Act") substitute—

"(1) The following provisions of this Part of this Act apply to any residential or other establishment the whole or a substantial part of whose function is to provide persons with such personal care or support, whether or not combined with board, and whether for reward or not, as may be required for the purposes of this Act.

(1A) For the purposes of subsection (1) above—

"establishment" does not include any establishment controlled or managed by a Government department or by a local authority or, subject to sections 61A and 63B below, required to be registered, or in respect of which a person is required to be registered, with a Government department or a local authority under any other enactment;

"personal care" includes the provision of appropriate help with physical and social needs; and

"support" means counselling or other help provided as part of a planned programme of care.".

(2) In subsection (2) of the said section 61, at the beginning insert "Subject to section 62(8) and (8A) below".

Voluntary registration

2.—(1) After the said section 61 of the 1968 Act insert—

"Voluntary registration

61A.—(1) Any grant-aided school or independent school within the meaning of section 135(1) of the Education (Scotland) Act 1980 (which defines terms used in that Act) which performs functions such as are described in section 61(1) above may, but shall not be required to, apply for registration under this Part of this Act in accordance with the provisions of this section.

(2) Where an application for registration of a grant-aided school or independent school is granted, the establishment shall be entered in

the register kept for the purposes of section 61(2) above by the local authority or, as the case may be, the Secretary of State.

(3) Any certificate of registration granted in respect of an establishment to which this section applies shall relate to the whole of the establishment, excepting any part thereof which is used exclusively for educational purposes.

(4) The provisions of this Part of this Act shall apply to establishments to which this section applies subject to the following—

   (a) section 61(2) and (3) shall not apply;

   (b) section 62(8) and (8A) shall not apply;

   (c) section 65 shall not apply;

   (d) the provisions of section 67(1) shall apply only where the person carrying on the establishment has been registered; and

   (e) section 67(2) shall not apply.".

(2) In the said section 135(1) of the Education (Scotland) Act 1980, in the definition of "school" the words "but does not include an establishment or residential establishment within the meaning of the Social Work (Scotland) Act 1968" shall be omitted.

Registration

3.—(1) For subsection (4) of section 62 of the 1968 Act (which provides for the cancellation of registration of persons in respect of establishments on certain grounds), substitute—

"(4) Without prejudice to subsection (2) of this section, where the person registered in respect of an establishment proposes to employ a manager, that is, a person engaged to run the establishment from day to day, he shall

   (a) include in the application for registration a note of the proposed manager's name; and

   (b) inform the authority, within 28 days in either case, of—

      (i) the departure of the manager presently employed, or

      (ii) the employment of a new manager.

(4A) Where any person registered in respect of an establishment employs a manager at the date when this enactment comes into force, he shall within 28 days of that date inform the local authority of the manager's name.

(4B) Where any person registered in respect of an establishment intends to cease to carry on the establishment, he shall give the local authority at least 28 days' notice of that fact.

(4C) The local authority may at any time cancel the registration of a person in respect of an establishment—

   (a) on any ground which would entitle them to refuse an application for the registration of that person in respect of an establishment; or

   (b) on the ground that that person—

      (i) has failed to notify the authority of a change in manager under subsection (4) above, or

      (ii) has been convicted of an offence against this section or against any regulations under this Part of this Act relating to the conduct of an establishment; or

   (c) on the ground that any other person has been convicted of such an offence as is mentioned in sub-paragraph (b)(ii) above in respect of that establishment; or

   (d) on the ground that the annual fee for the continuation of registration has not been paid on the due date.".

(2) For subsection (5) of the said section 62 substitute—

"(5) It shall be a condition of the registration of any person in respect of an establishment that he shall comply with such reasonable conditions with regard to the proper operation of the establishment as the local authority may impose, and such conditions shall include conditions as to—

(a) the maximum number of persons (excluding persons carrying on or employed in the establishment and their families) who may be accommodated at any one time in the establishment, and

(b) the categories of persons who may be admitted to the establishment.

(5A) The local authority may, at their own instance or at that of the person registered in respect of the establishment, at any time—

(a) impose any new condition with regard to the operation of the establishment; or

(b) vary any condition imposed under subsection (5) or paragraph (a) above.".

(3) In subsection (6) of the said section 62, for the words "condition imposed by or under the last foregoing subsection" substitute "condition, new condition or variation of a condition imposed by or under subsection (5) or (5A) above or section 63A(7) below".

(4) After the said subsection (6) insert—

"(6A) The certificate of registration issued under this section in respect of any premises shall include the following information—

(a) the name of the person registered in respect of the establishment;

(b) the name of any manager appointed by the person mentioned in paragraph (a) above;

(c) the address of the premises at which the establishment is to be carried on;

(d) the maximum number of persons who may be accommodated in the establishment under subsection (5)(a) above;

(e) the categories of persons who may be admitted to the establishment under subsection (5)(b) above,

and where any material change occurs in any of the information mentioned in this subsection the local authority shall issue a new certificate.

(6B) Where an establishment to which the provisions of this Part of this Act apply is being carried on on the date when this enactment comes into force the local authority shall, within 60 days of that date, issue to the person carrying on that establishment a new certificate including the information mentioned in subsection (6A) above.".

(5) After subsection (8) of the said section 62 (which makes provision for the carrying on of an establishment for a limited period without registration in the event of the death of the person registered) insert—

"(8A) Notwithstanding anything in subsection (1) of this section, where for any reason the person registered in respect of an establishment ceases to be so registered, the local authority may allow another person to carry on the establishment for such period not exceeding 60 days as the authority may sanction, and subject to such conditions as the authority think appropriate.".

Appeals against conditions imposed on registration or subsequently

4. After section 63 of the 1968 Act insert—

"**Appeals against conditions imposed on registration or subsequently**
63A.—(1) Not less than fourteen days before determining—

(a) the conditions intended to be imposed under section 62(5) above in respect of the registration of any person in respect of an establishment; or

(b) any new condition or variation of an existing condition
intended to be imposed under section 62(5A) above,
the Secretary of State or, as the case may be, the local authority shall
send by recorded delivery service to the applicant or the person
registered, as the case may be, notice of their intention.

(2) Every notice under subsection (1) above shall contain an
intimation that if within fourteen days after the receipt of the notice
the applicant or, as the case may be, the person registered informs
the authority or the Secretary of State in writing of his desire—

(a) to show cause, in person or by a representative, why the
proposed conditions, new conditions or variation of existing
conditions should not be imposed;

(b) to make representations as to what conditions, new conditions
or variation of conditions should be imposed in substitution for
those proposed,

the authority or the Secretary of State shall, before carrying out their
intention, afford him an opportunity so to do.

(3) The local authority or the Secretary of State, after giving the
applicant or the person registered, as the case may be, an opportunity
of being heard by them, shall send a notice to him by recorded
delivery service informing him of what conditions, new conditions or
variation of conditions they have decided to impose.

(4) A person aggrieved by a notice of a local authority or of the
Secretary of State under subsection (3) above may appeal to an appeal
tribunal established by Schedule 5 to this Act, and any such appeal
shall be brought within twenty-one days of the date of that notice.

(5) Where an appeal under subsection (4) above relates to the
imposition of conditions on the initial registration of a person in
respect of an establishment, the registration shall not take effect
until—

(a) the appeal has been determined; or

(b) the time for bringing an appeal has elapsed without—

(i) an appeal having been brought, or

(ii) an appeal which has been intimated having been
proceeded with,

and in either of the cases mentioned in paragraph (b) above the
registration shall be subject to the conditions proposed in the notice
sent to the applicant under subsection (3) above.

(6) Where an appeal under subsection (4) above relates to the
proposed imposition of new conditions or of a variation of existing
conditions, the new conditions or variation shall not take effect
until—

(a) the appeal has been determined; or

(b) the time for bringing an appeal has elapsed without—

(i) an appeal having been brought, or

(ii) an appeal which has been intimated having been
proceeded with.

(7) On any appeal under subsection (4) above the tribunal may
confirm or vary any condition, new condition or variation of a
condition against which the appeal is brought.".

Jointly registrable establishments

5.—(1) After section 63 of the 1968 Act insert—

"Special provisions for jointly registrable establishments

63B.—(1) Subject to the provisions of this section, where a person
registered or intending to be registered under section 1 of the Nursing
Homes Registration (Scotland) Act 1938 (which relates to the regis-

tration of nursing homes) in respect of an establishment intends that that establishment should also carry out functions in respect of which registration is required under this Act, the provisions of this Part of this Act shall apply in relation to the registration of that person for the purpose of carrying out those functions in that establishment.

(2) In this Part of this Act "jointly registrable establishment" means an establishment required to be registered under both this Part of this Act and the said Act of 1938.

(3) Any certificate of registration issued by a local authority to such a person as is described in subsection (1) above shall relate to the whole of the establishment, excepting any part thereof which is used exclusively for the purpose of carrying out functions under the said Act of 1938.

(4) Where a local authority cancel the registration of a jointly registrable establishment under section 62(4) above they shall inform the Health Board responsible under the 1938 Act for the registration of that establishment of the fact of and the reasons for the cancellation.

(5) Any person who, on the date when this enactment comes into force, is carrying on a jointly registrable establishment which is not registered under this Part of this Act shall within 3 months of that date apply for such registration.

(6) No fee shall be chargeable by a local authority under section 64A below in respect of any application made by virtue of subsection (5) above.".

(2) After section 2 of the Nursing Homes Registration (Scotland) Act 1938 insert—

"Special provisions for jointly registrable establishments

2A.—(1) Subject to the provisions of this section, where a person registered or intending to be registered under section 62 of the Social Work (Scotland) Act 1968 in respect of an establishment carrying out functions in respect of which registration is required under Part IV of that Act intends that that establishment should also carry out functions in respect of which registration is required under this Act, the provisions of this Act shall apply in relation to the registration of that person for the purpose of carrying out those functions in that establishment.

(2) In this Act "jointly registrable establishment" means an establishment required to be registered under both this Act and Part IV of the said Act of 1968.

(3) Any certificate of registration issued by a Health Board to such a person as is described in subsection (1) above shall relate to the whole of the establishment, excepting any part thereof which is used exclusively for the purpose of carrying out functions under Part IV of the said Act of 1968.

(4) Where a Health Board cancel the registration of a jointly registrable establishment under section 2 above they shall inform the local authority with which the establishment is registered of the fact of and the reasons for the cancellation.

(5) Any person who, on the date when this enactment comes into force, is carrying on a jointly registrable establishment which is not registered under this Act shall within 3 months of that date apply for such registration.

(6) No fee shall be chargeable by a Health Board under section 1A(a) above in respect of any application made by virtue of subsection (5) above.".

Registration fees

6.—(1) After section 64 of the 1968 Act insert—

"Registration fees

64A.—(1) Subject to the provisions of this section, a local authority shall impose fees in respect of—

(a) an application for registration made by any person in respect of the carrying on of any establishment to which this section applies;

(b) the annual continuation of any such registration;

(c) an application made by the person registered in respect of the establishment for a variation in any condition imposed under section 62(5) or (5A) of this Act; and

(d) the issuing of a new certificate following any change in the information mentioned in section 62(6A) above made at the instance of or resulting from an application by the person registered in respect of the establishment.

(2) This section applies to any establishment such as is mentioned in section 61(1) of this Act which is a residential establishment other than any establishment—

(a) the whole or a substantial part of whose function is to accommodate children for the purposes of this Act; or

(b) such as is mentioned in section 61A above.

(3) The Secretary of State may prescribe—

(a) the maximum fees which may be imposed by local authorities under this section; and

(b) the times at which fees may be charged.

(4) Subject to subsection 3(a) above, a local authority shall have regard to their reasonable expenses in carrying out their functions under this Part of this Act in fixing fees under this section:

Provided that where it appears to the authority to be appropriate they may charge a nominal fee, or remit the fee altogether.

(5) Where an application for registration in respect of an establishment has been made to a local authority before the coming into force of this section no fee shall be payable in respect of that registration.".

(2) In section 94(1) of the 1968 Act (which defines terms used in that Act)—

(a) in paragraph (c) of the definition of "prescribed", after "62(2)," insert "64A(3),"; and

(b) after the said paragraph (c) insert "and "prescribe" shall be construed accordingly.".

(3) After section 1 of the Nursing Homes Registration (Scotland) Act 1938 insert—

"Registration fees

1A.—A Health Board may impose fees, of such amounts and at such times as may be prescribed by the Secretary of State in regulations under this Act, in respect of—

(a) an application for registration made by any person in respect of the carrying on of a nursing home;

(b) the annual continuation of any such registration;

(c) an application made under section 1(3F) above by the person registered in respect of the home for a variation in any condition such as is mentioned in section 1(3D) or (3E) above which has effect in relation to the home; and

(d) the issuing under section 1(3) above of a new certificate following any variation, made as a result of an application under section 1(3F) above, in the conditions under section

1(3D) or (3E) above subject to which the registration has been granted.".

(4) In section 1(2) of the said Act of 1938 (which relates to the registration of nursing homes) the words "and shall be accompanied by such fee as may be so prescribed" shall cease to have effect.

Re-occupation of premises where residents removed

7.—(1) In section 65(4) of the 1968 Act (which provides for the removal of persons from establishments in certain circumstances)—
   (a) after the word "who" insert "—(a)";
   (b) after the word "subsection" insert "; or—
      (b) re-occupies the premises for the purpose of carrying on the establishment without any appeal under section 64 above having been decided in his favour,".

Citation, commencement and extent

8.—(1) This Act may be cited as the Registered Establishments (Scotland) Act 1987.

(2) This Act shall come into force on such day as the Secretary of State may appoint and different days may be so appointed for different provisions or different purposes.

(3) This Act applies to Scotland only.

CRIMINAL JUSTICE (SCOTLAND) ACT 1987*

(1987 c. 41)

ARRANGEMENT OF SECTIONS

PART I

CONFISCATION OF PROCEEDS OF DRUG TRAFFICKING ETC.

---

* Annotations by Christopher Gane, Lecturer in Law, University of Lancaster.

PART III

GENERAL

An Act to make provision for Scotland as regards the recovery of the proceeds of drug trafficking; to make further provision as regards criminal justice in Scotland; and for connected purposes.

[15th May 1987]

PARLIAMENTARY DEBATES

Hansard: H.L. Vol. 482, cols. 544, 1077; Vol. 483, col. 1053; Vol. 484, col. 997; Vol. 485, col. 354; Vol. 487, col. 774; H.C. Vol. 116, col. 206.

The Bill was considered by the Scottish Grand Committee on March 23, 1987, and by the First Scottish Standing Committee from April 7 to 30, 1987.

INTRODUCTION AND GENERAL NOTE

This Act is really two statutes rolled into one. Pt. I, which deals with the confiscation of the proceeds of drug trafficking, is essentially a Scottish adaptation of the Drug Trafficking Offences Act 1986. Pt. II of the Act is a "miscellaneous provisions" measure, dealing with a wide variety of matters, few of which have any direct relationship with the provisions of Pt. I. In summary, the Act provides as follows:

Part I

S.1 provides for the making of "confiscation orders" by the High Court, and sets out the pre-conditions for the making of such orders. S.2 provides for the postponement of the making of such orders in appropriate circumstances. S.3 states the grounds on which the proceeds of drug trafficking are to be assessed. S.4 makes provision in relation to statements made in connection with the assessment of the proceeds of drug trafficking and the valuation of property that might be realised under a confiscation order. S.5 states what property may be realised under a confiscation order, and includes therein property which has been transferred to a third party by way of "implicative gift". S.6 defines "implicative gift" for the purposes of Pt. I of the Act. Various provisions relating to the enforcement of fines are applied to confiscation orders by s.7. S.8 gives the Court of Session the power to make "restraint orders" in respect of property realisable under s.5, while s.9 sets out the nature and effect of such orders. S.10 gives a constable or person commissioned by the Commissioners of Customs and Excise power to seize property the subject of a restraint order to prevent its removal from Great Britain. S.11 makes provision for the inhibition of heritable property and the arrestment of moveable property subject to a restraint order or an interdict granted under s.12 of the Act. The latter section gives the Court of Session the power to interdict persons not subject to a restraint order from dealing with property subject to such an order. Ss.13 to 24 provide for the appointment of an "administrator" in respect of property realisable under Pt. I, and set out his powers and duties in respect of that property, including the satisfaction of the confiscation order. S.25 provides for the variation of confiscation orders on the application of a person in respect of whom a confiscation order has been made. The limited circumstances in which compensation may be payable to persons who have suffered "substantial loss or damage" as a result of actions taken under Pt. I of the Act are set out in s.26. Ss.27 and 28 provide for the recognition and enforcement in Scotland of orders made under the Drug Trafficking Offences Act 1986. S.29 deals with the enforcement in Scotland of orders made in Northern Ireland. S.30 makes provision for the registration and enforcement in Scotland of "external confiscation orders" made by the courts in a "designated country". This section also makes provision for the designation of countries by Order in Council for the purposes of s.30. S.31 amends the Drug Trafficking Offences Act 1986 to provide for the recognition and enforcement in England and Wales of orders made, and functions exercised, under Pt. I of this Act. S.32 relates to action which may be taken in a designated country in consequence of the making of a restraint order or a confiscation order. Ss.33 to 37 makes provision for possible conflicts between confiscation orders and proceedings in bankruptcy, the winding up of a company and related matters. Ss.38 to 41 makes special provision for the investigation of drug trafficking. Ss.42 to 44 create new offences in connection with the investigation and prosecution of drug trafficking, and make provision for the imposition of unlimited fines in respect of certain offences relating to controlled drugs. S.45 makes certain minor amendments in connection with drug trafficking. S.46 relates to the making of rule of court in connection with Pt. I. S.47 is an interpretation section for Pt. I.

Part II

This Part of the Act is appropriately, if unhelpfully, headed "Miscellaneous". Ss.48 to 50 deal with detention by customs officers and the rights of persons subject to detention. Ss.51 to 55 deal with the investigation of serious or complex fraud and, *inter alia*, confer on the Lord Advocate the power to make directions concerning the investigation of such fraud. S.56 makes further provision for the diversion of offences from the criminal courts by the introduction of the "conditional offer" of a fixed penalty by the procurator fiscal. S.57 makes provision in relation to sitting of the High Court, while s.58 increases the sentencing power of the sheriff in solemn proceedings. S.59 amends the Criminal Procedure (Scotland) Act 1975 ("the 1975 Act") by making provision for the detention of children found, or pleading, guilty before the sheriff in summary proceedings. S.60 provides for the certification of transcripts of tape recordings or police interviews with suspected persons. S.61 amends s.32 of the Criminal Justice (Scotland) Act 1980 ("the 1980 Act") which permits in certain circumstances the taking and admission of evidence on commission or by letter of request. S.62 amends s.328 of the 1975 Act (which deals with adjournment of summary proceedings for the purpose of making inquiries) so as to permit the court to ordain the accused to appear. S.63 allows the court to permit a witness to be present in court before giving evidence. Following recommendations from the Scottish Law Commission, s.64 makes provision for a statutory offence of aiding and abetting statutory offences. S.65 permits the court to combine a compensation order and probation by making compensation a requirement of the probation order. S.66 makes a number of additions to the provisions of the 1975 Act in respect of the "standard scale" in connection with offences created under subordinate legislation and also in connection with high maximum penalties. S.67 increases the periods of imprisonment for non-payment of fines of £50,000 and above. S.68 adds a new s.443A to the 1975 Act, permitting the suspension of orders of forfeiture, disqualification and the like pending the determination of any appeal against conviction or sentence.

Notwithstanding the short title, the Act contains a number of provisions which apply throughout the whole of, or to other parts of, the United Kingdom, including some which do not apply to Scotland at all. It would also be a mistake to assume from the title that the Act is of importance only in the criminal courts. The power to confiscate and realise property set out in Pt. I of the Act is likely in many instances to involve difficult questions of private property rights, a fact recognised in the allocation to the Court of Session of a number of important functions under the Act.

COMMENCEMENT

The following sections came into force on September 1, 1987: ss.57, 70 (as relating to the following parts of Scheds. 1 and 2); Sched. 1, paras. 1, 2, 4 to 6; Sched. 2, first to fifth items and from beginning of tenth item to "119" (Criminal Justice (Scotland) Act 1987 (Commencement No. 1) Order (S.I. 1987 No. 1468)).

The following sections came into force on October 1, 1987: ss.48, 49, 60, 64, 69; Sched. 1, paras. 3, 10(b), 11–14, 16–18, 19, Sched. 2 (repeal of Road Traffic Act 1974, Sched. 3 (part) and repeal of Criminal Procedure (Scotland) Act 1975, s.263(2) (part)) (Criminal Justice (Scotland) Act 1987 (Commencement No. 2) Order (S.I. 1987 No. 1594)).

The following sections came into force on January 1, 1988: ss.51–56, 61–63, 65, 68; Sched. 1, paras. 7 to 9, 10(a), Sched. 2 (part) (Criminal Justice (Scotland) Act 1987 (Commencement No. 3) Order (S.I. 1987 No. 2119)).

EXTENT

The Act applies to Scotland only (s.72(1)), except that:
  (a) the following sections apply to England and Wales as well as to Scotland: ss.4(5), 20(1), 33 to 37, 41(10) to (12), 45(2), (3) and (7)(c) and (f), 47, 55(a) and (b), 69, 72(4), and, in so far as relating to the Drug Trafficking Offences Act 1986, s.70(2) and Sched. 2;
  (b) the following sections apply to England and Wales and Northern Ireland as well as to Scotland: ss.51 to 53, 56(11) and 59;

(c) the following sections apply to England and Wales only: ss.31, 45(1), (4) and (7)(a), (b), (d) and (e);

(d) the following section applies to Northern Ireland only: s.55(c).

PART I

CONFISCATION OF PROCEEDS OF DRUG TRAFFICKING ETC.

GENERAL NOTE

Introduction

This part of the Act, like the Drug Trafficking Offences Act 1986, has its roots in recommendations contained in the Home Affairs Committee's Fifth Report, "Misuse of Hard Drugs—Interim Report" (H.C.P. 399, 1985). That Committee, in considering the general problems surrounding prevention and control of the abuse of "hard" drugs, paid particular attention to the profits to be made from trafficking in drugs. They noted with approval the American policy of giving the court "draconian powers" to strip drug dealers of all assets acquired from their dealing in drugs, including the power to confiscate the drug trafficker's assets where their connection with drug related offences is "probable" and the defendant is unable to prove the contrary. It is hardly surprising, then, that the Committee recommended ("Interim Report", para. 9) that "the civil and criminal law of the United Kingdom be amended to provide for the seizure and forfeiture of assets connected with drug traffic in accordance with American practice."

The power to make confiscation orders along these lines was given to the Crown Court in England and Wales by the Drug Trafficking Offences Act 1986. It was recognised during the passage of that Act through Parliament that similar measures would have to be made for Scotland. Pt. I of the Act confers on the High Court of Justiciary the power to make confiscation orders, and also establishes an elaborate mechanism for their enforcement.

The new procedures—an overview

The provisions relating to confiscation orders are complex. They introduce several new concepts into Scottish criminal law, and it may be useful at this stage to attempt a summary of the new procedures.

(a) *Confiscation*

Where a person is convicted in the High Court of any of the offences listed in s.1(2) of the Act, or is remitted to the High Court for sentence under s.104(1) of the 1975 Act in respect of any such offence, the High Court may make an order, known as a *confiscation order*, requiring him to pay what it assesses to be the value of the proceeds of his involvement in drug trafficking. The confiscation order is not restricted to the proceeds of the offence or offences of which he has been convicted, but extends to the proceeds of any involvement by the convicted person in drug trafficking.

(b) *Drug trafficking*

This is defined by s.1(6) so as to include activities which amount to offences under the Misuse of Drugs Act 1971. It is clear, however, that the idea of drug trafficking is not limited to such activities, but include activities which might loosely be described as the "laundering" of the proceeds of another person's drug trafficking activities.

(c) *Assessing the proceeds of drug trafficking*

Before the High Court can make a confiscation order, it must make an assessment of the proceeds of the convicted person's drug trafficking. S.3 of the Act provides that any payments or other rewards received by a person at any time (including payments or rewards received before the commencement of s.1 of the Act) in connection with drug trafficking carried on by him or another are to be treated as his proceeds of drug trafficking. In assessing the amount of those proceeds, the court is entitled to assume, *inter alia*, that property held by him at any time since his conviction, or transferred to him at any time during the six years preceding his being indicted, was received as a payment or reward in connection with drug trafficking carried on by him. It is for the convicted person to show that, in respect of any particular asset or assets, any assumption made by the court under s.3 is incorrect in his case.

(d) *Realisable property*

Only "realisable property" may be used to satisfy a confiscation order under s.1. It is important to notice that it is not only property held by the drug trafficker which is realisable. The whole estate of a person who has received what is termed an "implicative gift" from a drug trafficker is realisable under s.3. Nor is it necessary to wait for the trafficker to be convicted of an offence to which s.1 relates. The whole estate of a person suspected of, or charged with, an offence mentioned in s.1(2) becomes realisable once a warrant to arrest and commit him in respect of such an offence has been granted, or a "restraint order" has been made against him under s.8.

(e) *Restraint orders and interdict*

It is of course likely that persons against whom proceedings for offences in connection with controlled drugs are pending, or who are under investigation for such offences, will take steps to avoid the possible consequences of a confiscation order in the event of conviction. This might take the form of a distribution or concealment of their assets, or attempts to remove them from the jurisdiction.

In order to avoid such anticipatory evasion, the Court of Session (and *not* the High Court) may, on the application of the Lord Advocate, make a "restraint order", interdicting the person in respect of whom it is made from dealing with his property, or interdicting that person and any person who appears to have received an "implicative gift" from him, from dealing with their own or the other's property. The Court of Session is given additional powers, *inter alia*, to grant inhibition in respect of heritable realisable property, to grant warrant for arrestment of moveable realisable property, and to apply restraint orders to persons not named therein.

(f) *Implicative gifts*

It is clear that the impact of a confiscation order would be lessened considerably if it were to be applicable only to property presently held or owned by the drug trafficker. Pt. I of the Act therefore contains various provisions designed to enlarge the scope of the confiscation order by including within the scope of "realisable property" what are termed "implicative gifts". For these purposes, an "implicative" gift means any outright gift made not more than six years before the date on which proceedings in respect of an offence mentioned in s.1(2) were commenced against the donor, or on which a restraint order was made against him, or a gift made *at any time* if the gift was one of property received by the giver in connection with drug trafficking carried on by him or another, or of property which in the donor's hands represented property so received by him.

(g) *Administration of realisable property*

On the application of the Lord Advocate, the Court of Session may appoint a person to manage or otherwise deal with property affected by a restraint order. Where a confiscation order has been made the Court of Session may, again on the application of the Lord Advocate, appoint someone to realise the property of the trafficker (or any person to whom the trafficker has made an implicative gift). The person so appointed is to be known as the "administrator", and essentially his function is to take over and manage realisable property with a view, ultimately, of satisfying the confiscation order, after first having settled specified expenses.

(h) *Protection of third parties*

Given the scope of the powers conferred under Pt. I, it is clear that persons who have not themselves been involved in drug trafficking may suffer as a result of the operation of confiscation and restraint orders. The clear example of the drug trafficker's family springs to mind, but of course his creditors and other parties less closely connected with him may also be adversely affected. The Act does contain provisions whereby the rights and interests of third parties may be taken into account (see, for example, s.8(2)(b) in connection with the variation of restraint orders), but it must be said that the general tenor of the legislation is strict, and its policy is to strike severely at the drug trafficker, leaving little scope for the protection of the "innocent". This is particularly clear in relation to compensation for loss of damage suffered as a result of steps taken under Pt. I. S.26 makes it clear that such compensation will only exceptionally be payable, and the mere fact that an innocent third party has suffered such loss is not, in itself, sufficient ground for an award of compensation under that section.

The 1987 Act and Existing Forfeiture Powers

The powers conferred on the High Court by s.1 are additional to the existing powers of the Court to order forfeiture of, or otherwise strike at, the assets of drug offenders. At present this may be done directly by use of forfeiture powers contained in s.27(1) of the Misuse of Drugs Act 1971 or s.223 of the 1975 Act (s.436 in summary proceedings), or indirectly through the use of unlimited fines under s.193B of the 1975 Act (now repealed and re-enacted in s.44 of the present Act).

In practice, the existing powers of forfeiture have been fairly narrowly construed, with the result that they have not presented a serious threat to the assets of large-scale drug traffickers. Indeed, in *R.* v. *Cuthbertson* [1980] 2 All E.R. 401, Lord Diplock stated that s.27(1) of the 1971 Act should not be construed as if Parliament had intended it to be used as "a means of stripping professional drug traffickers . . . of the whole of their ill-gotten gains" (at p.403, and see also p.406). In line with this restrictive approach, the English courts have held that s.27 can only be used to order the forfeiture of tangible, moveable property (*R.* v. *Beard* [1974] 1 W.L.R. 1550; *R.* v. *Cuthbertson*, above) and cannot be applied to property situated abroad (*R.* v. *Cuthbertson*, above).

A rather broader approach has been adopted towards the use of general forfeiture powers (such as those contained in s.223 of the 1975 Act), at least in Scotland (compare, for example, *Donnelly* v. *H.M. Advocate*, 1984 S.C.C.R. 93 with *R.* v. *Ribeyre* (1984) 4 Cr.App.R.(S.) 165). But even using such powers it is clear that the courts are unlikely to go beyond the confiscation of such property found in the possession or control of the offender as quantities of drugs, the equipment associated with the consumption of, or trading in, drugs, and the drug trader's "working capital". The opportunity to attack the assets of the large-scale drug trafficker will be found in the provisions of Pt. I of the present Act.

Confiscation orders

Confiscation orders

1.—(1) Subject to the provisions of this Part of this Act, where a person is convicted in the High Court of, or is under section 104(1) of the 1975 Act remitted to that Court for sentence as regards, an offence to which this section relates the Court may, on the application of the prosecutor made when he moves for sentence (or, if the case is one so remitted, made before sentence is pronounced), make an order (in this Act referred to as a "confiscation order") requiring the person to pay such amount as the Court considers appropriate, being an amount not exceeding—

(a) subject to paragraph (b) below, what it assesses to be the value of the proceeds of the person's drug trafficking; or

(b) if the Court is satisfied that the property that might be realised in terms of this Part of this Act at the time the confiscation order is made has a value less than that of the proceeds of the person's drug trafficking, what it assesses to be the value of that property.

(2) This section relates to any of the following—

(a) an offence under section 4(2) (production, or being concerned in production, of controlled drug), 4(3) (supply of, or offer to supply, or being concerned in supply of, controlled drug), 5(3) (possession of controlled drug with intent to supply) or 20 (assisting in, or inducing commission of, certain drug related offences punishable under foreign law) of the Misuse of Drugs Act 1971;

(b) in connection with a prohibition or restriction on importation having effect by virtue of section 3 of the said Act of 1971, an offence under section 50(2) or (3) (improper importation), 68(2) (improper exportation) or 170 (fraudulent evasion of duty etc.) of the Customs and Excise Management Act 1979;

(c) an offence under section 43 of this Act;

(d) an offence of conspiring, inciting or attempting to commit an offence to which, by virtue of paragraph (a), (b) or (c) above, this section relates.

(3) The Court shall take account of the provisions of any order made by it under subsection (1) above in determining the amount of any fine

imposed on the person as regards the offence but not in determining any other matter as regards sentence.

(4) For the purposes of any appeal or review, a confiscation order is a sentence.

(5) No enactment restricting the power of a court dealing with a person in a particular way from dealing with him also in any other way shall by reason only of the making of an order under subsection (1) above (or the postponement of a decision as regards making such an order) restrict the High Court from dealing with a person in any way the Court considers appropriate in respect of an offence to which this section relates.

(6) In this Part of this Act, "drug trafficking" means doing or being concerned in any of the following, whether in Scotland or elsewhere—

(a) producing or supplying a controlled drug where the production or supply contravenes section 4(1) of the said Act of 1971;

(b) transporting or storing such a drug where possession of it contravenes section 5(1) of that Act;

(c) importing or exporting such a drug where the importation or exportation is prohibited by section 3(1) of that Act;

(d) producing, supplying, transporting, storing, importing or exporting such a drug in contravention of a corresponding law ("corresponding law" having the meaning assigned by section 36(1) of that Act);

and includes, whether in Scotland or elsewhere, entering into or being otherwise concerned in an arrangement whereby—

(i) the retention or control by or on behalf of another person of the other person's proceeds of drug trafficking is facilitated, or

(ii) the proceeds of drug trafficking by another person are used to secure that funds are placed at the other person's disposal or are used for the other person's benefit to acquire property by way of investment.

GENERAL NOTE

This section empowers the High Court, when passing sentence on a convicted offender, to make an order, known as a "confiscation order" requiring the convicted person to pay an amount determined by the court. The amount in question cannot exceed what the court assesses to be the value of the proceeds of the accused's drug trafficking. Where the value of the accused's realisable property is lower than the court's assessment of his drug trafficking proceeds, the courts may order confiscation of all of his realisable property.

Subs. (1)

An offence to which this subsection relates. A confiscation order may only be made under this section against a person who has been convicted of an offence listed in s.1(2).

The Court may. The High Court is not required to make a confiscation order, and it appears to be the Government's view that relatively few such orders will be made each year. The Government has estimated that the revenue from confiscated assets will be of the order of £0.3 million annually. (See the explanatory and financial memorandum to the Criminal Justice (Scotland) Bill as introduced into the House of Lords.)

The discretionary nature of the power conferred by s.1(1) should be contrasted with the position in England under s.1 of the Drug Trafficking Offences Act 1986. Under that section, where a person appears before the Crown Court to be sentenced in respect of a drug trafficking offence, the court must first determine whether he has benefitted from drug trafficking. If the court determines that he has so benefitted, then it is required, before dealing with the offender in any other way, to make a confiscation order.

On the application of the prosecutor. A confiscation order may be made when the accused has been convicted in the High Court or when he has been remitted to the High Court for sentence. In either case it is clear that an order cannot be made except on the application of the prosecutor. It is clear also that the prosecutor's application must be made before the sentence or any part of it has been pronounced.

Subs. (2)

This subsection lists the offences to which s.1 relates. It is important to note the relationship of subs. (2) to the concept of "drug trafficking" as defined by subs. (6). The offences listed in s.1(2) may be described as "triggering" offences. They operate so as to enable the court to make a confiscation order, but that order is not linked to the proceeds (if any) of these offences. The confiscation order is linked to the proceeds of the accused's "drug trafficking" as defined by subs. (6). Of course, subs. (6) so defines drug trafficking as to include within that term some of the offences listed in subs. (2), and the only drug trafficking activities of the accused may have been activities which have been the subject of his conviction. But this need not be so. Indeed, his drug trafficking activities need not have been the subject of *any* criminal proceedings whatsoever (see note to subs. (6) below).

Subs. (3)

A convicted person's ability to pay a fine is clearly going to be affected by the making of a confiscation order, especially where that order is of a substantial amount, and in some instances the imposition of a fine may well be pointless. Clearly, however, a confiscation order is unlikely to have a direct bearing on other sentencing options available to, and likely to be adopted by, the court in drugs cases. Certainly it would be invidious if those with substantial assets which could be confiscated could thereby hope to avoid other penalties such as imprisonment.

Subs. (4)

S.228(1) of the 1975 Act provides that any person convicted on indictment may appeal to the High Court against such conviction, against the sentence passed on such conviction, or against both conviction and sentence. Subs. (4) makes it clear that for these purposes a confiscation order counts as a sentence.

There was considerable discussion in the First Scottish Standing Committee as to the precise meaning of "review" in this context and as to how it might differ from an "appeal" (First Scottish Standing Committee, First Sitting, April 7, 1987). No clear answer was forthcoming from the Government spokesman. One might suggest, however, that the term "review" is apt to include such procedures as an application to the *nobile officium* or a Bill of Advocation.

Subs. (5)

Certain forms of disposal available to the criminal courts may not be used in conjunction with one another. Thus, for example, a community service order may be made along with an order for disqualification, forfeiture or caution or a compensation order, but not along with any other disposal (Community Service by Offenders (Scotland) Act 1978, s.1(7)). Subs. (5) makes it clear that a confiscation order under s.1(1) is exempt from such restrictions and thus in an appropriate case the court may impose another form of sentence at the same time as it makes a confiscation order.

Subs. (6)

This subsection defines "drug trafficking" for the purposes of Pt. I. A confiscation order may only be made in respect of the activities listed in this subsection, but may be made in respect of any of them. As was noted above, a confiscation order may be made in respect of activities which have not been the subject of a conviction, or, indeed, criminal proceedings. A very difficult question must therefore arise if the prosecutor seeks to include in a list of drug trafficking activities, activities which have been the subject of criminal proceedings resulting in the acquittal of the accused. Suppose, for example, that A is prosecuted on charges of producing and supplying controlled drugs. A conviction is obtained on the first charge but the second results in an acquittal. In these circumstances the court would have the power to make a confiscation order, but could it include therein the proceeds of the supply of the drugs? If the answer to this question is "yes", then a serious challenge is presented to the finality of the jury's verdict of acquittal. In effect the prosecutor may disregard it. But if the answer to the question is "no", then there is a clear incentive for prosecutors to avoid charging offences which would constitute drug trafficking where there is any doubt about securing a conviction. They can effectively avoid this hurdle by securing a conviction (of an offence listed in s.1(2)) which will enable them to have the more difficult matter disposed of as an instance of drug trafficking, the proceeds of which may be subject to a confiscation order.

Doing or being concerned in. While the meaning of "doing" is fairly clear, the same cannot be said of "being concerned in". Clearly this phrase covers someone who facilitates these activities, but does it cover the case of a person who incites them, or conspires to carry them out? Strictly, the answer to this ought to be "no", unless the activities are actually carried out. If they are not, then it is suggested that there is no proscribed activity in the doing of which one can be concerned. The same reasoning ought to apply to a failed attempt to do any of them.

Whether in Scotland or elsewhere. It seems that the intention here is to bring within the definition of drug trafficking activities carried on anywhere in the world, provided that they come within the descriptions contained in subs. (6)(a) to (d) and (i) and (ii). But is this what the subsection achieves? Arguably it does not, at least in the cases envisaged in paras. (a) to (c). Two examples may illustrate why not:

(1) A produces a controlled drug in an illicit laboratory in Fife. This clearly contravenes s.4(1) of the Misuse of Drugs Act 1971, and satisfies subs. (6)(a).

(2) B produces a controlled drug in an illicit laboratory in Paris. This may well violate French law, but does it contravene s.4(1) of the 1971 Act? Clearly not since s.4(1) has no extra-territorial effect. What the section intended, and should have said but did not, is "where the production or supply *would in Scotland* contravene s.4(1) etc. . ."

Postponed confiscation orders

2.—(1) The Court, if it considers that it requires further information before coming to any decision as regards making an order under section 1(1) of this Act, may subject to subsection (4) below postpone that decision for a period not exceeding six months after the date of conviction for the purpose of enabling that information to be obtained; but without prejudice to sections 179 and 219 of the 1975 Act may notwithstanding such postponement proceed, on the prosecutor's motion therefor, to sentence or to otherwise deal with the person in respect of the conviction:

Provided that no fine shall be imposed before the decision is taken.

(2) Where under subsection (1) above a decision has been postponed for a period, any intention to appeal under section 228 of the 1975 Act against conviction or against both conviction and any sentence passed during that period in respect of the conviction, shall be intimated under section 231(1) of that Act not within two weeks of the final determination of the proceedings but within two weeks of—

(a) in the case of an appeal against conviction where there has been no such sentence, the day on which the period of postponement commences;

(b) in any other case, the day on which such sentence is passed in open court.

(3) Notwithstanding any appeal of which intimation has been given by virtue of subsection (2) above, a person may appeal under the said section 228 against the confiscation order (if the decision is to make one) or against any other sentence passed, after the period of postponement, in respect of the conviction.

(4) If during the period of postponement—

(a) intimation is given by virtue of subsection (2) above by the person, the Court may, on the application of the prosecutor, extend that period to a date up to three months after the date of disposal of the appeal;

(b) the case is remitted under subsection (5) of section 3 of this Act, the Court may, on such application, extend that period to a date up to three months after the case is transmitted under that subsection by the Court of Session or, if there is an appeal against the decision of the Court of Session on such remit, the date of disposal of that appeal.

GENERAL NOTE

This section enables the court to postpone a decision in relation to the making of a confiscation order, normally for a period not exceeding six months after the date of conviction. The Court may only postpone the decision if it considers that it requires further information.

Subs. (1)

Ss.179 and 219 of the 1975 Act. S.179 of the 1975 Act includes within the power of the court to adjourn a case, the power to do so before sentence for the purpose of enabling inquiries to be made or of determining the most suitable method of dealing with the accused's case. S.219 provides for deferment of sentence after conviction.

Assessing the proceeds of drug trafficking

3.—(1) For the purposes of this Act—

  (a) any payments or other rewards received by a person at any time (whether before or after the commencement of section 1 of this Act) in connection with drug trafficking carried on by him or another are his proceeds of drug trafficking, and

  (b) the value of his proceeds of drug trafficking is the aggregate of the values of the payments or other rewards.

(2) Without prejudice to section 4 of this Act the Court may, in making an assessment as regards a person under section 1(1) of this Act, make the following assumptions, except in so far as any of them may be shown to be incorrect in that person's case—

  (a) that any property appearing to the Court—

    (i) to have been held by him at any time since his conviction, or

    (ii) to have been transferred to him at any time since a date six years before his being indicted,

  was received by him, at the earliest time at which he appears to the Court to have held it, as a payment or reward in connection with drug trafficking carried on by him,

  (b) that any expenditure of his since the date mentioned in paragraph (a)(ii) above was met out of payments received by him in connection with drug trafficking carried on by him, and

  (c) that, for the purpose of valuing any property received or assumed to have been received by him at any time as such a reward, he received the property free of any other interests in it.

(3) Subsection (2) above does not apply if the only offence by virtue of which the assessment is being made is an offence under section 43 of this Act.

(4) The Court shall, in making an assessment as regards a person under section 1(1) of this Act, leave out of account any of his proceeds of drug trafficking that are shown to the court to have been taken into account in a case where a confiscation order (whether under this Act or under and within the meaning of—

  (a) section 1 of the Drug Trafficking Offences Act 1986; or

  (b) any corresponding provision in Northern Ireland),

has previously been made against him.

(5) Where in making an assessment as regards a person under section 1(1) of this Act the Court at any stage is of the opinion that a difficult question of law or a question of fact of exceptional complexity is involved, it may of its own accord, or on the application of the prosecutor or of the person (or on their joint application), remit the case to the Court of Session for a decision as regards that question; and the Court of Session shall on deciding the question transmit the case to the High Court.

GENERAL NOTE

This section sets out the method by which the proceeds of the accused's drug trafficking are to be assessed. The central features of these procedures are (a) the assumptions that the court may make under subs. (2)(b) the onus placed on the person with regard to whom the assessment is being made (subs. (2)), and (c) the broad scope of the assessment, which includes property received even before the commencement of s.1 of the Act.

Subs. (1)

To the extent that payments or rewards received before the commencement of s.1 are included within the proceeds of drug trafficking, this section has retrospective effect. It does not appear, however, that the section violates the principle of legality in criminal law. Clearly it does not impose retrospective criminality, nor does it violate the rule that on conviction it is not permissible to impose a heavier penalty than that which was applicable at the time the offence was committed.

Subs. (2)

This subsection sets out the assumptions that the court may (but not "must") make in assessing the proceeds of the convicted persons drug trafficking. The court cannot make any assumption which is shown to be incorrect. The onus of demonstrating that any assumption is incorrect rests on the person in regard to whom it is made, but nothing is said about the standard of proof required to demonstrate that an assumption is wrong. At the highest it must, it is submitted, be the civil standard of "balance of probabilities" but there is presumably an argument in principle for saying that the convicted person should be given the benefit of any reasonable doubt in the matter.

The assumptions which may be made are (a) that any property which the accused has held since his conviction, or which he has received during the six years prior to his being indicted are the proceeds of drug trafficking; (b) any expenditure made by him during the six years prior to his being indicted was made out of payments received by him in connection with drug trafficking; and (c) any property received, or assumed to have been received, by him at any time as a reward for drug trafficking was received free of any other interest in it.

Subs. (3)

The assumptions set out in subs. (2) cannot be made if the accused has been convicted only of an offence under s.43 of the present Act, which deals with assisting another to retain the proceeds of drug trafficking.

Subs. (4)

This subsection excludes from the assessment of the proceeds of drug trafficking any such proceeds which have been taken into account in making an assessment of the proceeds of drug trafficking in criminal proceedings in England and Wales or Northern Ireland.

Subs. (5)

This subsection provides for the remission of a case to the Court of Session where a difficult question of law or a question of fact of exceptional complexity arises.

Statements relating to drug trafficking

4.—(1) Without prejudice to section 150 of the 1975 Act, where the prosecutor has, as regards a person, moved for an order under section 1(1) of this Act the prosecutor may lodge with the clerk of court a statement as to any matters relevant to the assessment of the value of that person's proceeds of drug trafficking and if the person accepts to any extent any allegation in the statement the Court may, for the purposes of that assessment, treat that acceptance as conclusive of the matters to which it relates.

(2) Where—
    (a) a statement is lodged under subsection (1) above, and
    (b) the Court is satisfied that a copy of that statement has been served on the person,
the Court may require the person to indicate, within such period as the Court may specify, to what extent he accepts each allegation in the statement and, in so far as he does not accept any such allegation, to indicate the basis of such non-acceptance.

(3) If the person fails in any respect to comply with a requirement under subsection (2) above, he may be treated for the purposes of this section as accepting every allegation in the statement apart from any allegation in respect of which he has complied with the requirement.

(4) Without prejudice to section 150 of the 1975 Act, where—

(a) there is lodged with the clerk of court by the person a statement as to any matters relevant to determining the amount that might be realised at the time the confiscation order is made, and

(b) the prosecutor accepts to any extent any allegation in the statement,

the Court may, for the purposes of that determination, treat that acceptance as conclusive of the matters to which it relates.

(5) No acceptance by the person under this section that any payment or other reward was received by him in connection with drug trafficking carried on by him or another shall be admissible in evidence in any proceedings, whether in Scotland or elsewhere, in respect of an offence.

GENERAL NOTE

This section deals with two separate issues. S.4(1) to (3) relates to the assessment of the value of the convicted person's proceeds of drug trafficking. S.4(4) relates to the determination of what might be realised under a confiscation order. Clearly the two are connected, but what might be realised under a confiscation order might well be a sum greater than, or less than, the proceeds of the offender's drug trafficking.

Subss. (1) to (3)

The prosecutor may tender statements of matters relevant to the assessment of the value of the proceeds of the accused's drug trafficking. If the accused accepts any allegation contained in such a statement his acceptance is conclusive of that allegation. The accused does not have the option of remaining silent in order to preserve his position since the court may require the accused to indicate whether or not he accepts any allegation, and where he does not, to state why not (subs. (2)). Failure to comply with such a requirement means that the accused may be treated for the purposes of this section as accepting *every* allegation in the statement which he has not on stated grounds rejected (subs. (3)).

Subs. (4)

The Court has no power, corresponding to that under subs. (2), to require the prosecutor to indicate whether or not he accepts any allegation contained in a statement tendered by the accused.

Subs. (5)

This subsection precludes the possibility of statements (or non-denials) made under this section being relied upon as evidence of an offence in a subsequent prosecution. But does the subsection exclude the possibility of such acceptances being relied upon in subsequent proceedings directed towards determining the value of the proceeds of a person's drug trafficking? Such proceedings are arguably not "proceedings . . . in respect of an offence" within the meaning of subs. (5) which is directed towards proceedings in the nature of, or connected with, a criminal prosecution.

Realisable property

5.—(1) Subject to subsection (3) below, the following property is realisable in terms of this Part of this Act—

(a) the whole estate of a person suspected of, or charged with, an offence to which section 1 of this Act relates, being an offence in respect of which (either or both)—

(i) warrant to arrest and commit him has been granted;

(ii) a restraint order has been made against him; and

(b) the whole estate of a person to whom any person whose whole estate is realisable by virtue of paragraph (a) above has (directly or indirectly and whether in one transaction or in a series of transactions) made an implicative gift,

if the proceedings as regards the offence have not been concluded.

(2) In subsection (1) above, "the whole estate of a person" means his whole estate, wherever situated, at the date on which, in respect of the suspected or charged person, the warrant to arrest and commit was

granted, or on which the restraint order was made (whichever first occurs), and includes—

  (a) any income or estate vesting in the holder of the realisable property on that date; and

  (b) the capacity to exercise, and to take proceedings for exercising, such powers in, over or in respect of any property as might have been exercised by the holder of the realisable property for his own benefit as at that date.

(3) Property is not realisable if—

  (a) held on trust by a person mentioned in subsection (1)(a) or (b) above for a person not so mentioned; or

  (b) an order under—

    (i) section 27 of the Misuse of Drugs Act 1971 (forfeiture orders), or

    (ii) section 223 or 436 of the 1975 Act (forfeiture of property), or

    (iii) section 43 of the Powers of Criminal Courts Act 1973 (deprivation orders), or

    (iv) any other statutory provision providing specifically for forfeiture in relation to an offence,

  is in force in respect of the property.

(4) Subject to subsection (7) below, for the purposes of sections 1(1)(b) and 4(4)(a) of this Act, the amount that might be realised at the time a confiscation order is made in respect of a person is the total value at that time of all realisable property owned, and all implicative gifts which have been made, by him; except that where there are obligations having priority at that time the amount that might be realised is the aforesaid total value less the total amount payable in pursuance of those obligations.

(5) In assessing, for the purposes of section 1(1)(b) of this Act, the value—

  (a) of realisable property (other than money) owned by a person in respect of whom it proposes to make a confiscation order, the High Court shall have regard to the market value of the property at the date on which the order would be made; but it may also have regard to any security or real burden which would require to be discharged in realising the property or to any other factors which might reduce the amount recoverable by such realisation;

  (b) of an implicative gift, the Court shall, subject to section 6(2) and (3) of this Act, take it to be—

    (i) the value of the gift when received, adjusted to take account of subsequent changes in the value of money, or

    (ii) where subsection (6) below applies, the value there mentioned,

    whichever is the greater.

(6) If at the date on which the order would be made the recipient holds—

  (a) the property which he received (not being cash), or

  (b) property which, in whole or in part, directly or indirectly represents in his hands the property which he received,

the value referred to in subsection (5)(b)(ii) above is, subject to section 6(2) and (3) of this Act, the value at that date of the property mentioned in paragraph (a) above or, as the case may be, of the property mentioned in paragraph (b) above so far as it represents the property which he received.

(7) Without prejudice to section 47(3) of this Act, the Court may, notwithstanding subsections (5)(b) and (6) above, for the purposes of section 1(1)(b) of this Act disregard the amount (or part of the amount) of an implicative gift if it considers it improbable that such amount (or part) could be realised.

(8) For the purposes of subsection (4) above, an obligation has priority at any time if it is an obligation of the person in respect of whom the confiscation order is made to—

    (a) pay an amount due in respect of—

        (i) a fine or order (not being a confiscation order or an order mentioned in sub-paragraph (ii) below) of a court, imposed or made on conviction of an offence, where the fine was imposed or order made before the confiscation order;

        (ii) a compensation order (within the meaning of the Criminal Justice (Scotland) Act 1980), made on conviction of an offence, where such order was made before, or in the same proceedings as, the confiscation order; or

    (b) pay any sum which would be included among—

        (i) the preferred debts (as defined in section 51(2) of the 1985 Act) were his estate being sequestrated in accordance with the provisions of that Act and were the date on which the confiscation order would be made the date of sequestration;

        (ii) the preferential debts (within the meaning given by section 386 of the Insolvency Act 1986) in the person's bankruptcy or winding up were that bankruptcy commencing on the date of the confiscation order or as the case may be were the winding up under an order of the court made on that date.

GENERAL NOTE

This section determines what property may be realised in order to satisfy a confiscation order. The significant points here are (a) that a person's property becomes realisable before conviction if the conditions set out in s.5(1)(a) are satisfied; (b) the property of a person who is not a suspect is also realisable if he or she has received from a person suspected of, or charged with, an offence listed in s.1(2), an "implicative gift"; (c) all forms of property, moveable or heritable, corporeal or incorporeal, are realisable; (d) property situated outside Scotland is realisable; and (e) only a limited list of exceptions is provided for, and the majority of these relate to property already the subject of forfeiture orders.

Subs. (1)

These provisions are central to the policy of the Act. Not only is the property of the convicted person liable to seizure under a confiscation order, but so also is the property of any third party to whom the convicted person has made an "implicative gift." This aspect of the Bill was severely criticised in the First Scottish Standing Committee on the ground that it was unfair to treat "someone who has been charged with no offence and who is not even suspected of an offence in the same way as a drug trafficker is to be treated" (First Scottish Standing Committee, Second Sitting, April 23, 1987, Mr. Clarke, col. 62). The Solicitor-General for Scotland did, however, confirm that a person's estate may be subject to confiscation in this way (*ibid.*, col. 66).

It is important to note, however, that where property is realisable by virtue of s.5(1)(b), the person's estate may be used to satisfy a confiscation order only to the value of the gift for the time being (s.23(3)).

Subs. (2)

This subsection defines the "whole estate of a person" for the purposes of subs. (1). One of the problems encountered in use of forfeiture powers under the Misuse of Drugs Act 1971 is, as we have seen (above, General Note to Pt. I) that the courts may not have the power to order the forfeiture of property situated abroad, and there is doubt as to whether intangible property, or heritable property may be seized. There can be no such doubts in relation to confiscation order in the light of the definition of the "whole estate of a person" which clearly extends to all categories of property, wherever situated. Of course there remains the problem of enforcement of confiscation orders outside Scotland. S.31, however, makes provisions for the enforcement of Scottish confiscation orders in England and Wales and s.32 contemplates the possible external effects of Scottish confiscation orders.

Subs. (4)

This subsection makes it clear that the making of an implicative gift does not diminish the value of the giver's realisable property. The subsection also provides that property is realisable subject to "obligations having priority." "Obligations having priority" are defined in subs. (8) as including obligations arising in respect of payment of a fine or order of a court, a compensation order, and the payment of preferred debts (within the meaning of s.51(2) of the Bankruptcy (Scotland) Act 1985 or preferential debts (within the meaning given by s.386 of the Insolvency Act 1986).

Subs. (5)

The general rule for determining the value of realisable property (other than money) is its market value at the date on which the confiscation order is made (subject to any relevant deduction such as the discharge of a security or real burden over the property). The value of an implicative gift is the greater of the following: (i) the value of the gift when received, adjusted to take account of changes in the value of money; or (ii) where, at the date of the confiscation order, the recipient still holds the gift (or property which represents in his hands that gift) then (subject to s.6(2) and (3), the value of the gift (or the representative property) on the date of the order.

Implicative gifts

6.—(1) Subject to subsection (4) below, in this Part of this Act references to an "implicative gift" are references to a gift (whether made before or after the commencement of section 1 of this Act)—

(a) made not more than six years before the date mentioned in section 5(2) of this Act; or

(b) made at any time if the gift was—

    (i) of property received by the giver in connection with drug trafficking carried on by him or another, or

    (ii) of property which, in whole or in part, directly or indirectly represented in the giver's hands property received by him in that connection.

(2) For the purposes of subsection (1) above, the circumstances in which a person is to be treated as making a gift shall include those of a case where he transfers an interest in property to another person, directly or indirectly, for a consideration significantly less than the value of that interest at the time of transfer. In subsection (3) below the said consideration is referred to as "consideration A" (or as "A") and the said value as "consideration B" (or as "B").

(3) In the case mentioned in subsection (2) above, section 5 of this Act shall apply as if the reference in sub-paragraph (i) of subsection (5)(b) of that section to "the value of the gift when received" were a reference to the amount by which consideration A is exceeded by consideration B and as if in sub-paragraph (ii) of the said subsection (5)(b) the reference to "the value there mentioned" were a reference to a value determined in accordance with the formula—

$$\frac{C\,(B-A)}{B}$$

where C is what the value referred to in the said sub-paragraph (ii) would be had the gift been an outright gift.

(4) A gift made for a charitable purpose to a person who is not an associate of the giver, being a gift which having regard to all the circumstances it was reasonable to make, is not an implicative gift.

(5) In subsection (4) above, "charitable purpose" means any charitable, benevolent or philanthropic purpose whether or not it is charitable within the meaning of any rule of law.

GENERAL NOTE

This section defines "implicative gift" for the purposes of Pt. I. The definition is complex, and three elements should be noted: subs. (1) states when a gift is to be considered "implicative"; subss. (2) and (3) extend the definition of gift to include the case where an interest in property is transferred by the giver to another person for a consideration significantly less than the value of that interest at the time of the transfer; subss. (4) and (5) exclude from the definition of implicative gift certain gifts made for "charitable purposes" as defined in subs. (5).

Subs. (1)

When are gifts "implicative"?
   Whether or not a gift is implicative may depend on a number of factors. Under para. (a) the crucial question is *when* the gift was made. Under para. (b) the central issue is the origin of the property which is the subject of the gift.

Para. (a)
   Under this paragraph, gifts made not more than six years before the date mentioned in s.5(2) of the Act are implicative. These are gifts made within the six years prior to the date on which (i) warrant to arrest and commit the accused was granted in respect of an offence to which s.1 relates, or (ii) within the six years prior to the date on which a restraint order was made against the accused (whichever first occurs).

Para. (b)
   Under this paragraph gifts made *at any time* are implicative if the gift was (i) of property received by the giver in connection with drug trafficking carried on by him or another, or (ii) of property which in whole or in part directly or indirectly represented in the giver's hands property received by him in that connection.

Subs. (2)
   The purpose of this subsection is to extend the definition of gift to include transfers which, although having the appearance of transfers for value, are in reality sham transactions designed to conceal the fact that property is being transferred for a consideration which does not bear a true relation to the value of the property.

Subs. (3)
   This subsection applies the notion introduced by subs. (2) to the valuation of an implicative gift for the purposes of s.5(5). This process only arises where the situation envisaged by s.6(2) applies. The following examples may clarify the operation of these provisions:
   (1) A makes an implicative gift to B which at the time of the gift is worth £5,000. B no longer has the property in question. Its value, therefore, is determined by s.5(5)(b)(i) and is the value of the gift *when received*, subject to adjustment to take account of changes in the value of money.
   (2) A makes an implicative gift to B, which at the time of the gift was worth £5,000. He still has the property, which has now risen in value to £7,500. Its value is determined according to s.5(6), and is the value of the property at the time of its receipt, or at the time of the confiscation order, whichever is the greater. In this case, £7,500.
   (3) A transfers property worth £10,000 to B for £2,500. This is the situation envisaged by section 6(2) and (3), and the value of the gift is determined in accordance with the formula in section 6(3).

Subss. (4) and (5)
   These subsections exclude from the definition of implicative gifts certain gifts made for charitable purposes. It is worth noting that although "charitable purpose" is given a very wide definition, it is not every gift for such a purpose which is exempt. Only gifts (a) made to a person who is not an associate of the giver and (b) which in all the circumstances it was reasonable to make are exempt. Whether or not a gift is reasonable will of course depend upon the circumstances, but clearly what is excluded here is the use of charitable donations to disguise or dissipate an estate consisting of realisable property.

Application of provisions relating to fines to enforcement of confiscation orders

   7.—(1) Sections 196 and 203 of the 1975 Act and, as applied by section 194 of that Act, the provisions of that Act specified in subsection (2) below shall, subject to the qualifications mentioned in subsection (2) below, apply in relation to confiscation orders as they apply in relation to fines; and section 91 of the Magistrates' Courts Act 1980 and Article 96 of the Magistrates' Courts (Northern Ireland) Order 1981 (provisions relating to transfer of fines from Scotland etc.) shall be construed accordingly.

(2) The provisions mentioned in subsection (1) above are—
section 396;
Provided that any allowance under that section (or section 397) of time (or further time) for payment shall be without prejudice to the exercise by any administrator appointed in relation to the confiscation order of his powers and duties under this Act; and the court may, pending such exercise, postpone any decision as to refusing or allowing time (or further time) for payment;
section 397;
section 398;
section 399;
Provided that any order of payment by instalments shall be without prejudice to such exercise as is above mentioned;
section 400;
section 401(2) and (3);
section 403, except that for the purposes of subsections (4) and (6) of that section "confiscation order" in subsection (1) above shall be construed as including such an order within the meaning of the Drug Trafficking Offences Act 1986 or of any corresponding provision in Northern Ireland;
section 404;
section 406;
section 407;
Provided that where a court imposes a period of imprisonment both in respect of a fine and of a confiscation order the amounts in respect of which the period is imposed shall, for the purposes of subsection (1A) of that section, be aggregated:
Provided also that before imposing a period of imprisonment to which there is a liability by virtue of that section the court shall, if an administrator has been appointed in relation to the confiscation order, require a report from him as to whether and in what way he is likely to exercise his powers and duties under this Act and shall take that report into account; and the court may, pending such exercise, postpone any decision as to such imposition;
section 408;
section 409, except that the reference in subsection (1) of that section to the person paying a sum to the governor of the prison under conditions prescribed by rules made under the Prisons (Scotland) Act 1952 shall be construed as including a reference to an administrator appointed in relation to the confiscation order making such payment under this Act in respect of the person;
section 411, except the proviso to subsection (3):
Provided that an order for recovery by civil diligence shall not be made under the section where an administrator is appointed in relation to the confiscation order;
Schedule 7.

(3) Where in any proceedings an order has been made under section 1(1) of this Act as regards a person and a period of imprisonment or detention is imposed on him in default of payment of its amount (or as the case may be of an instalment thereof), that period shall run from the expiry of any other period of imprisonment or detention (not being one of life imprisonment or detention for life) imposed on him in the proceedings.

(4) The reference in subsection (3) above to "any other period of imprisonment or detention imposed" includes (without prejudice to the generality of the expression) a reference to such a period on default of payment of a fine (or instalment thereof); but only where that default has occurred before the warrant for imprisonment is issued for the default in relation to the order.

GENERAL NOTE

This section applies to the enforcement of confiscation orders a series of provisions applicable to the enforcement of fines. Subject to the variations mentioned, the enforcement of confiscation orders is thus assimilated to the enforcement of fines.

Restraint orders and interdict

Cases in which restraint orders may be made

8.—(1) Where—

 (a) warrant to arrest and commit a person suspected of or charged with an offence to which section 1 of this Act relates has been granted and either—

  (i) notice has been served on him calling upon him to appear at a trial diet in the High Court or at a diet of that Court fixed for the purposes of section 102 of the 1975 Act (whether or not the trial has commenced, provided that the proceedings as regards the offence have not been concluded); or

  (ii) the Court of Session is satisfied that it is intended that any trial diet in respect of the suspected offence (or as the case may be the offence with which he has been charged) shall proceed in the High Court; or

 (b) the Court of Session is satisfied that a procurator fiscal proposes to petition within twenty-eight days for warrant to arrest and commit a person suspected of such an offence, that the suspicion is reasonable and that it is intended that any trial diet in respect of the suspected offence shall proceed in the High Court; or

 (c) an interlocutor has been pronounced under section 104(1)(b) of the 1975 Act remitting a person to the High Court for sentence in respect of such an offence,

the Court of Session may, on the application of the Lord Advocate, make in respect of the person such order (in this Act referred to as a "restraint order") as is described in section 9 of this Act. Any such application shal¹ be heard in chambers.

(2) Subject to subsection (3) below, the Court of Session may, at the instance of—

 (a) the Lord Advocate, at any time vary or recall a restraint order in relation to any person or to any property;

 (b) any person having an interest, at any time vary or recall a restraint order in relation to the person or to any property; and in particular may, on the application of a person named in a restraint order as having received an implicative gift, recall the order in relation to that person if satisfied—

  (i) that he received the gift not knowing, not suspecting and not having reasonable grounds to suspect that the giver was in any way concerned in drug trafficking; and

  (ii) that he is not, and has never been, an associate of the giver; and

  (iii) that he would suffer hardship were the order not to be recalled.

(3) The Court of Session may, where it has recalled a restraint order under subsection (2) above, order that property of the person at whose instance it was recalled shall cease to be realisable.

(4) Rules of court may provide that any application under subsection (2) above shall be made within such period of the applicant receiving notice of the restraint order as may be specified in the rules; and in the period between such application and any decision of the Court as regards recalling that order the powers of any administrator appointed as regards property of the applicant shall be subject to the restriction that the administrator shall not realise the property.

(5) Where, a restraint order having been made by virtue of—

    (a) paragraph (b) of subsection (1) above, the days mentioned in that paragraph expire without the petition having been presented; or

    (b) paragraph (a), (b) or (c) of that subsection, the proceedings as regards the offence are concluded,

the Lord Advocate shall forthwith apply to the Court of Session for recall of that order and the Court shall grant the application.

GENERAL NOTE

The purpose of this section and the section which follows is to ensure that property which might become realisable for the purpose of satisfying a compensation order is not dealt with in such a way as to frustrate any such order. S.8 sets out the cases in which restraint orders may be made for this purpose. S.9 sets out the nature and effect of a restraint order.

Subs. (1)

The Court of Session may, on the application of the Lord Advocate, make a restraint order where any of the cases in paras. (a) to (c) is satisfied. Para. (a) deals with two situations where warrant to arrest and commit a person suspected of or charged with an offence to which s.1(2) relates has been granted. Para. (b), however, permits an order to be made up to 28 days before a petition for warrant to arrest and commit is presented. Para. (c) relates to the situation where the accused has already been convicted before the Sheriff court.

Subs. (1) appears to suggest that the restraint order applies only to a person mentioned in paras. (a) to (c). But s.9(1) makes it clear that a restraint order may be applied to that person, or any person named therein as appearing to the court to have received from him or her an implicative gift.

Subs. (2)

This subsection provides for the variation or recall of a restraint order on the application of the Lord Advocate or any person having an interest. The conditions for the recall of an order as it affects a person named as having received an implicative gift are quite onerous. All three conditions must be satisfied. It is not enough that the gift was received innocently. It must also be shown that the recipient is not, and never has been an "associate" of the donor, and that he would suffer hardship were the order not to be recalled.

Restraint orders

    9.—(1) A restraint order is an order interdicting—

    (a) the person in respect of whom it is made from dealing with his realisable property; or

    (b) that person and any person named in the order as appearing to the Court of Session to have received from him an implicative gift from dealing with their own, or the other's, realisable property,

(whenever that property was acquired and whether it is described in the order or not); but, subject to subsection (5) below, the order may contain conditions and exceptions to which such interdict shall be subject.

(2) A restraint order shall provide for notice to be given to persons affected by the order.

(3) In subsection (1) above, the reference to "dealing with" property shall (without prejudice to the generality of the expression) be construed as including a reference—

(a) to making a payment in reduction of the amount of a debt; and

(b) to removing the property from Great Britain.

(4) If the restraint order is made by virtue of section 8(1)(b) of this Act, references in the foregoing provisions of this section to "realisable property" shall, in relation to any period before warrant to arrest and commit the person in respect of whom it was made is granted, be construed as references to property which would be realisable property had such warrant been granted immediately before the commencement of that period.

(5) Without prejudice to the generality of subsection (1) above, property in so far as it comprises reasonable legal expenses payable in relation to proceedings as regards the offence by virtue of which the restraint order has been made or as regards a confiscation order made on conviction thereof shall be excepted under that subsection from the interdict.

Seizure of property affected by restraint order

10.—(1) A constable or a person commissioned by the Commissioners of Customs and Excise may, for the purpose of preventing realisable property of a person subject to a restraint order (whether under this Act or under and within the meaning of the Drug Trafficking Offences Act 1986) from being removed from Great Britain, seize the property.

(2) Property seized under subsection (1) above shall be dealt with in accordance with the directions of the court which made the order.

Inhibition and arrestment of property affected by restraint order or by interdict under section 12

11.—(1) On the application of the Lord Advocate, the Court of Session may, in respect of—

(a) heritable realisable property in Scotland affected by a restraint order (whether such property generally or particular such property) grant warrant for inhibition against any person interdicted by the order or, in relation to that property, under section 12 of this Act;

(b) moveable realisable property so affected (whether such property generally or particular such property) grant warrant for arrestment if the property would be arrestable were the person entitled to it a debtor;

and, subject to the provisions of this Part of this Act, the warrant—

(i) shall have effect as if granted on the dependence of an action for debt at the instance of the Lord Advocate against the person and may be executed, recalled, loosed or restricted accordingly;

(ii) where granted under subsection (1)(a) above, shall have the effect of letters of inhibition and shall forthwith be registered by the Lord Advocate in the register of inhibitions and adjudications.

(2) Section 155 of the Titles to Land Consolidation (Scotland) Act 1868 (effective date of inhibition) shall apply in relation to an inhibition for which warrant has been granted under subsection (1)(a) above as that section applies to an inhibition by separate letters or contained in a summons.

(3) In the application of section 158 of the said Act of 1868 (recall of inhibition) to such inhibition as is mentioned in subsection (2) above, references in that section to a particular Lord Ordinary shall be construed as references to any Lord Ordinary.

(4) That an inhibition or arrestment has been executed under subsection (1) above in respect of property shall not prejudice the exercise of an

administrator's powers under or for the purposes of this Part of this Act in respect of that property.

(5) No inhibition or arrestment executed under subsection (1) above shall have effect once, or in so far as, the restraint order affecting the property in respect of which the warrant for such inhibition or arrestment has been granted has ceased to have effect in respect of that property; and the Lord Advocate shall—

(a) apply for the recall, or as the case may be restriction, of the inhibition or arrestment accordingly; and

(b) ensure that recall, or restriction, of an inhibition on such application is reflected in the register of inhibitions and adjudications.

(6) The foregoing provisions of this section shall apply in relation to an order made under section 8 of the Drug Trafficking Offences Act 1986 and registered under section 28 of this Act (a "relevant order") as they apply to a restraint order; but as if—

(a) for any reference to the Lord Advocate there were substituted a reference to the prosecutor or, in a case where the order was made by virtue of subsection (2) of section 7 of that Act and the information mentioned in that subsection has not yet been laid, to the person as regards whom the court which made the order was satisfied as is mentioned in subsection (3)(b) of that section;

(b) any reference to realisable property fell to be construed in accordance with section 5 of that Act (references in that section to the defendant, and to the time at which proceedings were instituted against him, being in such case as is mentioned in paragraph (a) above taken to be, respectively, references to the person as regards whom the court which made the order was satisfied as is mentioned in subsection (2) of the said section 7 and to the time immediately before the order was made);

(c) for any reference to a restraint order there were substituted a reference to a relevant order;

(d) in subsection (1)(a), for the words "interdicted by the order or, in relation to that property, under section 12 of this Act" there were substituted the words "with an interest in that property";

(e) in subsection (1), for the words "Part of this Act" there were substituted the word "section";

(f) in subsection (1)(i), after the word "and" there were inserted the words "subject to subsection (3A) below";

(g) after subsection (3) there were inserted the following subsection—

"(3A) Any power of the Court of Session to recall, loose or restrict inhibitions or arrestments shall, in relation to an inhibition or arrestment proceedings upon a warrant under this section and without prejudice to any other consideration lawfully applying to the exercise of the power, be exercised with a view to achieving the purposes specified in section 13 of the Drug Trafficking Offences Act 1986."; and

(h) in subsection (4)—

(i) for the reference to an administrator there were substituted a reference to a receiver; and

(ii) for the words "this Part of this Act" there were substituted the words "section 8, 11 or 12 of the said Act of 1986".

Interdict of person not subject to restraint order

12.—(1) The Court of Session may, where it has granted a restraint order, interdict a person not subject to that order from dealing with realisable property affected by it while it is in force; and the clerk of court shall, on the restraint order being recalled, forthwith so inform each person so interdicted.

(2) Subsection (2) of section 8 of this Act applies in relation to an interdict under subsection (1) above as the said subsection (2) applies in relation to a restraint order; and subsection (3) of section 9 thereof applies in relation to subsection (1) above as the said subsection (3) applies in relation to subsection (1) of the said section 9.

(3) An interdict under subsection (1) above shall not be effective against a person unless and until he is served with a copy both of it and of the restraint order.

GENERAL NOTE

This section gives the Court of Session the power to interdict a person from dealing with realisable property affected by a restraint order, even though that person is not named in the order. It is not clear how the question of interdict is to be brought before the Court. S.8 makes it clear that the Lord Advocate must apply for a restraint order, but there is no similar requirement in relation to s.12.

The provisions of s.8(2) relating to the variation or recall of a restraint order are, by s.12(2) applied to interdicts effective under s.12(1).

Administrators

Administrators

13.—(1) On the application of the Lord Advocate the Court of Session may as regards realisable property—

(a) affected by a restraint order, appoint a person to manage, or otherwise deal with, the property; or

(b) where a confiscation order has been made, appoint a person (or empower an appointee under paragraph (a) above) to realise the property,

in accordance with the Court's directions and may (whether on making the appointment or from time to time) require any person having possession of the property to give possession of it to the appointee (any such appointee being in this Act referred to as an "administrator").

(2) A requirement under subsection (1) above—

(a) subject to paragraph (b) below, may relate to the property generally or to particular such property and may be subject to such exceptions and conditions as may be specified by the Court;

(b) shall relate to property mentioned in paragraph (b) of section 5(1) of this Act only if expressly stated so to do and then only in so far as the person in whom such property is vested is named in the requirement as being subject to it.

(3) On a requirement being imposed under subsection (1) above—

(a) the clerk of court shall forthwith so notify—

(i) the person in respect of whom the restraint order, or as the case may be the confiscation order, has been made; and

(ii) any other person named in the requirement as being subject to it; and

(b) any dealing of or with such person in relation to the property shall be of no effect in a question with the administrator unless whoever dealt with the person had, at the time when the dealing occurred, no knowledge of the appointment.

(4) The Court of Session, at the instance of any person having an interest, may at any time—

(a) vary or withdraw a requirement imposed under subsection (1) above; or

(b) without prejudice to section 16 of this Act or to the powers and duties of an administrator pending a decision under this paragraph, on cause shown, remove the administrator from office.

(5) On the death or resignation of the administrator, or on his removal from office under subsection (4)(b) above or section 17 of this Act, the Court of Session shall appoint a new administrator. Such of the property (if any) as was, by virtue of section 14(3) of this Act, vested in the administrator who has died, resigned or been removed shall forthwith vest in the new administrator; and any requirement imposed under subsection (1) above shall, on the person subject to the requirement being notified in writing of the appointment by the appointee, apply in relation to the appointee instead of in relation to his predecessor.

(6) The administration of property by an administrator shall be deemed continuous notwithstanding any temporary vacancy in that office.

(7) Any appointment under this section shall be on such conditions as to caution as the accountant of court may think fit to impose; but the premium of any bond of caution or other security thereby required of the administrator shall be treated as part of his outlays in his actings as such.

(8) Without prejudice to section 17 of this Act, section 6 of the Judicial Factors (Scotland) Act 1889 (supervision of judicial factors) shall not apply in relation to an appointment under this section.

GENERAL NOTE
    This section, and those which follow, provide for the appointment of an administrator, and set out his powers and duties in respect of property realisable under this Act. Under the Drug Trafficking Offences Act 1986 the corresponding functions are carried out by a receiver appointed by the Court. Given the absence of a corresponding common law of receivers in Scotland it has proved necessary to make special provision for the administration and realisation of realisable property.

Subs. (1)
    The administrator's functions as regards realisable property differ according to whether or not a confiscation order has been made. Prior to the making of a confiscation order, an administrator may be appointed to manage or otherwise deal with realisable property, provided that it is affected by a restraint order (s.13(1)(a)). Once a confiscation order has been made, the function of the administrator under s.13(1)(b) is to realise the property.

Subs. (2)
    Property mentioned in paragraph (b) of section 5(1). This is the estate of a person who has received an "implicative gift" from a person suspected of or charged with an offence to which s.1 relates, and to whom the conditions in s.5(1)(a)(i) or (ii) apply.

Functions of administrators

    14.—(1) Subject to section 17 of this Act, an administrator—
      (a) shall be entitled to take possession of, and if appointed (or empowered) under paragraph (b) of section 13(1) of this Act shall as soon as practicable take possession of, the property as regards which he has been appointed and of any document which both—
         (i) is in the possession or control of the person (in this section referred to as "A") in whom the property is vested (or would be vested but for an order made under subsection (3) of this section); and
         (ii) relates to the property or to A's assets, business or financial affairs;
      (b) shall be entitled to have access to, and to copy, any document relating to the property or to A's assets, business or financial affairs and not in such possession or control as is mentioned in paragraph (a) above;
      (c) may bring, defend or continue any legal proceedings relating

to the property and, without prejudice to the generality of this paragraph, may sist himself in any case in the Court of Session which has been remitted under section 3(5) of this Act if the restraint order by virtue of which the administrator has been appointed interdicts the person whose case has been so remitted from dealing with the property;

(d) may borrow money in so far as it is necessary to do so to safeguard the property and may for the purposes of such borrowing create a security over any part of the property;

(e) may, if the administrator considers that to do so would be beneficial for the management or realisation of the property—
  (i) carry on any business of A;
  (ii) exercise any right of A as holder of securities in a company;
  (iii) grant a lease of the property or take on lease any other property; or
  (iv) enter into any contract, or execute any deed, as regards the property or as regards A's business;

(f) may, where any right, option or other power forms part of A's estate, make payments or incur liabilities with a view to—
  (i) obtaining property which is the subject of; or
  (ii) maintaining,
  the right, option or power;

(g) may effect or maintain insurance policies as regards the property or A's business;

(h) may, where A has an uncompleted title to any heritable estate, complete title thereto:
  Provided that completion of title in A's name shall not validate by accretion any unperfected right in favour of any person other than the administrator;

(j) may sell, purchase or exchange property or discharge any security for an obligation due to A:
  Provided that it shall be incompetent for the administrator or an associate of his to purchase any of A's property in pursuance of this paragraph;

(k) may claim, vote and draw dividends in the sequestration of the estate (or bankruptcy or liquidation) of a debtor of A and may accede to a voluntary trust deed for creditors of such a debtor;

(l) may discharge any of his functions through agents or employees:
  Provided that the administrator shall be personally liable to meet the fees and expenses of any such agent or employee out of such remuneration as is payable to the administrator by virtue of section 18(1) and (3) of this Act;

(m) may take such professional advice as he may consider requisite for the proper discharge of his functions;

(n) may at any time apply to the Court of Session for directions as regards the discharge of his functions;

(o) may exercise any power specifically conferred on him by the Court of Session, whether such conferral was at the time of his appointment or on his subsequent application to the Court in that regard; and

(p) may do anything incidental to the above powers and duties.

(2) Subject to the proviso to paragraph (j) of subsection (1) above—
  (a) a person dealing with an administrator in good faith and for value shall not require to determine whether the administrator is acting within the powers mentioned in that subsection; and

(b) the validity of any title shall not be challengeable by reason only of the administrator having acted outwith those powers.

(3) The exercise of a power mentioned in any of paragraphs (c) to (k) above shall be in A's name except where and in so far as an order made by the Court of Session under this subsection (either on its own motion or on the application of the administrator) has vested the property in the administrator (or in his predecessor in that office).

GENERAL NOTE

This section sets out the powers and duties of administrators appointed (or empowered) under s.13. Its is worth noting that if the administrator is appointed or empowered under s.13(1)(b) (*i.e.* where a confiscation order has already been made) he is obliged to take possession of the property as soon as practicable. In all other cases he has a discretion whether or not to do so.

In the performance of the functions conferred on him by the Act, the administrator is subject to the supervision of the accountant of court. Where an administrator without reasonable cause fails to perform a duty imposed on him under this Act, the Court of Session may remove him from office, censure him, or make such other order as the circumstances of the case may appear to the Court to require.

Paras. (c) to (p)

An administrator proposing to exercise the functions conferred by any of these paragraphs must first obtain the consent of the accountant of court (s.17(1)).

Money received by administrator

15.—(1) Subject to subsection (2) below, all money received by an administrator in the exercise of his functions shall be deposited by him, in the name (unless vested in the administrator by virtue of subsection (3) of section 14 of this Act) of the holder of the property realised, in an appropriate bank or institution.

(2) The administrator may at any time retain in his hands a sum not exceeding £200 or such other sum as may be prescribed by the Secretary of State by regulations made by statutory instrument.

(3) In subsection (1) above, "appropriate bank or institution" means a bank or institution mentioned in section 2(1) of the Banking Act 1979 or for the time being specified in Schedule 1 to that Act.

Application of proceeds of realisation and other sums

16.—(1) Subject to subsection (2) below, sums in the hands of an administrator which are—

(a) proceeds of a realisation of property under section 13 of this Act, and

(b) other property held by the person in respect of whom the confiscation order was made,

shall first be applied in payment of such expenses as are payable under section 37(2) of this Act and then shall, after such payments (if any) as the Court of Session may direct have been made out of those proceeds and sums, be applied on the person's behalf towards the satisfaction of the confiscation order.

(2) If, after the amount payable under the confiscation order has been fully paid, any such proceeds and sums remain in the hands of the administrator, he shall distribute them

(a) among such of those who held property which has been realised under this Act, and

(b) in such proportions,

as the Court of Session may, after giving such persons an opportunity to be heard as regards the matter, direct.

(3) The receipt of any sum by a sheriff clerk on account of an amount payable under a confiscation order shall reduce the amount so payable, but the sum—

(a) if not paid by an administrator under subsection (1) above, shall first be applied in payment of such expenses as are payable under section 37(2) of this Act;

(b) if so paid, shall first be applied in payment of the administrator's remuneration and expenses,

(c) subject to paragraphs (a) and (b) above, shall be applied in reimbursement of any sums paid by the Lord Advocate under section 20(2) of this Act,

and the balance shall be payable and recoverable (or as the case may be disposed of) under section 203 of the 1975 Act (fines payable to H.M. Exchequer) as applied by section 7 of this Act.

GENERAL NOTE

This section sets out the purposes for which the proceeds of a realisation and other sums may be applied, and the order in which they are to be applied. The section also makes provision for the distribution of any surplus remaining after the satisfaction of the confiscation order.

Subs. (1)

Sums in the hands of the administrator must first be applied in payment of such expenses as are payable under s.37(2) of this Act. S.37(1)(a) refers to the case where a person acting as an insolvency practitioner seizes or disposes of any property in relation to which his functions are, because that property is for the time being subject to a restraint order, not exerciseable. S.37(2) provides that any person who, acting as an insolvency practitioner, incurs expenses in respect of such property, and in doing so does not know and has no reasonable grounds to believe that the property is for the time being subject to a restraint order, shall be entitled to payment of those expenses under s.16(1) (or s.16(3)(a)) of the Act.

The next call on the sums in the hands of the administrator is such payment (if any) as the Court of Session may direct under s.16(1). No more specific indication is given, but this would presumably include incidental expenses incurred by the administrator in connection with the discharge of his functions where these are not otherwise provided for.

When the above calls have been satisfied the money and property in the hands of the administrator may be applied to the satisfaction of the confiscation order.

Subs. (2)

This subsection directs the manner in which any remaining proceeds and sums are to be distributed once the confiscation order has been fully paid.

Subs. (3)

This subsection directs the order in which sums paid on account of an amount payable under a confiscation order are to be applied, and the purpose to which they are to be applied. If the sums in question are not paid by an administrator, then the first call upon such sums is the satisfaction of such expenses as are payable under s.37(2) of this Act. If the sums are paid by an administrator, they must first be applied in payment of the administrator's remuneration and expenses. Subject to these prior calls, such sums paid on account are to be applied in reimbursement of any sums paid by the Lord Advocate under s.20(2) of the Act. S.20(2) provides that if no sum is available to be applied to the remuneration and expenses of an administrator under s.16(3)(b), then such remuneration and expenses shall be paid by the Lord Advocate.

Supervision of administrators

17.—(1) The accountant of court shall supervise the performance by administrators of the functions conferred on them by this Act; and in particular an administrator proposing to exercise functions conferred by any of paragraphs (c) to (p) of subsection (1) of section 14 of this Act shall first obtain the consent of the accountant of court to such exercise.

(2) If it appears to the accountant of court that an administrator has, without reasonable cause, failed to perform a duty imposed on him by any provision of this Part of this Act, he shall report the matter to the Court of Session which, after giving the administrator an opportunity to be heard as regards the matter, may remove the administrator from office, censure him or make such other order as the circumstances of the case may appear to the Court to require.

Accounts and remuneration of administrator

18.—(1) The administrator shall keep such accounts in relation to his intromissions with the property as regards which he is appointed as the Court of Session may require and shall lodge these accounts with the accountant of court at such times as may be fixed by the Court in that regard; and the accountant of court shall audit the accounts and issue a determination as to the amount of outlays and, on the basis mentioned in subsection (3) below, remuneration payable to the administrator in respect of those intromissions.

(2) Not later than two weeks after the issuing of a determination under subsection (1) above, the administrator or the Lord Advocate may appeal against it to the Court of Sessions.

(3) The basis for determining the amount of remuneration payable to the administrator shall be the value of the work reasonably undertaken by him, regard being had to the extent of the responsibilities involved.

(4) The accountant of court may authorise the administrator to pay without taxation an account in respect of legal services incurred by the administrator.

Effect of appointment under section 13 on diligence

19. Without prejudice to section 11 of this Act—

    (a) no arrestment or poinding of realisable property executed on or after an appointment as regards the property under section 13 of this Act shall be effectual to create a preference for the arrester or poinder and any such property so arrested or poinded, or the proceeds of sale thereof, shall be handed over to the administrator;

    (b) no poinding of the ground in respect of realisable property on or after such appointment shall be effectual in a question with the administrator except for the interest on the debt of a secured creditor, being interest for the current half-yearly term and arrears of interest for one year immediately before the commencement of that term;

    (c) it shall be incompetent on or after such appointment for any other person to raise or insist in an adjudication against the realisable property or to be confirmed as executor-creditor on that property; and

    (d) no inhibition on realisable property which takes effect on or after such appointment shall be effectual to create a preference for the inhibitor in a question with the administrator.

GENERAL NOTE

This section sets out the effect of the appointment of an administrator upon diligence effected in respect of realisable property on or after the appointment of the administrator. In general terms, s.19 operates against other creditors in favour of the administrator appointed under s.13. It does appear, however, that the precise operation of s.19 differs in this respect as between heritage and moveable property.

S.19(a) provides that no arrestment or poinding of realisable property on or after the appointment of the administrator is to be effectual to create a preference for the arrester or poinder. This suggests that the arrestment or poinding is to be completely ineffectual.

S.19(b), however, states that, subject to certain exceptions, a poinding of the ground shall only be effectual in a question with the administrator to the extent of the exceptions set out in that subsection. This raises the question of the effect of such poinding in a question with another creditor. Does the appointment of an administrator render such diligence ineffectual? It does not appear from the words of the section that this need be the case. Of course, the administrator is likely to consume the property in satisfaction of the confiscation order. But if no confiscation order is made, or if one is made which does not fully absorb the available property, then the effect of the appointment of an administrator on a conflict between two creditors may become a significant issue.

Further provision as to administrators

20.—(1) Where an administrator takes any action—

 (a) in relation to property which is not realisable property, being action which he would be entitled to take if it were such property,

 (b) believing, and having reasonable grounds for believing, that he is entitled to take that action in relation to that property,

he shall not be liable to any person in respect of any loss or damage resulting from his action except in so far as the loss or damage is caused by his negligence.

(2) Any amount due in respect of the remuneration and expenses of an administrator so appointed shall, if no sum is available to be applied in payment of it under section 16(3)(b) of this Act, be paid by the Lord Advocate.

GENERAL NOTE

This section provides a measure of security for administrators, in two senses. Subs. (1) protects the administrator who, in good faith, takes any action in relation to property which is not realisable property, thereby causing loss or damage to any person. In such a case the administrator is not liable to the person suffering loss except in so far as the loss or damage is caused by his negligence.

Subs. (2) provides that if the administrator's remuneration and expenses are not paid out of sums available under s.16(3)(b), then such costs must be paid by the Lord Advocate. (Payments made by the Lord Advocate in this respect may be reimbursed out of sums paid on account of a confiscation order under s.16(3)(c).)

Discharge of administrator

21. After an administrator has lodged his final accounts under section 18(1) of this Act, he may apply to the accountant of court to be discharged from office; and such discharge, if granted, shall have the effect of freeing him from all liability (other than liability arising from fraud) in respect of any act or omission of his in exercising the functions conferred on him by this Act.

Rules of court as regards accountant of court's supervision etc. of administrators

22. Without prejudice to section 16(i) of the Administration of Justice (Scotland) Act 1933 (power, in relation to certain statutory powers and duties, to regulate procedure etc. by Act of Sederunt), provision may be made by rules of court as regards (or as regards any matter incidental to) the accountant of court's powers and duties under this Act in relation to the functions of administrators.

Exercise of powers

Exercise of powers by Court of Session or administrator

23.—(1) The following provisions apply to the powers conferred on the Court of Session by sections 8, 11(1) to (5), 12 to 13, 16 and 24 of this

Act, or on an administrator appointed under subsection (1) of the said section 13.

(2) Subject to the following provisions of this section, the powers shall be exercised with a view to making available for satisfying a confiscation order the value for the time being of realisable property held by any person by the realisation of such property.

(3) In the case of a person who holds realisable property by virtue only of having received an implicative gift, the powers shall, so far as is reasonably attainable, be exercised so as to realise, interdict dealing with, or permit the seizure or taking possession of, property of a value no greater than the value for the time being of that gift.

(4) The powers shall be exercised with a view to allowing any person other than one mentioned in paragraph (a) or (b) of section 5(1) of this Act to retain or recover the value of any property held by him.

(5) An order may be made or other action taken in respect of a debt owed by the Crown.

(6) Subject to subsection (4) above and without prejudice to the power of the Court of Session to make an exception under section 9(1) or 13(2)(a) of this Act for the protection of a person or his family, in exercising those powers no account shall be taken of any obligation (other than an obligation having priority, within the meaning of section 5(8) of this Act) of a person holding realisable property if that obligation conflicts with the obligations to satisfy a confiscation order.

(7) Subsections (2) to (6) of section 13 of the Drug Trafficking Offences Act 1986 (exercise of powers by High Court etc.) shall apply as regards the powers conferred on the Court of Session by sections 27 and 28, or by virtue of section 11(6), of this Act as those subsections apply as regards the powers conferred on the High Court (within the meaning that expression has in relation to England and Wales) by the sections mentioned in subsection (1) of the said section 13.

GENERAL NOTE

This section sets out guidelines and objectives which are to govern the exercise of the powers conferred upon the Court of Session by ss.8, 11(1) to (5), 12, 13, 16 and 24 of this Act, and on the administrator appointed under s.13. In general these powers are to be exercised for the purpose of satisfying a confiscation order. This is to be done by making available for that purpose by a process of realisation, the value for the time being of realisable property.

Subs. (3)

This subsection imposes a restraint on the exercise of the powers in respect of a person whose property is realisable because he has received an implicative gift. This subsection recognises that to seize the whole of such a person's estate would in many cases be an extreme and unjust action. The section provides that powers mentioned in subs. (1) shall be exercised only in respect of property of a value no greater than the value for the time being of that gift.

Subs. (4)

This subsection contains a general provision directed in a sense to the protection of innocent third parties. It provides that the powers in question shall be exercised with a view to allowing any person affected to retain or recover that value of any property held by him. The only exceptions to this general rule are (a) a suspected or charged person whose property is realisable under s.5(1)(a), or (b) a person whose property is realisable under s.5(1)(b) by virtue of his having received an implicative gift.

Subs. (6)

This subsection protects the priority over other obligations accorded to the obligation to satisfy a confiscation order. This priority is, however, without prejudice to the power of the court to make an exception under s.9(1) (exceptions to a restraint order) or s.13(2)(a) (exceptions to the general powers of the administrator in relation to the property in question) "for the protection of a person or his family". This is one of the few provisions in the Act which is directly addressed to the issue of hardship to third parties resulting from the operation of the powers conferred under Pt. I.

Power to facilitate realisation

24.—(1) Without prejudice to any enactment or rule of law in respect of the recording of deeds relating to heritable property or the registration on interests therein, the Court of Session, to facilitate realisation under section 13 of this Act, may—

(a) order any person (in this section referred to as "A") holding an interest in property, not being such person (in this section referred to as "B") as is mentioned in paragraph (a) or (b) of section 5(1) of this Act, to make such payment to an administrator appointed to realise estate comprising an interest of B in that property as the Court may direct and may, subject to such payment being made—

    (i) authorise the administrator to transfer B's interest to A or to discharge it in favour of A; or

    (ii) itself by order so transfer or discharge B's interest; or

(b) by order—

    (i) transfer A's interest to B; or

    (ii) discharge it in favour of B,

on the administrator making such payment to A out of that estate in respect of A's interest as the Court may direct.

(2) The Court may make such incidental provision in relation to any exercise of powers conferred on it by subsection (1) above as it considers appropriate; but it shall not exercise those powers without giving such persons as hold an interest in the property reasonable opportunity to make representations to it in that regard.

Variation of confiscation orders

Variation of confiscation order

25.—(1) If, on an application by a person in respect of whom a confiscation order has been made, the Court of Session is satisfied that the realisable property is inadequate for the payment of any amount remaining to be recovered under that order, the Court shall issue a certificate to that effect giving the Court's reasons for being so satisfied.

(2) For the purposes of subsection (1) above the Court of Session—

(a) in the case of realisable property held by a person whose estate has been sequestrated, or who has been adjudged bankrupt in England and Wales or in Northern Ireland, shall take into account the extent to which any property held by him may be distributed among creditors; and

(b) may disregard any inadequacy in the realisable property if that inadequacy appears to the Court to be attributable wholly or partly to anything done by the person for the purpose of preserving such property from realisation under this Act.

(3) Where a certificate has been issued under subsection (1) above, the person may apply to the High Court for the amount to be recovered under the order to be reduced.

(4) The High Court shall, on an application under subsection (3) above—

(a) substitute for the amount to be recovered under the order such lesser amount as the High Court thinks just in all the circumstances of the case; and

(b) substitute for any period of imprisonment imposed under section 407 of the 1975 Act (or period of detention imposed under section

415(2) of that Act by virtue of the said section 407) in respect of the amount to be recovered under the order a shorter period, determined in accordance with subsection (1A) of the said section 407 (as it has effect by virtue of section 7 of this Act), in respect of the lesser amount.

Compensation

Compensation

26.—(1) Subject to subsection (2) below, if proceedings are instituted against a person for an offence to which section 1 of this Act relates and either—

(a) the proceedings do not result in his conviction for any such offence, or

(b) where he is convicted of one or more such offences, the conviction or convictions concerned are quashed (and no conviction for any such offence is substituted),

the Court of Session may, on an application by a person who held property which was realisable property, order compensation to be paid to the applicant; but this subsection is without prejudice to any right which may otherwise exist to institute proceedings in respect of delictual liability disclosed by such circumstances as are mentioned in paragraphs (a) and (b) of that subsection.

(2) The Court of Session shall not order compensation to be paid under subsection (1) above in any case unless satisfied—

(a) that there has been some serious default on the part of a person concerned in the investigation of the offence or offences concerned, being a person mentioned in subsection (4) below, and that, but for that default, the proceedings would not have been instituted or continued; and

(b) that the applicant has suffered substantial loss or damage in consequence of anything done in relation to the property under section 8, 11, 12, 13 or 24 of this Act or by virtue of section 24A of the Drug Trafficking Offences Act 1986 (recognition and enforcement in England and Wales of orders and functions under this part of this Act).

(3) The amount of compensation to be paid under this section shall be such as the Court of Session thinks just in all the circumstances of the case.

(4) Compensation payable under this section shall be paid, where the person in default was—

(a) a constable of a police force, by the police authority or joint police committee for the police area for which that force is maintained ("constable", "police force", "police authority", "joint police committee" and "police area" having the meanings assigned to these terms by the Police (Scotland) Act 1967);

(b) a constable other than is mentioned in paragraph (a) above, but with the powers of such a constable, by the body under whose authority he acts;

(c) a procurator fiscal or was acting on behalf of the Lord Advocate, by the Lord Advocate; and

(d) a person commissioned by the Commissioners of Customs and Excise, by those Commissioners.

GENERAL NOTE

This section sets out the circumstances in which compensation may be payable to a person who held realisable property and who has suffered loss or damage as a result of the exercise of powers under Pt. I. It must be said that the conditions under which such compensation is payable are very stringent indeed. The conditions, in summary are as follows:

(1) Proceedings must have been instituted in respect of an offence to which s.1 of the Act relates, and either no conviction has been obtained, or such conviction if obtained has been quashed on appeal (subs. (1)(a) and (b)).

(2) There must have been "serious default" on the part of a person concerned in the investigation of the offence concerned (for these purposes a police constable, a procurator fiscal or a person commissioned by the Commissioners of Customs and Excise) (subs. (2)(a) and (4)).

(3) That default must have caused the proceedings to be instituted or continued (subs. (2)(a)).

(4) The applicant must have suffered "substantial loss or damage" in consequence of anything done in relation to the property under ss.8, 11, 12, 13 or 24 of this Act or by virtue of s.2A of the Drug Trafficking Offences Act 1986.

The right to compensation set out in s.26 is stated to be without prejudice to any right which may otherwise exist to institute proceedings in respect of delictual liability disclosed by subs. (1)(a) or (b) but given the difficulties involved in bringing such an action against the parties mentioned in subs. (4) this reservation is unlikely to add to the protection of parties whose rights have been affected in the manner contemplated by s.26.

Reciprocal arrangements for enforcement of confiscation orders

Recognition and enforcement of orders under Drug Trafficking Offences Act 1986

27.—(1) An order to which this section applies shall, subject to this section and section 28 of this Act, have effect in the law of Scotland but shall be enforced in Scotland only in accordance with this section and that section.

(2) A receiver's functions under or for the purposes of section 8, 11 or 12 of the Drug Trafficking Offences Act 1986 shall, subject to this section and section 28 of this Act, have effect in the law of Scotland.

(3) If an order to which this section applies is registered under this section—

(a) the Court of Session shall have, in relation to its enforcement, the same power,

(b) proceedings for or with respect to its enforcement may be taken, and

(c) proceedings for or with respect to any contravention of such an order (whether before or after such registration) may be taken,

as if the order had originally been made in that Court.

(4) Nothing in this section enables any provision of an order which empowers a receiver to do anything in Scotland under section 11(3)(a) of the said Act of 1986 to have effect in the law of Scotland.

(5) The orders to which this section applies are orders of the High Court (within the meaning that expression has in relation to England and Wales)—

(a) made under section 8, 11, 12 or 30 of the said Act of 1986,

(b) relating to the exercise by that Court of its powers under those sections, or

(c) relating to receivers in the performance of their functions under section 8, 11 or 12 of that Act,

but not including an order in proceedings for enforcement of any such order.

(6) References in this section to an order under section 8 of the said Act of 1986 include references to a discharge under section 7(4) of that Act of such an order.

(7) In this section and in section 28 of this Act, "order" means any order, direction or judgment (by whatever name called).

(8) Nothing in any order of the High Court (within the meaning mentioned in subsection (5) above) under section 11(6) of the said Act of 1986 prejudices any enactment or rule of law in respect of the recording

of deeds relating to heritable property in Scotland or the registration of interests in such property.

Provisions supplementary to section 27

28.—(1) The Court of Session shall, on application made to it in accordance with rules of court for registration of an order to which section 27 of this Act applies, direct that the order shall, in accordance with such rules, be registered in that Court.

(2) Subsections (1) and (3) of section 27 of this Act and subsection (1) above are subject to any provision made by rules of court—

(a) as to the manner in which and conditions subject to which orders to which that section applies are to be enforced in Scotland,

(b) for the sisting of proceedings for enforcement of such an order,

(c) for the modification or cancellation of the registration of such an order if the order is modified or revoked or ceases to have effect.

(3) This section and section 27 of this Act are without prejudice to any enactment or rule of law as to the effect of notice or the want of it in relation to orders of the High Court (within the meaning mentioned in section 27(5) of this Act).

(4) The Court of Session shall have the like power to make an order under section 1 of the Administration of Justice (Scotland) Act 1972 (extended power to order inspection of documents etc.) in relation to proceedings brought or likely to be brought under the Drug Trafficking Offences Act 1986 in the High Court (within the meaning mentioned in section 27(5) of this Act) as if those proceedings had been brought or were likely to be brought in the Court of Session.

(5) The Court of Session may, additionally, for the purpose of—

(a) assisting the achievement in Scotland of the purposes of orders to which section 27 of this Act applies, or

(b) assisting receivers performing functions there under or for the purposes of section 8, 11 or 12 of the said Act of 1986,

make such orders and do otherwise as seems to it appropriate.

(6) A document purporting to be a copy of an order under or for the purposes of the Drug Trafficking Offences Act 1986 by the High Court (within the meaning mentioned in section 27(5) of this Act) and to be certified as such by a proper officer of that Court shall, in Scotland, be sufficient evidence of the order.

Enforcement of Northern Ireland orders

29.—(1) Her Majesty may by Order in Council provide that, for the purposes of sections 8 to 25 and 33 to 35 of this Act, this Act shall have effect as if—

(a) references to confiscation orders included a reference to orders made by courts in Northern Ireland which appear to Her Majesty to correspond to confiscation orders;

(b) references to offences to which section 1 of this Act relates included a reference to any offence under the law of Northern Ireland (not being an offence to which that section relates) which appears to Her Majesty to correspond to such an offence; and

(c) such other modifications were made as may be specified in the Order in Council, being modifications which appear to Her Majesty to be requisite or desirable having regard to procedural differences which may for the time being exist between Scotland and Northern Ireland; and without prejudice to the generality of this paragraph modifications may include provision as to the circumstances in which proceedings in Northern Ireland are to be treated for the purposes of those sections as instituted or as concluded.

(2) An Order in Council under this section may provide for the sections mentioned in subsection (1) above to have effect in relation to anything done or to be done in Northern Ireland subject to such further modifications as may be specified in the order.

(3) An Order in Council under this section may contain such incidental, consequential and transitional provisions as Her Majesty considers expedient.

(4) An Order in Council under this section shall not be made unless a draft of the order has been laid before Parliament and approved by resolution of each House of Parliament.

Enforcement of other external orders

30.—(1) Her Majesty may by Order in Council apply this section to any order made after the Order in Council comes into force by a court of a country or territory outside the United Kingdom, being an order—

    (a) of a description specified in the Order in Council, and

    (b) made for the purpose of recovering payments or other rewards received in connection with drug trafficking or their value.

(2) An order to which this section applies is referred to below in this section as an "external confiscation order"; and in this Act "designated country" means a country or territory outside the United Kingdom designated by an Order in Council under this section or under section 32 of this Act.

(3) Subject to subsection (4) below, the Court of Session may, on an application by or on behalf of the government of a designated country, register an external confiscation order made there.

(4) The Court of Session shall not register an external confiscation order unless the Court—

    (a) is satisfied that at the time of registration the order is in force in the designated country and is not subject to appeal in that country;

    (b) is satisfied, where the person in respect of whom the order is made did not appear in the proceedings, that he received notice of the proceedings in sufficient time to enable him to defend them; and

    (c) is of the opinion that enforcing the order in Scotland would not be contrary to the interests of justice.

(5) The Court of Session shall cancel the registration of an external confiscation order if it appears to the Court that the order has been satisfied (whether by payment of the amount due under the order, by the person in respect of whom the order is made serving imprisonment in default, or otherwise).

(6) In relation to an external confiscation order registered under this section, sections 8 to 25 and 33 to 35 of this Act shall have effect subject to such modifications as may be specified in an Order in Council under this section as they have effect in relation to a confiscation order.

(7) In subsection (4) above, "appeal" includes—

    (a) any proceedings by way of discharging or setting aside a judgment; or

    (b) an application for a new trial or a stay of execution.

(8) In any case where the Court of Session is satisfied, on an application by or on behalf of the government of a designated country, either—

    (a) that proceedings which might result in an external confiscation order being made against a person have been instituted in the designated country and have not been concluded; or

    (b) that such institution is imminent,

sections 8 and 10 to 12 of this Act shall have effect in relation to those proceedings—

    (i) where paragraph (a) above applies, as they would have effect in relation to proceedings instituted in Scotland against that person for an offence to which section 1 of this Act relates, being proceedings which have not been concluded and, where paragraph (b) above applies, as if the imminence of institution satisfied the Court of Session of the circumstances mentioned in subsection (1)(b) of the said section 8; and

  (ii) as if references to a confiscation order were references to an external confiscation order and references to an application by the Lord Advocate were references to an application by or on behalf of that government; and

  (iii) subject to such other modifications as may be specified in an Order in Council under this section.

(9) An Order in Council under this section may include such provision as Her Majesty considers expedient—

  (a) as to evidence or proof of any matter for the purposes of this section; and

  (b) as to the circumstances in which for those pruposes—

    (i) proceedings are to be treated as instituted or concluded; or

    (ii) the institution of proceedings is to be treated as imminent or such circumstances as are mentioned in paragraph (a) of section 8(5) of this Act are to be treated as having occurred.

(10) An Order in Council under this section may contain such incidental, consequential and transitional provisions as Her Majesty considers expedient.

(11) An Order in Council under this section may make different provision for different cases or classes of case.

(12) An Order in Council under this section shall not be made unless a draft of the order has been laid before Parliament and approved by resolution of each House of Parliament.

GENERAL NOTE

This section establishes a framework within which confiscation orders made outside Scotland may be registered with the Court of Session, and enforced within Scotland in the same manner as an order made by the High Court under s.1. Such orders may be registered with the Court of Session on the application of the government of a "designated country", that is, a country or territory outside the U.K. which has been designated by an order in Council under ss.30 or 32 of the Act.

Enforcement in England and Wales

31. The following section shall be inserted before section 25 of the Drug Trafficking Offences Act 1986—

"Recognition and enforcement of orders and functions under Part I of the Criminal Justice (Scotland) Act 1987

24A.—(1) Her Majesty may by Order in Council make such provision as Her Majesty considers expedient for the purpose—

  (a) of enabling property in England and Wales which is realisable property for the purposes of Part I of the Criminal Justice (Scotland) Act 1987 to be used or realised for the payment of any amount payable under a confiscation order made under that Part of that Act; and

  (b) of securing that, where no confiscation order has been made under that Part of that Act, property in England and Wales which is realisable property for the purposes of that Part of that Act is available, in the event that such an order is so made, to be used or realised for the payment of any amount payable under it.

(2) Without prejudice to the generality of the power conferred by subsection (1) above, an Order in Council under this section may—
  (a) provide that, subject to any specified conditions—
    (i) the functions of a person appointed under section 13 of the Criminal Justice (Scotland) Act 1987; and
    (ii) such descriptions of orders made under or for the purposes of Part I of the Criminal Justice (Scotland) Act 1987 as may be specified;
  shall have effect in the law of England and Wales;
  (b) make provision—
    (i) for the registration in the High Court of such descriptions of orders made under or for the purposes of that Part of that Act as may be specified; and
    (ii) for the High Court to have in relation to the enforcement of orders made under or for the purposes of that Part of that Act which are so registered such powers as may be specified; and
  (c) make provision as to the proof in England and Wales of orders made under or for the purposes of that Part of that Act.
(3) In subsection (2) above "specified" means specified in an Order in Council under this section.
(4) An Order in Council under this section may amend or apply, with or without modifications, any enactment.
(5) An Order in Council under this section may contain such incidental, consequential and transitional provisions as Her Majesty considers expedient.
(6) An Order in Council under this section shall not be made unless a draft of the Order has been laid before Parliament and approved by resolution of each House of Parliament.".

GENERAL NOTE
  This section provides for the recognition and enforcement in England and Wales of orders and functions under Pt. I of this Act. The section amends the Drug Trafficking Offences Act 1986 by inserting into it a new s.24A.

Order in Council as regards taking of action in designated country

32.—(1) Her Majesty may by Order in Council make such provision in connection with the taking of action in a designated country in consequence of the making of a restraint order or of a confiscation order as appears to Her Majesty to be expedient; and without prejudice to the generality of this subsection such provision may include a direction that in such circumstances as may be specified proceeds arising out of action taken in that country with a view to satisfying a confiscation order which are retained there shall nevertheless be treated as reducing the amount payable under the confiscation order to such extent as may be specified.
(2) Subsections (9)(a), (10), (11) and (12) of section 30 of this Act shall apply in respect of Orders in Council under this section as they apply in respect of Orders in Council under that section.

Sequestration etc. of estate comprising realisable property

GENERAL NOTE
  Ss.33 to 37 are directed towards regulating the relationship between the provisions of Pt. I, and the law relating to sequestration, insolvency and related matters. They are intended to avoid conflicts between the process of confiscation and procedures under the Bankruptcy (Scotland) Act 1985, the Insolvency Act 1986 and related legislation. The sections recognise that in certain cases an estate which includes realisable property may be sequestrated (or subjected to the corresponding English procedures) (ss.33 and 34) and exclude from the

debtor's estate certain categories of property, while at the same time placing the remainder of the debtor's estate beyond the reach of the procedures set out in Pt. I of this Act. S.35 makes similar provision in respect of the winding up of a company which holds realisable property, while s.36 deals with the case where property held subject to a floating charge is realisable property for the purposes of Pt. I.

Sequestration of person holding realisable property

33.—(1) Where the estate of a person who holds realisable property is sequestrated—

    (a) property for the time being subject to a restraint order made before the date of sequestration (within the meaning of section 12(4) of the 1985 Act); and

    (b) any proceeds of property realised by virtue of section 13(1) of this Act for the time being in the hands of an administrator appointed under that section,

is excluded from the debtor's estate for the purposes of that Act.

(2) Where an award of sequestration has been made, the powers conferred on the Court of Session by sections 8, 11 to 13, 16, 24, 27 and 28 of this Act or on an administrator appointed under subsection (1) of the said section 13 shall not be exercised in relation to—

    (a) property comprised in the whole estate of the debtor (within the meaning of section 31(8) of the 1985 Act); or

    (b) any income of the debtor which has been ordered, under subsection (2) of section 32 of that Act, to be paid to the permanent trustee or any estate which, under subsection (6) of that section, vests in the permanent trustee,

and it shall not be competent to submit a claim in relation to the confiscation order to the permanent trustee in accordance with section 48 of that Act.

(3) Nothing in the 1985 Act shall be taken as restricting, or enabling the restriction of, the exercise of the powers so conferred.

(4) Where, during the period before sequestration is awarded, an interim trustee stands appointed under the proviso to section 13(1) of the 1985 Act and any property in the debtor's estate is subject to a restraint order, the powers conferred on the interim trustee by virtue of that Act do not apply to property for the time being subject to the restraint order.

(5) Where the estate of a person is sequestrated and he has directly or indirectly made an implicative gift—

    (a) no decree shall, at any time when proceedings as regards an offence to which section 1 of this Act relates have been instituted against him and have not been concluded or when property of the person to whom the gift was made is subject to a restraint order, be granted under section 34 or 36 of the 1985 Act (gratuitous alienations and unfair preferences) in respect of the making of the gift; and

    (b) any decree granted under either of the said sections 34 and 36 after the conclusion of the proceedings shall take into account any realisation under this Act of property held by the person to whom the gift was made.

(6) In any case in which, notwithstanding the coming into force of the 1985 Act, the Bankruptcy (Scotland) Act 1913 applies to a sequestration, subsection (2) above shall have effect as if for paragraphs (a) and (b) thereof there were substituted the following paragraphs—

    "(a) property comprised in the whole property of the debtor which vests in the trustee under section 97 of the Bankruptcy (Scotland) Act 1913,

    (b) any income of the bankrupt which has been ordered, under subsection (2) of section 98 of that Act, to be paid to the trustee or any estate which, under subsection (1) of that section, vests in the trustee,";

and subsection (3) above shall have effect as if, for the reference in it to the 1985 Act, there were substituted a reference to the said Act of 1913.

GENERAL NOTE

This section makes provision for the possible conflict between the procedures set out in Pt. I of this Act and the process of sequestration under the Bankruptcy (Scotland) Act 1985 ("the 1985 Act") (and where appropriate under the Bankruptcy (Scotland) Act 1913). Subs. (1) excludes certain categories of property from the debtor's estate for the purposes of the 1985 Act. Conversely, subs. (2) excludes from the scope of certain Pt. I powers property which is included in the estate of the debtor for the purposes of sequestration.

Subs. (1)

Where the estate of a person who holds realisable property is sequestrated, this subsection excludes two categories of property from the debtor's estate for the purposes of the Bankruptcy (Scotland) Act 1985:

(1) Property which is subject to a restraint order made *before* the "date of sequestration" within the meaning of s.12(4) of the 1985 Act. For these purposes, the "date of sequestration" is either the date on which the sequestration is awarded (if the petition for sequestration is presented by the debtor) or, where the petition for sequestration is presented by a creditor or trustee acting under a trust deed, the date on which the court grants warrant to cite the debtor to appear before it to show cause why sequestration should not be awarded.

(2) Any proceeds of property realised by virtue of s.13(1) of the present Act, for the time being in the hands of an administrator appointed under that section.

Property included in (1) or (2) above forms no part of the debtor's estate for the purposes of the 1985 Act. It cannot, therefore, be included in "the whole estate of the debtor" within the meaning of s.31(8) of the 1985 Act. Thus property included in (1) or (2) above will not vest at the date of sequestration in the permanent trustee under s.31(1) of the 1985 Act.

Subs. (2)

Where an award of sequestration has been made, the powers conferred on the Court of Session by ss.8, 11 to 13, 16, 24, 27 and 28, or on an administrator under s.13(1) cannot be exercised in relation to:

(a) property comprised in the whole estate of the debtor (*i.e.* his whole estate at the date of sequestration, but not including property included in subs. (1)(a) or (b); or

(b) income of the debtor which has been ordered to be paid to the permanent trustee under s.32(2) of the 1985 Act. This is income in excess of any amount fixed by the sheriff for the aliment of the debtor and the debtor's "relevant obligations" (*i.e.*, any obligation of aliment owed by him within the meaning of the Family Law (Scotland) Act 1985, or an obligation to make a periodical allowance to a former spouse: 1985 Act, s.32(3)); or

(c) estate which, under s.32(6), vests in the permanent trustee (estate acquired by the debtor after the date of sequestration, or which would have vested in the permanent trustee if it had been part of the debtor's estate on the date of sequestration (1985 Act, s.32(6)).

Section 48 of that Act. In order to obtain an adjudication as to his entitlement to vote at non-statutory meetings of creditors, or to a dividend out of the debtor's estate, a creditor must submit a claim to the permanent trustee in accordance with s.48. This subsection makes it clear that the s.48 procedures cannot be invoked as a method of securing satisfaction of a confiscation order.

Subs. (4)

The proviso to s.13(1) provides for the appointment of an interim trustee before sequestration is awarded, if (a) the debtor consents, or (b) the Accountant in Bankruptcy, the trustee acting under the trust deed, or any creditor shows cause (1985 Act, s.13(1), provisos (a) and (b)).

Subs. (5)

Ss.34 and 36 of the 1985 Act deal with gratuitous alienations and unfair preferences respectively. Where it is established that the debtor has made such an alienation, or granted such a preference, the court may grant decree of reduction or for such restoration of property to the debtor's estate or other redress as may be appropriate. Where the estate of a person is sequestrated and he has, directly or indirectly, made an implicative gift, this subsection provides:

(i) that where proceedings as regards an offence to which s.1 of this Act relates have been instituted against him, and have not been concluded, no decree under s.34 or 36 may be granted in respect of the making of the implicative gift. In other words, an implicative gift will not, in these circumstances, be returned to the debtor's estate as a gratuitous alienation or fraudulent preference (para. (a));

(ii) that where property of the person to whom the gift was made is subject to a restraint order, no decree under s.34 or 36 may be made in respect of the making of the gift (para. (a));

(iii) that any decree granted under s.34 or 36 after the conclusion of the proceedings shall take into account any realisation under this Act of property held by the person to whom the gift was made.

Bankruptcy in England and Wales of person holding realisable property

34.—(1) Where a person who holds realisable property is adjudged bankrupt—

(a) property for the time being subject to a restraint order made before the order adjudging him bankrupt, and

(b) any proceeds of property realised by virtue of section 13(1) of this Act for the time being in the hands of an administrator appointed under that section;

is excluded from the bankrupt's estate for the purposes of Part IX of the Insolvency Act 1986.

(2) Where a person has been adjudged bankrupt, the powers conferred on the Court of Session by sections 8, 11 to 13, 16, 24, 27 and 28 of this Act or on an administrator appointed under subsection (1) of the said section 13 shall not be exercised in relation to—

(a) property for the time being comprised in the bankrupt's estate for the purposes of the said Part IX,

(b) property in respect of which his trustee in bankruptcy may (without leave of the court) serve a notice under section 307 or 308 of the Insolvency Act 1986 (after-acquired property and tools, clothes etc. exceeding value of reasonable replacement), and

(c) property which is to be applied for the benefit of creditors of the bankrupt by virtue of a condition imposed under section 280(2)(c) of the Insolvency Act 1986.

(3) Nothing in the Insolvency Act 1986 shall be taken as restricting, or enabling the restriction of, the exercise of the powers so conferred.

(4) Where, in the case of a debtor, an interim receiver stands appointed under section 286 of the Insolvency Act 1986 and any property of the debtor is subject to a restraint order the powers conferred on the receiver by virtue of that Act do not apply to property for the time being subject to the restraint order.

(5) Where a person is adjudged bankrupt and has directly or indirectly made an implicative gift—

(a) no order shall, at any time when proceedings for a drug trafficking offence have been instituted against him and have not been concluded or when property of the person to whom the gift was made is subject to a restraint order, be made under section 339 or 423 of the Insolvency Act 1986 (avoidance of certain transactions) in respect of the making of the gift, and

(b) any order made under either of those sections after the conclusion of the proceedings shall take into account any realisation under this Act of property held by the person to whom the gift was made.

(6) In any case in which a petition in bankruptcy was presented, or a receiving order or adjudication in bankruptcy was made, before the date on which the Insolvency Act 1986 came into force, subsections (2) to (5) above have effect with the following modifications—

(a) for references to the bankrupt's estate for the purposes of Part IX of that Act there are substituted references to the property of the bankrupt for the purposes of the Bankruptcy Act 1914,

(b) for references to the said Act of 1986 and to sections 280(2)(c), 286, 339, and 423 of that Act there are respectively substituted references to the said Act of 1914 and to sections 26(2), 8, 27 and 42 of that Act,

(c) the references in subsection (4) to an interim receiver appointed as there mentioned include, where a receiving order has been made, a reference to the receiver constituted by virtue of section 7 of the said Act of 1914, and

(d) subsections (2)(b) and (4) are omitted.

GENERAL NOTE

This section makes provisions, analogous to those contained in s.33, for the case where procedures under Pt. I conflict with English proceedings in bankruptcy. The pattern adopted in s.33 is generally followed, *viz.*,

(i) exclusion of certain property from the bankrupt's estate for the purposes of bankruptcy proceedings (subs. (1));

(ii) exclusion of property forming part of the bankrupt's estate from the operation of powers conferred under Pt. I of the present Act (subs. (2));

(iii) exclusion of property subject to a restraint order from the powers conferred on an interim receiver (subs. (3));

(iv) exclusion of implicative gifts from the category of "transactions at an undervalue" or "in defraud of creditors" within the meaning of ss.339 and 423 of the Insolvency Act 1986 (subs. (5));

(v) modifications to take account of proceedings in bankruptcy not governed by the Insolvency Act 1986 (subs. (6)).

Winding up company holding realisable property

35.—(1) Where realisable property is held by a company and an order for the winding up of the company has been made or a resolution has been passed by the company for the voluntary winding up, the functions of the liquidator (or any provisional liquidator) shall not be exercisable in relation to—

(a) property for the time being subject to a restraint order made before the relevant time, and

(b) any proceeds of property realised by virtue of section 13(1) of this Act for the time being in the hands of an administrator appointed under that section.

(2) Where, in the case of a company, such an order has been made or such a resolution has been passed, the powers conferred on the Court of Session by sections 8, 11 to 13, 16, 24, 27 and 28 of this Act or on an administrator appointed under subsection (1) of the said section 13 shall not be exercised in relation to any realisable property held by the company in relation to which the functions of the liquidator are exercisable—

(a) so as to inhibit the liquidator from exercising those functions for the purpose of distributing any property held by the company to the company's creditors, or

(b) so as to prevent the payment out of any property of expenses (including the remuneration of the liquidator or any provisional liquidator) properly incurred in the winding up in respect of the property.

(3) Nothing in the Insolvency Act 1986 shall be taken as restricting, or enabling the restriction of, the exercise of the powers so conferred.

(4) For the purposes of the application of Parts IV and V of the Insolvency Act 1986 (winding up of registered companies and winding up of unregistered companies) to a company which the Court of Session has jurisdiction to wind up, a person is not a creditor in so far as any sum due

to him by the company is due in respect of a confiscation order (whether under this Act or under and within the meaning of section 1 of the Drug Trafficking Offences Act 1986 or any corresponding provision in Northern Ireland).

(5) In this section—

"company" means any company which may be wound up under the Insolvency Act 1986; and

"the relevant time" means—

(a) where no order for the winding up of the company has been made, the time of the passing of the resolution for voluntary winding up,

(b) where such an order has been made and, before the presentation of the petition for the winding up of the company by the court, such a resolution had been passed by the company, the time of the passing of the resolution, and

(c) in any other case where such an order has been made, the time of the making of the order.

(6) In any case in which a winding up of a company commenced, or is treated as having commenced, before the date on which the Insolvency Act 1986 came into force, subsections (2) to (5) above have effect with the substitution for references to that Act of references to the Companies Act 1985.

GENERAL NOTE

This section makes provision, analogous to that contained in ss.33 and 34 to deal with possible conflicts between procedures under Pt. I and the winding up of a company which holds realisable property.

Property subject to floating charge

36.—(1) Where any property held subject to a floating charge by a company is realisable property and a receiver has been appointed by, or on the application of, the holder of the charge, the powers of the receiver in relation to the property so held shall not be exercisable in relation to—

(a) so much of it as is for the time being subject to a restraint order made before the appointment of the receiver, and

(b) any proceeds of property realised by virtue of section 13(1) of this Act for the time being in the hands of an administrator appointed under that section.

(2) Where, in the case of a company, such an appointment has been made, the powers conferred on the Court of Session by sections 8, 11 to 13, 16 and 24 of this Act or on an administrator appointed under subsection (1) of the said section 13 shall not be exercised in relation to any realisable property held by the company in relation to which the powers of the receiver are exercisable—

(a) so as to inhibit the receiver from exercising his powers for the purpose of distributing any property held by the company to the company's creditors, or

(b) so as to prevent the payment out of any property of expenses (including the remuneration of the receiver) properly incurred in the exercise of the receiver's powers in respect of the property.

(3) Nothing in the Insolvency Act 1986, shall be taken as restricting, or enabling the restriction of, the exercise of the powers so conferred.

(4) In this section—

"company" has the same meaning as in section 35 of this Act; and "floating charge" includes a floating charge within the meaning given by section 462 of the Companies Act 1985 (power of incorporated company to create floating charge).

(5) In any case in which a receiver was appointed as is mentioned in subsection (1) above before the date on which the Insolvency Act 1986 came into force, subsections (2) to (4) above have effect with the substitution for references to that Act of references to the Companies Act 1985.

GENERAL NOTE

This section provides for the case where property held subject to a floating charge is realisable property. The provisions are analogous, *mutatis mutandis*, to those contained in ss.33 to 35.

Insolvency practitioners dealing with property subject to restraint order

37.—(1) Without prejudice to the generality of any enactment contained in the Insolvency Act 1986 or in the 1985 Act, where—

(a) any person acting as an insolvency practitioner seizes or disposes of any property in relation to which his functions are, because that property is for the time being subject to a restraint order, not exercisable; and

(b) at the time of the seizure or disposal he believes, and has reasonable grounds for believing, that he is entitled (whether in pursuance of a court order or otherwise) to seize or dispose of that property,

he shall not be liable to any person in respect of any loss or damage resulting from the seizure or disposal except in so far as the loss or damage is caused by the insolvency practitioner's negligence; and the insolvency practitioner shall have a lien on the property, or the proceeds of its sale, for such of his expenses as were incurred in connection with the liquidation, sequestration or other proceedings in relation to which the seizure or disposal purported to take place and for so much of his remuneration as may reasonably be assigned for his actings in connection with those proceedings.

(2) Any person who, acting as an insolvency practitioner, incurs expenses—

(a) in respect of such property as is mentioned in paragraph (a) of subsection (1) above and in so doing does not know and has no reasonable grounds to believe that the property is for the time being subject to a restraint order; or

(b) other than in respect of such property as is so mentioned, being expenses which, but for the effect of a restraint order, might have been met by taking possession of and realising the property,

shall be entitled (whether or not he has seized or disposed of that property so as to have a lien under that subsection) to payment of those expenses under section 16(1) or (3)(a) of this Act.

(3) In the foregoing provisions of this section, the expression "acting as an insolvency practitioner" shall be construed in accordance with section 388 (interpretation) of the said Act of 1986 except that for the purposes of such construction the reference in subsection (2)(a) of that section to a permanent or interim trustee in a sequestration shall be taken to include a reference to a trustee in a sequestration and subsection (5) of that section (which provides that nothing in the section is to apply to anything done by the official receiver) shall be disregarded; and the expression shall also comprehend the official receiver acting as receiver or manager of the property.

GENERAL NOTE

This section provides two forms of protection for any person who, acting as an "insolvency practitioner", seizes or disposes of property which is for the time being subject to a restraint order, and therefore not part of the debtor's estate for the purposes of the law relating to sequestration, bankruptcy or the winding up of a company. Subs. (1) deals with the personal liability of the insolvency practitioner, and security for his expenses; subs. (2) deals with recovery of the insolvency practitioner's expenses from the proceeds of realisation and other sources.

Personal liability—subs. (1)
Where the property in question is seized or disposed of in good faith, the insolvency practitioner is liable only for loss or damage caused by his negligence.

Expenses
(1) *Security.* Subs. (1) provides that where the insolvency practitioner has seized or disposed of the relevant property in good faith, he shall have a lien on the property, or the proceeds of the sale, for so much of his expenses as were incurred in connection with the seizure or disposal, and for so much of his remuneration as is attributable to those transactions.
(2) *Recovery.* Subs. (2) provides that the insolvency practitioner who in good faith incurs expenses in respect of property subject to a restraint order, or who incurs expenses in respect of property not subject to a restraint order which, but for the effect of such an order, might have been met from the realising of that property, is entitled (under s.16(1) of this Act) to payment of those expenses from the proceeds of the realisation of the property or (under s.16(3)(a)) from sums received on account of an amount payable under a confiscation order.

Subs. (3)
S.388 of the Insolvency Act 1986 provides that a person acts as an insolvency practitioner (a) in relation to a company, by acting as its liquidator, provisional liquidator, administrator, administrative receiver, or as supervisor of a voluntary arrangement approved by it under Pt. I of that Act, and (b) in relation to an individual, by acting as his trustee in bankruptcy, or interim receiver of his property or as the permanent or interim trustee in the sequestration of his estate, as trustee under a deed of arrangement for the benefit of creditors or a trust deed for creditors, or as supervisor of a voluntary arrangement proposed by him and approved under Pt. VIII of the Insolvency Act 1986.

Investigations and disclosure of information

Order to make material available

38.—(1) The procurator fiscal may, for the purpose of an investigation into drug trafficking, apply to the sheriff for an order under subsection (2) below in relation to particular material or material of a particular description.
(2) If on such an application the sheriff is satisfied that the conditions in subsection (4) below are fulfilled, he may make an order that the person who appears to him to be in possession of the material to which the application relates shall—
    (a) produce it to a constable or person commissioned by the Commissioners of Customs and Excise for him to take away, or
    (b) give a constable or person so commissioned access to it,
within such period as the order may specify.
This subsection is subject to section 41(11) of this Act.
(3) The period to be specified in an order under subsection (2) above shall be seven days unless it appears to the sheriff that a longer or shorter period would be appropriate in the particular circumstances of the application.
(4) The conditions referred to in subsection (2) above are—
    (a) that there are reasonable grounds for suspecting that a specified person has carried on, or has derived financial or other rewards from, drug trafficking,
    (b) that there are reasonable grounds for suspecting that the material to which the application relates—
        (i) is likely to be of substantial value (whether by itself or

together with other material) to the investigation for the purpose of which the application is made, and

(ii) does not consist of or include items subject to legal privilege, and

(c) that there are reasonable grounds for believing that it is in the public interest, having regard—

(i) to the benefit likely to accrue to the investigation if the material is obtained, and

(ii) to the circumstances under which the person in possession of the material holds it,

that the material should be produced or that access to it should be given.

(5) Where the sheriff makes an order under subsection (2)(b) above in relation to material on any premises he may, on the application of the procurator fiscal, order any person who appears to him to be entitled to grant entry to the premises to allow a constable to enter the premises to obtain access to the material.

(6) Provision may be made by rules of court as to—

(a) the discharge and variation of orders under this section, and

(b) proceedings relating to such orders.

(7) Where the material to which an application under this section relates consists of information contained in a computer—

(a) an order under subsection (2)(a) above shall have effect as an order to produce the material in a form in which it can be taken away and in which it is visible and legible, and

(b) an order under subsection (2)(b) above shall have effect as an order to give access to the material in a form in which it is visible and legible.

(8) An order under subsection (2) above—

(a) shall not confer any right to production of, or access to, items subject to legal privilege,

(b) shall have effect notwithstanding any obligation as to secrecy or other restriction upon the disclosure of information imposed by statute or otherwise, and

(c) may be made in relation to material in the possession of an authorised government department.

GENERAL NOTE

Under this section the sheriff may, on the application of the procurator fiscal, make an order requiring a person to make available material likely to be of substantial value to the investigation of drug trafficking, provided certain conditions, set out in subs. (4), are satisfied.

Subs. (1)

For the purpose of an investigation into drug trafficking. This section relates specifically to the investigation of "drug trafficking", rather than the investigation of an offence to which s.1 relates (or any other offence in respect of controlled drugs). In many cases the investigation of drug trafficking will be conducted with a view to prosecution, but the investigation of drug trafficking may also be directed towards ascertaining the extent of a person's involvement in such activities whether or not a prosecution is contemplated. The prosecution may, for example, have obtained a conviction in respect of an offence to which s.1 relates, and the investigation may be directed towards information needed in connection with the making of a confiscation order. The section would thus apply to investigations directed towards assessing the proceeds of a person's drug trafficking (ss.3 and 4) or determining whether or not property was received in connection with drug trafficking for the purposes of the "implicative gifts" provisions (especially s.6(1)(b)).

Subs. (2)

If on such an application. No mention is made in the subsection of any opportunity being afforded to those in possession of the material to oppose, or even be represented at, such an application. If this were the ordinary case of an application for a warrant to search the premises or repositories of a suspected person then this would hardly be surprising. But s.38 contemplates the making of an order which might require a wholly innocent third party to give up material which may be of considerable value to that third party. The material may, for example, consist of books of account or other confidential or commercial records. They need not belong to the suspected person, and indeed they need not be *in themselves* indicative of drug trafficking activities on the part of the suspected person (see para. (4)(b)(i)). It is true that the conditions which must be satisfied before an order may be made are stringently drawn, but it would seem appropriate that in certain cases the person having possession of the material should have the right to be heard. If, for example, that person is not suspected of involvement in drug trafficking, and the material in question consists of commercial or other records not exclusively relating to the suspected party, then there would seem to be grounds for the person holding them to be heard on such questions as security and confidentiality. Subs. (6)(b) allows for the making of rules of court regarding proceedings relating to orders under subs. (2). These could, *inter alia,* set out arrangements whereby the legitimate interests of innocent third parties might be protected.

Subs. (4)
Before making an order the sheriff must be satisfied that *all* of the conditions in paras. (a) to (c) are satisfied.

Subs. (7)
This subsection deals with the situation where the material in question consists of information contained in a computer. In such circumstances, production of a computer disc or tape is not sufficient to comply with an order under subs. (2)(a). The information must be produced in a visible and legible form, and in a form which can be taken away (which would preclude display on a computer screen or monitor). Presumably what is required in this case is a print-out of the information. Where the order is simply one for access under subs. (2)(b), all that is required is that the information be produced in a form which is visible and legible. In this case simply projecting the information on the computer's screen would satisfy the requirements of the order.

Subs. (8)

Para. (a)
Items subject to legal privilege. These are defined by s.40.

Para. (b)
This subsection contemplates the disclosure and removal of material which is held subject to an obligation of secrecy or other restriction upon its disclosure "imposed by statute or otherwise". So far as concerns the "compellability" of such productions, the subsection makes little difference to the present law. There are only a few cases where a party who holds information subject to such an obligation can, on the basis of that obligation, refuse to testify in court or to produce documents or other material if required to do so by a court order. The special case of legal professional privilege is dealt with by para. (a) of this subsection, and the only other clearly established cases where a person may withhold information on the ground of confidentiality are those of communications between spouses and communication in between partners. The case of the journalist (or any other person) withholding information relating to his sources of information contained in a publication is perhaps analogous, but must be seen in the light of s.10 of the Contempt of Court Act 1981.

Imposed by statute. A clear example of such an obligation is to be found in the case of Commissioners of Inland Revenue and officers of the Inland Revenue who, in terms of s.6 and Sched. 1 of the Taxes Management Act 1970, are under a statutory obligation not to disclose information received in connection with their duties, except in connection with their duties.

Authority for search

39.—(1) The procurator fiscal may, for the purpose of an investigation into drug trafficking, apply to the sheriff for a warrant under this section in relation to specified premises.

(2) On such application the sheriff may issue a warrant authorising a constable, or person commissioned by the Commissioners of Customs and Excise, to enter and search the premises if the sheriff is satisfied—

(a) that an order made under section 38 of this Act in relation to material on the premises has not been complied with, or
(b) that the conditions in subsection (3) below are fulfilled, or
(c) that the conditions in subsection (4) below are fulfilled.
(3) The conditions referred to in subsection (2)(b) above are—
  (a) that there are reasonable grounds for suspecting that a specified person has carried on, or has derived financial or other rewards from, drug trafficking, and
  (b) that the conditions in section 38(4)(b) and (c) of this Act are fulfilled in relation to any material on the premises, and
  (c) that it would not be appropriate to make an order under that section in relation to the material because—
    (i) it is not practicable to communicate with any person entitled to produce the material, or
    (ii) it is not practicable to communicate with any person entitled to grant access to the material or entitled to grant entry to the premises on which the material is situated, or
    (iii) the investigation for the purposes of which the application is made might be seriously prejudiced unless a constable or person commissioned as aforesaid could secure immediate access to the material.
(4) The conditions referred to in subsection (2)(c) above are—
  (a) that there are reasonable grounds for suspecting that a specified person has carried on, or has derived financial or other rewards from, drug trafficking, and
  (b) that there are reasonable grounds for suspecting that there is on the premises material relating to the specified person or to drug trafficking which is likely to be of substantial value (whether by itself or together with other material) to the investigation for the purpose of which the application is made, but that the material cannot at the time of the application be particularised, and
  (c) that—
    (i) it is not practicable to communicate with any person entitled to grant entry to the premises, or
    (ii) entry to the premises will not be granted unless a warrant is produced, or
    (iii) the investigation for the purpose of which the application is made might be seriously prejudiced unless a constable or person commissioned as aforesaid arriving at the premises could secure immediate entry to them.
(5) Where a constable or person commissioned as aforesaid has entered premises in the execution of a warrant issued under this section, he may seize and retain any material, other than items subject to legal privilege, which is likely to be of substantial value (whether by itself or together with other material) to the investigation for the purpose of which the warrant was issued.

GENERAL NOTE
  This section enables the sheriff, on the application of the procurator fiscal, to issue a warrant authorising the search of specified premises, where an order under s.38 has not been complied with (subs. (2)(a)), or where it would not be appropriate to make such an order (subs. (3)) or where it would not be practicable to enforce such an order (subs. (4)).

Subs. (1)
  As in s.38(1) the purpose contemplated here is the investigation of "drug trafficking."

Subs. (2)

If the sheriff is satisfied that *any* of the circumstances set out in paras. (a) to (c) are present he may issue a warrant to enter and search the premises specified in the warrant.

Material on the premises. It is important to notice that the non-compliance with s.38 order referred to in s.39(2)(a) must relate to "material on the premises" specified in the warrant. Non-compliance in other respects does not permit the sheriff to issue a warrant in reliance on subs. (2)(a). Strictly speaking it appears that in order to obtain a warrant under this head, the procurator fiscal must show two things: (a) that an order under s.38(2) had not been complied with, and (b) that it related to property which is known to be on the premises to be specified in the warrant. A *belief* that the material is on the premises ought not to satisfy the terms of this paragraph, unless it is to be read as stating that "an order made under s.38 of this Act in relation to material *believed to be* on the premises has not been complied with." Compare, in this respect the provisions of subs. (4)(b) which deals with the case where the property is believed to be on the premises to be named in the warrant.

Subs. (3)

All of the conditions specified in this subsection (which include the conditions set out in s.38(4)(b) and (c)) must be satisfied before a warrant can be issued under subs. (2)(b) above.

Subs. (4)

Again, all of the conditions specified in paras. (a) to (c) must be satisfied before a search warrant may be issued under subs. (2)(c) above.

Interpretation of sections 38 and 39

40. In sections 38 and 39 of this Act—

   "items subject to legal privilege" means—

   (a) communications between a professional legal adviser and his client, or

   (b) communications made in connection with or in contemplation of legal proceedings and for the purposes of these proceedings,

   being communications which would in legal proceedings be protected from disclosure by virtue of any rule of law relating to the confidentiality of communications; and

   "premises" includes any place and, in particular, includes—

   (a) any vehicle, vessel, aircraft or hovercraft,

   (b) any offshore installation within the meaning of section 1 of the Mineral Workings (Offshore Installations) Act 1971, and

   (c) any tent or movable structure.

GENERAL NOTE

This section defines "items subject to legal privilege" and "premises" for the purposes of ss.38 and 39.

Items subject to legal privilege. It is important to note that not all communications of the kind envisaged in paras. (a) and (b) are items subject to legal privilege. The communications must also satisfy the test of being "protected from disclosure" in legal proceedings. In other words, they must also satisfy existing rules governing privileged communications. Thus while communications made between solicitor and client are privileged, even if not made in contemplation of legal proceedings (see, for example, *McCowan* v. *Wright* (1852) 15 D. 229) the privilege only extends to communications made in a professional context (see Hume, *Crimes*, II, p.350). It is also well-established that there is no privilege attaching to communications made for the purpose of obtaining advice or assistance in committing a crime or other illegal act (see, Walker and Walker, *The Law of Evidence in Scotland*, pp.413 *et seq.*, *McCowan* v. *Wright*, above, *Morrison* v. *Somerville* (1860) 23 D. 232).

Para. (b) of this section makes it clear that it is not only communications between an individual and his or her legal advisers which may be protected. Communications between any persons made in connection with or in contemplation of legal proceedings and for the purposes of these proceedings may also be subject to legal privilege, provided they satisfy the condition contained in the second half of the definition. In general, communications of this sort will attract confidentiality, although there are doubts about the precise limits of this privilege (Walker and Walker, *op cit.,* pp.417 *et seq.*). Statements made with a view to the settlement of a dispute likewise attract privilege, but this is not based on any notion of confidentiality, but on the public policy of promoting the settlement of disputes without recourse to litigation. Such statements do not, therefore, fall within the category of communications contemplated by s.40.

Disclosure of information held by government departments

41.—(1) Subject to subsection (4) below, the Court of Session may on an application by the Lord Advocate order any material mentioned in subsection (3) below which is in the possession of an authorised government department to be produced to the Court within such period as the Court may specify.

(2) The power to make an order under subsection (1) above is exercisable if—

(a) the powers conferred on the Court by subsection (1) of section 8 of this Act are exercisable by virtue of paragraph (a) thereof, or

(b) those powers are exercisable by virtue of paragraph (b) of subsection (1) of that section and the Court has made a restraint order which has not been recalled;

but, where the power to make an order under subsection (1) above is exercisable by virtue only of paragraph (b) above, subsection (4) of section 9 of this Act shall for the purposes of this section apply in relation to that order as the said subsection (4) applies, for the purposes of that section, in relation to a restraint order made by virtue of paragraph (b) of subsection (1) of the said section 8.

(3) The material referred to in subsection (1) above is any material which—

(a) has been submitted to an officer of an authorised government department by a person who holds, or has at any time held, realisable property,

(b) has been made by an officer of an authorised government department in relation to such a person, or

(c) is correspondence which passed between an officer of an authorised government department and such a person;

and an order under that subsection may require the production of all such material or of a particular description of such material, being material in the possession of the department concerned.

(4) An order under subsection (1) above shall not require the production of any material unless it appears to the Court of Session that the material is likely to contain information that would facilitate the exercise of the powers conferred on the Court by section 8, 13 or 24 of this Act or on an administrator appointed under subsection (1) of the said section 13.

(5) The Court may by order authorise the disclosure to such an administrator of any material produced under subsection (1) above or any part of such material; but the Court shall not make an order under this subsection unless a reasonable opportunity has been given for an officer of the department to make representations to the Court.

(6) Material disclosed in pursuance of an order under subsection (5) above may, subject to any conditions contained in the order, be further disclosed for the purposes of the functions under this Act of the administrator or the High Court.

(7) The Court of Session may by order authorise the disclosure to a person mentioned in subsection (8) below of any material produced under subsection (1) above or any part of such material; but the Court shall not make an order under this subsection unless—

(a) a reasonable opportunity has been given for an officer of the department to make representations to the Court, and

(b) it appears to the Court that the material is likely to be of substantial value in exercising functions relating to drug trafficking.

(8) The persons referred to in subsection (7) above are—
   (a) a constable,
   (b) the Lord Advocate or any procurator fiscal, and
   (c) a person commissioned by the Commissioners of Customs and Excise.

(9) Material disclosed in pursuance of an order under subsection (7) above may, subject to any conditions contained in the order, be further disclosed for the purposes of functions relating to drug trafficking.

(10) Material may be produced or disclosed in pursuance of this section notwithstanding any obligation as to secrecy or other restriction upon the disclosure of information imposed by statute or otherwise.

(11) An order under subsection (1) above and, in the case of material in the possession of an authorised government department, an order under section 38(2) of this Act may require any officer of the department (whether named in the order or not) who may for the time being be in possession of the material concerned to comply with such order; and any such order shall be served as if the proceedings were civil proceedings against the department.

(12) The person on whom an order under subsection (1) above is served—
   (a) shall take all reasonable steps to bring it to the attention of the officer concerned, and
   (b) if the order is not brought to that officer's attention within the period referred to in subsection (1) above, shall report the reasons for the failure to the Court of Session;

and it shall also be the duty of any other officer of the department in receipt of the order to take such steps as are mentioned in paragraph (a) above.

GENERAL NOTE

This section gives the Court of Session the power, on the application of the Lord Advocate, to require an authorised government department (as defined by s.47) to produce to the Court, material in its possession which is likely to contain information that would facilitate the exercise of the powers conferred on the Court by s.8 (restraint orders), s.13 (appointment of administrator, etc.) or s.24 (powers to facilitate realisation), or on an administrator appointed under s.13(1).

Subs. (2)

The power to make an order under subs. (1) is exercisable only if the Court has power to make a restraint order under s.8(1)(a) or (b). In the latter case a restraint order must actually have been made and must still be in force.

Subs. (4)

This subsection sets out the restrictions on the exercise of the power conferred by subs. (1). That power differs from the powers conferred on the sheriff by ss.38 and 39. Whereas the latter are intended to facilitate the investigation of drug trafficking, the power conferred on the Court of Session by subs. (1) above relates, at least primarily, to the exercise of powers conferred on the Court of Session or on an administrator appointed under s.13(1). It should be noted, however, that subss. (7) to (9) provide for further disclosure of material originally obtained under subs. (1), which will permit the use of such material "for the purpose of functions relating to drug trafficking."

Subs. (5)

This subsection permits the Court of Session to order disclosure to an administrator of material produced under subs. (1).

Subs. (6)

This subsection permits further disclosure of material disclosed under subs. (5). It is worth noting that in this subsection the person to whom the material may be disclosed is not specified. The *purposes* for which it may be disclosed are specified, *viz.*, "for the purposes of the functions under this Act of the administrator or the High Court." It is also worth noting that this subsection only permits the further disclosure of material which has already been disclosed to the administrator under subs. (5). It does not for example, permit the disclosure of material obtained under subs. (1) but not disclosed under subs. (5).

Subss. (7)–(9)

These subsections establish a procedure whereby material originally obtained under subs. (1) for the purposes set out in subs. (4) may be disclosed for other purposes. Provided that the conditions set out in paras. (a) and (b) of subs. (7) are satisfied, that subsection permits the disclosure to a person mentioned in subs. (8) of material obtained under subs. (1). Subs. (7) does not expressly state the purposes for which such disclosure may be authorised, but given the reference in para. (b) of that subsection it seems that the information should only be disclosed for functions relating to drug trafficking. Once material has been disclosed under subs. (7), it may be further disclosed for the purposes of functions relating to drug trafficking. Again, the persons to whom the material may be disclosed under this subsection are not specified, but might well include the police outside Scotland, and other agencies involved in the detection and prosecution of drug-traffickers.

The "functions relating to drug trafficking" referred to in subss. (7) and (9) are not defined or explained in the Act. Given the list of persons contained in subs. (8) it seems fair to suggest that these "functions" would include the investigation of drug trafficking. An interesting question arises as to whether the investigation of an offence to which s.1 relates is a function relating to drug trafficking for these purposes. Given that "drug trafficking" is clearly separated in the Act from what might be termed "drug offending", there is some argument for saying that the "functions" referred to do not include the prosecution of drug offences. On the other hand, ss.42 and 43 create specific offences linked to drug trafficking, and it might be difficult to argue that the investigation and prosecution of these offences is not a "function relating to drug trafficking". The answer is perhaps the following: The investigation of any offence which would amount to "drug trafficking" within the meaning of s.1(6) is a function relating to drug trafficking. So also is the investigation of an offence to which s.1 relates, even if the offence is not an example of "drug trafficking", since it is only on conviction for an offence to which s.1 relates that the power to confiscate the proceeds of drug trafficking arises. An investigation into an offence under s.42 is also a function relating to drug trafficking, even though that is not an offence to which s.1 relates, and the conduct struck at by that section would not amount to drug trafficking. It is, however, an offence directly related to drug trafficking, so that its investigation ought to be a function relating to drug trafficking.

Offences

Offence of prejudicing investigation

42.—(1) A person who, knowing or suspecting that an investigation into drug trafficking is taking place, does anything which is likely to prejudice the investigation is guilty of an offence.

(2) In proceedings against a person for an offence under subsection (1) above, it is a defence to prove—

(a) that he did not know or suspect, or have reasonable grounds to suspect, that by acting as he did he was likely to prejudice the investigation, or

(b) that he had lawful authority or reasonable excuse for acting as he did.

(3) A person guilty of an offence under subsection (1) above shall be liable—

(a) on conviction on indictment, to imprisonment for a term not exceeding five years or to a fine or to both, and

(b) on summary conviction, to imprisonment for a term not exceeding six months or to a fine not exceeding the statutory maximum or to both.

GENERAL NOTE

This section creates a new, and in certain respects ill-defined, offence of prejudicing an investigation into drug trafficking.

Subs. (1)

Does anything. Just what is included here is a matter of conjecture, or, less politely put, anybody's guess. Guesswork or conjecture, it can hardly be satisfactory that an offence carrying a maximum penalty of five years' imprisonment should be so ill-defined. During the House of Lords Committee stage of the Bill, Lord Morton suggested that marrying the person under investigation might well be enough to satisfy the requirement of doing "anything" (on the basis that as the suspect's spouse one's evidence could not be compelled). Probably that is going too far. Quite apart from any other consideration the example is open to the objection that it would not be the investigation of the offence but its prosecution which would be prejudiced. Nevertheless it does seem that a greater degree of precision might have been achieved in the drafting of this section. As Lord Morton pointed out, the equivalent English provision (s.31 of the Drug Trafficking Offences Act 1986) refers to the making of "any disclosure" and no satisfactory explanation was given as to why the Scottish offence had to be so much more widely drawn.

Presumably, since the offence requires the "doing" of something, it is not an offence under s.41(1) to fail to do something (such as disclose information relevant to the investigation). Presumably also it does not extend to doing something one is lawfully entitled to do, such as seeking legal advice as to one's own situation (even though in the eyes of some that might well be likely to prejudice the investigation).

Which is likely. It is clear that the "doing" of "anything" need not be accompanied by an intention to prejudice the investigation, or even recklessness as to that outcome. The test here is objective.

Subs. (2)

This subsection sets out two statutory defences to a charge under s.42(1). The burden of establishing these defences rests on the accused, presumably on a balance of probabilities given the use of the word "prove". Having regard to the terms of this subsection, and subsection (1), it would appear that the offence is structured as follows:

    (a) Subs. (1) requires that the accused knew or suspected that an investigation was taking place. On general principles it must be for the prosecutor to prove such knowledge or suspicion. Subs. (1) does not, however, require the prosecutor to prove that the accused intended to prejudice the investigation, or that he was reckless as to that consequence. The prosecutor need only show that that result was "likely".

    (b) Subs. (2) provides two statutory defences. The first of these, in para. (a), is a "good faith" or "excusable ignorance" defence. The second is one of "lawful authority or reasonable excuse".

    The structure of the former is one which has become familiar in recent years. It is clear that the accused may escape liability if he can show (how?) that he did not know or suspect that his conduct was likely to prejudice the investigation. He may also escape liability if he shows that he did not have reasonable grounds to suspect that his conduct was likely to prejudice the investigation. What is meant by this? Normally the "reasonableness" of a suspicion is relevant only where it is accepted that the suspicion was present in the individual's mind. But here, of course, we are considering the case where the accused claims he had no such suspicion. The most sensible way to read the defence is to say that he must prove that there were no grounds known to the accused on which he might reasonably have suspected that his conduct was likely to prejudice the investigation.

Subs. (3)

The offence under subs. (1) is not an offence to which s.1 of this Act relates, so that the provisions of s.44 relating to unlimited fines do not apply to offences under this section (ss.1(2) and 44(3)).

Offence of assisting another to retain the proceeds of drug trafficking

43.—(1) Subject to subsection (3)(b) below, a person shall be guilty of an offence if, knowing or suspecting that another person (in this section referred to as "A") is a person who carries on, or has carried on, or has derived financial or other rewards from, drug trafficking, he enters into, or is otherwise concerned in, an arrangement whereby—

    (a) the retention or control, by or on behalf of A, of A's proceeds of drug trafficking is facilitated (whether by concealment, removal from the jurisdiction, transfer to nominees or otherwise); or

(b) A's proceeds of drug trafficking—
    (i) are used to secure that funds are placed at A's disposal, or
    (ii) are used for A's benefit to acquire property by way of investment.

(2) In this section, references to proceeds of drug trafficking shall be construed as including any property which, whether in whole or in part, directly or indirectly constitutes such proceeds.

(3) Where a person discloses to a constable or to a person commissioned by the Commissioners of Customs and Excise a suspicion or belief that any funds or investments are derived from or used in connection with drug trafficking or any matter on which such a suspicion or belief is based—
  (a) the disclosure shall not be treated as a breach of any restriction imposed by contract on the disclosure of information; and
  (b) if the disclosure relates to an arrangement entry into which, or concern in which, by the person would (but for this paragraph) contravene subsection (1) above, he does not commit an offence under that subsection if—
    (i) the disclosure is made before, with the consent of the constable or as the case may be of the person so commissioned, he enters into, or becomes concerned in, that arrangement, or
    (ii) though made after he enters into, or becomes concerned in, that arrangement, it is made on his own initiative and as soon as it is reasonable for him to do so.

(4) In proceedings against a person for an offence under subsection (1) above, it shall be a defence to prove—
  (a) that he did not know or suspect that the arrangement related to any person's proceeds of drug trafficking; or
  (b) that he did not know or suspect that by the arrangement the retention or control by or on behalf of A of any property was facilitated or, as the case may be, that by the arrangement any property was used as mentioned in subsection (1) above; or
  (c) that—
    (i) he intended to disclose to a constable or to a person commissioned as aforesaid such a suspicion, belief or matter as is mentioned in subsection (3) above in relation to the arrangement, but
    (ii) there is reasonable excuse for his failure to make disclosure in accordance with paragraph (b) of that subsection.

(5) A person guilty of an offence under subsection (1) above shall be liable—
  (a) on conviction on indictment, to imprisonment for a term not exceeding fourteen years or to a fine or to both; and
  (b) on summary conviction, to imprisonment for a term not exceeding six months or to a fine not exceeding the statutory maximum or to both.

GENERAL NOTE

This section creates the offence of assisting another to retain the proceeds of that other's drug trafficking.

Subs. (1)

The variety of ways in which this offence may be committed is quite staggering. Under para. (a) alone it is possible to commit an offence by any of the following permutations:

The accused may { (i) know or
                        (ii) suspect

that A	(i) carries on (ii) has carried on (iii) has derived financial reward from (iv) has derived other reward from	drug trafficking
And with that knowledge or suspicion may	(i) enter into or (ii) be concerned in	an arrangement whereby
	(i) the retention (ii) the control	of the proceeds of A's drug trafficking
	(i) by A (ii) on behalf of A	is facilitated by
	(i) concealment (ii) removal from the jurisdiction (iii) transfer to nominees (iv) otherwise.	

Subs. (3)

Para. (a)

This paragraph protects a person who makes disclosures to a constable or person commissioned by the Commissioners of Customs and Excise (but not, apparently, a procurator fiscal) in circumstances where the person making the disclosure is under a contractual obligation not to disclose the information. A disclosure within the terms of this subsection will not be treated as a breach of that contractual restriction. An obvious example would be where information held by a bank, or by an accountant, about a customer or client's financial affairs is disclosed without the latter's consent. Para. (a) provides that such disclosure shall not be treated as a breach of the bank's or the accountant's *contractual* obligation of confidentiality.

Para. (b)

This paragraph provides an escape route for a person who has become involved in an arrangement of the type struck at by subs. (1). Sub-para. (i) deals with the situation where the person making the disclosure does so before he enters into or becomes concerned in the unlawful arrangement. Provided he enters into, or becomes concerned in the arrangement with the consent of the person to whom he makes the disclosure, then the person making the disclosure commits no offence under subs. (1). The paragraph, therefore, clearly contemplates the case where a party who may already be disposed to commit an offence enters into an arrangement with those responsible for the detection and prevention of crime whereby he will engage in what would otherwise be unlawful conduct, presumably for the purposes of facilitating the investigation into the activities of the drug trafficker. An interesting question arises as to the admissibility of any evidence provided by a person who has entered into such an arrangement. Can it be said that the information has been fairly obtained?

Sub-para. (ii) deals with the case of the person who, having entered into or become concerned in an arrangement of the kind struck at by subs. (1), subsequently makes a disclosure to the authorities. In this case no offence is committed provided he has made the disclosure as soon as is reasonable, and on his own initiative.

Subs. (5)

Fines

The offence contained in s.43 is an offence to which s.1 of this Act relates (see s.1(2)) with the result that the provisions of s.44 relating to unlimited fines apply to the offence of assisting another to retain the proceeds of drug trafficking.

Offences relating to controlled drugs: fines

44.—(1) Without prejudice to section 395(1) of the 1975 Act (fines) as applied by section 194 of that Act but subject to the proviso to subsection

(1) of section 2 of this Act, where a person is convicted on indictment of an offence to which this section relates and sentenced in respect of that offence to a period of imprisonment or detention, the Court where—

(a) paragraph (b) below does not apply shall, unless it is satisfied that for any reason it would be inappropriate to do so, also impose a fine;

(b) it makes an order under section 1(1) of this Act as regards the person, may also impose a fine.

(2) In determining the amount of a fine imposed under paragraph (a) of subsection (1) above, the Court shall have regard to any profits likely to have been made by the person from the crime in respect of which he has been convicted.

(3) This section relates to the same offences as does section 1 of this Act.

(4) Where in any proceedings a fine has been imposed by virtue of subsection (1) above as regards a person and a period of imprisonment or detention is imposed on him in default of payment of its amount (or as the case may be of an instalment thereof), that period shall run from the expiry of any other period of imprisonment or detention (not being one of life imprisonment or detention for life) imposed on him in the proceedings.

(5) The reference in subsection (4) above to "any other period of imprisonment or detention imposed" includes (without prejudice to the generality of the expression) a reference to such a period imposed on default of payment of a fine (or instalment thereof) or of a confiscation order (or instalment thereof); but only where that default has occurred before the warrant for imprisonment is issued for the default in relation to the fine imposed by virtue of subsection (1) of this section.

GENERAL NOTE

This section replaces, with modifications, s.193B of the 1975 Act, which was inserted therein by s.39 of the Law Reform (Miscellaneous Provisions) (Scotland) Act 1985 (now repealed by Sched. 2 to this Act).

Where a person is convicted on indictment of an offence to which this section relates (*viz.,* an offence to which s.1 of the Act relates (s.44(3)) and sentenced to a period of imprisonment, the Court is obliged to impose a fine, unless either it is satisfied that it would be inappropriate to do so, or it makes a confiscation order, in which case it may at its discretion impose a fine in addition to the confiscation order.

Subs. (1)

Without prejudice to section 395(1) of the 1975 Act. S.395(1) provides that in determining the amount of a fine the court must have regard to the means of the offender.

Subject to the proviso to section 2(1). S.2(1) of the present Act permits the High Court to postpone making a decision as regards making a confiscation order, and also permits the court to proceed to sentence or otherwise deal with the convicted person. However, the proviso to s.2(1) states that no fine may be imposed before the decision as regards the confiscation order is taken.

Paras. (a), (b)

Except where the court makes a confiscation order it has no discretion as regards the imposition of a fine. The court is obliged to impose a fine unless it is satisfied that for any reason it would be inappropriate to do so. Where the Court makes a confiscation order it has a discretion whether or not also to impose a fine.

Subs. (2)

S.44 is intended as a supplementary mechanism for seizing the assets of persons involved in drug offences, and the Court is expressly required to have regard to any profits likely to have been made by the convicted person from his involvement in drug offences. It is important to note, however, the limitations imposed by subs. (2). In the first place the Court may only have regard to the profits likely to have been made *by the convicted person,* and secondly, only those profits likely to have been made from the crime *in respect of which he has convicted* may be taken into account. It is, on the other hand, a mechanism which is available not only in the High Court, but also in solemn proceedings in the sheriff court.

Subs. (4)

Any period of imprisonment or detention for non-payment of a fine imposed under subs. (1) is to be served consecutively to, and not concurrently with, the period of detention or imprisonment initially imposed.

Minor amendments, service, notice and interpretation

Minor amendments in relation to drug trafficking

45.—(1) Section 28 of the Bankruptcy Act 1914 (effect of order of discharge) shall have effect as if amounts payable under confiscation orders were debts excepted under subsection (1)(a) of that section.

(2) In section 1(2)(a) of the Rehabilitation of Offenders Act 1974 (failure to pay fines etc. not to prevent person becoming rehabilitated) the reference to a fine or other sum adjudged to be paid by or on a conviction does not include a reference to an amount payable under a confiscation order.

(3) In subsection (4A) of section 18 of the Civil Jurisdiction and Judgments Act 1982 (exceptions as to enforcement of U.K. judgments in other parts of U.K.), at the end there shall be added the following words—

"; or as respects the enforcement in England and Wales of orders made by the Court of Session under or for the purposes of Part I of the Criminal Justice (Scotland) Act 1987".

(4) Section 281(4) of the Insolvency Act 1986 (discharge of bankrupt not to release him from liabilities in respect of fines, etc.) shall have effect as if the reference to a fine included a reference to a confiscation order.

(5) In the 1985 Act—

    (a) in section 5(4) (interpretation)—

        (i) after the words "future debts" there shall be inserted the words "or amounts payable under a confiscation order"; and

        (ii) at the end there shall be added the words "; and in the foregoing provisions of this subsection "confiscation order" has the meaning assigned by section 1(1) of the Criminal Justice (Scotland) Act 1987 or by section 1(8) of the Drug Trafficking Offences Act 1986";

    (b) in section 7(1) (constitution of apparent insolvency)—

        (i) in paragraph (b), at the beginning there shall be inserted the words "not being a person whose property is for the time being affected by a restraint order or subject to a confiscation, or charging, order,";

        (ii) in paragraph (c), after the words "became due" there shall be inserted the words "or that but for his property being affected by a restraint order or subject to a confiscation, or charging, order he would be able to do so"; and

        (iii) at the end there shall be added the words "In paragraph (d) above, "liquid debt" does not include a sum payable under a confiscation order; and in the foregoing provisions of this subsection—

            "charging order" has the meaning assigned by section 9(2) of the Drug Trafficking Offences Act 1986;

            "confiscation order" has the meaning assigned by section 1(1) of the Criminal Justice (Scotland) Act 1987 or by section 1(8) of the said Act of 1986; and

"restraint order" has the meaning assigned by section
9 of the said Act of 1987 or by section 8 of the said Act
of 1986."; and
(c) section 55(2) (discharge of debtor not to release him from
liabilities in respect of fines etc.) shall have effect as if the
reference to a fine included a reference to a confiscation order.
(6) In section 231 of the 1975 Act (intimation of intention to
appeal)—
(a) in subsection (1), after the words "236B(2) of this Act" there
shall be inserted the words "and to section 2(2) of the Criminal
Justice (Scotland) Act 1987 (postponed confiscation orders)";
(b) in subsection (4), at the beginning there shall be inserted the
words "Subject to subsection (5) below,"; and
(c) after subsection (4) there shall be added the following
subsection—
"(5) Without prejudice to subsection (2) of section 2 of
the said Act of 1987, the reference in subsection (4) above
to "the day on which sentence is passed in open court" shall,
in relation to any case in which, under subsection (1) of that
section, a decision has been postponed for a period, be
construed as a reference to the day on which that decision is
made (whether or not a confiscation order is then made or
any other sentence is then passed).".
(7) In the Drug Trafficking Offences Act 1986—
(a) at the end of section 2(5) (assessing the proceeds of drug
trafficking) there shall be inserted the words—
"References in this subsection to a confiscation order
include a reference to a confiscation order within the meaning
of Part I of the Criminal Justice (Scotland) Act 1987";
(b) in section 8 (restraint orders)—
(i) in subsection (8), for the words "the High Court has
made a restraint order" there shall be substituted the
words "a restraint order has been made" and at the end
of that subsection there shall be added the words—
"In this subsection, the reference to a restraint order
includes a reference to a restraint order within the
meaning of Part I of the Criminal Justice (Scotland)
Act 1987, and, in relation to such an order, "realisable
property" has the same meaning as in that Part"; and
(ii) in subsection (9), for the words "court's directions" there
shall be substituted the words "directions of the court
which made the order";
(c) in section 16 (sequestration of person holding realisable
property)—
(i) in subsection (2), at the end there shall be added the
words ", and it shall not be competent to submit a claim
in relation to the confiscation order to the permanent
trustee in accordance with section 48 of that Act."; and
(ii) in subsection (5), in paragraph (b)(ii), after the word
"disposal" there shall be inserted the words "and for so
much of his remuneration as may reasonably be assigned
for his actings in that connection"; and in paragraph (c),
for the words "a lien for any expenses (including his
remuneration) properly incurred in respect of the
property" there shall be substituted the words "any such
lien as is mentioned in paragraph (b)(ii) above";
(d) in section 19(2)(b)(ii) (compensation for loss in consequence
of anything done in relation to realisable property by or in

pursuance of order of Court of Session), for the words "20, 21 or 22 of this Act" there shall be substituted the words "11 (as applied by subsection (6) of that section), 27 or 28 of the Criminal Justice (Scotland) Act 1987 (inhibition and arrestment of property affected by restraint order and recognition and enforcement of orders under this Act)";

(e) in section 33 (power to inspect Land Register etc.)—
   (i) in subsection (2), after paragraph (c) there shall be inserted the words— ", or
      (d) the Lord Advocate or any person conducting a prosecution in Scotland on his behalf,";
   (ii) in subsection (4)—
      after the words "8 or 11 of this Act" there shall be inserted the words "or by an administrator appointed under section 13 of the Criminal Justice (Scotland) Act 1987 (comparable Scottish provisions)"; and
         in each of paragraphs (a) and (b), after the word "receiver" there shall be inserted the words "(or administrator)"; and

(f) in section 40(4)(b) (effect in Scotland), at the beginning there shall be inserted the words "section 3(6)".

Service and notice for purposes of Part I

46. Subject to the provisions of this Part of this Act, provision may be made by rules of court as to the giving of notice required for the purposes of this Part of this Act or the effecting of service so required; and different provision may be so made for different cases or classes of case and for different circumstances or classes of circumstance.

Interpretation of Part I

47.—(1) In this Part of this Act (except where the context otherwise requires)—

"administrator" shall be construed in accordance with section 13 of this Act;

"associate" shall be construed in accordance with section 74 of the 1985 Act;

"authorised government department" means a government department which is an authorised department for the purposes of the Crown Proceedings Act 1947;

"confiscation order" has the meaning assigned by section 1(1) of this Act;

"designated country" shall be construed in accordance with section 30(2) of this Act;

"drug trafficking" has the meaning assigned by section 1(6) of this Act;

"implicative gift" shall be construed in accordance with section 6 of this Act;

"realisable property" shall be construed in accordance with section 5 of this Act;

"restraint order" has the meaning assigned by section 9 of this Act; and

"the 1985 Act" means the Bankruptcy (Scotland) Act 1985.

(2) This Part of this Act shall (except where the context otherwise requires) be construed as one with the 1975 Act.

(3) This Part of this Act applies to property whether it is situated in Scotland or elsewhere.

(4) References in this Part of this Act—

    (a) to offences include a reference to offences committed before the commencement of section 1 of this Act; but nothing in this Act imposes any duty or confers any power on any court in or in connection with proceedings against a person for an offence to which that section relates instituted before the commencement of that section;

    (b) to anything received in connection with drug trafficking include a reference to anything received both in that connection and in some other connection; and

    (c) to property held by a person include a reference to property vested in the interim or permanent trustee in his sequestration or in his trustee in bankruptcy or liquidator.

(5) For the purposes of this Part of this Act (and subject to subsections (8) and (9) of section 30 of this Act), proceedings are concluded as regards an offence where—

    (a) the trial diet is deserted *simpliciter*;

    (b) the accused is acquitted or, under section 101 of the 1975 Act, discharged or liberated;

    (c) the High Court sentences or otherwise deals with him without making a confiscation order and without postponing a decision as regards making such an order;

    (d) after such postponement as is mentioned in paragraph (c) above, the High Court decides not to make a confiscation order;

    (e) his conviction is quashed; or

    (f) either the amount of a confiscation order made has been paid or there remains no liability to imprisonment in default of so much of that amount as is unpaid.

Part II

Miscellaneous

Detention by customs officers

GENERAL NOTE

    With appropriate modifications, ss.48 and 49 apply the provisions of ss.2 and 3 of the Criminal Justice (Scotland) Act 1980 to detention by a customs officer. S.48 sets out the circumstances in which a customs officer may detain a suspect without charge for up to six hours for the purpose of investigating an offence punishable with imprisonment. The section also sets out the duties of the customs officer in connection with detention, and some of the rights of the detainee. S.49 sets out the rights of the detainee in respect of his entitlement to have someone informed of the fact that he has been detained. Given the origin of these provisions it seems fair to assume that decisions on the construction of ss.2 and 3 of the 1980 Act will be directly relevant to ss.48 and 49, and reference is made to general considerations of ss.2 and 3 in Gordon, *The Criminal Justice (Scotland) Act 1980*, Gordon *Renton and Brown's Criminal Procedure* (5th ed., 1983), paras. 5.13 *et seq.* and Gane and Stoddart, *Criminal Procedure in Scotland: Cases and materials*, chap. 4.

Detention and questioning by customs officers

    48.—(1) Where an officer has reasonable grounds for suspecting that a person has committed or is committing an offence punishable by imprisonment relating to an assigned matter, the officer may, for the purpose of facilitating the carrying out of investigations—

    (a) into the offence; and

    (b) as to whether criminal proceedings should be instigated against the person, detain that person and take him as quickly as is reasonably practicable to a customs office or other premises and, subject to the following provisions of this section, the detention may continue there.

(2) Detention under subsection (1) above shall be terminated not more than six hours after it begins or (if earlier)—

    (a) when the person is arrested;

    (b) when he is detained in pursuance of any other enactment or subordinate instrument; or

    (c) where there are no longer such grounds as are mentioned in the said subsection (1),

and when a person has been detained under subsection (1) above, he shall be informed immediately upon the termination of his detention in accordance with this subsection that his detention has been terminated.

(3) Where a person has been released at the termination of a period of detention under subsection (1) above he shall not thereafter be detained, under that subsection, on the same grounds or on any grounds arising out of the same circumstances.

(4) Where a person has previously been detained in pursuance of any other enactment or subordinate instrument, he may not be detained under subsection (1) above on the same grounds or on grounds arising from the same circumstances as those which led to his earlier detention.

(5) At the time when an officer detains a person under subsection (1) above, he shall inform the person of his suspicion, of the general nature of the offence which he suspects has been or is being committed and of the reason for the detention; and there shall be recorded—

    (a) the place where detention begins and the customs office or other premises to which the person is taken;

    (b) the general nature of the suspected offence;

    (c) the time when detention under subsection (1) above begins and the time of the person's arrival at the customs office or other premises;

    (d) the time when the person is informed of his rights in terms of subsection (8) below and of section 49(1) of this Act and the identity of the officer so informing him;

    (e) where the person requests such intimation to be sent as is specified in section 49(1) of this Act, the time when such request is—

        (i) made;

        (ii) complied with; and

    (f) the time of the person's departure from the customs office or other premises or, where instead of being released he is—

        (i) further detained under section 50 of this Act, the time of commencement of the further detention; or

        (ii) arrested in respect of the alleged offence, the time of such arrest.

(6) Where a person is detained under subsection (1) above, an officer may—

    (a) without prejudice to any existing rule of law as regards the admissibility in evidence of any answer given, put questions to him in relation to the suspected offence;

    (b) exercise the same powers of search as are available following an arrest.

(7) An officer may use reasonable force in exercising any power conferred by subsection (1) or (6)(b) above.

(8) A person detained under subsection (1) above shall be under no obligation to answer any question other than to give his name and address, and an officer shall so inform him both on so detaining him and on arrival at the customs office or other premises.

(9) In this section and in sections 49 and 50 of this Act "assigned matter" and "officer" have the meanings given to them by section 1 of the

Customs and Excise Management Act 1979, and "customs office" means a place for the time being occupied by Her Majesty's Customs and Excise.

GENERAL NOTE

Subs. (1)

Assigned matter. This is defined in s.1 of the Customs and Excise Management Act 1979 as meaning "any matter in relation to which the Commissioners are for the time being required in pursuance of any enactment to perform any duties." This definition is applied to s.48 (and s.50) by s.48(9).

Subs. (4)

There is no corresponding provision in s.2 of the 1980 Act. Unfortunately no definition of detention is offered so that it is unclear whether the detention referred to in this subsection is restricted to detention of the kind envisaged under subs. (1), or whether it includes other forms of detention or even arrest. Would detention under s.23 of the Misuse of Drugs Act 1971 be included or detention under Pt. IV of the Police and Criminal Evidence Act 1984. There is nothing in the section to indicate that the prior detention need have been in Scotland.

Right to have someone informed when detained

49.—(1) Without prejudice to section 19 or 305 of the 1975 Act (intimation to solicitor following arrest), a person who, not being a person in respect of whose detention subsection (2) below applies, is being detained under section 48 of this Act at a customs office or other premises shall be entitled to have intimation of his detention and of the place where he is being detained sent to a solicitor and to one other person reasonably named by him without delay or, where some delay is necessary in the interest of the investigation or the prevention of crime or the apprehension of offenders, with no more delay than is so necessary; and the person shall be informed of such entitlement—

  (a) on arrival at the customs office or other premises; or

  (b) where he is not detained until after such arrival, on such detention.

(2) Without prejudice to the said section 19 or 305, an officer shall, where a person who is being detained as is mentioned in subsection (1) above appears to him to be a child, send without delay such intimation as is mentioned in that subsection to that person's parent if known; and the parent—

  (a) in a case where there is reasonable cause to suspect that he has been involved in the alleged offence in respect of which the person has been detained, may; and

  (b) in any other case shall,

be permitted access to the person.

(3) The nature and extent of any access permitted under subsection (2) above shall be subject to any restriction essential for the furtherance of the investigation or the well-being of the person.

(4) In subsection (2) above—

  (a) "child" means a person under 16 years of age; and

  (b) "parent" includes a guardian and any person who has the actual custody of a child.

Detention in connection with certain drug smuggling offences

50.—(1) Where an officer has reasonable grounds for suspecting—

  (a) that a person has committed or is committing a relevant offence; and

  (b) that, in connection with the commission of such an offence, a controlled drug is secreted in the person's body,

a superior officer may, notwithstanding that the person has been or is being detained in pursuance of any other enactment or subordinate instrument, authorise the detention of the person at a customs office or other premises in accordance with this section.

(2) Subject to subsection (7) below, where a person is detained under subsection (1) above or is further detained in pursuance of a warrant under subsection (4) below he shall—

(a) provide such specimens of blood or urine for analysis;

(b) submit to such intimate searches, to be carried out by a registered medical practitioner;

(c) submit to such other tests or examinations prescribed by the Secretary of State by regulations made under this paragraph to be carried out by, or under the supervision of, a registered medical practitioner,

as the officer may reasonably require; and regulations under paragraph (c) above shall be made by statutory instrument subject to annulment in pursuance of a resolution of either House of Parliament.

(3) Subject to subsection (4) below, detention under subsection (1) above shall be terminated not more than 24 hours after it begins, or (if earlier)—

(a) when the person is arrested;

(b) when he is detained in pursuance of any other enactment or subordinate instrument; or

(c) where there are no longer such grounds as are mentioned in subsection (1),

and, when a person has been detained under subsection (1), he shall, unless further detained in pursuance of a warrant under subsection (4) below, be informed immediately upon the termination of his detention in accordance with this subsection that his detention has been terminated.

(4) Where a person is detained under subsection (1) above and either—

(a) he has failed or refused—

(i) to provide a specimen in pursuance of paragraph (a) of subsection (2) above; or

(ii) to submit to any search, test or examination referred to in paragraph (b) or (c) of that subsection; or

(b) as a result of anything done in pursuance of the said subsection (2) the officer continues to have reasonable grounds for suspecting—

(i) that the person has committed or is committing a relevant offence; and

(ii) that a controlled drug is secreted in the person's body,

the procurator fiscal may, at the request of a superior officer, apply to the sheriff for a warrant for the further detention of the person at a customs office or other premises for an additional period of not more than 7 days; and if the sheriff is satisfied that there has been such failure or refusal as is mentioned in paragraph (a) above or, as the case may be, that there are reasonable grounds as mentioned in paragraph (b) above he may grant a warrant for such further detention.

(5) Detention in pursuance of a warrant under subsection (4) above shall be terminated at the end of the period of 7 days mentioned in that subsection or (if earlier)—

(a) when the person is arrested;

(b) when he is detained in pursuance of any other enactment or subordinate instrument; or

(c) where there are no longer such grounds as are mentioned in paragraph (b) of that subsection,

and when a person has been detained in pursuance of a warrant under subsection (4), he shall be informed immediately on the termination of his detention in accordance with this subsection that his detention has been terminated.

(6) Subject to subsection (7) below, the question whether it is to be a specimen of blood or a specimen of urine which is to be provided in pursuance of subsection (2) above shall be decided by the officer making the requirement.

(7) A person may be required, in pursuance of subsection (2) above—

(a) to provide a specimen of blood; or

(b) to submit to any search, test or examination,

only if a registered medical practitioner is of the opinion that there are no medical reasons for not making such a requirement; and, if a requirement to provide a specimen of blood is made, the specimen may be taken only by a registered medical practitioner.

(8) Subsections (3), (5), (6) and (8) of section 48 of this Act shall apply in respect of a person detained under this section as they apply in respect of a person detained under the said section 48; and, except as regards a requirement under subsection (2) above, an officer may use reasonable force in exercising any power conferred by this section.

(9) Section 49 of this Act shall, subject to the following modifications, apply in respect of a person detained under this section as it applies to a person detained under section 48 of this Act—

(a) any delay in informing a solicitor and one other person of such detention as is mentioned in subsection (1) of the said section 49 shall not extend longer than the period of 24 hours from the start of the detention, and shall only be permitted on the authorisation of a superior officer;

(b) the person detained shall be entitled to consult a solicitor at any time without delay, and he shall be informed of such entitlement at the commencement of the detention; but, if a superior officer considers it necessary in the interest of the investigation or the prevention of crime or the apprehension of offenders, he may authorise a delay not extending longer than the period of 24 hours from the start of the detention; and

(c) paragraph (a) of subsection (2) of the said section 49 shall cease to apply at the end of the period of 24 hours from the start of the detention,

but any delay authorised by virtue of this subsection shall be for no longer than is necessary in the interest of the investigation or the prevention of crime or the apprehension of offenders.

(10) Without prejudice to section 20(2) of the Interpretation Act 1978, the references in section 48(5) of this Act to section 49(1) of this Act shall be construed as including references to subsection (9) above; and the requirement to record certain matters under the said section 48(5) shall include a requirement to record the time when a person detained makes a request to consult a solicitor and the time when the solicitor is contacted for the purpose of arranging a consultation.

(11) In this section—

"intimate search" means a search which consists of the physical examination of a person's body orifices;

"relevant offence" means an offence involving a controlled drug under any of the following provisions of the Customs and Excise Management Act 1979—

(a) section 50(2) or (3) (importation etc. of prohibited goods;

(b) section 68(2) (exportation etc. of prohibited goods);

(c) section 170(1) (possessing or dealing with prohibited goods);

(d) section 170(2) (being concerned in evasion or attempt at evasion of a prohibition);

41–63

"superior officer" means an officer of the grade of senior executive officer or above.

GENERAL NOTE

This section provides for an entirely new power of detention in connection with certain drug smuggling offences. The section is designed to facilitate the investigation of persons suspected of smuggling drugs concealed within their bodies.

Subs. (1)

An officer. The powers conferred by this section can only be exercised by an "officer" who for these purposes is a person commissioned by the Commissioners of Customs and Excise (Customs and Excise Management Act 1979, s.1, as applied to s.50 by s.48(9)). The powers conferred by this section cannot, therefore, be exercised by a constable.

A relevant offence. This is defined in subs. (11) as meaning an offence involving a controlled drug under any of the following provisions of the Customs and Excise Management Act 1979 (s.50(2) or (3), 68(2), 170(1) and 170(2)).

A superior officer. This is defined in subs. (11) as an officer of the grade of senior executive officer or above.

Subs. (2)

Intimate searches. These are defined in subs. (11) as meaning a search which consists in the physical examination of a person's body orifices. An intimate search must be carried out by a registered medical practitioner. The provisions which permit the use of reasonable force by an officer in exercising a power conferred by this section do not apply to the conduct of intimate searches (s.50(8)). This would follow from the fact that an officer cannot conduct such a search but in any event the use of force in the conduct of such an examination would seem to be quite inappropriate.

Statutory provision for "intimate searches" was first made in the Police and Criminal Evidence Act 1984, s.55 of which permits such searches to be made for weapons and Class A drugs. The use of intimate searches under that Act is regulated by s.55 itself and the Code of Practice for the Detention, Treatment and Questioning of Persons by the Police. Para. 6 of Annex A to the Code states, for example, that during an intimate search "no person of the opposite sex who is not a medical practitioner or nurse shall be present nor shall anyone whose presence is unnecessary." Apart from the requirement that an intimate search be carried out by a registered medical practitioner, and the provisions of subs. (7) there are no corresponding safeguards in respect of the procedures envisaged by subs. (2)(b).

Subs. (4)

This subsection provides for the extension of the normal 24-hour period of detention for a period not exceeding seven days. The extension may only be granted by a sheriff on application by a procurator fiscal, and is subject to the sheriff being satisfied that the conditions of subs. (4)(a) or (b) are made out. The subsection appears to speak of only one extension, or at least refers only to the further detention of the suspect for "an additional period". It is not clear, therefore, whether it would be possible for a fiscal to apply for more than one extension provided that the maximum seven-day period has not been exceeded. If only one application were permitted, then this would probably result in applications for longer periods than might strictly be necessary. This could be avoided by construing the section so as to permit more than one additional period up to the maximum of seven days.

The extended period of detention is directed particularly at the detainee who is suspected of having concealed drugs in their body by packing them in a container (typically a condom) and swallowing them. The extended period of detention gives time for the drugs to be excreted from the body.

Subs. (7)

This subsection provides some safeguards in relation to requirements made under subs. (2), and in particular restricts the circumstances in which an intimate search may be carried out and also requires that a specimen of blood be taken only by a registered medical practitioner.

Investigation of serious or complex fraud

GENERAL NOTE

Ss.51 to 55 deal with the investigation of serious or complex fraud. S.51(1) gives the Lord Advocate the power to make directions for the investigation of the affairs of any person in connection with a suspected offence involving serious or complex fraud. S.51(2) provides for the appointment of a "nominated officer" who shall be entitled to exercise the powers and functions conferred by ss.52 to 54. S.52 sets out the powers of investigation which may be exercised by a nominated officer, and also makes provision for the granting of warrants by the sheriff to search for and seize documents relevant to an investigation under s.52. S.53 creates two new offences in relation to investigations under s.52. Under s.54 information disclosed by the Commissioners of Inland Revenue for the purposes of any prosecution of a revenue offence may be disclosed by the Lord Advocate for the purposes of any prosecution of an offence in respect of which a direction has been given under s.51(1)(a) of this Act, or an offence relating to inland revenue. S.55 provides for the winding up of a company or the disqualification of a person from acting as a director of a company on the basis of information obtained under s.52.

The Criminal Justice Act 1987 makes corresponding provision for England with the establishment, *inter alia*, of a serious fraud office with special powers of investigation to deal with the problem of major fraud which has, undoubtedly, been a problem in London and other financial centres. It is worth noting that the English provisions are based on a detailed examination of the law and practice relating to the prosecution of fraud by a committee under the chairmanship of Lord Roskill (*Fraud Trials Committee Report*, London, H.M.S.O., 1986) which made over 100 recommendations for changes in the law and practice governing the investigation and prosecution of serious fraud. Formalities of this kind can apparently be dispensed with so far as Scots law is concerned. The clauses which eventually became ss.51 to 55 only saw the light of day at the Report stage of the Bill in the House of Lords. They received less than two hours' consideration in that House, and just over 15 minutes consideration in the First Scottish Standing Committee. Nor can it be suggested that the problems relating to fraud in Scotland had already been aired elsewhere. The Roskill Committee Report devotes rather less than one page to Scots law, and then only on a general comparative basis.

Lord Advocate's direction

51.—(1) Where it appears to the Lord Advocate—
    (a) that a suspected offence may involve serious or complex fraud; and
    (b) that, for the purpose of investigating the affairs or any aspect of the affairs of any person, there is good reason to do so,
he may give a direction under this section.

(2) Where a direction is given under this section, sections 52 to 54 of this Act shall apply as regards the investigation of the offence; and any person (other than a constable) nominated by the Lord Advocate either generally or in respect of a particular case (in those sections referred to as "a nominated officer") shall be entitled to exercise the powers and functions conferred by those sections.

(3) A direction under this section shall be signed by the Lord Advocate.

Subs. (1)

Serious or complex fraud. No definition of these key terms is offered. This issue was raised in the Committee on Recommitment in the House of Lords and what might be described as the "elephant argument" was used to dispose of it—*i.e.*, that serious or complex fraud would be difficult to describe, but easy enough to recognise when one came face to face with it. But would it have been impossible to give some guidance? It is difficult to see why, for example, some financial limits could not have been suggested. The operation of s.51 could have been restricted, for example, to cases where sums in excess of a given figure were, or appeared to be, involved.

It would seem from the context that what is anticipated is large scale commercial fraud, but no doubt there are other frauds which would be capable of satisfying the epithet "serious" while not being particularly complex. This much could be said, for example, of the fairly common fraud which consists in obtaining access to residential property (usually occupied by elderly persons) by pretending to be a representative of the gas board or some similar body for the purpose of committing theft on the property. On criteria other than purely financial ones (and sometimes on these as well) a fraud of this kind has a claim to be described as "serious".

Nominated officer. During the House of Lords debates there was some discussion of the accountability of the "nominated officer". An attempt was made at one point to insert an amendment which would have resulted in the Lord Advocate being responsible for the actions of a nominated officer in the exercise of the powers and functions conferred on him. The Lord Advocate's position was that the nominated officer would normally be a member of the Crown Office staff, or the Crown Office Fraud Unit, or perhaps a procurator fiscal. The Lord Advocate also stated (*Hansard*, H.L. Vol. 485, col. 356) that "in so far as the officer is a person nominated by the Lord Advocate, who acts with the powers conferred upon him by the [section] and for the purposes of the particular investigation in respect of which the nomination is made then [the Lord Advocate] would clearly be answerable for anything that he might do or any omissions on his part because he would of course be acting on [the Lord Advocate's] behalf". His Lordship also stated (*ibid.*) that so far as concerns *ultra vires* conduct, the nominated officer would incur personal liability, and that the Lord Advocate would not be liable.

One problem which was not addressed, was the possibility of the Lord Advocate's authority conferring on the designated person a degree of *immunity*. Given that the functions to be carried out by the nominated officer (investigation of offences) are functions to which the Lord Advocate's immunity from civil action may extend (see, for example, *Hester* v. *MacDonald*, 1961 S.C. 370) there is at least an argument in favour of the view that the nominated officer may be protected from civil liability for loss or damage resulting from the exercise of his functions.

No particular qualifications are laid down in respect of the nominated officer, and during debate the Lord Advocate suggested that in an appropriate case a person with specialist knowledge, such as an accountant, could be appointed as a nominated officer.

Subs. (3)

This requirement reflects the view expressed during the Committee stage in the House of Lords that only a law officer should initiate directions under subs. (1). The original version of these provisions would have allowed the Lord Advocate one of his deputies to do so.

Powers of investigation

52.—(1) A nominated officer may by notice in writing require the person whose affairs are to be investigated ("the person under investigation") or any other person who he has reason to believe has relevant information to attend before a nominated officer at a specified time and place and answer questions or otherwise furnish information with respect to any matter relevant to the investigation.

(2) A nominated officer may by notice in writing require the person under investigation or any other person to produce at a specified time and place any specified documents which appear to a nominated officer to relate to any matter relevant to the investigation or any documents of a specified class which appear to him so to relate; and—

    (a) if any such documents are produced, a nominated officer may—
        (i) take copies or extracts from them;
        (ii) require the person producing them to provide an explanation of any of them;
    (b) if any such documents are not produced, a nominated officer may require the person who was required to produce them to state, to the best of his knowledge and belief, where they are.

(3) Where, on a petition presented by the procurator fiscal, the sheriff is satisfied, in relation to any documents, that there are reasonable grounds for believing—

    (a) that—
        (i) a person has failed to comply with an obligation under this section to produce them;
        (ii) it is not practicable to serve a notice under subsection (2) above in relation to them; or
        (iii) the service of such a notice in relation to them might seriously prejudice the investigation; and
    (b) that they are on premises specified in the petition,

he may issue such a warrant as is mentioned in subsection (4) below.

(4) The warrant referred to in subsection (3) above is a warrant authorising a constable together with any other persons named in the warrant—

(a) to enter (using such force as is reasonably necessary for the purpose) and search the premises; and

(b) to take possession of any documents appearing to be documents of the description specified in the petition or to take in relation to any documents so appearing any other steps which may appear to be necessary for preserving them and preventing interference with them.

(5) A statement by a person in response to a requirement imposed by virtue of this section may only be used in evidence against him in a prosecution for an offence under section 2 of the False Oaths (Scotland) Act 1933.

(6) A person shall not under this section be required to disclose any information or produce any document which is an item subject to legal privilege within the meaning of section 40 of this Act; except that a lawyer may be required to furnish the name and address of his client.

(7) No person shall be bound to comply with any requirement imposed by a person exercising power by virtue of a nomination under section 51(2) of this Act unless he has, if required to do so, produced evidence of his authority.

(8) In this section—

"documents" includes information recorded in any form and, in relation to information recorded otherwise than in legible form, references to its production include references to producing a copy of the information in legible form; and

"premises" has the same meaning as in section 40 of this Act.

(9) This section and sections 51 and 53 of this Act shall apply to England and Wales and Northern Ireland; and for the purposes of such application any reference—

(a) to the sheriff shall be construed as a reference to a justice of the peace; and

(b) to a petition presented by the procurator fiscal shall be construed—

(i) in England and Wales as a reference to an information laid by a nominated officer;

(ii) in Northern Ireland as a reference to a complaint laid by a nominated officer.

GENERAL NOTE

Subs. (1)

Or any other person. An attempt to limit this provision to the interrogation of the person under investigation was rejected by the Lord Advocate during the Committee on Recommitment. The Government's view was that to so limit the scope of the nominated officer's investigatory powers would be to "emasculate" the Act's provisions. As against the government view, however, it must be recognised that this section puts persons who are not themselves under investigation in the position of having to attend and answer questions under threat of criminal penalties for failing to do so. The Lord Advocate's answer to this point would appear to be that "It is a cardinal rule . . . that in general terms the ordinary individual has a duty to assist in providing information which, at the end of the day, may be relevant in bringing another person to justice" (*Hansard*, H.L. Vol. 485, col. 360). The problem with this argument is that at the pre-trial stage, and in the absence of an order from the court, the obligation is one which is best described as a "civic" rather than a "legal" duty, as indeed the Lord Advocate appears later to have recognised (*ibid.*).

Subs. (3)

It should be noted that the nominated officer cannot apply to the sheriff for a warrant under this subsection. The petition for the warrant must be presented by the procurator fiscal.

Subs. (3)

Conditions (a) and (b) must be satisfied before a warrant can be granted, but within (a) the three conditions stated are alternatives. Condition (iii) envisages the situation in which serving a notice would alert the person under investigation, or any other person upon whom a notice under subs. (2) might be served, to the fact of the investigation, thus giving them the opportunity to take steps to thwart the investigation.

Subs. (4)

Any other person named in the warrant. The obvious person to accompany the constable is the nominated officer, although this is not required by the section. An attempt to require the attendance of the nominated officer or his representative was made during the Committee on Recommitment, but this too was rejected by the Lord Advocate.

Subs. (5)

Statements made by a person in response to a requirement imposed under s.52 cannot generally be used as evidence against the person making them. They may, however, be relied upon in a prosecution for an offence under s.2 of the False Oaths (Scotland) Act 1933. That section makes it an offence, *inter alia*, knowingly and wilfully to make a statement, false in a material particular, in any oral declaration or answer which he is required by statute to make. It should be noted that this restriction on the use to which statements may be put does not apply to information contained in documents whose production has been required under subs. (2).

Offences in relation to investigations under section 52

   53.—(1) Where any person—
  (a) knows or suspects that an investigation under section 52 of this Act is being carried out or is likely to be carried out; and
  (b) falsifies, conceals, destroys or otherwise disposes of, or causes or permits the falsification, concealment, destruction or disposal of documents which he knows or suspects or has reasonable grounds to suspect are or would be relevant to such an investigation,
he shall be guilty of an offence.
   (2) In proceedings against a person for an offence under subsection (1) above, it shall be a defence to prove—
  (a) that he did not know or suspect that by acting as he did he was likely to prejudice the investigation; or
  (b) that he had lawful authority or reasonable excuse for acting as he did.
   (3) A person guilty of an offence under subsection (1) above shall be liable—
  (a) on conviction on indictment, to imprisonment for a term not exceeding seven years or to a fine or to both; and
  (b) on summary conviction, to imprisonment for a term not exceeding six months or to a fine not exceeding the statutory maximum or to both.
   (4) Any person who fails to comply with a requirement imposed on him under the said section 52 shall be guilty of an offence and liable on summary conviction to imprisonment for a term not exceeding six months or to a fine not exceeding level 5 on the standard scale or to both.
   (5) In proceedings against a person for an offence under subsection (4) above, it shall be a defence to prove that he had a reasonable excuse for acting as he did.

GENERAL NOTE

Subss. (1) and (2)

Subs. (1) creates two distinct types of offence in relation to documents relevant to an investigation under s.52. The offence may be committed by falsifying, etc., the documents, or by causing or permitting their falsification, etc., by a third party. The prosecutor must prove that the accused had the requisite knowledge or suspicion under para. (1)(a) (relating to the process of investigation) and also under para. (1)(b) relating to the relevance of the documents to the investigation. Subs. (2) provides two statutory defences: absence of knowledge or suspicion that by acting as he did the accused was likely to prejudice the investigation, and lawful authority or reasonable excuse for acting as he did. The onus of establishing these defences rests on the accused, and once again, although the Act is silent on the matter it seems likely that in order to establish his defence he would have to prove it on a balance of probabilities.

Disclosure of information

54.—(1) Where any information subject to an obligation of secrecy under the Taxes Management Act 1970 has been disclosed by the Commissioners of Inland Revenue or an officer of those Commissioners for the purposes of any prosecution of an offence relating to inland revenue, that information may be disclosed by the Lord Advocate for the purposes of any prosecution of an offence—

(a) in respect of which a direction has been given under section 51(1)(a) of this Act; or

(b) relating to inland revenue,

but not otherwise.

(2) Where any information is subject to an obligation of secrecy imposed by or under any enactment other than an enactment contained in the Taxes Management Act 1970, the obligation shall not have effect to prohibit the disclosure of that information to a nominated officer but any information disclosed by virtue of this subsection may only be disclosed by the Lord Advocate for the purpose of a prosecution in Scotland or elsewhere.

(3) Without prejudice to his power to enter into an agreement apart from this subsection, the Lord Advocate may enter into an agreement for the supply of information to or by him subject, in either case, to an obligation not to disclose the information concerned otherwise than for a specified purpose.

(4) Subject to subsections (1) and (2) above and to any provision of an agreement for the supply of information which restricts the disclosure of the information supplied, information obtained by a nominated officer may be disclosed—

(a) to any government department, or any Northern Ireland Department, or other authority or body discharging its functions on behalf of the Crown (including the Crown in right of Her Majesty's Government in Northern Ireland);

(b) to any competent authority;

(c) for the purposes of any prosecution in Scotland or elsewhere; and

(d) for the purposes of assisting any public or other authority for the time being designated for the purposes of this paragraph by an order made by the Secretary of State to discharge any functions which are specified in the order.

(5) The following are competent authorities for the purposes of subsection (4) above—

(a) an inspector appointed under Part XIV of the Companies Act 1985 or Part XV of the Companies (Northern Ireland) Order 1986;

(b) the Accountant in Bankruptcy;

(c) an Official Receiver;

(d) an Official Assignee;

(e) a person appointed to carry out an investigation under section 55 of the Building Societies Act 1986;

(f) a body administering a compensation scheme under section 54 of the Financial Services Act 1986;

(g) an inspector appointed under section 94 of that Act;

    (h) a person exercising powers by virtue of section 106 of that Act;

    (j) an inspector appointed under section 177 of that Act or any corresponding enactment having effect in Northern Ireland;

    (k) an inspector appointed under section 38 of the Banking Act 1987;

    (l) a person exercising powers by virtue of section 44(2) of the Insurance Companies Act 1982;

    (m) any body having supervisory, regulatory or disciplinary functions in relation to any profession or any area of commercial activity; and

    (n) any person or body having, under the law of any country or territory outside the United Kingdom, functions corresponding to any of the functions of any person or body mentioned in any of the foregoing paragraphs.

(6) An order under subsection (4)(d) above may impose conditions subject to which, and otherwise restrict the circumstances in which, information may be disclosed under that paragraph.

Power to petition for winding up etc. on information obtained under section 52

55. The words "or section 52 of the Criminal Justice (Scotland) Act 1987" shall be inserted—

    (a) in section 440 of the Companies Act 1985, after the words "that Act";

    (b) in section 8(1) of the Company Directors Disqualification Act 1986, after the words "the Financial Services Act 1986", in the second place where they occur; and

    (c) in Article 433 of the Companies (Northern Ireland) Order 1986, after the words "that Act".

Conditional offer by procurator fiscal

Conditional offer of fixed penalty by procurator fiscal

56.—(1) Where a procurator fiscal receives a report that a relevant offence has been committed he may send to the alleged offender a notice under this section (referred to in this section as a conditional offer); and where he issues a conditional offer the procurator fiscal shall notify the clerk of court specified in it of the issue of the conditional offer and of its terms.

(2) In this section "a relevant offence" means any offence in respect of which an alleged offender could competently be tried before a district court, but shall not include a fixed penalty offence within the meaning of section 27(5) as extended by section 42(3) of the Transport Act 1982.

(3) A conditional offer—

    (a) shall give such particulars of the circumstances alleged to constitute the offence to which it relates as are necessary for giving reasonable information about the alleged offence;

    (b) shall state—

        (i) the amount of the fixed penalty for that offence;

        (ii) the amount of the instalments by which the penalty may be paid; and

        (iii) the intervals at which such instalments should be paid;

    (c) shall indicate that if, within twenty-eight days of the date on which the conditional offer was issued, or such longer period as may be specified in the conditional offer, the alleged offender accepts the offer by making payment of the fixed penalty or of the first instalment thereof to the clerk of court specified in the conditional offer at the address therein mentioned, any liability to conviction of the offence shall be discharged;

(d) shall state that proceedings against the alleged offender shall not be commenced in respect of that offence until the end of a period of twenty-eight days from the date on which the conditional offer was issued, or such longer period as may be specified in the conditional offer; and

(e) shall state that acceptance of the offer in the manner described in paragraph (c) above by the alleged offender shall not be a conviction nor be recorded as such.

(4) Where payment of the fixed penalty or of the first instalment has not been made to the clerk of court, he shall, upon the expiry of the period of twenty-eight days referred to in subsection (3)(c) above or such longer period as may be specified in the conditional offer, notify the procurator fiscal who issued the conditional offer that no payment has been made.

(5) Proceedings shall not be brought against any person for the offence to which a conditional offer relates until the procurator fiscal receives notification from the clerk of court in accordance with subsection (4) above.

(6) Where an alleged offender makes payment of the fixed penalty or of the first instalment to the clerk of court specified in the conditional offer no proceedings shall be brought against the alleged offender for the offence.

(7) The fixed penalty under this section shall be such sum, not exceeding level 1 on the standard scale, as the Secretary of State may, by order made by statutory instrument subject to annulment in pursuance of a resolution of either House of Parliament determine; and an order under this subsection may contain provision as to the payment of the fixed penalty by instalments.

(8) Subject to subsection (9) below, where an alleged offender accepts a conditional offer by paying the first instalment of the fixed penalty, any amount of the penalty which is outstanding at any time shall be treated as if the penalty were a fine imposed by the court, the clerk of which is specified in the conditional offer.

(9) In the enforcement of a penalty which is to be treated as a fine in pursuance of subsection (8) above—

(a) any reference (howsoever expressed) in any enactment (whether passed or made before or after the coming into force of this section) to—

  (i) the imposition of imprisonment or detention in default of payment of a fine shall be construed as a reference to enforcement by means of civil diligence;

  (ii) the finding or order of the court imposing the fine shall be construed as a reference to a certificate given in pursuance of subsection (10) below;

  (iii) the offender shall be construed as a reference to the alleged offender;

  (iv) the conviction of the offender shall be construed as a reference to the acceptance of the conditional offer by the alleged offender;

(b) the following enactments shall not apply—

  (i) in the 1975 Act—

     section 395(1);
     section 395A(2);
     section 396(1) to (6);
     section 403(6);
     section 406;
     section 407, except subsection (1)(b);
     sections 408 and 409;

section 411(3); and

(ii) in the Criminal Justice (Scotland) Act 1980, section 52.

(10) For the purposes of any proceedings in connection with, or steps taken for, the enforcement of any amount of a fixed penalty which is outstanding, a document purporting to be a certificate signed by the clerk of court for the time being responsible for the collection or enforcement of the penalty as to any matter relating to the penalty shall be conclusive of the matter so certified.

(11) The Secretary of State may, by order made by statutory instrument subject to annulment in pursuance of a resolution of either House of Parliament, make such provision as he considers necessary for the enforcement in England and Wales or Northern Ireland of any penalty (treated, in pursuance of subsection (8) above, as a fine) which is transferred as a fine to a court in England and Wales or, as the case may be, Northern Ireland.

GENERAL NOTE

The fixed penalty system, as an alternative to prosecution, is well-established in relation to motoring offences. Under this section it becomes possible for a procurator fiscal to make a conditional offer of a fixed penalty in respect of any offence which would competently be tried before a district court (with the exception of a fixed penalty offence within the meaning of s.27(5) of the Transport Act 1982). If the alleged offender accepts the conditional offer of the fixed penalty by making payment of the penalty (or its first instalment) any liability to conviction is discharged. The fiscal is not obliged to make an offer of a fixed penalty in respect of any offence, and the option to prosecute is retained. But once a conditional offer has been made and accepted no proceedings can be taken. Where the penalty is payable by instalments, any outstanding amount shall be treated as a fine for the purposes of its recovery, but imprisonment or detention in default of payment is not competent. Under subs. (9) the appropriate method of enforcement is to civil diligence.

Sittings of the High Court

High Court sittings

57.—(1) For section 112 of the 1975 Act (sittings of the Court of Justiciary) there shall be substituted the following new section—

"Place of High Court sittings

112. Any crime or offence which is triable on indictment may be tried by the High Court sitting at any place in Scotland.".

(2) For section 114 of that Act (power of High Court to determine circuits etc.) there shall be substituted the following new section—

"Fixing of High Court sittings

114.—(1) The High Court shall sit at such times and places as the Lord Justice General, whom failing the Lord Justice Clerk, may, after consultation with the Lord Advocate, determine.

(2) Without prejudice to subsection (1) above, the High Court shall hold such additional sittings as the Lord Advocate may require.

(3) When an accused person has been cited to attend a sitting of the High Court, the prosecutor may, at any time before the commencement of his trial, apply to the Court to transfer the case to another sitting of the High Court; and a single judge of the High Court may,—

(a) after giving the accused or his counsel an opportunity to be heard; or

(b) on the joint application of all parties,

make an order for the transfer of the case.

(4) Where no cases have been indicted for a sitting of the High Court or if it is no longer expedient that a sitting should take place, it shall not be necessary for the sitting to take place.

(5) If any case remains indicted for a sitting which does not take place in pursuance of subsection (4) above, subsection (3) above shall apply in relation to the transfer of any such case to another sitting.".

Sentencing power of the sheriff

Sentencing power of sheriff in solemn procedure

58.—(1) In section 2 of the 1975 Act (which limits the term of imprisonment which the sheriff may impose on indictment)—

  (a) in subsection (2), for the words "two years" there shall be substituted the words "three years";

  (b) after subsection (2) there shall be inserted the following subsections—

    "(3) Subject to subsection (4) below, where under any enactment passed or made before the commencement of section 58 of the Criminal Justice (Scotland) Act 1987 an offence is punishable on conviction on indictment by imprisonment for a term exceeding two years but the enactment either expressly or impliedly restricts the power of the sheriff to impose a sentence of imprisonment for a term exceeding two years, it shall be competent for the sheriff to impose a sentence of imprisonment for a term exceeding two but not exceeding three years.

    (4) Nothing in subsection (3) above shall authorise the imposition by the sheriff of a sentence in excess of the sentence specified by the enactment as the maximum sentence which may be imposed on conviction of the offence.".

(2) In section 104 of the 1975 Act, after subsection (1) there shall be inserted the following new subsection—

  "(1A) Where under any enactment an offence is punishable on conviction on indictment by imprisonment for a term exceeding three years but the enactment either expressly or impliedly restricts the power of the sheriff to impose a sentence of imprisonment for a term exceeding three years, it shall be competent for the sheriff to remit the convicted person to the High Court for sentence under subsection (1) above; and it shall be competent for the High Court to pass any sentence which it could have passed if the person had been convicted before it.".

(3) In section 221(1) of that Act (abolition of penal servitude and hard labour), in the proviso, for the words "two years" there shall be substituted the words "three years".

General Note

  This section increases the sentencing power of the sheriff in solemn procedure. The sheriff may now impose up to three years' imprisonment where a period of imprisonment of that duration may competently be imposed in respect of an offence. The change in the law stems from proposals put forward by a review body on the use of judicial time in the superior courts in Scotland, chaired by Lord Maxwell, which in 1986 recommended a number of measures intended to ease pressure on the superior courts. Of these only this measure has been implemented (the others were, use of temporary judges, a single sift of summary appeals to the High Court, and the use of two-judge benches in the High Court to hear appeals against sentence).

Detention of children

Detention of children in summary proceedings

59.—(1) For section 413 of the 1975 Act (committal for residential training) there shall be substituted the following new section—

"Detention of children
413.—(1) Where a child appears before the sheriff in summary proceedings and pleads guilty to, or is found guilty of, an offence to which this section applies, the sheriff may order that he be detained in residential care by the appropriate local authority for such period, not exceeding one year, as the sheriff may determine in such place (in any part of the United Kingdom) as the local authority may, from time to time, consider appropriate.
(2) This section applies to any offence in respect of which it is competent to impose imprisonment on a person of the age of 21 years or more.
(3) In this section—
"the appropriate local authority" means—
(a) where the child usually resides in Scotland, the regional or islands council for the area in which he usually resides;
(b) in any other case, the regional or islands council for the area in which the offence was committed;
"care" shall be construed in accordance with section 32(3) of the 1968 Act, and the provisions of that Act specified in section 44(5) of that Act shall apply in respect of a child who is detained in residential care in pursuance of this section as they apply in respect of a child who is subject to a supervision requirement;
"the 1968 Act" means the Social Work (Scotland) Act 1968.
(4) Where a child in respect of whom an order is made under this section is also subject to a supervision requirement within the meaning of the 1968 Act, subject to subsection (6) below, the supervision requirement shall be of no effect during any period for which he is required to be detained under the order.
(5) The Secretary of State may, by regulations made by statutory instrument subject to annulment in pursuance of a resolution of either House of Parliament, make such provision as he considers necessary as regards the detention in secure accommodation (within the meaning of the 1968 Act) of children in respect of whom orders have been made under this section.
(6) Section 20A of the 1968 Act (review of children in care) shall apply to a child detained in residential care in pursuance of an order under this section as if the references to care in that section were references to care within the meaning of this section; and, without prejudice to their duty to do so by virtue of the said section 20A, the local authority may, at any time, review the case of such a child and may, in consequence of such a review and after having regard to the best interests of the child and the need to protect members of the public, release the child—
(a) for such period and on such conditions as they consider appropriate; or
(b) unconditionally,
and where a child who is released unconditionally is subject to a supervision requirement within the meaning of the 1968 Act, the effect of the supervision requirement shall, in the case of a supervision requirement imposed during the period of detention, commence or, in any other case, resume upon such release.

(7) Where a local authority consider it appropriate that a child in respect of whom an order has been made under subsection (1) above should be detained in a place in any part of the United Kingdom outside Scotland, the order shall be a like authority as in Scotland to the person in charge of the place to restrict the child's liberty to such an extent as that person may consider appropriate having regard to the terms of the order.".

(2) In section 463 of the 1975 Act—

(a) in subsection (1)(b) for the words "and 390" there shall be substituted the words ", 390 and 413"; and

(b) in subsection (1A) for the words "and 374" there shall be substituted the words ", 374 and 413".

(3) Notwithstanding the repeal by this Act of section 58A of the Children and Young Persons (Scotland) Act 1937, any child who, before the commencement of this section, has been ordered to be detained pursuant to the directions of the Secretary of State under section 413 of the 1975 Act—

(a) shall, while so detained after such commencement, continue to be deemed to be in legal custody; and

(b) may at any time be released conditionally or unconditionally by the Secretary of State, and any such child conditionally released shall be liable to recall on the directions of the Secretary of State and if he fails to comply with any condition of his release he may be apprehended without warrant and taken to the place from which he was released.

GENERAL NOTE

This section revises s.413 of the 1975 Act. That section gives the sheriff the power to impose residential training orders on children found guilty under summary proceedings of offences that would attract imprisonment for persons aged 21 or over. The new s.413 provides that the child should be detained in residential care by the appropriate local authority (rather than by the Secretary of State as under the old s.413) for a period not exceeding one year (rather than two as formerly).

Evidence

Transcript of police interview sufficient evidence

60.—(1) Subject to subsection (2) below, for the purposes of any criminal proceedings, a document certified by the person who made it as an accurate transcript made for the prosecutor of the contents of a tape (identified by means of a label) purporting to be a recording of an interview between a police officer and an accused person shall be received in evidence and be sufficient evidence of the making of the transcript and of its accuracy.

(2) Subsection (1) above shall not apply to a transcript—

(a) unless a copy of it has been served on the accused not less than 14 days before his trial; or

(b) if the accused, not less than six days before his trial, or by such later time before his trial as the court may in special circumstances allow, has served notice on the prosecutor that the accused challenges the making of the transcript or its accuracy.

(3) A copy of the transcript or a notice under subsection (2) above may be served personally or sent to the person on whom it is required to be served by registered post or by the recorded delivery service; and a written execution purporting to be signed by the person who served the transcript or notice, together with, where appropriate, a post office receipt for the relative registered or recorded delivery letter shall be sufficient evidence of such service.

(4) Where subsection (1) above does not apply to a transcript, if the person who made the transcript is called as a witness his evidence shall be sufficient evidence of the making of the transcript and of its accuracy.

GENERAL NOTE
This section provides for the certification of the transcripts of tape recordings of interviews between police officers and accused persons. Subject to subs. (2), a certified transcript will be received in evidence and be sufficient evidence of the making of the transcript and of its accuracy.
Subs. (2) provides that this general rule does not apply to a transcript (a) unless it has been served on the accused not less than 14 days before his trial, or, (b) if the accused within the time limits laid down in s.60(2)(b) challenges the making of the transcript or its accuracy.

Evidence on commission

61.—(1) Section 32 of the Criminal Justice (Scotland) Act 1980 (which permits, in certain circumstances, the taking and admission of evidence on commission or by letter of request) shall have effect subject to the amendments specified in subsections (2) and (3) below.
(2) In paragraph (b) of subsection (1)—
  (a) after the word "who" there shall be inserted "(i)"; and
  (b) at the end of the paragraph there shall be inserted the words "or
      (ii) is not ordinarily resident in, and is, at the time of the trial diet, unlikely to be present in, the United Kingdom, Channel Islands or the Isle of Man.".
(3) In subsection (4) at the end there shall be added the words "; and without prejudice to the generality of the power to make it, such an act of Adjournal may provide for the appointment of a person before whom evidence may be taken for the purposes of this section.".

GENERAL NOTE
S.32(1)(b) of the Criminal Justice (Scotland) Act 1980 provides for the taking of evidence on commission at any place in the United Kingdom, Channel Islands or Isle of Man from a witness who by reason of being ill or infirm is unable to attend the trial diet. S.61 of the present Act extends that provision so as to permit the taking of evidence on commission from a witness who is not ordinarily resident in, and at the time of the trial diet is unlikely to be present in the United Kingdom, the Channel Islands or the Isle of Man.

Miscellaneous

Ordaining to appear

62.—(1) In section 328 of the 1975 Act (adjournment for inquiry)—
  (a) after the words "liberate him on bail" there shall be inserted the words ", ordain him to appear"; and
  (b) in the proviso, after the words "allow bail" there shall be inserted the words "or to ordain a person to appear".
(2) In section 329(1) of the 1975 Act (remand and committal of persons under 21) after the words "released on bail" there shall be inserted the words "or ordained to appear".
(3) In paragraph (d) of section 337 of the 1975 Act (procedure following plea of not guilty by accused in custody) for the words from "either" there shall be substituted the following—
  "(i) if he is neither granted bail nor ordained to appear, or
  (ii) if he is granted bail on a condition imposed under section 1(3) of the Bail etc. (Scotland) Act 1980 that a sum of money is deposited in court, until the accused or a cautioner on his behalf has so deposited that sum.".
(4) In section 300 of the 1975 Act (bail appeals)—

(a) in subsection (1)—
>   (i) after the words "granted" there shall be inserted the words "or where the person is ordained to appear", and
>   (ii) after the words "amount fixed" there shall be inserted the words "or that such person has been ordained to appear"; and

(b) after subsection (4) there shall be inserted the following new subsection—
>   "(4A) When an appeal is taken by the prosecutor under this section against the fact that the person has been ordained to appear, subsection (4) above shall apply as it applies in the case of an appeal against the granting of bail or against the amount fixed.".

GENERAL NOTE

S.328 of the 1975 Act provides that a court of summary jurisdiction may, in order to allow time for inquiry, or for any other necessary cause continue the case for such time as is reasonable and necessary. In doing so the court may liberate the accused on bail or commit him to prison. S.62 now permits the Court simply to ordain the accused to appear. S.62(2) makes a consequential amendment to s.329. Similar consequential amendments are made by subs. (3) to s.337 of the 1975 Act, and by subs. (4) to s.300 of the 1975 Act.

Power to permit witness to be in court during trial

63. After each of sections 139 and 342 of the 1975 Act there shall be inserted the following new section where it shall be numbered respectively 139A and 342A—

"Power to permit witness to be in court during trial

The court may, on an application by any party to the proceedings, permit a witness to be in court during the proceedings or any part of the proceedings before he has given evidence if it appears to the court that the presence of the witness would not be contrary to the interests of justice.".

GENERAL NOTE

This is a curious provision. According to Lord Glenarthur (Minister of State at the Scottish Office) (*Hansard,* H.L. Vol. 482, col. 1080) this section "is designed to afford a remedy in cases where the defence agent cites the procurator fiscal as a witness in a trial, thereby preventing his attendance in court until after his evidence is given. This has resulted in fiscals having to spend an entire trial outside the court but on hand to give evidence without ever being called."

Aiding and abetting

64.—(1) In each of sections 216 and 428 of the 1975 Act for the words "statute or order" there shall be substituted the word "enactment"; and each of those sections as so amended shall be subsection (1) of that section and in each of those sections there shall be inserted the following subsection—

"(2) Without prejudice to subsection (1) above or to any express provision in any enactment having the like effect to this subsection, any person who aids, abets, counsels, procures or incites any other person to commit an offence against the provisions of any enactment shall be guilty of an offence and shall be liable on conviction, unless the enactment otherwise requires, to the same punishment as might be imposed on conviction of the first-mentioned offence.".

(2) Subsection (1) above shall not apply to an offence committed before the commencement of this section.

This provision follows recommendations of the Scottish Law Commission that there should be a general statutory offence of aiding, abetting, counselling, procuring or inciting the commission of a statutory offence. The section is intended to remove doubts concerning aiding and abetting in statutory offences and also to give some recognition to the differences in levels of participation in the commission of offences. The problems of art and part guilty in "special capacity" offences are removed by this provision (see, for examples *Robertsons* v. *Caird* (1885) 5 Couper 664, *Vaughan* v. *H.M. Advocate*, 1979 S.L.T. 49). For a general discussion of this problem, and the background to this section, see Scottish Law Commission, *Criminal Law: Art and Part Guilt of Statutory Offences* (Scot. Law Com. No. 93) (Cmnd. 9551, 1985).

Compensation requirement in probation order

65.—(1) In each of sections 183 and 384 of the 1975 Act (probation orders) after subsection (5A) there shall (subject to subsection (2) below) be inserted the following subsections—

"(5B) Without prejudice to the generality of subsection (4) above, where a court is considering making a probation order it may include in the probation order, in addition to any other requirement, a requirement that the offender shall pay compensation either in a lump sum or by instalments for any personal injury, loss or damage caused (whether directly or indirectly) by the acts which constituted the offence; and the following provisions of the Criminal Justice (Scotland) Act 1980 shall apply to such a requirement as if any reference in them to a compensation order included a reference to a requirement to pay compensation under this subsection—

section 58(2) and (3);
section 59 (except the proviso to subsection (1));
section 60;
section 62;
section 64 (except paragraph (a));
section 67.

(5C) Where the court imposes a requirement to pay compensation under subsection (5B) above—

(a) it shall be a condition of a probation order containing such a requirement that payment of the compensation shall be completed not more than eighteen months after the making of the order or not later than two months before the end of the period of probation whichever first occurs;

(b) the court, on the application of the offender or the officer of the local authority responsible for supervising the offender, may vary the terms of the requirement, including the amount of any instalments, in consequence of any change which may have occurred in the circumstances of the offender; and

(c) in any proceedings for breach of a probation order where the breach consists only in the failure to comply with a requirement to pay compensation, a document purporting to be a certificate signed by the clerk of the court for the time being having jurisdiction in relation to the order that the compensation or, where payment by instalments has been allowed, any instalment has not been paid shall be sufficient evidence of such breach.".

(2) In inserting the new subsection (5B)—

(a) into the said section 183, after the words "subsection (1)" in the reference in that new subsection to section 59 of the Criminal Justice (Scotland) Act 1980 there shall be added the words "and subsection (2)";

(b) into the said section 384, after the words "subsection (1)" in that reference there shall be added the words "and subsection (3)".

(3) In subsection (4) of each of the said sections 183 and 384 after the words "subsection (5A)" there shall be inserted the words "or (5B)."

(4) In subsection (6) of each of the said sections 183 and 384 for the words "or (5A)" there shall be substituted the words "(5A), (5B) or (5C)".

(5) In each of sections 186(2)(a) and 387(2)(a) of the 1975 Act (failure to comply with requirements of a probation order) at the beginning of the paragraph there shall be inserted the words "except in the case of a failure to comply with a requirement to pay compensation and".

GENERAL NOTE
This section permits a court, when considering making a probation order, to include in the probation order a requirement that the offender shall pay compensation for any personal injury, loss or damage caused by the acts which constituted the offence. Where a compensation requirement is made under this section, it is a condition of the probation order that the compensation be paid not more than 18 months after the making of the order or not later than two months before the end of the period of probation (whichever first occurs).

Penalties in respect of summary conviction for certain offences

66.—(1) In section 289G of the 1975 Act (which creates the standard scale and amends certain enactments accordingly), after subsection (9) there shall be added the following new subsections—

"(10) Subject to subsection (12) below, where under a relevant subordinate instrument the fine or maximum fine on conviction of a summary offence specified in the instrument is an amount shown in the second column of the standard scale, the reference in the instrument to the amount of the fine or maximum fine shall be construed as a reference to the level in the first column of the standard scale corresponding to that amount.

(11) In subsection (10) above, "relevant subordinate instrument" means any instrument made by virtue of an enactment after 30th April 1984 and before the commencement of section 66 of the Criminal Justice (Scotland) Act 1987.

(12) Subsection (10) above shall not affect so much of any instrument as (in whatever words) makes a person liable on summary conviction to a fine not exceeding a specified amount for each period of a specified length during which a continuing offence is continued after conviction or the occurrence of any other specified event.

(13) Where there is, under any enactment (however framed or worded) contained in an Act passed before the commencement of section 66 of the Criminal Justice (Scotland) Act 1987, a power to create summary offences by subordinate instrument, the maximum fine for a summary offence so created may be expressed as a fine not exceeding a level on the standard scale.

(14) Subsection (13) above has effect in relation to exercises of powers before as well as after the commencement of section 66 of the Criminal Justice (Scotland) Act 1987.".

(2) After section 289G of the 1975 Act there shall be inserted the following new sections—

"Statutory maximum as penalty in respect of summary conviction for offences in subordinate instruments

289GA.—(1) Where there is, under any enactment (however framed or worded) contained in an Act passed before the commencement of section 66 of the Criminal Justice (Scotland) Act 1987, a power by subordinate instrument to create a criminal offence triable either on indictment or summarily, the maximum fine which may, in the exercise of the power, be authorised on summary conviction shall, by virtue of this section, be the statutory maximum (unless some larger maximum fine can be authorised on summary conviction of such an offence by virtue of an enactment other than this subsection).

(2) Where there is, under any enactment (however framed or worded) contained in an Act passed before the commencement of section 66 of the Criminal Justice (Scotland) Act 1987, a power to create offences triable either on indictment or summarily by subordinate instrument, the maximum fine on summary conviction for such an offence may be expressed as a fine not exceeding the statutory maximum.

(3) Subsections (1) and (2) above shall have effect in relation to any exercise of such power before as well as after the commencement of section 66 of the Criminal Justice (Scotland) Act 1987.

(4) Where an offence created by a subordinate instrument made before the commencement of section 66 of the Criminal Justice (Scotland) Act 1987 may be tried either on indictment or summarily, the maximum fine which may be imposed on summary conviction shall by virtue of this subsection be the statutory maximum (unless the offence is one for which by virtue of the instrument a larger maximum fine may be imposed on summary conviction).

(5) Where a person summarily convicted of any offence to which subsection (4) above relates would, apart from this section, be liable to a fine or to a maximum fine of an amount in the case of a first conviction and of a different amount in the case of a second or subsequent conviction, subsection (4) above shall apply irrespective of whether the conviction is a first, second or subsequent one.

(6) Subsection (4) above shall not affect so much of any instrument as (in whatever words) makes a person liable on summary conviction to a fine not exceeding a specified amount for each period of a specified length during which a continuing offence is continued after conviction or the occurrence of any other specified event.

(7) Nothing in this section shall affect the punishment for an offence committed before the commencement of section 66 of the Criminal Justice (Scotland) Act 1987.

Exceptionally high maximum fines
289GB.—(1) The Secretary of State may by order amend an enactment or subordinate instrument specifying a sum to which this subsection applies so as to substitute for that sum such other sum as appears to him—

(a) to be justified by a change in the value of money appearing to him to have taken place since the last occasion on which the sum in question was fixed; or

(b) to be appropriate to take account of an order altering the standard scale which has been made or is proposed to be made.

(2) Subsection (1) above applies to any sum which—

(a) is higher than level 5 on the standard scale; and

(b) is specified as the fine or the maximum fine which may be imposed on conviction of an offence which is triable only summarily.

(3) The Secretary of State may by order amend an enactment or subordinate instrument specifying a sum to which this subsection applies so as to substitute for that sum such other sum as appears to him—

(a) to be justified by a change in the value of money appearing to him to have taken place since the last occasion on which the sum in question was fixed; or

(b) to be appropriate to take account of an order made or proposed to be made altering the statutory maximum.

(4) Subsection (3) above applies to any sum which—

    (a) is higher than the statutory maximum; and

    (b) is specified as the maximum fine which may be imposed on summary conviction of an offence triable either on indictment or summarily.

(5) An order under this section—

    (a) shall be made by statutory instrument subject to annulment in pursuance of a resolution of either House of Parliament; and

    (b) shall not affect the punishment for an offence committed before that order comes into force.

(6) In this section—

"enactment" includes an enactment contained in an Act passed after the Criminal Justice (Scotland) Act 1987; and

"subordinate instrument" includes an instrument made after the passing of that Act.".

Increases in periods of imprisonment for non-payment of fines etc.

67.—(1) In subsection (1A) of section 407 of the 1975 Act (periods of imprisonment for non-payment of fines), in the Table, for the entry relating to an amount exceeding £50,000 there shall be substituted the following entries—

"Exceeding £50,000 but not exceeding £100,000	2 years
Exceeding £100,000 but not exceeding £250,000	3 years
Exceeding £250,000 but not exceeding £1 million	5 years
Exceeding £1 million	10 years.".

(2) At the end of the said section 407 there shall be added the following subsection—

"(5) Where in any case—

(a) the sheriff considers that the imposition of imprisonment for the number of years for the time being specified in section 2(2) of this Act would be inadequate; and

(b) the maximum period of imprisonment which may be imposed under subsection (1) above (or under that subsection as read with either or both of sections 66(2) of the Criminal Justice (Scotland) Act 1980 and 7(2) of the Criminal Justice (Scotland) Act 1987) exceeds that number of years,

he shall remit the case to the High Court for sentence.".

Suspension of disqualification, forfeiture etc.

68.—(1) After section 443 of the 1975 Act there shall be inserted the following new section—

"Suspension of disqualification, forfeiture etc.

443A.—(1) Where upon conviction of any person—

(a) any disqualification, forfeiture or disability attaches to him by reason of such conviction; or

(b) any property, matters or things which are the subject of the prosecution or connected therewith are to be or may be ordered to be destroyed or forfeited,

if the court before which he was convicted thinks fit, the disqualification, forfeiture or disability or, as the case may be, destruction or forfeiture or order for destruction or forfeiture shall be suspended pending the determination of any appeal against conviction or sentence.

(2) Subsection (1) above does not apply in respect of any disqualification, forfeiture or, as the case may be, destruction or forfeiture or order for destruction or forfeiture under or by virtue of any enactment which contains express provision for the suspension of such disqualification, forfeiture or, as the case may be, destruction or forfeiture or order for destruction or forfeiture pending the determination of any appeal against conviction or sentence.".

(2) In section 264 of that Act (suspension of disqualification, forfeiture etc. in solemn proceedings) after subsection (2) there shall be inserted the following new subsection—

"(3) Subsections (1) and (2) above do not apply in respect of any disqualification, forfeiture or, as the case may be, destruction or forfeiture or order for destruction or forfeiture under or by virtue of any enactment which contains express provision for the suspension of such disqualification, forfeiture or, as the case may be, destruction or forfeiture or order for destruction or forfeiture pending the determination of any appeal against conviction or sentence.".

(3) Section 2 of the Act of Adjournal, Suspension of Disqualification from Driving Pending Appeal 1975 is hereby revoked.

PART III

GENERAL

Interpretation

69. In this Act—

"controlled drug" has the meaning assigned by section 2 of the Misuse of Drugs Act 1971; and

"the 1975 Act" means the Criminal Procedure (Scotland) Act 1975; and provision for the construction of the expressions "administrator", "associate", "authorised government department", "confiscation order", "drug trafficking", "implicative gift", "realisable property", "restraint order" and "the 1985 Act" is made by section 47(1) of this Act.

Amendments and repeals

70.—(1) The enactments mentioned in Schedule 1 to this Act shall have effect subject to the amendments respectively specified in that Schedule, being minor amendments and amendments consequential on the provisions of this Act.

(2) The enactments set out in columns 1 and 2 of Schedule 2 to this Act are hereby repealed to the extent specified in the third column of that Schedule.

Expenses

71. There shall be paid out of money provided by Parliament—

(a) any amount payable—
   (i) under section 20(2) of this Act in respect of remuneration or expenses of administrators; or
   (ii) as compensation under section 26(4)(c) of this Act;
(b) any administrative expenses incurred by the Secretary of State, or by the Lord Advocate, in consequence of this Act; and
(c) any increase attributable to this Act in the sums payable out of money so provided under any other Act.

Short title, commencement and extent

72.—(1) This Act may be cited as the Criminal Justice (Scotland) Act 1987; and subject to subsection (4) below it extends to Scotland only.

(2) This Act, except this section, shall come into force on such day as the Secretary of State may by order made by statutory instrument appoint; and different days may be so appointed for different purposes and for different provisions.

(3) An order under subsection (2) above may contain such transitional provisions and savings as appear to the Secretary of State necessary or expedient in connection with the provisions brought into force (whether wholly or partly) by the order.

(4) This section and sections 4(5), 20(1), 33 to 37, 41(10) to (12), 45(2), (3) and (7)(c) and (f), 47, 55(a) and (b) and 69 of, and, in so far as relating to the Drug Trafficking Offences Act 1986, section 70(2) of, and Schedule 2 to, this Act extend to England and Wales as well as to Scotland; sections 51 to 53, 56(11) and 59 extend to England and Wales and to Northern Ireland as well as to Scotland; sections 31 and 45(1), (4) and (7)(a), (b), (d) and (e) extend to England and Wales only; and section 55(c) extends to Northern Ireland only.

SCHEDULES

Section 70(1)   SCHEDULE 1

MINOR AND CONSEQUENTIAL AMENDMENTS

The Juries Act 1949 (c.27)

1. In paragraph (b) of section 25(1), for the words "on circuit" there shall be substituted the words "other than at Edinburgh".

The Judicial Offices (Salaries etc.) Act 1952 (c.12)

2. In section 2(1), for the words "circuit court expenses" there shall be substituted the words "expenses in connection with sittings of the High Court of Justiciary outwith Edinburgh".

The Road Traffic Act 1972 (c.20)

3. In section 101 (endorsement of licences) for subsection (8) there shall be substituted the following subsections—

"(8) Notwithstanding sections 311(5) and 357(1) of the Criminal Procedure (Scotland) Act 1975 (requirements as to notices of penalty and previous convictions), where a person is convicted in Scotland of an offence involving obligatory endorsement—

(a) where his licence is produced to the court, subsection (4A) above shall apply;

(b) where no such licence is produced, subject to subsection (8B) below, subsection (8A) below shall apply.

(8A) Where this subsection applies, it shall be competent for the court in determining what order to make in pursuance of such conviction as is mentioned in subsection (8) above to take into consideration particulars of—

(a) any previous conviction or disqualification pertaining to the person; and

(b) any penalty points ordered to be endorsed on any licence held by the person which have to be taken into account under section 19(3) of the Transport Act 1981,

specified in a document purporting to be a note of information contained in the driver licensing records maintained by the Secretary of State in connection with his functions under this Part of this Act.

(8B) Where the prosecutor decides to put before the court a document such as is mentioned in subsection (8A) above—

(a) if a plea of guilty is tendered, or if, after a plea of not guilty, the accused is convicted the prosecutor shall lay the document before the court and the court or the clerk of court shall ask the accused if he admits the accuracy of the particulars relating to him contained in the document and if such admission is made it shall be entered in the record of the proceedings;

(b) it shall not be necessary for the prosecutor to produce evidence of the particulars so admitted; and

(c) where the accused does not admit the accuracy of any such particular, the prosecutor unless he withdraws the particular shall adduce evidence in proof thereof either then or at any other diet.".

The Criminal Procedure (Scotland) Act 1975 (c.21)

4. In section 5(1) (crimes committed in different districts)—
(a) for the words "a court to be held in" there shall be substituted the words "the sheriff court of"; and
(b) the words ", whether that court is the High Court or the sheriff court" shall be omitted.

5. In section 86 (selection of jurors)—
(a) for the words "The High Court may by Act of Adjournal specify" there shall be substituted the words "The Lord Justice General, whom failing the Lord Justice Clerk, may give directions as to"; and
(b) for the words "in that court to be held in Edinburgh" there shall be substituted the words "to be held in the High Court",

and the section as amended shall be subsection (1); and there shall be added the following new subsection—

"(2) Where a sitting of the High Court is to be held at a town in which the High Court does not usually sit, the jury summoned to try any case in such a sitting shall be summoned from the general jury roll of the sheriff court district in which the town is situated.".

6. In section 113(2) (difference as to rotation of judges) at the end there shall be added the words "whom failing by the Lord Justice Clerk".

7. In section 129 (balloting of jurors), after the word "aside," there shall be inserted the words "or shall, before any evidence is led, be excused".

8. In each of sections 141(3) and 346(3) (which permit the prosecutor or an accused to call a co-accused as a witness)—
(a) after the words "guilty to" there shall be inserted the words "or been acquitted of";
(b) after the words "whether or not" there shall be inserted the words ", in a case where the co-accused has pleaded guilty to any charge,"; and
(c) after the word "sentenced)" there shall be inserted the words "or in respect of whom the diet has been deserted".

9. In section 149(1) (calling additional evidence)—
(a) for the words "after the close of that party's evidence and" there shall be substituted the words "at any time"; and
(b) in paragraph (b) for the words "party's evidence was closed" there shall be substituted the words "jury was sworn".

10. In each of sections 183(1) and 384(1) (probation orders)—
(a) after the word "offender" where it first occurs there shall be inserted the words "and having obtained a report as to the circumstances and character of the offender"; and
(b) for the word "one" there shall be substituted the words "six months".

11. In section 212(1) (recall to young offenders institution on reconviction)—
(a) the words "in a" shall be omitted; and
(b) for the words "an institution" there shall be substituted the word "detention".

12. In each of sections 215 and 426 (detention etc. deemed to be legal custody) for the words "Part I of the Criminal Justice (Scotland) Act 1980" there shall be substituted the words "any other enactment or any subordinate instrument".

13.—(1) In section 245(1) (quorum and sitting of the High Court in appeals), for the words "or other proceeding under this Part of this Act" there shall be substituted the words "under this Part of this Act or any proceeding connected therewith".

(2) In section 246 (arrangement of appeal sittings), after the words "section 247 of this Act)" there shall be inserted the words "for the purposes of hearing and determining any appeal under this Part of this Act or any proceeding connected therewith".

14.—(1) In section 268 (reckoning of time spent in custody pending appeal), for subsection (1) there shall be substituted the following subsection—

"(1) Subject to subsection (2) below, where an appellant is admitted to bail under section 238 of this Act the period beginning with the date of his admission to bail and ending on the date of his readmission to prison in consequence of the determination or abandonment of his appeal shall not be reckoned as part of any term of imprisonment under this sentence.".

(2) In subsection (2) of that section, after the word "appeal" there shall be inserted the words ", including any period spent in custody in consequence of the recall of his bail,".

(3) For subsection (3) of that section there shall be substituted the following subsection—

"(3) Subject to any direction which the High Court may give to the contrary, imprisonment of an appellant—

(a) who is in custody in consequence of the conviction or sentence appealed against shall be deemed to run as from the date on which the sentence was passed;

(b) who is in custody other than in consequence of such conviction or sentence shall be deemed to run or to be resumed as from the date on which his appeal was determined or abandoned;

(c) who is not in custody shall be deemed to run or to be resumed as from the date on which he is received into prison under the sentence.".

15. In section 289B—

(a) in subsection (7) for the words "Subsection (4) above" there shall be substituted the words "Section 289GA(1) of this Act"; and

(b) in subsection (8) for the words "subsection (4) above" there shall be substituted the words "section 289GA(1) of this Act".

The Criminal Justice (Scotland) Act 1980 (c.62)

16. In section 2 (police detention)—

(a) in subsection (2), the word "or" at the end of paragraph (a) shall be omitted and there shall be inserted the following new paragraph—

"(aa) when he is detained in pursuance of any other enactment or subordinate instrument; or";

(b) in that subsection, for the words "for a period of six hours, he shall be informed immediately upon expiry of this period" there shall be substituted the words "he shall be informed immediately upon the termination of his detention in accordance with this subsection"; and

(c) after subsection (3) there shall be inserted the following new subsection—

"(3A) Where a person has previously been detained in pursuance of any other enactment or subordinate instrument, he may not be detained under subsection (1) above on the same grounds or on grounds arising from the same circumstances as those which led to his earlier detention.".

17. In paragraph (b)(ii) of section 41(2) (construction of "detention" in England and Wales), after the words "England and Wales," there shall be inserted the words "a sentence of youth custody,".

18.—(1) In Schedule 1 (certificates as to proof of certain routine matters), as the first entry there shall be inserted—

"The Wireless Telegraphy Act 1949 (c.54). Section 1 in so far as it relates to the installation or use of apparatus designed for the purpose of receiving and exhibiting television programmes broadcast for general reception.	A person authorised to do so by the Secretary of State.	In relation to an address specified in the certificate, whether on a date so specified any television receiving licence (within the meaning of the Wireless Telegraphy (Broadcast Licence Charges and Exemption) Regulations 1984) was, in records maintained on behalf of the Secretary of State in relation to such licences, recorded as being in force; and, if so, particulars so specified of such record of that licence.".

(2) In that Schedule, in the entry relating to the Misuse of Drugs Act 1971, in column 3 (matters which may be certified) the word "and" shall be omitted and after the word "classification" there shall be inserted the words "purity, weight and description".

The Contempt of Court Act 1981 (c.49)

19.—(1) In section 15 (penalties for contempt of court in Scottish proceedings) after subsection (5) there shall be inserted the following subsection—

"(6) For the purposes of section 60 of the Criminal Justice Act 1967 (release on licence of prisoners serving determinate sentences) a penalty of a period of imprisonment imposed for contempt of court shall be treated as a sentence of imprisonment within the meaning of that Act.".

(2) Section 15, as amended, shall have effect as regards any penalty imposed before as well as after the coming into force of this paragraph.

Section 70(2)   SCHEDULE 2

REPEALS

Chapter	Short title	Extent of repeal
8 Anne c.16.	The Circuit Courts (Scotland) Act 1709.	The whole Act.
20 Geo. 2 c.43.	The Heritable Jurisdiction (Scotland) Act 1746.	Sections 32 to 34. Sections 36 and 37. Section 40.
9 Geo. 4 c.29.	The Circuit Courts (Scotland) Act 1828.	Section 15. Section 24.
11 & 12 Vict. c.79.	The Justiciary (Scotland) Act 1848.	Section 5.
61 & 62 Vict. c.40.	The Circuit Clerks (Scotland) Act 1898.	The whole Act.
1 Edw. 8 and 1 Geo. 6. c.37.	The Children and Young Persons (Scotland) Act 1937.	Section 58A.
1968 c.49.	The Social Work (Scotland) Act 1968.	In Schedule 2, paragraph 16.
1972 c.20.	The Road Traffic Act 1972.	In Schedule 4, Part I in the entry relating to section 1, the words "or, in the case of a conviction by a court in Scotland other than the High Court of Justiciary, 2 years.".
1974 c.50.	The Road Traffic Act 1974.	In Schedule 3, paragraph 10(4).
1975 c.21.	The Criminal Procedure (Scotland) Act 1975.	In section 5(1), the words ", whether that court is the High Court or the sheriff court". Sections 87 and 88. In section 113, subsection (3) and in the proviso to subsection (4) the words "in Edinburgh or on circuit". Sections 115 to 119. Section 193B. In section 263(2), the words ", or on any point arising on the case,". Section 289B(3) and (4). In section 289D, in subsection (1A), paragraphs (f) and (g); subsections (2) and (3); and in subsection (4) the words "or (2)". Section 300(5).
1976 c.67.	The Sexual Offences (Scotland) Act 1976.	In section 2D(5), in paragraph (a) the words "in the High Court of Justiciary"; and paragraph (b).
1978 c.49.	The Community Service by Offenders (Scotland) Act 1978.	In section 7, paragraph (c).
1985 c.73.	The Law Reform (Miscellaneous Provisions) (Scotland) Act 1985.	Section 39.

Chapter	Short title	Extent of repeal
1986 c.32.	The Drug Trafficking Offences Act 1986.	In each of sections 13(1), 15(2), 16(2) and 17(2) the words "or on the Court of Session by sections 20 to 22 of this Act". Sections 20 to 23. In section 27, in subsection (1), the words "or, in Scotland, the procurator fiscal" and "or, in Scotland, the sheriff"; in each of subsections (2) and (3) the words "or, as the case may be, the sheriff"; in subsection (5), the words "or, in Scotland, the procurator fiscal"; and in subsection (6), the words "or, as respects Scotland, rules of court". In section 28, in subsection (1), the words "or, in Scotland, the procurator fiscal" and "or, in Scotland, the sheriff,"; and in subsection (2), the words "or, as the case may be, the sheriff". Section 29(3). In section 33(2), the word "or" at the end of paragraph (b). In section 40(4), paragraph (a); in paragraph (b), the references to section 7(3), to section 8(8) and (9), to section 13, to section 24(3)(a) and to sections 27 to 29; and paragraph (c).